THEORIES OF COUNSELING AND PSYCHOTHERAPY

THEORIES OF COUNSELING AND PSYCHOTHERAPY

Systems, Strategies, and Skills

SECOND EDITION

Linda Seligman
Walden University
George Mason University

PEARSON

Merrill
Prentice Hall

Upper Saddle River, New Jersey
Columbus, Ohio

Library of Congress Cataloging-in-Publication Data

Seligman, Linda.
    Theories of counseling and psychotherapy : systems, strategies, and skills / Linda
Seligman.—2nd ed.
        p. cm.
    Rev. ed. of: Systems, strategies, and skills of counseling and psychotherapy.
    Includes bibliographical references and index.
    ISBN 0-13-114975-X
    1. Counseling—Textbooks. 2. Psychotherapy—Textbooks. I. Seligman, Linda.
Systems, strategies, and skills of counseling and psychotherapy. II. Title.
    BF637.C6S445 2006
    616.89'14—dc22

                                                                    2005003052

Vice President and Executive Publisher: Jeffery W. Johnston
Publisher: Kevin M. Davis
Editorial Assistant: Sarah Kenoyer
Production Editor: Mary Harlan
Production Coordinator: Thistle Hill Publishing Services, LLC
Design Coordinator: Diane C. Lorenzo
Cover Design: Terry Rohrbach
Cover Image: SuperStock
Text Design and Illustrations: Carlisle Communications, Ltd.
Production Manager: Laura Messerly
Director of Marketing: Ann Castel Davis
Marketing Manager: Autumn Purdy
Marketing Coordinator: Brian Mounts

This book was set in Berkeley by Carlisle Communications, Ltd. It was printed and bound by
R. R. Donnelley & Sons Company. The cover was printed by The Lehigh Press, Inc.

Previous edition titled *Systems, Strategies, and Skills of Counseling and Psychotherapy.*

Pearson Education Ltd.   Pearson Education Australia Pty. Limited
Pearson Education Singapore Pte. Ltd.   Pearson Education North Asia Ltd.
Pearson Education Canada, Ltd.   Pearson Educación de Mexico, S.A. de C.V.
Pearson Education–Japan   Pearson Education Malaysia Pte. Ltd.

10 9 8 7 6 5 4 3 2 1
ISBN: 0-13-114975-X

To all my clients and students who have taught me so much

Preface

I have made many changes in the second edition of this book, based on my own assessment of developments in counseling and psychology and on feedback and reviews I received from students and faculty who used this book in their courses. The basic structure of the book has been maintained, including the BETA format, descriptions of important treatment approaches, skill development sections, case studies, and exercises for large groups, small groups, and individuals. However, greater attention is paid in this edition to the use of each approach with diverse and multicultural clients. In addition, the discussion of relevant research, documenting the validity of each approach, has been expanded. Updated information is provided on all treatment approaches presented in the book, with considerably expanded information provided on narrative therapy, constructivist therapy, and feminist therapy. The chapter on transactional analysis has been omitted, although some information on that approach has been incorporated into the chapter on Gestalt therapy. Efforts have been made to clarify any confusing points in the first edition and to make the book even more user-friendly and relevant to the practice of counseling and psychotherapy.

Purposes of This Book

I have been a counselor educator for more than 25 years, have taught many courses on theories and strategies of counseling and psychotherapy, and have supervised hundreds of women and men seeking to become counselors or psychologists. Many of the students and professionals I taught and supervised complained that their years of training had left them ill-prepared for clinical work. To some extent, their concerns reflected the understandable self-doubts of beginning clinicians who recognize the importance of their work and want to help their clients as much as possible. However, I have also heard them worry about how to move from theory to practice, when to use the treatment approaches they have learned, and what they should actually do when facing clients.

I have designed this book to address those concerns. My goals include providing a clear, concise, meaningful, coherent, up-to-date, and useful overview of both well-established and emerging approaches to counseling and psychotherapy. In addition, I seek to bridge the gap between theory and practice and to teach salient skills associated with each treatment system. Rather than present each treatment approach in isolation, separating theory and practice, I group treatment systems according to whether their primary focus is on background, emotions, thoughts, or actions. These four areas of focus can be represented by the acronym BETA (background, emotions, thoughts, actions). Introductory chapters on each of these four areas help readers to understand the commonalities among theories in each group and determine which approach is best suited for them and their clients.

All but the last chapter include a skill development section that teaches one or more key skills associated with the treatment system under review. For example, chapter 3, which introduces theories emphasizing background, teaches readers how to conduct an intake interview; chapter 21, on solution-focused brief therapy, teaches goal setting; chapter 7, on ego psychologists, object relations theory, and self psychology, introduces interpretation; and chapter 14, covering thought-focused treatment approaches, teaches ways for clinicians to help people modify dysfunctional cognitions. By chapter 23, which teaches treatment termination, readers should have developed the basic clinical skills they need as counselors or psychotherapists.

This book focuses primarily on systems of counseling and psychotherapy that are designed for treatment of individuals. Many of these approaches, of course, are also useful in the treatment of groups and families, as I discuss throughout the book. However, treatment approaches that are used primarily in group or family counseling are beyond the scope of this book and should be covered in separate courses and texts on couples and family treatment and group therapy.

Organization of This Book

This book consists of 7 parts and 24 chapters. Later in this preface, I present a variety of ways to use this book in courses and training programs.

Part One, which includes chapters 1 and 2, presents the BETA format (background, emotions, thoughts, actions), around which this book is organized. These chapters introduce client and clinician characteristics associated with successful treatment, regardless of the clinician's theoretical approach, and discuss the importance of the therapeutic alliance. Ethical considerations essential to effective treatment also are presented. In addition, I introduce the Diaz family—Edie, her husband Roberto, and their daughter Ava—who appear throughout the book to illustrate treatment approaches and strategies. The skill development sections in *chapter 1* present the use of encouragers (e.g., restatement, paraphrase, summary). *Chapter 2* teaches skills associated with role induction and development of a sound therapeutic alliance and provides ways to help readers assess their own clinical skills.

Part Two focuses on systems of counseling and psychotherapy that emphasize background and context. Such treatment approaches maintain that, to promote positive change, practitioners must explore and promote clients' insight into their histories and early experiences. *Chapter 3* examines the importance of background in understanding and helping people and teaches readers the effective use of questions as well as how to conduct an intake interview to obtain background information. *Chapter 4* provides an overview of psychoanalysis as developed by Sigmund Freud. Skill development here focuses on using a lifeline to gather background information. *Chapter 5* considers individual psychology, developed by Alfred Adler, and teaches readers to use early recollections to gather information and promote self-awareness. *Chapter 6* introduces analytical psychology as developed by Carl Jung and considers the skill of Jungian dreamwork. *Chapter 7* discusses ego psychologists, object relations theorists, and self psychologists, including Anna

Freud, Karen Horney, Harry Stack Sullivan, Melanie Klein, Helene Deutsch, Heinz Kohut, and others who expanded and revised Freudian psychoanalysis. Understanding their contributions gives depth and breadth to clinicians' knowledge of treatment systems. This chapter also considers the skill of interpretation. *Chapter 8* provides information on brief psychodynamic psychotherapy and reviews the skill of identifying people's focal concerns.

Part Three focuses on systems of counseling and psychotherapy that emphasize identifying and changing emotions and sensations. *Chapter 9* considers the nature and importance of emotions in people's lives and teaches the skill of reflecting meaning and feelings. *Chapter 10* discusses person-centered counseling as developed by Carl Rogers and explores the skill of clinician self-disclosure. *Chapter 11* focuses on existential therapy and reviews the skill of values clarification. *Chapter 12* introduces Gestalt therapy, developed primarily by Fritz Perls. This chapter also presents information on transactional analysis. The skill development section offers information on the Gestalt approach to exploring dreams. *Chapter 13* reviews emerging approaches that emphasize emotions and sensation, including narrative therapy, feminist therapy, constructivist therapy, and transpersonal therapy, and considers the skill of using visualization.

Part Four focuses on treatment systems that emphasize identification and modification of dysfunctional thoughts. *Chapter 14* reviews the importance of cognitions in people's lives and discusses ways to help people identify and modify self-destructive cognitions. *Chapter 15* centers on cognitive therapy, developed primarily by Aaron Beck, and considers the beneficial use of homework in treatment, an essential skill of cognitive therapists. *Chapter 16* explores rational emotive behavior therapy, developed by Albert Ellis, and teaches the use of rational-emotive imagery. *Chapter 17* reviews emerging approaches emphasizing thoughts, including neurolinguistic programming, eye movement desensitization and reprocessing, and thought-field therapy, and considers the skill of anchoring.

Part Five discusses treatment systems targeting actions and behaviors and presents many strategies that are useful in changing behavior. *Chapter 18* gives an overview of the importance of actions and behavior in people's lives and describes ways to modify behaviors. *Chapter 19* focuses on both behavioral and cognitive-behavioral approaches to treatment and reviews systematic desensitization, a powerful tool for effecting behavioral change. *Chapter 20* describes reality therapy, developed primarily by William Glasser, and examines the skill of caring confrontation. *Chapter 21* reviews solution-focused brief therapy, along with the skill of goal setting, which is essential in successful treatment.

Part Six discusses eclectic and integrated treatment systems, which combine two or more theoretical approaches to help clinicians individualize treatment plans. *Chapter 22* presents an overview of integrated and eclectic treatment approaches, along with the skill of treatment planning. *Chapter 23* provides information about specific integrated and eclectic approaches, focusing particularly on multimodal therapy (developed by Arnold Lazarus) and dialectical counseling and therapy (developed primarily by Allen Ivey and Sandra Rigazio-DiGilio). This chapter includes the last skill development section in the book, providing information on effectively terminating treatment.

Part Seven concludes the book. *Chapter 24* discusses commonalities of effective treatment approaches, as well as current trends in treatment. It also synthesizes the contents of this book by reviewing the major treatment systems according to a structured format. Finally, it provides information on how clinicians select their preferred treatment approach and includes a questionnaire to help readers identify which approach best reflects their beliefs and personal style.

Special Features

Each chapter that presents a treatment system follows the same organization to facilitate comparison and ease of use. The chapter begins with a brief overview of the approach and a biographical sketch of its developer, highlighting any clear connections between the person's background and the theory. The next two sections present the treatment approach, describing its theoretical concepts as well as its goals, the therapeutic alliance, and specific strategies. Subsequent sections discuss the approach's application to diverse populations, research substantiating its value, its current use, its strengths and limitations, and its contributions to counseling and psychotherapy. A summary highlights important aspects of the approach, and the chapter ends with a list of recommended readings and other sources of information to continue learning.

Chapters 1 through 23 each include a skill development section. Initial chapters include basic skills such as encouragers, as well as skills that successfully launch the treatment process such as role induction and building a positive therapeutic alliance. Chapter 23 wraps up the learning of skills by familiarizing readers with effective ways to terminate treatment. Intervening chapters introduce most of the essential skills of successful treatment including reflection of feeling and meaning, identifying and modifying dysfunctional cognitions, and ways to help people change undesirable behaviors. Each skill is useful to clinicians from various theoretical orientations and also reflects the specific treatment approach described in that chapter.

Accompanying each chapter is a series of exercises divided into three categories: those for large groups, for small groups, and for individuals. The exercises are designed both to deepen thinking and understanding of each treatment approach and to encourage skill development. These exercises are useful in the classroom and also help individual readers develop self-awareness, knowledge, and skills.

Case illustrations are another useful feature. Members of the Diaz family illustrate the treatment approaches, showing readers how counseling and psychotherapy can be used with people of both genders, different ages, and different cultural backgrounds. Although each case study is complete in itself, reading all of them provides an overview of treatment for these family members.

Particular attention is given to the application of each treatment system to people from diverse backgrounds. Counselors and psychologists today must have multicultural skills and sensitivity, and this book is designed to foster those abilities. In addition, this book considers the appropriate use of each approach in the treatment of mental disorders as described in the American Psychological Association's *Diagnostic and Statistical Manual of Mental Disorders (2000)*. This should help clinicians develop successful treatment plans for their clients.

Effective Ways to Use This Book

This book has been designed for flexibility and ease of use. Although each college and university has its own curriculum and required courses, this book can be adapted to almost any curriculum in counseling and psychology and also can be used for training and staff development. A few suggestions for using the book follow:

1. The book is ideally suited for use in a two-semester or two-quarter course on theories and techniques of counseling and psychotherapy. Such a curriculum would provide students with an in-depth and comprehensive understanding of the fields of counseling and psychotherapy. The

first three parts (13 chapters covering introductory material, treatment systems focused on backgrounds, and treatment systems focused on emotions) could be covered in the first semester, with the remaining four parts (focusing on cognitive, behavioral, and eclectic treatment approaches) covered in the second semester. If each class session covers one chapter, then any remaining classes can be used for role-playing and exams.

2. The entire book also could be covered in a one-semester course, particularly courses for doctoral and advanced master's degree students in which depth of knowledge is prized. The following illustrates one way to cover this book in a 15-week semester:

Week 1—Chapters 1 and 2—Overview of the Book, Contexts of Effective Treatment

Week 2—Chapters 3 and 4—Overview of Background-Focused Treatment Systems, Freudian Psychoanalysis

Week 3—Chapters 5 and 6—Adler's Individual Psychology, Jung's Analytical Psychology

Week 4—Chapters 7 and 8—Freudian Revisionists, Brief Psychodynamic Therapy

Week 5—Chapters 9 and 10—Overview of Emotion-Focused Treatment Systems, Person-Centered Counseling

Week 6—Chapters 11 and 12—Existential Therapy, Gestalt Therapy

Week 7—Chapter 13—Emerging Approaches Emphasizing Emotions and Sensations

Week 8—Chapters 14 and 15—Overview of Thought-Focused Treatment Systems, Beck's Cognitive Therapy

Week 9—Chapters 16 and 17—Ellis's Rational Emotive Behavior Therapy, Emerging Approaches Emphasizing Thoughts

Week 10—Chapters 18 and 19—Overview of Action-Focused Treatment Systems, Behavior Therapy and Cognitive-Behavioral Therapy

Week 11—Chapter 20—Reality Therapy

Week 12—Chapter 21—Solution-Focused Brief Therapy

Week 13—Chapters 22 and 23—Overview of Integrated and Eclectic Treatment Systems, Theories of Integrated and Eclectic Treatment

Week 14—Chapter 24—Solidifying Understanding of Treatment Systems

Week 15—Conclusion, final examination

3. Chapters can easily and logically be selected and combined to create a course. For example, the following 15 selected chapters encompass the four types of clinical approaches in the BETA format (background, emotions, thoughts, actions) and constitute a one-semester course on established theories of counseling:

Chapter 1: Overview of the Book

Chapter 2: Contexts of Effective Treatment

Chapter 3: Overview of Background-Focused Treatment Systems

Chapter 4: Sigmund Freud and Psychoanalysis

Chapter 5: Alfred Adler and Individual Psychology

Chapter 9: Overview of Emotion-Focused Treatment Systems

Chapter 10: Carl Rogers and Person-Centered Counseling

Chapter 12: Gestalt Therapy

Chapter 14: Overview of Thought-Focused Treatment Systems

Chapter 15: Aaron Beck and Cognitive Therapy

Chapter 16: Albert Ellis and Rational Emotive Behavior Therapy

Chapter 18: Overview of Action-Focused Treatment Systems

Chapter 19: Behavior Therapy and Cognitive-Behavioral Therapy

Chapter 20: Reality Therapy

Chapter 24: Solidifying Understanding of Treatment Systems

In a 15-week semester, one chapter could be covered per week, providing a comprehensive picture of the major treatment approaches.

4. A variety of short courses or seminars can be created from the contents of this book. For example, Part Two could be used for a course on psychodynamic and psychoanalytic approaches to treatment; Part Six for a course on eclectic and integrated approaches to treatment; and chapters 8, 13, 17, 21, and 23 for a course on new and emerging approaches in counseling and psychotherapy.

5. The skill development sections in each chapter are designed to accompany the treatment system taught in that particular chapter. However, these sections can be used independently of the theoretical portions, perhaps taught in a subsequent semester following a course on theories of counseling and psychotherapy or used as part of a practicum or internship to facilitate skill development.

6. Like the skill development sections, the exercises are intended to accompany review of the treatment system in each chapter. However, they are designed to be used flexibly. Large-group exercises are appropriate for classroom discussion. Small-group exercises allow clusters of four learners to practice and improve their clinical skills with the benefit of peer feedback and support. Individual exercises offer people the opportunity to work alone and apply their learning to themselves, with their responses written in journals.

Faculty members, of course, can choose to use any or all of the exercises that accompany each chapter. Ideally, time should be allocated, either during or outside of class, for at least some of the large- and small-group exercises in each chapter. However, if time is limited, the individual exercises enable students to continue their learning and skill development outside of class. Although instructors may decide to review students' journals at the end of a course to determine whether they have completed the individual exercises, I encourage them not to grade or evaluate these journals so that students feel free to express themselves, try out new skills, and gain learning and self-awareness. Students should be told at the beginning of the course whether they will be required to share their journals in any way.

7. I have written another book organized according to the BETA format. That book, *Technical and Conceptual Skills for Mental Health Professionals* (2004b), focuses on skills rather than theories of counseling and psychotherapy. The first section of that book teaches the technical skills used by mental health professionals. It covers some of the same skills as *Theories of Counseling and Psychotherapy*, as well as additional technical skills, all covered in an in-depth and comprehensive way. The second part of *Technical and Conceptual Skills for Mental Health Professionals* teaches more

advanced conceptual skills needed by clinicians, such as case conceptualization, multicultural competency, and dealing with client crises. While these two books are intended to stand alone, they also can be used in combination. Ideally, learners will first use *Theories of Counseling and Psychotherapy*, developing understanding of the BETA format and the important treatment systems. In a subsequent course, they would use *Technical and Conceptual Skills for Mental Health Professionals*. Their familiarity with the BETA format and the treatment systems would facilitate their learning and accelerate their skill development.

Feel free to be creative and innovative in using this book—and, if you come up with some good ideas, please share them with me at LindaSeligman@aol.com.

Acknowledgments

I received a great deal of personal and professional support in writing this book. In addition, the efforts and contributions of those people who helped me write the first edition of this book still are evident in this edition. I am very grateful for the help I received from the following people:

- Michele Lewis, NCC, consultant, teacher, career counselor, and researcher, used her knowledge of both counseling and research to assist me in obtaining the most up-to-date information on the theories covered in this book.
- Diane Tuininga, MA, school psychologist in private practice and in the Manassas City, Virginia, Public Schools, and doctoral student at George Mason University, also provided high quality and up-to-date research and resources for many of the theories in this book.
- Terri Karol, teacher, editor, and virtual assistant, made sure that the manuscript was in proper order and patiently checked references and terminology. The high quality of her work enhanced the preparation of the book.
- Lynn Field, MA, PhD, LPC, psychotherapist in private practice, made an invaluable contribution to this book with her research and editing skills as well as her clear feedback.
- Carol J. Kaffenberger, MEd, PhD, currently associate professor in the Counseling and Development Program at George Mason University, contributed to the research for this book. She also helped me develop the structure of this book.
- Rosanne Shepler, LPC, trained at the C. G. Jung Institute of New York, and practicing counseling in Vienna, Virginia, offered helpful suggestions and additions to the chapter on Jungian analytical psychology.
- Janice Miner Holden, EdD, professor in the College of Education at the University of North Texas at Denton, carefully reviewed and made knowledgeable additions to the section on transpersonal therapy.
- Nancy Newport, LPC, LMFT, a psychotherapist in private practice in Fairfax, Virginia, and a trainer in brief therapy approaches, reviewed and made valuable suggestions for the chapter on solution-focused brief therapy.
- Francine Shapiro, PhD, who developed eye movement desensitization and reprocessing (EMDR), read and discussed with me the section on EMDR.
- Robert E. Wubbolding, EdD, director of the Center for Reality Therapy in Cincinnati, Ohio, training director at the William Glasser Institute, and faculty member at Xavier University in Cincinnati, reviewed and offered useful suggestions for the chapter on reality therapy.

- Many thanks are due to Kevin Davis, executive editor at Merrill/Prentice Hall, who invited me to write the book and provided much assistance and guidance along the way.
- And, special thanks to the reviewers for their helpful comments and suggestions: William A. Anderson, Minnesota State University, Mankato; James Archer, Jr., University of Florida; Andrew W. Beale, Virginia Commonwealth University; Linda Frye Campbell, University of Georgia; J. Kelly Coker, University of Nevada, Las Vegas; Dorothy L. Espelage, University of Illinois–Urbana-Champaign; Bette Katsekas, University of Southern Maine; Becky Liddle, Auburn University; E. Douglas Norton, University of North Texas, Denton; Aaron Rochlen, University of Texas–Austin; and Stephen R. Wester, University of Wisconsin–Milwaukee.
- Finally, special thanks to my husband, Robert M. Zeskind, who is always there to help me find balance and joy in my life.

Discover the Companion Website Accompanying This Book

The Prentice Hall Companion Website: A Virtual Learning Environment

Technology is a constantly growing and changing aspect of our field that is creating a need for content and resources. To address this emerging need, Prentice Hall has developed an online learning environment for students and professors alike—Companion Websites—to support our textbooks.

In creating a Companion Website, our goal is to build on and enhance what the textbook already offers. For this reason, the content for each user-friendly website is organized by chapter and provides the professor and student with a variety of meaningful resources.

For the Professor—

Every Companion Website integrates **Syllabus Manager**™, an online syllabus creation and management utility.

- **Syllabus Manager**™ provides you, the instructor, with an easy, step-by-step process to create and revise syllabi, with direct links into Companion Website and other online content without having to learn HTML.

- Students may logon to your syllabus during any study session. All they need to know is the web address for the Companion Website and the password you've assigned to your syllabus.

- After you have created a syllabus using **Syllabus Manager**™ students may enter the syllabus for their course section from any point in the Companion Website.

- Clicking on a date, the student is shown the list of activities for the assignment. The activities for each assignment are linked directly to actual content, saving time for students.

- Adding assignments consists of clicking on the desired due date, then filling in the details of the assignment—name of the assignment, instructions, and whether it is a one-time or repeating assignment.

- In addition, links to other activities can be created easily. If the activity is online, a URL can be entered in the space provided, and it will be linked automatically in the final syllabus.

- Your completed syllabus is hosted on our servers, allowing convenient updates from any computer on the Internet. Changes you make to your syllabus are immediately available to your students at their next logon.

For the Student—

Common Companion Website features for students include:

- **Chapter Objectives**—Outline key concepts from the text.
- **Interactive Self-quizzes**—Complete with hints and automatic grading that provide immediate feedback for students. After students submit their answers for the interactive self-quizzes, the Companion Website **Results Reporter** computes a percentage grade, provides a graphic representation of how many questions were answered correctly and incorrectly, and gives a question-by-question analysis of the quiz. Students are given the option to send their quiz to up to four e-mail addresses (professor, teaching assistant, study partner, etc.).
- **Web Destinations**—Links to www sites that relate to chapter content.
- **Message Board**—Virtual bulletin board to post or respond to questions or comments from a national audience.

To take advantage of the many available resources, please visit the *Theories of Counseling and Psychotherapy: Systems, Strategies, and Skills,* Second Edition, Companion Website at

www.prenhall.com/seligman

Research Navigator:
Research Made Simple!

www.ResearchNavigator.com

Merrill Education is pleased to introduce Research Navigator—a one-stop research solution for students that simplifies and streamlines the entire research process. At www.researchnavigator.com, students will find extensive resources to enhance their understanding of the research process so they can effectively complete research assignments. In addition, Research Navigator has three exclusive databases of credible and reliable source content to help students focus their research efforts and begin the research process.

How Will Research Navigator Enhance Your Course?

- Extensive content helps students understand the research process, including writing, Internet research, and citing sources.
- Step-by-step tutorial guides students through the entire research process from selecting a topic to revising a rough draft.
- Research Writing in the Disciplines section details the differences in research across disciplines.
- Three exclusive databases—EBSCO's ContentSelect Academic Journal Database, *The New York Times* Search by Subject Archive, and "Best of the Web" Link Library—allow students to easily find journal articles and sources.

What's the Cost?

A subscription to Research Navigator is $7.50 but is **free** when ordered in conjunction with this textbook. To obtain free passcodes for your students, simply contact your local Merrill/Prentice Hall sales representative, and your representative will send you the Evaluating Online Resource Guide, which contains the code to access Research Navigator as well as tips on how to use Research Navigator and how to evaluate research. To preview the value of this website to your students, please go to www.educatorlearningcenter.com and use the Login Name "Research" and the password "Demo."

About the Author

Linda Seligman is an educator, a writer and researcher, and a licensed psychologist and counselor with many years of clinical experience. Her three professional roles complement each other and are all reflected in this book.

Educator

Dr. Seligman presently is a faculty member at Walden University where she has a joint appointment in Clinical Psychology, Counseling Psychology, and Health Psychology. She also teaches at Johns Hopkins University and George Mason University.

Until 2002, Linda Seligman was a full professor at George Mason University in Fairfax, Virginia, where she was co-director of the doctoral program in education and served as coordinator of the counseling and development program. She taught a broad range of graduate courses and advised master's and doctoral students. She now is a professor emeritus at George Mason University.

Dr. Seligman has lectured throughout the world, primarily on diagnosis and treatment planning using the *Diagnostic and Statistical Manual of Mental Disorders (DSM)*. For many years, she traveled throughout the United States for the American Counseling Association, training clinicians in the use of the *DSM*. She continues to provide training to many schools, universities, businesses, and mental health agencies.

Writer/Researcher

Linda Seligman's primary research interests include diagnosis and treatment planning, the mind-body-spirit connection, counseling people with chronic and life-threatening illnesses, and theories and strategies of counseling and psychotherapy. She has written eleven books, including *Technical and Conceptual Skills for Mental Health Professionals, Selecting Effective Treatments, Diagnosis and Treatment Planning in Counseling,* and *Promoting a Fighting Spirit: Psychotherapy for Cancer Patients, Survivors, and Their Families,* as well as more than 75 professional articles and book chapters. Her book *Diagnosis and Treatment Planning in Counseling,* Third Edition, was a main selection of the Behavioral Sciences Book Club in 2004.

Clinician

A licensed psychologist and licensed professional counselor with a private practice in Fairfax, Virginia, Dr. Seligman specializes in treating people with chronic and life-threatening illnesses. Her practice also includes people who have experienced traumas, those with depression and anxiety, and those with relationship difficulties. Many of the cases in the book are drawn from her clinical experience (with clients' confidentiality protected). In addition, Dr. Seligman has worked in many clinical settings, including hospitals, mental health centers, substance abuse treatment programs, college counseling centers, foster care, and corrections.

Additional Information

Dr. Seligman received the PhD degree in Counseling Psychology from Columbia University. She has completed extensive post-graduate training in areas such as eye movement desensitization and reprocessing, cognitive-behavioral therapy, and complimentary and alternative approaches to medical treatment. Linda Seligman has served as editor of the *Journal of Mental Health Counseling* and as president of the Virginia Association of Mental Health Counselors. In 1986, her colleagues at George Mason University selected her as a Distinguished Professor; and in 1990, the American Mental Health Counselors Association designated her as Researcher of the Year.

Brief Contents

Contents

CHAPTER 19

Behavior Therapy and Cognitive-Behavioral Therapy   365

CHAPTER 20

Reality Therapy   392

Note: Every effort has been made to provide accurate and current Internet information in this book. However, the Internet and information posted on it are constantly changing, so it is inevitable that some of the Internet addresses listed in this textbook will change.

Part One

Providing Effective Counseling and Psychotherapy

CHAPTER 1

Overview of the Book

RATIONALE FOR THIS BOOK

I once overheard a conversation between two graduate students who were completing a course in theories of counseling. "Well," said the first one, "I know all about the theories of Freud and Adler and Rogers and Glasser, and I got an *A* on the exam, but I really don't know what to say or do when I'm with a client."

"I feel the same," said the second student. "Maybe we'll learn what to do in the next class."

Understanding, as well as wise application of theories of counseling and psychotherapy, is essential to the effectiveness of counselors and therapists. Consequently, learning of this information must be meaningful and useful to students. That is the goal of this book.

We focus in this book on systems, strategies, and skills of counseling and psychotherapy in ways that reflect current knowledge about effective treatment, promote intellectual understanding of theories and interventions, and also enhance readers' skill development, confidence, and professional development. By acquiring sound clinical skills, along with a cognitive grasp of treatment approaches, students as well as practicing counselors and psychotherapists will be prepared to help and collaborate with their clients.

1

TREATMENT IS EFFECTIVE

Psychotherapy and counseling are effective! Study after study has conclusively demonstrated the healing power of therapy. In his 1995 research, described as "the most extensive study of psychotherapy on record" (p. 969), Martin Seligman found that 87% of people who reported feeling "very poor" and 92% of those who said they felt "fairly poor" before therapy showed clear improvement by the end of treatment. In addition, this study found that improvement was long lasting and was reflected in changes in presenting concerns as well as improvement in occupational, social, and personal domains. Long-term treatment was generally superior to short-term treatment, especially when treatment was terminated prematurely due to limitations in insurance coverage. This effectiveness study is so important because it was a naturalistic and realistic study, providing information on how treatment is actually performed. This means that it continued until people were satisfied with their progress or left treatment prematurely because they were not getting the help they wanted, could no longer afford treatment, or encountered other reasons to leave treatment. Treatment methods and schedules were not artificially controlled but, rather, allowed for self-correction to improve treatment, encompassed a wide range of specific and integrated treatment approaches, and often addressed multiple concerns.

Lambert and Cattani-Thompson's (1996) review of the literature focused primarily on structured and planned efficacy studies but drew conclusions similar to those of Seligman. They stated, "Counseling is effective. . . . The effects of counseling seem to be relatively lasting. These effects are attained in relatively brief time periods, with the percentage of clients who show substantial improvement increasing as the number of counseling sessions increases" (p. 601).

More recent publications echo and synthesize these positive findings (Gabbard & Lazar, 1997; Howard, 1998; Lambert & Ogles, 2004). Approximately 80% of clients benefit significantly from counseling or psychotherapy. This improvement rate compares favorably to many medical procedures. These positive outcomes tend to endure.

Psychotherapy saves money by reducing the use of psychiatric inpatient services and medical visits and increasing work performance. For example, by extending psychotherapy coverage to military dependents, the United States government has apparently saved $200 million over 3 years through reductions in psychiatric hospitalizations.

Although differences in outcome among various forms of therapy are not strong, this does not detract from the importance of effectively using treatment approaches and strategies. Rather, this reflects the importance of multiple factors in determining treatment impact. Outcome depends on many factors including duration of treatment; therapeutic approaches and strategies; the client, the clinician, and their interaction; and social and environmental factors.

In this postmodern era of counseling and psychotherapy, clinicians and researchers no longer ask about the worth of treatment; that has been conclusively demonstrated. Now they ask more challenging and complex questions. What are the important ingredients of a successful therapeutic relationship? When is psychotherapy most likely to be effective? What are the characteristics of successful clinicians? What client traits, attitudes, and behaviors enhance treatment? How can these characteristics be fostered? What treatment systems and strategies are effective and under what circumstances? What skills are integral to effective counseling? These are only a few of the important questions that today's clinicians are asking that will be addressed in this book.

STRUCTURE OF THIS BOOK

This book is divided into seven parts designed to teach important theories and strategies of counseling and psychotherapy. It also presents information and exercises to help clinicians develop useful skills associated with these treatment approaches.

Part 1—Providing Effective Counseling and Psychotherapy includes chapters 1 and 2. These chapters introduce you to the purpose and structure of this book and present an overview of the elements of successful treatment. In addition to the clinician's theoretical approaches and intervention strategies, these elements include characteristics of the client, the clinician, and their relationship; multicultural counseling competence; and ethical practice. By discussing these factors early in this book, I hope readers will gain an appreciation for the many determinants that can affect treatment outcome and how to maximize their benefits. The key skills taught in part 1 are encouragers, self-assessment, role induction, and the development of a positive therapeutic alliance.

Parts 2 through 6 of this book cover the important treatment systems, strategies, and skills of psychotherapy and counseling. These parts are organized into the following four broad areas of focus:

1. Theories that emphasize the importance of BACKGROUND in treatment
2. Theories that emphasize the importance of EMOTIONS in treatment
3. Theories that emphasize the importance of THOUGHTS in treatment
4. Theories that emphasize the importance of ACTIONS in treatment

These four areas of emphasis can be represented by the acronym BETA (background, emotions, thoughts, actions). Remembering this acronym will make it easier for you to recall these four areas.

The organization of this book differs from the ways in which most books on theories of counseling and psychotherapy are organized. Some present the approaches in chronological order, while others have no clear structure. The grouping of treatment systems according to similarity of emphasis (background, emotions, thoughts, and actions) is designed to promote understanding of the various treatment approaches as well as their similarities and differences. This framework will also facilitate the teaching of theories of counseling and psychotherapy because it emphasizes underlying commonalities.

Nearly all clinicians and treatment approaches pay some attention to background, gathering information on people's histories including their previous emotional difficulties, their cultural and religious context, their family of origin, their important relationships, and their academic and employment experiences. However, clinicians advocating treatment approaches presented in **Part 2—Treatment Systems Emphasizing Background and Context** believe that people's early childhood years provide the key to their subsequent development. These approaches pay considerable attention to eliciting and promoting understanding of the nature and impact people's early experiences have had on them. For the theoreticians considered in part 2, this process is necessary to effect positive change. Treatment approaches presented in part 2 include:

- Freudian psychoanalysis
- Adler's individual psychology
- Jungian analytical psychology

- Freudian revisionists—Other developmental/psychodynamic (neo- and post-Freudian) approaches to treatment, including object relations theory as well as the theories of Karen Horney, Melanie Klein, Anna Freud, Helene Deutsch, Harry Stack Sullivan, and others
- Brief psychodynamic psychotherapy

The key skills taught in part 2 are widely used by clinicians with the above theoretical orientations, although most of these skills also are widely used by clinicians emphasizing other treatment approaches. These skills include asking effective questions; gathering background information; deepening understanding of background via lifelines and earliest recollections; identifying focal concerns; and making tentative interpretations.

Again, nearly all treatment approaches attend to clients' feelings. However, the humanistic and phenomenological treatment approaches covered in **Part 3—Treatment Systems Emphasizing Emotions and Sensations** take the stance that becoming aware of emotions and expressing them appropriately is essential to healing. Treatment systems presented in part 3 include:

- Carl Rogers's person-centered counseling
- Existential therapy
- Fritz Perls's Gestalt therapy
- Narrative, constructivist, and feminist therapies
- Some attention also will be paid to transactional analysis and transpersonal psychotherapy.

Key skills covered in part 3 include assessing emotions, communicating empathy, reflecting meaning and feeling, making helpful self-disclosures, using dreams and imagery in treatment, and promoting values clarification.

Part 4—Treatment Systems Emphasizing Thoughts focuses on approaches that emphasize the importance of cognitions in determining emotional well-being. These treatment systems include:

- Aaron Beck's cognitive therapy
- Albert Ellis's rational emotive behavior therapy
- Attention also is paid to Francine Shapiro's eye movement desensitization and reprocessing as well as to other innovative approaches emphasizing thoughts.

Key skills presented in part 4 include analysis and modification of dysfunctional cognitions, use of homework with clients, rational emotive imagery, and anchoring. These skills are used by a broad range of clinicians but are especially important to those advocating cognitive approaches.

Part 5—Treatment Systems Emphasizing Actions addresses theories emphasizing the importance of actions and behavioral change strategies. Approaches presented here include:

- Behavior therapy
- Cognitive-behavioral therapy
- Reality therapy
- Solution-focused brief therapy

Key skills included in part 5 are planning and implementing behavioral change, systematic desensitization, caring confrontation, and goal setting.

Parts 2 through 5 each begin with an introductory chapter providing an overview of the common focus (background, emotions, thoughts, or actions) discussed in that section. Individual chapters then follow, focusing on each of the treatment theories sharing that common focus. Discussion of each treatment approach is organized according to the following outline:

- Introduction to the theory of counseling or psychotherapy
- Information on the people who developed or contributed greatly to its development
- Overview of the evolution of the theory
- Important theoretical concepts
- The treatment process, including typical goals, the nature of the therapeutic alliance, and both general strategies associated with this treatment approach (basic strategies consistently used during treatment) and specific strategies (associated with the approach but used only with particular problems or clients)
- Application of the theoretical approach, including information on the multicultural, diagnostic, and other groups for which its use is indicated
- Information on current use of the approach
- Evaluation of the treatment approach, including both research and theoretical information on its limitations, strengths, and contributions
- Presentation of one or two skills associated with the treatment approach
- Illustration of the use of this treatment approach with a case study (a member of the Diaz family, introduced later in this chapter)
- Exercises designed to promote learning and application of the treatment system, including large-group (in-class), small-group, and individual activities
- Summary of the chapter
- Recommended readings and Internet resources

Research shows that most clinicians today do not adhere strictly to only one treatment approach but instead describe the treatment they provide as primarily integrated or eclectic. **Part 6—Integrated and Eclectic Treatment Systems** discusses the nature, strengths, and shortcomings of such approaches and reviews important efforts to develop systematic eclectic and integrated approaches. This includes Arnold Lazarus's multimodal therapy and Allen Ivey and Sandra Rigazio-Digilio's developmental counseling and therapy, as well as other integrated and eclectic treatment approaches. Skill development focuses on treatment planning and use of the BASIC I.D. assessment format of multimodal therapy. Although part 6 considers a range of treatment approaches, the structure of its chapters generally follows the format previously outlined.

Finally, **Part 7—Solidifying Understanding of Treatment Systems** helps readers to solidify and clarify their understanding of theories of counseling and psychotherapy. Tables in part 7 facilitate structured comparisons of the major treatment approaches discussed in this book. A questionnaire helps readers identify their own preferred styles of treatment. The key skill covered is termination of the treatment process.

EXERCISES TO PROMOTE LEARNING

As mentioned previously, I include exercises at the end of each chapter to help readers learn more about treatment systems, strategies, and skills. To maximize flexibility and ease of use, this book includes three categories of exercises: those for large groups or an entire class, those for small groups (generally four participants), and those for individuals. The formats for the exercises vary: Some entail discussion and analysis, some promote skill development via role playing, and others call for written responses. The following instructions, along with information provided throughout this book, will help readers use these exercises.

Large-Group Exercises: General Instructions

The large-group exercises have been designed for use in a classroom or with a group of at least five people. They are crafted to help readers understand and process new material, share ideas, and discuss clinical problems and thought-provoking questions. Although these exercises are generally self-explanatory, participants will benefit from the involvement of a teacher or a leader who structures and guides the discussion.

Small-Group Exercises: General Instructions

Small-group exercises are designed for groups of four students or participants, usually divided into two dyads. These exercises afford participants an opportunity to practice and improve their skills. Because group members need to develop rapport with one another and become comfortable about sharing feedback, the composition of the small groups should change no more than once, if at all, during a semester or quarter. Information is provided below and in subsequent chapters on helpful ways to give and receive feedback and promote a supportive learning environment in small groups. When planning the small group exercises, time should be allowed, if possible, for each member to assume both client and clinician roles in the exercise.

Giving and Receiving Feedback   To facilitate learning, group members should tape-record all small-group exercises, including both their role plays and the feedback they receive from other members. People sometimes have difficulty absorbing feedback. Taping allows participants to review the exercises later and think about ways to improve their skills. Videotaped recordings are ideal because they provide information on nonverbal communications. However, audiotaping is a satisfactory substitute if logistics prevent videotaping.

While two members of the group are engaged in a simulated counseling session, the other two should observe and take notes so that they can provide clear and specific feedback. One of the two observers should also serve as time-keeper, making sure that the exercise is completed in the allotted time. Once the role play has finished, the person in the clinician role should initiate the feedback process by assessing his or her own performance, focusing on strengths as well as areas for improvement. Feedback from the person in the client role should come next. Finally, the two observers should provide their feedback.

Feedback is most helpful if it is specific and constructive, focusing on behaviors. Strengths should be emphasized first and then suggestions can be made for ways to address weaknesses. People receiving feedback should have an opportunity to share their reactions to the feedback and obtain clarification if needed. The process should be helpful and promote growth and learning; it should never make people feel attacked or humiliated.

Individual Exercises: General Instructions

The individual exercises are designed to promote introspection and self-awareness. Because they require considerable self-disclosure, I recommend that participants have the right to maintain the privacy of their responses to these exercises. However, if instructors decide to have people share their responses to these exercises or want to review written replies to the individual exercises, they should make their intentions clear before participants complete the exercises so that they can decide how much to share about themselves. Pass/fail rather than letter grades are recommended if people's responses to the individual exercises are graded; this should facilitate openness and promote personal and professional growth.

Readers will probably benefit most from the individual exercises if they keep their responses in a journal or a notebook. In this way, they will have a record of their ideas and can review them throughout their training. Looking back at these journal entries in future years is likely to be interesting and enlightening, giving readers the opportunity to see how their thoughts and perceptions have evolved over time.

CASE STUDIES AND EXAMPLES

Because this book promotes both theoretical understanding and skill development, extensive clinical examples are provided. Readers will become acquainted with many clients, via this book, representing diverse backgrounds in terms of age, gender, socioeconomic status, culture and ethnicity, sexual orientation, and other variables.

The clients that will become most familiar to readers are the Diaz family, used at the end of each chapter to illustrate an aspect of the treatment approach discussed in that chapter. I use a three-person family to illustrate the treatment approaches so that readers can become familiar with the application of interventions to both genders, to adults and children, and to people of different cultural groups. This family includes Edie Diaz, her husband Roberto, and their daughter Ava. Family members present a range of concerns. However, many avenues are available to help them improve their lives, as the case examples will illustrate. By studying these examples, readers will learn to apply the systems, strategies, and skills presented in the chapters.

Edie Diaz

Edie Diaz initiated the family's request for treatment. Now age 38, she is a white Jewish woman. She was born in Brooklyn, New York, and spent her early years living with her biological parents and older sister. Her father was an accountant, and initially her mother stayed at home with the children. When Edie was four, her mother discovered that Edie's father was having an extramarital affair and insisted on a divorce. At that point, the father, who had been very close to Edie, withdrew from the family.

After her parents separated, Edie's mother found employment as a sales clerk in a department store to support her family and, with her two daughters, moved in with her parents. Edie's maternal grandparents cared for the children while their mother worked. The grandmother resented her caretaker role and was very critical of the children, especially Edie. The grandfather abused both Edie and her sister. Both grandparents are now deceased, but Edie has clear memories of the mistreatment she received and continues to experience strong resentment toward her grandparents.

When Edie was 10 years old, she was diagnosed with cancer. She had to undergo chemotherapy, which caused her to lose her hair and gain weight. Teasing from her classmates contributed to her already low self-esteem. However, a positive aspect of her illness was her increased involvement with her father. He visited her regularly in the hospital, brought her gifts, and gave her a sense of family once again. Edie and her father have continued to have contact and they presently see each other at least once a month.

Although Edie's prognosis for recovery from cancer was poor, she has been in good health since her treatment. However, her treatment raised questions about whether she could ever become pregnant and created a sense of anxiety and foreboding that never left her.

When Edie was 14, her mother remarried. Edie described her stepfather as physically and emotionally abusive. He yelled at the children, told them they were worthless, and frequently hit them. Edie dealt with this by avoiding her stepfather as much as possible. She was afraid to complain to her mother about the stepfather's behavior, thinking that her mother would become angry and punish her.

Edie continued to live with her mother and stepfather until she was 18. She had always been a good student and was able to earn a college scholarship. After college, she received a master's degree in library science and worked as a librarian until Ava's birth.

Edie had not dated much before she met Roberto. He had installed a computer system in the library where she worked and then asked Edie out for lunch. After dating for six months, Roberto proposed marriage, and Edie accepted. They were married when Edie was 24 and Roberto 28. Although their relationship was initially very close, with many shared interests and activities, their lengthy efforts to conceive a child had an adverse effect on the marriage. Finally, after a year of infertility treatments, Edie became pregnant and then gave birth to Ava. Despite subsequent fertility treatments, she has not been able to become pregnant a second time, a source of great sadness to her.

Edie reported marital and emotional difficulties since her initial efforts to become pregnant. When Ava was born, Edie left her job to care for her child. She missed her rewarding and successful career but felt that she had to do everything in her power to safeguard her only child. Edie reported long-standing and increasing symptoms of sadness, loneliness, and discouragement. Since her marriage, she has gained more than 50 pounds and finds little joy or intimacy in her relationship with Roberto. Finally, last year when Ava was 9, Edie resumed work as a librarian. However, she is now experiencing strong feelings of self-doubt, guilt, and worry about Ava.

Edie has maintained contact with her mother and sister, as well as with her father. Her mother is still married to the stepfather who mistreated Edie. She finds it painful to be in his presence and never lets Ava spend time alone with him. Edie and her sister communicate frequently by e-mail but see little of each other because of geographic distance. Her sister has had a series of unrewarding relationships with men and now has an intimate relationship with a woman—her best relationship so far.

Roberto Diaz

Roberto's background is very different from Edie's. Roberto's grandparents and parents came to the United States from Puerto Rico. Roberto was born in New York City, the fifth of eight children. Although he always had frequent contact with both his mother and father, his parents separated when he was young. Nevertheless, he describes his family as warm and loving, always ready to help.

Roberto's neighborhood was rough, and he became involved with street gangs at an early age. His father taught him to defend himself with both fists and weapons. Because he was tall and stocky and had few fears, Roberto became a leader among his peers.

Roberto had little interest in school, preferring to teach himself. When he was 17, he left school to learn about computers. He received a GED as well as some specialized training in computers and now has a job he enjoys, installing Internet systems. He takes great pride in his abilities and his success in earning a good income for his family.

Roberto had two brief marriages and many relationships before he met Edie. He was impressed by her intelligence, stability, and caring and hoped that by marrying her he would find the committed and loving relationship he was seeking. He stated that, although he was very attached to his family, he was disheartened by Edie's long period of unhappiness. He reported that they were rarely intimate and no longer had a rewarding relationship. He told the therapist that he was "almost at the end of his rope" and that Edie had better make some changes fast if this marriage were to continue. At age 42, he was eager to get his life back on track.

Ava Diaz

Ava, age 10, is a tall girl who resembles her father both physically and temperamentally. She has recently been misbehaving at school, and her teacher describes her as a bully. A good student, Ava has excelled in English and history but seems to be losing interest in school. She has one close friend in the neighborhood but otherwise socializes with a wide variety of children.

Through this book, you will learn more about the Diaz family and their strengths and difficulties. You will also learn effective ways to help Edie, Roberto, and Ava, as well as your own clients.

DEVELOPMENT OF THEORIES OF COUNSELING AND PSYCHOTHERAPY

Before we begin to consider theories of counseling and psychotherapy, we pave the way by providing some information on the history and nature of these approaches. Prior to the late 19th century, people had little understanding of emotional difficulties and mental disorders. Many people with severe symptoms were forcibly confined in institutions and exposed to largely ineffective treatments while those with mild or moderate difficulties typically received no professional help.

The development of psychodynamic approaches to psychotherapy, spearheaded by the work of Sigmund Freud, led to the emergence of what has been called the first force of psychotherapy (Ivey, Ivey, & Simek-Morgan, 1997). Viewing past experiences as the source of people's present emotional difficulties and emphasizing unconscious processes and long-term treatment, psychodynamic approaches provided a solid foundation for the field of psychotherapy, but that approach had clear limitations.

The research and practice of B. F. Skinner as well as more modern theorists such as Albert Ellis, Aaron Beck, William Glasser, and Donald Meichenbaum led to the emergence of the second force: cognitive and behavioral theories and interventions. Behavioral treatment approaches, widely used in the 1970s, have been integrated with cognitive approaches, developed primarily in the 1980s, leading to the cognitive-behavioral approaches that received considerable attention and empirical support in the 1990s. Cognitive and behavioral treatment systems emphasize the influence of thoughts and actions on emotions. They use interventions that generally focus on the present and seek to minimize dysfunctional cognitions and behaviors while replacing them with more helpful and positive thoughts and actions.

Carl Rogers's innovative work emerged in the 1960s and led to the development of the third force, existential-humanistic psychotherapy. The work of Fritz Perls, Viktor Frankl, and others contributed to this force, which emphasizes the importance of emotions and sensations and of people taking charge of and finding meaning in their own lives. These approaches also drew attention to the importance of the therapeutic alliance.

4th Force

Now, at the beginning of the 21st century, clinicians are entering the era of the fourth force. Elements of first-, second-, and third-force treatment approaches are integrated into a comprehensive and holistic effort to understand people as fully as possible. Clinicians' awareness and understanding of gender, culture, age, and other aspects of people facilitate development of positive therapeutic relationships and effective treatment plans. Joining with clients and grasping their multiple perspectives of themselves and their world are essential to today's clinicians. Networking and collaboration with other mental health professionals, providers of community resources, and important people in clients' lives are now viewed as integral to treatment. Theories of counseling and psychotherapy, as well as their implementation, have changed in response to the fourth force. New approaches such as eye movement desensitization and reprocessing and narrative therapy provide powerful ways to understand people's experiences more fully and help them play an active and powerful role in changing their emotions and perceptions.

UNDERSTANDING THEORIES OF COUNSELING AND PSYCHOTHERAPY

Theories of counseling and psychotherapy also have been referred to as treatment systems, treatment theories, treatment approaches, and theories of change, as well as by other terms. In this book, these terms will be used interchangeably to refer to an integrated set of concepts that provide explanations for and descriptions of:

- Stages, patterns, and important factors in people's emotional development
- Healthy emotional development, as well as problematic or abnormal emotional development
- How to help people develop in positive ways and reduce symptoms that are distressing and/or cause impairment in functioning
- The role of the clinician and how that role contributes to treatment
- Strategies for putting the theory into practice (e.g., identifying and modifying cognitive distortions, reflecting feelings, developing a clear plan for behavioral change)
- Specific skills or interventions that can enhance implementation of the treatment approach (e.g., use of earliest recollections, analysis of dreams, diaphragmatic breathing)
- Information on people who are likely to benefit from this treatment approach; this information might include their ages, cultural background, symptoms, mental disorders, treatment settings, and other factors

According to Stuart (1998), treatment approaches that have proven their value over time are theoretically "robust, . . . reasonably well validated . . . and have clearly defined pragmatic roles in intervention practice" (p. 7). According to Hansen, Stevic, and Warner (1986), an effective theory is also "clear, easily understood, and communicable . . . coherent and not contradictory . . . comprehensive, encompassing explanations for a wide variety of phenomena . . . explicit, generating research" (p. 356). Effective theories are grounded in an understanding of human development. They provide a framework for gathering and organizing information and exploring personality. They present a theory of development and change that helps us understand people and their concerns. They provide steps and interventions that encourage learning and growth and that allow for evaluation of progress and modification of treatment plans if needed. They provide reassurance and direction. They lend themselves to development of testable hypotheses that can be investigated to determine the validity and usefulness of the approach and they promote further study and improvement of the treatment process.

Ingredients in Positive Change

Although more than 350 forms of counseling and psychotherapy have been identified and described (Corsini & Wedding, 1995), successful treatments have common ingredients that promote change:

- A therapeutic relationship characterized by collaboration, trust, mutual investment in the therapeutic process, shared respect, genuineness, positive emotional feelings, and a holistic understanding of clients and their backgrounds and environments
- A safe, supportive, and healing context
- Goals and a sense of direction, preferably explicit but sometimes implicit
- A shared understanding between clinicians and clients about the nature of the problems and concerns to be addressed in treatment and the change processes that will be used to resolve them
- Therapeutic learning, typically including feedback and corrective experiences
- Encouragement of self-awareness and insight
- Improvement in clients' ability to identify, express constructively, and modify their emotions
- Improvement in clients' ability to identify, assess the validity of, and modify their thoughts
- Improvement in clients' ability to assess and change dysfunctional behaviors as well as acquire new and more effective behaviors that promote coping, impulse control, sound relationships, and good emotional and physical health

Successful treatment is reflected in attitudinal shifts. According to Weissmark and Giacomo (1998), these include "significant changes from beginning to end of treatment in the patients' assessments from external to internal, from reactive to selective, and from unconditional to conditional" (p. 107). Successful treatment promotes realistic hope and optimism as well as feelings of mastery and self-efficacy (Kleinke, 1994).

UNDERSTANDING MENTAL HEALTH

Just as it is important for clinicians to be aware of the breadth of factors in positive change as a backdrop to studying systems and strategies of treatment, so is it useful for them to have a concept of mental health. Witmer and Sweeney (1992) advanced a holistic model for optimal health and functioning that delineates five important aspects of people's lives:

- Spirituality (values, beliefs, ethics, purpose and direction, optimism, inner peace)
- Self-regulation (sense of worth, mastery of one's own life, spontaneity and emotional responsiveness, sense of humor, creativity, awareness of reality, physical health)
- Work (including paid employment, volunteer experiences, child rearing, homemaking, and education) that provides psychological, social, and other rewards
- Friendship (positive interpersonal relationships and social supports that provide rewarding activities and interactions)
- Love (intimate, trusting, sharing, and cooperative long-term relationships)

type chart

These five areas serve as a map of healthy functioning. More important, for purposes of this book, they delineate areas for assessment. Deficits in any of these five areas are likely to impair functioning, cause distress, require help, and be an appropriate focus for treatment. Knowledge of treatment systems, strategies, and skills enable clinicians to help their clients make changes that will move them toward healthy functioning.

IMPORTANCE OF UNDERSTANDING THEORIES OF COUNSELING AND PSYCHOTHERAPY

This book reviews those systems of counseling and psychotherapy that should be part of the repertoire of today's clinicians. Whether clinicians describe themselves as eclectic, as do more than 75% of current therapists (Walborn, 1996), or affiliate with a particular theoretical model, these treatment approaches all shed light on people's challenges and change processes and provide skills that promote emotional health. Clinicians no longer seek the one right theory but, rather, the concepts and skills they need to form a sound therapeutic alliance with clients and develop treatment plans that are likely to ameliorate difficulties and improve growth and development.

But systems and strategies of counseling and psychotherapy are only part of the treatment process. Current research suggests that treatment approaches and interventions are just one factor in producing change. Miller, Duncan, and Hubble (1997) found that clients attributed 40% of the change they experienced in treatment to *extratherapeutic factors* (including people's internal resources and events in their lives), 30% to the *therapist-client relationship*, 15% to particular *techniques and interventions*, and 15% percent to their *hope and expectation of positive change*.

Several important points emerge from this finding. First, clinicians may not be as powerful as they might think; clients' experiences and inner resources seem to be the most powerful factor in change. Consequently, clinicians must take the time to know and understand their clients, to grasp their perspectives on the world, to hear their stories, and to learn about their lives so that the clinicians can help them to make the most of those extratherapeutic factors. Second, the therapeutic alliance is of great importance. Promoting a positive relationship characterized by conditions and interactions that encourage desired changes can make a significant difference in the success of the treatment process. Chapter 2 provides more information on the importance of the client, the clinician, and their alliance in the success of the treatment process.

Observing that interventions represent only 15% of the factors contributing to change, readers may be tempted to ask, "Why, then, pay so much attention to learning treatment systems and strategies?" In reality, 60% or more of client change can be attributed to treatment approaches. In addition to the direct influence of the approach (15%), the skills and strategies of the clinician are largely responsible for the development of the therapeutic alliance (30% of the source of change) and for engendering hope and positive expectations in clients (15% of the source of change). Furthermore, counseling and psychotherapy can also make a difference in people's ability to make positive use of extratherapeutic factors such as support systems, community resources, and educational programs. Thus, treatment systems and strategies are important not only for their direct impact on symptoms and problems but also for their indirect impact on the treatment alliance as well as on client attitudes and behaviors associated with successful treatment.

SKILL DEVELOPMENT AND EXERCISES: ENCOURAGERS

One of the most important and challenging roles of the clinician is facilitating client self-disclosure: encouraging people to talk about their perceptions of themselves; their background, thoughts, emotions, and actions; the important people in their lives; their concerns and joys; and their hopes. Even people who are self-referred for treatment may be reluctant to talk at length about themselves. They may feel uncomfortable and awkward in the treatment setting, mistrust the clinician, worry about being judged or criticized, lack facility in talking about themselves, or simply need coaching on how to use their sessions productively. Some beginning clinicians have a misconception that most clients will immediately share personal and intimate details of their lives. Often, however, people approach treatment cautiously and need help in talking about themselves.

In this first Skill Development section of the book, we introduce the use of encouragers. These basic skills are invaluable in helping clinicians maintain a productive dialog with their clients and promote client self-expression. We focus here on four encouragers: minimal encouragers, restatement, paraphrase, and summarization.

Skilled clinicians can review transcripts of their sessions and not only explain their goals for each session but also clarify the purpose of each intervention they made. Without such a clear vision, encouragers can simply fill up air space and promote conversation. When used deliberately and with care, however, encouragers can focus communication, facilitate assessment, promote client self-awareness, and maximize the benefits of treatment. Encouragers are not designed to modify or interpret client's words but only to focus and promote client self-disclosure and self-exploration.

Minimal Encouragers

Minimal encouragers are well named; they are brief interventions in which clinicians demonstrate that they are listening, encourage clients to keep talking, and perhaps channel the clients' words. When using minimal encouragers, clinicians deliberately maintain a low profile; they want to focus on the client and do not want their interventions to disrupt or intrude on the process.

The following are three types of minimal encouragers:

1. *Umm-hmm.* This is the classic minimal encourager, a supportive murmur from the clinician accompanied by a nod of the head and an attentive posture. If clients are talking about themselves easily and using their time productively, this may be all they need to continue that process.

2. *Repetition of a word.* Here, the clinician repeats or underscores a client's spoken word or phrase. This narrows the client's attention and generally encourages the client to elaborate further. Although this intervention is very brief, it can have a considerable impact on the direction of treatment, as the following examples show.

Example A
Client: I went home for the holidays and had quite a surprise.
Clinician: You went home?
Client: Yes, I still think of my parents' house as my home. It meant a great deal to me and to them to spend the holidays together, so I braved the Thanksgiving Day traffic and drove down to see them. Nothing could have kept me away.

Example B

Client: I went home for the holidays and had quite a surprise.

Clinician: A surprise?

Client: Yes, my brother, the great family man, is getting a divorce. That should change my parents' opinion of him.

Each dialog provides important information about the client's values and suggests a useful focus of treatment. However, the conversations go in different directions as a result of the minimal encouragers.

3. *How so?* Although this brief phrase is really a question, it functions like a minimal encourager in that it prompts the client to hone in on a particular point and explore it in greater depth, as the following example (a continuation of the previous dialog) shows.

Client: That should change my parents' opinion of my brother.

Clinician: How so?

Client: They've always seen him as the good son; he went to college, he got married, he had kids. Just because I haven't gotten married and had kids doesn't mean I'm not as good as he is. Maybe they'll finally appreciate me.

Restatement

Restatement involves repeating or underscoring a longer phrase or sentence that the client has spoken. It can be thought of as an expanded version of a minimal encourager and serves the same purpose: focusing the client's attention and promoting self-expression without adding to, changing, or interpreting the client's words.

In the following example, the client talks about both himself and his brother. Restatement is used to encourage the client to focus on himself.

Client: I've always resented my brother. He got it all . . . good looks, attention from my parents, girlfriends, athletic skills, and brains too. I tried hard to succeed. But whatever I did, my brother did better.

Clinician: You tried really hard to succeed.

Client: Yes, I figured out how to please people and then tried to do it—get good grades for my parents, volunteer in class for my teachers, look good for the girls. But somehow it never worked out for me like it did for my brother.

Clinician: Never worked out for you?

Client: No, I was a mediocre student and a social loser. Nobody noticed me.

Paraphrase

In a paraphrase, clinicians feed back to clients the essence of what they have said. Although clinicians use different words from those of the client, they do not seek to interpret, analyze, or add depth to a client's statement. Rather, they simply give clients an opportunity to hear what they have said. Paraphrases let clients know that the clinician is listening and understanding them, and encourage clients to keep talking. The following is a series of paraphrases used with the previous client.

Client: Maybe they'll finally appreciate me.

Clinician: You're hoping your parents will see you in a more positive light.

Client: Yes, I have good relationships now, I have a respectable job, I vote; but just because I'm not married, they act like I'm a failure.

Clinician: So in your eyes you have really accomplished something, even though your parents seem to have a different viewpoint.

Client: I *have* accomplished something. I really know how to reach children, even the tough ones who act like they couldn't care less.

Clinician: Your success as a teacher is very important to you.

Summarization

A summarization pulls together and synthesizes a group of client statements. Summarizations are useful for focusing a session, bringing closure to a topic, wrapping up a session, and helping clients reflect on what they have said. Like paraphrases, summarizations are not interpretive or analytical but simply feed back in a concise and coherent way what clients have said.

The following is an example of a summary statement that is used to focus a session.

Clinician: You've talked about many things so far in today's session—your relationships with your parents, your competitive feelings toward your brother, your wish for recognition, and your concern about being single. Sounds like you have quite a few concerns on your mind. Which one of these issues would you like to be our initial focus?

Mastering encouragers may seem simple. However, these interventions are powerful. They can contribute a great deal to the development of rapport in the session and to the overall direction and value of treatment.

Exercise in the Use of Encouragers

Each participant should have a partner for this exercise. I suggest you pair with someone you do not know well. In that way, you will be sharing new information as is usually done in an initial counseling or psychotherapy session. Decide who will assume the client role first; the other person will initially assume the clinician role. If time allows after you have completed all steps of the exercise, switch roles and follow the steps in the exercise again.

- The task of the person in the clinician role is to initiate and develop a discussion with the person in the client role about that person's professional role (e.g., student, practicing clinician, worker in another field). The clinician should make thoughtful use of encouragers to promote and develop the discussion, which should last about five minutes.
- The person in the client role should be reasonably cooperative but should not make the clinician's job too easy! Avoid lengthy monologues. Rather, allow the clinician the opportunity to prompt and guide your description of your professional role.
- Following this role play, the two participants should spend 5–10 minutes discussing the following questions:
  - What was the "client's" experience of that role?
  - What was the "clinician's" experience of that role?

- How would the clinician describe his or her use of encouragers? For example, did they flow smoothly or feel awkward? Did they seem to enhance or detract from the conversation?
- How would the client describe the clinician's use of encouragers?
- What does each participant view as the strengths of this simulated counseling interview?
- What suggestions does each participant have for improving the interview and increasing personal comfort, ease of communication, and amount and depth of information shared?

SUMMARY

This chapter provided an overview of the book, including information on the BETA framework, the structure of each chapter, ways to use the exercises for greatest benefit, and a description of the three clients who will be used for many of the case illustrations. In addition, we considered the development of theories of counseling and psychotherapy, the elements of a useful theory, a model for mental health, and some of the treatment ingredients that facilitate positive change. The first skill development section in the book focused on use of encouragers. An exercise offered an opportunity for people to practice and receive feedback on their use of encouragers.

CHAPTER 2

Contexts of Effective Treatment

A s you learned in chapter 1, skillful application of appropriate treatment approaches and intervention strategies is a requisite of effective treatment. However, many other factors also have a strong relationship to treatment outcome. This chapter focuses on many of those factors, including the following:

- Characteristics of successful clients
- The therapeutic alliance
- Essential conditions of effective therapeutic relationships
- The training, skills, and experience of effective clinicians
- Personal and professional characteristics of the clinician
- Treatment setting
- Ethical guidelines and standards

The final section of this chapter focuses on self-assessment and the important clinical skills of role induction and developing a positive therapeutic alliance.

CHARACTERISTICS OF SUCCESSFUL CLIENTS

Both the personal qualities and the backgrounds of clients help determine the success of their treatment. Clinicians can maximize the positive influence of these factors in three ways:

- First, they need to be aware of those client characteristics that are likely to correlate with therapeutic outcome.
- Second, they need an in-depth understanding of each client, paying attention to that person's history; family composition and interactions; culture, religion and spirituality; relationships; socioeconomic status; physical health; abilities; and other relevant attributes. This understanding helps clinicians view the world through their clients' eyes and determine interventions that are likely to be well received and effective.
- Finally, clinicians can instill or develop in clients those qualities that are typically associated with a positive therapeutic outcome—in a sense, socializing the person to treatment (Walborn, 1996). This process, called role induction, will be discussed later in this chapter.

The client's personality understandably plays a significant role in determining treatment outcome (Asay & Lambert, 1999). The following client characteristics bear a particularly strong relationship to outcome:

Maturity   People whose lives are reasonably well-organized and who are responsible and knowledgeable about the world seem better able to engage in productive treatment than people who lack these characteristics (Asay & Lambert, 1999). Clients who are mature also are more likely to make a commitment to treatment and to follow through on agreed upon steps to help themselves.

Capacity for Relationships   Interpersonal qualities such as good communication skills, an ability to invest energy and caring in personal relationships, and the capacity to form stable and close relationships are important client strengths (Gelso & Carter, 1985). Kivlighan, Patton, and Foote (1998) suggest that "the client's ability to form relationships (attachment style) moderates the relationship between counseling experience and working alliance" (p. 274). They describe those clients who can form positive relationships as having a "need for intimacy, trust in others, and freedom from the fear of abandonment." People who have a good capacity to develop relationships outside of the treatment setting are more likely to collaborate with the clinician in the development of a positive therapeutic alliance (Joyce & Piper, 1998). In addition, clients who can use role models, support, and the caring of others to help themselves are likely to benefit from treatment.

Ability to Establish Appropriate Interpersonal Boundaries   An important aspect of people's capacity for relationships is the boundaries they establish in those relationships. People who have good self-esteem and a sense of control over their lives are likely to establish appropriate boundaries both within and outside of the therapeutic relationship. On the other hand, people who have inordinate needs for affiliation may seek an overinvolved and dependent relationship with the clinician, while people who have extreme needs for separateness and independence may reject the clinician's social influence and guidance.

High reactance in clients is a personality variable that is particularly likely to interfere with the establishment of appropriate boundaries in the therapeutic relationship. People who are high in reactance typically have strong impulses or motivation to regain lost or threatened freedom and resist any suggestions or interventions that are perceived as curtailing that freedom. Strong needs for independence, control, autonomy, and dominance also are associated with high levels of reactance. According to Seibel and Dowd (1999), "Our results indicate that psychological reactance is associated with a host of in-session behaviors that may be inimical to the course and outcome of therapy. These can be summarized as client behaviors that attempt to control and direct the amount of therapeutic or interpersonal influence" (p. 377).

Introspection and Psychological-Mindedness   People who are accustomed to looking within themselves and thinking in insightful ways about people and relationships are more likely to continue in treatment and have better outcomes (McCallum, Piper, & Joyce, 1992). The process of self-examination usually associated with counseling and psychotherapy will probably be comfortable and rewarding for them.

High Frustration Tolerance   People who have reasonably good ego strength, are patient, can tolerate ambiguity, and delay gratification probably are good candidates for psychotherapy. On the other hand, people who tend to be impulsive and have a high need for novelty and stimulation often leave treatment prematurely and may not benefit substantially from that process (Wingerson et al., 1993).

Role of the Client

Both pretreatment characteristics, such as those just reviewed, and those qualities that clients manifest in treatment have a strong impact on outcome. The following within-session client behaviors and attitudes play an important part in the treatment process.

Motivation   The term *motivation* is a broad one that clinicians use to describe a range of client behaviors associated with readiness for treatment and ability to engage productively in that process (Orlinsky, Grawe, & Parks, 1994). Particularly important aspects of client motivation include engagement in and cooperation with treatment and a willingness to self-disclose, confront problems, put forth effort to change, and, if necessary, experience some temporary anxiety and discomfort in the hope of eventual benefit (Hanna & Ritchie, 1995; Orlinsky et al., 1994; Paulson, Truscott, & Stuart, 1999). Other signs of strong client motivation include low levels of defensiveness and a belief that treatment is necessary and important. Not surprisingly, self-referred clients are less likely to terminate treatment prematurely than are clients referred by others.

Positive but Realistic Expectations for Treatment   People who have a clear and accurate understanding of psychotherapy and its strengths and limitations, and who expect to benefit from that process, are more likely to have successful treatment outcomes (Sabourin, Gendreau, & Frenette, 1987; Silverman & Beech, 1979). Pretreatment preparation of clients via role induction (discussed later in this chapter) can make a considerable difference in people's expectations for treatment and correspondingly in their commitment to treatment, willingness to self-disclose, and alliance with the clinician (Acosta, Yamamoto, Evans, & Skilbeck, 1983; Lawe, Horne, & Taylor, 1983). Similarly, effective engagement of the client in the very first session has been shown to make a positive contribution to successful treatment (Odell & Quinn, 1998).

Full Participation in Treatment   Clients who succeed in treatment freely present their concerns, collaborate with the clinician in a mutual endeavor, and take steps to improve their lives. They develop a problem-solving attitude and maintain positive expectations of change (Sexton & Whiston, 1991). They recognize that at least some of their difficulties come from within themselves and believe they have the power to improve their situation. They view the need for personal change as significant and can identify a specific problem (Lambert & Cattani-Thompson, 1996). According to Asay and Lambert (1999), "Clients who do better in psychotherapy and maintain treatment gains believe that the changes made in therapy were primarily a result of their own efforts" (p. 32). These people probably feel empowered as a result of their treatment successes and are optimistic that they can continue to make positive changes and choices, even after treatment has ended.

Other Characteristics   Some research has found a positive correlation of client intelligence, education, socioeconomic level, and initial symptoms of depression or anxiety with likelihood of positive outcome. Client gender and age seem unrelated to outcome.

Client Diversity

The diversity of people seeking counseling has increased enormously in the past 40 years. During the 1960s, most people seeking treatment came from middle-class and majority cultural backgrounds. The professional literature paid little attention to the needs of people who did not fit that mold. By the 1970s, most clinicians were aware of the need to adapt treatment to the ethnic and cultural backgrounds of their clients. Clinicians became more aware of their own biases and the importance of respecting clients' values. However, much of the research during the 1970s and 1980s oversimplified treatment issues related to client diversity and sought to match treatment approaches to clients' cultural and ethnic backgrounds.

Understanding of diversity became more sophisticated in the 1990s. The concept of diversity itself expanded to include not only people's racial, ethnic, and cultural group memberships but also their age, abilities, socioeconomic status, gender, sexual orientation, and other attributes. The literature now recognized that each person has multiple perspectives, stemming from a wide variety of personal characteristics and background experiences. Even people who are similar in age, gender, and cultural background can have very different worldviews and respond best to very different treatment approaches.

The importance of considering people's worldviews and multiple perspectives will increase as the population becomes even more diverse. In the United States, the white population is expected to show little growth while Asian American, Pacific Islander, African American, and Hispanic populations are likely to show considerable growth (Edmunds, Martinson, & Goldberg, 1990).

Rates of premature termination of treatment are significantly higher for people from lower socioeconomic or ethnic minority groups (Reis & Brown, 1999). In light of this, as well as the anticipated growth in client diversity, clinicians must maintain awareness of the multiple perspectives of their clients as well as clinicians' own preconceptions about those clients. Clinicians need to be aware of how people's cultural, ethnic, socioeconomic, and family backgrounds have shaped their views of personal problems and mental illness and of counseling as a way to address those concerns. For example, attitudes toward treatment of a woman whose family recently emigrated to the United States from rural Africa are likely to differ greatly from those of a man with an upper-middle class, white, Anglo-Saxon, Protestant background whose family has been living in Los Angeles for many years. The importance of clinicians' awareness of clients' contexts and perspectives can hardly be overemphasized. This awareness should facilitate clinicians' efforts to broach discussion of clients' worldviews and multicultural characteristics, to successfully adapt treatment to the special needs of each person, and to provide effective and diversity-sensitive treatment.

THE THERAPEUTIC ALLIANCE

Research indicates, with increasing clarity, "that therapist relationship skills and strength of the therapeutic alliance are the most powerful predictors of client outcome across many therapeutic orientations" (Green & Herget, 1991, p. 321). Therefore, it is imperative that clinicians acquire a sound understanding of the elements of a positive therapeutic alliance, develop the skills and strategies they need to create successful working relationships with their clients, and be able to adapt their treatment style to individual clients to help them participate in and appreciate the value of the therapeutic alliance.

Both the clinician and the client, of course, determine the formation of a positive therapeutic alliance. Clients who perceive their clinicians as empathic, caring, and credible and who feel understood by them are likely to progress in treatment, while those who have a negative perception of their clinicians, whether or not that perception is grounded in reality, are less likely to make progress.

Mutuality can enhance the therapeutic relationship. Feelings of shared warmth, affection, affirmation, and respect contribute to a positive therapeutic outcome (Waterhouse & Strupp, 1984). Clients who identify with their clinicians also are more likely to have positive outcomes. The interaction of client and clinician makes a difference in clients' feelings of mutuality and their ability to identify with their clinician.

Similarity between client and clinician also is associated with the development of a positive therapeutic alliance and with successful treatment. Kelly and Strupp (1992) found that compatibility of overall values contributed positively to the treatment process. In multicultural counseling, most of the research supports similarity in culture and values as enhancing the therapeutic relationship and increasing the likelihood that clients will remain in treatment (Beutler, Machado, & Neufeldt, 1994; Gibbs & Huang, 1989). Dorothy Beck (1988) found that most people prefer clinicians who are relatively close to them in age; and Coleman, Wampold, and Casali (1995) stated that people who had not been well assimilated into the culture in which they were living preferred clinicians whose cultural background was similar to their own. These findings suggest that clients should be asked about any qualities or characteristic they might prefer in a clinician. If possible, they should be matched with a clinician who fits that profile.

Having a shared vision of the treatment process and its goals is another important element in the therapeutic alliance (Hill & O'Brien, 1999; Tallman & Bohart, 1999). If client and clinician view themselves as engaged in an important shared endeavor that is likely to be successful (Kolden, Howard, & Maling, 1994), have clear and mutually established goals in mind, and agree on the tasks and procedures that will be used to achieve those goals, their collaboration is likely to be smooth and efficient.

Although the client-clinician relationship evolves over time and can improve throughout the treatment process, clients' perceptions of the quality of the therapeutic alliance form early and tend to be stable. Walborn (1996) concluded that a positive therapeutic alliance must develop by the fifth session if treatment is to be successful. The treatment approaches discussed throughout this book provide clinicians with many skills and strategies that they can use to develop and enhance the all-important clinician-client relationship and thereby maximize the likelihood of a successful treatment outcome.

Clarkson (1990) delineated five types of therapeutic alliances:

1. *Working alliances,* focused on shared goals and an agreement to engage in certain tasks to achieve those goals
2. *Transferential/countertransferential relationships,* in which clinicians communicate little of their own lives and personality but seek to foster and analyze transference relationships
3. *Reparative/developmentally needed relationships,* most often used with severely damaged clients, offer reparenting and nurturing in an effort to compensate for deprivation in early relationships
4. *I-you relationships,* emphasize immediacy and mutuality in the therapeutic relationship, with the clinician serving as a role model and an instrument for healing
5. *Transpersonal relationships,* characterized by the healing presence of the clinician, view therapy as a shared journey toward personal growth and increased spirituality

This classification system is useful in enabling clinicians to examine the nature of their therapeutic relationships. Few clinician-client relationships represent a pure version of any one of these five types; most incorporate elements of two or more. Being conscious of the nature of their therapeutic alliances can help clinicians be more intentional and thoughtful in their efforts to form helpful alliances.

Objective measures of the therapeutic alliance usually indicate that clinicians' and clients' perceptions of that relationship are congruent. However, this is not always the case. When clients' and clinicians' views of the therapeutic alliance differ, research suggests that clients' perceptions of the nature and quality of the therapeutic alliance make the difference in treatment effectiveness. Consequently, clinicians need to not only meet their own standards for a successful therapeutic alliance but be sure that clients also have a positive view of that interaction. Clinicians should be attuned to their clients' verbal and nonverbal messages, ask them for feedback and reactions to their treatment, and address any barriers to the establishment of a positive alliance. In assessing and developing the therapeutic relationship, then, clinicians should look at what they and their clients bring into treatment as well as the effectiveness of the treatment process.

ESSENTIAL CONDITIONS OF EFFECTIVE THERAPEUTIC RELATIONSHIPS

Carl Rogers's person-centered counseling, discussed in part 3 of this book, emphasizes the importance of some essential therapist characteristics that he believed would promote client self-esteem and self-efficacy. Most other approaches to counseling and psychotherapy have come to recognize the importance of these growth-facilitating qualities in all therapeutic relationships, regardless of the clinician's theoretical orientation. The ability of the counselor or psychotherapist to communicate these qualities can have a great impact on treatment and its outcome and may exceed the impact made by any specific technique or approach. As Neukrug and Williams (1993) stated, "We all seem to want a therapist who is viewed as competent, caring, warm, and trustworthy and who has a good amount of clinical orientation" (p. 60). Although specific interventions can effect significant change in problem areas, the presence of the following essential conditions of the therapeutic relationship make it likely that those interventions will succeed.

Empathy is the clinician's ability to see the world through the client's eyes and to communicate that understanding so that the client feels heard and validated. Empathy helps clients feel that their clinicians can relate to their experiences and are with them emotionally. According to Lambert and Cattani-Thompson (1996), empathy, or the feeling of being understood by one's therapist, is strongly associated with positive change and may be an even better predictor of treatment outcome than are treatment interventions.

Trustworthiness communicates to clients that the clinician can be relied on to behave in ethical ways, possess the knowledge and skills needed to provide effective treatment, protect the client from harm and humiliation during treatment, show respect for the client, and advocate for what is best for the client. Clinicians foster trust when they honor commitments to clients, including being on time and keeping scheduled appointments; are clear about fees and payment schedules; help clients deal effectively with third-party payors; return clients' telephone calls; remember information that clients share with them; and follow up on clients' homework and unfinished discussions from a previous session. Clinician stability and reliability are essential ingredients in most therapeutic relationships and can offset some of the confusion and chaos that many clients experience in their lives.

Caring gives clients the message that they matter to the clinician and that the clinician is concerned about them and their lives. Caring is transmitted through emotional warmth, appropriate reassurance, interventions that communicate positive regard for and confidence in the client, an interest in what is important to the client, and therapeutic activities that empower the client. Caring clinicians do not use clients to satisfy their own emotional needs or try to control clients' thoughts, emotions, or behaviors. Clinicians who are warm and caring have a higher likelihood of a positive outcome than do those who are aggressive and confrontational (Lambert & Cattani-Thompson, 1996).

Genuineness, sincerity, and congruence have not received clear support in the research literature but continue to be viewed as important to the establishment of a positive therapeutic relationship (Jinks, 1999). Clinicians with these qualities give clients clear, accurate, unambiguous, and honest, yet sensitive, messages. The clinician is not verbalizing concern while counting the minutes until lunch. If clinicians believe clients are making harmful or self-destructive choices, they provide feedback and clarification and show clients possible ways to change but never coerce, attack, or humiliate clients.

Persuasiveness (social influence) is the process of encouraging clients to take reasonable and growth-promoting risks, to make thoughtful decisions and healthy choices, to disclose and process troubling feelings and experiences, and to move forward toward their goals. Clinicians whom clients perceive as credible and admirable are more likely to have a positive persuasive influence and to become role models for their clients. Persuasiveness in clinicians is a positive force that provides clients with the information, tools, models, and sense of empowerment they need to make good choices for themselves (Wanigaratne & Barker, 1995).

As with other essential conditions of treatment, clinicians must be careful that they do not move beyond encouraging positive change into an authoritarian role in which they tell clients how they should be and make value judgments of the clients' thoughts, feelings, and actions. Occasionally, clients present a danger to themselves or others, and clinicians must intervene forcefully to prevent a suicide or physical injury. However, under most circumstances, clinicians must protect the clients' right to decide what is best for themselves.

Hope or optimism is the final essential condition of treatment that we will consider. Therapy and counseling are hard work for both clients and clinicians. For people to persist in that process and tolerate the increased anxiety it often causes, as well as the commitment of time and finances, they must believe that treatment has something positive to offer them and that, at the end of that process, they will be better off than they were before treatment.

The essential conditions of psychotherapy are intertwined and build on each other. Consequently, empathy, trustworthiness, caring, genuineness, and persuasiveness all facilitate the development of hope in our clients as do support, encouragement, and affirmation (Odell & Quinn, 1998). In addition, clear and mutually agreed upon goals and procedures, the clinician's communication of direction and optimism, emphasis on the client's strengths, ability to address problematic client behaviors and attitudes, and a collaborative client-clinician relationship all can build the client's positive expectation of change (Foreman & Marmar, 1985; Green & Herget, 1991; Kivlighan & Schmitz, 1992).

IMPORTANT CLINICIAN SKILLS, TRAINING, AND EXPERIENCE

Training and experience make a difference in clinician effectiveness. Martin Seligman (1995) found that psychologists, psychiatrists, and social workers all had a similar overall level of effectiveness and were more effective than "long-term family doctoring" (p. 965). Crits-Cristoph et al. (1991) found that inexperienced therapists had more varied and often less successful outcomes than experienced therapists did. However, research has not always given clear support to either the importance of advanced training in counseling and psychotherapy or the value of experience (Beck, 1988). In part, that may be because the helping professions have not reached a consensus on which skills and training experiences are most important and because clinicians do not all benefit equally from their training and experience.

Agreement on essential clinical skills may not be far off. Recent research has been moving toward a consensus on necessary skills and experiences (Sexton, 1995a). A review of the literature suggests that clinician training should include the following areas of preparation and competence (Seligman, 2004a):[1]

- *Professional Orientation, Identity and Ethics*   Includes knowledge of the history of our profession, roles and functions of mental health professionals, relevant professional organizations and credentials, ethical and legal guidelines, and the use of technology to enhance one's professional roles
- *Social and Cultural Foundations of the Profession*   Includes multicultural sensitivity, appreciation, knowledge, and competence; understanding of social problems, their causes and remedies; and skills in outreach, prevention, social change, advocacy, coalition building, and community organization and intervention
- *Human Growth and Development*   Includes knowledge of theories of individual development, family development, personality development, cognitive development, and sexual development; capability of distinguishing between healthy and unhealthy growth and development; and ability to provide information on and facilitate healthy development
- *Lifestyle and Career Development*   Includes understanding of the economic and occupational arenas and their meaning to society, individuals, and families; knowledge of career development; and skill in using counseling, information, inventories, technology, and other resources to promote rewarding and healthy career development and decisions

[1] Adapted from Seligman, L. (2004). *Diagnosis and treatment planning in counseling* (3rd ed.). New York: Plenum. Used by permission.

- *Theories of Counseling and Psychotherapy*   Includes the ability to establish a positive therapeutic alliance; knowledge of a broad range of well-accepted treatment approaches and their use and implementation; ability to conduct effective interviews, formulate appropriate treatment goals, develop sound treatment plans, and help clients in crisis; and consultation skills
- *Group Counseling and Psychotherapy*   Includes understanding of group development and dynamics, the various types of groups, and leader and member roles and functions; knowledge of effective approaches to group treatment; and awareness of the benefits, drawbacks, and appropriate use of these approaches
- *Assessment and Appraisal*   Includes knowledge of a broad range of assessment tools (e.g., inventories to assess personality, ability, career development) as well as their appropriate use; skills in presenting, planning, and integrating assessment into the treatment process; ability to conduct intake interviews, mental status examinations, and observations; understanding of statistical concepts relevant to assessment and of ways to demonstrate multicultural competence in assessment; and awareness of when and how to make referrals for assessment
- *Research and Program Evaluation*   Includes knowledge of the importance of research and of statistical, technological, and other procedures essential to conducting sound research; skills in planning and conducting research; and understanding of relevant research studies and how to use them to enhance professional effectiveness
- *Diagnosis and Psychopathology*   Includes knowledge of the hallmarks of healthy and pathological personality and functioning; familiarity with the current edition of the *Diagnostic and Statistical Manual of Mental Disorders;* ability to formulate a case conceptualization and make an accurate multiaxial assessment; awareness of ways to assess and address dangerousness and risk in clients; and awareness of when clients should be referred for psychiatric, neurological, or other evaluations

A study by Sexton (1995b) indicated that, when clinicians rated the importance of their skills, two of the most important were knowledge of theories of counseling and psychotherapy and an understanding of intervention strategies used in individual treatment. These two competencies reflect the primary focus of this book. The skill rated as most important, understanding abnormal behavior, also has considerable relevance to using systems and strategies of counseling and psychotherapy successfully and will be discussed in part 7 of this book.

The broad and extensive array of skills and competencies described in this chapter may seem daunting. However, novice clinicians already possess some of these abilities when they begin their training. Most of these skills are taught in graduate school, while others are developed when clinicians embark on their internships and postgraduate employment. In addition, these competencies develop and improve with experience.

PERSONAL AND PROFESSIONAL CHARACTERISTICS OF THE EFFECTIVE CLINICIAN

As we have discussed, communicating empathy, trustworthiness, caring, genuineness, persuasiveness, and the ability to instill hope are important for a clinician. The literature also suggests personal and professional qualities in clinicians that contribute to treatment effectiveness. Many are the same qualities that most of us value in friends and colleagues. The profile of the effective clinician is, in many respects, comparable to a profile of an emotionally healthy person (Bachelor & Horvath, 1999; Jinks, 1999; Odell & Quinn, 1998). Effective clinicians typically are:

- Characterized by strong interpersonal skills, including patience, warmth, caring, a sense of humor, and friendliness (Najavits & Weiss, 1994)
- Genuine, sincere, and authentic; able to make appropriate self-disclosures, provide useful feedback, and acknowledge their mistakes and limitations
- Emotionally stable, mature, and responsible
- Well-adjusted and fulfilled, self-aware, with positive and realistic self-esteem, good relationships, a sense of direction, and a rewarding lifestyle
- Able to acknowledge their mistakes and limitations
- Capable of high levels of thinking and conceptualizing
- In possession of good insight into themselves and others
- Aware of, sensitive to, and respectful of multicultural characteristics and differences
- Engaged in and appreciative of the value of personal and professional growth and learning
- Ethical, objective, and fair
- Flexible and open to change and new experiences, willing to take reasonable risks
- Affirming and encouraging of others
- Clear and effective in both oral and written communication

Walborn (1996) suggested that many people seek to become clinicians because they know what it is like to feel lonely and to experience emotional pain. At the same time, effective clinicians are likely to manifest emotional health and well-being as well as the ability to put their own needs aside at least temporarily so they can understand, support, and help others. Apparently, having personal difficulties in the past does not prohibit people from later becoming emotionally healthy and effective clinicians. In fact, the process of honestly looking at and bravely tackling their own issues and concerns may help people develop the positive traits often found in successful clinicians.

Clinicians' values also seem linked to treatment outcome. Lafferty, Beutler, and Crago (1989) found that effective therapists placed significantly less importance on having prosperous and exciting lives and more importance on being intelligent and reflective than did clinicians with weaker skills.

Excellent clinicians manage their lives well, keep their personal needs from intruding on the treatment process, are well-integrated, and value themselves and their lives (Van Wagoner, Gelso, Hayes, & Diemer, 1991). In general, clinicians who are emotionally stable, well-adjusted, and optimistic are more likely to be effective than those who lack these characteristics (Sexton & Whiston, 1991).

Research has not clearly demonstrated that a particular age, gender, professional orientation, or background is associated with successful treatment outcomes. However, clients often express strong preferences for clinicians in a certain age group, of one gender or the other, or with a particular cultural or religious affiliation. For example, most women prefer a female therapist (Pikus & Heavey, 1996). When clients receive the sort of treatment they prefer, they have more confidence that treatment will help them (Devine & Fernald, 1973; Wanigaratne & Barker, 1995). Respecting and honoring client preferences in a clinician, whenever possible, usually enhances the therapeutic alliance as well as the effectiveness of treatment.

THE IMPACT OF SETTING ON THE TREATMENT PROCESS

The setting in which treatment occurs is another important influence on counseling and psychotherapy. Treatment programs typically limit the range of clients and problems they address. In addition, they may set guidelines for the number and frequency of sessions and even determine the treatment approach used. Counseling in a high school, for example, will differ greatly from psychotherapy in a private practice specializing in treating people who have survived abuse or in an inpatient program treating people with severe depression and psychotic disorders.

Treatment settings also have a strong impact on client expectations. The person seeking help from a career counseling center will almost always have different expectations and wants than a person contacting a community mental health center.

Clinicians must be aware of the guidelines and requirements of the setting in which they practice as well as typical clients seen for treatment in that setting. Of course, clinicians' primary goal is to provide people with the help they need. However, sometimes a referral is indicated because clients cannot receive the help they need from the first treatment program they consult.

ETHICAL GUIDELINES AND STANDARDS

Each professional association for clinicians, including the American Psychological Association (APA) and the American Counseling Association (ACA), has its own set of ethical guidelines and standards. Familiarizing oneself with and abiding by those ethical standards is essential to sound clinical practice for many reasons including (Seligman, 2004a):

- Ethical standards give strength and credibility to the mental health professions
- Ethical guidelines help clinicians make sound decisions
- Providing clients with information on when clinicians can and cannot maintain confidentiality, as well as on other important ethical guidelines, affords clients safety and predictability and enables them to make informed choices about their treatment
- Practicing in accord with established ethical standards can protect clinicians in the event of malpractice suits or other challenges to their competence
- Demonstrated knowledge of relevant ethical and legal standards is required for licensure and certification as a counselor, psychologist, or social worker

Clinicians are responsible not only for acting in ethical ways themselves but also for helping their colleagues to become aware of and adhere to these standards. Clinicians who believe a colleague is acting unethically should first discuss this matter with the colleague and provide any needed information. If clinicians believe that the colleague is still acting unethically, clinicians should consider reporting this matter to the appropriate licensing board and professional association.

Although a detailed discussion of the ethical standards for each of the mental health professions is beyond the scope of this book, an overview of these standards is presented here because of their importance and relevance to clinicians practicing counseling and psychotherapy. The ethical standards of the various mental health professions have far more similarities than differences. Underlying these guidelines are the following general ethical and moral principles (Herlihy & Corey, 1996):

- *Autonomy*—Clinicians help people develop the skills and strengths they need to make wise choices for themselves. Inherent in this guideline is the mandate that clinicians understand, respect, and appreciate diversity.
- *Nonmaleficence (Do No Harm)* and *Beneficence*—Clinicians should always keep in mind the importance of actively promoting the well-being of their clients and acting in the best interests of their clients.
- *Justice*—Fairness is an essential ingredient of clinicians' professional relationships and interactions, whether they are with clients, colleagues, students, or others.
- *Fidelity*—Clinicians "maintain their commitments to their profession and to their clients. They are reliable and responsible, nurture and sustain trust in their relationships, value and protect the therapeutic alliance, and are truthful and congruent in their communications" (Seligman, 2004a, p. 356).

In addition to these general principles, the following ethical guidelines, with headings adapted from the ACA Code of Ethics (1995, p. 1), are among the most important:

- *The Counseling Relationship*—As stated previously, clinicians always act in the best interests of their clients. They competently develop treatment plans and use approaches and interventions that are likely to be helpful. If they believe their services are no longer beneficial to a client, they refer that person to more appropriate sources of help. They avoid potentially harmful dual relationships (e.g., client and student, client and family member) and do not engage in sexual intimacies with current or former clients, following the guidelines of the clinicians' professional associations. They provide clients with written information about their services and charge fees that reflect common practice in their area. Respect for and appreciation of diversity, as well as for people's rights and dignity, is reflected in all their professional interactions.

- *Confidentiality*—Clinicians inform clients about the clinicians' obligation to maintain confidentiality, as well as about exceptions to that guideline. Under most circumstances, they maintain their clients' confidentiality and take steps to ensure that their employees also follow this ethical guideline. If clinicians are working with minors, with people who present a danger to themselves or another person, or who engage in abuse of children, the elderly, or people with disabilities, clinicians may need to break confidentiality but always do so with thought and care. Court orders and clients' requests also may require clinicians to disclose otherwise confidential information.

- *Professional Responsibility*—Clinicians practice only within their areas of competence. They engage in professional development in order to maintain and improve their skills and are active in their professional associations. They have sound relationships with other professionals, make good use of consultation and collaboration, present themselves and their credentials accurately, and never exploit clients or employees.

- *Evaluation, Assessment, and Interpretation*—Clinicians make knowledgeable, professional, and helpful use of diagnosis and assessment. They use strategies and tools that are within their range of competence and are appropriate for the client and the concern. Selection, administration, scoring, and interpretation of inventories is in keeping with established procedures and reflects multicultural competence.

- *Teaching, Training, and Supervision*—Educators and supervisors maintain standards similar to those of clinicians. They have clear policies and ensure that their students and supervisees are informed of those policies and procedures. Educators and supervisors provide those they teach and supervise with clear and useful feedback on their performance, offer referrals for help with educational and emotional difficulties if needed, and have recourse available if students or supervisees believe that unfair or erroneous decisions were made about their professional development. Educators and supervisors ensure that their students and supervisees know and abide by the ethical guidelines for their profession.

- *Research and Publication*—Writers and researchers in mental health fields also are subject to ethical guidelines. They must be sure not to harm research participants. They provide opportunity for voluntary consent whenever possible, make available to participants and colleagues clear information on their work, and follow guidelines for submission of manuscripts to professional journals. They appropriately acknowledge any help they received from colleagues and students.

SKILL DEVELOPMENT AND EXERCISES

This chapter has emphasized the importance of the therapeutic alliance and the personal characteristics of the clinician in determining treatment outcome. The following sections include information to help you develop and explore three skills that are relevant to both the contents of this chapter and your development as effective clinicians:

1. Role induction
2. Self-assessment
3. Building a positive therapeutic alliance

Role Induction

Role induction is the process of orienting people to treatment so they are more likely to become successful clients who understand and can make good use of the therapeutic process. Role induction can help both client and clinician engage productively in a common endeavor and can contribute greatly to the efficiency and success of the process. Acosta, Yamamoto, Evans, and Skilbeck (1983) found that clients who received pretreatment preparation were more motivated, had a better understanding of treatment and their role in the process, seemed more optimistic about making positive changes, and demonstrated greater willingness to self-disclose and talk about their concerns.

Role induction typically entails discussing the following topics with clients early in the therapeutic relationship and ensuring that clients understand and are comfortable with the information that has been discussed:

- The nature of the treatment process
- How treatment promotes positive change
- The kinds of issues and concerns that usually respond well to counseling and psychotherapy
- The collaborative nature of the client-clinician relationship
- The roles and responsibilities of the clinician
- The roles and responsibilities of the client
- The importance of honesty and self-disclosure on the part of the client

- Ethical aspects of the therapeutic relationship, especially guidelines for maintaining and breaking confidentiality
- Ways to contact the clinician and what to do in the event of a client emergency
- Obtaining third-party payments (e.g., from managed care, health insurance)
- Clinician's fees and appointment schedules
- The kinds of changes people can realistically expect from treatment
- Risks inherent in treatment

Exercises in Role Induction

Classroom/Large-Group Exercise   Discuss the meaning and importance of each of the items on the list you have just read. Decide if any items should be added to or omitted from the list. Explore positive and negative ways to communicate to clients information about these items.

Small-Group Exercise   General instructions on conducting small-group exercises appear in chapter 1. Review that explanation before beginning this exercise.

Form into groups of four people. One participant should role-play one of the three clients introduced in chapter 1: Edie, Roberto, or Ava. A second participant should assume the clinician role and conduct a role induction with this client. Assume that this is taking place in an initial session.

The other participants should observe the role play and provide feedback on the topics and questions that follow. Remember that feedback should be specific and constructive; therefore, observers should take notes during the role play so that they can remember important statements to be discussed. Suggesting alternative statements or procedures will make feedback especially useful. Keep the focus on the content and the process, not on the person, and be sure to pay attention to strengths in the role play first before addressing areas needing improvement.

- Consider whether the important items in the role induction were presented clearly. Were some items omitted? What items were described particularly well? What changes would you suggest in the role induction?
- Discuss the clinician's nonverbal communications, including tone of voice, rate of speech, eye contact, and posture. How did these affect the role induction process?
- How did the client seem to react to the role induction? Should the process have been modified in any way to fit this person's needs?

Building a Positive Therapeutic Alliance

Building rapport and a positive therapeutic alliance are gradual processes that evolve throughout treatment. However, the first few sessions form the foundation for that alliance. If the therapeutic relationship does not begin well, clients may terminate treatment prematurely, precluding future efforts to form a sound working alliance. Consequently, counselors and therapists must actively engender rapport and collaboration from the first moment of contact with the client.

Guidelines for Building a Positive Therapeutic Alliance   Following are some procedures and interventions that can promote rapport and development of a positive therapeutic alliance:

- Facilitate the client's efforts to begin treatment by providing a role induction (described previously). Be sure that clinician and client have a shared understanding of how treatment will proceed.

- Support the client's decision to seek treatment by discussing the importance of taking a first step and the courage that is involved in seeking help.
- Establish and consistently follow the session guidelines, including starting and ending times; follow up on homework tasks; promote active client participation; ensure that sessions have a productive structure; and clarify fee collection.
- Discuss the client's expectations for treatment, encouraging realistic hope for positive change. This can be accomplished by acknowledging the person's difficulties and discussing ways in which treatment usually can help with such concerns.
- Develop with the client shared and specific goals that reflect those hopes and expectations and are meaningful to the client.
- Understand and value the client's perspectives on the world.
- Communicate warmth and concern in a professional manner, showing empathy for the client's feelings and experiences.
- Demonstrate congruence and genuineness in verbal and nonverbal messages. Sometimes sharing a small piece of information about yourself, especially if it establishes a commonality between you and the client, can convey genuineness. Examples would be a brief mention of a visit you made to the client's hometown or your shared enjoyment of the client's favorite hobby. Be careful not to focus too much on yourself or share very personal material.
- Engage the client actively in the therapeutic process and begin to engender both a sense of empowerment in the client and confidence in the treatment. This can be accomplished by suggesting small, manageable, helpful steps or activities that the person can do between sessions.
- Be sure to acknowledge and build on successes and support networks that the person has already established.

Exercises in Building a Positive Therapeutic Alliance

Large-Group Discussion   Edie and Roberto come from very different backgrounds. Edie grew up in a middle-class, white, Jewish family, living in the suburbs, while Roberto grew up in a lower middle-class Roman Catholic Latino family, living in an urban area. These differences in their backgrounds are likely to affect their expectations for and attitudes toward counseling. Discuss the following:

- How would you go about understanding and addressing the impact of their background differences on their orientations toward treatment?
- In what ways might you individualize treatment for Edie and for Roberto in order to increase the likelihood of developing a positive therapeutic alliance with each of them?

Large- or Small-Group Exercise in Building a Positive Therapeutic Alliance   Assume that you have had an individual counseling session with each of the members of the Diaz family (introduced in chapter 1). Here are their opening statements to you:

Edie: This is going to be very hard for me. I'm not used to talking about myself and I don't feel ready to tell you some of the things that have happened to me.

Roberto: I can't take this much longer. If things don't go back to the way they used to be, I'm walking. How long do you think it will take you to fix Edie's problems?

Ava: I'm not sure why my mom wanted me to talk to you.

Each statement reflects some possible barriers to the establishment of a positive therapeutic alliance. Discuss each of the statements, drawing on what you already know about Edie, Roberto, and Ava from chapter 1. Consider the possible barriers to successful treatment and what strategies and skills you might use to facilitate the establishment of a positive therapeutic relationship with each person. Use the previous list of ways to develop a positive therapeutic alliance to give you ideas.

Exercises in Self-Assessment

Individual Exercises   General instructions on individual exercises appear in chapter 1. Review that explanation before beginning these exercises. Your responses should be written in your journal.

1. Previously in this chapter, we identified six essential characteristics of effective therapeutic relationships: empathy, trustworthiness, caring, congruence/genuineness, persuasiveness, and hope. List each of these characteristics on a piece of paper. Then select at least one (but no more than three) which you believe is already a strength for you. For each, write out your rationale for believing you would be successful in transmitting that quality to a client. For example, you might perceive yourself as strong in persuasiveness because you can easily engage people in conversations, are articulate and well spoken, and have extensive knowledge of mental disorders and their treatment. You might believe clients are likely to view you as trustworthy because you almost always remember your commitments and are well organized.

    For each of the items you did not select, write down one change you might make to maximize your ability to transmit that characteristic to clients. For example, you might try to communicate more caring to others by deliberately acknowledging positive statements they have made about themselves. To improve your ability to communicate hope, you might focus on making fewer judgmental statements and instead look for new possibilities.

2. List some of the important perspectives or viewpoints you would bring with you if you were a client. Write briefly about how you would like a clinician to adapt treatment to meet your needs. What can you learn from this about your own work as a clinician?

SUMMARY

This chapter has presented important information about the nature of a positive therapeutic alliance, client and clinician characteristics and abilities associated with successful treatment, and important ethical standards. Exercises and skill development sections focused on role induction, the development of a sound therapeutic alliance, and self-assessment.

Part Two

Treatment Systems Emphasizing Background and Context

CHAPTER 3

Overview of Background-Focused Treatment Systems

We are our histories, our families, the events in our lives, our joys and losses, our dreams, and more. All our experiences have shaped and continue to shape us. Most clinicians agree that we cannot fully understand our clients and their concerns unless we learn about their backgrounds and contexts.

However, clinicians disagree on the amount of time they spend exploring clients' histories, on the importance of past experiences in determining present functioning, and on the ways clinicians should focus on those past experiences in relieving present concerns and promoting mental health. This chapter focuses on approaches to counseling and psychotherapy that emphasize understanding and working through unresolved problems and issues in the client's past. Clinicians advocating these approaches believe that unless treatment facilitates healing of past wounds and relieves developmental blocks, people will continue to repeat harmful and dysfunctional patterns.

According to treatment approaches that emphasize the past, a young man with a seductive and unreliable mother probably will mistrust women and will have difficulty in forming healthy intimate relationships. Similarly, the woman who, as a child, saw the blood, pain, and grief associated with her mother's sudden miscarriage may fear becoming pregnant, whether or not she can link her fears to her mother's loss. These examples reflect the potential impact of the past on the present. Whether clinicians emphasize the past or focus almost entirely on the present, they need some understanding of their clients' backgrounds to make accurate diagnoses and plan successful treatments.

Chapter 4 begins the discussion of treatment approaches that emphasize background with a consideration of Sigmund Freud's psychoanalysis. Although many theories of human development and psychotherapy have been advanced since Freud's work began more than 100 years ago, he is generally regarded as the father of psychotherapy. His ideas and strategies continue to inform and contribute to treatment in the 21st century. Alfred Adler and Carl Jung were Freud's colleagues early in their careers but ultimately developed their own theories, discussed in chapters 5 and 6. The ideas of the Freudian revisionists, including Anna Freud, Melanie Klein, Karen Horney, Helene Deutsch, Harry Stack Sullivan, and the object relations theorists, all of whose work was inspired and influenced by Freud's, are considered in chapter 7. Finally, a modern psychodynamic approach, brief psychodynamic psychotherapy (developed by Malan, Sifneos, and others), is presented in chapter 8.

IMPORTANCE OF PAST EXPERIENCES IN TREATMENT

Incorporating the discussion and processing of past experiences into treatment can greatly enhance its impact. Following are some of the important reasons for exploring a client's history.

Most of us view our pasts as important to making us who we are. Most people who seek treatment expect to discuss their histories. By showing interest in clients' families, school experiences, and other aspects of their backgrounds, clinicians can communicate a genuine interest in truly knowing and understanding their clients. Viewing clients as unique individuals who merit that in-depth understanding conveys caring and can help develop rapport.

Many people find it easier to talk about the past than the present, especially if they are currently in emotional pain. Allowing people to spend some time describing their past can give them a respite from the sadness and anxiety associated with their present concerns. Focusing on past successes, in particular, can engender hope, optimism, and self-confidence.

Psychodynamic theorists believe that the roots of current problems lie in the past and that exploration and interpretation of past experiences are essential to alleviating current concerns. Whether or not readers share that point of view, some understanding of the past can shed light on the nature and dynamics of people's current concerns and provide a context for understanding them more fully. Repetitive patterns can be identified, as can possible precipitants of current and future difficulties. For example, the adolescent who was insolent to his teacher can be better understood by knowing whether he has longstanding difficulty with authority figures or whether this is an isolated and uncharacteristic incident.

People's presenting problems are not always their most significant concerns. Embarassment, guilt, distorted perceptions, limited self-awareness, or other factors can lead clients to focus initially on minor concerns while withholding information on more significant issues. An example is a young woman who sought help in dealing with the end of a recent relationship; history-taking revealed a background of abuse by her father and brother, as well as a series of subsequent self-destructive relationships.

Diagnosis, using the *Diagnostic and Statistical Manual of Mental Disorders* (American Psychiatric Association, 2000) is an important aspect of the clinician's role. Making an accurate diagnosis often depends on knowing the duration of a person's symptoms and whether and how often that person has experienced the same or other symptoms in the past. Taking a careful history is essential when making a diagnosis.

Similarly, the likelihood of developing an effective treatment plan can be greatly enhanced if clinicians have knowledge of their clients' histories. Consider the example of two men who sought counseling following automobile accidents. The first man had no history of accidents or self-harm and no prior difficulty with alcohol abuse. However, on the day of the accident, he had been fired from his job, was worried about his ability to support his family, and had four beers "to calm himself" before driving home. This man probably does not have a mental disorder but would benefit from some brief treatment, with an emphasis on career counseling and coping skills. The second man had a different history, including multiple accidents and suicidal ideation. His mother committed suicide when he was a child. This man probably has a mood disorder; his treatment might combine cognitive-behavioral therapy, psychodynamic therapy, and medication. Only by understanding the differing backgrounds of the two men can accurate diagnoses and treatment plans be formulated.

In this post-modern era of counseling and psychotherapy, most clinicians recognize the importance of taking a holistic approach to understanding their clients. This involves learning about people's development, their cultural and socioeconomic backgrounds, their families, their abilities, and other important aspects of their lives. Each person has a story to tell, and by listening to these stories and learning about people's lives, clinicians can see the world through their clients' eyes as much as possible. This can help clinicians to minimize their biases and preconceptions and truly know, appreciate, and respond to each person as a special individual.

In light of the many reasons why knowledge of clients' histories is essential to effective treatment, I strongly encourage all counselors and psychotherapists to engage in at least a cursory exploration of clients' pasts. How much time and attention the clinician devotes to this depends on the preferences of the clinician and the openness, concerns, and background of the client. Some readers may adopt a psychodynamic theoretical orientation and focus extensively on background, while others may prefer to integrate a discussion of background into another theoretical approach. Regardless of theoretical orientation, history-taking is an essential clinical tool. The skills presented in this chapter, asking questions and conducting intake interviews, were selected to provide tools, as well as a structure, that facilitate gathering information on people's histories.

SKILL DEVELOPMENT AND EXERCISES

This chapter introduces two important skills: asking questions and conducting an intake interview. Questions are used by all clinicians, regardless of their theoretical orientations. They use questions throughout the treatment process to elicit information and to promote client self-exploration, self-awareness, and self-expression. However, questions are especially important in eliciting background information.

Questions are the primary intervention used in conducting an intake interview. Many mental health agencies use a structured intake interview as a way to systematically gather information on clients. This helps clinicians to be consistent and thorough in the information they seek and increases the likelihood of obtaining information that is essential to understanding each client. Although counselors and psychotherapists in schools, private practices, and career counseling settings may not conduct formal intake interviews, those clinicians, too, can benefit from bearing in mind the topics that are usually covered in these interviews, although they might elicit that information from their clients in less structured ways.

Asking Helpful Questions

Questions are a powerful intervention. They can focus the treatment on core issues, elicit information, promote exploration, and deepen awareness and understanding. Questions can also exaggerate the power imbalance between clinician and client; lead people to feel judged, attacked, and demeaned; and turn a treatment session into an inquisition. Consider the following example of a client statement followed by four questions posed by clinicians:

Client:	I got a speeding ticket on my way to our session today.
Intervention 1:	What happened?
Intervention 2:	How did you feel about that?
Intervention 3:	Why did you do *that?*
Intervention 4:	How fast were you going?

Each of the four clinician interventions moves the session in a different direction, some more positive than others. The first two responses are likely to be helpful. Intervention 1 gives the client an opportunity to describe and process the incident, perhaps leading to recognition of difficulties with behavior and impulse control; while intervention 2 encourages exploration of feelings, perhaps leading to a discussion of emotions related to the client's treatment. Neither intervention is judgmental, and both give the client many possible ways in which to respond. Interventions 3 and 4, however, are unlikely to have a positive impact on the therapeutic process. The third question may be interpreted by the client as suggesting that he made poor choices and perhaps deserves punishment. The fourth question focuses on a specific piece of information. While this information may be relevant to the discussion, asking immediately for the speed may suggest that it is the most important aspect of the incident. If, indeed, the person was going at a high speed, having to disclose that information to the clinician may be embarrassing and may even lead the client to withhold accurate information. Clearly, the nature and timing of a question are instrumental in both building rapport and achieving treatment goals.

Purposeful Questioning   When clinicians make an intervention or respond to clients, they consider the direction in which they want to move the session and the impact they want their words to have on the client. To beginning clinicians, having such a high level of awareness and direction may seem almost impossible. However, with training and experience, that sort of clinical thinking becomes rapid and almost automatic. Even new clinicians should be able to look at a transcript of a treatment session and discuss the probable intention and impact of an intervention.

When formulating questions, clinicians should consider:

- What information they want to elicit
- How that information will advance the therapeutic process
- What they want to focus on or emphasize with their question
- What tone they want to establish in the session

Open and Closed Questions   Questions can be open or closed. An open question is usually designed to elicit narration, perhaps about the client's feelings, thoughts, behaviors, or experiences. Open questions encourage people to talk at greater length or depth than do closed questions and generally are more powerful and productive. Open questions are broad and give clients responsibility and flexibility in how they might respond. Open questions often begin with "how," "could," "what," and "why" but may have other openers. Interventions 1, 2, and 3 in the previous example are open questions, encouraging the person to respond with at least a few sentences. Clinicians rely much more on open rather than closed questions because they are more likely to promote client self-awareness and exploration.

Closed questions ask for a specific piece of information, often a fact, and invite a limited response of only a few words. Closed questions often begin with "who," "when," "where," "are," "do," and "is." Closed questions can make people feel like they are on the spot. Intervention 4 in the previous example is a closed question.

However, closed questions do have a place in counseling and psychotherapy. Questions such as, "Do you have siblings?" "Would you like to schedule an appointment for next week?" and "Where were you born?" yield important information. In addition, closed questions can help narrow the focus of a session that is drifting or can help a confused or highly emotional client present clearer information. For example, the clinician might say, "It sounds like your experience of being robbed was terrifying and overwhelming. I'd like to get a better idea of what happened. When did you first realize you were being followed? . . . What did the thief say to you? . . . When did you decide to give him your money? . . . Who was the first person you told about the robbery?" Although focusing on emotions is generally helpful to clients, closed questions can help people who are overwhelmed and distraught to ground themselves in the facts before focusing on feelings.

Phrasing Questions   As with most interventions, questions should be phrased so that they are clear, concise, and easily understood. They should encourage and empower, moving treatment toward its goals. In general, questions that begin with "what" and "how" promote exploration and are well received by clients, while questions that begin with "why" can sound negative and accusatory (as in intervention 3 on page 36).

Questions may end in a question mark or may be a statement that suggests a question, such as, "Tell me more about the robbery." These implied or indirect questions should follow the same guidelines as direct questions.

Pacing of Questions   An uninterrupted series of questions can have a negative impact on the treatment process. Like questions beginning with "why," this pattern can increase a person's defensiveness and exaggerate the clinician's power. Even in an initial or intake session, clinicians should not deliver a barrage of questions. Instead, other interventions, such as reflections of feeling and meaning (discussed later in this book), should be interspersed among or combined with the questions so that the session has the flow of a dialog, preserving the collaborative nature of the treatment. The following example demonstrates how a series of questions can be softened by varying the nature of the questions and including other interventions:

Client:	Yesterday, I got so anxious, I thought I would pass out.
Clinician:	That must have been frightening to you. What seemed to trigger your anxiety?
Client:	I guess it was a telephone call I received.
Clinician:	Telephone call?
Client:	Yes, from my brother. We've been out of touch for years. And then he suddenly calls to invite me to his daughter's wedding.
Clinician:	That must have brought up all sorts of feelings.
Client:	You're right. I felt shocked and angry, but also relieved to hear from him. I hadn't even known if he was still alive.
Clinician:	A mix of positive and negative emotions! What thoughts did you have about the call?

Subject Matter of Questions   Of course, just as the format and the pacing of questions have an impact on the development of the therapeutic relationship, so does the content of the questions. Although no topics are unacceptable in counseling and psychotherapy, clinicians should introduce topics when they believe clients will be fairly comfortable discussing them. For example, initiating discussion of a client's history of abuse during the first 10 minutes of an initial session usually is unwise; discussing that information with the client after some rapport has developed, however, is probably essential to effective treatment.

Questions usually should be presented so that they do not cause great discomfort. Asking questions about areas that the client is reluctant to discuss, as well as about painful memories or other highly charged subjects, should be done with extreme caution.

Questions generally yield more useful information when they focus on the client rather than on people who are not involved in the treatment. For example, asking, "What thoughts did you have when your mother left your father?" is likely to be more productive than, "What was your mother's reason for leaving your father?" The first question keeps the focus on the client and encourages self-exploration, while the second shifts the focus away from the client and asks for mind reading. Exercises at the end of this chapter are designed to improve your questioning skills and give you an opportunity to apply some of the concepts covered in this section.

Conducting an Intake Interview

An intake interview may be a formal process that precedes the referral of a client to another clinician, a structured interview that occurs during the first session or two of treatment, or simply the informal get-acquainted process that occurs during the early sessions of counseling. Intake or initial interviews differ greatly, depending on client, clinician, and context. For example, school counselors rarely conduct structured intake interviews but, rather, gradually acquire information about their students over many brief meetings. Intake interviewers in hospital emergency rooms generally focus on the present, assessing the urgency and dangerousness of a client's symptoms. In community mental health centers, structured and comprehensive intake interviews are the norm.

The primary purpose of a comprehensive intake interview is for clinicians to obtain enough information on clients' history, current situation, presenting concerns, and characteristics to formulate an accurate diagnosis and develop a treatment plan that is likely to succeed. Clinicians also need to assess whether clients are at risk of harming themselves or others. Because the intake interview occurs during the first few sessions of the therapeutic relationship, clinicians must also orient clients to treatment (role induction, discussed in chapter 2) and promote rapport and a collaborative therapeutic alliance.

Although clients may complete forms to provide some information, the intake process is primarily a dialog between client and clinician. Questions are the major vehicle for eliciting information; but as we have discussed, a barrage of questions is unlikely to be productive either in eliciting important personal material or developing rapport. Clinicians should follow the guidelines for formulating questions (presented in the previous section) when conducting an intake interview.

Content of the Intake Interview   A comprehensive intake interview generally covers the following topics, with questions, sequence of subjects, and depth of interview adapted to the client's age, concerns, motivation for help, and level of self-disclosure, as well as to the setting and the theoretical orientation of the clinician (Seligman, 2004a):

- Demographic and identifying information, including age, relationship status, and living situation

- Presenting problems, including reasons for seeking help now, symptoms, onset and duration of difficulties, the impact of concerns on the person's lifestyle, and previous efforts to obtain help
- Prior and additional emotional difficulties
- Current life situation, including important relationships, occupational and educational activities, social and leisure activities, stressors, and sources of gratification
- Ethnic, cultural, religious, and socioeconomic information
- Family background, including information on the composition of family of origin and current families, relationships within the families, parenting styles, parental role models and messages, family values, family strengths and difficulties
- Developmental history
- Career and educational history
- Medical history, including significant past and current illnesses, medical treatments, and medications
- Health-related behaviors, including use of drugs and alcohol, exercise, diet, and overall self-care

In addition, clients should have the opportunity to provide information that was not covered in the intake interview but that they view as important.

EXAMPLE OF AN INTAKE INTERVIEW

The following intake interview is with Edie Diaz. Edie sought counseling from a community mental health center close to her home. Her therapist is a woman, about 10 years older than Edie. Assume that Edie has already been provided with information about the nature of treatment and her role as a client.

When reading this transcript, pay particular attention to how questions are used in the interview. Look at whether they are open or closed and how they are integrated with other kinds of interventions. Think about what the therapist's intent might have been in asking each question. Also, compare the content of this interview with the list of topics usually covered in an intake interview. An initial interview may not cover all topics. Are important aspects of this client's life ignored? Should these areas have been discussed in this session, or are they better left for exploration after Edie and her therapist build some rapport? Consider whether some topics or questions were particularly fruitful, and whether others had a negative impact on the session. How would you have improved this intake interview?

Therapist: Edie, we've gone over the consent-to-treatment forms and talked about the counseling process. Do you have any further questions about that information?

Edie: No, it all seems pretty clear.

Therapist: Well, feel free to ask any questions that come up during our work together.

Edie: Thank you. I will.

Therapist: I can see from the forms you completed that you are 38 years old and live with your husband Roberto and your daughter Ava.

Edie: Yes, that's right.

Therapist: What prompted you to seek some help at this time?

Edie: A lot of things. It's hard to know where to begin.

Therapist: We can start almost anywhere, and probably one issue will lead us to talk about another. But often people have a specific concern in mind when they actually pick up the phone to make an appointment. I wonder if that happened for you?

Edie: Well, yes, I guess it did. Ava will be 10 in a few weeks, and she and I were planning her birthday party. After she went to bed, I started to think about when I was 10. That was such a hard time for me.

Therapist: I can see even thinking about it brings up strong feelings. What made that such a hard time for you?

Edie: I was diagnosed with cancer when I was 10. It was awful. I had chemotherapy, lost all my hair, even my eyebrows, and gained lots of weight. Can you imagine what that's like for a child? I felt like such a freak. And everybody was acting like I was going to die. *Almost* everybody. . . .

Therapist: That must have been a terrible experience for you. Very frightening.

Edie: Yes, it was. And I'm so afraid it's going to happen to Ava. She means the world to me. I couldn't stand it if she had to go through what I went through. And I still worry about my health too. The doctors told me years ago that I was cured, but it's hard for me to believe that.

Therapist: So not only are you worrying about Ava, who means so much to you, but also about yourself. . . . When you were talking about having had cancer, it sounded like someone came into your mind who had been optimistic about your prognosis.

Edie: Yes, my father.

Therapist: How did that affect your experience with cancer?

Edie: It made an enormous difference. It was the one good thing that came out of that whole mess. You see, my parents divorced when I was about four. My mother told me my father had been involved with another woman, so she divorced him and tried to keep me and my sister away from him. I didn't see much of him for about six years. Then, when I was diagnosed with cancer, he insisted on seeing me. We formed a relationship for the first time. He would take me out for ice cream and talk with me about what was happening to me. No one else would. He was there for me. And we've been close ever since.

Therapist: Sounds like you really value your relationship with him.

Edie: I do. I wish Roberto and Ava could have that kind of bond.

Therapist: We'll certainly talk more about your experience with cancer, but maybe this is a good time to talk about your family. How do you perceive the relationship between Roberto and Ava?

Edie: It's interesting because they look alike, both tall and big boned. They even have similar personalities, but they often conflict. Both of them are pretty headstrong. Roberto is really a workaholic. If he's not actually at work, he's glued to the computer, trying out some new piece of software or surfing the Net. He's good at his work and thrives on new challenges, but he almost feels like a visitor in our home.

Therapist: How does that affect you?

Edie: I feel a real sense of loss. Roberto and I were so happy when we married. It felt like we couldn't be together enough. We would take walks and go dancing and go to the beach. Anything we did together was wonderful. And then gradually things changed.

Therapist: Changed?

Edie: Yes, I guess it started when we decided to have a baby. That cursed cancer came into the picture again. The doctors told me that I probably couldn't become pregnant because of all the medical treatments I had. But I was determined. We saw every specialist I could find, and after many months of trying I did become pregnant with Ava. But all that took a toll on our marriage. Even sex went on a time schedule, trying to do everything we could to conceive. It was worth it to have Ava, but things have been difficult ever since.

Therapist: So, having Ava was a great joy for you, but it sounds like you had to pay quite a price.

Edie: Yes, and then when we tried to have a second child, things got even worse. Years of trying. I guess we have given up on that now. Ava is wonderful, but I still wish I had a second child.

Therapist: I hear your sadness and longing.

Edie: Yes.

Therapist: We'll want to talk more about those feelings, too. But I'd like to broaden the picture and talk about other parts of your life. What would a typical day be like for you?

Edie: Not very exciting. I get up early, get dressed, wake Ava and Roberto, make breakfast, and help Ava get ready for school. After they both leave, if I don't have to go to work, I might clean the house, do some shopping, plan dinner, and then I make sure to be home when Ava gets back from school. If I have any extra time, I read or watch television. Last year I went back to work part-time. I'm employed as a librarian, working two days a week.

Therapist: How do you feel about the way you spend your time?

Edie: It's all right. We have a beautiful home, and I want to be there for Ava. Lately I've started to think about working more hours, though. I loved being home with Ava, but I missed having a job and being in more contact with the world. I was out of work so long that I worried about learning the new library computer systems, but I've managed so far.

Therapist: So for now, your time is focused on caring for your family and working part time. Let's look at some other aspects of your current life. In addition to your father, what contact do you have with other family members?

Edie: I see my mother fairly often. She comes over at least once a week, usually after Ava comes home from school, so they can have some time together.

Therapist: What is your time with your mother like?

Edie: We get along all right most of the time.

Therapist: I hear some mixed feelings there.

Edie: I just can't respect the choices my mother made, and it makes me angry. My mother remarried when I was about 14. I don't like to say this about anyone, but I really hate my stepfather. I lived with him and my mother for four years, and I don't think he ever said a kind word to me. Any little thing I did wrong, like leave my schoolbooks on the table, he would yell at me and hit me. And he treated my mother that way too. Still does. I don't know why she stays with him.

Therapist: Sounds like you have a lot of anger at your stepfather. How do you handle those feelings?

Edie: I try not to think about him much. I rarely see him; and of course, I won't let Ava be alone with him. But things still happen that make me angry. Last week, my mother was visiting, and we were going to take Ava shopping for a dress for her party. We were heading out the door when he calls, saying he doesn't have to work late after all, and my mother should come home and make dinner. And off she goes without a second thought.

Therapist: So you had some bad feelings about your relationship with your mother as well as anger at your stepfather. How do those feelings affect your relationship with your mother?

Edie: I used to tell her how I felt. And when I was a teenager, I sure let her know how unhappy I was. But it didn't seem to make any difference to her, so I just gave up. She knows how I feel, but she won't change. It's a barrier between us.

Therapist: It sounds like you've found a way to maintain a relationship with your mother but you wish it could be better.

Edie: Yes, I do.

Therapist: That might be another aspect of your life that we could work on.

Edie: Yes, I'd like that.

Therapist: Besides your mother and father, I know you have an older sister. What is your relationship with her like?

Edie: That's another relationship that has had problems over the years. We used to be very close when we were children. She's four years older than I am, and she would try to protect me from . . . things.

Therapist: Protect you?

Edie: We had some problems with my grandparents, but I don't want to talk about that.

Therapist: That's up to you. Perhaps as we continue to work together, you will want to talk about that but that's your decision. How do you and your sister get along now?

Edie: We don't see each other much. She lives in Las Vegas, likes the fast track. Beth's had lots of problems with men, drugs, and gambling. I try to talk to her and helped her out with money a couple of times. Actually,

she has settled down some lately. She's living with a woman. . . . I guess she's a lesbian. At first I was real uncomfortable with that, but whenever I call her, she seems okay. This sounds like her best relationship yet.

Therapist: So there has been a sort of reversal in your relationship with your sister. When you were younger, she tried to protect you from some difficult situations, but as adults, you have tried to protect her.

Edie: True, but neither of us was really able to protect the other one.

Therapist: You wish it had been different?

Edie: Yes, I do. But Beth is doing better.

Therapist: And that must be a relief for you. I wonder what your own use of drugs and alcohol is like?

Edie: No problems there for me. I had all the drugs I wanted when I had cancer. I never drank much, but I had to stop drinking for so long when I was trying to become pregnant that I just never started again.

Therapist: You've told me about your history of cancer, but what is your current medical condition like?

Edie: The doctors say I'm doing well, though they think I might go into menopause early because of the chemotherapy. I have gained a lot of weight though, nearly 50 pounds since before I was pregnant. I feel tired a lot . . . maybe because of the extra weight.

Therapist: Tell me about your sleeping and eating.

Edie: I have trouble falling asleep most nights, and then I'm tired for the rest of the day because I get up early. My eating isn't very good either. I try to make nutritious meals for my family, but I snack during the day . . . peanut butter, cookies, whatever is around. I know I should do something about my weight and get some exercise, but I've been saying that for years and haven't done anything. Maybe you can help me with that too.

Therapist: We can certainly talk about ways to address those concerns. There are a few more areas I want to cover before we finish our session today. I know you are employed as a librarian, but I'd like to hear more about your education and work.

Edie: I was always a good student and enjoyed school. I guess it was an escape for me from all the problems at home. The only time when school got bad was during my cancer treatments; all the kids would tease me, and I hated to go to school. I was never very social or popular, and I guess I withdrew even more after that. But I still got good grades. My goal was to get a scholarship so I could go away to college. And I did! So I left home when I finished high school and went to the state university, majored in English. I like to read, so that major made sense to me. But after I graduated, I really didn't know what to do. I worked in sales for a while, but that was definitely not right for me. After a year or so, I decided to get my master's in library science. I borrowed some money from my dad and went to graduate school. I got a good job with the New York Public Library right after I got my degree, paid my father back for the loan, and was moving up in the system when Roberto and I got married. I guess my priorities shifted then. I focused more on my marriage and trying to become pregnant, but work was still rewarding for me. I felt like I had found my niche there.

Therapist: So your academic work and your job as a librarian have been great sources of success and pride to you.

Edie: Well, you're putting it more strongly than I would, but I guess you're right. In some ways, I feel more contented in the library than anywhere else I've ever been.

Therapist: So it also is a source of comfort for you. There is almost a spiritual quality to your talk about the library, and that makes me wonder about the place of religion and spirituality in your life.

Edie: Formal religion doesn't mean much to me anymore. Both of my parents are Jewish, but we hardly ever went to synagogue, just on the high holidays. I never had any religious education either. I still put down Jewish on forms that ask for your religion, but I don't practice the religion. And Roberto isn't Jewish. His family is Catholic. They used to go to church, but he hasn't gone in years. I worry about Ava's lack of religious education, but she doesn't seem to miss it. I do talk to her about God, though. I think believing in God comforted me as a child, and I want her to have that feeling too. When she was little, I taught her prayers to say at bedtime, but I don't think she prays anymore. I gave you a long answer to your question, but I guess this is a part of my life that confuses me. I have always felt a connection to God, to a spiritual side of myself, but then I wonder if I'm being a hypocrite because I don't follow any organized religion. Maybe that's something we can talk about, too, but it's pretty far down on the list.

Therapist: We can get back to that, though. I'd like to hear some more about your childhood years. We've talked about your parents' divorce, your relationships with your sister and your parents, your stepfather, your treatment for cancer, and your enjoyment of most of your school years. What else stands out as important during those years?

Edie: Not too much. My mother says I was precocious as a baby, walking and talking early. I had a few friends in the neighborhood, but I've always been kind of shy and was never very popular. I only dated three or four guys very briefly before I met Roberto. I guess I haven't told you about my grandparents, my mother's parents. . . .

Therapist: What do you want to tell me about them?

Edie: They took care of us when my mother went back to work after the divorce. I don't want to talk about them any more right now.

Therapist: All right. Let's put that topic on the shelf until you want to take it down. What other parts of your life might be important to talk about?

Edie: I do want to mention my friend, Sandi. She lived near me and had her first child when I was pregnant with Ava. Our children played together, and we became good friends. Three years ago she moved to California. I really miss her, but we're still in touch; e-mail is great for that.

Therapist: So Sandi is another important person in your life, but here's another relationship that has involved loss. What else do you want to be sure to mention before we finish our session?

Edie: I think that's about it. I didn't think I would have so much to say!

Therapist: Yes, you did cover a lot of ground. I can see that trying to get some help through counseling is really important to you and that you are already involved in that process. We'll get back to most of these topics again and probably also find some important areas we overlooked, but it's time to stop for today. How did you feel about our first session?

Edie: I liked talking to you; I wasn't sure I would. Where do we go from here?

Therapist: Let's schedule another appointment and try to hone in on some goals.

Exercises

The following exercises are designed to help you learn more about both asking questions and conducting an intake interview. In addition to working on these specific exercises, try to be more conscious of the questions you ask in your everyday activities, particularly when you meet a new person. Do you tend to ask open or closed questions? Are your questions just part of making conversation, or are you consciously trying to get to know the person you have met? Are you receiving the responses you want? If not, what might you do differently?

Exercises in Questioning: Large-Group Exercise   Read the following three client statements and the four clinician responses to each client statement. The client is a 42-year-old woman whose husband died recently. Consider the following aspects of each clinician response and then discuss which seems to be the best intervention in response to each client statement.

- Whether the question is open or closed
- The information you expect will be elicited by each question
- The focus of each question (e.g., the direction in which it moves the session)
- The tone of each question and the impact it is likely to have on the client

Client Statement 1

Client:	It's been three months since my husband died and two months since I began counseling, but I miss him even more than I did right after his death.
Counselor A:	Why do you think that is?
Counselor B:	Do you think I am doing something wrong in counseling you?
Counselor C:	What prevents you from getting over his death?
Counselor D:	What feelings come up for you as you think about missing him?

Client Statement 2

Client:	Even though I miss George, I have gone back to work, and I'm concentrating fairly well.
Counselor A:	How are you managing to do that?
Counselor B:	How do you feel that?
Counselor C:	Do you think you are ready to stop counseling now?
Counselor D:	Is your work still as demanding as it was?

Client Statement 3

Client:	I know I should get out and meet new people, but I just feel stuck.
Counselor A:	Where are you stuck?
Counselor B:	Did you sign up for the art class as we agreed?
Counselor C:	What has helped you when you have felt stuck before?
Counselor D:	Do you think you could be sabotaging your efforts to change?

Exercises in Questioning: Small- or Large-Group Exercise   Your client is a 12-year-old boy who is having difficulties related to socialization and self-esteem. For each client statement, write a question that you think will have a positive impact on the treatment process. Then share your questions with your group or class. For each of your questions, consider:

- Whether the question is open or closed
- The information you expect will be elicited by each question
- The focus of each question (e.g., the direction in which it moves the session)
- The tone of each question and the impact it is likely to have on the client

Client Statements

1. No matter how hard I try to make friends, it just doesn't work. There must really be something wrong with me.
2. I tried to talk to my dad about my problem. He said, "You just need to develop an interest in sports, and then you'll fit in fine with the other boys."
3. Roger asked me to sit with him at lunch. I really wanted to, but I felt so scared. I just said, "No, thanks," and walked away.

Small-Group Exercise in Conducting an Intake Interview   General directions for the small-group exercises are included in chapter 1. Review those directions before beginning this exercise.

Now that you have improved your ability to make good use of questions, try out that skill via an intake interview. Divide into your groups of four people, and then break each of those groups into two dyads. Each pair should take a turn conducting an interview; one person should assume the role of the clinician, while the other becomes the client. Use the interview topics listed previously in this chapter to structure your interview. Record this interview to facilitate analysis and feedback.

When you are in the client role, think about a comfortable way to approach the intake process. You can assume a persona, making believe you are someone you know well and presenting information as that person might. Details can be changed to protect the person you are role playing. You might also choose to talk about yourself if that feels comfortable. Like any client, keep in mind that you do not need to answer all the clinician's questions, and it is your right to disclose as much or as little as you choose. However, because this is a learning experience, try to approach this exercise in a way that allows you to be a cooperative and collaborative client who will not present the clinician with too great a challenge. Allow approximately 20 minutes for the interview and 10 minutes for feedback.

While one pair is engaged in an intake interview, the other pair should observe and take notes, preparing to provide feedback. Remember to emphasize strengths when giving feedback. When identifying weaknesses in the role play, be sure to suggest alternatives that might have been more successful. Feedback should cover the following topics:

- The overall tone of the interview
- How well important areas of information were covered in the interview
- The nature of the questions that were asked (open or closed, implied or direct)
- The focus of each question (e.g., the direction in which it moved the session)
- The tone of each question and the impact it had on the client
- The strengths of the interview
- Ways in which the interview might have been improved

SUMMARY

This chapter has reviewed the importance of background in understanding people. It also has provided guidelines, examples, and exercises to teach readers how to ask helpful questions and to conduct an intake interview that will obtain background information while building rapport. Chapter 4 will present ideas and approaches to treatment developed by Sigmund Freud, a master at using past history to help people change in positive ways.

CHAPTER 4

Sigmund Freud and Psychoanalysis

In 1993, *Time Magazine* asked, "Is Freud dead?" The question of whether psychoanalysis, reflecting the ideas of Sigmund Freud, is obsolete has often been explored. However, even the frequent revisiting of this question testifies to the strength and influence of Freud's ideas. In 1998–1999, for example, the Library of Congress in Washington, DC, hosted a large exhibit titled *Sigmund Freud: Conflict and Culture*. Prochaska and Norcross (2003) reported that, among American psychotherapists, 18 percent of clinical psychologists, 15 percent of counseling psychologists, 35 percent of psychiatrists, 33 percent of social workers, and 11 percent of counselors viewed their primary theoretical orientation as psychoanalytic or psychodynamic. Freud established the foundation for today's counseling and psychotherapy; he succeeded in bringing our knowledge of personality, human development, and psychological symptoms into the modern age. Many of Freud's concepts, including the unconscious, defense mechanisms, and the ego, have become so widely accepted that we sometimes forget they began with Freud.

Freud's efforts required great courage; he disagreed radically with the thinking of his peers, withstood years of verbal and written attacks, and worked prodigiously to advance his ideas. Because of Freud's contributions, efforts to advance people's psychological growth and reduce emotional difficulties are much more successful.

SIGMUND FREUD

Sigmund Freud was born in Freiberg, Moravia, on May 6, 1856. His father was 40 years old, a widower with two sons, when he married his second wife, who was only 19 at the time. Freud was the couple's first child, born two years after his parents' marriage. As the firstborn and reportedly his mother's favorite (Jones, 1953), Freud had a special place in his family, although his mother gave birth to 7 more children in the next 10 years. His father, a busy merchant with a commanding but gentle disposition, seems to have been a role model for his son. When Freud was 19 months old, his 8-month-old brother Julius died. Freud recalled early feelings of jealousy and resentment toward his brother and later reproached himself when his brother died. Memories such as these probably contributed to Freud's emphasis on the formative power of early childhood experiences.

Freud's family was Jewish, and this cultural and religious background affected him throughout his life. His Jewish heritage, with its emphasis on learning and family, contributed to Freud's appreciation for study, family history, and in-depth analysis. It also influenced his place of residence and his career choice, probably colored the reception his work received, and eventually led him to flee from Austria when Hitler came into power.

When Freud was a child, the ill-treatment of Jews in many parts of Europe prompted his family to move to Vienna, Austria (at that time a relatively safe place for Jews), where he spent most of his life. Freud was a diligent student, studying at the University of Vienna between 1873 and 1881, when he completed medical school. Jones (1953) reported that career choices open to Jews in Vienna at that time included business, law, and medicine. Although Freud felt drawn to politics or social work, he chose medicine as the best available option. He was interested in learning about the mind and did his residency in neurology, beginning his medical career in theoretical medical work.

In 1884, Freud began studying and experimenting with cocaine as a tool to heighten mental powers (Mahoney, 1998). However, evidence of the negative impact of this substance on his colleagues dampened his enthusiasm for the drug.

Love was an important influence on Freud's career. He became engaged to Martha Bernays, daughter of the chief rabbi of Hamburg, in 1882. To earn enough money to marry and support a family, Freud took a position at a psychiatric clinic. Over their 4-year engagement, Freud wrote more than 900 letters to his wife-to-be, providing her with the details of his daily life.

Freud married Martha Bernays in 1886 and, about the same time, opened a private practice in neuropathology in Vienna. Growing up in a large family probably influenced him to have a large family himself and to value and feel comfortable with family around him. The couple had six children during the first 10 years of their marriage. Martha's sister, Minna, also was a part of the family, living with them from 1896 until her death in 1941, helping Martha and offering emotional support to Freud.

Freud's work and his family were the most important parts of his life. Jones (1955, p. 386) speaks of the "unshakable devotion and a perfect harmony of understanding" between Freud and his wife and of Freud's efforts to raise his children in an atmosphere that would minimize anxiety, limitations, and criticism, and allow personalities to develop freely. Although he often saw 10 patients a day, Freud found time for his hobbies, especially collecting antiquities, reading biographies and other literature, studying mushrooms and rare wildflowers, and traveling. He was much affected by family joys and sorrows; his letters reflect the profound impact of the military involvement of his three sons, the capture of one during World War I, the death of his daughter Sophie in 1920, and the death of a grandson in 1923.

In that same year, Freud was diagnosed with cancer, probably related to the many cigars he smoked each day. During his remaining years, he had 33 operations on his jaw and palate, which prolonged his life but caused him considerable pain. In his later years, he wore a prosthesis in his mouth and wrote frequently of the severe discomfort caused by this apparatus and his many surgeries. Despite this, Freud continued to see patients and to write until the year of his death. We consider his work in the next section of this chapter.

In March 1938, the Nazis invaded Austria. Although he was 82 years old and seriously ill, Freud decided that he must leave Austria. His daughter Anna and his son Martin had already been questioned by the Nazis, and the family members believed that they would not survive long in Vienna. Freud, his wife, and his daughter Anna left Vienna and went to England, where he was welcomed by friends. He tried to bring his four sisters with him. Unfortunately, they were not permitted to leave the country, and Freud was only allowed to leave money for their welfare. All four sisters died in concentration camps during the next five years.

Despite additional surgery in England, Freud's cancer was deemed incurable. Because he wanted to continue writing and seeing patients as long as possible, he put off taking the pain killers that might cloud his mind until 4 months before his death. He died on September 23, 1939, leaving a legacy that many of his followers have shaped into modern psychotherapy.

THE DEVELOPMENT OF PSYCHOANALYSIS

Freud's early work focused on the study of neurology. His research on the brain and spinal cord was his first notable contribution to the field. During the 1880s, he became interested in the work of Josef Breuer, a well-known physician in Vienna. Breuer used hypnosis and verbal expression to treat emotional disorders. His famous case of Anna O., a woman who experienced conversion symptoms (paralysis of limbs, as well as disturbances of sight, eating, and speech) and dissociative symptoms in relation to the death of her father, captured Freud's attention. He became increasingly interested in psychological disorders and their treatment (Freud, 1938). He studied hypnosis with Charcot and investigated the use of electrotherapy, baths, and massage treatments for people with emotional difficulties. Although Freud sometimes used hypnosis, none of these other strategies seemed effective to him. Experimentation led him to initiate what he called the concentration technique, in which patients lay down with their eyes closed while Freud placed his hand on their foreheads and urged them to say whatever thoughts arose. He used questions to elicit material and promote self-exploration. This was an early version of modern psychotherapy. Although Freud later stopped touching his patients in this way because of its erotic possibilities, he continued to emphasize the importance of patient self-expression and free association.

Freud first used the term *psychoanalysis* in an 1896 paper. His writings during the 1890s reflected growing awareness of the importance of sexuality in people's lives. He initially believed that symptoms of hysteria and neurosis were due to childhood sexual experiences, perhaps traumatic sexual abuse such as seduction of the child by the father. A combination of difficulty in substantiating this idea and the negative reactions it elicited led Freud to change his ideas. He subsequently focused more on infantile sexuality and fantasies rather than actual sexual experiences as instrumental in determining emotional difficulties. In retrospect, Freud probably was wiser than even he knew. More than 100 years later, clinicians are now well-aware of the high incidence of child sexual abuse. Probably at least some of his patients who described early sexual experiences to Freud did indeed have those experiences.

The combination of Freud's interest in understanding the human psyche and an effort to address difficulties he experienced in his own life led him to explore the meaning of his dreams and fantasies, as well as his childhood sexual feelings toward his mother and anger toward his father. His major work, *Interpretation of Dreams* (Freud, 1938), was completed in 1899 and advanced the powerful concepts that dreams reflect repressed wishes and that mental and physical processes are intertwined. Freud's ideas were largely ignored or rejected when the book was published. However, again he expressed ideas that ultimately gained widespread acceptance: the close connection between the mind and the body.

Despite the mixed reactions to his work, Freud moved forward to collaborate with colleagues who shared his viewpoints. In 1902, he suggested to Alfred Adler and several others that they meet to discuss Freud's work. This became the Vienna Psycho-Analytical Society, which met weekly at Freud's home. In 1910, Freud designated Carl Jung as president of the International Psycho-Analytical Association. Adler and Jung eventually separated from the Psycho-Analytical Association and went on to make their own important contributions to psychotherapy, discussed in chapters 5 and 6 of this book.

Growing international recognition of his work led to Freud's first visit to the United States in 1909, where he lectured at Clark University at the invitation of its president, Stanley Hall. Hall was a pioneer in experimental psychology and viewed Freud's work as a major contribution. Published as *Five Lectures on Psycho-Analysis,* these lectures presented Freud's ideas in a comprehensible way. They were widely read and broadened awareness of his work.

By this time, Freud had replaced hypnosis with free association in his work and encouraged analysts to experience their own analysis, a requirement still maintained by programs that train psychoanalysts. He also believed that patients needed to lie on a couch during treatment in order to relax them, facilitate self-expression, allow transference reactions to develop, and enable analysts to think freely without worrying about their nonverbal messages. Patients were told never to withhold any thoughts so that Freud could understand the unconscious, often reflected in sexually related fantasies stemming from early childhood experiences, that had produced symptoms.

Freud's writings during these years included not only his theoretical works but also lengthy case studies, reflecting his ideas. *Dora* (Decker, 1998) was the report of an 11-week analysis that Freud performed on an 18-year-old woman whose father was having an affair. Her father's lover befriended Dora, while the woman's husband made sexual advances toward her, creating a situation that would cause many people to have emotional difficulties. *Little Hans* (Freud, 1936) was Freud's analysis of a five-year-old boy who would not leave his house because he feared being bitten by a horse. Freud conducted the analysis secondhand, meeting only with the boy's father, and enabled the father to help his son use Freud's insights into the boy's displacement of his fear of his father onto horses. Fourteen years later, the boy visited Freud to report that Freud had cured him of his phobia of horses. Other important cases include the so-called *Man with Rats,* who had what Freud termed an obsessional neurosis characterized by doubts and compulsions as well as terrifying dreams involving rats. This 11-month analysis was also successful. Another patient, Wolf Man, sought help from Freud when the patient was 23 years old and incapacitated by his compulsions. Freud believed this man may have witnessed parental intercourse as a child, exacerbating his ambivalent feelings toward his father. After four years of treatment, this patient, too, was free of serious symptoms.

By World War I, Freud saw 12 to 13 patients a day, each for 55 minutes with 5 minutes in between. His services were sought by the rich and famous. He reportedly cured the conductor Bruno Walter of partial paralysis of his right arm in six sessions and required only four sessions to relieve composer Gustav Mahler of a problem with impotence by exploring its psychodynamic origins (Jones, 1957).

Freud's interests broadened during the war years. He became interested in what was then called shell shock or traumatic neurosis, symptoms that developed after exposure to war experiences. The primary treatment for this disorder had been electrical stimulation of the skin and muscles. According to Freud, psychoanalysis, not electricity, was the proper treatment for this disorder, which he believed reflected an emotional conflict between the desire to escape and to honor one's sense of duty. Freud's thinking paved the way for our modern understanding of posttraumatic stress disorder.

Freud also became interested in understanding homosexuality, writing, "homosexuality is assuredly no advantage, but it is nothing to be ashamed of, no vice, no degradation, it cannot be classified as an illness" (Jones, 1957, p. 195). Here, too, Freud's ideas were very advanced—not until the 1970s did the American Psychiatric Association and the American Psychological Association officially determine that homosexuality is not a mental disorder.

Freud was less astute in his understanding of women, a controversial aspect of his theory. This will be discussed in detail later in this chapter.

Freud continued to broaden his interests in his later writings, which addressed not only the human psyche but also art, religion, anthropology, sociology, biology, and literature. He placed greater emphasis on context and society and acknowledged the important ways in which they both reflected and shaped human development. He expanded his definition of the unconscious, viewing it as containing more than repressed material, and also broadened his definition of sexuality, describing it as a great source of energy. In addition, he expressed approval of "lay analysts"—people such as his daughter Anna Freud, who had been trained in analysis and had themselves been analyzed, but had not received an M.D. degree. We may think of these lay analysts as the forerunners of today's non-medical clinicians: the psychologists, counselors, social workers, and psychiatric nurses who are our primary providers of psychotherapy.

IMPORTANT THEORETICAL CONCEPTS

Freud began his work as a theoretician, and it is through his comprehensive theory of personality that he has made his major contributions. This section reviews the most important aspects of his theory, including his concepts of human nature, the three structures of the personality, how personality develops, levels of consciousness, and the meaning of symptoms. Freud's ideas, like those of many of the theorists discussed in this book, have great depth and complexity and this book can only provide an overview of those ideas. Readers are strongly encouraged to read more about all of these theorists.

View of Human Nature

Freud placed great emphasis on the influence of biology and of early childhood experiences. He believed that, because of their biology, people go through predictable stages of psychosocial development and must struggle to find a balance between their strong sexual drives and their need to behave in socially acceptable ways. According to Freud, biological processes are mediated by early patterns of attachment, as well as by how people negotiate the stages of development.

Freud also recognized the importance of context. For example, he viewed people as seeking to win love and approval by acting in ways that reflected the dictates of their families and societies. This perspective is compatible with current thinking on diversity and multiculturalism.

Freud has been criticized for taking a deterministic stance, emphasizing irrational and instinctual forces in shaping people. Certainly, he viewed those forces as important, but perhaps the essential message in his work is that people need not be the victims of biology. Rather, we can use psychotherapy and other sources of help and personal growth to gain insight, lessen the power of the unconscious, and free ourselves to make conscious and healthy choices. Understanding early development, as well as the pressures of the libido and the superego, and strengthening our egos can enable us to lead the sorts of lives and have the sorts of relationships that we desire. Freud himself achieved much both personally and professionally, apparently reflecting his own success in balancing the competing pressures inside him.

Personality Structure

According to Freud, the personality is comprised of three systems: the id, the superego, and the ego. These structures often overlap and intertwine and are not discrete entities, although each has distinctive properties. Keep in mind that Freud's concept of the id (the biological component), the ego (the psychological component), and the superego (the social component) is simply a sort of map designed to clarify the nature of the personality. Just as states and countries are separated by artificial boundaries, so are these structures of the personality separated into artificial constructs. In reality, they operate together as the internal forces that form our personalities. However, using this theoretical structure can facilitate understanding of strengths and areas of difficulties in a personality.

The Id   The *id* is the first system of the personality. Present at birth, it encompasses all the inherited systems, including the instincts, and is largely unconscious. The id derives its energy from bodily processes and is in close touch with the needs and messages of the body, seeking to satisfy them when possible. The id is subjective and emotional and, in its pure form, is not moderated by the external world. Simply put, the id wants what it wants when it wants it. The id, like the infant in which it originates, is intolerant of tension, pain, and discomfort and seeks to avoid them by pursuing pleasure and gratification (the pleasure principle). It is demanding and its needs, rather than logic, morality, or the constraints of society, determine the direction of its wants.

The id has two important strategies for obtaining pleasure: reflex actions and primary process. Reflex actions include automatic processes such as coughing and blinking, which reduce tensions, especially those of a biological nature such as a tickle in the throat or a speck in the eye.

Primary process is more complex; it allows people to form a mental image of a remedy for their discomfort, a wish fulfillment. Freud believed that dreams served this function, offering a wish-fulfillment image. Although the image may assuage some of the discomfort, it also can cause frustration in failing to resolve the problem. It is the ego, discussed later in this section, that helps people truly find wish fulfillment and reduce discomfort in realistic ways.

Freud believed that people have both life instincts and death or destructive instincts. Life instincts, reflecting the needs of the id, lead us to pursue pleasure and avoid pain. The *libido,* present at birth, is an important aspect of the life instinct. This was originally defined by Freud as sexual desire, but its meaning has been broadened over the years to refer to energy and vitality, a zest for life. A desire for sexual fulfillment is only one facet of the life instinct, but it is an essential one because it leads people to procreate and continue the human race. Although Freud's concept of a death instinct has not received much support over the years, recognizing the possible presence of this force can help us to understand human development.

The Superego   The *superego* can be thought of as the opposite of the id. The superego is a sort of rigid conscience that internalizes the rules and guidelines of a person's world. Messages from parents, teachers, and society as well as racial, cultural, and national traditions are important contributors to the development of a person's superego. The moral code of the superego is perfectionistic, diligently discriminating between good and bad, right and wrong. The formation of the superego allows self-control to take the place of parental control. When people follow the idealistic dictates of their superego, they typically feel proud and righteous but may sacrifice pleasure and gratification. On the other hand, when they ignore the superego, shame, guilt, and anxiety may result. The superego serves an essential function in curtailing the drives of the id; but like the id, the superego is too controlling and extreme in its directives.

The Ego   The *ego,* like the superego, becomes differentiated from the id as the child develops, although energy from the id provides the power for both the ego and the superego. The ego is not present at birth but evolves as the baby realizes its separateness from the mother.

The ego is aware of both the pressures of the id and the constraints of the superego and seeks to moderate both while still meeting their needs. The ego has been described as "the mental agent of rational and self-conscious selfhood" (Brunner, 1998, p. 83). It is a mediator and organizer. Guided by the reality principle or reality testing, the ego has considerable power; it can effect changes in the environment, postpone or suppress instinctual demands, and encourage sound moral judgment and flexibility. Using logic, intelligence, objectivity, and awareness of external reality, a healthy ego considers, modifies, and integrates both internal and external pressures on a person; decides when and how the person should respond to those demands; and identifies wise choices and behaviors that promote self-preservation.

Stages of Development

Freud believed that people develop according to predictable stages, with those during the first 5 years of life being the most important. The nature of a person's development during those early years is a major factor in determining the later emotional health of that person.

The Oral Stage   The *oral stage* makes up the first year or so of a child's life. The mouth is the most important zone of the body for the infant, with sucking and eating providing the nurturance that will sustain the child's life during the oral-incorporative phase. Biting is a way for the child to express aggression during the subsequent oral-aggressive period. The mouth also becomes the child's first erotic zone (Stafford-Clark, 1965). Freud believed that developmental problems at this point could later manifest themselves in symbolic and sublimated forms through symptoms such as gullibility (swallowing anything), overeating, and argumentativeness (oral aggressiveness).

Erik Erikson (1963) built on Freud's stages of development in Erikson's own delineation of developmental stages. Erikson's linking of personal and social development to Freud's concept of psychosexual development increased the importance and relevance of Freud's work. According to Erikson, issues of dependency and trust are particularly important during the initial or oral stage which he believed focused on basic trust versus basic mistrust. Children who develop a stable attachment to a nurturing and trustworthy caregiver who meets their important needs during these early years are more able to develop healthy, close, and trusting relationships with others later on.

The Anal Stage   Freud termed the second stage of development, between the ages of one and three, the *anal stage* because of the importance of toilet training and the process of elimination during those years. In this second stage, the focus of gratification shifts from the oral functions to the social pleasure of impressing the parents and the physical pleasure of emptying the bowels. According to psychoanalytic theory, parents who use punitive and restrictive means to develop children's bowel and bladder control are likely to promote stingy, compulsive, controlling, and withholding characteristics in their children; those who reward and praise their children lavishly for appropriate elimination are likely to foster creativity. Feelings about the body and its functions also are shaped during these years. Understanding the relationships between children's bodily functions and their subsequent personality development can help define healthy parenting as well as provide insight into emotional difficulties that may stem from early developmental problems.

According to Erikson (1963), issues of autonomy versus shame and doubt typically arise during this period as children test limits, try out new behaviors, and make mistakes while learning skills that give them independence and control over their lives. Children who are allowed to acquire age-appropriate independence and learn from their mistakes without being shamed or berated are more likely to become independent, competent, and self-confident adults.

The Phallic Stage   The third stage, between ages three and five, is known as the *phallic stage*. According to Freud, this complex stage is strongly related to our adult sexual relationships. During these years, feelings of pleasure become associated with the genitals, and masturbation and sexual fantasies develop.

Freud believed that at this age children harbor unconscious sexual desires for the parent of the other gender along with an unconscious wish to eliminate the parent of the same gender, perceived as standing in the way of the child's desires. In boys, this is termed the *Oedipus complex,* referring to a man who, according to the literature of ancient Greece, unknowingly married his mother. According to Freud, fear of retribution from the father causes boys to develop castration anxiety, which, in turn, allows them to repress their desire for their mother and resolve their feelings appropriately through identification with the father.

In girls, the parallel situation is referred to as the *Electra complex,* named after a woman in Greek literature who had strong feelings of love and devotion toward her father. Freud hypothesized that the female equivalent of castration anxiety is penis envy, in which girls become jealous and resentful because of their lack of a penis. He believed that girls, like boys, typically resolve this phase by identifying with their same-gender parent.

Modern psychoanalysts acknowledge the possibility that a girl may experience penis envy but also believe that a boy may have womb or breast envy. However, they downplay the importance of both patterns, viewing them as only one of many internal and external experiences that may be important in children's development. In addition, although Freud saw many parallels between the ways in which both boys and girls passed through this stage, many modern theorists emphasize that, for both genders, the mother is typically the first love and source of nurturance. Mothers are, of course, the same gender as their daughters but not as their sons. Most girls, then, must shift the primary source of their attachment from women to men while most boys do not make this shift, probably an important difference in their development of love and attachments.

Many aspects of emotional development evolve during the phallic years, including self-esteem and self-image, sexuality, need for love and approval, feelings toward authority figures, and sense of initiative. According to Erikson (1963), this stage focuses on initiative versus guilt. Positive development entails forming healthy attachments to parents of both genders as well as identification with the same-sex parent. This enables children to develop feelings of competence, to make and trust their own decisions, and to take the initiative in moving forward with their lives. Those who do not resolve this stage successfully may be troubled by guilt, difficulty in intimate relationships, and a negative or confused sense of self.

The Latency Stage   Freud viewed the time between ages 5 and 11 as a relatively quiet period in a child's sexual development; therefore, he called these years the *latency stage*. Sexual drives become less important, while social interests increase. Children turn outward, form relationships, progress through school, and develop rewarding hobbies and activities. Emotional development focuses on their ability to take on and succeed in new challenges and endeavors and to set and achieve realistic goals. Children who negotiate this stage successfully typically develop feelings of empowerment and have initiative, while those who cannot deal with the demands of this stage may experience low self-esteem.

Freud's latency stage parallels Erikson's fourth stage, industry versus inferiority, occurring between the ages of 6 and 12. Positive development during these years entails achievement of social and academic success. Children learn good work habits and become productive and able to meet new challenges. As they mature, this is reflected in their ability to become responsible and competent to successfully cope with obstacles and difficulties.

The Genital Stage   The final stage in Freud's model is the *genital stage,* which follows the latency stage and continues throughout the life span. During this stage, adolescents and adults solidify their personal identities, develop caring and altruistic feelings toward others, establish positive loving and sexual relationships, and progress in successful careers. Each stage builds on and integrates the growth and learning of the previous stage and ideally results in the development of an emotionally healthy adult.

Paralleling the first part of Freud's genital stage is Erikson's stage of identity versus role confusion, occurring between ages 12 and 18. During the adolescent years, young people develop identities and formulate self-images that will greatly influence their ability to love and work. Those who develop a clear and positive sense of themselves and their roles are more likely, according to Erikson, to find later fulfillment in both relationships and careers.

Erikson's Additional Stages   Although Freud's concept of the developmental stages ended with the fifth or genital stage, Erikson's model includes the following additional stages that reflect awareness of the lifelong nature of development:

Stage 6. Intimacy versus isolation is the focus of this stage, extending from age 18 to 35. According to Erikson, the primary goals of healthy development during young adulthood include forming meaningful relationships and becoming part of a community.

Stage 7. Generativity versus stagnation is the emphasis of the middle adult years, extending from ages 35–60. Successful passage through these years is marked by feelings of productivity, achieved through parenting, career accomplishments, or achievements in other areas of one's life.

Stage 8. Integrity versus despair is the focal issue of the later years. Healthy development, according to Erikson, occurs when people take stock of their lives, feel worthwhile, and have a sense of fulfillment and ego integrity as they approach the end of their lives.

Levels of Consciousness

Most people have few, if any, memories of times before the age of three or four. In addition, we all have had experiences we either cannot recall at all or that only come into awareness when something reminds us of them, triggering their recall. What has happened to those memories?

According to Freud, we have three levels of consciousness: the conscious, the preconscious, and the unconscious. The *conscious* is material in awareness, always available to us. The *preconscious* holds information that may not be part of current awareness but which can be readily accessed. This material may be benign, such as the memory of a person we knew years ago but do not think of until we see her again in the grocery store; or it may be aversive, such as the memory of a car accident that returns to us each time we hear the screech of car brakes applied in a hurry. The *unconscious* holds memories that are highly charged, including repressed drives and impulses (such as a child's sexual feelings toward a parent), and recollections of experiences that may be too painful or unacceptable to be allowed into the conscious or preconscious. Freud believed that the unconscious held many times more memories than were in the preconscious or the conscious. Psychoanalysis can bring memories from the unconscious into the conscious. However, without benefit of therapy, those memories may either remain in the unconscious or emerge into consciousness in symbolic or distorted ways, perhaps via dreams or symptoms.

Dreams and Other Reflections of the Unconscious

Freud believed that dreams, symptoms, and errors all reflect the unconscious and its fantasies. His writings, *Psychopathology of Everyday Life* (1938) and *The Interpretation of Dreams* (1938), discuss in depth the process by which the unconscious is revealed. Freud believed that all dreams are meaningful and that dream analysis may be the most important way to understand people. He viewed dreams as fulfilling wishes or impulses that could not be allowed into awareness, providing a vehicle for working through disturbing thoughts and feelings. Although people may recall the manifest content of dreams, the defenses of the ego displace and condense the underlying significance of a dream so that it is disguised. Unconscious events and emotions may be represented in dreams by items or experiences that seem unimportant but may nevertheless cause anxiety because of their latent meaning.

The following abbreviated example of a dream of one of my clients reflects Freud's concepts. (Keep in mind that dream analysis usually is a complex and challenging process.) A young woman had a dream of herself frolicking in the park with a dog. Earlier that day, she had taken a walk in a park and had come upon a couple embracing. Discussion suggested that the dog represented a married co-worker of her father's whom she found attractive. Freud might also have believed this reflected an attraction to her father. The park was a place where she had seen sexual behavior taking place. The dream, then, may well have reflected the fulfillment of her repressed wish to have a sexual relationship with her father's friend and perhaps also reflected her childhood desire for her father.

For Freud, errors, omissions, slips, and poorly performed tasks also had latent meaning, and the term *Freudian slip* has come to mean a misstatement that reveals an unconscious wish or feeling. For example, a man who was attracted to his next-door neighbor, a woman called Lou, left her a note about a package that had been delivered to him by mistake. However, he addressed the note to "Dear Love" rather than "Dear Lou."

Defense Mechanisms

Many of us have experienced frequent and painful episodes of anxiety. According to Freud, people have an innate drive toward reduction of tension and anxiety. Freud was particularly interested in what he labelled *signal anxiety,* the anxiety that results from a conflict between internal wishes or drives and constraints that come from either internalized prohibitions or external reality. He believed that signal anxiety would automatically trigger ego defense mechanisms, usually learned during early childhood and developed as a way of dealing with inner conflict, anxiety, pain, shame, sorrow, and other negative emotions.

Everyone has defenses. Some are healthy, mature defenses that promote adjustment and enable people to transform undesirable wishes into ones that can be fulfilled. For example, sublimation is a defense mechanism that can change a self-destructive sexual desire into the drive to create a work of art. On the other hand, some defenses distort reality and interfere with efforts to build relationships. An example is splitting, in which people view themselves and others as being either all good or all bad and vacillate from idealization to devaluation of themselves and others. Which defense mechanism people use at a particular time depends on their level of development and the degree of anxiety they are experiencing.

The literature identifies and describes over 40 defense mechanisms. These have been categorized in various ways including the following:

- *Primary vs. secondary defense mechanisms*—Primary or fundamental defense mechanisms include repression and denial, which keep unacceptable thoughts or impulses from consciousness. Secondary defense mechanisms are outgrowths of the primary ones; examples are projection, sublimation, and reaction formation.
- *Relationship to developmental stage*—Defense mechanisms associated with the oral stage include primitive defenses such as denial and distortion. Regression, undoing, and reaction formation are some of the defense mechanisms linked to the anal stage. Most sophisticated defense mechanisms are associated with later stages of development. For example, intellectualization has been associated with the phallic stage and sublimation, with the latency stage.
- *Psychotic vs. neurotic defenses*—Psychotic defenses are most likely to be evident in children, in dreams, and in people with psychotic disorders. Examples include distortion, denial, and delusional projection, all of which reflect a loss of contact with reality. Neurotic defenses are far more common, although they, too, are typically associated with emotional difficulties. Among these defenses are rationalization, intellectualization, and displacement.

- *Immature vs. healthy defenses*—Immature defenses are common in adolescents as well as in people with mood, personality, and impulse control disorders. Included in this group are such defenses as projection, splitting, and acting out. On the other hand, examples of healthy defenses are humor, altruism, sublimation, and conscious suppression.

The following is a list of some of the most common defense mechanisms, along with brief definitions (American Psychiatric Association, 2000):

Healthy, Adaptive Defense Mechanisms

- *Affiliation*—turning to others for help and support, but retaining responsibility for one's own difficulties
- *Altruism*—deriving satisfaction from investing heavily in helping others
- *Anticipation*—reducing anxiety by considering the probable consequences of future events and finding ways to address them effectively
- *Humor*—focusing on the amusing aspects of situations
- *Sublimation*—redirecting potentially harmful emotions or impulses into socially acceptable ones
- *Suppression*—intentionally avoiding paying attention to nonproductive and troubling issues, experiences, and emotions

Maladaptive Defense Mechanisms

- *Acting out*—exhibiting negative behaviors rather than using thoughts or emotions to deal with a situation
- *Avoidance*—refusing to deal with troubling situations or experiences
- *Denial*—refusing to acknowledge an aspect of reality that is evident to others
- *Displacement*—transferring strong feelings from the situation in which they originated to a less threatening situation (e.g., expressing anger toward one's dog rather than one's supervisor)
- *Dissociation*—temporarily disconnecting from a situation via memory loss or loss of awareness
- *Help-rejecting complaining*—constantly complaining and requesting help which is then rejected when offered
- *Idealization*—exaggerating the positive and ignoring the negative aspects of a person or situation
- *Identification*—modeling oneself after another person in order to gain approval
- *Intellectualization*—avoiding emotions by focusing on thoughts and abstractions
- *Isolation*—disconnecting thoughts and emotions
- *Passive aggression*—expressing anger and hostility in indirect ways (e.g., "accidentally" breaking a person's heirloom vase)
- *Projection*—attributing one's own unacceptable thoughts, emotions, or actions to another
- *Rationalization*—justifying one's choices in self-serving but invalid ways
- *Reaction formation*—replacing unacceptable thoughts and emotions with their opposite to overcompensate
- *Regression*—reverting to a lower developmental level in thoughts, emotions, and behavior

- *Repression*—relegating disturbing thoughts and feelings to the unconscious rather than dealing with them effectively
- *Resistance*—blocking memories, insights, or avenues to positive change
- *Somatization*—channeling conflicts into physical symptoms
- *Splitting*—perceiving the self and others as either all good or all bad
- *Undoing*—negating or invalidating unacceptable thoughts, emotions, or actions

The study of people's use of defense mechanisms is a fruitful line of inquiry today and provides insight into ways in which clinicians can help people cope with anxiety and other emotional difficulties. For example, a study by Snarey, Son, Kuehne, Hauser, and Vaillant (1987) focused on how men in early adulthood coped with infertility. Those who redirected their needs into substitute parent-like activities such as mentoring a child or leading a youth group were most likely to eventually adopt a child and remain married. However, those men whose defense mechanisms led them to use self-centered substitution styles such as focusing on themselves or their possessions were more likely to divorce and least likely to achieve later fulfillment of their generativity needs. In another study, ego defense mechanisms, assessed via the Ego Defense Scale, distinguished between suicidal and non-suicidal adolescents (Apter et al., 1997). The suicidal young people scored higher on denial, displacement, repression, regression, projection, introjection, and total defenses and lower on sublimation.

Research suggests that the construct of defense mechanisms is relevant in multicultural groups. Tori and Bilmes (2002) found that these concepts were relevant to an Asian population.

TREATMENT USING PSYCHOANALYSIS

Extensive supervision and training is required to master the rich array of treatment strategies associated with psychoanalysis. This book presents an overview of these strategies, but readers should bear in mind that additional training is needed before they can be used skillfully.

Goals of Psychoanalysis

The overall goal of psychoanalysis is "the best possible psychological equilibrium for the functioning of the ego" (Stafford-Clark, 1965, p. 213). Specific treatment objectives include the following (Baker, 1985):

- Improving the ego's conscious and mature control over irrational and harmful impulses and instincts
- Enriching the nature and variety of the ego defense mechanisms so that they are more effective, mature, and adaptable
- Encouraging development of perspectives that are grounded in an accurate and clear assessment of reality and that promote adjustment
- Developing a capacity for healthy and rewarding intimate relationships along with the ability to express oneself in rewarding ways
- Reducing the perfectionism, rigidity, and punitiveness of the superego

Freud's writings offer a rich array of approaches to achieving these goals.

Therapeutic Alliance

Psychoanalysis, as performed by Freud as well as by modern therapists, usually is a long-term, intensive process. People are typically seen for treatment from 2 to 5 times a week for 3 to 5 years. Freud advocated having the patient lie on a couch while the therapist sat in a chair positioned behind the patient's head so the therapist could not be observed during the session. This was designed to both relax and reduce distractions for the patient and to allow the therapist to remain as anonymous as possible. Therapist neutrality is important in fostering the development of transference.

Although clients do most of the talking in psychoanalysis, therapists actively guide the sessions in meaningful directions and promote the uncovering of repressed material. They can be described as listening with a third ear attuned to underlying meanings, symbols, contradictions, and important omissions that may point the way to unlocking the unconscious. Questions, interpretations, and free association are common interventions that psychoanalysts use in their work.

Transference and Countertransference

In transference the client projects onto the therapist characteristics of another person, usually a parent, and reacts to the therapist as though he or she really does possess those characteristics. Transference involves a distortion or misperception of the therapist and is not a direct response to the way the therapist actually is. The unobserved and neutral psychoanalyst is more likely to elicit transference reactions than is a therapist who engages in self-disclosure and interacts more actively with clients.

Transference can be positive, negative, or mixed. For example, a client may project onto the therapist the seductive but loving traits of his mother (mixed), the angry and rejecting attitude of his father (negative), or the warm and nurturing characteristics of his grandmother (positive). Freud saw the establishment of transference as a key component of successful treatment. Some degree of emotional health and a capacity to form relationships is necessary for people to establish a transference. That is one reason why Freud's approach works best for people with neurotic (e.g., depressive disorders, anxiety disorders) rather than psychotic disorders and who maintain contact with reality.

Three stages are involved in the lengthy process of working through a transference. Once the transference develops, it is further established and explored in order to elicit repressed material. Gradually, the original dysfunctional pattern reemerges, now in terms of the transference to the therapist. Finally, the origins of the transference are understood and resolved, strengthening the ego and freeing the client to relate to others in healthier ways.

Although countertransference was not a salient part of Freud's work, many therapists today from both psychoanalytic and other theoretical orientations pay attention to it. In countertransference, a clinician projects onto a client characteristics of important people in the clinician's past. A therapist with a mother who exhibited passive-aggressive behaviors might berate a client who was delayed by a traffic jam, projecting feelings toward the mother onto the client. Clinicians should not assume that they are too skilled or insightful to develop countertransference reactions but should carefully monitor any strong emotional reactions they have to clients for the possibility of countertransference. The importance of clinicians having awareness of their reactions is one of the primary reasons personal analysis is a required part of training in psychoanalysis.

Free Association

Freud used many approaches to access repressed material, including analysis of dreams and transference as well as free association. The process of free association reflects the most important rule of psychoanalysis: People should say whatever comes into their minds without censoring or judging. Free association is the automatic linking of one thought to another, which we all experience. We may hear a song that reminds us of the dance we attended when we first heard it, reminding us of our date for the dance, reminding us of the rage a parent expressed when we returned home after curfew, reminding us of the beatings we received from that parent, reminding us of our repressed impulse to attack the parent. A song, then, through a chain of association, can bring up strong feelings of anxiety because of its link to emotions that we have been unable to accept and process successfully. Freud encouraged free association in his patients to facilitate their recall of past material and release intense feelings. Blocks in the chain of association are another source of information about repressed material.

Abreaction

Although Freud placed primary emphasis on uncovering repressed material, he also recognized the importance of emotions, discussed in depth in part 3 of this book. He believed that affect needs to accompany the recall of past material in order for people to successfully understand and work through the importance that material has for them. To facilitate this link between emotions and the recall of repressed information, Freud often encouraged abreaction in his patients. Abreaction entails recalling a painful experience that had been repressed, working through that painful experience and the conflicts it created by reliving in memory the experience and its associated emotions, analyzing that experience, and achieving an emotional release as the culmination of that process. This technique is used today not only in psychoanalytic treatment but also in other treatment approaches that help people cope with strong emotional reactions to past events.

Interpretation and Analysis

The most fundamental techniques in Freudian psychotherapy are analysis and interpretation designed to promote awareness and insight. Whether his focus was on dreams, slips, transference, free association, or symptoms, the tools of analysis and interpretation enabled Freud to bring unconscious material into consciousness. Once this had occurred, people could gain insight into and work through previously repressed material and make connections between that material and their present difficulties, resulting in positive change.

Analysis is the process of thoroughly exploring and understanding the unconscious representations in the material people present in treatment. For example, in analyzing the dream of the young woman in the park (presented earlier in this chapter), Freud would explore with her the meaning of each item in the dream, including the park, the dog, and the woman herself. She would be encouraged to free-associate to the dream, to talk about both the emotions reflected in the dream and those she experienced upon awakening and recalling the dream, and to discuss events in the recent past that might have triggered the dream. Emphasis would be on the wish fulfillment represented by the dream and on suggestions of repressed, unacceptable sexual or other urges.

Interpretation is the process of elucidating the unconscious meaning of the symbols in material that clients present and of linking those new insights to their present concerns and blocks. Cognitively and emotionally working through material previously housed in the unconscious enables people to understand the influence the past has had on them and to use the mature defenses and strategies of the ego to make choices that are wiser and freer of the negative impact of unconscious material.

APPLICATION OF FREUDIAN PSYCHOANALYSIS

Freud himself recognized that his approach was only suitable for a limited group of people. In light of the length and depth of the psychoanalytic process, readers might be tempted to conclude that it is designed for only those people with severe mental disorders. In fact, the opposite is true.

Application to Diagnostic Groups

During Freud's time, mental disorders were categorized into two broad groups: psychoses and neuroses. *Psychoses* involve a loss of contact with reality, a significant disturbance in a person's ability to accurately perceive and interpret both internal and external experiences. Because they are likely to be experiencing delusions, hallucinations, and other perceptual distortions, people with psychoses cannot engage in the sort of self-examination that is required in psychoanalysis. They are unlikely to benefit from this mode of treatment.

People with *neuroses,* on the other hand, experience disorders of thoughts, emotions, and behaviors that interfere with their capacity for healthy functioning. Although their defenses and difficulties may lead to some confusion and misunderstanding about the meaning of their experiences, they have a capacity to form relationships, can engage in productive analysis, and can distinguish dreams and fantasies from reality. In Freud's time, six major neuroses had been identified (Stafford-Clark, 1965):

1. Hysteria, (now known as conversion disorder), involving a loss or disturbance of the senses or motor ability such as blindness or paralysis without medical cause
2. Anxiety states, including phobias and generalized anxiety disorders, both involving unreasonable fears
3. Obsessional disorders, now called obsessive-compulsive disorders, involving anxiety as well as repetitive thoughts and behaviors
4. Depression, especially the melancholic (nonreactive) type
5. Paranoid attitudes, comparable to today's paranoid personality disorder, involving pervasive suspiciousness, hypersensitivity, and sometimes jealousy
6. Sexual perversions, now called paraphilias

Freud divided the neuroses into two categories: transference neuroses, which involved a conflict between the id and the ego; and narcissistic neuroses, involving a conflict between the superego and the ego. He believed that only transference neuroses, (including the first four in the previous list) were treatable by psychoanalysis, although today most psychoanalysts view all nonpsychotic disorders as potentially treatable by psychoanalysis.

Application to Women

Jones (1955) quoted Freud as asking, "What does a woman want?" Jones concluded, "There is little doubt that Freud found the psychology of women more enigmatic than that of men" (p. 421). Unfortunately, despite his admission that his understanding of women was limited, Freud advanced some erroneous and harmful ideas about women. Because they typically are children's primary caregivers, he blamed mothers, and largely exonerated fathers, for their children's emotional distress (Enns, 1993). He distinguished between vaginal orgasm (experienced during intercourse) and clitoral orgasm and stated that vaginal orgasms reflected sexual maturity in women (Matlin, 1996). He suggested that women experience penis envy that can be at least partially resolved by giving birth. Freud seemed to view men as emotionally healthier than women (Stafford-Clark, 1965), whom he viewed as suffering from greater narcissism, masochism, shame, and envy.

Dispelling these mistaken beliefs took many years and probably did harm to women. We now know that taking a holistic and family systems approach is essential in understanding the causes of children's distress; that only one type of orgasm exists, no matter how it is achieved; that any envy that girls and women experience toward males can stem from many factors including preferential treatment they perceive males as receiving; and that men are not healthier overall than women. Indeed, Freud was guilty of what Gilligan (1993) referred to as observational bias, using the ". . . male life form as the norm" and trying "to fashion women out of a masculine cloth" (p. 6).

Reading about Freud's misconceptions about women may bring up feelings of anger and you may tend to dismiss his entire theory. However, keep in mind that these represent only a small fraction of Freud's ideas and that Freud lived in an era when women and their roles were very different from those of today. Freud always valued women, including his wife; his daughter Anna, who will be discussed later in this book; and his women patients, colleagues, and supporters. His later work advanced a more contemporary view of women, perceiving them as more personal and emotional in their decisions than men are and as having a more flexible superego.

In addition, recent feminist writings have recognized an underlying similarity of purpose between feminism and Freud's writings about women that outweigh their differences. Buhle (1998), for example, credits Freud with launching the sexual liberation of women and observes that both feminist therapy and modern psycholanalysis urge women to engage in self-discovery that will lead to unfolding of the personality and freeing of untapped psychic and sexual potential. Chodrow (1989), too, sees similarity between the goals of the two groups, with both feminist therapy and psychoanalysis correctly acknowledging the importance of gender and advocating women's self-actualization.

Application to Multicultural Groups

Many reasons exist for questioning the appropriateness of using traditional psychoanalysis with a diverse population. Psychoanalysis encourages anonymity in the therapist, and it seems to view the importance of self-satisfaction and individual development as greater than that of social and family involvement and dedication. With its emphasis on talk, analysis, and uncovering, psychoanalysis is also a very western or Eurocentric approach. These perspectives and others may well be incompatible with the viewpoints of people from diverse multicultural backgrounds and therefore may not be well received by people from some cultural backgrounds.

On the other hand, contemporary psychoanalysis, with its increased flexibility, more collaborative treatment alliance, and recognition of the importance of cultural backgrounds and messages, may be appropriate for use with a multicultural population. In recent years, articles such as that of Altman (2003) have discussed ways to make effective use of psychoanalysis with diverse clients. Contemporary psychoanalysis, discussed later in this chapter, has greatly enhanced the relevance and multicultural sensitivity of psychoanalytic treatment.

Application to Other Groups

Despite the broad applicability of Freudian psychoanalysis from diagnostic and feminist perspectives, other constraints limit the use and appropriateness of this approach. Few people have the time, financial resources, and inclination to engage in such intensive treatment. In addition, the slowly paced nature of the process; the relatively passive role of the client on the couch; and the emphasis on sexuality, early childhood, and the unconscious make the approach a poor choice for many people. Those in crisis, those who want to play a more active and equal role in their treatment, and those who are uncomfortable with or do not believe in Freud's focus on infantile sexuality are unlikely to respond well to psychoanalysis.

Traditional psychoanalysis seems best suited to treatment of people with at least moderate ego strength who have already achieved some success and satisfaction in life via relationships and occupational and leisure activities. Such people are in reasonable contact with reality and, on the surface, may seem to lead normal lives and to be fairly functional. In fact, however, these people are significantly impaired by long-standing symptoms such as depression, anxiety, and sexual or physical symptoms without any identified medical cause. Their lives may be constricted, they may have repeated failures in relationships or work that are caused by their own self-destructive behaviors, they may have pervasive and harmful personality patterns, and have not succeeded in ameliorating their difficulties.

CURRENT USE

Despite the limited application of psychoanalysis, schools to train analysts flourish in New York City, Washington DC, and other large cities. Not only do people seek training in this approach, but clients seek psychoanalysis from both these training facilities and psychoanalysts in independent practice. Few modern psychoanalysts, however, draw exclusively on the ideas of Freud. Rather, they use his ideas as the basis for their work but incorporate into their therapy the ideas of his followers as well as more recent theorists in psychoanalysis and psychodynamic psychotherapy.

Particularly important to understanding the current use of psychoanalysis is the evolution of this approach. Although some clinicians practice traditional psychoanalysis, many of those who embrace the basic tenets of Freud's work have gravitated toward what is being called Contemporary Psychoanalysis. A key shift in this approach is in the role of the therapist. No longer is the analyst aloof and anonymous. Rather, contemporary psychoanalysis assumes that the therapist cannot be objective and neutral but that both therapist and client each view the world through their own cultural lens. Together, they collaborate in determining whether and what kind of treatment is appropriate and how it will be structured for a particular person, couple, or family. Practitioners of contemporary psychoanalysis recognize that people are a product of their life experiences and that culture must be considered in understanding people. These practitioners assert that their approach is well-suited for working with people from diverse cultural, ethnic, and racial groups because of the flexibility and attention to culture inherent in this treatment model.

EVALUATION OF FREUDIAN PSYCHOANALYSIS

The continued attention to Freud's ideas reflects the important and enduring contributions of his work. Freud provided a solid foundation for future theorists who elaborated and expanded on his work. Their contributions will be discussed in the remaining chapters in part 2 of this book.

Limitations

Psychoanalysis does have limitations, many of which stem from its lengthy and costly format. In addition, the approach is not designed to help people with urgent concerns, may not pay adequate attention to multicultural dimensions, and says little about developing healthy adult lifestyles.

The research substantiating the value of this approach is limited, partly because the lengthy and intense nature of the treatment means that each analyst works with only a small number of people and that each treatment process is unique. Some contend that psychoanalysis can never demonstrate its value because it does not lend itself to empirical research. However, others, like Edelson (1985), disagree. Edelson insists that alternative approaches to research including matched samples and single subject studies can and have demonstrated the value of psychoanalysis. For example, the Psychotherapy Research Project of the Menninger Foundation collected data between 1954 and 1984 on the use of psychoanalysis and psychoanalytic psychotherapy with 42 clients (Wallerstein, 1986). Approximately 60% experienced good or moderate outcomes, with most continuing to improve after treatment.

Although these results are encouraging, they do not demonstrate that lengthy psychoanalysis is superior to other treatment approaches at ameliorating difficulties. As with most systems of psychotherapy and counseling, additional research, particularly of a comparative nature, is needed.

Strengths and Contributions

Probably Freud's most important contribution is the profound impact his thinking had on our understanding of human development. Most of us acknowledge the importance of childhood experiences, understand the major role that sexuality plays in development, recognize the powerful influence of parent figures in our lives, assume that dreams and slips are often meaningful, accept the existence of the unconscious, and acknowledge that internal conflicts commonly occur within our personalities. We also recognize the healing power of the therapeutic relationship, believe that talk therapy can be a powerful vehicle for promoting positive change, and are optimistic that treatment can help most people to lead more productive and rewarding lives. Whether or not we agree with the psychoanalytic model of treatment or with an emphasis on infantile sexuality, Freud's profound contributions to our understanding of psychological development and knowledge of psychotherapy is undeniable. Although few readers will go on to become psychoanalysts, all will find that their conceptions of mental health and mental illness and their approaches to treatment are colored by their knowledge of Freudian psychoanalysis.

SKILL DEVELOPMENT: THE LIFELINE

An earlier section of this chapter presented the developmental stages proposed by Freud and Erikson. Both theorists emphasize the profound impact that negotiation of these stages has on a person's subsequent development. Erikson's model is used for this skill development exercise rather than Freud's because of its consideration of the entire life span, its focus on positive growth experiences, and its ease of use without extensive training in psychoanalysis. In addition, it is more appropriate for group discussion because it addresses overall development rather than emphasizing the role of sexuality and the early childhood years in development.

Using developmental-stage perspectives to examine both our own lives and those of our clients can be very productive, and the systematic exploration of each stage can promote awareness of patterns and insight into milestones and turning points. The specialized skill in this chapter, the lifeline, is a tool that you can use for self-exploration as well as with your clients. Before you complete this exercise on analyzing life patterns, review the information on Erikson's stages presented earlier in this chapter and read the following instructions on preparing a lifeline. Then read the case illustration, which presents a lifeline of Roberto Diaz. This will guide you in developing and analyzing your own lifeline.

Instructions for Creating a Lifeline

Draw a long line that reflects your life. Divide the line into eight parts, reflecting Erikson's eight stages, and mark out the corresponding ages on the line. For the first five stages, list each year individually. Beyond that, you may list years in groups of five if you prefer. Think back over your life and also think ahead to the years to come. Complete the lifeline so that it reflects your life in the following ways:

1. For each stage you have completed or are completing, list important events at the age at which they occurred. You may need to talk with family members to gather information about your early milestones. You might list events such as a death or divorce in your family, a family relocation, an illness in you or a family member, the birth of a younger sibling, or events that may seem less important but that made a great difference in your life such as bringing home a lost kitten, making a special friend, and learning to ride a bicycle.

2. For those stages that lie ahead, list in parentheses events that you are hoping for and looking forward to next to the age at which you would like the event to occur. Such events might include entering a committed relationship, having a child, traveling to Europe, buying a home, finishing graduate school and obtaining a job, or retiring to a tropical island.

3. Go through the lifeline a second time. This time draw in peaks and valleys to reflect the highs and lows that you have had or expect to have. They should be linked to the events you have listed.

4. Go through the lifeline a third time. For each of the eight stages, write down a positive word or phrase and a negative word or phrase to describe your actual or anticipated passage through that stage. For example, for the industry versus inferiority (latency) stage, you might write, "Loved school, especially reading," and "Few friends, felt different."

5. Go through the lifeline a fourth time. This time, for each of the eight stages, write a statement indicating your assessment of your negotiation of that stage. For example, for the identity versus role confusion (genital) stage, you might write, "Developing a good personal sense of myself but still confused about who I am as a worker."

6. Take a final tour through your lifeline, reviewing all the information you have gathered about yourself and your life. Look for patterns or recurrent themes that might reflect areas of concern or problems that may arise in the future. For example, you might observe that all your successes are in the academic and occupational area, while most of your important disappointments are in the personal realm. Make a list of the patterns you observe. If you completed this exercise while in counseling, the information would probably provide direction for the treatment process as well as considerable insight into ways in which the past has influenced the present in your life. Think about that for yourself.

CASE ILLUSTRATION

Roberto prepared the following lifeline as part of his treatment (see Figure 4.1).

Stage 1: Basic Trust versus Basic Mistrust (Freud's Oral Stage)

Important events: Just survived; a lot of kids in my neighborhood didn't. I was a big baby; always wanted to be fed.

Positive and negative descriptors: Maybe I needed a lot of attention and that's why I always wanted to be fed. I wonder if I got much attention with all those other kids around; but knowing me, I yelled the loudest and got what I needed.

Assessment: I always knew my parents and grandparents loved me, and I have a lot of trust in my family, but I sure don't trust other people much.

Stage 2: Autonomy versus Shame and Doubt (Freud's Anal Stage)

Important events: My younger sister was born. My older brother was hit by a car. I don't remember this stuff, but my parents told me about it. When we were toilet training Ava, I wondered about my own toilet training. I asked my mom, but she didn't really remember. I guess it wasn't much of a problem.

Positive and negative descriptors: I think I became self-sufficient really fast with so much going on in my family, but sometimes I feel angry without knowing why. I used to feel ashamed of how I looked, always tall and big. I wonder if some of those bad feelings go back to that time period.

Assessment: Well, I got toilet trained! Seriously, I bet I just toilet trained myself; that's how things usually went in my family. I wonder if the anger has to do with that. And I'm not very neat; that's a conflict between me and Edie.

Stage 3: Initiative versus Guilt (Freud's Phallic Stage)

Important events: Twin sisters were born. I can remember my parents bringing them home. No big deal though; they were numbers seven and eight. I started preschool at that time, some kind of special program. You know, my parents spoke Spanish at home and my English wasn't very good, so I got put in something like the Head Start programs they have now. I remember my dad really well from those years. He used to watch sports on TV—boxing, I think. I thought he was tough, just like those guys.

Positive and negative descriptors: Time with Dad was great, but I didn't like school.

Assessment: I can see myself maturing, using my father as a role model. He didn't think much of school either.

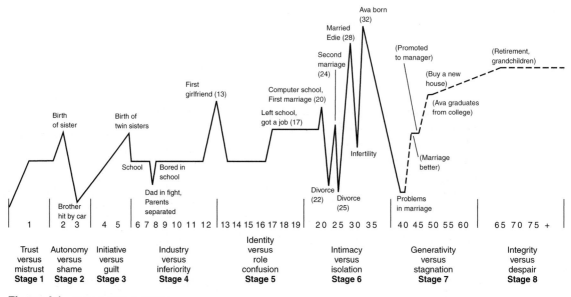

Figure 4.1   Roberto Diaz's lifeline.

Stage 4: Industry versus Inferiority (Freud's Latency Stage)

Important events: Started public school. Dad got into a fight and came home all bloody; that scared me. The major thing, of course, was that my parents separated.

Positive and negative descriptors: Needed to be real self-sufficient, and I was. I still didn't like school.

Assessment: I learned to take care of myself, started fixing cars with my brothers, and I was good at it. I couldn't get that school stuff though . . . acted like I didn't care, but I did.

Stage 5: Identity versus Role Confusion (Freud's Genital Stage)

Important events: Had my first girlfriend and my first sexual relationship. Dropped out of high school and went to work fixing cars.

Positive and negative descriptors: I really felt important; sex and money did it. Work was harder than I thought; maybe leaving school wasn't such a great idea.

Assessment: I had a sense of identity, but I was full of myself; didn't really see I was going nowhere.

Stage 6: Intimacy versus Isolation

Important events: Lots of things here. Got my GED and went to computer school, smartest thing I ever did. Involved with lots of women. Married and divorced twice. Met Edie, got married. The big event: Ava was born. Started to make some real money; bought a house.

Positive and negative descriptors: Lots of mistakes, but at 35 I was on top of the world at home and at work.

Assessment: Really turned my life around and figured out who I was and what I wanted.

Stage 7: Generativity versus Stagnation

Important events: I guess this is where I am now. Big problems in the marriage. Started therapy. (Hopefully, marriage gets better; I move into management at work; Ava goes to college. Probably bad stuff too. . . parents getting sick, dying.)

Positive and negative descriptors: I'm doing my best to keep my family together; but that anger keeps coming up for me, especially when I feel trapped. If my marriage doesn't make it, I guess I just can't do this relationship thing.

Assessment: A real crossroads. I've come so far, but it could all fall apart.

Stage 8: Integrity versus Despair

Important events: I retire with a good pension. Edie and I live at the beach. Ava gets married, and I become a grandpa. That's what I hope for.

Positive and negative descriptors: I hope I feel great about what I've done, rebuilt my marriage, turned out a terrific kid, left work at the top. I guess the down side is getting sick, losing people I love. If Edie and I don't make it, I could just be a lonely old man.

Assessment: I can see the possibilities here, and I'm going to make the good ones happen.

Patterns

- I always had a great appetite: food, women, money. Sometimes I get too hungry and don't really think about the consequences.
- My anger gets me in trouble just like it did my dad. I have his toughness and I'm good with my hands like him, but we both fly off the handle.

- Kids mean a lot to my parents and to me. Too bad we only had the one, but she's great.
- I made lots of mistakes but never let them get me down. Knock me down, and I get up fighting. I guess that's really helped me.

Analysis

Clearly, Roberto has shared a great deal of himself in this lifeline. In-depth analysis in treatment might focus on the following three areas:

1. Patterns of impulsivity and impulse control: does his ego have difficulty controlling the demands of the id?
2. His difficult relationships with women, perhaps stemming from early issues with his mother.
3. His identification with the aggressive side of his father and his expression of his own aggressive impulses.

Insight and change in these areas, as well as others that might arise during the course of treatment, are likely to help Roberto improve his capacity for intimacy.

EXERCISES

Large-Group Exercises

1. As a class, develop a hypothetical lifeline for Edie based on the information about her provided in chapters 1, 2, and 3. You may add additional details on Edie's life to enrich your knowledge of her as long as it is consistent with information you already have.
2. Review the list of ego defense mechanisms provided earlier in this chapter. Identify two or three defense mechanisms that you believe would characterize Edie's way of coping with anxiety. Identify two or three defense mechanisms that you believe would characterize Roberto's way of coping with anxiety. Be sure to provide a rationale for your conclusions.
3. Discuss your predictions for the future of psychoanalysis. Be sure to provide a rationale for all your points.

Small-Group Exercises

Form into your groups of two dyads. Each dyad should take a turn conducting an interview on early childhood experiences, with one person in the dyad being the interviewer, the other the interviewee. Using the interview skills you learned in chapter 3, spend 10–15 minutes asking your partner about his or her recollections of any or all of the following:

- Being fed by a caregiver
- Being toilet trained

- Developing an identification with the same-sex parent or caregiver
- Early experiences of independence and taking initiative

After each role play, group members should give the interviewer some feedback, using the guidelines in chapter 1. Feedback should include (but not be limited) to (1) use of questions, (2) ability to elicit information, (3) client-clinician rapport, and (4) eye contact and other nonverbal behaviors.

Be sure to take care of yourself during this exercise and during all exercises in this book. You can choose what you do or do not want to reveal about your early childhood experiences. If you find strong emotions or troubling memories coming up for you, be cautious about sharing them. Remember that this is an exercise, not a counseling session. If any exercises are very troubling for you, consider the possibility that counseling might help you better understand and handle those feelings.

Individual Exercises

1. Now that you have an understanding of the id, the superego, and the ego, the three structures of the personality, you can be more aware of the dynamics of some of your inner conflicts. Write briefly about a time when you experienced a conflict between your id and your superego and how you resolved that conflict.
2. We all make mistakes, make slips, and forget commitments. Try to be more conscious of these processes in your own life for the next week. Each time you notice one of these errors, think about whether it is a random occurrence or whether it might reflect a wish or another psychological process.
3. Create and analyze your own lifeline based on Erikson's eight stages, following the directions in the "Skill Development" section.

SUMMARY

This chapter reviewed psychoanalytic theory and strategies as developed by Sigmund Freud. It also provided information about Freud's background and on the development of his concepts, which form the foundation for modern conceptions of psychological development, mental health, and the treatment of mental disorders. This chapter also presented Erikson's eight stages of development. Freud's theory emphasizes the three structures of the personality (id, superego, and ego), the five stages of psychosexual development (oral, anal, phallic, latency, and genital), defense mechanisms, and levels of consciousness (unconscious, preconscious, and conscious). Treatment focuses on promoting insight by analysis of dreams and other clues to the unconscious; interpretation, working through, and abreaction; and the development of transference.

RECOMMENDED READINGS

Erikson, E. H. (1963). *Childhood and society*. New York: Norton.

Freud, S. (1938). *The basic writings of Sigmund Freud*. (A. A. Brill, Trans.) New York: Modern Library.

Jones, E. (1953, 1955, 1957). *The life and works of Sigmund Freud*. (3 vols.). New York: Basic Books.

Roth, M. S. (Ed.) (1998). *Freud: Conflict and culture*. New York: Alfred A. Knopf.

Stafford-Clark, D. (1965). *What Freud really said*. New York: Schocken.

ADDITIONAL SOURCES OF INFORMATION

The New York Psychoanalytic Institute and Society and information on their journal, the *Journal of Clinical Psychoanalysis,* can be accessed at http://users.rcn.com/brill/jcp/html

International Psychoanalytic Association, based in England, can be accesssed at http://www.ipa.org.uk

Information on the *International Journal of Psychoanalysis* can be accessed at http://www.ijpa.org/

Information on the American Psychoanalytic Association and the *Journal of the American Psychoanalytic Association* can be accessed at http://www.apsa.org/. This also is a good resource for information on training in psychoanalysis.

CHAPTER 5

Alfred Adler and Individual Psychology

Alfred Adler initially shared Freud's perspectives on human development and psychotherapy. However, as Adler's thinking evolved, he came to disagree with the emphasis Freud placed on biological and physiological determinants of psychological development. Adler believed that early childhood experiences played an integral part in future development, but he viewed Freud's concepts as too deterministic and limited. Adler eventually established his own theory of human development and psychotherapy, which he called *Individual Psychology*.

Adler's ideas are compatible with current thinking about mental health. Adlerian therapy pays considerable attention to social context, family dynamics, and child rearing. This approach is phenomenological, empowering, and oriented toward both present and future. As a result, Adler's ideas have experienced a resurgence of popularity during the past 25 years or so and are currently viewed as an important approach to psychotherapy, especially for clinicians working with children and their families.

ALFRED ADLER

Alfred Adler was born on February 7, 1870, in Vienna, Austria, the third of six children. His father, Leopold Adler, was a merchant. Alfred Adler had a difficult childhood. When he was three years old, a brother died in the bed they shared (Orgler, 1963). Adler himself was prone to accidents and illnesses. Twice he was run over in the streets; he had pneumonia, suffered from rickets and poor eyesight, and was sickly and delicate. Because of his medical problems, Adler was pampered, especially by his mother. However, when his younger brother was born, Adler felt dethroned as his mother shifted her attention from him to her new baby. This led Adler to transfer his attention to his father and to his peers, from whom he learned "courage, comradeliness, and social interest" (Orgler, 1963, p. 3). Adler's subsequent interest in birth order, inferiority, and parental overprotectiveness may have originated in his own childhood experiences.

Adler was initially not a good student; a teacher suggested that Adler's father apprentice his son to a shoemaker rather than encouraging his academic pursuits. However, Adler subsequently became a strong student, demonstrating in his own life that people can change their goals and their lives. From childhood on, Adler was interested in psychology and social issues. Even in his first professional position (an eye specialist) after he completed medical school, Adler was interested in the total person; he sought to understand the connection between mental and physical processes and their impact on people's work and social lives. Adler found his next position as a general physician more rewarding because it meshed with his beliefs. However, he was troubled by feelings of helplessness when treating people with terminal illnesses. This led Adler to another career change; he entered the field of neurology while continuing to study psychology and social science in an effort to understand people more fully.

Adler's insights into personality development brought him recognition in his field and probably helped capture Freud's attention. In 1902, Freud wrote to Adler and several other leaders in the fields of neurology and psychology, suggesting they meet to discuss his work. This led to Adler's involvement in the Vienna Psycho-Analytical Society.

Descriptions of Adler's personal style are mixed. Orgler's (1963) research suggests that Adler was warm and friendly, while Jones, Freud's biographer, describes Adler as "morose, cantankerous, contentious, and sulky" (1955, p. 130). Perhaps these descriptions reflect aspects of Adler's personality as well as his displeasure with Freud's belief that sexual impulses are basic determinants of psychological development.

This rift finally led Adler to separate himself from the Psycho-Analytical Society, where he had achieved power and leadership, to form the Society for Individual Psychology. His work for the rest of his life had the goals of deepening his understanding of people and finding better ways to help them. Adler's strong social interest prompted him to write and speak on child rearing and educational practices; establish child guidance clinics in the Viennese public schools; and initiate programs to train teachers, social workers, physicians, and other professionals in ways to promote children's mental health. Using live demonstrations and writing books for the general public, he made his ideas and techniques accessible to a wide audience, which was important to him. His wife Raissa, described as a "strong feminist and political activist," was an ardent supporter of Adler's social activism (Sherman & Nwaorgu, 2002, p. 181). Beginning in the 1920s, Adler traveled frequently to the United States, where he generated considerable interest in his work. His tireless involvement in his work continued until his death. On May 28, 1937, while preparing for a lecture in Scotland, he died of a heart attack.

THE DEVELOPMENT OF INDIVIDUAL PSYCHOLOGY

Adler's professional development falls roughly into four time periods. The first phase of his career followed his completion of medical school. Neither his initial work as a physician nor his subsequent work in neurological research seemed right for him, although he made contributions in both areas. His great interest was the mind rather than the body.

When he joined forces with Freud to further the field of psychoanalysis, Adler entered the second phase and seemed, at least temporarily, to have found his place. His focus finally was on promoting healthy emotional development. However, before long, he felt stifled by the apparent rigidity of some of Freud's beliefs and his limited interest in the whole person.

Adler's disengagement from Freud signaled the third period in his professional development. This freed Adler to move forward with his own ideas. According to Ansbacher and Ansbacher (1956), Adler replaced "biological, external, objective causal explanation with psychological, internal, subjective causal explanation" (p. 9). He replaced the concept of the sexual drive and the libido with the drive to gain power and become a fully functioning adult. The goal of Adler's Individual Psychology was to comprehend and help the unique individual, a departure from what he perceived as Freud's overgeneralized ideas.

A final stage in Adler's career came after his service as a psychiatrist in World War I. Seeing the bonds among soldiers during their war experiences convinced him that the drive toward social interest was even stronger than the drive for superiority and power. He proposed that people's basic motivation is "an innate predisposition for social interest" (Grey, 1998, p. 8) and viewed people as driven primarily by needs for significance, self-worth, and social involvement. Adler's thinking moved in directions that are compatible with what many now view as the fundamental purpose of therapy: to help people feel empowered and self-actualized and build rewarding social involvement and relationships.

IMPORTANT THEORETICAL CONCEPTS

Adler's theories, like Freud's, have considerable depth and richness. Adler's concepts emphasize the unity and uniqueness of each individual. He believed that understanding people grew from knowledge of their goals and drives, their family constellations, their social contexts, and their styles of life. Sweeney (1998) described Adler's theories as socio-teleo-analytic:

- *Socio.* This reflects Adler's emphasis on social interest (his belief that people have a basic need to belong to a social whole) and his concern with the betterment of people.
- *Teleo.* This denotes his belief in the goal-striving nature of people, with behavior being purposeful and intended to help people achieve their goals. According to Sweeney (1998, p. 10), "the teleological aspects of Adler's theory reveal the optimistic, encouraging nature of his position." According to Adler, people are not victims of biology or circumstance but can choose to change both their goals and their behaviors.
- *Analytic.* Adler shared Freud's belief that much of what determines the direction of people's lives is unconscious and needs to be analyzed to bring their goals and lifestyles into conscious awareness.

View of Human Nature

Adler, like Freud, acknowledged the importance of the first five years of life in influencing people's future development. However, Adler's view was less deterministic. He believed that biological and physiological factors provided probabilities for future growth but that, "the self, with creative power as part of its inner nature, is the important intervening variable" (Ansbacher & Ansbacher, 1956, p. 179).

For Adler, those characteristics of the person that were determined by heredity and early upbringing were less important than what the person made of them. He believed that behavior is purposeful and goal-directed, and that we can channel our behavior in ways that promote growth. Adler believed that what matters to people is developing and working to achieve meaningful and rewarding goals, along with a lifestyle that leads to a positive sense of ourselves, connectedness to other people and our communities, and satisfying work (Adler, 1963a).

The Importance of Feelings of Inferiority

Adler (1963b) believed that feelings of inferiority during the early childhood years have a great impact on development. Nearly all children experience these feelings, perceiving themselves as small and powerless in relation to their parents and older siblings. How young children are treated and how they deal with their feelings of inferiority are important in shaping them. Children who succeed in reducing their feelings of difference and low self-esteem by social involvement, building their strengths and abilities, making wise and creative choices, and striving in healthy ways toward growth and power are likely to develop in positive ways. On the other hand, children who are pampered or neglected and whose efforts toward empowerment are thwarted are far less likely to experience positive growth and development. Adler believed that pampered children often grow up expecting others to care for them and so do not develop their own resources, while neglected children may become discouraged and hopeless when their efforts to overcome an inferior role are ignored or rejected.

Family Constellation and Birth Order

Adler paid considerable attention to other early influences on development including people's family constellations and birth order. This is in keeping with Adler's emphasis on the social nature of human problems. He believed that, through an examination of the family constellation, we can understand people's lifestyles. Conversely, by understanding their outlooks on life, we can understand the roles people have in their families (Dreikurs, 1973).

A person's family constellation includes the composition of the family, each person's roles, and the reciprocal transactions that a person has, during the early formative years, with siblings and parents. The child is not a passive recipient of these transactions; rather, children influence how parents and siblings respond to them. Each child comes to play a role in the family that is determined by the interactions and transactions within that family (Adler, 1963b).

Children are affected by both their similarities to and differences from their families. According to Adler, siblings who are most different from us influence us most. That difference gives us the opportunity to compare and contrast ourselves with others, see new possibilities, and rethink the choices and roles we have taken on in our own lives.

Birth order is another aspect of families that, according to Adler (1963b), has a profound impact on development. Five psychological positions in the family, described by Adler, and characteristics believed to be associated with each position include (see Figure 5.1):

1. *Oldest children* tend to be the most intelligent and achieving of the five groups. Their verbal skills are especially strong. Firstborns, who initially grow up in a family of adults, tend to be dependable, well-organized, and responsible. They generally are well-behaved and cooperative, conforming to societal expectations and being fairly traditional. Their many strengths often help them attain positions of leadership.

While firstborns are the only child in the family, they tend to be the center of attention and sometimes are spoiled. However, when siblings are born, oldest children tend to feel dethroned and may feel threatened, angry, fearful, and jealous in response to losing their special role as only child. Dealing successfully with the birth of a sibling can help firstborns to become more affiliative and self-confident.

2. The *second child* feels pressure to catch up and compete with the oldest child. Because second-born children usually realize they cannot outdo the successes the firstborn has already achieved, they gravitate toward endeavors in which the older sibling is either unskilled or uninterested. A common pattern is for a firstborn to excel in a traditional area such as English or mathematics and for the second-born to seek success in a more creative and less conventional area such as singing or drawing and to emphasize social rather than academic success. The more successful the firstborn, the more likely it is that the second-born will move in directions opposite to those of the typically well-behaved and achievement-oriented firstborn. Second-born children tend to be more caring, friendly, and expressive than their older siblings.

3. The *middle child* is often the second child and is likely to manifest many of the strengths of the second-born. However, some middle children feel squeezed between older children who have already found their place and younger children who seem to receive more love and attention. Middle children sometimes have difficulty finding a way to become special and can become discouraged, viewing themselves as unloved and neglected. This pattern is usually less evident in large families where two or more children share the role of middle child but is particularly likely in families with only three children. With encouragement and positive parenting, however, middle children often become well-adjusted, friendly, creative, and ambitious, prizing their individual strengths.

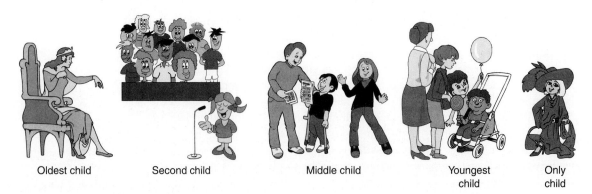

| Oldest child | Second child | Middle child | Youngest child | Only child |

Figure 5.1   Drawings of birth order.

4. *Youngest children* encounter three common pitfalls: They may be pampered and spoiled by the rest of the family, they may feel a need to go at top speed at all times just to keep up with their older siblings, and they may become discouraged about competing with their brothers and sisters. Decisions may be made for them, and they may not need to take on much responsibility for themselves or others. Adler expressed concern that these children would experience strong feelings of inferiority. However, last-born children also can acquire considerable power in the family and thrive on the special attention they receive. They often become adventurous, easygoing, empathic, sociable, and innovative. They typically pursue interests that are all their own to avoid competition with siblings. Their most likely ally is the oldest, who also has feelings of being different.

5. *Only children* have much in common with both firstborn and last-born children. They seek achievement like firstborns and usually enjoy being the center of attention like the youngest. They may become pampered and spoiled, focusing only on their own needs, but also may integrate the achievement-orientation of the firstborn with the creativity of later-born children. Because other family members are all adults, these children typically mature early and learn to cooperate and deal well with adults. However, if their parents are insecure, only children may adopt parental worries and insecurities.

Research has validated many of Adler's assumptions about the impact of birth order on personality, but some discrepant results suggest the importance of caution when drawing conclusions about the connections between personality and birth order (Grey, 1998; Herrera, Zajonc, Wieczorkowska, & Cichomski, 2003; Lombardi, 1996; Parker, 1998). Variables within families can have a complex impact on these patterns. For example, when twins are born, families tend to treat one child as older than the other, artificially determining their birth order. When a firstborn is a girl or is impaired in some way, families may inadvertently promote the second child into the position of firstborn. High expectations will be held for that child, while the firstborn will be treated like a second-born. Large families may operate as though they have more than one group of children, with each group having a child who functions as the oldest, one who functions as the youngest, and children in the middle. This is especially likely in families in which many years separate groups of children. In addition, the way in which children respond to their positions will have an impact on their personalities and behaviors.

Clinicians should not stereotype people according to birth order. At the same time, exploring birth order and the influence it has on the development of an individual's personality can facilitate understanding of that person. Inventories such as the White-Campbell Psychological Birth Order Inventory (White, Campbell, & Steward, 1995) can facilitate accurate assessment of the impact birth order has had on a person.

Lifestyle

The composition and interactions of people's families exert the major influence on the development of their lifestyle, another important concept in Adler's theory. According to Starr, (1973), "Adler concluded that each child in the family, out of his own inner capacities and his appraisal of the outer environment, experiences a different situation. He joins these attitudes into a characteristic pattern of behavior [lifestyle]" (p. 95). Grey (1998) views lifestyle as the most fundamental of Adler's concepts, describing it as "the sum total of all the individual's attitudes and aspirations, a striving which leads him in the direction toward his goal of believing he has significance in the eyes of others" (p. 37). Lifestyle is "the creative and created self" (Sherman & Nwaorgu, 2002, p. 183).

Similar to the personality or the self, lifestyle encompasses four ingredients: (1) the person's subjective worldview, including beliefs about the self and others, values, inner narratives, expectations, and attitudes, (2) goals, (3) behavioral strategies that the person uses to achieve goals and negotiate the life journey, and (4) the outcomes or consequences of those behaviors. Lifestyle can be assessed informally via exploration of these four areas or can be explored through the use of an inventory.

Lifestyle, then, is the unique way in which each of us seeks to overcome feelings of inferiority and to achieve our goals. These goals nearly always involve achievement of significance, superiority, competence, and mastery. Each person has an image, usually unconscious, of what life will be like when those goals have been reached. Adler originally used the term *fictional finalism* to describe the imagined central goal or ideal that guides our behavior but later referred to it as the *guiding self-ideal* and the *goal of perfection* (Watts & Holden, 1994). He believed that this goal is firmly established between the ages of 6 and 8 and remains constant throughout a person's life. Our *private logic* is the route that takes us from our feelings of inferiority to the development of a lifestyle that we believe will enable us to reach our self-ideal. Dreikurs (1973), who contributed greatly to Adler's work, described private logic as the inner rationale we use for justifying our lifestyle and the way to achieve our goals.

Goals

Adler viewed the healthy, well-functioning adult as a person who is independent, emotionally and physically self-reliant, useful and productive, and able to cooperate with others for both personal and social benefit. The "inadequate responses of envy, greed, competition and sabotage" arise in people who have not developed these characteristics (Beecher & Beecher, 1973, p. 2).

Through psychotherapy and education, Adler sought to help people realize that feelings of pain and inadequacy are caused not by others but by their own faulty logic and the behaviors and attitudes that stem from that logic. By enabling people to become aware of their faulty logic; to establish healthy, realistic and rewarding goals; and to align their lifestyles, their thinking, and their behavior with those goals, therapists can help people overcome their feelings of inferiority, dependency, and inordinate fears of failure. They can then develop the self-confidence and social interest they need to achieve a healthier adjustment and a more rewarding lifestyle.

These concepts can be applied to Edie Diaz, the woman discussed throughout this book. Edie developed a guiding self-ideal, early in life, of being wife and mother in a caring and supportive family. Her short- and long-range goals all focused on that ideal as did many elements of her lifestyle. However, the abuse and neglect she experienced during childhood have made it difficult for her to overcome her feelings of inferiority; she does not know how to realize her goals, to become part of a family and community, and to appreciate herself. She is working, in counseling, to develop an effective private logic and lifestyle and to align her lifestyle with her self-ideal.

Social Interest

Adler had a clear idea of emotional health. He distinguished between well-adjusted and maladjusted people on the basis of their goals and their lifestyles. People who are well-adjusted have a private logic that reflects common sense as well as social interest; they perceive themselves as part of a community and appreciate individual differences. Those who are maladjusted focus only on their own needs and fail to recognize the importance of their social context and the needs of others.

This idea reflects Adler's (1963a) belief that development can be explained primarily by psychosocial rather than psychosexual dynamics. He believed that people are, by nature, social beings interested in belonging to a group and desiring to solve the problems of their society. Through awareness that we are part of the human community, as well as through the development of social interest, our feelings of inferiority, alienation, and anxiety diminish; and we develop feelings of belonging and happiness. We no longer view ourselves as alone, seeking to diminish others to advance ourselves. Instead, we recognize that the goods and ills in our society all have an impact on us and that we can best achieve our own goals of significance and competence by contributing to the greater good. Adler's emphasis on social connectedness is very timely and congruent with the importance to clinicians of multicultural competence and appreciation of diversity.

People's social interest is best reflected in their accomplishment of what Adler viewed as the three life tasks: occupation, sexual love, and friendship (Ferguson, 2003). Social interest can be assessed by how successfully people are able to negotiate relationships, the degree of closeness they maintain in those relationships, and their connectedness and contributions to society. Although Freud acknowledged the importance of love and work, Adler added friendship to the important areas of our lives. Although Adler viewed early childhood experiences as important in determining the nature of our social interest, he believed that social interest could be taught and developed in later life, conveying optimism not only for the individual but also for our society.

Phenomenological Perspective

Another viewpoint compatible with current thinking on human development and change is Adler's emphasis on a person's perception of reality, not what actually is or what others perceive. For Adler, the internal and subjective were more important than the external and objective. His theory can be thought of as *phenomenological,* meaning that he focused on a person's inner reality, the way that person perceived the world. Adler saw each person as a unique individual and believed that only by understanding that person's perceptions of the world, private logic, lifestyle, and goals can we really make sense of and know that person. This is the essence of Adler's Individual Psychology.

TREATMENT USING INDIVIDUAL PSYCHOLOGY

Adler's theory is an optimistic, growth-oriented and educational one. Adler believed that people could change their goals and lifestyles in order to achieve happier and more fulfilled lives. His ideas have endured because they draw on the important concepts of Freudian psychoanalysis; incorporate many elements of modern cognitive, behavioral, and humanistic treatment approaches; and add their own valuable and useful ideas.

Therapeutic Alliance

Adler departed from the ideas of Freud in his conception of the clinician-client relationship. Adler emphasized the importance of a cooperative interaction that involves establishment of shared goals as well as mutual trust and respect. This view is consistent with the aims of his treatment; he sought to foster responsibility and social interest and saw the establishment of a therapeutic relationship in which client and clinician collaborated to achieve goals they had formulated together as important in promoting client growth.

Clinicians following Adler's approach have a complex role that calls for the application of a broad range of skills. These clinicians are educators, fostering social interest and teaching people ways to modify their lifestyles, behaviors, and goals. They are analysts who identify faulty logic and assumptions. They explore and interpret the meaning and impact of clients' birth order, dreams, early recollections, and drives. They are role models, demonstrating ways to think clearly, search for meaning, collaborate with others, and establish and reach meaningful goals. And they are supportive and encouraging, urging clients to take risks and helping them accept their own mistakes and imperfections.

Thoughts and behaviors, as well as background, are primary targets of the Adlerian clinicians' efforts. Private logic, lifestyle, and the guiding self-ideal all stem from heredity and early experiences. Helping people understand these constructs can enable them to challenge and modify their beliefs and develop new and more rewarding goals, a modified lifestyle, and constructive and positive social interest and behaviors.

Stages of Treatment

Although they often merge and overlap, four treatment phases can be identified in Adler's model: (1) establishment of a collaborative therapeutic relationship and a shared view of the treatment goals, (2) assessment, analysis, and understanding of the person and the problem, (3) encouragement of change through reeducation, reorientation, and development of insight, and (4) reinforcement of change, evaluation, termination and follow-up (Milliren, & Barrett-Kruse, 2002; Sherman & Nwaorgu, 2002).

Phase 1: Establishing the Therapeutic Relationship and Setting Goals   Adler was ahead of his time in emphasizing the importance of a positive therapeutic relationship. He advocated many of the approaches later described by Carl Rogers to build that relationship (see chapter 10). Adler believed in the importance of true caring and involvement, the use of empathy, and both verbal and nonverbal techniques of listening to overcome the feelings of inferiority and fear that many clients bring with them into treatment. Initial questions explore clients' expectations for treatment, their views of their problems, how they have tried to improve their lives, and what has led them to seek treatment at the present time.

Encouragement is an essential component of this initial phase of treatment and is used throughout treatment to counter clients' discouragement. Sweeney (1998) described seven actions that can be used in counseling as well as in other relationships to provide encouragement:

- Focus on what people are doing rather than evaluate their performance. Asking, "What did you do to pass all your courses?" is more encouraging than "Did you get the best grades in your class?"
- Focus on the present more than the past or the future.
- Focus on behavior rather than the person. "Your careful driving really helped you deal with the sudden snowstorm" is more encouraging than "You're a great driver."

- Focus on the effort rather than the outcome. "Sounds like you really feel good about developing your skating skills" is more encouraging than "Sounds like your skills are almost good enough to make the team."
- Focus on motivation from within (intrinsic) rather than from the outside (extrinsic). "You must have felt a great sense of satisfaction, knowing that all your studying resulted in success on the bar exam" is more encouraging than "You finally passed the bar. Now you'll get that raise."
- Focus on what is being learned rather than the lack of learning. "What did you learn from this challenging relationship?" is more encouraging than "You really need to make better choices in your friends."
- Focus on what is positive rather than what is negative. "So the odds are on your side" is more encouraging than "So the physician said there is a 40 percent chance that your disease will recur."

Counseling and psychotherapy offer clinicians many opportunities to encourage clients and to show them genuine caring and concern. A telephone call to a client in crisis, a note to a client in the hospital, sharing an article on home buying with a client who is purchasing a first home are all appropriate ways for clinicians to form partnerships with clients and provide support and encouragement.

As client and clinician build a collaborative, democratic, and trusting relationship, they can work together to formulate a clear statement of the problem, as well as meaningful and realistic goals. They also can discuss and negotiate agreement on the structure of the treatment process and the guidelines and procedures for their work.

Phase 2: Assessment, Analysis, and Understanding of the Person and the Problem   The goals of this phase of treatment are understanding clients' family background, lifestyles, private logic and goals, and identifying self-destructive behaviors and faulty logic. To accomplish this, Adler led clients on an in-depth exploration of their lives. He paid particular attention to the family constellation, clients' birth order, their dreams, their earliest recollections, and their motives or priorities.

Lifestyle assessment. Acting as what Mozdzierz, Lisiecki, Bitter, and Williams (1986) referred to as psychological explorers or lifestyle investigators, clinicians conduct a systematic exploration of clients' lifestyles. Focusing primarily on how people have addressed the tasks of love, work, and friendship, clinicians seek holistic understanding of their clients and comprehension of their goals and private logic. Particularly important are assessing people's levels of satisfaction with themselves, their relationships, and their lives and looking for examples of faulty logic. Structured guidelines are available to help clinicians conduct comprehensive and informative lifestyle assessments. Among these are *Understanding Life-Style: The Psycho-Clarity Process* (Power & Griffith, 1987), *The Individual Psychology Client Workbook* (Powers & Griffith, 1986), the *BASIS-A Interpretive Manual* (Kern, Wheeler, & Curlette, 1997), and the *Manual for Life Style Assessment* (Shulman & Mosak, 1988).

Family constellation and birth order. An understanding of the impact of the family constellation on a person comes from both objective and subjective sources. Objective information includes people's birth order, the number of children in the family, the gender of each child, the number of years between the births of each child, and any special circumstances such as the death of a child or the presence of a physical or intellectual disability in any of the children. Subjective information includes people's perceptions of themselves as children, how their parents felt about and treated each child, clients' relationships with their parents and siblings, ways in which they resembled and differed from their siblings, and patterns of rivalry and cooperation within the family. Additional information on birth order is presented earlier in this chapter.

Dreams. Although Adler did not emphasize understanding dreams as Freud did, he, too, used them as a vehicle for promoting self-awareness. De-emphasizing symbolism, Adler viewed dreams as providing important information on lifestyle and current concerns. He believed that both past and current dreams were useful sources of information, with recurrent dreams and recurrent themes within dreams being particularly important.

Earliest recollections. Adler viewed people's earliest recollections as important sources of information on their current lifestyles. According to Adler (1931), whether memories are recalled accurately is unimportant. Rather, he believed that people only retained early memories that were consistent with their views of themselves. Consequently, what mattered were people's reports of their memories.

Adlerian therapists usually elicit at least three early memories so that they can identify recurrent themes and patterns. Once the memories have been elicited and written down, each memory is explored with the client. The clinician usually asks about the age when the person believes the recalled events occurred and the thoughts and emotions associated with the recollections. Exploration of the client's role in the memories, as well as his or her relationships and interactions with other people in the memories, are believed to reflect the person's lifestyle. More information on analyzing earliest recollections is provided in the skill development section of this chapter.

Priorities and ways of behaving. People's behaviors also provide a rich and endless source of information about their lifestyles. Inquiring in detail about a person's behavior over a period of time or looking at a series of choices and actions can reveal consistent and repetitive behavioral patterns that reflect lifestyle. Adler and his associates (Adler, 1956; Mosak, 1971) identified the following common lifestyles, reflected in ways in which people orient themselves toward the world:

- Ruling and dominating others
- Avoiding interpersonal and other challenges
- Pleasing and seeking approval from others
- Controlling and managing
- Depending on others and needing to be cared for
- Pursuing superiority and perfection
- Seeking achievement
- Being a martyr or victim
- Seeking comfort
- Promoting social welfare and progress

Summarizing findings. After an extensive process of exploration, assessment, and analysis, clinicians formulate hypotheses about the nature of clients' lifestyles as well as the faulty assumptions and self-destructive thoughts and behaviors that interfere with their efforts to achieve their goals. This information is presented to clients for discussion and revision, paving the way for the third phase of treatment.

Phase 3: Reeducation, Insight, and Reorientation   Phase 3 can be especially difficult for clinicians because they need to be both encouraging and challenging. While remaining supportive, they use interpretation and confrontation to help people gain awareness of their lifestyles, recognize the covert reasons behind their behaviors, appreciate the negative consequences of those behaviors, and move toward positive change. Several strategies help clinicians remain caring through this phase of treatment:

- They focus on the present rather than the past.
- They are more concerned with consequences than with unconscious motivation.
- They present their interpretations in ways that are likely to be accepted by clients.

Rather than being dogmatic or authoritarian, clinicians state interpretations as guesses or hunches. They might say, "I have a hunch that you threw your brother's hat in the sewer because you wanted more attention from your parents," or "I wonder if you have refused to set a more realistic sale price for your house because the house represents part of your ideal self." With gentle interpretations such as these, clinicians seek to educate clients and to promote self-awareness, insight, and discussion rather than to persuade clients to agree with them.

Reorientation. Clinicians continue to play an active role during this phase of treatment, presenting alternate possibilities, providing information, and helping people weigh their options and make decisions. Emphasis is on beliefs, attitudes, and perceptions because, according to Adler, if these are changed, then behavioral change will follow (Dinkmeyer, Dinkmeyer, & Sperry, 1987).

Once clients have gained some insight and modified their distorted beliefs, they are ready to reorient their lives and initiate new ideas and patterns of behaviors. Clients now view their lives from different perspectives and can make more rewarding choices. Clinicians foster this outcome by helping people become full participants in their social system, shift their roles and interactions, and take positive actions to achieve their revised goals. Throughout, clinicians model and nurture optimism and flexibility; they support clients in developing the courage to be imperfect and take on rewarding challenges.

The reorientation phase can be divided into four parts (Sweeney, 1998):

1. Clients clarify their goals and determine whether they are realistic.
2. Common sense and clear thinking are applied to clients' feelings, beliefs, and goals. Although clients are reminded that their choices are their own, clinicians help them use common sense to evaluate and, if necessary, modify their thinking.
3. New learning is applied to the clients' lives.
4. Any barriers to progress are addressed and removed.

Phase 4: Reinforcement, Evaluation, Termination, and Follow-Up   This final phase of treatment enables people to solidify the gains they have made and move forward with their lives in healthier and more fulfilling ways. Clinicians continue to provide education, teach skills, and make interpretations. However, their primary role is reinforcing positive changes. Clients and clinicians collaborate in evaluating progress, strengthening social interest and healthy and rewarding beliefs, and planning future steps toward goal attainment. Together, they determine when the client is ready to complete treatment and agree on follow-up procedures to ensure that clients stay on track and continue their positive growth and forward movement.

Interventions

Adler's Individual Psychology offers a wide range of creative and useful interventions. Many have already been discussed in this chapter, such as the use of earliest recollections and analysis of family constellation and birth order. Additional interventions include the following:

- *Acting as if* is a technique in which clinicians suggest to clients that they act as if they could accomplish something they do not believe they can do. A woman who is intimidated by her verbally abusive husband, for example, might act as if she had the courage to stand up to him and to leave the room if he continues to berate and belittle her.

- *Avoiding the tar baby* is an intervention designed to help people avoid those traps and pitfalls where they frequently get stuck. Rather than participating in repetitive patterns, clinicians respond in unexpected ways in order to change the client's persistent self-destructive behaviors. For example, a client spent many fruitless evenings poring over his bills and feeling sorry for himself. Rather than encouraging him to work harder at this task, the clinician suggested that the client spend an evening with friends and pay only one bill a day.

- *Catching oneself* encourages people to be more conscious of their repetitive faulty goals and thoughts. Clinicians facilitate this by identifying warning signs of difficulties and encouraging clients to view them as stop signs that remind them to pause and redirect themselves. This concrete approach helps people develop self-awareness and monitor themselves without being self-critical. For example, a man who often lost his temper and became inappropriately angry recognized that his whole body became tense before he exploded. He was taught to identify signs of physical tension, view them as stop signs, and use deep breathing as a quick and effective way to diffuse his anger.

- *Pushing the button* is designed to help people become more aware of the control they can have over their emotions, rather than allowing their emotions to control them. Clinicians encourage people to alternately imagine pleasant and unpleasant experiences, observe the emotions that accompany each image, and recognize that they can determine which button to push. A young woman who frequently consumed too much alcohol at social events imagined the pride she took in remaining sober (pleasant experience) as well as the embarrassment and physical discomfort she felt after becoming intoxicated (unpleasant experience). Vivid images of these two contrasting experiences helped her abstain from alcohol (push the healthy button).

- In *spitting in the client's soup,* clinicians identify the underlying motivations behind clients' self-defeating behaviors and then spoil their imagined payoff by making it unappealing. This is illustrated in the following dialog:

> Client: I feel so awful that Dana broke up with me, I've thought about killing myself.
>
> Clinician: I guess you want to make her feel guilty. But if you kill yourself, you won't be around to see how she's feeling. . . or go to college or buy that car you were talking about. You'll just be lying in the ground.

In addition to these specific techniques associated with Adlerian therapy, clinicians who follow this theoretical model also use many other techniques. Some of these, including encouragement, interpretation, and use of questions, have been discussed previously in this book. Others include the following:

- *Immediacy* focuses the session on the interaction between the client and the clinician, often because it is a mirror of the client's interactions outside of the session. For example, a client accused the clinician of disliking him when the clinician provided information on parenting that differed from the client's style of parenting. The clinician helped the client see that when people disagreed with him, he viewed it as evidence that they disliked him.

- *Confrontation* involves pointing out discrepancies in the material that clients present. For example, a counselor might say, "Help me understand your decision to spend $1,000 on a wedding gown when you've told me that you're concerned about being able to make the down payment on the house you want to buy."

- *Task assignments* are used throughout the treatment process. Client and clinician agree that the client will engage in a planned activity such as observing and listing times when he feels angry or exercising three times a week. Not only do the specific tasks advance the treatment, but the process of coming to an agreement on tasks, making a commitment to complete them, and planning and executing the tasks can promote feelings of competence and responsibility.

- *Humor, silence, advice, and reflection of feeling* are other techniques in the repertoire of the Adlerian psychotherapist. The many types of interventions associated with this treatment approach offer clinicians many avenues to build rapport with their clients, promote insight and self-awareness, and encourage positive change.

APPLICATION AND CURRENT USE OF INDIVIDUAL PSYCHOLOGY

Adler's model of Individual Psychology is used with a broad range of situations and clients. Not only is it used for treatment of individuals, couples, families, and groups, it also is used in career development, education, training, supervision, consultation, and organizational development.

Application to Children

Adler's Individual Psychology is well suited for use with children and has been adopted by many school counselors as well as clinicians who treat children. Adler's approach offers counselors a flexible yet structured approach that lends itself well to treatment of both immediate and long-standing concerns of young people. His emphasis on cooperation, character building, and development of self-esteem (overcoming inferiority, according to Adler) are compatible with current emphases in treatment of children and adolescence.

Nicoll (1994) developed classroom guidance programs based on Adler's theories. Nicoll proposed the following five-stage model for classroom use:

1. Increase awareness and appreciation of individual differences
2. Teach about the range of human emotions, promote awareness of our own feelings, clarify the impact our actions have on other people's feelings, and encourage the development of empathy
3. Foster good communication skills
4. Promote cooperation and collaboration skills
5. Encourage responsibility and use natural consequences

Rudolf Dreikurs, a therapist and writer, spread awareness of Adler's ideas among educators and parents. Dreikurs drew on Adler's ideas in his writings on effective parenting. *Children: The Challenge* (Dreikurs & Stoltz, 1964) has become a classic and is still used in parenting classes. Dreikurs suggested that children's misbehavior is a reflection of their goals and lifestyle. He identified four possible motives behind such misbehavior (Dreikurs & Cassel, 1972):

- Attention getting
- Power
- Revenge
- Display of inadequacy

Teachers and parents typically have negative responses to these behaviors. However, their automatic reactions often reinforce an undesirable behavior. For example, they may engage in a power struggle with the child who wants to be in charge or may reprimand an attention-seeking child, inadvertently providing the desired attention. Dreikurs suggested that, by understanding the goal of a child's misbehavior, people can address it more successfully. For example, teachers and parents should attend to and reinforce only the positive behaviors of an attention-seeking child and acknowledge the power of a child who wants to be in charge, encouraging cooperation and responsibility as part of his or her leadership role.

Don Dinkmeyer (1982) contributed further to the use of Adler's concepts in schools through his program called Developing Understanding of Self and Others (DUSO). DUSO has been used in elementary schools to promote self-awareness, positive socialization, and feelings of competence in children and to raise awareness of the importance of using encouragement to promote children's development.

Adlerian play therapy is yet another extension of Adler's work. According to Kottman and Johnson (1993), its purpose is to "build relationships with children; to explore the ways children view themselves, others, and the world; to help children understand the ways they gain significance in their families and in school; and to help them explore new ways of gaining significance in interacting with others" (p. 42). Interventions used by Adlerian play therapists to effect positive change in children include:

- Encouragement
- Play and stories used as therapeutic metaphors
- Limit setting
- Analysis of early recollections and lifestyle
- Discussion of family constellation and atmosphere
- Verbal tracking
- Sharing of hypotheses to promote self-awareness
- Teaching new behaviors

Application to Parenting

Adler's ideas, especially as interpreted by Dreikurs, Dinkmeyer, and others, can provide a solid foundation for teaching parenting skills, improving family functioning, and helping parents to raise healthy children. Dreikurs had a vision of families that emphasized communication, respect, encouragement, teaching, the use of natural and logical consequences, and the expectation that children should assume age-appropriate responsibilities. He also recognized the importance of families having fun together, an aspect of family life often forgotten in our busy society. Dreikurs advocated the use of a family council in which all family members convene at the same time each week to talk about their family and address any concerns or difficulties. Even young children should be involved in these meetings and should have the opportunity to express themselves. This process can improve family functioning, empower each family member, and instill early the importance of the social group (Zuckerman, Zuckerman, Costa, & Yura, 1978).

Several structured parent education programs, including Active Parenting and Systematic Training for Effective Parenting (STEP), have evolved from Adler's ideas. Developed by Dinkmeyer and McKay (1997), the STEP parenting system offers guidelines on motivating, disciplining, understanding, communicating with, and encouraging children. This educational program emphasizes the use of natural and reasonable consequences, teaches reflective listening, and promotes the use of birth order as a vehicle for better understanding children.

Programs that provide training in Adler's Individual Psychology typically emphasize education and offer community presentations to teach parenting and other interpersonal skills. A popular format involves a clinician interviewing members of one family while other families observe and then provide feedback and discuss ways in which they could apply to their own families the information that emerged in the interviews.

Application to Couples

Counseling with couples is another of the many applications of Adler's work. Carlson and Dinkmeyer (2002) created a program called Time for a Better Marriage that uses Adler's ideas to help couples improve their relationships. Designed for use as either a self-help manual or an adjunct to treatment, this program helps partners to understand each other's goals, provide encouragement, assume responsibility, and communicate effectively. Worksheets and skill cards help couples put learning into action. Dinkmeyer's view of marital happiness as a combination of self-esteem, social interest, and sense of humor is a concise reflection of Adler's concepts.

Application to Assessment

Adlerian theory, with its emphasis on understanding lifestyle and private logic, lends itself to the development of tools to facilitate assessment. Many useful inventories have been developed to aid clinicians in implementing this theory. Wickers (1988) developed the Misbehavior Reaction Checklist to help teachers and parents understand the purpose of a child's misbehavior. Several tools are useful in lifestyle assessment. For example, the Kern Lifestyle Scale (Kern, 1992) is a self-scoring instrument designed to obtain lifestyle information and promote self-awareness in career, personal, and relationship counseling as well as in business settings. This and many other inventories, audiotapes, booklets, and other materials based on Adler's ideas, are published by CMTI Press ([800] 584-1733). All enhance the work of the Adlerian clinician.

Application to Diagnostic Groups

Most of the common problems and mental disorders seen in counseling and psychotherapy are amenable to treatment via Adlerian therapy (Sperry & Carlson, 1996). According to Sherman and Nwaorgu (2002, p. 192), this approach addresses a broad spectrum of problems from individual "mistakes that lead to negative lifestyles to a whole breadth of social problems such as racial conflict, . . . discrimination, war, poverty, drugs, issues of democracy, and inadequate parenting. Conceptualized in this way, everyone has a problem, and this remains part of the human condition."

The literature documents the use of this approach with "all the major categories of psychopathology" (Sherman & Nwaorgu, 2002, p. 193). Certainly, this approach seems useful with people who have mood, anxiety, or personality disorders; people with these disorders typically engage in thoughts and behaviors that are ineffectual and unrewarding and that reflect an excessive focus on their own needs rather than their place in society and their family. Most of these clients are capable of engaging in the self-examination, self-awareness, and learning that are integral to the Adlerian approach.

The literature also provides many examples and descriptions of the use of Individual Psychology with other disorders and problems. Strauch (2001), for example, proposed that this approach, with its emphasis on understanding lifestyle and social involvement, could be useful to people having dysfunctional responses to traumatic experiences. People with low self-esteem and social and relationship concerns also seem likely to benefit from Adlerian therapy. Children with behavioral problems are, of course, well suited to treatment via this approach. Even people with drug and alcohol problems, criminal behavior, and other impulse control disorders can be understood and helped through Adler's model; they are failing to meet their needs for power and belonging in positive ways (Adler, 1979; Dinkmeyer, Dinkmeyer, & Sperry, 1987). Carroll (1999) found Adlerian theory compatible with Alcoholics Anonymous and other 12-step programs and concluded that this approach was appropriate for treating people with substance use disorders.

Although people with psychotic disorders may not be able to engage in the kind of self-examination that Adlerian therapy requires, they can be better understood through Adler's ideas. Mosak and Goldman (1995), for example, wrote about the unrealistic superiority goals of people with psychotic disorders, reflected in their irrational and nonconstructive thinking. Individual Psychology can help make sense of the loss of contact with reality experienced by these people and suggest useful ways to help them.

Application to Multicultural Groups

Individual Psychology not only has much that would appeal to a diverse and multicultural population, but it actively seeks to address problems of discrimination and disenfranchisement. According to Sherman and Nwaorgu (2002, p. 193), "Adlerians take seriously social discrimination based on ethnicity, gender, poverty, religion, and education level as issues for consideration in the treatment of clients."

The emphasis on culture (broadly defined to include ethnicity, class, religion, community, gender, age, and lifestyle), social interest, and the family constellation, as well as the importance of collaboration, have wide appeal. According to Adlerians, prejudice, racism, and gender discrimination grow out of misguided efforts to gain superiority by degrading others (Hanna, 1998). True self-esteem comes not from oppressing others but from working cooperatively to contribute to the common good, empowering ourselves as well as others, and facing life's challenges together (Ferguson, 2000).

Adler's approach has particular relevance to people with disabilities. He wrote of the feelings of discouragement and inferiority and the efforts toward compensation that often emerge in people with disabilities. His understanding of this dynamic, as well as his emphasis on understanding maladjustment and promoting healthy empowerment, responsibility, and realistic self-esteem, should be helpful in treatment of people who are having difficulty coping with physical and mental challenges (Livneh & Sherwood, 1991). Of course, clinicians should be cautious not to overgeneralize and assume that all people with disabilities experience feelings of inferiority.

A logical extension of Adler's insights into people with disabilities is to people with other potential challenges in their lives, such as recent immigrants, people who grow up in one-parent homes, those who experienced poverty or abuse, and those who feel disenfranchised for any reason. Adler's understanding of the connection between early experiences and the development of lifestyles and goals provides insight into ways in which people with difficult backgrounds cope with their lives, as well as ways to help and empower them.

Although Adler's theories seem compatible with multicultural competence, clinicians still must exercise caution when using Individual Psychology. Adler's approach in its traditional form is an in-depth, lengthy one that is not well suited to people in crisis or those who have little patience or motivation for self-analysis. His emphasis on individual responsibility and power as well as his exploration of early recollections also may be incompatible with the thinking of some people from nonwestern cultures. Consequently, the approach may need to be adapted to such clients.

EVALUATION OF INDIVIDUAL PSYCHOLOGY

The strengths in Adler's treatment system far outnumber its shortcomings and weaknesses. Although developed over 75 years ago, his ideas seem remarkably timely and relevant today.

Limitations

Like other approaches focused on background, Adlerian therapy suffers from a dearth of empirical research. A few efforts have been made to provide research support for Adler's concepts. For example, some empirical validation of Adler's ideas on the impact of birth order has been done (Lombardi, 1996). A study of the Adlerian Lifestyle Inventory to assess lifestyles of Native American women residing on a reservation provided some support for the broad usefulness of lifestyle assessment (Roberts, Harper, Caldwell, & Decora, 2003). However, more empirical research is needed to fully support the growing importance of Individual Psychology. In addition, many of Adler's concepts such as fictional finalism and superiority are not well defined and risk oversimplification.

Strengths and Contributions

Adler's contributions, not only to the current practice of psychotherapy, but also to the thinking of some of the other leaders in our field, is enormous. Rollo May, Viktor Frankl, Carl Rogers, and Abraham Maslow all acknowledged their debt to Adler (Hoffman, 1994). The development of existentialism, cognitive therapy, reality therapy, person-centered counseling, and Gestalt approaches to treatment have been influenced by Adler's ideas. His work drew attention to the human spirit and people's need to be special. Whether or not clinicians describe themselves as followers of Adler's approach, nearly all counseling and psychotherapy now reflects some of his concepts, including:

- The impact of early experiences and family constellation on current functioning
- The importance of taking a holistic approach that considers mind, body, and spirit

- The need to view people in their family, social, and cultural contexts
- The recognition that thinking influences emotions and behavior
- The emphasis on strengths, optimism, encouragement, empowerment, and support
- The relevance of lifestyle and goals
- The need to identify, understand the purpose of, and modify repetitive self-defeating behaviors
- The importance of a collaborative therapeutic alliance
- The benefits of having a therapist and client with realistic and mutually agreed-on goals
- The recognition that having problems and differences is a normal part of life and that these can be viewed as opportunities for growth rather than as pathology
- The view of therapy as an educational and growth-promoting process as well as a remedial one

Watts (2000, p. 26) wrote, "The beauty of Individual Psychology is its flexibility: Adlerian practitioners can be both theoretically integrative and technically eclectic." Individual Psychology can easily and effectively be combined with many contemporary treatment approaches. Its emphasis on beliefs and behavior is compatible with cognitive-behavioral therapy. Adlerian lifestyle assessment has much in common with narrative therapy's emphasis on stories that provide the structure of life. Of course, the attention to early memories and childhood experiences is psychoanalytic in origin while the emphasis on the therapeutic alliance reflects elements of humanistic approaches.

Many of Adler's ideas have become more important than ever in light of some of the pervasive problems in our society today (Hoffman, 1994). Our growing awareness of the widespread abuse of children and the enduring harm that can result has focused attention on the significance to adults of their early childhood experiences and memories. Adler's call for changes in the "debilitating gender roles within the family and the workplace" (Hoffman, 1994, p. 329) still needs attention in our society. His emphasis on responsibility, resilience, character building, and social interest seems especially relevant in light of the many incidents of violence in our society. The importance of fathers and of sibling relationships are other areas of current attention. Probably of greatest importance are Adler's emphasis on respect for individual differences and the importance of each of us becoming a contributing part of a larger social system.

SKILL DEVELOPMENT: ANALYZING EARLIEST RECOLLECTIONS

Eliciting and analyzing people's earliest recollections can provide understanding of their lifestyles and how they view the world. The following four-step procedure, followed by examples, will help you learn to use early recollections in treatment. Exercises later in this chapter give you the opportunity to practice these skills.

1. *Eliciting the recollections.* Begin by inviting people to think back to their childhood, as early as they can remember, and describe at least three incidents that they recall. They should come up with experiences that included them and that they actually remember clearly rather than family stories or events. The clinician should write down each recollection as it is described.

2. *Processing each memory.* Ask about the person's feelings during the memory; discuss any actions or movements in the memory, especially transactions between the client and others; ask what part of the memory seems most vivid or important; and ask what meaning the memory has for the teller.

3. *Analyzing the memories.* Looking particularly for commonalities among the three or more recollections, consider the role of the client in the memories, the emotions associated with the memories, who else is present and how they are interacting with the client, the nature of the situations recalled, and the way in which the client responded to the events and interactions in the memories.

4. *Interpretation and application.* Develop a hypothesis or hunch, based on the common themes and patterns in the recollections, as to what these memories disclose about the person's goals and lifestyle. Present this hypothesis to the client for discussion and clarification.

Consider the following three recollections provided by a 27-year-old single woman:

Recollection 1: I remember being in my crib. It was very dark and I felt afraid. I was crying. Then my father came into the room. He picked me up and held me. He said something like, "What's the matter? Everything is all right now."

Recollection 2: I was in a department store. Somehow I got separated from my mother. I looked around, and I couldn't see her. I didn't know what to do, and I started to scream. This man came over, a salesperson or a manager in the store. He took me into a little room—an office, I guess—and he said he would help me find my mommy. He asked my name and then I heard something about a lost child over the loudspeaker. The man gave me some candy and kept talking to me. It seemed like a long time, but finally my mother came. She was crying too. I was so happy to see her.

Recollection 3: I was riding a tricycle, and I fell down. Nobody was around to help me. My knee was bleeding. I was crying and hurt, but nobody came. Finally, a neighbor heard me. He came out to see what the problem was, and then he called my mother. I felt better as soon as there was somebody to help me.

Analysis: In all three recollections, the woman is scared and perceives herself as needing help. Through crying, she is able to let others know that she needs help but is not able to otherwise help herself. In all three instances, she is rescued by caring men. They reassure her and provide the help she needs. Although her mother subsequently provides help in two of the memories, it is the men who are there when the woman really needs help. Discussion revealed that this woman often felt fearful and doubted her own ability to move ahead in her career and cope with her life. She had been engaged twice and was eager to marry, but both times her fiancés had broken the engagement, telling her that she was too needy and dependent. The woman became aware that, although she was a successful teacher, she expected to get into trouble in some way and was hoping to be rescued from the demands of her career by marriage. At the same time, she indicated that she didn't trust people very much, especially women, and that she often felt overwhelmed by the day-to-day demands of her life. By assuming a needy and helpless role, she was actually undermining her relationships but believed that the way to find a man to rescue her was to become as needy as possible: the child crying loudly for help. This information played an important part in her treatment.

CASE ILLUSTRATION

Ava, age 10, is Edie and Roberto's daughter. The family's counselor decided to have some individual sessions with Ava to get to know her and her role in the family better and to develop a positive relationship with her. In addition, both Edie and Roberto expressed concerns about Ava's behavior. They described her as always being willful and independent, with these problems worsening in recent months. They reported that Ava is disobedient, both at home and at school, and that her teacher told them that some of the children do not want to play with her because she is "bossy." In addition, Ava's grades have been declining.

Ava was willing to meet with the counselor for an individual session. Ava was quite open and started off the session by describing how much she enjoyed seeing the cartoon version of the movie *Tarzan*. She had been particularly impressed by Tarzan's ability to swing through the trees, overcome the "bad guys," and help all the animals. Ava also talked about some of her concerns related to her family. She described her mother as "crying a lot and moping around" while her father worked long hours and "just yells about everything." She also reported a dream that she compared to *Alice's Adventures in Wonderland* in which her mother was getting smaller while Ava was getting larger. As Ava talked, the counselor began to formulate hypotheses about Ava's lifestyle, her goals and the reasons for her misbehavior.

Toward the end of the session, the counselor asked Ava to describe three early recollections:

Recollection 1: Ava recalled that when she was about four years old she became afraid of spiders. Once, while taking a walk with her father, she noticed a spider on her shoe and became upset. Her father brushed the spider off and squashed it. Ava was so impressed by this that she began squashing every bug she saw until her mother discouraged this.

Recollection 2: Another memory from a year or so later involved an incident when the mother of her friend Lori took Ava and Lori swimming. When Ava got out of the car, she swung her car door into another car and chipped the paint. The person sitting in the car complained to Lori's mother,

but she just told him "not to make a big deal out of nothing" and took the children into the pool.

Recollection 3: The last memory involved a fight between her parents when Ava was in kindergarten. Her mother had burned the meatloaf that was to be served for dinner. When Roberto arrived home, he yelled at Edie for being careless. Edie began to cry, but Roberto just went into the other room and ordered pizza. Ava remembered thinking that the pizza was much better than the meatloaf would have been.

In all three memories, Ava's initial role is observer. Although her own behavior is a factor in the first two memories, what she recalled most sharply were the actions of the adults who used strength and anger to gain power and control. In the last two memories, other people's feelings are disregarded. Roberto and the friend's mother seem admirable to Ava while her own mother is viewed as weak.

These memories confirmed many of the counselor's hypotheses. Ava's misbehavior seemed to be a misguided attempt to gain power. She wanted to be in charge and wanted other people to stop controlling her. Her recollections suggest that she believes the way to obtain power is to become dominating, telling other people what to do as she has observed her father and others do. Her mother, who has a very different style, is devalued in Ava's mind because she seems to lack power. This has carried over to Ava's loss of interest in school, which her mother highly values. Ava's behavior is harming her relationships with both her peers and her parents.

Future sessions will involve both play therapy and talking to help Ava recognize her self-destructive efforts to obtain power and to change both her private logic and her repertoire of behaviors so that she finds more rewarding ways to gain power. Discussion would include exploration of Ava's roles and relationships with family members, basic messages and coping behaviors she learned as a child, her current lifestyle, and whether her beliefs and behavior are helping her to achieve the central goals of her life. This information also will be used in sessions with Roberto and Edie to help them parent Ava more effectively.

EXERCISES

Large-Group Exercises

1. Ask for two or three volunteers from the class who are willing to share their earliest recollections. Taking one person at a time, list that person's memories on the board and then process and analyze them according to the guidelines in the "Skill Development" section. Encourage the person with the memories to play an active part in the analysis. Discuss the relationship of the patterns that emerge from the recollections to the person's lifestyle.

2. Refer to the history of Roberto as presented in previous chapters. Ask for two volunteers—one to play Roberto and one to serve as the interviewer. The person assuming the role of Roberto should feel free to be creative and add information as long as it is consistent with what is already known about Roberto. Engage in a role-played interview that will shed light on Roberto's lifestyle. The interviewer might ask about family constellation and birth order, earliest recollections, successes and disappointments both in childhood and as an adult, goals and values, and social involvement and relationships. After the role-play, discuss the interview and try to identify Roberto's private logic, goals, priorities, and lifestyle. Allow at least 45 minutes for this exercise.

3. Divide the participants into four groups based on their birth order. Groups should be formed for oldest, youngest, middle, and only children. Have each group meet for 15–20 minutes and discuss the following questions:

- What are the common characteristics of people with your birth order?
- What important differences emerged among the people in your group?
- What are common misconceptions or stereotypes about people in your birth position?
- What preconceptions do you have about the characteristics of people in the other three birth order positions?

Each group should select a spokesperson who will present the group's conclusions to the class as a whole.

Small-Group Exercises

1. In previous chapters, you gained experience in conducting interviews and using open questions. You build on those skills in this exercise. Form into your groups of four people, but this time change partners so you are interviewing a different person than the one you interviewed in previous exercises. Spend about 15 minutes conducting an interview with that person, focusing particularly on the following four areas:

- Childhood behavior and misbehavior
- Family constellation
- Important values and goals
- Ways in which the person has sought to achieve those goals

Next the interviewer should lead the interviewee in a discussion of the patterns that emerged. Remember to be encouraging and to help your partner feel comfortable.

At the conclusion of each role play, spend 5–10 minutes providing feedback to the person in the interviewer role on the following aspects of the exercise:

- Therapeutic alliance
- Use of open questions
- Ability to elicit relevant information on the four topics
- Use of encouragement

2. In your groups of four, discuss memories of times when you misbehaved as a child. Help each other determine whether the motive of the misbehavior was power, attention, revenge, or display of inadequacy. Then discuss helpful responses that your teachers or parents might have made to your misbehavior.

Individual Exercises

1. List at least three of your earliest memories. Process and analyze them according to the guidelines in the "Skill Development" section. What patterns emerge? What sorts of goals and lifestyle do they suggest? How does this information relate to your image of yourself? Write your memories and responses to these questions in your journal (described in chapter 1).
2. Identify a challenge you are facing that you are not sure you can handle successfully. Imagine yourself capable of dealing with that challenge. Be sure the image of yourself is clear and vivid in your mind. Now think about how the person reflected by this image of yourself would handle the challenge. As you address this issue in your life, act as if you are that image of yourself and keep reminding yourself that you can handle the situation. After you have made some progress, monitor your success. Think about how well this technique is working and how you might improve on this intervention. Write a summary of this experience in your journal.

SUMMARY

Adler's Individual Psychology has made an important contribution to counseling and psychology and continues to be widely practiced. His model is useful with a broad range of people and difficulties. Adler's emphasis on encouragement and logic rather than pathology, power and importance rather than sexuality, and family and society rather than the unconscious are appealing and contribute to people's empowerment. Many of Adler's concepts, including goals, private logic, priorities, and lifestyle, provide a useful framework for understanding people. In addition, the interventions and tools that have grown out of his model help clini-cians use his ideas to assess, educate, and encourage change in their clients.

Many opportunities exist for further education on Adler's work. The North American Society of Adlerian Psychology, the International Association for Individual Psychology, and the Rudolf Dreikurs Institute all hold annual conventions. Ongoing training can be obtained at Bowie State University in Bowie, Maryland, as well as the Alfred Adler Institutes in many cities, including Boca Raton, Florida; Chicago; and New York City. Information on these programs can be obtained from the North American Society of Adlerian Psychology.

RECOMMENDED READINGS

Adler, A. (1963). *The practice and theory of individual psychology*. Paterson, NJ: Littlefield, Adams.

Dreikurs, R., & Stoltz, V. (1964). *Children: The challenge*. New York: Meredith.

Grey, L. (1998). *Alfred Adler, the forgotten prophet: A vision for the 21st century*. Westport, CT: Praeger.

Hoffman, E. (1994). *The drive for self: Alfred Adler and the founding of individual psychology*. Reading, MA: Addison-Wesley.

Individual Psychology: Journal of Adlerian Theory, Research, and Practice.

Sherman, R., & Nwaorgu, A. (2002). Adlerian therapy: A century of tradition and research. In F. W. Kaslow (Ed.), *Comprehensive handbook of psychotherapy: Interpersonal/ humanistic/existential*. New York: John Wiley & Sons.

Sperry, L., & Carlson, J. (1996). *Psychopathology and psychotherapy*. Washington, DC: Accelerated Development.

ADDITIONAL SOURCES OF INFORMATION

http://www.alfredadler.org—The website for the North American Society of Adlerian Psychology.

http://www.emicrotraining.com/adlerian.html—Resources for Adlerian therapists.

http://www.iaiponline.org—The website for the International Association of Individual Psychology (IAIP)

http://www.nyinstitute.com/adler.htm—The website for the New York Institute for Adlerian therapists, including information on training and resources.

CHAPTER 6

Carl Jung and Jungian Analytical Psychology

C arl Jung spent part of his career as a close colleague of Sigmund Freud and was strongly influenced by the concepts of Freudian psychoanalysis. However, like Adler, Jung eventually went on to develop his own innovative ideas.

Although Jung's work continues through training institutes, current publications, and the practice of Jungian analysts, its complex and esoteric nature has prevented it from achieving the widespread acceptance that Adler's work has received. Nevertheless, Jung's interest in the ancestral roots of our psyche, dreams and symbols, and the development of wholeness through the integration of the conscious and the unconscious have captured the imagination and loyalty of many clinicians who thrive on the depth and challenge of his ideas. In addition, those ideas have served as the basis for the Myers-Briggs Type Indicator, a widely used personality inventory (discussed later in this chapter), and have influenced both art therapy and the incorporation of spirituality into clinical work.

CARL JUNG

Carl Gustav Jung was born on July 26, 1875, in Kesswyl, Switzerland. His father was a minister descended from a long line of clergy associated with the Swiss Reformed Church. Although Jung had two siblings, one died in infancy before Jung was born, and the other, a sister, was born nine years after Jung (Ellenberger, 1970). Jung was apparently a lonely and introverted child who began experiencing terrifying dreams at an early age (Ewen, 1993; Jung, 1963).

Jung's impressions of his parents had a great impact on his thinking, as his work reflects. His father disappointed Jung because of the father's inability to fully experience his faith; Jung placed great emphasis on the experience of spirituality and viewed that as an important part of our inner world (Schwartz, 1995). Just as his father seemed paradoxical (the minister who was a disbeliever), so did his mother, a woman who followed socially accepted and often repressive standards in her outward behavior but had a different and almost clairvoyant inner self.

From adolescence, Jung was an avid reader who studied philosophy, anthropology, the occult, and parapsychology on his own. Sedgwick (2001, pp. 20–21) described Jung as, ". . . a thinking and intuitive kind of person, with a near-visionary capacity and proclivity for mystical experience. Though romantic and somewhat combustible in his intimate relations, he was also capable of a coolness in feeling with others . . . "

Despite his strong personality and breadth of interests, Jung's formal education was fairly traditional. He attended medical school at the University of Basel where he initially specialized in internal medicine, but his independent and original ideas made this a poor fit. He subsequently shifted his focus to psychiatry and obtained a position at a psychiatric hospital in Zurich, working under the supervision of Eugen Bleuler, a pioneer in the study of schizophrenia. Jung studied and administered word association tests, one of the first experimental efforts to learn more about the unconscious origins of mental illness.

When he was in his 20s, Jung completed his military service and married Emma Rauschenbach, daughter of a wealthy industrialist. Their marriage gave him some financial freedom and a full family life; the couple had four daughters and a son.

An important turning point occurred for Jung in 1907 when he defended Freud against an attack by a professor at the University of Heidelberg (Kelly, 1990). This led Freud to welcome Jung as his disciple and eventually as his successor, not recognizing the important differences in their ideas (Jones, 1955). The two worked closely for six years. During that time, Jung accompanied Freud to lecture at Clark University in the United States. However, in 1913, Jung resigned as both president and member of the International Psychoanalytic Association because of his conviction that delusions and hallucinations frequently reflected universal archetypes rather than repressed memories.

Jung was a prolific theorist and writer throughout his life, with his work filling 18 volumes. Nevertheless, throughout his career, he had many periods in which he questioned himself and sought to resolve his doubts by immersing himself in his unconscious, using vehicles such as sand play, dialogs with figures in his dreams, and art to develop his understanding of the unconscious. Jung (1964) viewed his psyche as his greatest instrument: "My life is what I have done, my scientific work; the one is inseparable from the other. The work is the expression of inner development" (Jung, 1963, p. 211).

Despite a heart attack and a near-death experience in 1944 and the unjust accusation of being pro-Nazi and anti-Semitic, Jung worked productively in his later years (Ewen, 1993). His work reflects his belief that the years from midlife on are the time when creativity and personality integration are at their height. Jung died on June 6, 1961, at the age of 85, having lived long enough to witness the considerable impact of his work.

THE DEVELOPMENT OF JUNG'S THEORIES

Jung's ideas, like those of most important theoreticians, went through many phases during the 60 years of his professional life. He gained renown early in his career because of his writings on mental disorders, especially *The Psychology of Dementia Praecox* (Jung, 1907). During the early years of his collaboration with Freud, Jung's writings focused primarily on his experimental studies of word association, memory, and physiological responses to emotional changes. The publication of *Symbols of Transformation* (Jung, 1912) led to the end of his association with Freud and marked a shift in his writings.

During the subsequent 20 years, Jung's work continued to address many of the concepts that had grown out of psychoanalysis, notably analytical psychology, the ego, the conscious, and the unconscious. However, his view of these concepts was quite different from Freud's. Jung also wrote about art, literature, and culture during these years.

The focus of his writing shifted again during the last 25 years of his life. His work became increasingly spiritual, and he developed many of the constructs that make his work unique, including archetypes, the collective unconscious, anima and animus, the shadow, and the symbol of the mandala. (All will be discussed later in the chapter.) One of the most provocative works of this period was *Aion: Researches into the Phenomenology of the Self* (Jung, 1959) in which Jung drew connections among Christ, the ego, the shadow, the anima-animus relationship, the historical and alchemical significance of the fish symbol, gnostic symbols, and the structure and dynamics of the self.

During his later years, Jung not only continued his writing but maintained a psychotherapy practice and lectured throughout the world. He received many honors and considerable professional recognition. His work has been continued by others. Particularly important is the International Association for Analytical Psychology, founded in Zurich in 1966 as a training and accreditation center for people interested in learning and practicing according to Jung's model of treatment (Kirsch, 1996). Interestingly, many of the early Jungian analysts in the United States were women.

IMPORTANT THEORETICAL CONCEPTS

Jung's theory, known as analytical psychology, rests on his concept of the psyche. His concept of psychotherapy, in turn, focuses on helping people integrate and make conscious aspects of the psyche or personality.

The Components of the Psyche

Jung's concept of the psyche is much more complex than that of Freud. Figure 6.1 offers a simplified picture of Jung's conception of the psyche.

The Conscious Mind

According to Jung, psychic functioning includes three levels: the conscious mind, the collective unconscious, and the personal unconscious. Jung believed as did Freud that the conscious

Conscious Mind
Ego
Persona
Two Attitudes (Extraversion and Introversion)
Four Functions (Thinking, Feeling, Sensation, Intuition)

Unconscious Mind	
Collective Unconscious	**Personal Unconscious**
Archetypes	Repressed or Forgotten Memories
Self	Complexes
Shadow	Archetypes
Other Images, Myths, Symbols	Shadow

Figure 6.1   Jung's conception of the psyche.

mind was only a small fraction of the psyche, including the ego, the persona, two attitudes and four functions.

The Ego   The ego is the center of the conscious mind. The ego gives us our sense of the world and our reality. It therefore exerts considerable influence over our transactions with our environment. It is formed of perceptions, memories, thoughts, and feelings that are within our awareness and give us a sense of identity (Strean, 1994). The development of the ego, along with our bodily sensations, allows us to differentiate ourselves from others. Although the ego is relatively weak in relation to other parts of the psyche, it can protect itself by consigning threatening material to the personal unconscious through the process of repression. In this way, it connects and integrates the conscious and unconscious levels of personality.

The Persona   The persona is the idealized side of ourselves that we show to the outside world, the face of the collective psyche. This mask or protective facade conceals our problems and sorrows but enables us to function well in society, deal with other people, and pursue our daily needs and activities. Our persona may change in an effort to adapt to social situations and is affected by the group or person we are with at a particular time. The persona is a sort of compromise. It is inauthentic in that it usually does not reflect our true thoughts and emotions which might not be socially acceptable. At the same time, it usually captures enough of who we are and what we need to make us comfortable with it.

Attitudes and Functions   The two attitudes are *extraversion* and *introversion*. The four functions *include thinking and its opposite, feeling; sensation and its opposite, intuition.* People tend to interact with the world through one of the four functions, termed their primary or superior function. Its opposite function is the least developed, inferior function and is most problematic. For example, if someone's primary or superior function were thinking, this would guide most of his or her decisions. Its opposite, feeling, would probably not be well developed and the person would have difficulty giving emotions much weight in their decisions. Opposites in the personality provide psychic energy and, in the well-functioning person, are in balance. The attitudes and functions form the basis for the Myers-Briggs Type Indicator (discussed in the case illustration).

The Unconscious Mind

Freud and Jung agreed on the nature of the unconscious up to a point. Both believed that it was a large and powerful part of the psyche and contained repressed material. However, Jung presented a more complex and potentially positive view of the unconscious, viewing it as a source of creativity and spiritual and emotional growth, as well as of confusion and symptoms. The unconscious includes fantasies, knowledge and learning, memories of experiences and relationships, and subjective reactions to events and people (Sedgwick, 2001). According to Jung, these are housed in the personal unconscious and the collective unconscious, the two levels of the unconscious mind. The personal unconscious reflects the history of the individual while the collective unconscious "pertains to world history, . . . to the evolutionary history" of the human mind (Sedgwick, 2001, p. 32).

The Collective Unconscious   The collective unconscious has been described as the storehouse of latent memory traces inherited from the past that predispose people to react to the world in certain ways. The collective unconscious transcends individual experience and includes primordial motives or images passed on from our ancestors (Kelly, 1990; Strean, 1994). Fear of the dark and fear of snakes are examples of reactions that Jung believed originated in the collective unconscious, reflecting archaic remains.

The collective unconscious also includes a wealth of myths, images, and symbols of which *archetypes* are especially important examples. Archetypes are unconscious universal energies that result from repeated human experience and predispose people to view the world and organize their perceptions in particular ways. Archetypes are innate and have been transmitted through cultures and generations; they do not develop anew for each person but exist in and of themselves (Herman, 1975). Archetypes reflect endless repetition of typical situations that have engraved forms and images in our psyches. They might be thought of as stereotypes or prototypes. Examples include the wise old man, the mother, the father, the child, the wife, the husband, the hero, the trickster, the prophet, the disciple, rebirth or reincarnation, and the Self (the ultimate goal of the individuation process) (Ewen, 1993). Archetypes appear in dreams and fantasies, often through symbols, and influence how we think, feel, and behave throughout our lives. Jung wrote extensively about certain well-developed archetypes.

Modern perspectives of archetypes have been presented by Adams (2002) and Knox (2001). Adams suggests that the collective unconscious includes both cultural and archetypal factors and is strongly affected by cultural background. Knox (2001, p. 628) compares archetypes to innate structures of the mind that are "a direct expression of genetic codes, a set of hard-wired information processing instructions about how to attend to and prioritize stimuli" which can be dynamic and evolving. Knox's experimental research has given preliminary support to the existence of such innate mechanisms.

The Self. The Self, a central archetype, is the regulating center of the personality, integrating and balancing the needs and messages of the conscious, the personal unconscious, and the collective unconscious. Primarily located in the collective unconscious, the Self can emerge through dreams, symbols, perceptions, and images. It rarely emerges before the second half of our lives and is reflected in our spiritual and philosophical attitudes. The Self gives the personality unity, equilibrium, and stability (Jung, 1953, 1960). It is the goal of personality development, approached but rarely reached.

Anima/Animus. The anima is the psychological feminine component in a man, while the animus is the psychological masculine component in a woman (Schwartz, 1995). The anima and animus are archetypes that have evolved from generations of experience. They have two functions: they are a part of the Self and are also projected onto others. These archetypes influence how we feel about and present the masculine and feminine sides of ourselves. The anima and animus also shape our relationships, especially with the other gender. For example, a man with feminine archetypes of the evil seductress, the self-sacrificing mother, and dutiful daughter may project these images onto a woman with whom he is forming a relationship, making it difficult for him to see who this woman really is. The anima also allows the man to incorporate typically feminine attributes such as tenderness and devotion into his own personality to balance his typically masculine attributes.

Similarly, the woman projects the animus onto men with whom she has relationships. This process, in its negative form, may lead her to view men as overbearing and dominating while its positive form casts men in the role of knights in shining armor.

Awareness of the anima and animus can have a positive impact on our self-awareness, development, and relationships. However, people who are overly identified with their persona—that is, too concerned about the impressions they make on others—are likely to be unaware of their anima or animus and to project it onto others in ways that misrepresent people and relationships (Jung, 1953).

The shadow. The shadow originates in ancestral archetypes but can be manifested in both the collective and the personal unconscious. It is our dark side that we do not wish to acknowledge, so we attempt to hide it from ourselves and others. The shadow includes morally objectionable traits and instincts and has the potential to create thoughts, feelings, and actions that are socially unacceptable, shameful, and evil. At the same time, the shadow's unrestrained and primitive nature is a wellspring of energy, creativity, and vitality. The shadow is, in a sense, the opposite of the persona. The persona seeks social acceptance and approval, while the shadow embraces the socially undesirable.

The shadow includes a person's unlived and unexperienced aspects. It generally reflects negative qualities and attributes, although it may also encompass the golden shadow—positive qualities that were not affirmed or allowed to come into existence while the person was growing up.

Determining the nature of the shadow is difficult, especially for ourselves. However, we have several places to look for information on our shadows. The shadow is easier to observe in the manifestations of the personal unconscious than in archetypes of the collective unconscious, where its negative side may be too troubling for us to apprehend. Because the characteristics of our shadows are so unacceptable to us, they are the characteristics we are most likely to find objectionable in others and even to project onto people who do not possess them. Our own areas of moral weakness, difficulties in adaptation, and socially unacceptable behavior provide other clues to the nature of our shadows. Great efforts at self-knowledge are needed to comprehend our shadows, but the reward can be the ability to channel the obsessive and powerful attributes of the shadow into expanded creativity and power.

The Personal Unconscious   The personal unconscious is unique to each individual and forms over that person's lifetime. It includes memories of thoughts, feelings, and experiences that were forgotten or repressed; have lost their intensity and importance over time; or never had enough energic charge to enter consciousness. Jung agreed with Freud that the unconscious exerted considerable influence over our current thoughts, emotions, and behaviors. He also believed that bringing unconscious material into consciousness was an important part of both individuation and psychotherapy. However, he viewed the personal unconscious as not only holding negative and unacceptable memories but also providing a source of creativity and guidance as well as a drive for health and growth.

Images from the personal unconscious can be triggered by daily stimuli. For example, a view of a child riding on a pony can bring back a long forgotten image of oneself as a young child being led around a ring on a pony. Memories that have merely been forgotten or deposited in the personal unconscious because of their lack of importance may be recalled clearly or in fragments when something triggers their entry into consciousness. Repressed material, however, will generally emerge from the personal unconscious in incomplete or disguised forms, via dreams or symbols.

Complexes. Complexes are dynamic structures of the personality, located in the personal unconscious. They have an archetype at their core that has attracted a related and emotionally charged collection of feelings, thoughts, perceptions, and memories. Complexes have an impact on our daily lives but, because they are located in the unconscious, are generally out of our awareness.

Complexes that have been discussed extensively in the literature include the Oedipus complex and the mother complex. The mother complex has as its nucleus an archetype of the mother. Through psychic energy, this complex emerges in and is reflected by life experiences and images related to the maternal archetype. In this way, it exerts considerable influence over a person. For example, it might lead a man to search for his repressed ideal of the mother figure in all his relationships with women, thus preventing his establishment of a healthy adult sexual relationship. Complexes can also relate to such issues as guilt, finances, the self-image (inferiority complex), and traumatic events. Complexes are often reflected in peoples' presenting concerns when they enter treatment.

Jung discovered complexes through his experimentation with word association tests. He found that key words triggered chains of thoughts and associations that reflected the complexes.

Concept of Human Development

Jung envisioned people's lives as divided into two periods (Strean, 1994). During the first half of life, we find our place and accomplish the basic tasks of developing values and interests, finding a partner, and making career choices. During the second half of life, with our foundation in place, we progress toward individuation. This begins with a transition period, a sort of second puberty, during the mid- to late 30s (Ewen, 1993). The search for individuation is a lifelong process in which a person becomes "a psychological individual, that is, a separate indivisibility or whole" (Jung, 1953, p. 383). As part of the process, the whole personality develops. We gain greater access to the unconscious and our latent potentials; we move toward a state of greater balance, harmony, and equilibrium; and we clarify who we are in relation to others. We become more our own person and less a reflection of the ways in which we have been programmed throughout our lives. During the second half of life, the Self evolves, the persona is weakened, the shadow is better integrated and understood, and archetypes emerge that empower us. Our values shift from materialism, sexuality, and procreation to spiritual, social, and cultural values. Our visions of our purpose and the meaning of our lives become clearer.

Jung's theory of development is an optimistic one, emphasizing growth that can accelerate throughout the life span. Part of the appeal of his ideas rests in his positive view of human development in the second half of life. The link between Jung's theories and existentialism is evident in his emphasis on finding meaning in our lives.

Balance and Polarities

To Jung, life consists of opposites—polarities—with their balance determining the psychological health and development of the person. He viewed extremes as harmful because they prevent the opposite construct from being realized and gaining satisfactory expression. A consequence of imbalance is the tendency of any extreme emotion to turn into its opposite over time. For example, idealizing, unrealistic love can be transformed into hatred if the love object fails to live up to the ideal image.

People have inborn self-regulating systems that govern energy flow and help maintain balance. These include the principle of equivalence, which states that energy lost in one system will reappear in another system, with the sum total of energy remaining constant; and the principle of entropy, in which the libido (defined broadly by Jung as total psychic energy) tends to flow from a more intense to a less intense component to prevent the overload of energy in any one area. Self-regulation is also facilitated by transcendent functions, which allow us to make the transition from one dimension of our personalities to another (Kelly, 1990).

Dimensions of Personality

Jung attributed individual differences in personality to two dimensions: (1) the typical ways in which people take in and understand internal and external stimuli, and (2) the characteristic directions of their libidos (Jung, 1921).

The Four Functions   Four functions determine how people process internal and external stimuli:

1. *Thinking*. People whose thinking function is dominant react cognitively and intellectually, seeking to interpret and understand a stimulus.
2. *Feeling*. The feeling function is the opposite of the thinking function. People whose feeling function is primary react emotionally, focusing on pleasure, dislike, anger, and other emotions raised by a stimulus.
3. *Sensation*. Sensation involves receiving and identifying physical stimuli through the senses and relaying them to consciousness. People who have sensation as their dominant function look at the facts and the substance of a stimulus, seeking concrete evidence of its meaning and value.
4. *Intuition*. Intuition is the opposite of sensation. People whose intuition is their dominant function rely on hunches about where a stimulus has come from, where it is going, and what the possibilities are, to determine their reactions and decisions related to the stimulus.

Each person has a dominant or superior function that organizes experiences and perceptions as well as an inferior function that is closer to the unconscious. We have the least control over the inferior function, which causes us the most discomfort. Having balance or access to all functions can enable people to operate fully in a range of situations.

One role of the unconscious is to compensate for the dominance of the superior function by encouraging the opposite tendencies. A personality that remains overly one-sided despite efforts of the unconscious benefits from psychotherapy to restore balance.

The Two Attitudes   The second determinant of personality is the libido's (or energy's) direction of movement. For each person, energy moves primarily in one of the two following ways:

1. *Extraversion.* People in whom this attitude dominates direct their energy toward the outside world; they tend to be outgoing and adapt easily to external change. They are energized by social and interpersonal situations rather than by solitude.
2. *Introversion.* This is the opposite of extraversion. People in whom introversion dominates are most comfortable channeling their libido inward. Although they may have good social skills, they tend to be introspective and replenish their energy by being alone. Crowds of people exhaust them.

Each of the four functions of the first dimension can be paired with each of the two attitudes of the second dimension, making eight possible personality types (e.g., Thinking and Introversion, Thinking and Extraversion, Feeling and Extraversion). The functions and attitudes may sound familiar because they form the basis for the Myers-Briggs Type Indicator (discussed later in the chapter).

TREATMENT USING JUNGIAN ANALYTICAL PSYCHOLOGY

Like Freudian psychoanalysts, Jungian analysts view treatment as a lengthy and intensive process. Ideally, people are seen at least twice a week, usually with client and clinician facing one another (Schwartz, 1995).

Goals of Psychotherapy

Jungian analysis is deep and intensive, encouraging the emergence and understanding of material from both the personal and the collective unconscious. Regression facilitates access to the unconscious and is followed by progression, as the painful and unacceptable elements of the unconscious are made conscious, acceptable, and meaningful. This ultimately leads to resolution of inner conflicts, greater balance and integration in the person, individuation, growth in creativity and energy, and the expansion of spiritual feelings. Jung does not seek to bring people happiness but, rather, to enable them to cope with the inevitable pain and suffering of life and to find a balance between joy and sorrow. He also views therapy as helping people develop "a self-correcting homeostatic relationship between conscious life and the unconscious reaction to it" (Sedgwick, 2001, p. 38), a balance between the conscious and the unconscious.

Jungian treatment typically has four stages (Ewen, 1993):

1. *Catharsis and emotional cleansing.* Strong emotions are discharged while the therapeutic alliance forms. People begin to understand their pasts but do not need to relive them; Jung saw the reliving of past traumas as undesirable. Rather, catharsis and an understanding of both past and present allow people to ameliorate their present difficulties without increasing their pain.

2. *Elucidation.* The meaning of symptoms, the anima and animus, the shadow, and the person's current life situation and difficulties are clarified. In addition, people work through the

childhood origins of their emotional difficulties, as well as their immature and unrealistic thoughts and fantasies. Transference and countertransference are explored and analyzed; Jung believed that both can inform and guide treatment.

3. *Education.* Education can help remedy any gaps in development or maturation that have resulted from maladjustment or imbalances. During this stage, the clinician is supportive and encouraging, helping people take risks to improve their lives. Many people stop treatment at this point, but some continue on to the fourth stage.

4. *Transformation.* This occurs when people have achieved an in-depth access to the collective unconscious and the archetypes. Transformation facilitates an ego-Self dialog, leading to further emergence of the Self and greater balance. This in turn promotes individuation and self-realization (Dehing, 1992).

Therapeutic Alliance

Jungian analysts take an active part in the treatment process. They are not only analysts but also educators and collaborators in the therapeutic endeavor. Through interventions (discussed in the next section), clinicians promote awareness and analysis of the unconscious, usually beginning with the recognition of the anima and the animus as well as the personal unconscious and the shadow. With awareness, these elements of the personality can become integrated and their impact on the person better understood and modified, leading to greater social awareness and personal transformation.

Jung saw transference as an inevitable and crucial experience in therapy, but conceptualized transference in his own way. Jungians speak of "working in the transference" rather than analyzing the transference (Proner, 2002). Jung viewed the client-clinician relationship as one of "extraordinary intimacy and meaning" (Proner, 2002, p. 384) and believed that new developments in the psyche would take place in the context of the relationship itself. Analysts, with their life-affirming qualities, could serve as models and agents of transformation for people. To facilitate that, Jung encouraged analysts to avoid disclosing information about themselves to their clients and minimize contact with clients outside of the sessions. Jung believed that, although transference could promote self-healing, it also could promote undue dependence on the clinician (Allan & Lawton-Speert, 1993). Thus, objectivity on the parts of both clinician and client are important.

Jung placed great emphasis on the person of the clinician, not only as a transference object but as an individual. He believed that both client and clinician have an unconscious influence on each other that can facilitate treatment. Therapy, for Jung, was a reciprocal process in which both client and therapist experienced healing and growth, with each participant benefiting from the positive changes in the other. So that the emotional growth of the clinician did not create a barrier to treatment, Jung insisted that every clinician following his treatment approach undergo personal analysis.

Jung also emphasized the special atmosphere of the psychotherapy process. Viewing it as a sort of sacred place, he thought of psychotherapy itself as archetypal, providing healing, comfort, and guidance (Sedgwick, 2001).

Interventions

Jungian psychotherapy begins by focusing on the conscious, building a therapeutic alliance, and laying the groundwork for safe and productive exploration of the unconscious. Once that groundwork is established, Jungian analysts use a range of techniques to provide access to the contents of the unconscious. Initially, the threshold of consciousness is lowered, permitting the unconscious to emerge through the client's material, including dreams, images, fantasies, and symbols. When contents of the unconscious are brought into consciousness, they are explored, clarified, interpreted, and ultimately understood. Then the material can be integrated into the overall psyche of the person and further meaning found until the integration feels complete and natural and the person can instinctively use the knowledge from the unconscious.

Other than the following interventions and an exploration of the person's personality in terms of the four functions and two attitudes, Jung's theory does not devote much attention to techniques. In this approach, the material for analysis (dreams, visions, fantasies, and perceptions) is broad rather than the tools used to explore the material.

Use of Symbols   Jung's model of the psyche rests on his concepts of the Self and the archetypes. Therefore, Jungian work stresses the capacity to think symbolically and see the underlying dynamics and patterns driving clients' thoughts, feelings, and actions. These patterns may appear in symbolic and indirect forms in people's dreams, symptoms, fantasies, and other material. Clinicians' ability to understand this psychological subtext can be enhanced by knowledge of the wide range of symbols found in myths, fairy tales, art, literature, and religions, which are our cultural storehouses.

Dream Interpretation   Jung (1964) saw dreams as providing easiest access to the unconscious and viewed them as reflecting people's inner lives as well as their unconscious responses. Jung took a broader view of dreams than did Freud; Jung believed they not only represented wishes and fears but also fantasies, memories, experiences, visions, truths, and more. Jungian dream interpretation involves retelling the recalled dream; describing its impact on consciousness; exploring events that may have triggered the dream; investigating the dream's objective and subjective content for archaic images and symbols of the unconscious; and assimilating the dream into consciousness, having made sense of it.

Amplification is a tool used to explore the meaning of dreams and includes both subjective and objective processes. With the help of the clinician, the dreamer first engages in subjective amplification, exploring the personal meaning of each element of the dream. Then objective amplification is used to elucidate the collective or universal meaning of the dream by connecting the elements of the dream to universal and symbolic images from such sources as fairy tales and myths (Jacobi, 1973).

For example, a client named Diana had a dream about Athena, the virgin goddess of wisdom, war and peace, and the arts, and acknowledged that she identified with Athena. According to Greek mythology, Athena came into the world by leaping from her father Zeus's head. Athena had the capacity to aim and concentrate and could be a torch bearer for those in the dark. Diana had little sense of her own feminine nature and overidentified with her father's thoughts and ideas. Like Athena, she had, in a way, emerged from the head of her father and was now caught in her own father complex. Awareness of this pattern allowed the analyst to identify the imbalance in Diana and determine a helpful way to focus treatment. By working on her shadow (the unexperienced aspects of herself), Diana was able to experience herself differently and to interact with the world in a more embodied, genuine, and feeling manner.

Word Association Tests   In word association tests, the clinician reads single words, one at a time, to the client, who replies with the first word that comes into mind. Unusual responses, repeated responses, hesitations, and physiological changes such as flushing and visible tension all provide clues to the presence of complexes and other unconscious material. Associations also are used to explore the meaning of dreams.

Rituals   Jung recognized the importance of religious and secular rituals such as confirmations, weddings, and retirement celebrations in facilitating people's growth and passage from one phase of life to another, although he was skeptical about the value of rigid and entrenched rituals (Al-Krenawi, 1999). Jung sometimes incorporated rites and rituals into therapy and some modern Jungian analysts have embraced this intervention. Incorporating rich and meaningful interventions into Jungian analysis can enhance that process and increase its individual and cultural relevance and impact.

APPLICATION OF JUNGIAN ANALYTICAL PSYCHOLOGY

Jung conceptualized his work as having broad application. However, in determining the application of Jungian analysis, we must consider several factors including typical people whom Jung treated, Jung's writings on the application of his theory, and how his approach is presently used.

Application to Clients and Diagnostic Groups

Jung's typical patients were sophisticated and relatively well-functioning people who sought greater self-awareness and self-realization. Most were in mid-life or older and craved a deeper meaning in their lives. Some had tried other treatment approaches without success and consulted Jung in the hope that his ideas and strategies would be more meaningful and effective. According to Sedgwick (2001, p. 23), "Jung's approaches were encouraging to those seeking and creating deeper, sometimes uniquely spiritual meaning in their lives, and their Jungian paths sometimes involved direct transpersonal experience through introspection and imagination."

Although many of Jung's patients were not experiencing severe pathology, Jung believed that his concepts could apply equally well to other client groups. Because he viewed hallucinations as linked to the collective unconscious, he saw his approach as appropriate for people diagnosed with psychoses, as well as those with milder disorders characterized by depression and anxiety. In addition, modern Jungian analysts perceive their approach as helpful to people dealing with day-to-day problems (R. Shepler, personal communication, November 15, 1999), although its long-term, esoteric, and in-depth nature makes it generally unsuitable for treatment of urgent problems.

It is the growth-promoting aspects of this approach that are particularly compelling. Jungian analytical psychology is most appropriately thought of as a method for achieving personal growth and self-awareness for people who feel unfulfilled. This approach, then, seems best suited for people who already are fairly healthy but who believe that greater access to their spiritual dimension as well as greater understanding of their unconscious can bring them more integrated, balanced, and fulfilling lives.

Application to Multicultural Groups

Jung's concepts offer an alternative to conventional therapy that may be more compatible with the spiritual and cultural beliefs and behaviors of many multicultural clients. Jung's attention to spirituality and universal symbols is likely to have relevance to people from a broad range of cultures. Al-Krenawi (1999) views the flexible use of rituals as another element of Jungian analysis that gives this approach multicultural relevance. According to Al-Krenawi (1999, p. 11), "The accepted therapeutic use of ritual, its freedom from stigma and its legitimacy as a healing device in traditional cultures can help circumvent their members' suspicion of insight-oriented 'talking therapy.' . . . The use of rituals may reduce the novelty of Western therapy by connecting it to the clients' values and beliefs." The use of rituals also casts the therapist in a role resembling that of the traditional healer and this, too, may promote acceptance of this approach. Its emphasis on social context, as well as its view of dreams and archetypes from cultural perspectives, are other ingredients that enhance the multicultural relevance of Jungian analysis.

CURRENT USE

Since Jung's death, the number of Jungian analysts has increased considerably. These practitioners can be categorized into four groups, based on the emphasis of their work: classical, developmental, archetypal, and relational (influenced by self psychology discussed in the next chapter) (Sedgwick, 2001). The developmental and relational orientations are the newest, although the four overlap.

During most of his career, Jung focused on individual analysis. However, in his later years, he also acknowledged the benefits of both play therapy (focused on children's acting out) and group therapy. Modern Jungian analysts have applied Jung's work to group therapy, viewing it as an adjunct to individual treatment that can teach people to operate more successfully as social beings (Allan & Lawton-Speert, 1993; Day & Mathes, 1992). In addition, Jung's ideas are evident in many recent writings, discussed in the next section.

Despite its long-term in-depth orientation, Jungian analysis continues to have a small but loyal following among clinicians, as well as clients who seek Jungian analysis. It has never achieved the wide-spread use of Freudian psychoanalysis or the growing popularity of Adler's Individual Psychology, but Jungian analysis maintains its place among theories of psychotherapy.

EVALUATION OF JUNGIAN ANALYTICAL PSYCHOLOGY

Perceptions of Jung's work vary widely. According to Ewen (1993),

> Jung's emphasis on our spiritual and religious longings has provoked considerable controversy. Proponents claim that Jung has justifiably extended the scope of psychology by calling attention to a vital area of human functioning. Critics argue that a scientific psychology cannot deal with such arcane issues as the nature of God and the existence of the supernatural, or that Jung's synthesis is shallow and unsuccessful (p. 14).

Evaluating Jungian analytical psychology is difficult for several reasons. Jung's concepts are complex, ill-defined, and sometimes seem contradictory. His treatment approach entails few specific interventions and is presented in broad and global terms. Similarly, the outcomes that Jung views as desirable involve such elusive constructs as self-realization and balance and rarely address amelioration of specific symptoms. Jung's ideas fail to meet the criteria for a useful, sound, and testable theory. Consequently, any discussion of limitations, strengths, and contributions must have as a backdrop the serious shortcomings of Jung's theory.

Limitations

Despite growing attention to his ideas, Jung's work has not been well researched. His writing is dense and challenging, complicated by specialized terminology. His treatment approach is a lengthy one that pays little attention to immediate crises. Jung does not offer much in the way of readily accessible tools and techniques, and the practice of Jungian analysis requires extensive training and supervision.

Many clinicians have difficulty understanding Jung's work as well as appreciating its value to their clients. As Sedgwick (2001, p. 8) stated, ". . . the Jungian student faces the puzzle of how to create a Jungian psychotherapeutic theory out of Jung's basically atheoretical position." Although proponents of this approach attest to its positive impact, the literature provides little in the way of either empirical research or case studies that offer clear and replicable treatment steps and procedures. These shortcomings suggest that clinicians drawn to Jungian analysis should give careful thought to their decision.

Strengths and Contributions

Despite the esoteric nature of his theory, Jung's approach has left its mark. His work has contributed to the thinking of the existentialists, the humanists, the Gestalt therapists, and others and can be integrated with these and many other approaches. His belief in synchronicity, the idea that nothing happens without having meaning and purpose, is reflected in the thinking of many transpersonal clinicians (see chapter 13). Jung's awareness that people have a strong need for meaning in their lives and his belief that people have an inherent teleological (purposive) tendency toward individuation and self-realization (Ewen, 1993) are reflected in existential thought. Jung's emphasis on spirituality and the universality of people's images and experiences are very much in keeping with modern psychological thought.

Current practice reflects several applications of Jung's work. The Myers-Briggs Type Indicator, a widely used personality inventory, is based on Jung's work. His concept of the collective unconscious places our lives in a broad context and further contributes to the meaning and historical continuity of our lives. Jung was the first to use the term "individuation," referring to the process of becoming one's unique self. This concept has become integrated into psychotherapy and provides a positive and empowering view of people as has Jung's view of pathology as an unsuccessful attempt at growth. Some see his view of symptoms as messages from the unconscious about emotional needs or difficulties as useful in counteracting an overemphasis on pathology. His emphasis on the therapeutic alliance was ahead of its time and is increasingly supported by current research. Similarly, Jung's attention to countertransference and the positive impact of therapy on the clinician are widely accepted. Jung was among the first to recognize the importance of play therapy and group therapy, both important treatment modalities (Allan & Lawton-Speert, 1993; Day & Mathes, 1992).

Several recent writers and theorists have drawn on Jung's ideas in their work. Their popularity attests to the continuing influence and importance of Jung's work. Marion Woodman, a controversial psychologist, has taken Jung's concept of symbols further and suggests that the body also carries the messages of the psyche. Without proper attention and release of bodily energies, the psychic promptings can manifest themselves as illnesses and addictions (McDonald, 1996). Woodman's (1982) writings focus particularly on women's issues. She applies Jungian thought to topics such as perfectionism, eating disorders, and creativity in women and has collaborated with Robert Bly, poet and leader of the men's movement.

Joseph Campbell's works also derive from Jungian thought. Campbell focused his attention on myths, stating that myths embody the eternal essence of life and are about identity and the unrealized parts of the self (Ellwood, 1999). The influence of Campbell's writings about the mythological hero are reportedly evident in the Star Wars films. Another important and timely concept advanced by Campbell is the spiritual unity of culture and myths. Although Campbell's work, like Woodman's, is controversial, his writings have received considerable attention.

As further evidence of the relevance of Jung's work, consider the bestseller *Women Who Run with the Wolves: Myths and Stories of the Wild Woman Archetype* by Clarissa Pinkola Estes (1992), a Jungian analyst. Like Woodman, Estes used Jungian concepts to promote empowerment of women.

Although Jung has a relatively small group of devoted followers, his work has not been embraced by most clinicians except in their use of the Myers-Briggs Type Indicator (MBTI). However, many people have manifested interest in his concepts of symbols and archetypes, as people increasingly recognize the importance of spirituality in their lives. The thought-provoking nature of his work and the originality and depth of his concepts continue to lead people to become Jungian analysts and to read Jung's works.

SKILL DEVELOPMENT: JUNGIAN DREAMWORK AND THE MBTI

Jung thought of dreams as a way to view current situations from new perspectives. He believed that in this way dreams could compensate for the blind spots of consciousness. Through analyzing dreams, clinicians can link symbolic images and patterns to the dreamer's personal experiences and situations.

Whitmont and Perera (1989), Jungian analysts, presented a four-step approach to dream analysis using the Jungian model:

1. *Obtain an overview* of the dream, clarifying the action in the dream ego (central character), as well as that of the other characters. Look for any polarizations, dissonances, or repetitions.

2. *Examine the dramatic structure.* Dreams, like ancient Greek plays, have a sequence of unfolding elements, including the *exposition* (setting), the *development of the action,* the *crisis,* and the *lysis* (resolution).

The exposition (setting). Every dream is set in a particular time and place with particular people. The setting is key to understanding the motif of the dream. Does it take place in the client's childhood home because a past dynamic is occurring in the present? Who are the people in the dream? Unknown people in the dream who are the same gender as the dreamer are usually shadow figures (representing unacceptable and unexpressed aspects of the Self). Opposite gender figures can be representations of the anima or animus or can be related to parental complexes as well as images of the Self. Through associations, clinicians can explore the meaning of these figures with the dreamer.

Development of the action. The plot begins to thicken, and the story unfolds. Look at any discrepancies. For example, if the dream ego is not afraid in a terrifying situation, ask the dreamer how he or she would react if this event really occurred. Clinicians may want to look for situations in the dreamer's waking life that reflect a similar dynamic—for example, in which the client is not in touch with fear when he or she should be.

While a dream may be related to an external situation involving other people, it is also an image of what is going on in the inner landscape of the dreamer. For example, a woman dreams that her male supervisor is being harsh and demanding. That may well be an accurate reflection of her work environment; but more important, it reflects an inner dynamic as well—the woman's tendency to be harsh and demanding of herself. Considering the dream's connection to both inner and outer experience allows clients to explore hidden aspects of the psyche.

Crisis and lysis (resolution). The crisis of the dream occurs when the conflict comes to a head and something good or ill happens to resolve the deadlock (lysis). Often, a dream will end with no resolution, which means that the issue is still unfinished. Jung used the technique of active imagination with his clients in which they imagined themselves going back into the dream and allowing the action to develop to see how the situation might resolve itself. Jung also might suggest that the client have a dialog with a character in the dream to obtain more information. Such approaches usually bring up unconscious material and offer other avenues to exploring dreams.

3. *Identify the images that need elucidation.* Eliciting the dreamer's emotionally charged associations, explanations, and amplifications of aspects of the dream are the key to linking the conscious and unconscious and provide meaning and understanding. The significance of dream motifs is never fixed. Therefore, the only reliable criterion is clients' own recognition of what aspects of the dream mean to them. Analysts are careful not to impose their own interpretations on the client or the dream material. Jung once stated that clinicians should discard book learning and assume a stance of curiosity and ignorance when working with dreams.

Associations. Examine any ideas, feelings, reactions, or memories that come into the dreamer's mind when exploring dream images. By finding the emotional core of the associations, clinician and dreamer can ground the dream in the dreamer's current reality.

Explanations. Explanations provide a rational meaning for the images in the dream and also indicate what they represent in terms of their function or significance. Explanations can be objective as well as subjective. The image of a desk in a dream, for example, might have the objective explanation of a place to study and work. The desk might also have a subjective explanation, if it were the desk given to the dreamer by a loving and caring grandparent. Associations to that person would be pertinent as well.

Amplifications. The personal content of a dream often has a corresponding motif in fairy tales, myths, or other sources (e.g., the dream about Athena described previously). The analyst may recognize these motifs. However, unless the dreamer links a myth or fairy tale to the dream, the analyst should not rush the client toward discovery of the connection. That may interfere with the client's own process of discovery and lead to intellectualizing and avoidance of the emotional core. On the other hand, if the client spontaneously connects the motifs in the dream with stories or images, exploration of that connection can be a fruitful source of information for the client.

4. *Formulate a psychological understanding* of the dream, knowing that it will be tentative until the dreamer identifies and accepts the meaning of the dream.

Illustration of a Jungian Dream Analysis

The following example provides a brief illustration of a Jungian dream analysis. A 35-year-old man presented a dream: "The dream starts with my sports car beginning to go down a steep embankment, and it rolls over and over and over. I am terrified. Then I am outside and above the car looking down at my dead body."

In his associations to the dream images, the client connected his sports car to aspects of his personality. He liked the sense of power the car gave him and stated that it enhanced his feelings of importance at work. In looking at the car rolling, the client said that he felt like his life was going around and around. He felt out of control and confused about his relationship to his wife. He didn't know why he felt so distant from her. (Note the absence of females in the dream.) To his dead body, the client associated the feelings "eerie and upsetting." In the dream, he didn't know what to do and felt helpless and scared.

The client had separated from his wife and had invested his energy in his work. However, the dream suggested that he was not in control and that some aspect of himself that had been in power too long had to "die." This led to many sessions spent in discussing his confusion, fear, and lack of relatedness in his life until he was able to understand his situation more clearly and identify steps he could take to regain a sense of control.

Readers should be aware that, although Jungian dream analysis may seem to be an intriguing and relatively straightforward intervention, in reality it requires considerable training and expertise. Keep the strategies discussed here in mind but use them with great caution. A related and somewhat less complex strategy for dream analysis, reflecting Gestalt approaches to using dreams in treatment, will be presented in chapter 12. Dreams are a powerful source of information and insight and are frequently presented by people in counseling and psychotherapy. Both of these approaches should provide some avenues for productive exploration of dreams.

CASE ILLUSTRATION

Because of the extensive training required to successfully understand and practice Jung's approach, and because it does not offer many tools to the typical clinician, I have chosen to illustrate what is probably the best known contribution of Jung's work to modern therapy: the Myers-Briggs Type Indicator (MBTI) (Myers, McCaulley, Quenk, & Hammer, 1994). Based on Jung's concept of psychological functions and attitudes, the MBTI was initially developed by Katharine Briggs and her daughter Isabel Briggs Myers. One of the most widely used personality inventories, it has an extensive range of uses and is especially appropriate for people who are emotionally healthy or have only mild difficulties. The MBTI is helpful in promoting personal growth, self-awareness, leadership skills, team building, and career development, and in enhancing interpersonal skills (Seligman, 1994). It is used with individuals, in couples counseling, and in work settings.

This inventory yields scores on four bipolar dimensions: introversion-extraversion, sensing-intuition, thinking-feeling, and judging-perceiving. Combinations of these scores yield 16 personality types. A children's version of the MBTI, the Murphy-Meisgeier Type Indicator for Children, is available for those in grades 2–8. All preferences on these inventories are considered equally desirable; the inventory is not designed to diagnose pathology but rather to promote self-awareness. The definitions of the first six dimensions have been discussed on pages 101–102 in this chapter. The remaining two, judging and perceiving, can be defined as follows:

- *Judging.* People whose personality profile reflects a strong judging component value planning, organization, order, and security. They may have a high need for

achievement and generally are viewed as responsible and hard-working.
- *Perceiving.* People with high perceiving scores prefer to be spontaneous and flexible so that they can take advantage of opportunities. They tend to be casual and resourceful and typically make last-minute decisions rather than long-range plans.

Roberto and Edie both completed the MBTI as a way of increasing their self-awareness as well as their understanding of their interactions and the strengths and weaknesses in their marriage. Edie's MBTI type was ISFJ (introversion, sensing, feeling, judging), while Roberto's was ESTJ (extraversion, sensing, thinking, judging). His thinking score was especially strong, while Edie's feeling score was her highest. A large gap was evident between Edie's introversion score and Roberto's extraversion score as well as between her feeling score and his thinking score.

Each of the MBTI types reflects potential strengths as well as potential weaknesses. People with an MBTI type of ISFJ (like Edie) tend to be caring, sensitive, quiet, practical, and conscientious (Myers, 1998). If they feel unappreciated, they can become resentful and complaining. They may have difficulty asserting themselves and maintaining objectivity.

On the other hand, people with an MBTI type of ESTJ (like Roberto) tend to be decisive and self-confident, outgoing, and concerned with outcome rather than process. They can be impatient, overbearing, and insensitive to the feelings of others.

An examination of Edie's and Roberto's MBTI types sheds light on their difficulties. Roberto tends to devalue Edie's feelings, particularly because, with her strong introversion, she has difficulty articulating her feelings directly.

On the other hand, Edie tends to devalue Roberto's need for socialization and results, and accuses him of being shallow and uncaring. Because both share sensing and judging preferences, they tend to have difficulty with spontaneity, flexibility, and change, and are likely to spend too much time on work and chores, neglecting the pleasurable side of their lives. At the same time, they both value organization and planning as well as concrete information.

Exploration of some of their similarities and differences helped the couple identify ways to make positive changes. For example, Roberto agreed to work on his tendency to be critical of Edie and Ava, while Edie agreed to work on articulating her feelings and needs more clearly. Both recognized the importance of having more fun as a couple and as a family.

EXERCISES

Large-Group Exercises

Understanding Jungian concepts such as the following can be challenging:

- Animus/anima
- Shadow
- Collective unconscious/personal unconscious
- Self
- Persona
- Archetype

Discuss these concepts in class, exploring the meaning of each, how the concepts can be used in counseling and psychotherapy, and whether you believe they have validity.

Small-Group Exercises

1. Complete the Myers-Briggs Type Indicator. One member of your small group should score your inventory and explain your results to you, while the other group members observe this process. Discuss with your group partner your understanding of your inventoried MBTI type and how it reflects or is inconsistent with what you already know about yourself. After each interpretation, both participants and observers should provide feedback to the interviewer and the interviewee. Feedback should focus on but not be limited to the following areas:
   - Use of open questions
   - Clarity of information presented
   - Adequacy of opportunity for the interviewee to react to the information
2. In your small group, take turns sharing a recent dream. Be sure to select a dream that you are comfortable presenting to your group and keep in mind that you can redirect or stop discussion of the dream at any time. After each dream is described, the group as a whole should analyze the dream according to Whitman and Perera's four-step approach to dream analysis previously presented:
   - Obtain an overview of the dream
   - Examine the dramatic structure (exposition or setting, development of the action, crisis, and lysis or resolution)
   - Identify the key images in the dream and explore their associations, explanations, and amplifications
   - Formulate a psychological understanding of the dream

Individual Exercises

1. Write in your journal about the expression of the six Jungian concepts (listed in the large-group exercise) in your own life. Consider how each concept has manifested itself. For example, think about how your persona affects your social behavior and how your anima or animus has affected your relationships with the other gender.
2. Identify a fairy tale or a myth that seems meaningful to you. Do you relate to Beauty and the Beast, the Ugly Duckling, Bacchus, Demeter, Robin Hood, or another well-known story or legendary figure? Write about how this reflects your own psyche and your view of yourself.
3. Analyze one of your own dreams, following the four-step process previously described. Write down your analysis in your journal.

SUMMARY

Jung's analytical psychotherapy is grounded in Freudian psychoanalytic thinking. However, Jung's innovative ideas have called attention to the innate patterns and images that influence psychological development, the importance of spirituality in our lives, our need for wholeness and balance, and the levels of the unconscious. As a clinician and educator, Jung sought to help people find knowledge, meaning, and fulfillment, as well as individuation and self-realization by developing and accessing awareness of their psyches.

RECOMMENDED READINGS

The Journal of Analytical Psychology

Christopher, E., & Solomon, H. M. (Eds.) (2003). *Contemporary Jungian clinical practice.* London: Karnac Books.

Jung, C. G. (1961). *Memories, dreams, reflections.* New York: Pantheon.

Jung, C. G. (1964). *Man and his symbols.* Garden City, NY: Doubleday.

Kelly, W. L. (1990). *Psychology of the unconscious: Mesmer, Janet, Freud, Jung, and current issues.* New York: Prometheus.

Sedgwick, D. (2001). *Introduction to Jungian psychotherapy: The therapeutic relationship.* New York: Brunner-Routledge.

ADDITIONAL SOURCES OF INFORMATION

Specialized training in Jung's analytical psychology can be obtained from institutes and societies throughout the world. Jungian training facilities in the United States include the C. G. Jung Institutes in New York City, Los Angeles, and Chicago. Jungian seminars are conducted by the CGJ Foundation, which can be reached at (800) 258-3533 or http://www.jungianseminars.org. Additional relevant websites include:

http://www.cgjungpage.org/—This website includes information on Jung and his theories, resources, and articles.

http://www.ship.edu/~cgboeree/jung.html—This is another website with information on Jung and his theories.

http://www.jungchicago/org/—This website for the C. G. Jung Institute of Chicago includes information about relevant publications as well as services and training opportunities provided by the Institute.

CHAPTER 7

Freudian Revisionists: Ego Psychologists, Object Relations Theorists, Self Psychologists, and Others

One of Freud's greatest contributions was his ability to attract to his ideas people who were, themselves, brilliant and innovative thinkers with a deep interest in human development and psychology. Adler and Jung, discussed in chapters 5 and 6, are probably the two who had the greatest impact. However, many others played significant roles in the evolution of counseling and psychotherapy. These might be called the Freudian revisionists, men and women who initially accepted the tenets of Freudian psychoanalysis but then moved forward to develop their own innovative and influential ideas. They can be loosely categorized into the following three groups:

- *Ego Psychologists*—Helene Deutsch, Karen Horney, Harry Stack Sullivan, and Anna Freud
- *Object Relations Theorists*—Melanie Klein, W. R. D. Fairbairn, D. W. Winnicott, Otto Kernberg, John Bowlby, and others
- *Self Psychologists*—Heinz Kohut and others

The skill development section later in the chapter introduces interpretation, a technique associated with these theorists.

THE EGO PSYCHOLOGISTS

Linking the ego psychologists is a shift away from Freud's emphasis on the drives and the id to a focus on the development of the ego. Most of these theorists took a broader perspective than did Freud, focusing on development over the lifespan, and emphasizing the importance of both the self-image and relationships. Beyond that, these theorists differ considerably and those differences sometimes led to rifts in the profession.

Helene Deutsch

Helene Deutsch contributed important ideas about the psychological development of women. Over her lengthy career, she shaped and modified many of Freud's ideas so that they reflected the special characteristics of women's development and took account of the importance of both the mother-daughter bond and women's maternal role. Although Deutsch's ideas may seem dated today, readers should view her in the context of her time; she served as a bridge between Freud's limited understanding of female development and our present understanding of women.

Biography of Helene Deutsch   Born Helene Rosenbach on October 9, 1884, in Przemysl, Poland, Deutsch was the youngest of four children. Reportedly, she adored her father but had a negative relationship with her mother (Sayers, 1991; Thompson, 1987). This early closeness with her father was later reflected in her relationship with Freud, who became an admired father figure (Webster, 1985).

Deutsch was a pioneer. She was one of the first female medical students at the University of Vienna, where she pursued her interests in pediatric medicine and children with intellectual and emotional disabilities. But by the time of her marriage to Felix Deutsch and her graduation from medical school, her interests had shifted, and she joined the staff of the University of Vienna's psychiatric clinic.

Deutsch was frustrated here by both the low standing of psychiatry in Vienna and the many limitations on the roles of women physicians. Consequently, in 1918, she became one of the first women to join the Vienna Psycho-Analytical Society and began a year of psychoanalysis with Freud. The two worked closely until 1933 (Williams, 1987).

In 1935, Deutsch, her husband, and their child emigrated to the United States where she taught at Boston University, practiced at Massachusetts General Hospital, and was active in the Boston Psychoanalytic Institute. She wrote, taught, and practiced until her death in 1982. At the age of 89, she published her memoirs, *Confrontations With Myself: An Epilogue* (1973), a cap to her productive life.

Helene Deutsch's Theories   Deutsch's contributions are primarily theoretical. As a practicing analyst, she adopted most of Freud's strategies. However, she understood her clients differently, and therein lies her important contribution.

Deutsch's revisions of Freudian Psychoanalysis. Deutsch was uncomfortable with Freud's patriarchal emphasis, particularly his concepts of penis envy and the Oedipal conflict. Her work revised both of these key concepts.

According to Deutsch, Freud's belief that girls suffer from a castration complex was too narrow. Although she believed in the existence of what she called the genital trauma, she did not think that it always played a fundamental part in girls' development and their adult conflicts. She broadened Freud's concept of penis envy to refer to a general tendency toward envy, which she believed was experienced by all children when they think others receive love, attention, or other qualities they desire.

Deutsch also suggested that the genital trauma (girl's discovery that she does not have a penis) could be a positive force, contributing to the development of women's sexual and maternal drives (Roazen, 1985). She believed that intercourse, pregnancy, motherhood, and breast feeding all enabled women to resolve the genital trauma and achieve emotional health and fulfillment. Identification with children also helped them overcome the trauma of their own birth (Thompson, 1987).

In addition, while Freud emphasized the Oedipus complex and the impact on development of the son's fear and envy of the father, Deutsch focused on children's connections with the mother. She believed that girls needed to establish a bond with the mother that was close and that served as a basis for the girls' own development, but that was not overly restrictive. According to Deutsch, emotional disorders often resulted when a girl's tie to the mother restricted her freedom to develop and failed to offer her a role model and guide for positive development.

The Feminine Core. Deutsch emphasized biology and constitutional predispositions. She suggested that women inherently have a feminine core composed of three traits: narcissism, passivity, and masochism (Wimpfheimer & Schafer, 1977).

Today *narcissism* has negative connotations. However, as Deutsch used the term, it could be either positive or negative. Healthy narcissism involved loving and valuing the self, having self-esteem and self-respect, and being inner-directed rather than allowing others to control one's life. Unhealthy narcissism, on the other hand, was characterized by self-centeredness, insecurity, feelings of inferiority, intolerance of criticism, and a constant need for approval and affirmation. Deutsch believed that people with unhealthy narcissism have particular difficulty handling rejection or disappointments in intimate relationships (Wisdom, 1990).

Healthy narcissism is especially important during adolescence; it facilitates development of a strong ego as well as the individuation and integration of the personality. Healthy narcissism serves an important protective function: It promotes the instincts for self-preservation, contributes to women's strong intuitive powers, and guards women against the dangers of excessive masochism.

For Deutsch, *passivity* was a central attribute of femininity—an attitude of receptive waiting and expectancy (Williams, 1987). Her emphasis on this characteristic stemmed both from the biological (the man entering the woman during sexual intercourse) and the social (the man being the initiator and pursuer who provided the woman with financial and social status, typical in Deutsch's era). Deutsch credited women's passivity with the development of their concern with relationships, their ability to make judgments based on emotions, their sensitivity, their capacity for love and tenderness, their insight and intuition, their emphasis on harmony rather than conflict, and their propensity for fantasy. Today, important thinkers such as Carol Gilligan (1993) and Mary Phipher have affirmed these positive traits in girls and women as well as Deutsch's belief that females and males have fundamental differences in personality that must be kept in mind and understood by clinicians, teachers, and others.

Feminine *masochism,* according to Deutsch, allows women to accept more suffering than men can, enabling women to endure childbirth, menstruation, and other uncomfortable experiences. According to Deutsch, masochism is linked to an inhibition of aggression but does *not* encompass a wish to experience punishment, suffering, guilt, or humiliation. Healthy narcissism serves the function of guarding women against excessive masochism and preventing unnecessary suffering.

Clinicians today might dislike and question Deutsch's terminology. However, her concepts have validity and are compatible with current research on female development.

Female development. Deutsch believed that the primary goal of women's development was to become a mother and that women had maternal instincts and love that enabled them to be successful and happy in that role (Sayers, 1991). Healthy development throughout the life span enabled women not only to become mothers but to preserve their self-esteem and individuality and to establish full and rewarding lives.

As young children, important developmental tasks for girls include individuating from the mother while still retaining a positive and loving connection to her, establishing a positive relationship with the father, and channeling the active-aggressive components of their personalities into directions that enhance their adult development (Deutsch, 1944). Girls who identify with an active and empowered image of their mothers seem particularly likely to develop self-esteem (Sayers, 1991). Some identification with males also is desirable, especially in helping girls develop their rational capacities and balance the feminine core. According to Deutsch, people who failed to establish close attachments to parental figures tend not to develop adequate superegos and instead form what Deutsch called "as if" personalities that are unstable, other-directed, and lacking in a solid sense of self (Sayers, 1991).

Puberty revives girls' early sexual and bisexual feelings toward both parents, feelings that need further resolution in adolescence. Forming rewarding friendships with other girls during childhood and adolescence is important in resolving these feelings.

Deutsch paid considerable attention to women's biological milestones and responses, including menstruation, intercourse, orgasm, pregnancy, childbirth, breast feeding, and menopause, which she believed was a difficult transition. She wanted women to participate actively in the birth process and disapproved of medication which dulled women's awareness during delivery. Despite the great value Deutsch placed on motherhood, she acknowledged that many women had achievement-oriented goals and addressed the importance of integrating these with their maternal goals. In her forthright discussion of such topics, she was ahead of her time and paved the way for our current understanding of women's development and conflicts.

Current Status   Best known for her two-volume *The Psychology of Women* (1944), Deutsch has made an impact not only on psychoanalysis but on our understanding of women's development. Clinicians, as well as scholars, continue to study and research Deutsch's work. Her concepts are compatible with feminist therapy and so are of particular interest to those who practice either feminist therapy or psychodynamic treatment. Consistent with her view of healthy female development, Helene Deutsch made an important contribution to her field while being a wife and mother.

Karen Horney

Like Helene Deutsch, Karen Horney initially believed in the ideas of Freud. However, as her clinical experience grew, she developed her own ideas that laid the groundwork for important concepts of human development and psychotherapy.

Biography of Karen Horney   Karen Horney was born in Hamburg, Germany, on September 16, 1885. She received her medical degree from the University of Berlin, trained as a psychoanalyst, and began a practice in 1919. Her own analysis was with Karl Abraham and Hans Sachs, leaders in their field. In 1909, Horney married and subsequently had three daughters.

Like Deutsch, Horney broke ground for women in psychoanalysis. She was the first woman teacher at the Berlin Psychoanalytic Institute (Sayers, 1991). Between 1923 and 1935, she wrote a series of papers that critically examined the relevance of Freud's theories to women's psychosocial development. During the 1960s, these papers were embraced by proponents of the feminist movement because of their enlightened view of women (Eckardt, 1991).

In 1932, Horney moved to the United States to become the assistant director of the newly established Psychoanalytic Institute of Chicago and subsequently became involved with the New York Psychoanalytic Institute. A complicated person who elicited strong and often conflicting reactions from others, Horney directly challenged Freud's work in her book *New Ways in Psychoanalysis* (1939), which apparently led to her disqualification as instructor and analyst at the New York Psychoanalytic Institute (Eckardt, 1984; Ewen, 1993). In response, she resigned from the institute and formed the American Institute of Psychoanalysis. Horney served as dean of this organization, which is still in existence.

Horney died of cancer on December 4, 1952. She left a substantial body of work reflecting her broad and timely interests in topics such as women's development and social and cultural influences.

Karen Horney's Theories   Horney's early works presented an analysis of Freud's theories with her own revisions. This ultimately evolved into her mature work, which explored human nature and development in both men and women and paid particular attention to culture.

Human nature and self-realization. Horney's view of human nature is positive and optimistic, more consistent with humanistic theorists than with Freud's ideas. She suggested that the purpose of life was actualization of the real self, the repository of the healthy conscience and values that promoted the best interests of all humanity (Paris, 1994). Self-realization involved developing one's innate capacities, emotions, and interests. Horney believed that people who achieve self-realization are self-aware, responsible, and able to make sound judgments. They seek healthy relationships and care about the welfare of others while maintaining their own integrity.

According to Horney, our potential for growth and self-actualization is present at birth. Children whose environments are nurturing and harmonious, promoting their healthy development, move toward self-realization (Williams, 1987). However, children raised in aversive environments, especially those that do not provide security, are likely to develop in unhealthy directions. They may develop unrealistic and idealized self-images rather than fulfilling their inherent potential.

Neurosis and basic anxiety. The drive for security, according to Horney, is a more powerful force than either the sexual or the aggressive drive. She believed that hostile, threatening, and unfriendly environments compound children's natural insecurity and lead them to develop a basic anxiety, including feelings of helplessness, isolation, and anger. This, in turn, leads to neurotic conflicts involving a repressed and apparently insoluble dilemma (Horney, 1945). For example, a person might want close relationships yet believe that people are untrustworthy. Neurotic conflicts are expressed indirectly through characteristics such as inconsistency, indecisiveness, fear of change, shyness, sadistic and vindictive behavior, and unexplained fatigue.

Horney (1945) believed that, in an effort to cope with their conflicts, people gravitate toward one of three styles of relating to others:

1. *Moving toward people* involves seeking safety through the protection of others, becoming compliant and self-effacing to please others, blaming ourselves for our interpersonal difficulties, and suppressing our own needs.

2. *Moving against people* is characterized by seeking mastery and domination over others, externalizing blame, being arrogant and vindictive, caring only about ourselves, exploiting and manipulating others, and feeling superior.
3. *Moving away from people* is reflected by avoidance of interpersonal contact, withdrawal and detachment, feelings of differentness, pursuit of self-sufficiency, numbing of emotions, and disregard of rules and restrictions.

Extreme versions of these styles are unsatisfying because they restrict growth and lead to impoverished relationships and self-hatred (Williams, 1987). Emotionally healthy people do not need to use exaggerated and inflexible styles of relating to others but deal with the world in balanced and integrated ways that promote positive self-esteem, rewarding relationships, and personal development.

Selves and self-image. Horney believed that people have four competing selves (Paris, 1994):

1. The real or potential self
2. The idealized or impossible self
3. The despised self, which results from recognizing that we fall short of the idealized self
4. The actual self, all we are at a given time

The more self-actualizing we are, the more congruent are the real self, the idealized self, and the actual self.

For people without good self-esteem and a sense of wholeness, the idealized image typically dominates. Designed to enhance feelings of worth and provide a sense of identity, the idealized self-image actually leads people to feelings of self-contempt because of their failure to live up to this image.

Although efforts to achieve the idealized self-image inevitably fail, people develop strong guidelines about what they must do in their efforts to reach this goal. Horney spoke of the "tyranny of the should" (Horney, 1950; Paris, 1994, 1996), designed to make us over into our idealized selves. (This concept surfaces again in Albert Ellis's work, discussed in chapter 16.) Horney described four patterns of shoulds (1950):

• Self-effacing people believe they should be grateful, humble, trusting, and giving.
• Arrogant-vindictive people believe they should be in charge and independent, attack before being attacked, and distrust others.
• Narcissistic people think they should be supremely competent, admired by all, and accept no limitations.
• Detached people believe they should not need or expect anything out of life.

Female development. Horney, like Deutsch, paid considerable attention to the development of girls and women. However, Horney's work emphasized women's current personality structures and their social context rather than their early childhood experiences. She believed that change could be effected by empowering women and modifying their social roles (Symonds, 1991). Horney focused more on the female's desire for love, sex, and motherhood than on envy of the male anatomy (Horney, 1967).

In addition, Horney (1935) believed that masochism arose from conflicts related to the subordinate role of women in society and was culturally rather than biologically determined. Unlike Deutsch, she believed that healthy development in women was not characterized by masochism.

Impact of culture and society. Horney emphasized the role of culture and environment in shaping personality, as well as the importance of understanding people in context. She believed that people's innate characteristics were not fixed but were possibilities shaped through reciprocal interaction with their environments (Williams, 1987). Conflicts could arise because of inconsistencies in a culture, transmitted from parent to child (Strean, 1994). For example, conflicts in American society include competition versus love of humankind and autonomy versus rules and laws.

Horney's psychotherapy. Horney's system of psychotherapy is an optimistic one. She believed that through treatment people can resolve deeply repressed inner conflicts and free their innate constructive forces to grow and develop. She suggested that, with help, people could give up their idealized images and find satisfaction in seeking actualization of their real selves (Ewen, 1993).

Horney viewed the the clinician's role as helping people become aware of their conflicts without being overwhelmed by them (Rossano, 1996), facilitating both emotional and intellectual insight, and reawakening a person's capacity for self-realization and joy. To accomplish this, the clinician works collaboratively with the client (Strean, 1994). Techniques of free association, analysis of dreams, countertransference and transference, empathy, and education are important in both recovering the past and unraveling the personality structure. Horney's approach also pays considerable attention to exploring the social and family context and life situation of the client.

Current Status   Horney's theories are probably more studied than practiced. However, she broke ground in many important ways, and the Association for Advancement of Psychoanalysis (AAP), which she founded, still promotes her ideas. Horney's definition of emotional health, "a state of inner freedom in which the full capacities are available for use," is compatible with our views today (Paris, 1994, p. 115). Her analysis of women's development as separate and distinctive from men's is similarly up-to-date (Miccolis, 1996; Rubin, 1991). So are her emphases on cultural and interpersonal factors and her focus on development throughout life. In addition, many of her concepts, such as the tyranny of the shoulds, self-actualization, the idealized self-image, basic anxiety, and neurotic styles of relating to the world, influenced the development of humanistic psychology and continue to facilitate our understanding of people. As Rubin (1991) said,

> Perhaps Horney's greatest contribution was and remains her wonderful optimism as regards the human condition. Horney believed that people are basically "good." She believed that sickness made them "bad" to themselves and others. She believed that people could get better, that is, healthier. She believed that people have the capacity to change and to grow in a healthy direction all of their lives. (p. 316)

Harry Stack Sullivan

Harry Stack Sullivan is the first American-born clinician discussed in this book. Although his ideas, like those of the others in this chapter, draw heavily on Freud's (Grey, 1988), his emphasis on relationships and concern with the relevance of psychoanalysis led him to develop concepts and approaches that reflect fast-paced, interactive American society more than European culture (Mitchell, 1986).

Biography of Harry Stack Sullivan   Harry Stack Sullivan was born on February 21, 1892, in Norwich, New York, the only child of a Catholic family living in a Protestant community. He experienced many personal difficulties, culminating in what he viewed as a schizophrenic episode during his freshman year in college (Ewen, 1993). He recovered and went on to receive his medical degree in 1917 from Valparaiso University of Indiana. After serving in the medical corps during World War I, he worked in government and psychiatric hospitals where he focused on treatment of people with schizophrenia. This had a great influence on his theories.

In 1931, Sullivan moved to New York to further his training in psychoanalysis and to establish a successful practice, modifying traditional analysis according to his own ideas. He served as president of the William Alanson White Foundation, founded the still-thriving Washington School of Psychiatry, and initiated the journal *Psychiatry*. Because his ideas were new and controversial, many psychoanalysts felt they needed to choose whether to align themselves with Sullivan or Freud. Sullivan died on January 14, 1949. Although his writings fill seven volumes, most of them were published posthumously.

Harry Stack Sullivan's Theories   Sullivan valued the contributions of Freud but disagreed with him in fundamental ways. For Sullivan, Freud was too pessimistic, too inflexible, too quick to theorize without supporting data, and too prone to overlook the importance of relationships. Sullivan developed his own school of psychoanalysis—called Interpersonal Psychoanalysis—to address these shortcomings and communicate his own ideas.

Interpersonal relationships. Sullivan's theory can be thought of as a drive theory, with the search for relatedness being people's primary drive. Intimacy, according to Sullivan, is as strong an interpersonal drive as sexual desire (Chapman, 1978). Both can bring people together in powerful unions that relieve anxiety and provide gratification. Intimacy occurs when people feel that the welfare of another individual is as important to them as their own well-being.

Sullivan believed that relationships proceed according to what he called the *principle of reciprocal emotions* in which the reciprocity of behaviors and attitudes determines the course of the relationship. He viewed pathology as resulting from unhealthy relationships (Sullivan, 1953). Excessive maternal anxiety, loneliness, failure to find satisfactory childhood friendships, and other relationship problems can impair self-esteem and the development of healthy relationships in adulthood.

Anxiety, tension, security, and euphoria. Sullivan believed that what he called euphoria, a state of total well-being and equilibrium, was the ideal human condition, while tension was the polar opposite (Ewen, 1993). Anxiety, caused primarily by disturbances in relationships, creates tension that disrupts equilibrium (Williams, 1994). Anxiety propels people to seek security in order to minimize tension and create feelings of safety, comfort, and self-esteem. According to Sullivan, safe relationships are people's primary source of security.

Personality development. Sullivan, like Horney, had a positive view of human nature, seeing it as pliable and adaptive. He believed that people have a natural tendency toward mental health, which he defined as achieving a balance between the pursuit of satisfaction and the pursuit of security (Ewen, 1993). Sullivan described several important components of the personality:

- *The self-system* includes all the security systems and maneuvers a person usually employs to defend against emotional discomfort and anxiety (Chapman, 1978). Security measures evaluate aspects of the self as good-me (those that provide positive feelings), bad-me (those that were punished or disapproved of in childhood), and not-me (parts of the self that were ignored or neglected). These evaluations are based on perceptions, derived from how others regard us, and form our personalities.

- *Personifications* are mental images of ourselves and others that stem from our interpersonal experiences (Strean, 1994). Although they are often inaccurate, these images help us organize and make sense of our experiences. Stereotypes are examples of personifications.
- *Dynamisms* are enduring patterns of energy transformation that characterize people's relationships and emotional functioning and are intended to reduce anxiety and increase satisfaction. These habitual reactions have a physiological origin but flow through interpersonal actions (Chapman, 1978). A hungry child asking to be fed reflects a dynamism, as does a person making sexual overtures toward another person.

Stages of development. According to Sullivan, development before adulthood consists of six stages reflected primarily in social maturation (Strean, 1994). According to Sullivan, healthy development through the following stages enables people to form relationships that will reduce anxiety and increase security:

1. *Infancy.* The self-system, personifications, and autonomy begin.
2. *Childhood.* The self-system becomes more coherent. Children recognize that not everyone will treat them well.
3. *Orientation in living.* Children become part of groups, learn to cooperate and compete, and begin to develop ideals and insight.
4. *Juvenile stage.* Children acquire confidants of the same gender as their good friends.
5. *Early adolescence.* Heterosexual activity and sexual desire develop, leading to conflicts between opposing needs.
6. *Late adolescence.* Privileges, responsibilities, and satisfaction in interpersonal living all are important as the person develops more mature relationships.

Strategies of Psychotherapy Sullivan viewed all psychological dysfunction as resulting from faulty interpersonal processes. Consequently, he focused his treatment on correcting people's harmful perceptions through the interpersonal process of psychotherapy (Strean, 1994). The relationship of the client and the clinician is a primary component of his approach.

According to Sullivan (1954), clinicians should have a sincere desire to help, great respect and empathy for their clients, as well as a strong interest in them. Clinicians should ensure that sessions progress well, that meaningful work takes place, and that clients keep their anxiety at manageable levels.

Awareness is one of the primary goals of Interpersonal Psychoanalysis. Sullivan believed that if people have a good understanding of their interpersonal relationships and the reciprocal processes in those relationships, they can lead reasonably satisfying lives. Developing that awareness involves examination of clients' life histories from varying viewpoints, so that clinicians and clients can reach a consensus. This brings thoughts and feelings to the surface and facilitates clear thinking as well as new insights, perceptions, experiences, and ways of relating. In other words, "The goal is for the patient to abandon sick dynamisms and to substitute healthy ones in their place" (Chapman, 1978, p. 101).

Sullivan placed emphasis on drawing conclusions based on solid data and observations, and this is reflected in his use of consensus to determine meaning. Achieving consensual validation was necessary to reduce what he called *parataxic distortion,* occurring when people's perceptions and actions are colored and distorted by their unhealthy early childhood relationships and their private logic and images (Sullivan, 1947). Treatment helps people explore these distortions, especially those that are reflected in the clinician-client interaction, so that they can shift from parataxic to syntaxic modes of perceiving that are less influenced by early childhood experiences.

Many aspects of Sullivan's theory are innovative and contemporary. He stressed the importance of the therapeutic alliance and viewed therapy as a learning process. He believed that his task was to remove obstacles so that people could realize their natural tendencies toward health, and he emphasized the importance of nonverbal communication. In addition, Sullivan paid attention to cultural background and differences, avoided giving advice, and recognized that brief therapy and flexible treatment schedules could be beneficial. He advocated short and simple interpretations and believed that clinicians should thoroughly understand what they were doing and what their goal was—in effect, plan the treatment (Shainess, 1978). According to Sullivan, when people's views of themselves were consistent with the consensually validated viewpoints that had evolved during their sessions, treatment was complete and people could now use their own resources to pursue more rewarding lives (Levenson, 1992).

Current Status   Sullivan is considered one of the most influential figures in psychoanalysis (Greenberg & Mitchell, 1983). His work has had an impact on ego psychology, self psychology, phenomenological approaches, and family systems therapy (Siegel, 1987). He maintained a deep respect for the uniqueness and power of the individual and for the limitations of psychotherapy. De-emphasizing the importance of dreams, free association, the libido, and transference in treatment, he focused on relationships, perceptions, anxiety, and learning, all important in treatment today.

Anna Freud

Anna Freud, daughter of Sigmund Freud, was her father's colleague and later his caregiver. She was also an innovative theorist and clinician who focused on child development and analysis and the ego defense mechanisms. Her study of the impact of trauma on children is particularly relevant today.

Biography of Anna Freud   Anna Freud was born on December 3, 1895, the youngest of Sigmund Freud's six children and the only one to become a psychoanalyst. She first worked as a teacher but quickly shifted her interest to psychoanalysis. In 1922, she qualified to become a psychoanalyst. Current ethical standards were not in place when Anna Freud began to practice; she was psychoanalyzed by her father and treated the children of family friends.

Initially, Anna Freud focused her practice on adults. However, her involvement in teaching, rescue work with children and families during World War I, and care of her nephew after her sister's death led her to focus on treating children and adolescents. Anna Freud believed in direct observation and assessment of children, the need to understand child development, and the importance of social interest, as well as the necessity of working with both healthy and troubled children. She combined these interests when she established an experimental nursery designed to serve Vienna's poorest families and provide a vehicle for study of the second year of life and the initial separation of the child from the mother (Sayers, 1991). Freud continued her work in London, where she opened a nursery for children who had been orphaned or separated from their families during World War II. Subsequently, she developed the Hampstead Child Therapy Clinic for both research and treatment.

Although Freud's training was primarily experiential rather than academic, she wrote numerous books on subjects such as family law and the impact of war on children. Her most important book may be *The Ego and the Mechanisms of Defense* (Freud, 1946), an 80th birthday present for her father.

During her long life, Anna Freud witnessed the growing influence and importance of her own work as well as her father's. She died on October 9, 1982.

Anna Freud's Theories   Anna Freud's areas of specialization were child development and the ego defenses. Because she did not believe that traditional analysis was effective with young children, she emphasized a supportive and educational approach rather than an analytical one.

Child development. Developmental thinking was fundamental to Freud's work. She believed that children mature along a basic trajectory—from the infant's dependency on the mother to the adult's emotional self-reliance. Periods of imbalance or regression can signal problems in maturation, although Freud saw adolescent turmoil as normal, usually requiring time rather than psychotherapy (Crain, 1992).

The strengthening of the ego so that it gradually gains control over the id allows children to mature from primary process, instinctual, id-governed behavior to the secondary process, ego-driven behaviors and experiences of adults. Freud believed that the role of the mother, especially during the second half of the child's first year of life, is critical in ego development. She asserted that the presence of a constant maternal object and a reciprocal mother-infant relationship were essential for development of the child's healthy capacity for attachment (Tyson & Tyson, 1990). Thus, Freud suggested that orphaned or displaced children should reside with relatives or foster families rather than in institutions and that hospitalized children should be allowed to have a parent stay with them.

Child psychoanalysis. Freud conceived of child psychoanalysis as a method of understanding and asking questions, leading to the emergence of the child's inner experiences and internal world (Mayes & Cohen, 1996). She recognized that children rarely have an active wish for treatment. Rather, they cooperate with treatment primarily for three reasons (Freud, 1965):

1. They trust and believe in an adult whom they perceive as helpful and interested.
2. They wish to please the clinician.
3. They view the clinician as a sort of understanding and safe parent.

These attitudes needed to be nurtured in order to address children's reluctance to engage in treatment (Edgcumbe, 1985).

Freud viewed child analysis as different from adult analysis in important respects. She believed that children often cannot benefit from direct interpretation but can gain more from the use of stories about toys or other children. She recognized that behavior that appears maladaptive might reflect a child's best effort to cope with environmental stressors. In addition, what might be resistance in an adult may be a developmentally appropriate response in a child. The clinician has to take an active role to facilitate children's self-expression and to clarify the connection between their symptoms and the content of sessions. Freud's treatment of children usually focused on current life events rather than transference and repressed material.

Role of environment. Anna Freud believed that clinicians must pay attention to children's environment. She emphasized the need to establish a treatment alliance with the child's parents and to understand the child's social and family situation.

Freud believed that analysis should be used primarily to treat internal and internalized conflicts, not problems due essentially to external causes (Mayes & Cohen, 1996; Sayers, 1991). Freud saw the impact of environmental factors on children who had been separated from their parents during World War II. She had great compassion for these children and sought to help them, but did not view analysis as the best treatment for such externally caused difficulties. According to Freud, efforts to change the environment, as well as supportive interventions, were often more appropriate to facilitate development and address the aftereffects of external events such as inadequate parenting and environmental traumas.

Assessment. Freud believed strongly in the assessment of both emotionally healthy and troubled children as a way of identifying the hallmarks of age-appropriate development. She maintained a flexible concept of healthy development, recognizing that individual variations and fluctuations in development were often normal. She sought to obtain a balanced picture of children's development, focusing on areas of positive growth and adjustment as well as areas of impairment. To enhance her work, Freud developed several tools and assessment procedures, including the Diagnostic or Metapsychological Profile and the Hampstead Psychoanalytic Index, which systematized the process of gathering information on children's development (Sandler, 1996; Solnit, 1983).

Ego defenses. Freud's work focused on the ego. However, she believed that an effective clinician stayed equidistant from the id, the ego, and the superego, allowing all three components to surface without making judgments or choices (Strean, 1994). One of Freud's major contributions was her comprehensive description of ego defense mechanisms (Sandler & Freud, 1985). She believed that people used defense mechanisms to cope with anxiety stimulated by either unacceptable drives from the id or harmful threats and commands from the superego. Freud shifted the emphasis of her approach from the drives to the ego defenses, which, according to Gabbard (1990), "anticipated the movement of psychoanalysis and dynamic psychiatry away from neurotic symptom formation and toward character pathology" (p. 22).

Strategies of intervention. Although Freud's work has particular relevance to the treatment of young people, she believed that psychoanalysis of adults could be enhanced by understanding and reconstructing childhood developmental issues (Yorke, 1983). Consequently, her work has meaning for all clinicians.

Freud's concept of therapy emphasized several perspectives that are compatible with treatment today. She believed in the importance of the therapeutic alliance, saying, "To be in contact is so important, and to interpret does not always mean to be in contact" (Freud, 1983, p. 119). She advocated an optimistic and holistic perspective: "In treatment, you work with the healthy side of the child and you work with the ill side—you don't only work with the ill side, but you trust that the healthy side will come to your assistance, although it may not be there or it may not be strong enough" (p. 125). She emphasized the importance of clinician flexibility, letting treatment follow the needs of the child and perhaps suggesting a game to reduce a child's anxiety.

Current Status   Anna Freud's moderate and realistic stance led to her great influence in the field of child analysis; even today, her methods are widely used in the western world and continue to be consistent with current thinking about children and their appropriate treatment. (Sayers, 1991).

Anna Freud's ideas paved the way for other theorists and clinicians to focus on the bond between the child and the parent. Particularly important is research on attachment theory, increasingly acknowledged as a key variable in human development. The object relations theorists, including John Bowlby and his important work on attachment theory (Bowlby, 1978; Greenberg & Mitchell, 1983), are discussed next.

According to Sayers (1991), Anna Freud "left a legacy of child analysis, ego psychology, and psychoanalytic observations on pediatrics, developmental assessment, and childcare policy" (p. 198). Furthermore, "Her innovative thinking and active collaboration in child care and health and in education and the law, in addition to her extraordinary capacity to be practical in providing care for children caught up in 'experiments' of nature and man-made catastrophes were brilliant applications of psychoanalytic theory in the service of children and their parents" (Solnit, 1997, p. 7).

Anna Freud's ideas and writings have left their mark. Her writings on child rearing include *Beyond the Best Interests of the Child* (Goldstein, Freud, & Solnit, 1973) and *Before the Best Interests of the Child* (Goldstein, Freud, & Solnit, 1979); those on the impact of war on children include *War and Children* (Freud & Burlingham, 1943) and *Infants Without Families* (Freud & Burlingham, 1944). Also important are her pioneering works on child and adolescent analysis and development; her emphasis on health and on the ego and its defenses; her belief that all people dealing with children must have practical as well as theoretical training; and her appreciation of the importance of the therapeutic alliance, healthy early attachment, the family system, and context.

OBJECT RELATIONS THEORISTS

Although object relations theory may seem complicated, it offers clinicians many useful tools and concepts. In general, object relations theorists attend to the past by exploring people's early childhood relationships and attend to the present through the development of the client-clinician relationship. Observing what is occurring in that interaction can give clinicians information about what clients have experienced in past relationships, while understanding of the past can shed light on present interactions.

Overview of Object Relations Theory

The central concept of object relations theory is that development and individuation depend on the nature of people's early relationships, particularly the relationship the child has with the mother or primary caregiver. According to this theory, the infant is driven to attach to an "object," defined not as another person but as the internal mental structure that the infant forms of that person through introjection. This internal mental structure or representation is based on both actual and fantasized experiences that involved an investment of emotions and energy. The mother usually is the first internal object, but others evolve over time.

As the infant forms these internal mental structures, feelings will inevitably arise that the infant cannot tolerate. Anger toward the mother is one of these feelings. Because experiencing these feelings might jeopardize the child's emotional gratification and safety, the child splits off and represses these unacceptable emotions. These are dealt with via projective identification, in which the split off parts of the self are projected onto another person with whom the self can then identify.

In healthy infant development, where consistent and nurturing parenting has been provided throughout the child's life, the infant becomes able to reclaim the unacceptable feelings at about 8 months of age as he or she begins to individuate and separate from the caregiver. The infant then can accept the notion that the self and the caregiver each have both positive and negative emotions. Object relations theory sees the early mother (or primary caretaker) and child experience as the template for relationship patterns that follow. For these theorists, then, the critical events that shape people's lives occur not at 5 or 6 years, but at 5 or 6 months.

Impact of Internalized Objects on Relationships   These internal representations affect people's later sense of themselves as well as their perceptions of and capacity for forming external relationships. Object relations theorists believe that symptoms such as anxiety, depression, and impaired relationships reflect the nature of people's problems with object relations and corresponding threats to their sense of self.

Fox (1996) offers the example of a woman experiencing depression who received the message, as a child, that women should not be ambitious. She split off this part of herself, eventually projecting it onto her husband who was not, by nature, an ambitious man. This led to conflicts between the two, with the woman interpreting her husband's lack of ambition as a rejection of her; in effect, he failed to meet her need to realize her ambitions through him. In treatment, this dynamic was explored, repressed material arose and was interpreted, and therapy moved toward helping the woman reclaim her own ambitious feelings and her need for achievement.

Intervention Strategies   Freudian psychoanalysis forms the backdrop for object relations therapists. Many of their approaches stem from his school of thought, and their work typically entails long-term and intensive analysis. However, changes in emphasis, application, and technique distinguish object relations therapists from traditional Freudian analysts. In addition, significant differences of opinion characterize the object relations theorists discussed later in this chapter. The British Psychoanalytic Group responded to these differences by dividing their curriculum into the A group (Freudian) and the B group (Kleinian). Winnicott began the C group, which saw value in both of the other groups. Object relations theorists were also divided according to national lines. For example, the British group (including Klein, Fairbairn, and Winnicott) emphasized transference and countertransference, while the American group (including Mahler and Kernberg) was more interested in ego functioning and adaptation (Scharff & Scharff, 1992).

Projective identification. All three groups viewed the process of projective identification, along with its exploration and analysis, as essential treatment ingredients. Projective identification should be distinguished from transference. In transference, the clinician is viewed inaccurately as having characteristics of significant people in the client's early life; for example, the clinician may be seen as an angry and judgmental parent. In projective identification, a part of the internalized object or the self is projected onto the therapist. The internal object relationship is then re-created in the clinician-client relationship, where it can be reworked to allow modification of the internalized object (Scharff & Scharff, 1992). For example, the depressed woman in the previous example might project onto the therapist the wish for the woman to excel in her profession; this reflects the woman's underlying fear of her own ambition.

Therapeutic alliance. Establishing a positive therapeutic alliance is much more important to object relations theorists than it was to traditional psychoanalysts. Just as an important element in the mother's role is to provide nurturing and care, so are those elements perceived as important in the therapeutic process. According to object relations theory, clinicians should deliberately introduce these and other elements into therapy to facilitate transference and projective identification. In a sense, the therapist becomes a good-enough mother, providing a holding environment for people who may never have had adequate parenting. Affective exchanges between clinician and client bring the internal object relationships into the here and now, allow the client to reexperience those relationships, and promote insight and change.

Resistance. Resistance in clients is viewed as reflecting a rigid transference, growing out of the client's strong need for a particular type of object relationship. Resistance leads to the client's inability to relate to the clinician in ways that are flexible and reflective of present relationships. Resistance is a way for people to keep painful emotions and fantasies buried in the unconscious to protect the self from the threat these pose. Clinicians can reduce resistance by acknowledging and accepting clients' internal worlds and by being patient, consistent, safe, and available.

Countertransference. Understanding countertransference as well as transference and projective identification are important in object relations theory. Countertransference is viewed as inevitable in the interaction between the client and the therapist and a source of important clues to the nature of the transference relationship (Greenberg & Mitchell, 1983). In understanding and dealing with their countertransference reactions, clinicians should be clear about whether those reactions stem largely from interactions with a client or from the clinicians' own issues and experiences.

Assessment. The clinician, in collaboration with the client, assesses the person's development; unconscious patterns; internalized object relationships; and underlying anxieties, defenses, and projective identifications. A thorough assessment is necessary to pave the way for well-timed and accurate interpretations that will make a difference.

Interpretation. Interpretation is a primary route to change. Through analysis and interpretation of transference, projective identification and countertransference, past and present experiences, and the manifestations of the unconscious, people work through their internalized and unconscious emotions and relationships. *Working through* is the process of obtaining clarification and resolution of projective identification patterns by experiencing them over and over at progressively higher levels of development (Scharff & Scharff, 1992). This enables people to develop the capacity to transcend old patterns and have genuine emotional contact with others. As Fairbairn (cited in Greenberg & Mitchell, 1983) stated, "The analytic process is understood not as consisting of a resolution of unconscious conflict over pleasure-seeking impulses, but as a process through which the capacity for making direct and full contact with real other human beings is restored" (p. 156). When this is accomplished, and when people can have loving relationships, cooperate with and perceive others accurately, have empathy and concern for others, and manage their own stress, they are ready for their analysis to terminate.

The Object Relations Theorists

Many names are associated with the development of object relations theory. This section offers an overview of the backgrounds and ideas of some of the most important, including Melanie Klein, W. R. D. Fairbairn, D. W. Winnicott, Otto Kernberg, and John Bowlby. Others who contributed to the development of object relations theory include Margaret Mahler, Edith Jacobson, Henry Guntrip and Ivan Boszormenyi-Nagy.

Melanie Klein   Melanie Klein is regarded as the mother of object relations theory (Cashdan, 1988). Her work as an analyst grew out of her fascination with Sigmund Freud's work and her own experience in analysis. Like Anna Freud, Klein focused her work on treating children. After practicing in Budapest and Berlin, she relocated to England where she wrote and practiced until her death in 1960 (Greenberg & Mitchell, 1983).

Klein was a transitional figure, who shifted the focus of psychoanalysis away from Sigmund Freud's drive theory and toward the importance of early relationships. Although her failure to successfully integrate drive theory and object relations theory probably explains why most of her ideas are not currently accepted, she contributed several important concepts to psychoanalysis.

Klein suggested that when the child is 3 to 6 months of age, the infant develops the capacity to internalize objects and integrate fragmented perceptions of the caregiver. Klein believed that these mechanisms, as well as introjection, splitting, projection, and projective identification, were used by infants to avoid fears of death and their own destructive impulses. Internalized objects color people's later relationships. Fantasies and anxieties stemming from people's internal object world form the basis for their later moods, behaviors, and self-images. The roots of modern object relations theory are evident in this concept.

According to Klein, people have two fundamental positions: paranoid-schizoid and depressive (Schafer, 1994). The *paranoid-schizoid* position stems from infants' natural fearfulness or paranoia. In an attempt to ward off danger, infants separate good objects and feelings from bad objects and feelings. Klein termed this pattern *splitting,* referring to splits in the ego as well as in the conceptual and emotional organization of the self. In the paranoid-schizoid position, people's emotional focus is on aggression and other-directed destructiveness, manifested through envy and grandiosity, and characterized by defenses such as splitting and projective identification. Splitting is currently viewed as a defense, common among people with borderline personality disorders, in which they view themselves, others, and their life experience in extremes: as either all good or all bad.

The *depressive* position reflects people's concern that images of and connections with the internalized objects are threatened by internal conflicts. The depressive position is characterized by the defense of regression; people in this position focus on emotions such as love, understanding, empathy, and reparation of the internalized object.

How these positions are manifested vary throughout a person's life. Mature people primarily manifest the depressive position, which is never fully overcome (Scharff & Scharff, 1992).

Klein also believed that play in children is comparable to free association in adults, reflecting unconscious material. This viewpoint is now well accepted in child psychoanalysis (Weisberg, 1994).

W. R. D. Fairbairn   W. R. D. Fairbairn is another object relations theorist of some importance. Fairbairn's writings during the 1940s were influential because of their clear description of the shift in psychoanalysis from the drive model to the relational model (Greenberg & Mitchell, 1983). He modified the work of both Sigmund Freud and Melanie Klein. According to Cashdan (1988),

> Fairbairn's object relations are more purely relational than Klein's in that real interactions rather than fantasy are afforded primary consideration. Despite his retention of traditional analytic terminology, Fairbairn was one of the first to give meaning to the object relational contention that an ego or true self never develops outside the context of interpersonal relationships. (p. 12)

Fairbairn suggested that the infant was not so much "pleasure-seeking as object-seeking" (Summers, 1993, p. 226). He disagreed with Klein and emphasized dependency needs rather than destructive fantasies in a child's relationship with the mother. According to Fairbairn, human experience and behavior derive primarily from the search for and maintenance of contacts with others (Greenberg & Mitchell, 1983). Emotional development is characterized by a maturational sequence of relationships. Pathology can occur when the ego seeks to perpetuate the old hopes and ties of the internalized object, when strong attachments to bad objects are in place, and when fragmentation of the ego occurs. On the other hand, emotional health is reflected in an ego that retains a sense of wholeness and achieves positive relationships with real people rather than fantasies or distortions.

D. W. Winnicott   D. W. Winnicott was a British pediatrician and child psychiatrist. His contributions center around the struggle of the self to establish both individuality and intimate contact with others. Winnicott emphasized the importance of the child's relationship with the mother. He believed that the presence of good-enough mothering was necessary for mental health. Adequate mothering allows the emergence of a healthy creative self and facilitates the shift from the infant dependency to independence.

The mother serves many functions for the infant. She provides a *holding environment* that contains and experiences the infant; in this environment, the mother offers security and serves as an object for the child's love and aggression. The physical holding of the child allows the baby to become psychologically organized as it sorts and reacts to physical touch. The mother also *mirrors* the child's experiences, validating them and allowing the development of a stable and unique self. In a *moment of illusion,* the infant experiences a oneness with the need-gratifying mother, giving the child a sense of omnipotence that contributes to healthy and integrated development. Also promoting the child's individuation and independence is *transitional space,* the growing physical distance between the mother and the child that allows the child opportunity to discover and learn, and *transitional objects,* such as blankets and teddy bears, which represent the mother and afford the child a sense of control and contact with the internalized mother while being physically separate from her. Transitional objects are used now in treatment to ease separation and facilitate individuation in clients, especially those who are dealing with experiences of abuse.

The mothering experience can promote maladjustment as well as health. According to Winnicott, unhealthy maternal expectations can lead to the emergence of a false self in the child based on illusion and fragmentation, which both conceals and protects the true self. Regression can also result when the parenting is inadequate, leading the child to search for needed but missed relationship experiences.

Otto Kernberg   Kernberg's work emphasized the interactive nature of the self and the importance of relational factors in shaping the person. He believed that people are innately object-related and social from early development onward. Kernberg theorized that people have three kinds of internalization systems that shape who they are:

1. *Introjection,* which is the earliest and most primitive system
2. *Identification,* in which an image of the self is colored by taking on perceived characteristics of another person
3. *Ego identity,* in which the introjections and identifications are organized in a coherent and integrated way to provide a sense of self

Kernberg's approach is interpretive, focusing on basic issues such as anger, envy, self-sufficiency, and demands of the self and others in reality and in transference. His writings have made a strong contribution to our understanding of personality disorders, particularly borderline and narcissistic personality disorders (Kernberg, 1985). He reported using a modified psychoanalytic approach with some success to help clients develop a more accurate sense of reality.

John Bowlby   John Bowlby is currently one of the best-known object relations theorists because of his development of attachment theory. Bowlby hypothesized the existence of a universal human need to form close emotional bonds (Fonagy, 1999). Child and caregiver form a system in which the attachment behaviors of the infant (e.g., smiling, clinging) are ideally reciprocated by adult attachment behaviors (e.g., touching, soothing, feeding). This provides security and emotional regulation. Bowlby believed that a strong causal relationship existed between children's attachment to their parents and their later capacity to form affectional bonds and experience positive emotional development (Bowlby, 1988). The main variable in this connection is the extent to which children's parents provide them with a secure base that allows growth and exploration.

Bowlby's clinical approach reflected his emphasis on attachment. He believed that, like a good parent, clinicians need to respect and encourage clients' desire to explore the world and make their own decisions. According to Bowlby (1988), therapists applying attachment theory provide the following conditions:

- A secure base from which people can explore painful and unhappy aspects of their lives
- Help and encouragement with this exploratory process, facilitating people's efforts to understand the connections between patterns in their current relationships and those in unconscious and internalized images
- Encouragement for people to consider whether and how their current perceptions, expectations, emotions, and actions may be the products of childhood experiences and messages, especially those connected to their parents
- A therapeutic alliance that can be analyzed and understood in light of clients' new insights and information
- Help in assessing the appropriateness, accuracy, and helpfulness of people's models of themselves and others

Bowlby believed that the essence of treatment was to help people understand the nature and development of representational models of attachment figures that were governing their perceptions, expectations, and actions and, if indicated, to help them modify those in light of more recent experience (Bowlby, 1978).

Bowlby's ideas have provided the basis for many articles and research studies supporting and extending his concept of attachment. For example, McClure and Teyber (1996) used Bowlby's work on attachment as the basis for what they called the multicultural-relational approach, emphasizing the importance of a sound and sensitive therapeutic relationship with a diverse client population.

In a study of adult romantic relationships, Hazan and Shaver (1987) found a correlation between attachment style and patterns in current relationships. Research showed that children with a history of secure attachment are more likely than those without this sort of attachment to manifest many positive personal characteristics including resilience, self-reliance, empathy, social interest, and ability to form close intimate relationships (Fonagy, 1999). Attachment relationships also figure prominently in transgenerational transmission of deprivation; secure adults are more likely to have children who are securely attached to them than those who have not had their own secure attachments.

Mary Ainsworth (Ainsworth, Blehar, Waters, & Walls, 1978) conducted what is probably the most important and best-known research based on Bowlby's concepts. Ainsworth and her colleagues created what they termed the "strange situation" in which infants were observed before, during, and after a brief period of time in which they were separated from their caregivers and left with a stranger in an unfamiliar environment. The infants' responses were classified into the following four categories:

1. *Secure* —Children demonstrated curiosity and comfort in the presence of their care-giver, became anxious and distressed in the presence of the stranger, and sought and accepted comfort when the caregiver returned, soon resuming exploration.
2. *Anxious/Avoidant* —These children were less anxious with the stranger, did not seek comfort from the caregiver, and did not seem to prefer the caregiver over the stranger. These children probably had experiences in which the caregiver did not help them regulate their emotions; consequently, they over-regulate emotions and avoid troubling situations.
3. *Anxious/Resistant* —Children in this group engaged in little exploration, were highly distressed during the separation, but had difficulty accepting comfort from the caregiver and continued to manifest anxiety or anger.
4. *Disorganized/Disoriented* —Children in this group manifested confusing and undi-rected behavior such as head banging and a wish to escape, even after the caregiver had returned. Ainsworth suggested that the caregivers of these children had evoked both fear and comfort. A history of neglect or abuse often is associated with this pattern.

With the findings of Ainsworth and her colleagues as a basis, researchers have developed the Adult Attachment Interview, a structured clinical instrument designed to elicit narratives of child-hood attachment relationships. Scoring classifies respondents as Secure/Autonomous, Inse-cure/Dismissing, Insecure/Preoccupied, or Unresolved in terms of their attachments as adults (George, Kaplan, & Main, 1996).

Current Status

Modern clinicians are aware of weaknesses in the ideas of the early object relations theorists. Prob-ably most glaring is their lack of emphasis on the role of the father. However, when these theo-ries were developed, traditional family patterns with the mother as a child's primary caregiver were the norm. In addition, the birth process as well as breast feeding gave the mother an essen-tial role in the child's life. Other shortcomings of object relations theory include:

- Complex ideas and vocabulary, sometimes compounded by a lack of clarity in definitions and the many differences of opinion among theorists
- An excessively narrow focus on issues of infantile dependence and inadequate mothering that downplays the impact of individual differences and incompatibilities between mother-child dyads
- A view of people as relatively passive victims of parental deficiency

On the other hand, objects relations theories have made many important contributions to counseling and psychotherapy and remain important to these professions. Research by Bowlby (1978, 1988) and others has affirmed object relations theorists' emphasis on the child's attach-ment to the caregiver. Many believe that attachment problems in western society are becoming more prevalent because of the high divorce rate, high stress in our daily lives, and demanding and busy schedules which make parents less able to meet children's attachment needs. This, in turn, has been implicated as a factor in the growing rates of youth violence and family instability.

Other contributions of object relations theory to modern counseling and psychotherapy include

- The link it established between developmental theory and psychoanalytic practice (Weisberg, 1994)
- The emphasis it placed on ensuring that the therapeutic situation is a safe place, a holding environment, and a place of containment, that enables people to meet the challenges of emotional growth without being engulfed by troubling emotions
- The recognition of the importance of both countertransference and transference, the person of the therapist, the therapeutic alliance, and attention to the here-and-now clinical situation

Object relations therapy is being used with individuals, couples, and families (Scharff, 1989); in play therapy, art therapy, and group therapy; and for treatment of substance misuse, anorexia nervosa, personality disorders (especially borderline personality disorder), and even psychosis (Scharff & Scharff, 1992). Thomas and Garske (1995) advocated the use of this model for people with disabilities, believing it could provide insight into barriers to adjustment and ways to help people deal effectively with disabilities.

HEINZ KOHUT AND SELF PSYCHOLOGY

Heinz Kohut's work grew out of Freudian psychoanalysis (as did the work of everyone discussed in this chapter) and was strongly influenced by object relations theory. Kohut's self psychology moved the field toward its next major phase of development: humanistic, existential, and other theories that focus on emotion and sensation (see part 3). Kohut's emphasis on empathy, self-image, current experience, and the importance of taking a holistic view of people, as well as his groundbreaking work on narcissism, made essential contributions to counseling and psychotherapy.

Biography of Heinz Kohut

Born in Vienna, Austria, in 1913, Kohut was an only child. After a brief psychoanalysis, he focused his work on psychiatry and neurology. He completed his residency at the University of Chicago and became a U.S. citizen in 1945. In 1948, he married Betty Meyer, a social worker.

During the 1950s, Kohut established a successful clinical practice, which provided the basis for his ideas. He has been described as meticulous but playful; he had the ability to invest himself heavily in his work as a clinician, teacher, researcher, writer, and leader in his field but also to set limits and to enjoy the moment (Stozier, 1985). Until 1965, Kohut was a spokesperson for Freudian psychoanalysis. However, his ideas about narcissism and his book *The Analysis of the Self* (1971) created a rift between him and other leading analysts of his time. This, coupled with his mother's development of paranoid delusions and her death in 1972, led him to engage in considerable self-analysis and creative thought and writing. Kohut died in 1981, leaving behind a considerable body of work.

Kohut's Theories

Lynch (1991) described Kohut's self psychology as follows:

> The patient needs to verbalize and experience fully the core deficits of the self structure (as exemplified in the kind of transferential response which develops). The therapist needs to take the transferential response and remain empathically immersed with the patient to learn fully about the nature and extent of the deficits and their genetic origins. Through the process of understanding and explaining, the therapist helps the patient achieve a new and lasting level of strength and maturity for what once was an enfeebled, vulnerable psychological self. (p. 25)

This quotation captures the essence of self psychology: Using empathy and interpretation, clinicians explore early developmental deficits, reflected in the transference relationship, to help people emerge from their unhappy conditions and find joy and empowerment.

The Self   Kohut emphasized the importance of establishing meaningful goals and of the attachment of young children to their parents. He conceived of the self as evolving out of this relationship. For Kohut, the observable self was the focus of analysis rather than Freud's ego, id, and superego (Cocks, 1994). Kohut believed that a strong self allows us to tolerate and successfully handle successes and failures, while a deficient self is developmentally frozen and prone to fragmentation (Gabbard, 1990; Kohut & Wolf, 1978). He described the self structure, which begins at 18 months of age, as having three poles (Lynch, 1991):

1. The *grandiose self,* which needs confirmation, validation, and mirroring responses from others
2. The *idealizing self,* which reflects the internalized and idealized selfobject derived from early relationships and leads to formation of goals and ideals for the self
3. The *twinship sector,* which seeks mutuality and equality in relationships with others as well as sharing of values and preferences

Kohut's concept of the selfobject is broader than the internalized object discussed by the object relations theorists. They referred primarily to children's internalization of their image of the mother, while Kohut used *selfobject* as a generic term for our intrapsychic experiences of others, our mental representations of them experienced as part of the self or in service of the self. Selfobjects are needed throughout our lives. These internalized images constantly change and mature to provide us with a sense of ourselves, self-esteem, soothing, and validation, and to meet our needs for mirroring, idealizing, and twinship (Gabbard, 1990). Maturation and emotional health are reflected by our ability to use more appropriate and growth-promoting selfobjects.

View of People   Self psychology is based not on efforts to contain the drives but on understanding and promoting people's development in the context of a responsive environment so that they can achieve their positive potentials (Lachmann & Beebe, 1995). For Kohut, feelings of sexuality and aggression, appropriately moderated, are part of our normal development and integral parts of ourselves, not the primary source of our difficulties.

According to Kohut (1982), traditional psychoanalysis views a person with emotional difficulties as the "guilty man"—a person trapped in a conflict between the drives of the id and the constraints of the superego. Instead, Kohut speaks of the "tragic man," "attempting, and never quite succeeding, to realize the program laid down in his depth during the span of his life," his failures overshadowing his successes (p. 402). Kohut viewed the tragic man as typically the product of an unempathic mother and an absent father. A representation of both men and women with emotional difficulties, the tragic man has the potential for growth, joy, adjustment, and fulfillment but consistently fails to reach that potential (Cocks, 1994).

Empathy, providing affirmation and mirroring, is essential to development of the healthy self. Initially, children need empathy from their parents to promote the development of the children's psychological strengths (Cocks, 1994). However, people later seek empathy from others. Empathy is an essential ingredient of the therapeutic relationship. This thinking reflects Kohut's emphasis on the present—what he called the *experience near* (as distinguished from the *experience far,* which refers to the id, ego, and superego and to early childhood experiences). Kohut believed that, although past experiences have a profound impact on our development, it is the present or here-and-now experiences that lead to their resolution.

Narcissism and Other Clinical Syndromes   Kohut perceived narcissism, one of the central concepts of his later work, as existing on a continuum (Nicholson, 1991). Healthy narcissism allows people to value themselves and their needs and to have self-confidence. Pathological narcissism often results when healthy development of a cohesive self is blocked. Unhealthy narcissism involves an unstable self-concept, grandiose fantasies of self-importance, a sense of entitlement, and an inability to think of others as anything but need-gratifying objects. Pathological narcissism can be reflected in a broad range of symptoms, including depression, anxiety, hypochondriasis, misuse of drugs, acting out, and dysfunctional sexual experiences, as well as fragmentation of the self and lack of a zest for life (Wolf, 1994). Kohut believed that this sort of narcissism was at the root of many people's emotional difficulties and that it could be modified through treatment.

Kohut also identified clinical syndromes that he often saw in treatment, including the fragmented self, the overstimulated self, the overburdened self, and the understimulated self (Nicholson, 1991). In addition, he described some character or personality types, including the mirror hungry, ideal hungry, alter-ego hungry, contact shunning, and merger hungry. Kohut linked these syndromes and character types to particular early experiences and symptoms and suggested treatment strategies for each. This information is useful in helping clinicians understand personality disorders and other longstanding and pervasive unhealthy patterns that clients manifest, and facilitates efforts to treat these challenging disorders.

Intervention Strategies

In self psychology, treatment focuses on a client's subjective experiences and meanings, enabling the clinician to enter the client's world (Donner, 1991). From that vantage point, clinicians address the condition of the self, including symptoms, developmental deficits, intrapsychic conflicts, and relational and behavioral difficulties. The ultimate goal is development of a healthy and cohesive self.

Empathy   Kohut viewed empathy as essential to effective treatment. Self psychology theorists believe that clinicians should take a nurturing role; emphasize active and open listening; and provide acceptance, understanding, and explanations or interpretations to facilitate the unfolding of the client's subjective world. Clinicians constantly reflect the essence of what clients have said, and clients' confirmation or rejection of these reflections allows clinicians to truly understand clients' inner reality.

Clinicians practicing self psychology avoid judging and view even narcissistic needs as developmentally understandable rather than immature and self-centered. Resistance as well as symptoms are viewed as efforts to protect the vulnerable self and maintain some internal cohesion. Clinicians' obvious interest in clients and their valuing of clients' words increase client investment in treatment and encourage disclosure of painful and unacceptable material.

Transference   Clinicians' empathy for clients facilitates the development of transference. In an idealizing selfobject transference, the vulnerable client perceives the clinician as a source of strength and safety who is able to respond to unmet developmental needs, including mirroring, idealizing, and twinship (Lachmann, 1993). Clients' needs reflect those that were frustrated in the course of development, and the transference is viewed as a reactivation of the selfobject experience. Empathy allows clinicians to contain and rebuild the early selfobject reflected in the transference relationship. Techniques such as *optimal frustration* and *optimal responsiveness* allow clients to change their internalizations, incorporating the skills provided by the clinician, so that clients develop an inner sense of self-competence that allows them to deal successfully with frustrations and nurture themselves. Kohut discusses this process in *The Restoration of the Self* (1977) and *How Does Analysis Cure?* (1984).

Current Status

During the 1980s and 1990s, Kohut's concepts were expanded on and substantiated through empirical research on infant development (Lachmann & Beebe, 1995). In addition, his work also has gained in influence because of our increasing attention to personality disorders and the sound ideas that his work provides for treating them (Meares, 1996). Kohut's work also has demonstrated its value in treating depression and anxiety (Nicholson, 1991), eating disorders (Bachar, 1998), and the impact of abuse (Hirschman, 1997). In addition, self psychology seems to have value in treating people with psychoses and borderline personality disorders, although the approach needs to be adapted to treatment of people with these disorders.

Although research on the application of self psychology to a diverse client population is limited, some studies suggest that this approach has broad relevance and application. Elliott, Uswatte, Lewis, and Palmatier (2000), for example, studied Kohut's idea that optimal adjustment during life transitions depended on people's capacity for pursuing meaningful goals and achieving a stable sense of self. They found that people's adjustment to and acceptance of recent disabilities, as well as their subjective well-being and life satisfaction, were indeed related to meaningful goal orientation and sense of self. Kim (2002) found that, among male Korean immigrants, their concepts of God and their religious leaders provided them mirroring, idealing, and twinship self objects. In another study, Lesser (2000) found that group therapy based on self psychology promoted helpful self-awareness in women. Although more research is needed on the multicultural application of self psychology, these and other recent studies suggest that, used with flexibility, this approach probably can be used with a diverse population.

Kohut's emphasis on empathy and the importance of the clinician-client collaboration, his understanding of narcissism and the role it often plays in emotional disorders, and his phenomenological perspective, emphasizing people's subjective reality, are important contributions to the practice of depth psychotherapy and also to the development of humanistic approaches to counseling and psychotherapy. His work forms a bridge between Freudian psychoanalysis and the person-centered and existential counseling approaches discussed in part 3. Kohut provides a way of understanding and helping people that is analytical in nature but at the same time consistent with the current clinical emphasis on early attachments; subjective reality; and the importance of promoting resilience, optimism, and empowerment in clients. Kohut's view of the tragic man captures the pitfalls of our ambitious and hurried society and enhances the timeliness of his theory.

SKILL DEVELOPMENT: INTERPRETATION

Interpretation is one of the fundamental skills of psychoanalysis and is employed by all of the clinicians discussed in this chapter. Interpretations provide people with an alternative frame of reference for viewing a problem or situation. Interpretations can link a current reaction that may appear unimportant to a past experience that has considerable depth and significance, thereby providing clients new understanding and routes to change.

Interpretations often reflect insights that clinicians have into clients' motives and behaviors that may not yet be in clients' awareness. For that reason, practitioners must deliver interpretations with great care. Ideally, questioning and information-giving can be used to help clients make their own interpretations. Timing is another critical variable in effective interpretations; they should be presented when people are ready to accept and understand them. Clinicians also should be clear about what they hope to accomplish in making an interpretation. Although it may enhance clinicians' self-esteem to realize that they are insightful and have drawn important connections between pieces of information that clients have presented, interpretations, of course, should never be self-serving or primarily for the purpose of demonstrating the clinician's skills. Rather, they should be used to move clients forward in positive ways such as helping them gain insights that will enhance their self-esteem, empower them, help them make better choices, facilitate their efforts to manage and change their emotions, and improve their interpersonal and other behaviors. Finally, presentation of interpretations should never create an adversarial situation in which clinician and client are in conflict or engaged in a debate about who is right. Generally, interpretations are most successful if they are presented tentatively as information for clients to think about and discuss. If interpretations are not meaningful to clients, they should have the right to reject them without being made to feel as though they are cowardly, unintelligent, or fearful of change. Using language carefully and thoughtfully can contribute to the successful delivery of interpretations.

CASE ILLUSTRATION

Consider the following dialog between Roberto and his counselor. Think about the strengths and weaknesses in the dialog and what you can learn from it about the use of interpretations. Notice the clinician's efforts to deliver interpretations in ways that are meaningful and acceptable to Roberto. The exercises in the next section will give you an opportunity to analyze this dialog.

Dialog Demonstrating Use of Interpretation

Roberto: I just don't understand what's wrong with Edie. She has a wonderful daughter and husband. Why can't she be contented?

Clinician: I wonder how Edie's role compares with the one your mother took when she had young children?

Roberto: Oh, my mother was very different from Edie. She devoted her whole life to her children. Me especially. I think I'm her favorite. She was so happy with her family. I don't understand why Edie doesn't feel that way.

Clinician: So the nurturing you received from your own mother and the joy she took in her role as mother make it especially hard for you to understand Edie.

Roberto: Yes, I guess that's true. But Edie loves Ava, and she's so sad that we can't have more children. Shouldn't she feel happy that she has a home and family?

Clinician: I can understand that this would puzzle you and maybe even make you angry sometimes because Edie doesn't seem to be the kind of mother you think she should be.

Roberto: Yes, I guess I don't want to admit that to Edie, but I suppose she senses my anger. I'm trying to help her find herself, and I realize that times have changed and not all women feel like my mother did, but it still bothers me sometimes. I want Ava to have the best possible mother . . . like I did.

Clinician: I can hear you really struggling with a conflict inside yourself. On the one hand, you want to help Edie figure out what would make her happy; but on the other hand, you are concerned that it might keep Ava from having the good mothering you had.

Roberto: Yes, that's really it.

Clinician: Could it also be that sometimes you feel angry and almost deprived because Edie is not giving you the caring that your mother taught you to expect from a woman?

Roberto: Well, . . . I don't know. . . . I mean, I'm a grown man; I don't need anybody to mother me anymore. I can take care of myself.

Clinician: You have become very self-sufficient. Yet sometimes most of us still feel that little child inside us who wants a loving mother to ease our fears and tell us how special we are.

Roberto: Isn't there something wrong with a grown man having those feelings?

Clinician: I don't think so, especially if we can recognize those feelings and use them in ways that help us.

Roberto: Well, I guess I do feel that way sometimes. Every once in a while I get this feeling like I'm a scared kid, like I just skinned my knee, and I want somebody to tell me it's all right. But that's a fantasy; there's nobody to wipe my eyes and wash my knee and make everything all right. And my problems now go way beyond a skinned knee.

Clinician: It sounds like it's hard for you to let yourself talk about those feelings and even to have those feelings. But from what you're saying, they are there sometimes, and maybe they have an impact on your relationship with Edie and your expectations of her.

Roberto: You may have something there. I never thought about any connection between my feelings toward Edie and the kind of mother I have. What can I do about that?

EXERCISES

Large-Group Exercises

1. Discuss the dialog you just read. Consider the following dimensions of the delivery of the dialog: content, language, purpose, timing, impact on clinician-client relationship, how large a part the client played in the interpretation process, and overall effectiveness. Consider ways in which the dialog might have been improved.

2. Consider what you know about Roberto's history from this dialog as well as from information provided in previous chapters. Select one of the theoretical approaches described in this chapter that might provide understanding of Roberto's development, his current difficulties, and ways to help him. Discuss the application of that approach to Roberto, being sure to link past and present and generate ideas for his treatment.

3. Have each student list what he or she perceives as the three greatest contributions of the theories presented in this chapter as well as the three concepts that seem least acceptable. List these on the board, identifying areas of agreement among students. Discuss the thinking behind the choices.

4. The leading thinkers in psychoanalysis disagreed among themselves. Stage the following discussion. Participating students are encouraged to do some research on the theorists whose ideas they will represent:

   Select three people to represent Sigmund Freud's ideas. Select three people to represent the ideas of the object relations and self psychology theorists. The two groups should debate the respective merits of their ideas, focusing especially on the importance of drives versus relationships in human development.

Small-Group Exercises

Divide into your groups of four students. One dyad should assume the roles of clinician and client, with the client being Edie or Ava. Do a 10-minute role play in which the client discusses her early relationships with her parents and her current social and self-esteem difficulties. Using information already available about Edie and Ava, the clinician should make at least two interpretations, linking the past and the present.

The two observers should take notes on the effectiveness of the interpretations and of the role play as a whole. Then the four group members should discuss the nature, language, timing, purpose, and impact of the interpretations, focusing particularly on how they might be improved.

Individual Exercises

1. Think about your relationships with your parents. What kind of parents do you think they were when you were very young? You may be particularly likely to have some insights into this if you observed them parenting your younger siblings or if you completed the exercise on early recollections in chapter 5. Write a paragraph in your journal in which you discuss ways in which the parenting you received as a young child might be affecting your current expectations and behaviors in relationships.
2. As you have learned in this chapter, Harry Stack Sullivan suggested that people go through a series of stages in their interpersonal development. Think about your development during each of the stages that Sullivan identified (p. 121) and list an experience you had during each stage that was typical of your relationships at that time. Write about the progression of interpersonal stages in your own life and how your present relationships might be a logical outgrowth of those patterns.

SUMMARY

This chapter reviewed three groups of what might be called Freudian revisionists: the ego psychologists, the object relations theorists, and the self psychologists. Nearly all of the theorists discussed in this chapter initially embraced the ideas of Sigmund Freud, but later developed their own ideas. All deemphasized the role of drives in human development and placed considerable emphasis on the ego or self and on early parent-child relationships and attachment. Most believed that children internalize images of their parents and that those images have a signifi-

cant impact on the children's sense of themselves and their subsequent relationships. Although most of these theorists continued to view the transference relationship as important, they also believed in the collaboration of clinician and client and advocated the use of empathy, acceptance, and other affective and humanistic interventions to enhance treatment. Nearly all of these theorists continue to be read and studied. Their influence has been great, not only on psychoanalysis but on other theories that will be discussed in this book.

RECOMMENDED READINGS

Helene Deutsch

Wimpfheimer, M. J., & Schafer, R. (1977). Psychoanalytic methodology in Helene Deutsch's *The Psychology of Women. Psychoanalytic Quarterly, 46,* 287–318.

Karen Horney

Paris, B. J. (1994). *Karen Horney: A psychoanalyst's search for understanding.* New Haven: Yale University Press.

Harry Stack Sullivan

Chapman, A. H. (1978). *The treatment techniques of Harry Stack Sullivan.* New York: Brunner/Mazel.

Grey, A. L. (1988). Sullivan's contributions to psychoanalysis: An overview. *Contemporary Psychoanalysis, 24,* 548–576.

Anna Freud

Sandler, A. (1996). The psychoanalytic legacy of Anna Freud. *Psychoanalytic Study of the Child, 51,* 270–284.

Object Relations Theorists

Cashdan, S. (1988). *Object relations therapy: Using the relationship.* New York: Norton.

Kernberg, O. F., & Clarkin, J. F. (1992). Treatment of personality disorders. *International Journal of Mental Health, 21,* 53–76.

Scharff, J. S., & Scharff, D. E. (1992). *Scharff notes: A primer of object relations therapy.* Northvale, NJ: Aronson.

Weisberg, I. (1994). Linking theory to practice: Melanie Klein and the relational revolution. *International Journal of Communicative Psychoanalysis and Psychotherapy, 9,* 77–84.

Heinz Kohut and Self Psychology

Kohut, H., & Wolf, E. S. (1978). The disorders of the self and their treatment: An outline. *International Journal of Psycho-Analysis, 59,* 413–425.

Lachmann, F. M. (1993). Self psychology: Origins and overview. *British Journal of Psychotherapy, 10,* 226–231.

Other References

Sayers, J. (1991). *Mothers of psychoanalysis: Helene Deutsch, Karen Horney, Anna Freud, Melanie Klein.* New York: Norton.

ADDITIONAL SOURCES OF INFORMATION

http://www.annafreudcentre.org/—A web page created by the London-based Anna Freud Center which seeks to educate others about Anna Freud's work.

www.webster.edu/-woolflm/—Information on Helene Deutsch and Karen Horney.

www.object-relations.com—Resources and information on object relations therapy.

www.sonoma.edu/users/d/daniles/objectrelations.html— More information on object relations therapy.

http://www.johnbowlby.com—Information on attachment theory and on John Bowlby.

http://www.psychologyoftheself.com/—Website of the International Council of Psychoanalytic Self Psychology, including an eJournal.

http://selfpsychology.com—Information on Heinz Kohut and self psychology.

CHAPTER 8

Brief Psychodynamic Therapy

The final theory to be discussed in part 2 is brief psychodynamic therapy (BPT). Like all of the theories reviewed in this part of the book, BPT is anchored in Freudian psychoanalysis. In fact, Freud, himself, often did brief therapy. BPT also has been influenced by Anna Freud's ego psychology, developmental psychology, object relations theories, Kohut's self psychology, Sullivan's interpersonal theories, and family systems concepts (Strupp, 1992).

Compared to traditional psychoanalysis, BPT is much more compatible with today's clinical emphasis on the establishment of specific goals, efficiency of treatment, and an interactive and often reparative clinician-client relationship. BPT usually is time-limited, focuses on a specific crisis or problem, establishes circumscribed goals, and uses a broad and flexible array of interventions. What makes this approach psychodynamic is the assumption that a person's focal problem reflects or repeats earlier issues in that person's family of origin (Messer & Warren, 1995). Clinicians who practice BPT believe that, by addressing in treatment both the current focal conflict and its origins, people's presenting concerns can be resolved and they can improve their ability to deal with similar issues in the future.

BPT is an important treatment approach that is widely used. According to Levenson and Strupp (1999, p. 386), ". . . a considerable amount of brief therapy is being conducted by psychodynamically trained therapists." In a survey of members of the American Psychological Association, 25% identified their theoretical orientation as psychodynamic, the most popular orientation after eclectic. In addition, extensive research supports the value of BPT in treating a broad range of people and mental disorders. Of course, this approach is not appropriate for all people or problems; it requires careful assessment to determine whether people are suitable for treatment by BPT.

THE DEVELOPMENT OF BRIEF PSYCHODYNAMIC THERAPY

Several names are associated with the early development of BPT including Sandor Ferenczi and Franz Alexander. Ferenczi, from Budapest, was one of Freud's followers. However, Ferenczi objected to the passive stance assumed by traditional psychoanalysts and sought a more active, efficient approach to treatment (Messer & Warren, 1995). He encouraged clients to face their fears, advocated a narrower focus of clinical attention, and believed that clinicians should assume an active role in the treatment process.

Alexander, practicing at the Chicago Institute for Psychoanalysis in the 1940s, viewed therapy as a "corrective emotional experience" designed to promote new learning (Weisberg, 1993, p. 106). Rather than seeking to elicit transference, he suggested that clinicians behave in ways opposite to those likely to provoke transference. This could provide people with an experience designed to heal rather than reopen old wounds (Messer & Warren, 1995). Alexander experimented with short-term treatment, focused on current life problems. He believed that treatment should enable people to apply what they learned to their lives outside of therapy.

Many names are associated with modern applications of BPT (Demos & Prout, 1993). In the 1960s and 1970s, notable advances in BPT were made by Habib Davanloo (intensive short-term dynamic psychotherapy) and Peter Sifneos (short-term anxiety-provoking therapy). Current leaders in development of BPT include:

- David Malan (Tavistock system of short-term dynamic psychotherapy)
- Lester Luborsky (time-limited dynamic supportive-expressive psychotherapy)
- James Mann (time-limited psychotherapy)
- Hans Strupp and Hanna Levenson (time-limited dynamic psychotherapy)
- Gerald Klerman (interpersonal psychotherapy)

We will consider the distinguishing features and contributions of some of these approaches later in the chapter, once we have reviewed the commonalities of BPT. However, the names of these approaches in themselves reflect their nature. They are brief, intensive, and active and pay considerable attention to emotions and relationships.

IMPORTANT THEORETICAL CONCEPTS

Although BPT can be "dynamic and uncovering" (Messer, 2001; Weisberg, 1993, p. 105), it differs from traditional psychoanalysis in some important ways:

- Strict criteria are employed for selection of suitable clients.
- BPT is relatively brief, with a time limit, a specific termination date, or number of sessions often fixed at the start of therapy. Treatment is rarely longer than 1 year with treatment typically taking 10–25 sessions (Demos & Prout, 1993).
- The focus is on specific intrapsychic conflicts identified early in treatment.
- Goals are established to clarify treatment priorities.
- The clinician is active and sometimes challenging, using interpretation but discouraging regression. Client and clinician sit face to face to promote interaction in a reality-based relationship that de-emphasizes transference but promotes a corrective emotional experience.
- Termination, with its issues of loss, separation, and ending, receives considerable attention.

Underlying Theory

According to BPT, emotional difficulties often result from people's inability to deal successfully with unacceptable feelings or impulses. When their ego defenses fail to mediate between their drives and the demands of external reality to suppress or modify unacceptable feelings, problematic anxiety arises. Clinicians using BPT believe that early interactions and intrapsychic experiences form enduring patterns in the mind and that these patterns show up in current difficulties, which typically reflect a repetition of early childhood issues (Strupp, 1992).

For example, a woman might find herself frequently attracted to married men who either reject her or take advantage of her. This may re-create her early relationship with her father, who was both seductive and rejecting, and her own inability to move beyond that relationship. Her ego defenses have been unsuccessful in mediating between her drive toward an intimate relationship with her father and the social unacceptability of such a relationship. Because these feelings have not been suppressed or modified in positive ways, the woman is caught in a conflict. She sabotages her efforts to find a rewarding relationship and is unhappy and frustrated about this pattern, but she is unable to alter her impulses so that she can establish a healthy relationship with an appropriate partner.

According to most BPT approaches, by strengthening the ego so that it can control self-destructive impulses, helping people gain insight and resolve conflicts, and using the therapeutic relationship to teach effective ways of relating to others, clinicians can help clients break out of their repetitive dysfunctional patterns and grow in healthy ways. Important ingredients for change include emotional release, a corrective emotional experience with the clinician, and acquisition of greater insight. As people succeed in connecting with their clinicians, expressing their emotions, and understanding themselves better, energy that has been bound up in defensive and self-protective maneuvers is now freed to enable them to move forward.

Selection of Appropriate Clients

Advocates of BPT seem to agree that their approach is suitable only for people who meet predetermined selection criteria. Davanloo (1980), for example, found that only 30 to 35% of people seeking treatment in outpatient settings were good candidates for his version of BPT. To determine whether a person is likely to benefit from BPT, a thorough initial assessment is essential. Some clinicians meet with a prospective client for an extensive history taking and evaluation that may last for up to 3 hours and make some trial interpretations before deciding whether to accept that person for treatment.

The following 10 qualities contribute to a person's suitability for BPT (Demos & Prout, 1993; Horowitz, et al., 1984; Messer & Warren, 1995):

1. Psychological-mindedness, or the ability to be introspective, report thoughts and feelings, recognize that symptoms are psychological in nature, and gain insight
2. Above-average intelligence and a capacity for new learning
3. Presentation of a circumscribed chief complaint, understandable through BPT
4. Motivation toward change and growth, not just motivation toward symptom relief
5. A history of at least one trusting, meaningful relationship in childhood
6. Capacity to form a flexible and collaborative relationship with the clinician
7. Ability to handle strong emotions and anxiety-provoking material
8. Flexible defenses, at least some of which are mature ones
9. Ability to listen to, consider, and make use of interpretations
10. Capacity to be open, honest, and curious

The Process of BPT

Messer (2001) and others identified two triads that are important areas of focus in BPT. The first, the *triangle of insights* (also known as the *impulse–defense triad*), includes current and recent relationships, past real or imagined relationships (especially parents and siblings), and the relationship with the clinician. The second, the *triangle of conflict,* includes impulses and emotions, the anxiety and guilt associated with impulses, and the defenses used to reduce anxiety that arises from impulses. Exploration of these triads, leading to insight into their nature, can promote new learning and positive changes in people's lives.

Phases of BPT

Sifneos (1979a) identified five phases of treatment that are typical of most models of BPT:

1. *Patient-therapist encounter.* Client and clinician develop rapport and build a therapeutic alliance. They identify a feasible and mutually agreeable focus of treatment, an emotional problem that is related to the client's core difficulties. The clinician begins to develop a psychodynamic formulation to explain the difficulty, generally reflected in repetitive dysfunctional relational patterns stemming from childhood. Client and clinician might prepare a written statement of goals and probable accomplishments through treatment.

2. *Early treatment.* This phase emphasizes the importance of reality in BPT. Clients' positive transference reactions are confronted to curtail regression, while clients are encouraged to distinguish magical and wishful thinking from reality.

3. *Height of treatment.* The primary thrust of this phase is to link present problems to the past. Although the past is explored in BPT, it is only examined in relation to the current focal problem. Anger and anxiety toward the clinician are common during this phase, leading to manifestations of resistance. Transference may be explored, when resistance is evident, to facilitate understanding of clients' discomfort and reduce their resistance. More commonly, the therapeutic relationship will be a source of information on dysfunctional relational patterns and a venue for trying out new ways of interaction. Clients are encouraged to make increasing use of new ways to solve problems.

4. *Evidence of change.* Clients become able to generalize and apply what they have learned through treatment. Positive changes may be noted including symptom reduction, improved problem solving, and enhanced interpersonal skills and relationships.

5. *Termination.* Initial goals have been sufficiently met for client and clinician to determine that treatment should end. Efforts are not made to expand goals or to effect significant personality change; clinicians remain aware of the limitations of treatment. Attention is paid to addressing issues of loss and separation as treatment ends. Clients are congratulated on their efforts and accomplishments, and treatment is brought to a close with clients' awareness of work they can continue on their own.

TREATMENT USING BRIEF PSYCHODYNAMIC THERAPY

Brief psychodynamic therapy is not associated with a broad range of distinctive techniques. Rather, it draws heavily on analysis, interpretation, and other strategies associated with traditional analysis. Modern practitioners of BPT also make extensive use of strategies associated with other treatment models such as cognitive therapy. However, some generalizations can be made about approaches associated with BPT.

Goals

BPT seeks to resolve presenting problems as well as promote overall growth. Specific goals typically target the resolution of a focal conflict such as independence versus dependence, activity versus passivity, diminished versus positive self-esteem, and unresolved versus resolved grief (Mann & Goldman, 1982). Growth-related goals include promoting understanding and change in people's inner experiences, increasing positive feelings toward the self, and facilitating application of learning so people can live their lives more successfully (Strupp, 1992). In addition, clinicians seek to give people the insight and tools they need to continue exploration of their conflicts and their interpersonal contexts in order to address them more effectively (Weisberg, 1993).

Therapeutic Alliance

Strupp (1992) said of BPT, "What may be the most therapeutic is the patient's experience of the therapist as a significant other whose feelings, attitudes, and values are *introjected*, thus effecting *corrections* of the patient's experience with significant others in his or her early life" (p. 25). Formation of a positive relationship with the clinician can help people to reexperience and handle successfully experiences they had not handled well in the past, thereby enabling them to change maladaptive patterns. The corrective experience of the therapeutic alliance can enable them to compensate for deficits in their early childhood relationships and form healthier relationships in the present. In addition, internalization of the clinicians' attitudes and behaviors toward them can help clients treat themselves more positively. A great deal of responsibility rests on the clinician in this model; consequently, personal therapy is recommended for those who practice BPT.

Although BPT acknowledges that transference and countertransference responses may need to be addressed in treatment, traditional interpretations of transference, focused on childhood attachment issues, are used sparingly. When transference and countertransference do occur, these theorists generally think of those processes in new ways. According to Levenson (2003, p. 305), ". . . transference is not considered a distortion but rather the patient's plausible perceptions of the therapist's behavior and intent, and countertransference does not indicate a failure on the part of the therapist but rather represents his or her natural reactions to the pushes and pulls from interacting with the patient." The goal of exploring transference is not insight into early childhood attachment experiences, but providing a corrective emotional experience. Rather than encouraging transference responses, clinicians "resist the pull to respond to the client's interpersonal orientation in a complementary manner, so as not to reinforce the client's rigid way of approaching relationships" (Bernier & Dozier, 2002, p. 39). Instead, clinicians actively use client behaviors and reactions to the therapist as a way to increase clients' awareness of their habitual dysfunctional relationship patterns and promote more effective relationship skills.

In addition to providing a corrective emotional experience, clinicians should also be skilled in empathic listening, caring and compassion, understanding, interpretation, confrontation, and teaching. Clinicians play an active and collaborative role in this model, developing rapport quickly to gain some influence in treatment (Koss & Butcher, 1986).

SPECIFIC MODELS OF BPT

Many names are associated with the development of BPT. Describing all varieties of BPT is beyond the scope of this chapter. However, we present expanded information on two approaches, along with brief summaries of additional important approaches to BPT. The two that are highlighted here include interpersonal psychotherapy, developed by Gerald Klerman and his associates, and time-limited dynamic psychotherapy (TLDP), developed by Hans Strupp and recently enhanced by the work of Hanna Levenson.

Klerman's Interpersonal Psychotherapy

Interpersonal Psychotherapy (IPT) is a form of brief psychodynamic therapy designed specifically for treating depression (Klerman, Weissman, Rounsaville, & Chevron, 1984). Influenced by Harry Stack Sullivan's ideas, IPT emphasizes social and interpersonal experiences. It recognizes the importance of the unconscious and of early childhood interactions but gives more attention to current relationships and patterns, social roles, and coping skills.

Research has given considerable support to IPT. In a large study conducted by the National Institutes of Mental Health, IPT was found as effective as antidepressant medication and cognitive-behavior therapy in the amelioration of depressive symptoms (Elkin et al., 1989). Several studies also indicated that IPT reduced depression in people who were HIV-positive (Levenson, Butler, & Beitman, 1997).

According to IPT, "A disrupted, unloving relationship between a child and its parent or parent substitute can increase the child's vulnerability to depression as an adult" (Levenson, Butler, & Beitman, 1997, p. 55). Once the vulnerability has been established, stressful interpersonal experiences in adulthood can lead to the onset or recurrence of depression. IPT postulates that strong social bonds reduce the likelihood of depression.

IPT is a focused, time-limited treatment approach in which client and clinician typically meet for 14 to 18 weekly sessions. Treatment focus is on "(1) interpersonal relations (social roles and interactions among people) versus object relations or intrapsychic phenomena, (2) role expectations and disputes versus internal conflicts and wishes, and (3) here-and-now transactions versus childhood or past experiences" (p. 58). Treatment seeks to both ameliorate symptoms and improve interpersonal functioning.

Treatment via IPT includes three phases:

1. *Initial sessions* —Treatment objectives of phase 1 include assessment of symptoms and identification of one or two interpersonal difficulties linked to the symptoms such as grief, interpersonal conflicts, role transitions, or interpersonal deficits. In addition, clinicians explain IPT and help clients recognize that their symptoms represent a disorder which can be ameliorated through treatment.
2. *Intermediate phase* —Focus of this phase is on the problem or interpersonal difficulty identified in phase 1. Goals are established and strategies are used to achieve those goals. IPT encourages use of a variety of strategies including support, questions to elicit emotion and content, interpretation, identification of patterns, advice giving, education, clarification, feedback on communication, teaching of decision-making skills, behavior-change techniques, role playing, and use of the therapeutic relationship. Although clinicians play an active role, clients are encouraged to take as much responsibility as possible for their treatment.
3. *Termination phase* —Termination is planned and carefully processed, beginning at least two to four sessions before the conclusion of treatment. Client's feelings of anger, sadness, loss, and grief are accepted and discussed. Clinicians give clients the message that they are now capable of handling these feelings and moving ahead in their lives.

Common concerns that benefit from treatment via IPT include depression (particularly when it occurs in conjunction with medical conditions), abnormal grief, conflicts in interpersonal roles and relationships, role transitions such as divorce and parenthood, and interpersonal skill deficits.

Time-Limited Dynamic Psychotherapy

Hans Strupp, working with his colleagues at Vanderbilt University, drew heavily on both object relations theory and the work of Harry Stack Sullivan in formulating time-limited dynamic psychotherapy (TLDP). Recent writings by Hanna Levenson (2003) expanded upon and clarified the nature of TLDP. According to Levenson (2003, p. 301), "TLDP is an interpersonal, time-sensitive approach for patients with chronic, pervasive, dysfunctional ways of relating to others." These clients typically have personality disorders, reflecting patterns of dependency, negativism, or externalization of blame, along with long-standing interpersonal difficulties. Research on the use of

TLDP to treat people diagnosed with personality disorders indicated that 60% achieved positive outcomes after an average of 14 sessions.

The primary goal of TLDP is to change patterns of interpersonal interactions that probably stem from childhood relationships with caregivers. The therapeutic relationship is the primary vehicle for change. According to TLDP, clients interact with their clinicians in the same ways they have interacted with others throughout their lives. By identifying these persistent and problematic ways of relating and helping clients develop both understanding and new ways of interacting through the corrective emotional experience of the therapeutic alliance, clinicians help people improve their relationships (Najavits & Strupp, 1994; Strupp, 1992).

Initially, treatment concentrates on present relationship patterns, but it shifts to exploring early origins of difficulties once current patterns have been identified and understood (Levenson, Butler, & Beitman, 1997, p. 84). Once these have been clarified, clinicians help their clients to understand that, although their patterns of relating may have been adaptive at one time, they are no longer helpful to them. This paves the way for revision in interpersonal patterns, as well as development of new skills.

The role of the clinician is exploratory and positive. Strupp and his associates found that the quality of the therapeutic alliance in this approach is strongly related to outcome; therapists who are perceived as warm, affirming, and protective of their clients have more positive outcomes.

Other Models of BPT

• *Davanloo's Intensive Short-Term Dynamic Psychotherapy* Davanloo's approach to BPT, an early model, is closest to traditional psychoanalysis (Davanloo, 1979, 1980). His version of BPT emphasizes interpretation of drives and defenses. Davanloo uses active techniques to elicit underlying thoughts and feelings and reveal the unconscious and the triangle of insights.

• *Luborsky's Time-Limited Dynamic Supportive-Expressive Psychotherapy* Luborsky and his colleagues (Luborsky, 1984; Messer & Warren, 1995) focus on the conflict between people's interpersonal wishes and their fears of expected outcomes, leading to the identification of a *core conflictual relationship theme* (CCRT). The CCRT reflects habitual and problematic ways in which people view and interact with others. This approach is supportive; interpretations are delivered only when people seem ready to hear and understand them, and symptoms are viewed as efforts to cope and solve problems.

• *Malan's Tavistock System of Short-Term Dynamic Psychotherapy* Malan's approach, too, is characterized by the identification of a central focus. He views the transference-parent link as important in providing information and treatment direction (Demos & Prout, 1993).

• *Mann's Time-Limited Psychotherapy* Mann's approach resembles object relations theory and self psychology (Demos & Prout, 1993). Treatment emphasizes the connection between early separation issues and present concerns. Goals include improvement of self-esteem and self-reliance. Support and empathy to enhance self-esteem are important in this 12-session model.

• *Sifneos's Short-Term Anxiety-Provoking Therapy* Sifneos focused on treating people with a wide range of anxiety disorders, interpersonal problems, and physical problems with an emotional cause (Sifneos, 1979b, 1984). People with unresolved issues of early separation and loss seem to respond especially well to this model. A written agreement, including a hypothesis about the nature of the client's difficulties as well as outcome criteria, is used to guide treatment. Sifneos's treatment involves intense and direct interpretations that can initially raise anxiety, hence the name of this approach. Education about emotional difficulties and their resolution is also an important treatment component.

APPLICATION OF BRIEF PSYCHODYNAMIC THERAPY

Brief psychodynamic therapy is a major approach to treatment that is in widespread use in one form or another. BPT has many strengths. It is a flexible approach, which is active and optimistic (Levenson, 2003). It encourages integration of treatment strategies from other theoretical perspectives. It is a brief and efficient treatment approach, meeting both client needs for rapid symptom relief and the requirements of managed care. Much is known about its use in treating various mental disorders but knowledge about its multicultural application still is limited.

Application to Diagnostic Groups

BPT is a sound treatment approach for many disorders of moderate severity. Research has substantiated its value in treating depressive disorders, personality disorders, trauma-related disorders, grief, substance use disorders, physical complaints of psychological origin, and others. Of course, not all approaches to BPT are effective in treating all of these disorders. Matching of client to type of BPT should increase the likelihood of effective treatments. Time-limited dynamic psychotherapy, for example, is directed particularly at people with chronic and pervasive interpersonal difficulties while interpersonal psychotherapy is especially effective in treatment of depression.

BPT is not suitable for all people or all disorders. According to Messer (2001, p. 9), "Contraindications include serious suicide attempts or potential; a history of alcohol or other drug addiction; severe depression; poor impulse control; incapacitating, chronic obsessional or phobic symptoms; some psychosomatic conditions such as ulcerative colitis; and poor reality testing. Used alone, BPT usually is not the best approach for people with psychotic disorders, bipolar disorders, and severe personality and substance use disorders. However, BPT is a flexible approach. Combined with medication and other treatment approaches such as cognitive therapy, it may well have a place in treatment even for these disorders.

Application to Multicultural Groups

BPT is currently being used with people of all ages. The literature has described its effective use with children, adolescents, elderly people, and other adults (Messer, 2001).

Research has begun to investigate its usefulness with culturally diverse clients. One study of Asian American students (Wong, Kim, Zane, Kim, & Huang, 2003), for example, found that those with low White identity and strong independent self-concepts found cognitive therapy more credible than BPT. Cultural variables, as well as self-image, then, seem to play a role in people's acceptance of BPT.

Whether BPT is appropriate for people from non-western cultures is an unanswered question. Some will be uncomfortable with the probing, interpretation, and exploration of early childhood issues that are part of most versions of BPT. However, because clinicians who practice BPT typically also emphasize empathy, support, and the importance of the clinician-client relationship, BPT is likely to appeal to a wide range of clients. In addition, although BPT does not say much about the importance of culture, its emphasis on relationships and on problem solving enables practitioners to incorporate into treatment attention to cultural context as well as family. More research is needed on the use of BPT with a culturally diverse population.

Overall Application

Clinicians should keep in mind the selection criteria listed previously in this chapter when deciding whether to use BPT with a client. Particularly suitable for BPT are people who are intelligent, insightful, interested in increasing their self-awareness, and open to change. Good candidates for BPT also have mature defenses, a focal complaint that is central to their concerns, and a history of at least one close, positive relationship (Horowitz et al., 1984). In other words, people who are relatively healthy and well functioning seem to respond particularly well to this approach.

EVALUATION OF BPT

BPT is a treatment approach that is growing in importance through both practice and research. It has many strengths as well as some limitations.

Limitations of BPT

Some concerns and criticisms have been voiced about BPT. BPTs sometimes confrontational and authoritarian nature and its emphasis on early childhood issues can elicit anger, dependency, and even regression. Its short-term nature can result in a superficial sort of treatment that ameliorates symptoms but does not sufficiently address underlying concerns. In addition, the research of Najavits and Strupp (1994) suggests that the quality of the clinician-client relationship and the interpersonal qualities of the clinician may be at least as important in BPT as specific concepts and interventions.

Levenson and Strupp (1999) found that training usually provided on BPT does not seem to be adequate. They observed that therapists often have difficulty grasping the brief therapy paradigm that requires setting specific and circumscribed goals, adhering to the focal concern, and quickly developing a therapeutic alliance. Levenson and Strupp recommend increased training opportunities, including the use of videotapes to provide models and facilitate feedback, the use of treatment manuals, and attention to clinicians' conceptions of treatment.

Risks also are inherent in the process of interpretation as used in BPT. Hoglend (2003) found infrequent use of transference interpretation was more effective than extensive use of these interpretations and that accuracy of interpretation also was positively associated with treatment outcome (Messer, 2001).

Strengths and Contributions of BPT

Theorists who developed BPT have made an important contribution through their efforts to build on the strengths of Freudian psychoanalysis and enhance that model through approaches that make it more efficient, more acceptable to many people, and more compatible with modern counseling and psychotherapy's emphasis on brief treatment and on relationships. One of the greatest contributions of BPT is the strong commitment of its proponents to research in order to improve and determine the value of this approach.

Numerous studies have been conducted on various approaches to BPT (Levenson, Butler, & Beitman, 1997), with many of them substantiating its value (Demos & Prout, 1993). APA's Division 12 Task Force on empirically validated therapies lists BPT as "probably efficacious" in the treatment of opiate dependency, bulimia, and depression (Messer, 2001). Malan's approach to BPT has been found as effective as long-term psychoanalysis in the treatment of anxiety, depression, and mild to moderate personality problems. An NIMH study demonstrating the effectiveness of interpersonal psychotherapy in treating depression seems to have contributed greatly to the use and importance of this model. Crits-Christoph (1992) conducted a meta-analysis of 11 studies of BPT that lasted at least 12 sessions. That review found that people treated with BPT showed considerable reduction in symptoms compared to people on a waiting list for treatment. This finding applied to people with a broad range of difficulties.

According to Weisberg (1993), BPT works as well as conventional/classical psychoanalytic therapy; saves time and money; and is more suitable for people in crisis as well as for people with interpersonal problems, career concerns, difficult decisions, and disorders of mood and anxiety. As Messer and Warren (1995) state, we have "good evidence for the efficacy of BPT" (p. 103).

The development of BPT continues. Research is ongoing to provide further information on the effective therapeutic ingredients of this model and the conditions under which BPT is most likely to be helpful. In addition, specific approaches to BPT are being developed and refined to treat specific groups of disorders. Tailoring the application of this rich and flexible approach should enhance its value and application even further over time. BPT promises to be one of the important treatment approaches of the 21st century.

SKILL DEVELOPMENT: IDENTIFYING A FOCAL CONCERN

Identifying a focal concern is important in BPT. This strategy also can improve effectiveness and clarify the direction of other approaches to treatment. The focal issue in BPT usually reflects dysfunctional interpersonal interactions and patterns that occur repeatedly in a person's life. These patterns are often linked to early childhood experiences, especially formative aspects of people's lives such as their early childhood attachment to and separation from their primary caregivers.

Whether or not clinicians seek an early childhood origin for focal concerns, analysis of present interactions can provide understanding of the dysfunctional patterns these concerns perpetuate. Luborsky and Mark (1991) sought to identify what they called the core conflictual relationship theme (CCRT), their version of the focal concern, by listening for patterns in three key areas: "the patient's wishes from the other person, the other person's actual or expected responses, and how the patient responds" (p. 119). By eliciting examples of relationship difficulties and examining these three areas for similarities, clinicians can make a tentative formulation about the nature of people's focal interpersonal concerns. This can be shared with clients, modified if necessary, and written down as a statement of the focus of treatment.

The following example illustrates the identification of a focal concern or CCRT for Julie, a divorced woman with a 5-year-old son named Danny. Julie sought counseling for interpersonal problems, especially in relationships with her parents, her ex-husband, and her boyfriend. Julie complained that these people did not really seem to care about her and treated her unfairly. When she was asked for examples of her relationship difficulties, Julie produced the following, with accompanying analysis according to the three key areas identified by Luborsky and Mark:

1. *Example 1: Asking my parents for financial help*
   - *What I wish for from the other person:* I had worked up a detailed budget of my monthly expenses. It took me a long time to do that. It clearly showed that I needed at least $1,000 more a month. I wanted my parents to provide that.
   - *The actual or expected response:* Although I thought my parents would make up the difference between what I got from my ex and what my expenses were, instead they said I should get a part-time job. All they agreed to do is pay for after-school child care and gas for my car until I found a job.
   - *My reaction:* I feel really hurt and angry. I don't know if I can manage a job and a child. My parents don't understand how hard it is to be a single parent, and they don't seem to care. They had it easy. They always had each other and never had to struggle like this. If I didn't need them to baby-sit so I could take a break every once in a while, I wouldn't even let them see Danny. Then they would feel sorry.
2. *Example 2: Telling Danny to clean up his room before bedtime*
   - *What I wish for from the other person:* I think he should just do it. You know that T-shirt that says, "Because I'm the mom." Well, that's what I want. I tell him to clean up his room, and he should do it.
   - *The actual or expected response:* Oh no, not Danny; he always has to give me a hard time. I think he's putting things away; and then as soon as I leave his room to make a phone call or something, he's playing with his toys.
   - *My reaction:* Who does he think I am? His slave? I've sacrificed a lot for that kid, and the least he can do is obey me. So I yelled at him and gave him a time out.
3. *Example 3: Learning that before the divorce my husband loaned his brother some money without discussing it with me*
   - *What I wish for from the other person:* I said to my husband, "Where are your priorities? Your own family needs money, and you lend it to your brother so he can start another business that will fail." I wanted him to see he had made a mistake and that he should try to get the money back.
   - *The actual or expected response:* Well, I didn't know if he would really ask for the money back, but at the very least I thought he would see he was wrong and promise not to do it again. No way! He just said, "I didn't tell you because I knew what you would say, and I really wanted to help my brother."
   - *My reaction:* I knew what really happened. He wanted his parents to think he was so great. He was more concerned with pleasing them than with helping us. I was really mad, so I took some money out of the checking account and bought an expensive dress. Then when he asked me about it, I said, "You think you can do whatever you want with our money. Well, so can I."

Although more information should be obtained to conclusively establish the presence of patterns, these three examples provide enough information to allow the development of a hypothesis about Julie's focal conflict or CCRT. These examples suggest that, on one level, Julie views herself as special and deserving of treatment that reflects her specialness. When people do not treat her as special, particularly when she asks for something and is refused, she becomes angry and even punitive. Conflict arises because, under the surface, she seems to have considerable self-doubt. She questions her ability to be both a parent and an employee, perceives her husband as valuing his parents' opinions more than hers, and even feels powerless in her role as mother. Behind her unrealistic demands and expectations is a woman who needs others to reassure her of her importance. Not surprisingly, as a young child, Julie apparently received little affirmation and affection from her parents. The primary way in which she got attention was by throwing a temper tantrum, paralleling her current behavior. In addition, Julie's transference relationship with her clinician reflected her need for special treatment to counteract her doubts. She requested telephone conversations between sessions as well as reduced fees.

Analysis of Julie's CCRT and the similarities in the triad of her current relationships, her past relationships, and her transference to the clinician all shed light on patterns related to her focal relationship concern. Once these patterns have been understood and worked through, Julie might be able to make changes that will improve her relationships and help her feel better about herself.

CASE ILLUSTRATION

The following dialog between Roberto and his counselor illustrates several aspects of brief psychodynamic therapy:

- The stance of the therapist as supportive but also confrontational, analytical, and educational
- The clinician's efforts to identify a focal conflict reflecting dysfunctional relationship patterns
- Recognition of commonalities among Roberto's past relationships, his present relationships, and his relationship with the clinician

Clinician: Roberto, you look very upset.

Roberto: Yes, I am. Edie and I had another one of those fights. I give her everything she wants. . . . I don't know what more I can do.

Clinician: Tell me about what happened.

Roberto: We were having a birthday party for Ava. Edie's family and my family were coming for dinner, and Edie had been cooking all day. I had asked her the day before what I could do to help, and I did everything she told me. I went to the jeweler to pick up the gift Edie had ordered, I got the wine and some of the groceries, I even vacuumed the house. So that morning I sat down to read my e-mail, and next thing I know she's standing there screaming at me: "I do all the work around here. Who do you think you are? Glued to your computer as usual." Yada, yada, yada. So I said to her, "Look, just give me 15 minutes to finish this, and then I'll come down." Not good enough for her. She goes off again. So I just left before I really lost it.

Clinician: Sounds like you felt angry that she expected you to do even more than you had already done and wouldn't give you a few minutes for yourself.

Roberto: Yeah, e-mail is part of my work. If I don't take care of that, no job, no money.

Clinician: So Edie's behavior doesn't make sense to you. This reminds me of our discussion of how much your mother expected of you and how unreasonable it seemed.

Roberto: Yeah, I can see that. I would be trying to get my homework done and the younger kids would be screaming, and she'd say, "Roberto, would you feed the baby and then take your brothers out to play so I can get something done around here?" What about me? When was I going to get my homework done? Yeah, I didn't like that either, but I just did it.

Clinician: So in both cases, you were doing a lot to help a woman, but it felt like there was no time for your needs.

Roberto: Yeah, I'm always supposed to be the strong one. Roberto, fix this, do that, pay this bill. And I do it. But when is it my turn?

Clinician: Yet in a way, it must feel good to be the strong one. I wonder if you might give people the message that you can handle anything because you enjoy having them see you as very capable?

Roberto: I guess so. It's like I'm strong and they're weak and they really need me. But then it gets to be too much.

Clinician: Perhaps we saw a similar pattern in our work together. A couple of times when the phone rang here, you said, "Go ahead, doc, get the phone. It's okay." And when I was sick for a few weeks and had to cancel our sessions and I asked you how you felt about it, you said that it was fine; but I noticed that you seemed irritated and less open in the next few sessions. It seems hard for you to acknowledge that you have any needs, but you do; and they can build up and come out in ways that hurt you and other people.

Roberto: Well, everybody has needs, but I've always been able to take care of myself.

Clinician: Yes, you have been very self-sufficient and take great pride in that. But maybe sometimes your need to be strong backfires and hurts you and those you care about.

Roberto: That could be right, but I don't want to turn into a wimp. I like who I am. Are you telling me to be different?

Clinician: I'm certainly not telling you to be a wimp! I don't think you could do that if you tried. But, you know, sometimes part of being strong is recognizing that we can't do everything ourselves and letting other people know what we need.

Roberto: That's a new way to think about things. How could I have handled the problems around Ava's party differently?

At this point in the session, Roberto has gained insight into patterns that have shown up in old relationships, current relationships, and his relationship with his clinician. He has information to help him view his need to be strong in a different light. He is now ready to explore these patterns further and to consider ways to make some shifts that allow him to maintain his image of himself as a strong caretaker but also will help him articulate his own needs appropriately. Accomplishing this should lead to more mutuality in his relationships and enable him to avoid the anger and frustration he experiences when his needs are ignored for too long.

EXERCISES

Large-Group Exercises

1. Discuss and list the differences and similarities between traditional psychoanalysis and brief psychodynamic therapy. Then select five participants to represent the traditional model and five to represent BPT. Have the two groups engage in a debate of the question, "Which of these two approaches has more to offer today's clinicians?"

2. Conduct a group interview of Edie. One participant should assume the role of Edie and should sit or stand in front of the class. Each student should then have the opportunity to ask Edie one or two questions. The goal of the interview should be an identification of Edie's focal conflict or CCRT. After the round-robin interview has been completed, analyze the information elicited from Edie, focusing on the following:
   - The *triangle of insights* (*impulse-defense triad*), including current and recent relationships, past real or imagined relationships, and the transference relationship
   - The *triangle of conflict,* including the aim or impulse, the injunction or threat that makes the aim dangerous or unacceptable, and the defense used to reduce the anxiety arising from the impulse
   - The *focal conflict*

3. Consider the criteria described in this chapter that indicate whether a person is likely to be a good candidate for BPT. Apply them to Edie to determine whether she would be appropriate for treatment via this model.

Small-Group Exercises

Divide into your groups composed of two dyads. Role-play a 15–20 minute interview designed to identify your partner's focal conflict or issue. At the end of each role-play, all four participants should engage in identifying the repeated patterns that emerged and defining the focal issue. Take time to provide feedback to the interviewers about the following:

- Ability to elicit a focal conflict
- Interactions between client and clinician
- Use of open questions and other intervention strategies
- Strengths of the role play and suggestions for improvement

Individual Exercises

1. In this chapter, you learned to identify a core conflictual relationship theme (CCRT). Identify and list three important interactions you have had with others, at least one of which occurred at least five years ago. Next, examine the patterns used in the "Skill Development" section's example of Julie. Analyze your interactions in a similar way. For each, consider the following:
   - What you wish for from the other person
   - The actual or expected response
   - Your reaction

   Now try to identify common patterns among these three areas and develop a written hypothesis about the nature of your CCRT.

2. Brief, time-limited treatment has elicited much debate among mental health professionals. If you were to enter counseling, would you prefer open-ended, extended treatment or brief, time-limited treatment? Write about what you think your treatment would be like in each case, highlighting benefits and limitations you would expect with each type.

SUMMARY

Brief psychodynamic therapy, derived from traditional Freudian psychoanalysis, grew out of the work of Alexander, Ferenczi, and others, who found that length and depth of analysis were not clearly correlated with amount and stability of gains (Horowitz et al., 1984). BPT is typically much shorter than traditional analysis, often has a fixed time limit, and centers on a focal concern or core relationship pattern that is linked to the person's symptoms. While clinicians practicing BPT assume that early childhood experiences, especially attachment to and separation from caregivers, are related to current relationship issues and do pay attention to transference, their primary focus is on the therapeutic alliance, present relationships, and ways to help people lead more rewarding lives. Goals are clear and circumscribed; clinicians are active and flexible; and strategies are designed not only to promote insight but also to elicit feelings, promote new learning, and change behavior. Research supports the value of this approach in treating a broad range of mild to moderately severe difficulties, notably depression.

RECOMMENDED READINGS

Demos, V. C., & Prout, M. F. (1993). A comparison of seven approaches to brief psychotherapy. *International Journal of Short-Term Psychotherapy, 8,* 3–22.

Klerman, G. L., Weissman, M. M., Rounsaville, B. J., & Chevron, E. S. (1984). *Interpersonal psychotherapy of depression.* New York: Basic Books.

Levenson, H., Butler, S. F., & Beitman, B. D. (1997). *Concise guide to brief dynamic psychotherapy.* Washington, DC: American Psychiatric Press.

Messer, S. B. (2001). What makes brief psychodynamic therapy time efficient. *Clinical Psychology: Science & Practice, 8,* 5–22.

Messer, S. B., & Warren, S. (1995). *Models of brief psychodynamic therapy.* New York: Guilford.

ADDITIONAL SOURCES OF INFORMATION

http://www.guidetopsychology.com/brieftx.htm—This website provides information on and case examples of BPT.

http://www.geocities.com/~nwidp/course/assbrief.htm—This website provides an introduction to BPT.

Levenson Institute for Training in Brief Therapy, 2323 Sacramento Street, San Francisco, CA 94115, (510) 547-1245.

Part Three

Treatment Systems Emphasizing Emotions and Sensations

CHAPTER 9

Overview of Emotion-Focused Treatment Systems

Part 3 of this book focuses on treatment approaches that emphasize emotions. This introductory chapter provides an overview of emotions and their characteristics. In addition, the information, examples, and exercises in this chapter introduce you to some of the skills that are essential in helping clinicians identify and understand emotions as well as promote their clients' emotional well-being and ability to manage their emotions.

"How are you?" Most of us hear this question many times each day—when we arrive at work, when we see our friends at school, when we answer the telephone, when we return home, and at many points in between. People all around us ask about our feelings. We don't always answer this question honestly; we may simply participate in a ritual and respond, "I'm fine. How are you?" However, sometimes we give an honest answer, at least to ourselves, and talk and think about our feelings.

We express our feelings, either intentionally or inadvertently, many times a day; and many more times a day we have feelings that we do not disclose. Our emotions are an essential part of who we are. Expressions of emotion can bring people closer or drive them apart; they contribute to our professional success and can be part of the reason we fail at a job. Emotions such as guilt, hopelessness, and anxiety can be symptoms of mental disorders, while those such as joy, pride, and love may reflect our mental health.

Although troubling emotions often lead people to seek help, clinicians differ on the importance of dealing with feelings in treatment, just as they disagree on the importance of dealing with past experiences (discussed in part 2). Some clinicians and theorists believe that helping people identify, express, understand, and manage their emotions and sensations is the key to successful treatment, while others believe that emotions are governed by thoughts and that treatment will be most productive if clinicians de-emphasize feelings and focus on cognitions. Whether you believe thoughts produce feelings or feelings produce thoughts, emotions play an important part in treatment.

In part 1 you learned about the BETA model, which reflects the four important areas of focus in counseling and psychotherapy (background, emotions, thoughts, actions) and provides the structure of this book. Part 2 focused on treatment approaches that emphasize the importance of background. Although those approaches do not ignore clients' emotions, they are viewed primarily as a route to identifying longstanding patterns stemming from early attachments.

Treatment systems presented in part 3 not only pay particular attention to emotions and sensations but also are experiential; they view as important what people have observed, encountered, and experienced. These approaches are phenomenological because of the importance they ascribe to how people view themselves and their world.

Carl Rogers, more than anyone else, made emotions an important focus of treatment; we consider his theory, person-centered counseling, in chapter 10. Chapter 11 focuses on existentialism. At least as much philosophy as psychotherapy, this approach, developed by Viktor Frankl, Rollo May, and others, emphasizes the importance of feeling that our lives are meaningful and that we have a purpose. We consider Fritz Perls's approach, Gestalt therapy, in chapter 12, along with information on its integration with transactional analysis. Gestalt therapy pays particular attention to physical sensations and the messages they give. Chapter 13 introduces narrative therapy, constructivist therapy, feminist therapy, and transpersonal psychotherapy. These treatment approaches are relatively new but already are having a significant impact. Familiarizing ourselves with these emerging approaches enriches our work as clinicians, helps us deal more productively with our clients' feelings, and contributes to our understanding of new directions in counseling and psychotherapy.

DIMENSIONS OF EMOTIONS AND SENSATIONS

Feelings take many forms. They can be experienced primarily as *emotions,* as *physical sensations,* or, most often, as a combination of the two. Examples of emotions include sadness, apprehension, grief, anger, and discouragement. Examples of physical sensations include queasiness, headaches, muscle tension, and chills. Physical and emotional feelings often go together. For example, when we feel sad, we sometimes lose our appetite, feel tired and heavy, and have no sexual desire. When we feel happy, we may feel buoyant, relaxed, and alert.

Feelings can be *overt or covert* or a combination of the two. Overt feelings are evident to other people through either words or nonverbal clues. For example, a person can express anger by saying, "You make me really mad when you do that," or by scowling, shouting, or making an obscene gesture. Covert feelings are concealed. Sometimes when we attend a social event or go into a situation such as a dissertation defense where we believe others will judge us, we experience anxiety and tension. However, we often hide those feelings so we can make a positive impression. Fear of rejection and disapproval, shame about our feelings, and lack of awareness of our emotions may lead us to conceal or even deny our feelings.

Feelings may be both overt and covert—for example, when we share only a part of our feelings. Before a final examination begins, nearly everyone feels apprehension and anxiety. However, some students conceal the enormity of their feelings so that they do not seem more fearful than most of the others.

Feelings can be *positive, negative, or neutral*. Some emotions such as affection, happiness, and amusement usually are positive. Others such as worry, rage, and disappointment generally are negative. Still others such as curiosity and sleepiness may be neutral. Of course, this categorization often is more complex. Emotions may be experienced differently by different people. For example, George enjoyed feeling rage; it gave him a sense of power and control, and he liked to intimidate others. Sharon, on the other hand, viewed anger as a negative emotion; she had been brought up to be self-effacing and was afraid that people would disapprove if she expressed even mild annoyance. Emotions may also be both positive and negative. For example, Karen disliked the sadness and lethargy she felt when she was depressed, but she did enjoy the attention she received.

Intensity of emotions varies greatly depending on the person and the circumstances. Our anger may be mild when someone takes a parking spot that was justifiably ours but intense when we discover that our home has been burglarized. Be sure to consider intensity when assessing people's feelings. Emotions themselves may be appropriate, yet their intensity can cause misunderstandings and relationship difficulties.

People may be *aware or unaware* of their emotions and sensations. For example, Fred felt envious of Charleton, his supervisor, but had difficulty recognizing those feelings and admitting them to himself. However, Fred spoke negatively of Charleton to others, avoided working late, and fabricated excuses to miss meetings with his supervisor. Charleton sensed Fred's displeasure and tried to discuss it, but the conversation was not productive. Fred received a satisfactory performance evaluation but was not recommended for a promotion; his lack of understanding of the reasons for this contributed further to his resentment toward Charleton.

Emotions that, like Fred's, are evident to others and guide our behaviors and reactions but are largely out of our awareness are especially challenging in treatment. Such emotions may not emerge or be available for discussion until a strong therapeutic alliance has been established. Clinicians who hurry clients' awareness of their emotions may alienate the clients and inhibit successful treatment.

Appropriateness of feelings is another important dimension, affecting how we are perceived by others and our relationships with them. A wedding, for example, provides a context that can elicit a variety of emotions, both appropriate and inappropriate. The nostalgic tears of the mother of the bride, the pride of her father, the love of the groom, the joy of the bride, the shared happiness of the wedding party, and the pleasure, perhaps coupled with some mild envy, experienced by some of the guests are all classic and appropriate emotions. Inappropriate emotions such as the groom's obvious anger at the cost of the wedding, the noisy grieving of the bride's former suitor, or the rudeness of the servers are particularly intrusive because of the context of the wedding. Contexts, as well as precipitants for emotions, determine the appropriateness and impact of the emotions.

Congruence is another variable to consider. When feelings are expressed congruently, verbal and nonverbal clues to emotions all give the same message. A person expressing words of love will speak softly, maintain good eye contact, and have an open and welcoming posture. However, if that person verbalizes love but has poor eye contact, an angry tone of voice, or a tense and closed posture, conflicting and confusing emotions are communicated. The receiver may not know what to believe, only pay attention to part of the message, misinterpret the message, or discredit the message because of its delivery. People sometimes unknowingly sabotage their efforts to communicate with others by giving mixed and confusing messages. Self-observation and feedback can help people to increase the congruence, clarity, and impact of their emotional messages.

Finally, emotions may *help or hurt* people, depending on the variables we have discussed. Expressing emotions can enhance our lives and our relationships, move us toward achievement of our goals, and increase pleasure in our lives. Expressing emotions can also do harm and can contribute to failed relationships, physical symptoms, unsatisfying careers, and unrewarding and unsuccessful lives. When assessing emotions, our own as well as those of our clients, family, friends, and associates, consider the eight dimensions of expression of feelings:

1. Primarily emotional, physical, or a combination
2. Overt, covert, or a combination
3. Positive, negative, or neutral
4. In or out of awareness
5. Level of intensity
6. Appropriateness for context and stimulus
7. Congruence
8. Helpful or harmful

Awareness of these dimensions can help us to better understand the nature and impact of feelings and to find ways to modify unhelpful emotions.

MULTICULTURAL FACTORS AND EMOTIONS

Clinicians seeking to understand clients' emotions need to keep multicultural factors in mind. Research demonstrates that cultural background, gender, and age all affect the nature and intensity of people's experienced and expressed emotions.

Gender and Emotions

In a study of sex roles, Jakupcak, Salters, Gratz, and Roemer (2003) found that gender differences in intensity of affect and recognition of others' emotions are consistent with gender stereotypes. Although men and women may experience similar emotional reactions to events, women express emotions more strongly and freely. Women are more attuned to emotions in others, especially the meaning of their facial expressions. Men are more fearful than women of expressing emotions, particularly anger, positive emotions, and sadness. This pattern is particularly prominent in men with traditional views of masculinity. Men's avoidance of strong emotions may well be related to an overall fear of being out of control, seeming weak, and losing composure. Of course, considerable variability exists in how men and women express emotions.

Content of emotions also is linked to gender (MacGeorge, 2003). Men are more likely than women to follow an "ethic of justice," emphasizing blame and responsibility in their reactions to themselves and others. Women, on the other hand, maintain an "ethic of care" and are more likely than men to seek help for being victimized and mistreated.

Hutson-Comeaux and Kelly (2002) found that people react differently to the same emotions in men and women, depending on whether those emotions are gender-consistent. Strong emotional reactions that conform to gender stereotypes, such as happiness in women and anger in men, are viewed as less sincere than emotions that are counter to type (e.g., happiness in men and anger in women). Clinicians should monitor their own reactions for such instances of gender bias.

Age and Emotions

Both generational and age differences affect expression of emotion, with research disputing the idea that depression increases with age. Charles, Mather, and Carstensen (2003, p. 310) concluded, "Currently a growing number of empirical studies have revealed an age-related pattern better characterized by relatively positive emotional experience and improved emotional control." This seems related to the tendency for people to "place increasingly more value on emotionally meaningful goals." Older adults report experiencing less anxiety and depression, more contentment, and shorter periods of negative mood than younger adults do. Older adults also recall relatively more positive information than do younger adults.

Generational differences suggest that younger men and women have patterns of emotional expression that differ from those of their elders. For example, younger men tend to have more androgynous gender roles, probably associated with greater facility in emotional expression.

Culture and Emotions

Culture is yet another variable that has an impact on emotional experiences and expression. Mesquita and Walder (2002, p. 789), for example, observed that, "In order to judge an excess or deficit in emotion, one needs to be aware of the 'normal amount' of emotion . . . Thus cross-cultural assessment of emotional disturbances requires the consideration of standard—i.e. modal and normative—emotion practices." In addition, emotions that are compatible with a cultural model are more likely to be activated while those that are not well accepted in the culture are less likely to be experienced. For example, American culture values happiness and includes an abundance of awards, celebrations, and expressions of praise designed to evoke pleasure. Anger and disapproval are other emotions that are congruent with American culture. On the other hand, in Japanese and other cultures that devalue anger and encourage maintenance of relationships, self-blame is a more common emotion. Knowledge of cultural models and values helps clinicians distinguish between unhealthy emotions and those that may seem dysfunctional in American culture but are compatible with a person's culture of origin.

THE IMPORTANCE OF EMOTIONS IN COUNSELING AND PSYCHOTHERAPY

The most common disorders treated in both inpatient and outpatient mental health settings are mood disorders, primarily those characterized by depression. People typically seek treatment because they have feelings that are uncomfortable, painful, or confusing and they want clinicians to help them feel better. Emotions, then, are usually what motivates people to seek help. Even in their initial telephone call to schedule an appointment, people will explain, "I feel so bad. I'm thinking about killing myself," or "I worry all the time," or "My husband says I need to stop being so angry," or "My stomach hurts, and the physicians can't find anything wrong with me. Can counseling help?"

Even when people's presenting concerns focus on actual or anticipated events, feelings typically underlie those experiences. For example, the woman who says, "My boss is threatening to fire me if I don't shape up," is probably thinking, "I'm terrified that I will lose my job, but I'm also furious at my supervisor." The man who asks, "How can I get my wife off my back about my drinking? I've got it under control," may be feeling angry at his wife and ashamed of his drinking. The teenager who complains, "My parents are from Korea and don't understand what it's like to be a young person in America," may feel caught between his longing for peer acceptance and his love and respect for his parents.

Because emotions typically lead people into treatment, clinicians' recognition and acknowledgment of those feelings can engender hope and optimism in clients, even in the first few minutes of treatment. Consider the following two openings:

Example 1

Client: I called for an appointment because I've been feeling very depressed and discouraged. Nothing seems to be going right.

Clinician: What specifically led you to make an appointment at this time?

Example 2

Client: I called for an appointment because I've been feeling very depressed and discouraged. Nothing seems to be going right.

Clinician: Sounds like you're feeling pretty hopeless. I wonder what specifically led you to make an appointment now?

Even though both clinicians ask the same exploratory question, the second clinician shows empathy and acknowledges the person's feelings. The second clinician's use of the word "hopeless" will probably lead the client to reflect further on his or her feelings and perhaps understand them better. The first clinician, on the other hand, sounds very businesslike and, by failing to attend to emotions, may seem uncaring and disinterested.

Recognizing and dealing productively with feelings in treatment can accomplish the following goals:

- Clients feel heard and understood.
- Clinicians build rapport and join with their clients in a collaborative relationship focused on helping the clients.
- Clients who believe that their clinicians hear and understand them are more likely to have confidence in those clinicians and to feel optimistic that treatment can help them. This, in turn, enhances the therapeutic alliance, perhaps the most important ingredient in effective treatment. (More information on this is provided in chapter 2.)
- Clinicians who attend to their clients' emotions and sensations are likely to feel more caring toward them; to know, as fully as possible, the pain and unhappiness that the clients are experiencing; and to appreciate them as unique human beings.
- By assessing the nature and intensity of people's feelings, clinicians can formulate specific treatment goals and interventions and can measure progress.

- Many people not only experience painful emotions but also berate themselves for having those feelings. Discovering that their feelings are normal and understandable can be very reassuring.
- Promoting clients' expression and understanding of painful feelings can enable them to change the antecedents, the personal meaning, the nature, and the expression of those feelings, leading to relief of symptoms.

SKILL DEVELOPMENT: ANALYZING AND RESPONDING TO EMOTIONS

Many skills are useful in helping clinicians analyze and respond effectively to their clients' emotions. Three of these skills are presented here, selected because they are interrelated and because they provide clinicians a solid basis for beginning to grasp and respond in helpful ways to clients' emotions:

- Analysis of the nature and dimensions of emotions
- Reflection of feeling and meaning
- Communication of empathy

Analysis of Emotions

Previously, we discussed the following eight dimensions of emotions:

1. Primarily emotional, physical, or a combination
2. Overt, covert, or a combination
3. Positive, negative, or neutral
4. In or out of awareness
5. Level of intensity
6. Appropriateness to context and stimulus
7. Congruence
8. Helpful or harmful

The following example illustrates how the expression of a feeling can be analyzed according to these dimensions.

Edie: Roberto and I had another big blow-up yesterday. We were expecting his family for dinner in an hour, and I had tons more to do. I had asked him to help but, there he was, locked away in his office with his computer. I marched down to the basement, pounded on the door, threw it open, and then told him off. I was so mad that I knocked all the books and papers off his desk. I guess I got through to him because he shut off his computer right away and ran for the vacuum to help clean up the house. He really did work hard for that last hour. But somehow it didn't make me feel any better. I just felt like crying.

Nature of Edie's Feelings: Anger, Sadness

1. *Emotional, physical, or a combination.* Edie's anger is emotional (feels mad) and physical (pounds on door, yells, pushes books and papers off desk). Sadness also is both emotional and physical (feels like crying).
2. *Overt, covert, or a combination.* Anger is overt. Sadness initially is covert but then surfaces.
3. *Positive, negative, or neutral.* Both emotions are negative.
4. *In or out of awareness.* Edie is aware of both emotions but has little understanding of the sadness underlying her anger.
5. *Level of intensity.* Anger was very intense. Sadness was moderate.
6. *Appropriate to context and stimulus.* Edie's anger seems to be an overreaction to the situation and probably reflects pent-up rage related to past conflicts and disappointments. The stimulus for the sadness is unclear and needs exploration. The underlying unexpressed sadness probably contributed to the intensity of the anger.
7. *Congruence.* Although Edie's verbal and nonverbal expressions of anger were congruent, her anger and sadness seem in conflict and confuse her.
8. *Helpful or harmful.* Although Edie succeeded in getting Roberto's immediate help and attention, the intensity of her anger was destructive to their relationship.

This analysis suggests the following ways in which counseling could help Edie deal with her emotions:

- Developing her awareness of warning signs of her rage so that she can choose to express it differently
- Promoting her awareness of the complexity of her feelings, especially the link between her anger and her sadness, so that she can pay more attention to the sadness and perhaps express her feelings more fully
- Helping her recognize the potentially harmful nature of her expression of emotion
- Enabling her to gain insight into the intensity and incongruence of her emotions, probably reflecting sources of anger and sadness beyond the present context
- Teaching her more constructive ways to manage and express her anger and communicate her concerns to Roberto

The exercises later in the chapter give you an opportunity to analyze emotions according to these eight dimensions and, based on that analysis, to generate ways to help people better manage and express their emotions.

Reflection of Feeling and Meaning

Reflection is a process that identifies people's emotions and experiences and feeds back to them the underlying or important meaning that those emotions and experiences have for them. Reflections, using words different from those used by the client, give another perspective on emotions and experiences. Reflections are intended to deepen people's awareness of their feelings and experiences, promote thought and insight, let people know that they are heard and understood, and encourage further discussion and self-exploration.

Reflections of feelings differ from reflections of meaning. The following examples clarify the nature of these two types of reflections:

Client:	For the first time, I handed in my assignment on schedule. Even though I worked very hard and followed the plan we developed, I didn't think I could do it, but I did!
Reflection of feeling:	I can hear that you feel very proud of yourself.
Reflection of meaning:	This sounds like a real milestone for you.

Both of the interventions are potentially effective because they do not simply repeat the client's words but use language that enhances his awareness and demonstrates that the clinician is attuned to the client. The reflection of feeling contains the word "proud" that labels the client's emotion. The reflection of meaning captures the significance this experience has for the client: succeeding, at least once, in overcoming his procrastination. Although the two interventions probably will take the session in different directions, both reinforce the client's accomplishment, help him feel good about his success, and raise his awareness of how he achieved this milestone and could generalize his positive behaviors to other experiences.

The effectiveness of these reflections becomes particularly clear when they are contrasted with other types of interventions that clinicians might have used with this client, such as the following:

Open question:	How did you manage to do that?
Closed question:	When did this happen?
Suggestion:	I suggest you write down exactly how you did this so that you can try to repeat this success.
Self-disclosure:	I'm really impressed!
Interpretation:	It seems that once you became comfortable seeing yourself as a success, your behavior started to change.
Restatement:	So you worked hard and finally met the deadline.

Previous chapters familiarized you with open and closed questions, restatements, and interpretations. Suggestions and self-disclosure are discussed in later "Skill Development" sections of this book. All six types of interventions are potentially therapeutic and helpful. However, none of them accomplishes the purpose of reinforcing the client's gains quite as well as the reflections do. Although the other responses might be good as follow-up interventions, a reflection with a positive emphasis seems most powerful in this case.

Although reflections, as well as communicating empathy considered next, may seem simple and straightforward, formulating accurate responses that can easily be understood and absorbed by a client is challenging, even to experienced clinicians. What if a reflection is not on target and does not really capture the client's emotions? That happens to the best clinicians, no matter how carefully they are listening. Usually, a reflection that is not accurate does no harm as long as the clinician-client relationship is open and supportive enough so that the client can correct the reflection. Consider the following interaction:

Client:	For the first time, I handed in my assignment on schedule. Even though I worked very hard and followed the plan we had developed, I didn't think I could do it, but I did!
Clinician:	Sounds like you feel elated that you were able to work so hard.

Client:	Well, that's not exactly it. I usually work hard, but most of the time it just feels like I'm spinning my wheels. Somehow this time I set a reasonable schedule for myself, I didn't get into that perfectionistic thinking, I did a good enough job, and I was able to finish on time.
Clinician:	So hard work wasn't really what made the difference. It was setting realistic expectations for yourself that led to your success.
Client:	Yes, that's it.

Although the clinician missed the mark slightly in her first intervention, the intervention was still helpful. It prompted the client to think about what had contributed to his success, express that to the clinician, and hear a second intervention that demonstrated the understanding he wanted. In addition, exchanges such as these can give people practice in making themselves clear to others and ensuring that they are understood.

Communicating Empathy

Communicating empathy is probably the most important benefit of making sensitive and accurate reflections of meaning and emotions. Empathy involves feeling deeply connected to people, being sensitive to the nuances in their words and nonverbal cues, sensing and almost experiencing their emotions, and successfully communicating that awareness to them. Empathy is very important in building rapport between client and clinician and establishing a collaborative therapeutic alliance. Typically, people who feel that their clinicians understand and care about them are more optimistic about their treatment, more willing to disclose personal information, more agreeable to trying new experiences and behaviors, and more likely to achieve their treatment goals. As we discussed in chapter 2, empathy is an important aspect of the clinical relationship and plays a vital part in determining the success of the treatment.

Empathy and sympathy are sometimes confused. Sympathy is characterized by feeling sorry for people. This can make them feel pitiful, helpless, and hopeless. Empathy, on the other hand, gives people the message that their feelings can be understood and accepted, which is empowering rather than demeaning.

Although reflections of meaning and reflections of feelings, designed to communicate empathy as well as promote self-awareness, are only one of many interventions that clinicians use, they are an essential part of their repertoire of skills. Becoming familiar with ways to begin and structure empathic responses can help you learn this skill. A common format for such a response is the following:

- *Sentence stem + name of emotion + link to context = empathic response*

An illustration of this is:

- *You must have felt* (sentence stem) *terrified* (name of emotion) *when your daughter fell in the lake* (context) = empathic response

The following sentence stems are useful ways to being an empathic response:

- Sounds like you're feeling. . .
- You seem. . .

- You look. . .
- You sound. . .
- You must have felt. . .
- That must have been. . .
- I'm hearing feelings of. . .

The following dialog with Ava provides examples of reflections to communicate empathy:

Ava: My mom and dad told me I should meet with you today. I don't really know why.

Clinician: You sound a little apprehensive about coming in to talk with me.

Ava: Yes, I guess I am. I've seen movies about therapists, and they usually had a couch. I was afraid I would have to lie down on a couch, but you don't even have one here.

Clinician: So this is different from what you expected and maybe not quite so scary.

Ava: Yes. But I still don't know what to do.

Clinician: This is all kind of a mystery to you.

Ava: Yes. My mom said I should talk about my family. I guess I could do that.

Clinician: Sounds like that might be a comfortable place for you to start.

Ava: I know my mom and dad have been seeing you for a while. They fight a lot. I just try to stay out of the way. I go to my room, but I wish I could make them stop fighting.

Clinician: It must be pretty upsetting to you when they fight.

Ava: Yes, I worry that they might get a divorce. My friend Carrie's mom and dad got a divorce, and it was awful. I never know whose house she's at when I want to call her.

Clinician: So divorce looks like a pretty bad thing to you, and you wish you could do something to make sure your mom and dad don't get divorced.

Ava: Yes, but when I ask my mom about it, she just says, "Don't worry about it. We both love you, and we'll always take good care of you." What kind of an answer is that?

Clinician: You sound angry that your parents are not really telling you what's going on.

Ava: That's true. I'm not a baby anymore. I just had my 10th birthday. I could understand what's going on, and maybe I could help them. I could earn more money mowing lawns; I could do better in school; I could bother them less. If they would only tell me what to do, I would do it.

Clinician: I can hear how much you love your parents and wish with all your heart that you could help them to be happier together.

Ava: (tearfully) Yes, that's exactly how I feel.

This dialog demonstrates how using reflections of feeling and meaning to communicate empathy can help people become comfortable in treatment, share feelings that are hard for them to talk about, feel understood, and begin to make good use of the treatment process. Staying with a person's emotions and showing awareness, acceptance, and understanding of those feelings can go a long way toward helping.

EXERCISES

Large-Group Exercises

1. Analyze the following statement of feelings according to each of the eight dimensions discussed previously in this chapter:

   Roberto: (speaking in a loud voice and occasionally banging his fist on the table) I really love Edie, but I just can't get through to her. I do everything I can to show her how much I care. I work hard; I help around the house; I'm a good father to Ava; I don't drink; I don't run around with other women. I said all this to her, but no, it's not enough for her. She says, "But you don't understand my feelings." So I say, "I don't know what you're talking about. I love you. That's *my* feeling. You don't understand my feelings either."

2. Based on your analysis of Roberto's feelings, how do you think treatment focused on his emotions could be helpful to him? Identify at least three goals that you would have for helping him deal with the emotions he has expressed in this example.

3. Write reflections of meaning and reflections of feeling in response to the following five statements. Then discuss your responses as a group, listing two or three helpful responses to each statement. For each of the five statements, discuss whether a reflection of feeling or a reflection of meaning would be more helpful to the client.

   Client A: Losing my job was the last straw. What else is going to happen? I feel like I'm jinxed.

   Client B: I didn't have a good time at the party. I felt like everyone was watching me, waiting for me to do something stupid. That's the last time I'll put myself in a situation like that.

   Client C: You know, it meant a great deal to me when you called me after my surgery. I was feeling pretty scared, but somehow knowing that you were there and wanted to talk to me really turned things around, and my situation didn't look so bad after all.

   Client D: I love to be outside in the springtime, to get away from the mess at home. It makes me forget about all my problems. I get this sort of religious feeling.

   Client E: I've been telling my wife for years that she doesn't make me feel special, that she takes me for granted. She never seemed to hear me. Then out of the blue, she makes me a surprise birthday party. Well, I couldn't believe it. It was like I was king for a day.

Small-Group Exercises

Divide into your groups of four, composed of two dyads. Each dyad should engage in a 10–15 minute, role-played, counseling interview. The person playing the client should talk about how he or she spent the previous weekend, emphasizing expression of feelings. The person in the clinician role should facilitate the discussion, relying as much as possible on reflection of feeling and reflection of meaning to promote the client's self-awareness and expression of emotion. Record the interview and then play back the recorded interview so that the group can identify whether each intervention is a reflection of meaning or feeling and can discuss the impact of each intervention.

Individual Exercises

1. We express emotions many times throughout each day. Listen to yourself for several hours and write down in your journal at least three statements of feelings that you heard yourself make. Then select one of them—ideally, an expression of emotions accompanied by some discomfort—and prepare a written analysis of your statement according to the eight dimensions of feelings. What did you learn from this about yourself and the ways in which you express your feelings? Be your own counselor and suggest at least two ways you might have improved on your expression of feelings in order to communicate your emotions more clearly to others.
2. Select a 2-hour time period in the next few days in which you will make a conscious effort to use more reflections of feeling and reflections of meaning in your everyday conversations. Be aware of how it feels to use these skills, whether your reflections seem to produce any changes in your interactions with others, and the kinds of responses your use of reflection elicits. Write about this experience in your journal.

SUMMARY

This chapter reviewed the place and importance of emotions and sensations in counseling and psychotherapy. It also provided a list of eight dimensions that can help clinicians understand and analyze feelings. Skill development included analyzing expressions of emotion, using reflections of meaning and reflections of feelings, and communicating empathy.

CHAPTER 10

Carl Rogers and Person-Centered Counseling

Carl Rogers, more than anyone else, is associated with theories of counseling and psychotherapy that emphasize emotions. As much a philosophy as a treatment approach, Rogers's person-centered counseling was built on a strong humanistic base. Humanism views people as capable and autonomous, with the ability to resolve their difficulties, realize their potential, and change their lives in positive ways. The person-centered clinician seeks to build a relationship with clients that will promote their self-esteem, enable them to become more authentic and actualized, and empower them to use their strengths and flourish.

CARL ROGERS

Carl Rogers was born in 1902 and spent his childhood in the Midwest. He described his family as religious fundamentalists (Rogers, 1980). Rogers was raised to be judgmental of behaviors and attitudes that conflicted with his parents' values. His family rarely shared personal thoughts and feelings. Rogers reported that he had little social contact with children other than his brothers and viewed himself as distant and aloof. Rogers's later ideas about emotional health seem to be the converse of what he experienced while growing up.

Rogers's family instilled in him the importance of hard work, the scientific method, and a sense of responsibility, values that were reflected in his academic pursuits. He was an outstanding student who prized academic accomplishment. College and graduate school, however, were periods of great transition for him. Initially majoring in agriculture, Rogers soon realized that following the career path reflected by his family background was not right for him, and he changed his focus first to history, then to religion, and finally to clinical psychology. Rogers completed his undergraduate work at the University of Wisconsin and began study for the ministry at Union Theological Seminary but transferred to Columbia University, where he received a Ph.D. in psychology in 1931.

These shifts in career direction parallel Rogers's growing awareness of the importance of social relationships and of sharing thoughts and feelings. His experiences as a camp counselor and on a trip to China as part of the World Student Christian Federation Conference, his dating experiences, and his marriage immediately after college all contributed to his evolution from a person with a rigid and judgmental view of others to one who appreciated the individuality of each person while believing strongly in the importance of world peace and the interconnections of all humankind.

Rogers's career reflected a growing involvement with people and the evolution of his theory of counseling and psychotherapy. He initially worked with children in Rochester, New York, and later was a faculty member at Ohio State University and at the University of Chicago. From 1963 until the end of his life, Rogers promoted his ideas through the Center for Studies of the Person in La Jolla, California. During his later years, he focused on using person-centered approaches to reduce interracial tensions, resolve intergroup conflicts, and promote world peace and social justice. He led workshops and encounter groups around the world (Kirschenbaum, 2004). By bringing together groups in conflict such as the Catholics and Protestants from Northern Ireland and Blacks and Whites in South Africa, he sought to promote communication and understanding and reduce antagonism. Rogers was nominated for a Nobel Peace Prize although he did not receive that award.

In 1987, Rogers broke his hip in a fall, underwent surgery, but died of heart failure several days later. Rogers was a strong and influential leader in his profession until his death. His own words capture the life he led: "I do not know when I will die, but I do know that I will have lived a full and exciting eighty-five years!" (Rogers, 1987, p. 152).

According to Cain (1987), Rogers was the embodiment of the theory he developed, "the most attentive, careful, and sensitive listener" he had ever known (p. 284). Rogers's habits of hard work, self-discipline, organization, and concentration continued throughout his life. He enhanced these strengths with his optimism, his sense of self-actualization, and his ability to be open to experience and live in the moment. He was not afraid to express ideas that were new and innovative and was deeply committed to improving the world. His life and his ideas are inseparable. As

Rogers (1961, pp. 23–24) stated, "Experience is, for me, the highest authority. The touchstone of validity is my own experience. No other person's ideas, and none of my own ideas, are as authoritative as my experience. It is to experience that I must return again and again, to discover a closer approximation to truth as it is in the process of becoming in me."

THE DEVELOPMENT OF PERSON-CENTERED COUNSELING

According to Seeman (1990), the evolution of Rogers's theories closely mirrored his personal development, with his ideas growing richer as his insight, personality, and compassion deepened. His conceptual development seems to fall into time periods: the 1940s, the 1950s, the 1960s, and the 1970s and 1980s (Zimring & Raskin, 1992).

When Carl Rogers published his first major work, *Counseling and Psychotherapy* (1942), the field was dominated by two systems of treatment: psychoanalytic/psychodynamic approaches and behavioral approaches. Rogers criticized both for their lack of scientific method and for their assumption that clinicians know best and should tell clients how they should change. Instead, he proposed what he called *nondirective counseling,* in which the primary role of the clinician is to help people express, clarify, and gain insight into their emotions. According to Rogers, acceptance, reflection, and genuineness are a clinician's primary tools; he avoided elaborate interventions and diagnostic procedures because of their lack of proven validity and the power they gave clinicians over clients. Even theory was minimized in Rogers's early writings; practice and experience were what mattered.

Rogers's second stage of development was marked by the publication of *Client-Centered Therapy* (1951). Although Rogers maintained his emphasis on the importance of people's emotions, the book signaled several important changes in his thinking. He renamed his approach *client-centered therapy,* reflecting his realization that treatment cannot, and probably should not, be completely nondirective. Rogers now saw the clinician's role as more active and important and believed that by communicating accurate empathy, congruence, and acceptance, clinicians could create an environment conducive to helping people make positive changes. These three core facilitative conditions—empathy, congruence, and acceptance (also known as unconditional positive regard)—became hallmarks of Rogers's work.

In the 1960s, Rogers began his third developmental period (Zimring & Raskin, 1992), again signaled by the publication of a major work, *On Becoming a Person* (1961). That book introduced Rogers's conception of healthy and fully functioning people: those who are open to experience, appreciate and trust themselves, and are guided by an inner locus of control rather than by an effort to please or impress others. Such people view their lives as a process and value lifelong growth. Rogers's interest in promoting people's healthy development led him to extend his reach beyond the clinical setting. For example, he promoted the idea of student-centered teaching. Encounter groups based on Rogers's ideas became widely used to promote positive development (Rogers, 1970). His work during the 1960s also reflected his interest in research. Rogers pioneered efforts to identify those elements of the client-clinician relationship and the therapeutic process that are most likely to facilitate positive change.

The last two decades of Rogers's life, the 1970s and 1980s, reflected a continued broadening of his ideas and their application. The term *client-centered* was replaced by *person-centered.* Because Rogers's focus was no longer only on the clinical relationship, the new term better represented his concern with all of humanity. His methods were now used not only in treatment of individuals but also in families, business and administration, education, crosscultural settings, conflict resolution, and, perhaps most important to Rogers, the promotion of world peace.

Throughout his career, Rogers sought to help people feel powerful and in control of their lives while encouraging them to respect the right of others to have their own feelings of power and competence. His person-centered theory evolved out of the belief that people have within themselves "vast resources for self-understanding" for developing their self-concepts and their self-direction, but "these resources can be tapped only if a definable climate of facilitative psychological attitudes can be provided" (Rogers, 1980, p. 49).

IMPORTANT THEORETICAL CONCEPTS

For Carl Rogers, understanding, appreciating, and relating to others in positive ways were the ultimate goals. The theory of person-centered counseling reflects this.

Person-Centered Theory and Humanism

Humanism has been defined as "a style of thought or attitude which makes the human central, important, valuable, crucial, pivotal, wonderful, powerful—even miraculous" (Barton, 1992, p. 332). According to Kirschenbaum (2004), humanism or humanistic psychology differed from psychoanalysis and behaviorism in three major ways:

- Humanism is phenomenological, focusing on people's own frames of reference and the personal meaning of their experiences.
- It optimistically promotes wellness, personal growth, and achievement of one's potential, encouraging development of what Rogers called the fully functioning person.
- It emphasizes qualities such as choice, freedom, values, and goals that distinguish humans from other species.

Rogers's ideas embody the humanistic perspective. He perceived people as strong and capable and trusted their ability to handle their difficulties, grow and develop, and realize their potential. Consistent with this point of view, he believed that the goal of treatment was to affirm and empower people so that they have enough trust and confidence in themselves to make use of their inner resources.

Human Potential and Actualization

Implicit in person-centered theory is a strong belief in the dignity and worth of each individual. Practitioners believe that people must be appreciated and accepted for themselves, not shaped to fit a mold. They believe that people have a right to their own thoughts and opinions, should be free to construct their own lives, and are fundamentally good and trustworthy. They believe in the human potential—in the inherent tendency of people to develop in positive ways that enhance and maintain themselves as well as humanity (Cain, 1987).

An important aspect of the human potential is people's natural inclination toward actualization, expansion, growth, and health. Rogers's concept of actualization is similar to ideas advanced by Karen Horney (discussed in chapter 7) and Abraham Maslow (discussed in chapter 11). However, only person-centered counseling views encouragement of actualization to be a practical and functional treatment goal (Bozarth & Brodley, 1991). Rogers believed that actualizing occurs as people develop in holistic and unified ways. Actualizing is a constant process, manifesting itself throughout life; it is a directional movement toward intrinsic goals, self-realization and fulfillment, involving autonomy and self-regulation. Although actualizing is a universal tendency, each person's efforts are unique.

Conditions of Worth

According to person-centered theory, children's self-concepts are shaped through interactions with important people in their lives and the messages they receive from those people (Rogers, 1961). If children experience *conditions of worth,* judgmental and critical messages that they are only worthwhile and lovable if they think, feel, and act in ways that meet the needs of others, their self-images and growth may be impaired (Barton, 1992; Dolliver, 1995). Environments that are overprotective, dominating, or intimidating exert a particularly negative influence on children's development and make it difficult for them to feel free and powerful.

Children in negative environments typically internalize the criticisms they receive, perceiving aspects of themselves as worthy or unworthy. They tend to devalue, shut down, and inhibit what they perceive as the unworthy aspects of themselves. This creates inner conflicts and incongruities and curtails their natural tendency toward growth. According to Rogers, messages of conditional worth restrict authenticity so that people cannot respond with honesty in their emotions, thoughts, or behaviors. They have not learned to value the self, the total organism, and so they become fragmented. Children such as these have a high likelihood of developing into adults who are timid, inhibited, and conformist or angry and defensive.

On the other hand, children who receive unconditional positive regard—the message that they are special and wonderful just because of who they are, not because of their importance to another or the children's specific behaviors or characteristics—are far more likely to become actualizing and fully functioning adults. This does not mean that parents need to be permissive and condone children's harmful behaviors. However, they should correct undesirable behavior in such a way as to affirm both the child's worth and the parents' worth.

Consider the case of Maddy who is fearful of innoculations and reacts to her parents' efforts to take her to the physician by kicking and hitting them. Parents who apply conditions of worth to their children might say, "I don't like you when you hit me. Stop acting like such a baby over a little shot." Parents who seek to affirm the child but shape the behavior might say, "I can understand that you are scared of the shot and are angry that I am taking you to the doctor, but you hurt my leg when you kicked me. I love you and we can find ways to help you with your feelings, but I need you to stop kicking me."

Although Rogers (1980) acknowledged the harm that an aversive background can do to a person's development, he was ever optimistic: "Individuals have within themselves vast resources for self-understanding and for altering their self-concepts, basic attitudes, and self-directed behavior; these resources can be tapped if a definable climate of facilitative psychological attitudes can be provided" (p. 115). The goal of person-centered treatment is to provide that climate of acceptance and unconditional positive regard, counteract negative messages that people have received, and enable them to develop positive self-esteem and realize their potential as actualizing and fully functioning people.

The Fully Functioning Person

In describing the fully functioning person, Rogers (1961, pp. 104–105) wrote, "The person comes to *be* what he *is* . . . in awareness as well as in experience, a complete and fully functioning human organism." Such people have authenticity and can respond with congruence and honesty. They reflect what Rogers referred to as the *organismic valuing process* (OVP), defined as follows (Sheldon, Arndt, & Houser-Marko, 2003, p. 836): "The OVP refers to peoples' innate ability to know what is important to them, what is essential for a more fulfilling life. The presumption is that people automatically evaluate their experiences and actions to ascertain whether they are actualizing and if they are not, a 'nagging sense that something isn't right' results which can motivate corrective action."

Rogers's concept of the fully functioning person reflects his ideal of emotional health. Three personality dimensions are particularly characteristic of the fully functioning person: openness to experience, living with a sense of meaning and purpose, and trust in self and others (Bozarth & Brodley, 1991). People with these personality traits move and grow in positive directions, have a sense of their place in the world, feel comfortable with and connected to other people, have an internal source of evaluation, and channel their lives in productive and rewarding ways. They are not driven by a need to please or outdo others but strive to meet their own high standards. They manage their lives well, have positive self-esteem, are proud of who they are, and are actualized.

Rogers's image of the fully functioning person has considerable importance in person-centered treatment, and helping people become fully functioning is a fundamental treatment goal. Clinicians can educate their clients about the nature and importance of becoming a fully functioning person and establish goals and plan interventions that will move people toward becoming fully functioning. In addition, Rogers believed that clinicians, too, should move toward becoming fully functioning. This concept can help us to lead our own lives in positive ways and become role models for our clients.

Phenomenological Perspective

Person-centered theorists are phenomenological in their thinking. They believe that each person has his or her unique perception of the world. That perception determines the person's beliefs, behaviors, emotions, and relationships. According to Rogers (1951), "The organism reacts to the field as it is experienced and perceived. This perceptual field is, for the individual, reality" (pp. 483–484).

Because all the choices we make in our lives stem from our perceptions, we are, in effect, the focus of our universe. Rogers believed that each person exists at the center of a constantly changing world of experience. Even when we believe we are being objective, our subjective perceptions determine the direction of our lives.

For example, assume that a group of people in an office hears a loud noise. Timi, who delights in social gatherings, believes the noise is a balloon bursting at a nearby party and wishes she were there. Kahing attributes the noise to a car backfiring and is reminded that his own car needs repair. Tom, who experienced combat in the military, thinks the noise might be gunfire and feels apprehensive, while Alice is so immersed in her work that she does not even hear the noise. This example illustrates how people can distort, interpret, and organize objective information based on their perceptions of the world, with those perceptions leading to thoughts ("I really should get my car repaired"), behaviors ("I'm going to check out that party"), and emotions ("I feel afraid").

Every moment of the day, we have perceptions that evolve out of our experiences and influence all aspects of our lives. Understanding ourselves, our relationships, and our clients depends on our awareness and acceptance of these subjective perceptions. Only by understanding people's perceptions of reality can we fully appreciate them and the ways in which they direct and organize their lives.

Consistent with his strong emphasis on phenomenology and people's internal frames of reference, Rogers wanted nothing but clients' own experience to inform their treatment (Dolliver, 1995). He believed that no authority, including the clinician's, should take precedence over clients' direct experience. Correspondingly, Rogers drew heavily on his own experience and perceptions, both in his interactions with clients and in the development of his theories. He believed that self-disclosure, used carefully and deliberately, could enhance the therapeutic alliance and advance treatment. More information on the effective use of self-disclosure is provided in the Skill Development section of this chapter.

TREATMENT USING PERSON-CENTERED COUNSELING

Although the use of specific strategies is not an important part of person-centered counseling, setting goals and creating a sound therapeutic alliance are both vital. Person-centered counseling is primarily a way of being with clients and providing therapeutic conditions that will facilitate change. As Fernald (2000, p. 174) stated, "When certain conditions (empathy, unconditional positive regard, genuineness) are present, actualizing forces take over, denial and distortions of experience diminish, and the person becomes a more fully functioning human organism."

Goals

In the early 1960s, Rogers became interested in bettering his understanding of the process of person-centered counseling. To do this, he spent many hours listening "as naively as possible" to recorded sessions (Rogers, 1961, p. 128). He found that, early in treatment, people were characterized by remoteness, rigidity, and a limited awareness of their inner selves. By the end of treatment, however, people were able to live in and experience the present and trust both themselves and the therapeutic process.

A central goal of person-centered counseling, then, is to facilitate people's trust and their ability to be in the present moment. This enables them to become more honest with themselves and their clinician and to express fully their emotions and thoughts, even those that are painful and viewed as unacceptable by others. Additional treatment goals include promoting self-awareness, empowerment, optimism, self-esteem, responsibility, congruence, and autonomy. Development of these strengths, in turn, helps people build an internal locus of control, become more aware of external reality, make better use of their potential, gain the ability to manage their lives and resolve their concerns, and become more actualized. Rogers's approach does not focus on the resolution of specific presenting problems but on developing fully functioning people who are capable of creating rewarding lives and dealing successfully with life's joys and challenges.

Therapeutic Alliance

Study after study has indicated the importance of the therapeutic alliance in treatment. In a meta-analysis, Horvath and Symonds (1991) concluded that the effects of that alliance were very robust. Glauser and Bozarth (2001, p. 142) stated, "The variables most related to success in counseling outcome research are the client-counselor relationship and the personal and situational resources of the client . . . " More studies supporting this conclusion are cited in chapter 2. The person of the clinician and the relationship of the client and the clinician are essential ingredients for change (Barton, 1992). Not only do clinicians need to establish a positive therapeutic alliance, but they also need to communicate the core therapeutic conditions, which we discuss in this section.

Role of the Clinician   Person-centered clinicians view people in a positive light. They appreciate and accept their clients on their own terms. They believe that people are capable and powerful, possessing the abilities they need to resolve their difficulties. These clinicians assume that people have a natural tendency toward growth, self-regulation, and self-knowledge (Bozarth & Brodley, 1991). They focus on their clients' strengths rather than their deficiencies, their successes rather than their failures, encouraging them to move forward so that they become more actualized and fully functioning.

Because person-centered clinicians have faith in their clients, they do not need to probe the unconscious, direct people's activities, point out their errors, or even teach an array of new skills. Instead, they create an environment that allows people to trust themselves and make good use of their potential. Clinicians' acceptance, understanding, and valuing of their clients; their respect for clients' subjective experiences; and their full and active participation in the treatment process empower those clients. Clinicians may challenge, encourage, and promote self-exploration but are always supportive, caring, and trusting of the client's natural tendencies toward growth and actualization. The trust their counselors have in them is contagious, and clients begin to feel more self-confident themselves, enabling them to find and use their strengths and abilities to help themselves. As Rogers (1961) stated, "If I can provide a certain type of relationship, the other person will discover within himself or herself the capacity to use that relationship for growth and change, and personal development will occur" (p. 33).

The role of the person-centered clinician is a rewarding but demanding one. Clinicians must have great self-awareness as well as the ability to be fully present and use themselves as an instrument of change. According to Barton (1992), "Rogerian technique and attitude liberate therapists to become a full, resonating, affective, thinking, imagining, listening, and speaking presence. They come to inhabit fully their client's worlds" (p. 334).

Client-Clinician Relationship   Rogers (1967) stated, "Significant positive personality change does not occur except in a relationship" (p. 73). His view of this relationship evolved over many years (Rogers, 1961). In his early writings, he described a distant and impersonal therapeutic relationship, perhaps reflecting his own upbringing. However, in 1955, he wrote, "I launch myself into a relationship. . . . I risk myself. . . . I let myself go into the immediacy of the relationship where it is my total organism which takes over" (Rogers, 1955, p. 269). By the 1960s, he acknowledged that while he initially feared being trapped by a close and loving involvement with his clients, he now found a close client-clinician relationship to be something that added to the lives of both participants (Rogers, 1961). Clinician and client are conceived of as two equal and capable human beings who become collaborators in a shared journey in which both grow and are enriched by the process.

Facilitative Conditions

Consistent with the emphasis Rogers placed on the importance of the clinician in the therapeutic process is his belief that effective clinicians have certain qualities that they communicate to their clients. These qualities help create a positive client-clinician relationship and promote clients' self-esteem and ability to direct their lives in positive ways. The most important of these are congruence, unconditional positive regard, and empathy but other qualities also enhance treatment.

Congruence   Congruence refers to clinicians' ability to be genuine and authentic, well integrated, and aware of themselves and how they are perceived by others. People who are congruent transmit messages that are clear and coherent; their inner and outer selves are consistent. Clinicians' genuineness and consistency promotes clients' trust and openness, establishes a relationship that is free of deception and hidden agendas, and provides a positive role model. For some clients, this sort of relationship is new and can help them see that such relationships are possible in other settings.

This does not mean that clinicians should share their personal stories and experiences with clients; instead, it means that what they do share with clients comes from the heart and is both relevant and helpful to the client. For example, a clinician might say, "I am concerned that you may not have thought about all aspects of that decision," or "I can really share your joy in that accomplishment." This gives the client the opportunity to consider another perspective and receive feedback.

Incongruent communications, on the other hand, are difficult to decipher because they may be dishonest and contain mixed messages and inconsistencies. This can lead to confusion and mistrust and can damage relationships. If clients cannot count on their clinicians to be consistent and clear, the clients may have difficulty knowing how to act and what to disclose about themselves. Their own messages may become increasingly incongruent as they strive to address all possible meanings in the clinicians' unclear messages.

The following example illustrates the difference between congruent and incongruent communication. In a congruent message of affection at the end of a date, a person might say, "I really enjoyed spending time with you," while smiling, looking directly into the other person's eyes, and extending a hand. An invitation to get together again might follow. In an incongruent message, the words might reflect liking, but the body language might involve poor eye contact and a tense posture. In addition, the person may not initiate further contact.

Congruence in the treatment process requires sensitivity, openness, and self-awareness on the part of clinicians. To maximize their ability to be genuine and congruent and to participate in clients' experiences, clinicians must be in the present moment, aware of and attuned to their environment and interactions. Particularly important in person-centered counseling are present interchanges between client and clinician.

Clinicians should be aware that clients' subjective interpretation of information may lead to misinterpretation. For example, clients may believe that a yawning counselor is bored with them. While clinicians may not be able to suppress their yawns, they can be aware of the possible impact of their sleepiness and say something like, "I noticed you looked dismayed when I yawned. I'm sorry to be yawning. The thunderstorm kept me awake last night. How did you react when I yawned?" Clinicians need to be aware of both their verbal and their nonverbal messages, maintain consistency between the two, and address clients' reactions if clinicians inadvertently give confusing or potentially negative messages.

Unconditional Positive Regard   Rogers's writings emphasize the importance of what he called unconditional positive regard: caring about, respecting, liking, and accepting people for who they are without placing any requirements on them to act, feel, or think in certain ways to please their clinicians. Rogers viewed people as inherently worthy, although he recognized that people have both positive and negative impulses and feelings (Kirschenbaum, 2004). Communication of warmth and positive regard is essential to helping people like themselves, emphasize their positive impulses and emotions, feel powerful enough to successfully cope with their difficulties, and become more fully functioning.

Unconditional positive regard does not mean that clinicians view everything people do or think as wise and appropriate but simply that clinicians see people as doing the best they can at the present time. Person-centered clinicians are consistent in their acceptance of and confidence in the person, although they might express concern about that person's choices. Rather than saying, "You seem to be an angry person," they might say, "You sounded angry when I could not change our appointment time." This perspective is reflected in current child-rearing practices that advocate focusing feedback and evaluation on the behavior, not on the child. Parents are encouraged to say, "You did a great job picking up your toys," rather than, "You're such a good girl for cleaning your room."

Communication of acceptance and unconditional positive regard helps people believe that they are worthy and can trust their own feelings and thoughts. It can counter devaluing messages they have received throughout their lives. It allows people to recognize that they can change undesirable behaviors, thoughts, and feelings while still viewing themselves as likable and worthwhile. Knowing that they will be accepted no matter what also enables people to disclose to clinicians aspects of themselves that cause them shame or discomfort. Rogers (1980) believed that the more clinicians prize and value people for who they are, the more likely it is that they will make positive changes.

Empathy   Rogers (1959, p. 210) defined empathy as, ". . . to perceive the internal frame of reference of another person with accuracy and with the emotional components and meanings which pertain thereto, as if one were the other person, but without losing the 'as if' condition." He further stated (1980, p. 50), "Simply to listen understandingly to a client and to attempt to convey that understanding are potent forces for individuals' therapeutic change." This kind of listening is empathic understanding: the accurate sensing of what people are experiencing, feeling, and communicating and the ability to let people know they are heard in this way. Rogers viewed sensitive, accurate, and active listening; deeply grasping the subjective world of another person and transmitting understanding of that world to enhance a person's own self-awareness; as the most powerful force for change.

Empathy is very close to reflection (described in chapter 9), although empathy usually refers to understanding emotions while reflection is broader. However, empathy is not close to sympathy. Sympathy can make people feel pitiful and can communicate a distance between the sympathizer and the other person, while empathy brings people closer together in a shared experience. Empathy opens the door for further discussion, usually at a deeper level, and is empowering. Sympathy, on the other hand, encourages people to view themselves as wounded victims and limits productive conversation. The following example illustrates the difference:

Client: I can't believe the terrible grade I got on the exam. I hope no one finds out.
Sympathy: I'm sorry you did so poorly on the test.
Empathy: I can hear the deep sense of shame you feel about your grade.

The dialog with the sympathetic clinician is likely to further entrench the client's negative self-evaluation. That dialog might continue like this:

Client: I can't believe the terrible grade I got on the exam. I hope no one finds out.
Clinician: I'm sorry you did poorly on the test.
Client: Yes, I am too. I guess I'm just too dumb to learn physics. I better give up on going to med school.
Clinician: That's really a shame.
Client: Yes, I don't know how I'll ever tell my parents.
Clinician: How unfortunate that you might have to do that.

In this dialog, the client seems to be in a downward spiral and has no sense of empowerment or competence.

Empathic understanding, on the other hand, often leads clients and clinicians to develop hypotheses that promote self-awareness and positive change. For example, the conversation with the empathic clinician might continue as follows:

Client: I can't believe the terrible grade I got on the exam. I hope no one finds out.
Clinician: You seem to feel a deep sense of shame about your grade.
Client: Yes, I do feel ashamed. I just always screw things up.
Clinician: You're sounding very angry with yourself.
Client: Yes, I am. I mean, it's not just school. I screwed up my relationship with Judy. I screwed up my job by getting that report in late.
Clinician: You're blaming yourself for all those things. Help me understand that better. I wonder if you ever felt like you screwed things up in our work together?
Client: Yes, I did. Remember when I paged you when you were on vacation? I was so upset about my father's heart attack and so much wanted to talk to you that I forgot you were away. I felt ashamed then too.
Clinician: Sounds like you felt you were imposing on me and weren't worth a few minutes of my time. I wonder how you thought I reacted to your call?
Client: Well, you didn't sound annoyed and really tried to help me. Somehow I still felt I had done a dumb thing.

The use of empathy, as well as congruence and unconditional positive regard, has enabled the client to disclose feelings of low self-esteem. The clinician can now generate some hypotheses about the client's view of the world and himself and the impact this has on his relationships. Awareness of his phenomenological field or worldview, along with the facilitative conditions communicated by the clinician, can encourage the client's positive change.

Other Strategies   Many of the systems of psychotherapy and counseling discussed in this book rely heavily on specialized strategies such as word association, dream analysis, and modification of cognitive distortions to further the treatment. Because the heart of person-centered counseling is the therapeutic relationship, clinicians rarely use strategies such as these, nor do they use elaborate diagnostic and assessment tools. They are viewed as unnecessary and as detracting from the client-clinician relationship. All interventions in person-centered treatment should promote the therapeutic relationship and enhance the client's awareness and empowerment (Kelly, 1997). Strategies that promote and deepen communication and that reflect the clinician's caring and interest probably are the most useful interventions in person-centered counseling. These include open questions, reflections of emotion and meaning, paraphrases, and encouragers such as "umm-hmm," "how so?," and repetition of a key word.

Nondirectiveness Updated

Rogers originally called his approach *nondirective counseling,* emphasizing the importance of the client taking the lead and being the focus of the treatment process. Although Rogers later changed the name of this approach to client-centered counseling and then to person-centered counseling, the nondirective aspects of this approach still merit attention.

Grant (1990) described two types of nondirective counseling, instrumental and principled nondirectiveness. *Instrumental nondirectiveness* is the technique of allowing clients to take charge of the therapeutic process. Although person-centered counselors sometimes use this approach, most seem to believe it is more realistic and helpful to play an active part in the treatment.

Grant views *principled nondirectiveness* as integral to person-centered treatment. He defines this as not forcing self-expression, insight, or change in clients but providing "the therapeutic conditions in the belief that they are expressions of respect and with the hope that the client will make use of them" (p. 78). Person-centered clinicians do not manipulate change; rather, they create a favorable psychological environment that is conducive to change. Although they are always respectful of and responsive to the needs of their clients, they are not simply passive recipients of client input but are active in developing conditions that are conducive to client growth. According to Grant, principled nondirectiveness, rather than instrumental nondirectiveness, is compatible with Rogers's vision of person-centered counseling.

APPLICATION OF PERSON-CENTERED COUNSELING

Person-centered counseling has continued to evolve since Rogers's death in 1987, with changes in both its popularity and its application. In the years shortly before and after his death, this approach declined in popularity, with many viewing it as simplistic and inadequate to help people with severe emotional difficulties. However, recognition of the broad application of this approach and its ease of integration into other treatment models, led to a resurgence of interest in person-centered work. This is largely due to two factors.

One of these is the widespread appreciation for the importance of conditions such as congruence, unconditional positive regard, and empathy in the therapeutic relationship. According to Hill and Nakayama (2000, p. 870), ". . . the facilitative conditions have permeated other orientations and are oftentimes a precursor to other types of interventions. Even behaviorally oriented therapists now recognize the need to establish a therapeutic relationship before moving to behavioral change." The importance of nurturing a positive therapeutic relationship as described by Rogers has both empirical and common sense support. Most people benefit from being treated with re-

spect and viewed as worthy and competent. When this is operationalized via the facilitative conditions, clients are more likely to participate actively in treatment and believe that it can help them.

A second reason for the ongoing interest in the person-centered model is a trend toward integrating treatment approaches. (More information on this will be provided in chapters 22 and
23). Rogers's approach blends easily with a broad range of approaches.

Motivational Interviewing

Miller and Rollnick (2002) have developed motivational interviewing, based on the principles of
person-centered counseling. Originally intended to promote behavioral change in people who
misused drugs and alcohol, this approach now is being used with a broad range of clients. More
directive and behaviorally-focused than Rogers's person-centered counseling, motivational interviewing uses reflection, open questions, and other strategies to help reduce barriers to progress,
help people recognize and express their concerns, and make positive changes.

Carkhuff's Human Technology

A noteworthy example of integrating person-centered counseling with other approaches is Human
Technology (HT), developed primarily by Robert Carkhuff (Aspy, Aspy, Russel, & Wedel, 2000).
According to the tenets of HT, learning progresses through three phases: exploration, understanding, and action. Drawing heavily on person-centered concepts and approaches in the first phase of
HT, practitioners build a positive therapeutic alliance and promote exploration and self-awareness.
Communication of empathy via "interchangeable responses" is critical during this phase. The second phase of HT relies most on psychodynamic interventions to develop people's insight and understanding. Finally, behavioral approaches are used to encourage initiative and constructive
action. In addition to his development of HT, Carkhuff's (2000) manuals, designed to improve
people's helping skills, have contributed greatly to the teaching of the facilitative conditions.

Application to Diagnostic Groups

Because Rogers viewed the diagnosis of people's mental disorders as potentially detrimental to the
treatment process, little information can be gleaned from Rogers's writings on the application of
person-centered theory to diagnostic groups. However, more recent writings, coupled with the
move toward integrating this approach with other treatment models, do provide some understanding of this issue.

A pure version of person-centered counseling seems best suited to people who have fairly
good emotional resources, hampered by low self-esteem, lack of confidence in themselves and
others, and negative and distorted views of the world. These people are not in crisis, nor do they
have severe mental disorders; but they do believe that they can find more fulfillment in their lives
through personal growth and self-awareness. In addition, research (Greenberg, Elliott, & Lietaer,
1994) suggests that people with high reactance and an internal coping style are particularly likely
to benefit from a pure version of person-centered treatment.

On the other hand, many people enter treatment seeking solutions to their problems. They
view clinicians as the experts and expect to receive information and direction. People with this
frame of reference may be disappointed with the slow pace and unstructured nature of a pure

person-centered approach and may question the competence of clinicians who use it. For such people, a more active and focused model that integrates person-centered and other strategies will probably better meet their needs and increase the likelihood that they will make a commitment to and benefit from treatment.

Nowadays, a pure person-centered model is rarely used. Combining person-centered counseling with other approaches to treatment usually expands and enhances its usefulness. An active version of person-centered counseling can help build rapport and increase motivation in people who are reluctant to engage in treatment. Kensit (2000) concluded that the empathic, nonjudgmental, and supportive stance of person-centered clinicians could even be helpful in ameliorating the hostility and suspiciousness of people diagnosed with schizophrenia. Apparently, given the right combination of person-centered and other treatment interventions, this approach can be helpful to nearly all clients.

Application to Multicultural Groups

The respectful and accepting nature of person-centered counseling, coupled with its phenomenological perspective, makes it an appropriate part of treatment for people from a wide range of ethnic, cultural, and socioeconomic backgrounds. Person-centered theory emphasizes the importance of valuing and understanding people, of viewing them from their own frame of reference, of building a positive client-clinician relationship, and of attending to the client's world through that person's perspective (Glauser & Bozarth, 2001). Because of these attributes, people from diverse cultural backgrounds are likely to accept and respond well to person-centered treatment.

Some research supports this point. Abdel-Tawab and Roter (2002), for example, studied the communication styles of personnel in family planning clinics in Egypt. They found that a "patient-centered" model of care delivery involving such qualities as reassurance, approval, empathy, concern, and partnership was associated with better patient follow-through and satisfaction than a more authoritarian model. The authors of this study observed that, even in a developing culture with a hierarchical perspective, person-centered methods proved their value. Chang and Page (1991) noted the similarity between Rogers's concept of the actualized person and personality traits such as openness to experience, closeness to nature, and independence in thought and action that are valued in eastern cultures and in Buddhism and Taoism. In addition, person-centered approaches have demonstrated their value with such diverse groups as prison inmates, children, and high school students (Landreth, Baggerly, & Tyndall-Lind, 1999). Clinicians in other countries have perhaps become even more enthusiastic about person-centered theory than have clinicians in the United States. This approach has become a leading treatment system in Europe, especially in the emerging democracies of Eastern Europe, as well as in Latin America (Kirschenbaum, 2004). Many Asian clinicians also have embraced this approach. Of course, person-centered theory served as the foundation for Rogers's efforts to promote intergroup communication and peace in our world.

CURRENT USE

Clinicians who now describe themselves as primarily person-centered probably use a broader array of interventions than Rogers described in his writings. This is due, at least in part, to the increasing severity of problems that most clinicians confront. No longer are counselors and psychotherapists focusing primarily on issues of personal growth and fulfillment; now they are dealing with physical and sexual abuse, drug and alcohol problems, violence, and incapacitating depression and anxiety. Cognitive and behavioral techniques (discussed in parts 4 and 5) have demonstrated their effectiveness in ameliorating such problems, while person-centered counseling has not. However, research and theory strongly suggest that an integration into treatment of those conditions developed and espoused by Rogers is essential to development of a healthy therapeutic alliance as well as to treatment effectiveness. The genuineness, acceptance, and empathy that characterize person-centered treatment have left their mark on the field and have been incorporated into a wide range of other approaches to treatment.

Prochaska and Norcross (2003), for example, reported that the combination of humanistic and cognitive approaches was the second-most frequent combination of theoretical orientations and the combination of humanistic and behavioral approaches was fourth. In addition, person-centered principles have been used in career counseling, play therapy, couples and family counseling, group therapy, and management training. Student-centered schools have been developed, based on these principles.

Facility of integration and breadth of application are not the only reflections of the continuing importance of person-centered theory. Several relatively new and emerging approaches to treatment are based on this approach. Carkhuff's HT, discussed previously, is one example. In addition, some clinicians espouse what is called relationship-centered counseling, an approach with roots in humanism and person-centered counseling but which employs a broader and more eclectic array of clinician interventions (Kelly, 1997). Experiential approaches, such as that developed by Greenberg et al. (1994), also incorporate and have furthered principles of person-centered work including viewing people as oriented toward growth, seeing them as the experts on their own experiences, and emphasizing the curative power of a positive therapeutic alliance.

EVALUATION OF PERSON-CENTERED COUNSELING

Rogers's person-centered theory has made an immeasurable contribution to counseling and psychotherapy. As Cain (1987) stated, Rogers's views of the human potential and the role of the clinician "literally shook the beliefs of therapists of many persuasions and professions" (p. 286). His vision of a collaborative therapeutic alliance and a genuine, supportive, accepting, empathic clinician provided an important alternative to the anonymity of the Freudian analysts and the directiveness of the early behaviorists. Rogers humanized clinicians and taught us that the clinician's use of the facilitative conditions in a positive therapeutic alliance is the most important strategy for change.

Limitations

Despite its enormous contribution, Rogers's theory has some limitations. The following criticisms have been raised about a pure approach to person-centered treatment:

- It is too simplistic and unrealistically optimistic.
- Person-centered counseling fails to draw on developmental, psychodynamic, behavioral, and other approaches that enhance understanding of people.
- Listening and caring are not enough.
- This approach is inappropriate for people who are not motivated toward change or do not have the capacity for or interest in making productive use of their sessions.

- It is not useful with people manifesting significant pathology.
- Acceptance of clients may further entrench their self-destructive thoughts, emotions, and behaviors and lead to passivity and complacency.
- The unconditionally positive clinical relationship fails to prepare people to deal with the real world.
- This approach is too leisurely and unfocused; people who are in crisis or prefer a more active, structured, and efficient approach may feel uncomfortable or disappointed.
- Person-centered theory lacks techniques to help people solve their problems.
- The emphasis on individual, internal evaluation, and the facilitative conditions may make this model unsuitable for people from cultures that emphasize the community, hierarchy, and external evaluation and do not value collaboration with authority figures.
- Although this approach claims to value the uniqueness of each individual, it promotes a picture of the fully functioning person that may mold people in a predetermined direction.
- Research on the effectiveness of this model has been inconclusive, limited, and methodologically flawed.

These criticisms all contain some truth. However, many stem from a limited, superficial, and dated understanding of person-centered theory. Most, if not all, of these limitations can be avoided by skilled clinicians who truly understand and embody Rogers's vision of a facilitative clinician, appreciate the importance of the therapeutic alliance, adapt this approach to the needs of the individual client, and integrate person-centered treatment with other approaches. Although more research on the effectiveness and appropriate use of person-centered treatment is needed, Hill and Nakayama (2000, p. 870) concluded, ". . . we have evidence that client-centered therapy indeed is effective and is comparable to other therapies in terms of efficacy."

Strengths and Contributions

Rogers's belief in the dignity and worth of each individual and in people's motivation toward actualization and growth offers a perspective that is up-to-date and optimistic. Although person-centered theory and treatment do reflect American ideals of independence, self-direction, and individuality, many aspects of this approach also are relevant to a diverse and multicultural society (Freeman, 1993). These include:

- The emphasis on people's right to their own opinions and thoughts
- The importance it places on respect, genuineness, acceptance, and empathy
- The focus on people's own experience and frame of reference
- Its emphasis on the need for clinicians to listen and truly understand their clients
- Its encouragement of clinicians to take a responsive stance toward clients
- Its interest in relationships and commonalities among people
- The attention this approach pays to the immediacy of the counseling situation

These perspectives are pertinent to all people, regardless of cultural background.

Rogers's work also was important in demystifying psychotherapy. As he stated, person-centered counseling revolutionized treatment by opening the "field of psychotherapy to public scrutiny and research investigation" (Rogers, 1980, p. 48). Rogers was the first to record and publish complete transcripts of psychotherapy cases (Kirschenbaum, 2004). Through his extensive writings for both mental health professionals and the general population; demonstrations, tapes, and transcripts of his sessions; research on the process of treatment; and his emphasis on education and the widespread need for person-centered relationships, Rogers gave us an accessible and comprehensible brand of counseling. Rogers's ideas have found wide appeal because they explain "basic aspects of the way in which the person's own capacity for change can be released and ways in which relationships can foster or defeat such self-directed change" (Rogers, 1980, p. 50).

Rogers's ideal of the client-clinician relationship has infiltrated and influenced all theories of counseling and psychotherapy. Stiles et al. (1996), for example, found that support, provided through the therapeutic relationship, is the clinical intervention that is most highly rated by both psychodynamic-interpersonal and cognitive-behavioral clinicians. Similarly, person-centered theory's humanistic and phenomenological emphases, reflecting great appreciation of individuality and diversity, have been incorporated into many treatment approaches.

Research, such as that discussed in chapter 2, continues to substantiate the importance of the client-clinician relationship, particularly the client's perception of that relationship, in effecting positive change. Rogers gave clinicians the guidelines and tools they need to establish positive and growth-promoting relationships with clients. Although thousands of clinicians have been influenced by Rogers, relatively few now view themselves as primarily person-centered clinicians (Prochaska & Norcross, 2003). However, Rogers's ideas live on in the relationships most clinicians seek to have with their clients, even though their treatment may be further enhanced by interventions and ideas derived from other approaches.

Rogers's work is well known internationally. His writings have been translated into many languages, and he is viewed not only as a leader in counseling and psychology but also as a peacemaker. His ideas formed the basis for the work of Thomas Gordon, founder of Effectiveness Training, Inc., used in training well over one million parents, teachers, adolescents, and leaders throughout the world using Parent Effectiveness Training (Gordon, 1970), Teacher Effectiveness Training (Gordon & Burch, 1974), and Leader Effectiveness Training (Gordon, 1983). In addition, organizations such as the Center for Studies of the Person in La Jolla, California, continue to promote and teach Rogers's ideas. As Rogers (1980) said, he "expressed an idea whose time had come" (p. 49).

SKILL DEVELOPMENT: CLINICIAN SELF-DISCLOSURE

Because person-centered counseling encourages clinicians to be fully human and present in the moment, practitioners using this approach often engage in self-disclosure. Although self-disclosure is less common in most other models of counseling and psychotherapy, all clinicians use this intervention at one time or another.

Using self-disclosure is risky for many reasons. It can shift the focus away from the client and onto the clinician, damage the client-clinician relationship, and give clients the message that the clinician's needs are more important than those of the client.

However, research has found that many benefits can result from judicious and purposeful self-disclosure. According to Knox, Hess, Petersen, and Hill (1997), clinician self-disclosure received high client ratings for helpfulness. It enhanced the therapeutic alliance and enabled clients to feel less alone, more hopeful, and less troubled. It encouraged the use of clinicians as role models and led clients to share more of themselves in sessions. Self-disclosure increased clients' appreciation of clinicians' humanness and did not result in loss of status for the clinicians.

Beneficial Uses of Self-Disclosure

The purpose of a self-disclosure should always be to advance the progress of treatment. The following lists many helpful purposes for clinician self-disclosure; each is followed by an example:

- *Enhance the collaborative nature of the client-clinician relationship.* Working along with you on your concerns has been very rewarding to me because you put so much effort into helping yourself.
- *Provide useful feedback.* Your sense of humor is a strength you use well!
- *Normalize a client's reactions.* I would have been pretty angry, too, if that had happened to me.
- *Provide a different perspective.* I understand you believe your husband was justified in hitting you when you were late picking him up. However, I would have felt angry and upset if he treated me that way. Even hearing about what he did to you troubles me.
- *Communicate empathy.* I felt afraid just hearing about the terrifying experiences you had in the war.
- *Letting the client know the clinician belongs to the same invisible group.* Yes, I recall how difficult it was for me also when I told my family that my roommate was really my life partner and that we are gay.

Harmful and Inappropriate Uses of Self-Disclosure

Just as there are many positive reasons for using self-disclosure, so are there harmful and self-serving reasons for using this strategy. The following are some examples:

- *Obtaining information to meet the clinician's personal needs.* I understand you work for a roofing company. What do you think I should do about that leak in the ceiling?
- *Working out the clinician's own problems.* You know, I had a date stand me up not long ago also. Let me tell you about that, so we can figure out how I should have handled the situation.
- *Offering advice that curtails the client's self-determination.* I confronted my father about his abuse, and it really improved our relationship. I think you should confront your father too. I'm sure it will help you.
- *Just making conversation or filling up time.* Terrible weather, isn't it? Do you think that hurricane will hit us?

Guidelines for Helpful Use of Self-Disclosure

- When contemplating making a self-disclosure, be aware of exactly why you are using this strategy and what you expect it to accomplish. *Being purposeful and deliberate* about self-disclosures will help avoid risks. If in doubt about a self-disclosure, the safest choice is to find another way to accomplish your purpose.
- *Conciseness and brevity* are essential in self-disclosures. Lengthy stories about oneself can detract from the client's train of thought and shift the focus from client to clinician. If more in-

formation needs to be provided, that can be done in a follow-up statement, but make the initial self-disclosure statement brief and assess its impact before proceeding.

• *Timing of a self-disclosure is important,* as it is with any intervention. The self-disclosure should fit in smoothly with the conversation and be clearly linked to the immediate focus of the session, unless the clinician has the specific purpose of disconcerting or redirecting the client. Self-disclosures can distract and can interrupt the flow of the session. If an opportunity for a contemplated self-disclosure has passed, wait for another opportunity or use another type of intervention rather than intrude on the session.

• *Focus is another important aspect* of self-disclosure. If clinicians sense that the focus is shifting away from the client, they need to restore attention to the client.

• Self-disclosures should be *relatively impersonal,* although there are exceptions to this guideline. Some clinical settings deliberately employ clinicians who have dealt successfully with problems similar to those faced by clients in that setting. This is common in drug and alcohol treatment programs. Under these circumstances, clinicians serve as role models and talk about their efforts to overcome their own difficulties. In most clinical settings, however, clinicians do not talk at length about their personal problems. In general, self-disclosure should primarily include clinicians' immediate reactions to material presented by the client or relatively neutral and superficial information about clinicians such as their difficulty resisting chocolate or the hometown they have in common with the client. Clinicians do not usually reveal highly charged and personal issues such as current conflicts in their relationships or their history of sexual abuse.

• *The facilitative conditions discussed by Rogers should be evident in self-disclosures.* In other words, clinicians should demonstrate genuineness and congruence in their self-disclosures and always communicate acceptance and empathy for their clients.

• Conclude each self-disclosure by *returning the focus of discussion to the client.* This helps prevent the focus from being diverted to the clinician.

The exercises later in this chapter will give you an opportunity to refine your skills in self-disclosure.

CASE ILLUSTRATION

The following dialog between Edie and her counselor illustrates many hallmarks of person-centered treatment, including active listening, communicating empathy, valuing and empowering the client, modeling genuineness and congruence, and focusing on the present. In order to demonstrate the clinician's use of person-centered approaches, Edie's responses are abbreviated, although person-centered clinicians typically talk much less than do their clients. Edie is working on her relationship with her mother and stepfather:

Edie: I feel so angry at my mother! Ava and I were visiting her and in came Pete, her husband. I could smell the liquor across the room. And my mother said nothing. How could she be like that?

Clinician: You're feeling pretty frustrated that she can't assert herself.

Edie: Yes, and to expose Ava to that. . . .

Clinician: You wish she would have done something to protect Ava.

Edie: Yes, but she never does.

Clinician: Never?

Edie: Yes, she's always been like that.

Clinician: I wonder if you are thinking about her failure to protect you from your stepfather and the pain that caused you.

Edie: Yes, it's affected my whole life.

Clinician: I can sense the very deep hurt that's still there for you.

Edie: I feel like crying just thinking about that. How could anyone abuse a helpless child?

Clinician: I have trouble understanding that too. We may never be able to understand why you were abused. But perhaps we can find a way for you to protect Ava.

Edie: You know how much I want to, but I don't know where to start.

Clinician: Even thinking about what happened must make you feel like that helpless child again. But you have accomplished so much in your life . . . coping with cancer, succeeding in school, having a family. . . . Perhaps you can find a way to protect Ava.

Edie: I have thought about it.

Clinician: So you did have some ideas?

Edie: Yes, several. One idea was not to see my mother or her husband anymore. That would protect Ava, but it seems so drastic.

Clinician: Part of you would like to just get away from this situation, but that seems to you like too big a step.

Edie: Yes, sometimes I do feel like never seeing them again, but that seems very childish. My mother is Pete's victim, just as I was. I also thought about setting some limits, telling her that if Pete is angry or drunk, I'll just have to leave, even if it seems rude.

Clinician: It sounds difficult for you to think about anything that might hurt your mother's feelings, and yet I agree with you that protecting Ava is essential.

Edie: I know it is. But somehow it's very hard for me to stand up to my mother. I can't imagine myself telling her what I just told you.

Clinician: It really frightens you to stand up to her. Yet I have seen you assert yourself successfully with Roberto in ways that let him know what you needed but still conveyed your love. How would it feel to speak to your mother in that same way?

Edie: Well, I would be scared, but maybe I can do it. It's for Ava.

Clinician: Yes, and maybe for you too. I suspect you would feel very proud of yourself if you could follow through on this plan.

Edie: That's true. I am starting to feel that I can protect Ava, stand up for myself, and still have a close relationship with my mother. Wouldn't that be something?

EXERCISES

Large-Group Exercises

1. Discuss the strengths and limitations of the dialog in the case illustration. What would you change, if anything, to improve on this segment of a treatment session?

2. Identify, in the dialog, examples of the following key elements of person-centered counseling:

   - Active listening
   - Empathy
   - Reflection of feeling
   - Reflection of meaning
   - Valuing and empowering the client
   - Genuineness
   - Focusing on the present
   - Self-disclosure

3. Create a round-robin dialog. One person, teacher or student, stands or sits in front of the class and assumes the role of Roberto or another hypothetical client. This client should engage in a dialog with the class about a time when he or she had very strong

emotions. Each student in turn should make one comment or intervention. Interventions should reflect person-centered treatment, with each successive intervention building on the previous one. Following the dialog, the class should discuss the role-played interview and its strengths and limitations.

Small-Group Exercises

1. Divide into groups of four students. Each dyad should engage in a 10-minute client-clinician role-play, building on previous dialogs that they have had together. Use self-disclosure at least twice and try to communicate empathy often when assuming the role of clinician.

   After each dialog, the group of four should discuss the dialog and its strengths and limitations, providing feedback to each clinician on the following:

   - The nature and effectiveness of the self-disclosures
   - Communication of empathy
   - Therapeutic alliance
   - Strengths of the role play
   - Ways in which it might have been improved

2. Most clinicians agree that pure person-centered counseling is not appropriate for treating all people. Discuss how you would screen people to determine their suitability for this mode of treatment. Develop a list of 5–10 questions you would use to help you decide whether this approach is suitable for a particular person. Then develop a list of 5–10 criteria that suggest a client's suitability for person-centered treatment.

If you were a practicing clinician and realized that a particular person was not a good candidate for a pure person-centered approach, you might then consider how to integrate this treatment approach with other approaches to develop a better way to help that person. However, because you are not yet familiar with many of the established theories of treatment, that step will not be made part of this exercise.

Individual Exercises

1. Develop and write in your journal an appropriate clinician self-disclosure in response to the following client statements and questions:

   Client A: There must be something really wrong with me. Everybody else seems to love parties, but I hate going into a big room full of strangers.

   Client B: I finally had a great weekend. I woke up early, took a walk, had brunch with a friend, and then went to that great Georgia O'Keeffe exhibit at the museum.

   Client C: I feel embarrassed that my parents found out I had too much to drink last night and had to have someone drive me home. Did anything like that ever happen to you when you were younger?

Client D: My older brother hits me and pushes me whenever we are alone. Yesterday, when he pushed me, I fell down and really hurt myself. I don't know what to do. I'm afraid he'll get into trouble if I tell anyone.

Client E: It feels like once I let people know I'm a lesbian, that changes all their reactions to me and they don't see me as a person anymore. Sometimes I think that happened here too. When I told you my partner was a woman, your expression changed, and I sensed that you disapproved of me.

2. Listening is something we often take for granted, not realizing that it is an art. For the next hour of time when you are interacting with people, be conscious of your listening skills. Use reflection and empathy to let people know you hear and grasp the meaning of what they are saying. Maintain good eye contact. Monitor your verbal and nonverbal messages to be sure they are congruent and that you are genuine, caring, and accepting. Write about this experience in your journal.

SUMMARY

Carl Rogers's person-centered counseling, first developed in the 1940s and 1950s, is a humanistic and phenomenological approach to treatment that prizes the dignity and worth of all people as well as their potential to resolve their difficulties. The primary source of healing in person-centered treatment is the therapeutic alliance. By demonstrating facilitative conditions such as empathy, caring and acceptance, genuineness, and congruence, clinicians promote people's empowerment and self-esteem and enable them to help themselves. Ideally, treatment moves people along a path of growth toward actualization of potential, helping people to become more fully functioning. This approach, which emphasizes the present rather than past problems, revolutionized thinking about counseling and psychotherapy. Although person-centered treatment is no longer widely used as a primary treatment approach, it frequently is integrated with other treatment approaches to make a powerful treatment package. Rogers's ideas influenced nearly all current approaches to psychotherapy and have helped us recognize that the success of any approach to treatment is strongly linked to a positive client-clinician collaboration.

RECOMMENDED READINGS

Cain, D. J. (1987). Carl R. Rogers: The man, his vision, his impact. *Person-Centered Review, 2(3),* 283–288.

Carkhuff, R. R. (2000). *The art of helping in the 21st century.* Amhearst, MA: Human Resource Development Press, Inc.

Hill, C. E., & Nakayama, E. Y. (2000). Client-centered therapy: Where has it been and where is it going? A comment on Hathaway (1948). *Journal of Clinical Psychology, 56,* 861–875.

Kirschenbaum, H. (2004). Carl Rogers's life and work: An assessment on the 100th anniversary of his birth. *Journal of Counseling and Development, 82,* 116–124.

Rogers, C. R. (1951). *Client-centered therapy: Its current practice, implications and theory.* Boston: Houghton Mifflin.

Rogers, C. R. (1961). *On becoming a person.* Boston: Houghton Mifflin.

Rogers, C. R. (1980). *A way of being.* Boston: Houghton Mifflin.

ADDITIONAL SOURCES OF INFORMATION

http://www.psy.pdx.edu/PsiCafe/KeyTheorists/Rogers.htm—Website provides information about Rogers's life, his theories, his writings, and his contributions.

http://www.ahpweb.org/—This website for the Association for Humanistic Psychology promotes the values reflected in Rogers's work.

http://www.infed.org/thinkers/et-rogers.htm—Information on Rogers's life, his influence on education, and the facilitative conditions are featured in this website.

http://www.nrogers.com/carlrogers/html—This website focuses on Carl Rogers and his daughter Natalie who provides information on her father's life and vision.

http://adpca.org—This website of the Association for the Development of the Person-Centered Approach, Inc. (ADPCA) promotes Rogers's work through publications such as the *Person-Centered Journal,* annual meetings, continuing education, training, and supervision in the person-centered approach.

CHAPTER 11

Existential Therapy

Existential therapy embodies many of the values and viewpoints of Carl Rogers's person-centered counseling discussed in the previous chapter. However, according to Vontress (Epp, 1998), "Existential philosophy for me fills in where Rogers left off. It defines the issues that must be broached in counseling in broad strokes: love, death, suffering, and meaning" (p. 3).

Existential therapy is more a philosophy than a structured treatment system. It seeks to enable people to face the anxieties and uncertainties of life, make wise and responsible choices, and create meaning in their lives. Existential therapy helps people become more actualized, make rewarding use of their potential, and experience a deep, perhaps spiritual, connection with other people and their world. These goals are accomplished primarily through the special relationship between the clinician and the client, an essential vehicle for change in existential therapy, as it is in person-centered counseling. Events of the early years of the 21st century, including terrorist attacks and wars, have established a climate of heightened anxiety, fears of death, and a sharpened sense of loneliness. Existential therapy seems well suited to addressing these concerns.

THE PEOPLE WHO DEVELOPED EXISTENTIAL THERAPY

Many names are associated with the development of existential therapy, including Viktor Frankl, Rollo May, Irvin Yalom, James Bugental, Ludwig Binswanger, and Medard Boss. The ideas of theoreticians and philosophers such as Abraham Maslow, Sören Kierkegaard, Friedrich Nietzsche, Martin Heidegger, Paul Tillich, and Martin Buber also were key to the development of this approach. In addition, writers including Albert Camus, Jean-Paul Sartre, Franz Kafka, and others helped shape existentialism. Following are brief biographies of the three men—Viktor Frankl, Rollo May, and Irvin Yalom—who are most strongly associated with existential therapy today. Information on several other contributors to this approach also is included.

Viktor Frankl

Viktor Frankl was born in 1905 in Vienna, Austria, and received both M.D. and Ph.D. degrees from the University of Vienna. Before the Second World War, he was a practicing physician. Between 1942 and 1945, however, he was a prisoner in the Nazi concentration camps in Dachau and Auschwitz. His mother and father, his brother, and his first wife and their children all perished in the camps. Of course, these experiences had a profound impact on Frankl's thinking. Although his interest in existential thought began before his imprisonment, his difficult years in the concentration camps led him to conclude that the will to create meaning and purpose is the prime human motivator (Bauman & Waldo, 1998). For Frankl, his purpose became surviving his imprisonment so that he could tell others about those experiences and the terrible impact of war and hatred. *Man's Search for Meaning* (Frankl, 1963) is a powerful description of his experiences, his existential struggles, and what he learned from them (Wawrytko, 1989). In that book, Frankl quotes Nietzsche: "He who has a why to live for can bear with almost any how" (p. 121) and "That which does not kill me, makes me stronger" (p. 130). These quotations reflect Frankl's own triumph over tragedy, his ability to make meaningful the terrible losses and experiences he endured.

Frankl called his treatment approach *logotherapy*—therapy through meaning. Barton (1992) said of logotherapy, "It presupposes that the freedom to make meanings belongs to the human world essentially, and that all human beings have regions in which they can take up freedom and make meaning" (p. 338). Frankl believed that, even under extreme circumstances, people have choices. The tasks of the clinician are to help people:

- Discover and notice where they possess freedom and the potential for meaning
- Actualize those potentials to transform and make meaning of their lives
- Honor meanings realized in the past (Lantz, 2000)

For Frankl, as for most existentialist clinicians, the central ingredient in treatment is the use of the treatment relationship to accomplish these goals.

Frankl's writings as well as his lectures throughout the world certainly made his life a meaningful one. In addition, he married again in the late 1940s and reportedly found personal as well as professional success. Frankl lived until 1997, continuing to write throughout his life about the most important aspects of all our lives, including meaning, love, work, and society (Frankl, 1978, 1987, 1992).

Rollo May

Rollo May was born in 1909 into a family of six children and spent his childhood in Ohio and Michigan. A practicing psychoanalyst, he studied with Alfred Adler in Vienna and was influenced by Adler and European existential thought. In addition, May's own difficult life, including an unhappy childhood, two unsuccessful marriages, and serious illness, contributed to the development of his ideas.

May's writings brought existentialism to the United States (May, Angel, & Ellenberger, 1958). His work initially focused on the anxiety he believed all people experience as we struggle with the difficulties of growth and change, our aloneness in the world, our apprehensions about death, and the courage required to pursue goals of independence and growth (May, 1950). Also important to him were people's roles in and relationships with their society, reflecting Adler's emphasis on social responsibility. May believed that often people avoid difficult conflicts and confrontations, such as those with culture and destiny (including death), leading us to neglect the potentials for meaning in our lives. Many of May's landmark writings and studies addressed fundamental human experiences such as these. Several of his books, including *Love and Will* (May, 1969), became popular and increased general awareness of existential concepts that May saw as relevant to all our lives. As he stated (May, 1990a), "I do not believe there is a special school of therapy to be put in a category of 'existential.' I think existential, rather, refers to an attitude toward human beings and a set of presuppositions about these human beings" (p. 49).

Like Frankl, Rollo May lived a long and productive life, dying in 1994 at the age of 85. In his obituary for Rollo May, Bugental (1996, p. 418) said of May's contribution, ". . . so much of what he contributed has entered into our general discourse about such conceptual areas as human nature, the major life issues and dimensions that we confront as individuals and as scientists and professionals . . . "

Irvin Yalom

Born in 1931 in Washington, DC, Irvin Yalom grew up in a small apartment over his parents' grocery store. His escape from the poverty and danger of his inner-city neighborhood was the library, where he developed an enduring love of reading. Yalom was trained as a psychiatrist and completed his residency at Johns Hopkins University. After some years in the army, he became a professor of psychiatry at Stanford University School of Medicine. Yalom and his wife Marilyn, a scholar of women's studies and French literature, have four children and many grandchildren.

Yalom is a prolific writer on both existentialism and group psychotherapy with his ideas influenced by both European and American existential thought. His book *Existential Psychotherapy* (Yalom, 1980) contributed greatly to understanding of this approach, particularly in the United States. Yalom also has written books for the general reader, describing his therapy with people coping with existential issues. In *Love's Executioner and Other Tales of Psychotherapy*, Yalom (1989) stated, "I have found that four givens are particularly relevant to psychotherapy: the inevitability of death for each of us and for those we love; the freedom to make our lives as we will; our ultimate aloneness; and, finally, the absence of any obvious meaning or sense to life. However grim these givens may seem, they contain the seeds of wisdom and redemption" (pp. 4–5).

In clarifying the nature of existentialism, Yalom (1980) identified the basic difference between Freudian psychoanalysis and Yalom's concept of existentialism. Freud viewed people as struggling with a conflict between the instinctual strivings of the id and the socialized forces of the ego and superego, while Yalom saw our conflicts as stemming "from the dilemma of a meaning-seeking creature who is thrown into a universe that has no meaning" (p. 9). He continues to lecture and write about his ideas as well as his practice of psychotherapy, as reflected in his book, *Momma and the Meaning of Life: Tales of Psychotherapy* (1999).

Two Other American Existential Therapists: Bugental and Vontress

Because of their groundbreaking and prolific writing, Rollo May and Irvin Yalom have become the best known American existential therapists. However, James Bugental and Clemmont Vontress are two other important existential therapists in the United States.

Since the 1970s, Bugental sought to clarify the implementation of existential therapy (Miars, 2002). He provided information on the therapeutic alliance, the values inherent in existential therapy, and the skills and stance reflective of existentially-oriented clinicians. Important in Bugental's theory is the self-and-world construct system, defined as "the conception each of us holds about who and what we are and how our world operates" (Miars, 2002, p. 219). Bugental likened this construct to a spacesuit that helps people navigate through their lives. Existential therapy can help people examine their self-and-world constructs and configure them in more life-enabling ways.

Clemmont Vontress, an African American and a leading advocate of the existential approach to counseling, taught for many years at George Washington University. His work has been important in promoting awareness of the holistic and spiritual aspects of existentialism, as well as of its relevance to a diverse population. This will be addressed further later in this chapter.

THE DEVELOPMENT OF EXISTENTIAL THERAPY

Although existentialism as a philosophy has evolved since the 19th century, existential therapy arose in Europe during the 1940s and 1950s. Social, political, and scientific events during those years contributed to the development of this approach. According to Bauman and Waldo (1998), World War I and World War II led to a "pervasive sense of alienation and meaninglessness." Growing industrialization and urbanization of society, as well as scientific advances, added to this dehumanization. Even psychology, dominated at that time by psychoanalysis, seemed to "conceptualize the person as an assemblage of parts often struggling against one another" (p. 15). People needed a force that would restore their sense of humanness as well as help them cope with their concerns about the meaning of life in the face of the devastation, isolation, and death that resulted from the wars. Existentialism, along with its close relative, humanistic psychology, evolved in response to those needs.

The works of Frankl and May were widely read in the United States during the 1950s and 1960s. Interest in existential therapy has been kept alive by the more recent writings of Yalom, Bugental, Vontress, and others, although attention to the approach seems to have declined since the 1960s. This may be due to the emphasis on accountability in treatment and the corresponding growth of more structured and empirically validated approaches such as cognitive and behavior therapy.

Although relatively few clinicians select existential therapy as their primary theoretical orientation, existentialism continues to exert an influence today, particularly on our conception of the clinician's role and the realization that, for many people, counseling and psychotherapy are not just tools for solving problems but ways to give meaning to lives that lack purpose and fulfillment.

IMPORTANT THEORETICAL CONCEPTS

The theory underlying existential therapy focuses not on the treatment process but on exploring the universal issues that people face and ways for people to address them that are life-enhancing and actualizing. Through their understanding of these issues, clinicians can connect with people on a deep and personal level and help them change their lives so that they have more meaning and fulfillment.

Ultimate Concerns of the Human Condition

For the existentialists, life has no inherent meaning and is replete with challenges. Unless people meet these challenges with awareness, openness, and courage, their emotional development can become blocked or delayed. Existentialist theory suggests that the following four ultimate concerns of the human condition are typically at the root of emotional difficulties:

- *Inevitability of death.* From childhood, we realize that our death is inevitable, as are the deaths of our loved ones. No matter how gifted we are, no matter how special our lives are, death is the outcome for everyone. The fear of our ultimate nonbeing can cast a pall over people's lives and make them seem pointless.

- *Isolation.* Although we may surround ourselves with colleagues, friends, and family, we are ultimately alone. No one can truly understand us or sense our thoughts and feelings as we do. No one can rescue us from the inevitability of death and other losses we will experience in our lives. Some people seek to fuse with and become dependent on others in an effort to counteract their sense of alienation and loneliness, but those efforts inevitably fail because they detract even further from people's sense of themselves and the purpose of their lives. In fact, loneliness can be most acute when we are with others and are aware of our lack of a true connection with them.

- *Meaninglessness.* According to existential theory, "Meaninglessness is the dreaded answer to the existential questions 'What is the meaning of life?' 'What difference do I really make?' 'What is the purpose of the struggles?' " (Frank, 1995, p. 217). The inherent meaninglessness of life can lead to hopelessness, discouragement, and a sense of emptiness. The only certainties in our lives are birth and death. Beyond that, life seems to be a random process. On the other hand, that very lack of inherent meaning gives people the opportunity to make sense of their lives. Just as Viktor Frankl found meaning in his efforts to survive the concentration camp so that he could share his ideas with the world, we can create goals and purposes that make our lives worthwhile and meaningful to us.

> • *Freedom and responsibility.* Modern society presents people with an overwhelming and constantly increasing array of choices: choices of lifestyles, choices of experiences, choices of acquisitions, and others. We have both the freedom and the responsibility to make choices that create a worthwhile existence for ourselves in the limited time we have on earth. That is a daunting prospect for most of us!

Existential and Neurotic Anxiety

Everyone experiences the four ultimate concerns of the human condition and, according to existentialist theory, that creates feelings of anxiety in everyone. However, the theory distinguishes between existential (normal) anxiety and neurotic anxiety. Existential anxiety is viewed as an inevitable part of the human condition. It is deeper than anxiety about one's career or health. Rather, it is "a deep feeling of unease that arises from our awareness of the givens: our existence is finite, we are mortal, and there is no purpose but the ones we create for ourselves" (Bauman & Waldo, 1998, p. 19). Existential anxiety is a positive sign rather than a pathological state; it indicates that people recognize the need to accept responsibility for their lives and are engaged in efforts to create a worthwhile and meaningful existence. Such people are living *authentic* lives in which they are aware of their self-in-world construct, strive to make wise choices, and take responsibility for their decisions.

Existential guilt and neurotic anxiety result when we lack awareness of our physical world, our relationships, and our psychological world; fail to take responsibility for making our lives meaningful and worthwhile; and realize that we have not become what we might have. It reflects our awareness that we have not fully realized ourselves as human beings and have allowed our lives to be controlled by chance and circumstance. We may not understand or be able to articulate the reasons for our feelings of guilt but, for many, an underlying sense of deep guilt and regret pervades our lives.

Depression often is the result of efforts to defend against existential guilt and anxiety and avoid the task of making our lives meaningful. Yalom (1980) found, for example, that among people nearing death, depression was greatest in those who had not created meaningful lives, while those who felt satisfied with the lives they had created for themselves were more able to accept death.

Human Development and the Development of Emotional Difficulties

Existential therapists do not dispute the importance of early development and the child-parent relationship. However, they link those to existential concerns. Frankl, for example, believed that so-called neurotic difficulties often stem from an upbringing in which parents were punitive and deprived children of freedom (Barton, 1992).

Similarly, existential therapists think of the unconscious in ways that reflect the tenets of existentialism. They concentrate on the unconscious conflict between people's wish to escape the givens of the human condition and lose themselves in lethargy and denial and their wish to achieve fulfillment despite the challenges and responsibilities that achievement entails. For the existentialists, emotional difficulties stem from failure to deal successfully with the inevitabilities of the human condition and to transcend them by creating a meaningful and authentic life for oneself.

Existential therapists pay attention to development throughout the life span and do not limit their focus to early childhood. They view life as a process of creating our own histories, with each choice and phase shaping and contributing to the next. Existence is never static; people are always becoming something new, striving to move toward their possibilities, and making their lives worthwhile.

Dasein

Existentialists speak of *dasein*—defined as being present, being in the world. According to Bauman and Waldo (1998, p. 16), "The term dasein acknowledges that human beings exist, have consciousness, and are responsible for their own existence." According to May, "Man (or Dasein) is the particular being who has to be aware of himself, be responsible for himself, if he is to become himself. He also is that particular being who knows that at some future moment he will not be: he is the being who is always in dialectical relation with non-being death." (May et al., 1958, p. 42). The concept of dasein is complex and elusive but reflects people's ability to simultaneously live in the present, be conscious, and take responsibility for making their lives meaningful, while realizing fully that death will inevitably end their efforts. It reflects potential and becoming rather than a fixed state.

Concept of Mental Health

Vontress defined mental health as "being in balance and harmony with one's inner-self; with one's friends, family and colleagues; with one's physical environment; and with one's spirituality" (Epp, 1998, p. 9). Existential therapists emphasize the importance of experiencing the unity of self and world. They also believe that people who are not simply passive victims of circumstances but become the architects of their own lives reflect emotional health. As Paul Tillich (1961), an existential philosopher, stated, "Man becomes truly human only at the moment of decision" (p. 39). Whatever difficulties we encounter in our lives, we always have choices. According to May (1990b), "No matter how great the forces victimizing the human being, man has the capacity to know that he is being victimized and thus to influence in some way how he will relate to his fate" (p. 270).

Potentials of the Human Condition

The inevitable concerns of the human condition, discussed previously, seem to present a bleak picture of life. However, existential therapy is an optimistic and hopeful approach, especially in its perspective that all people have the potential to transcend those inevitabilities and its recognitions of people's many strengths including the following.

Awareness   People have the capacity for awareness of both themselves and the world. The greater our awareness, the more possibilities that are open to us and the more successfully we can address our fears and anxieties. Although awareness will not always bring us pleasure or peace, it allows us to recognize the limitations and challenges of our lives and make wise choices that can make our lives worthwhile.

Years ago, people often were not told when they had a terminal illness because of the belief that they were better off not knowing about their condition. However, that decision deprived them of the capacity to make meaningful choices about how they would live out their lives and encouraged inauthenticity and deceptive relationships. Now people are almost always told the truth about their medical conditions so they can make choices such as whether to take medication that may hasten their deaths but relieve their pain.

Authenticity   Authenticity has been described as "the kind of existence human beings have when they accept the responsibility for choosing the direction of their lives and they base those choices on values determined through increasing self-awareness" (Bauman & Waldo, 1998, p. 19). In *The Search for Authenticity* (1965), Bugental described three essential features of authenticity:

1. People are aware of themselves and their relationships with the world.
2. They make choices, knowing that decisions are the inevitable consequences of responsibility.
3. They take responsibility for their choices, recognizing that awareness is imperfect, and sometimes leads to unanticipated results.

Taking responsibility for making choices based on awareness reflects authenticity and allows people to live more fully in the present and be themselves in their relationships. People whose decisions are based on denial, the wishes of others, or dependence are not truly living in the present; they may be driven by past losses or acting out of a hope for future gains. In addition, they are wearing a "mask of inauthenticity" that prevents others from really knowing who they are (Frank, 1995, p. 214).

Freedom and Responsibility   Freedom can be viewed as consisting of four aspects: awareness, choice, action, and change. Once people accept that they have freedom, no matter what their circumstances are, they have the responsibility:

- To be aware of their past history, their current options, and their future potential
- To make choices that give meaning to their lives
- To exercise courage and thought in taking action toward life-enhancing change

Once we see that we have freedom, we can no longer view our decisions and behaviors as purposeless and accidental, make excuses for ourselves, and shift blame for our unhappiness to others. We must assume responsibility and recognize that ultimately we alone are in charge of our lives. The enormity of that realization can be frightening but also can be empowering, if only we can use our freedom in positive and growthful ways.

Actualization   Actualization is an important concept for existential therapists, as it is for person-centered clinicians. Abraham Maslow (1954, 1968) probably best described the nature of actualization. He advanced the idea that each person has an essential nature, part of which is universal and part of which is unique to that individual. Maslow (1954) believed "that full healthy and normal and desirable development consists in actualizing this nature, in fulfilling these potentialities, and in developing into maturity along the lines that this . . . essential nature dictates, growing from within rather than being shaped from without" (p. 340). The will toward actualization is an innate and natural process that leads people toward realization of their potentials and toward growth and fulfillment.

Actualization can be blocked by many factors including a cultural or family background that inhibits creativity, a repressive environment, and overwhelming fear and guilt. People who fail to move toward actualization typically experience shame, defeat, anxiety, and a perception of life as meaningless (Frank, 1995; Yalom, 1980).

Making Meaning   Existential therapists believe that life has the potential to be meaningful if people use their capacities to bring purpose and worth into their lives. According to May (1969), our will to love and to live gives us meaning. Our awareness, our recognition that we have freedom, our authenticity, and our will toward actualization all enable us to know and confront disturbing aspects of ourselves and our world, such as the inevitability of death and our ultimate aloneness, and to transcend them by creating meaning in our lives.

Meaning is the purpose and logic of our lives and often is reflected in choices people make. Dreams, visions, and fantasies also provide clues to meaning. Some people have social goals, such as Carl Rogers's efforts to increase world peace; others have competitive goals, such as breaking a world record, or creative goals, such as writing a novel. But most people find meaning in daily activities such as raising healthy children, planting gardens, helping others, and establishing a rewarding business.

Because life itself is a process, we are in a constant state of emerging and evolving, becoming more fully ourselves, and making meaning of each day as well as of the entirety of our lives. According to the existentialists, it is this journey that makes us human.

TREATMENT USING EXISTENTIAL THERAPY

Existential therapy is a process in which two people, client and clinician, embark on a journey to help the client cope more effectively with the inevitable conditions of life and make better use of the potentials of humankind. This approach makes minimal use of techniques but relies heavily on the clinician to effect change.

Goals

The fundamental goal of existential therapy is helping people find value, meaning, and purpose in their lives. Treatment does not specifically seek to ameliorate symptoms. In other words, "The purpose of psychotherapy is not to 'cure' the clients in the conventional sense, but to help them become aware of what they are doing and to get them out of the victim role" (May, 1981, p. 210).

To reach this goal, existential therapists help people confront their deepest fears and anxieties about the inevitable challenges of life including death, isolation, and meaninglessness. Reviewing and reflecting on clients' histories can facilitate this process, especially if it helps them identify barriers that impede their movement toward an authentic and personally meaningful life. In addition, treatment helps people become aware of the freedom they do have, recognize their options, and make choices that help them become more actualized and able to lead a life that reflects their values and priorities.

Therapeutic Alliance

As the primary vehicle for facilitating change, clinicians who practice existential therapy have considerable responsibility. Their own values are very much a part of the treatment process and clinician self-disclosure is important. Therapists advocate freedom and responsibility (Barton,

1992), encourage people to confront their fears, and promote their efforts to make meaningful choices. In keeping with their emphasis on personal freedom, existential clinicians do not hold back their views. They express their values and beliefs, give advice, use humor, and make suggestions and interpretations but always allow clients the freedom to determine how they will use this input. As Bugental (1987) put it, "The therapeutic alliance is the powerful joining of forces which energizes and supports the long, difficult, and frequently painful work of life-changing psychotherapy" (p. 49).

Existential therapists are companions and co-explorers with their clients. Available and empathic, these clinicians experience clients' pain without losing their sense of themselves. To understand their clients' deepest thoughts and feelings about issues such as death, isolation, and guilt, existential therapists need to be with their clients as fully as possible and to listen with both eyes and ears. According to Yalom (1980), clinicians should, "implicitly and explicitly, wonder about the patient's belief systems, inquire deeply into the loving of another, ask about long-range hopes and goals, and explore creative interests and pursuits" (p. 471). They communicate respect, support, encouragement, and concern and are genuine, open, and caring. They have no expectations for outcome, no mandates for client behavior, but simply join people in their quest to use their freedom to craft a meaningful and rewarding life. Their focus is on process, rather than on content.

Martin Buber (1970) believed that relationships can reflect several possible levels:

1. I to I relationships, in which other people are almost irrelevant; I am all that matters
2. I to it relationships, in which people are viewed as objects in transient interactions
3. It to it relationships, in which people have little sense of self
4. We to we relationships, involving a lack of individuality and primarily characterizing children's relationships
5. Us to them relationships, in which others are viewed as either chosen or rejected, special or lacking, in or out of favor; us (those in good favor) are all that matters
6. I to you relationships, involving two people who view each other as separate individuals
7. I to thou relationships, in which people have the deepest respect for each other as well as a great sense of relatedness

I to thou relationships are the most profound and meaningful kind. Therapists who can create this type of relationship with their clients are truly sharing a journey with them and empowering their clients through the strong and honoring connection between client and therapist (Bugental, 1978).

Maintaining relationships of this magnitude and intensity can be very demanding of clinicians. As Frank (1995) stated, "Making several such painful journeys with clients is bound to affect practitioners at a very personal level. . . . Being an existential counselor or therapist means being open to continued learning and awareness because existential helping operates at an intense level of involvement" (p. 222).

The Process of Treatment

Because existential therapy is not problem- or crisis-focused and involves the establishment of a deep relationship between client and clinician, it is almost never time-limited or rushed. Typically, treatment has no clear stages or transitions.

However, the process generally begins by developing clinicians' understanding of their clients and clients' awareness of themselves and their world. Clients are encouraged to describe their values, beliefs, and assumptions; their histories and backgrounds; and the choices they have made, as well as the choices they believe they cannot make. Clinicians listen closely so they can comprehend the clients' views of the world and gradually help them express their deepest fears and take greater responsibility for their lives.

The middle phase of treatment enables people to use the information they have shared to find purpose, meaning, and value in their lives. Therapist interventions encourage client authenticity during this process.

Treatment moves toward a close when people can implement their awareness of themselves and move forward to establish more meaningful lives. They have learned that they cannot eliminate anxiety from their lives but have found ways to live full lives despite anxiety about the inevitabilities of the human condition. In addition, they are progressing along a path that seems natural and right for them and is helping them become actualized.

An important and challenging aspect of concluding treatment is the client's separation from the clinician. This can be a reminder of the inescapable endings in life and is often difficult for both client and clinician. However, if both can be present in the moment, authentic, and aware of their reactions to the end of treatment, that process itself can foster growth, helping people face and cope effectively with their fears.

Specific Intervention Strategies

The primary interventions in existential therapy—use of the person of the clinician and the client-clinician relationship—have already been discussed. However, the approach also uses some other interventions.

Being in the World   May (May et al., 1958) used the term *being in the world* to refer to the importance of clinicians' understanding as fully as possible both clients' objective world and their subjective one. The term includes three modes of being: being in the physical world, being in the world of interpersonal relationships, and being in the personal and psychological world. May believed that therapy needs to focus on the interaction of these three modes, helping people to keep them in balance. Being in the world is compromised for both client and clinician if one mode is overemphasized while the others are excluded from attention.

Symbolic Growth Experience   Both Frankl (1963) and Maslow (1968) described the learning and growth that came from intense experiences. Maslow referred to these as peak experiences but some of them might also be viewed as cathartic experiences. Frick, building on the ideas of Frankl and Maslow, described a model, the Symbolic Growth Experience (SGE), to explain the relationship between experience and the discovery of meaning. Frick (1987) defined the SGE as "the conscious recognition and interpretation of the symbolic dimensions of an immediate experience leading to heightened awareness, discovery of meaning, and personal worth" (p. 36). The exploration of an SGE has four steps:

1. People are educated about the concept of the SGE.
2. They select a salient past experience and explore its importance and symbolism in their lives.

3. They are helped to understand the meaning embedded in the experience.
4. They have a clearer sense of that meaning and are able to repeat their use of these strategies to grasp the significance of other experiences.

We will explore an SGE in more detail later in this chapter.

Frankl's Logotherapy and Paradoxical Intention   Viktor Frankl (1978) termed his version of existential therapy *logotherapy*—"therapy through meaning" (p. 19). He believed that even well-functioning people sometimes perceive life as meaningless and experience a sense of emptiness. He referred to this as "the unheard cry for meaning" (p. 20). Through treatment, he helped people recognize the depth of their need for meaning, reassured them that all people can create meaning in their lives, and supported them in their efforts to find purpose and meaning.

Frankl described a cycle in which fears evoke symptoms that in turn increase the fears. For example, a person who fears heights avoids them; because of the avoidance, anticipatory anxiety develops, the heights become increasingly frightening in the person's mind, and the avoidance as well as the fears increase. As Frankl (1978) put it, "The fear of fear increases fear" (p. 116).

To break this pattern, he recommended a technique called *paradoxical intention* in which clinicians encourage clients to do or wish for the very thing they fear most. For example, a woman was afraid to leave her house lest she faint. Frankl instructed her to go outside and try her best to faint. Not surprisingly, she was unable to faint. His intervention succeeded in both reducing her fear and strengthening her courage by changing the meaning of her fear. She could now accept her fear, as well as the slight possibility that she might faint. As Yalom (1980) stated, "When we take ourselves out of the lie and become distant spectators, things cease to matter" (p. 478).

Yalom (1980) believed that this principle extended to people's search for meaning: "I believe that the search for meaning is similarly paradoxical: the more we rationally seek it, the less we find it; the questions that one can pose about meaning will always outlast the answers" (p. 482). Finding meaning is a lifelong process of facing our fears, developing awareness, and making choices. Paradoxical intention is one technique that can help people in that process.

Dereflection   *Dereflection* is a type of paradoxical intervention that can help people deal with feelings of meaningless. Developed by Frankl, it involves telling people to focus less on themselves and more on finding meaning outside of themselves (Yalom, 1980). Encouraging people to focus on something other than themselves helps to reduce self-absorption and anxiety and facilitates their efforts to find meaning in their lives.

Addressing the Four Dimensions of the Human Condition   Presented earlier in this chapter are the four dimensions of the human condition that typically underlie emotional difficulties: death, isolation, meaninglessness, and freedom. Theorists have suggested responses to concerns about these four conditions, such as the following (Bauman & Waldo, 1998).

- Faith in our own existence in the present can ameliorate fears of death.
- Love is the authentic response to isolation.
- Drawing on our inner creativity, to find ways to realize our potential, can counteract the inherent meaninglessness of life.
- Responsibility and commitment, making choices and staying with them, help us cope with our overabundance of freedom.

APPLICATION OF EXISTENTIAL THERAPY

Existential therapy is a useful approach with many problems and people. The following describes its application, as reflected in theory and research.

Application to Diagnostic Groups

Because of its lack of specific interventions, its focus on philosophical issues rather than on concrete problems, and its emphasis on the client-clinician relationship and thoughtful and open dialog, existential therapy seems most appropriate for people who are coping with relatively mild disorders that do not need rapid relief. People with longstanding, pervasive anxiety (generalized anxiety disorder) or depression (dysthymic disorder) seem especially likely to benefit from this approach to treatment, probably combined with interventions designed to reduce specific symptoms. People with other anxiety disorders such as posttraumatic stress disorder, agoraphobia, and panic disorder also may respond well to the existential clinician's efforts to help them explore and understand the meaning of their fears so that they can take more control of their lives. In addition, people with the milder personality disorders such as dependent, avoidant, narcissistic, and histrionic personality disorders also might benefit from this approach, probably after they have made some progress via other modes of treatment. Looking at how they have made choices and the meaning of their lives so far might enable people with these disorders to live their lives more deliberately, create more meaning for themselves, and be more authentic and connected in their relationships.

Existential therapy also might be helpful to people with chronic or recurrent mental disorders such as major depressive disorder, bipolar disorders, schizophrenia, and substance use disorders, at times when their symptoms are not prominent. For these people, too, looking at their lives, perhaps seeing and addressing their need for meaning, might enable them to better cope with their difficulties and make the most of their lives.

Application to Culturally Diverse Groups

Some have questioned the appropriateness of existential therapy in treating a multicultural population because of its European origins, its abstract and theoretical nature, and its lack of focus on solving immediate problems. Vontress, however, argues that existential treatment is suitable for people from all cultural backgrounds (Epp, 1998). He reminds us that philosophers from Asia and other non-western areas have addressed issues of the meaning of life for many more years than have western philosophers. Vontress believes that because of its focus on issues that all people face such as death, suffering, love, and loneliness, existential counseling can help all people "find meaning and harmony in their lives" (p. 2) and is, indeed, "a universal philosophy of humankind" (p. 7).

Bauman and Waldo (1998, p. 24) agree. They observe that the phenomenological perspective of the existential clinician allows "the counselor to move away from the Western notion of cause and effect and to accept clients' experience within their cultural context."

Application to Other Groups

Studies have looked at the impact of existential therapy on specific client groups. Although the scope and sample size of these studies are insufficient to firmly establish the approach's effectiveness, research does suggest broad application for existential therapy.

Eisenberg (1989), for example, used Frankl's logotherapy as well as other humanistic and emotionally oriented interventions (e.g., Rogers's facilitative conditions, meditation, relaxation) to treat people in an Israeli prison. Participants were helped to increase their awareness, find meaning and alternatives in all situations, and use their guilt as a catalyst for positive change. They were encouraged to make a conscious choice to "straighten themselves out" (p. 90) and to be more open and authentic. A theme of treatment was the existential message: "Place one thing above everything else: To master life under all circumstances. This foremost self-transcending endeavor immunizes against despair. By forgetting yourself, by transcending yourself, you become truly human" (p. 90). The treatment approach yielded positive results and still is used in this setting.

Schwartzberg (1993) applied existential concepts to HIV-positive gay men, a group of people likely to be struggling with fears of death and the meaning of life. Common issues of irreparable loss, isolation, powerlessness, and punishment, as well as clients' efforts to find spiritual growth and meaning in the face of their diagnosis, suggested that existential concepts and therapy would be relevant to such a population.

Lantz and Gregoire presented two studies that reflect the beneficial impact of an existential approach on couples. Twenty-seven couples dealing with breast cancer, treated via an existential approach, showed significant positive change on two clinical measures (Lantz & Gregoire, 2000). Similarly, 53 Vietnam veteran couples all showed improvement, as indicated by self-report as well as measures of marital adjustment. In describing the treatment, Lantz and Gregoire (2000, p. 317) wrote, "The therapist pays close attention to the importance of the treatment encounter, to freedom and responsibility, to opportunities for growth to be found in tragedy and crisis, and to the central human desire to notice, actualize, and honor the meanings and meaning potentials in marital and family life."

Existential therapy also lends itself to use in group counseling. Garrow and Walker (2001) describe the use of this approach with a group of older adults dealing with issues of death and dying. Particularly useful in counteracting participants' sense of meaningless and isolation was the opportunity to connect with others with similar losses and to help each other. The group leader was able to build on this experience in encouraging group members to help people outside of the group.

These studies reflect the type of person and situation for whom existential therapy seems best suited:

- People coping with life-threatening and chronic illnesses
- Those whose lives have challenging limitations, such as people who are incarcerated, people with disabilities, and people living in poverty
- Those who have suffered important losses, such as bereavement, disappointments in relationships, and failure to achieve their goals
- People who have had traumatic experiences
- People with long-standing mild-to-moderate anxiety or depression
- People at a crossroads in their lives who are looking for direction, such as those who are recently divorced, retired, or graduated from college

Although existential therapy seems especially relevant to these six groups, the existential approach has relevance to all of us, whether or not we are actively struggling with issues of meaning. Nearly all people, at one time or another, reflect on the significance of their lives, on who they really are and who they want to become, and on issues of closeness and authenticity in relationships. Whether or not existential therapy is used as the primary mode of intervention with a given person, its concepts have a place in all client-clinician relationships, especially with people who are open to new ideas and who are struggling with issues addressed by existential thinkers.

CURRENT USE OF EXISTENTIAL TREATMENT

Existential therapy's themes of meaningfulness, authenticity, freedom, and responsibility continue to have great relevance and broad application. The more our lives seem controlled by technology, the more we hear about terrorism and school violence, and the more we are troubled by our own overcommitted lifestyles, the more many of us search for meaning and purpose in what we do and struggle to maintain a sense of freedom and authenticity.

In recent years, spirituality has emerged as an acceptable and important topic in counseling and psychotherapy. This emphasis on spirituality is consistent with an existential viewpoint. Although existentialism does not advocate any specific religious beliefs, it reminds us of the importance of having a sense of meaning that transcends our immediate and finite lives. Whether that meaning comes from traditional religion, the spirituality of nature, watching a child grow, or another source, it can help people cope with the challenges of the 21st century.

Although a pure form of existential treatment has never been widely practiced, clinicians seem to recognize and appreciate the value of an existential perspective in their work. Particularly with some of the groups of people described in the previous section, an existential approach, either alone or in combination with more problem-focused treatments, has much to recommend it.

EVALUATION OF EXISTENTIAL THERAPY

Like all approaches to counseling and psychotherapy, existential therapy has both strengths and limitations. In addition, we must keep in mind that research on this approach has been limited primarily to small groups of clients in studies lacking control groups and structured treatment conditions.

Limitations

Existential therapy relies heavily on developing a strong client-clinician relationship and on verbal communication. It is an individualized approach in which the clinician offers little structure or direction. This approach takes a stance that responsibility, choice, and self-determination are desirable but does not offer specific steps and has few strategies for intervention. Treatment may be a leisurely and lengthy process. Because of these limitations, many people may be skeptical of its value, reluctant or unable to engage in the thinking and self-exploration that it requires, and find its underlying philosophy unacceptable. Of course, clinicians need to respect those feelings and select carefully the people for whom existential therapy is recommended.

In addition, this approach does not seek to directly ameliorate symptoms and its practitioners acknowledge that symptoms may or may not abate after existential treatment. People struggling with prominent symptoms such as drug or alcohol dependence or mania probably are not good candidates for this approach.

Strengths and Contributions

The existential approach to treatment does have many strengths. Its greatest contribution is probably not as a separate approach to psychotherapy and counseling but as a philosophy of human development that can be infused into other treatment systems. This idea was advanced by May and Yalom (1995), who stated that their primary objective was the integration of the theory's goals and concepts into all approaches to psychotherapy. They wanted all clinicians to become aware of the importance of choice, meaning, actualization, and the therapeutic alliance. May and Yalom believed that this process was already well underway. Certainly, few would argue with the premise that counseling should promote people's overall wellness, help them live fully and authentically, and encourage them to take responsibility for their lives, make more positive and deliberate choices, and create meaning for themselves (Bauman & Waldo, 1998).

Existential therapy has made many important contributions to the fields of counseling and psychotherapy. Like person-centered counseling, it emphasizes the importance of a collaborative, respectful, and authentic client-clinician relationship. Current research has given ample support to the connection between the treatment alliance and the outcome of treatment.

Existential therapy has broadened the reaches of psychotherapy beyond pathology and symptoms and legitimized inclusion in the treatment process of deep and philosophical issues such as existential anxiety, isolation, fear of death, actualization, freedom, and the meaning of life. It is a holistic and growth-promoting approach that de-emphasizes pathology and has relevance to everyone.

Although it was developed over 50 years ago, existential therapy is compatible with current trends in counseling and psychotherapy. It affirms the importance of spirituality in our lives and takes a broad perspective on the meaning of spirituality. It is phenomenological and emphasizes the importance of meaning making. While espousing an emphasis on people's commonalities, existential therapy also attends to the importance of each person's experience within his or her cultural context. It acknowledges the importance of people's thoughts and values flexibility and creativity in thinking. Existential treatment also encourages balance in our lives, another important contemporary value.

Although existential therapy de-emphasizes techniques, Frankl's paradoxical intention has attracted the attention of clinicians from many theoretical perspectives. Family therapists and cognitive behavioral counselors, in particular, use this intervention in their work and find it to be a powerful tool for change, although one that must be used carefully.

Inventories and assessment scales developed by existential thinkers provide other potentially useful tools. Some of these are:

- Reker's (1994) Life Attitude Profile for assessing meaning and purpose in life
- The Sources of Meaning Profile, also developed by Reker, measuring how meaningful people find aspects of their lives
- Purpose in Life Test (Bauman & Waldo, 1998) which measures level of existential meaning and future time perspective

Inventories such as these can promote discussion and awareness, helping people give meaning to their lives.

Existential therapy is a hopeful, optimistic, and timely approach. Its many strengths support Vontress's contention that, through existential treatment, ". . . the results of counseling will be more enduring than the haphazard work on the issues the client struggles with at the moment" (Epp, 1998, p.3).

SKILL DEVELOPMENT: VALUES CLARIFICATION

Understanding people's values is relevant to existential therapy as well as to other treatment approaches. Our values are an important aspect of our identities and affect the choices we make. Our success in leading lives that are consistent with our values is strongly connected to the meaningfulness of our lives and our sense of fulfillment. Values can be expressed, manifested in our daily activities, and assessed via inventories. Ideally, people's expressed, manifest, and assessed values all will be congruent. However, sometimes discrepancies emerge, particularly between expressed and manifest values. This can lead people to feel unfulfilled and unmotivated.

Wanda, for example, reported that she valued close interpersonal relationships, spending time in nature, and demonstrating her creativity. However, her manifest values were different. She worked long hours as a bank manager and made a high salary but had little time for friends and leisure activities. In addition, she lived in a small apartment in an urban setting. Her place of residence did not allow her to grow a garden, make space for her painting, or have much contact with the beauty of nature. Not surprisingly, Wanda reported that she was unhappy with her life and felt unmotivated at work.

Seeing the discrepancy between her expressed and manifest values prompted her to take a more honest look at her values. She realized that the security and income of her job were important values to her but that she was neglecting the interpersonal and creative values that also mattered. She was able to transfer to a bank in a more rural area and purchased a small house. These changes allowed her more time and opportunity for hiking, painting, and gardening. Although Wanda did take a cut in pay, she was able to maintain an adequate and stable income and decided that the loss in income was more than offset by her ability to realize some of her other values.

Expressed Values

Looking at values from several perspectives can provide useful information. The usual place to start is with people's expressed values. This might involve asking questions such as the following:

- What do you view as the most important and meaningful parts of your life?
- What accomplishments have you had that make you particularly proud?
- If you had only one year to live, how would you want to use your time?
- What do you view as your three most important values?
- If you were to write a brief biography of yourself for publication in a national magazine, what information would you include?

Of course, these questions can be modified and adapted to ensure that they are well received by a particular client.

Manifest Values

Manifest values are reflected in how people lead their lives, including their personal and professional activities, the distribution of their time, their lifestyles, their objective accomplishments, and neglected areas of their lives. Questions such as the following can elicit manifest values:

- Describe a typical day (or week or month) in your life.
- If someone who did not know you read a biography of your life, what would that person view as your greatest accomplishments? Your greatest disappointments?

- Assume that you have 16 waking hours each day. Tell me the number of hours you typically spend in each of the following roles and what you usually do in that role:
  - Spouse/partner/friend
  - Parent
  - Career person
  - Leisurite
  - Life manager (e.g., shopping, cleaning, paying bills)
  - Other roles
- If you could redistribute your time among these roles, what changes would you make?
- How have your activities and the ways in which you spend your time changed during the past 5–10 years?
- When you awaken in the morning, what parts of your life do you look forward to and engage in as much as possible and what parts do you avoid whenever you can?
- What do you enjoy doing when you are on vacation?

Inventoried Values

Many inventories, both standardized and nonstandardized, are available to assess values. Sometimes paper-and-pencil or computerized inventories elicit more objective responses than do discussion questions such as those just listed. The following is a simple written assessment of values that can provide another perspective on what is important to a person. Either of the two sets of instructions can be used with the accompanying list of values, depending on which seems more likely to engage a person's interest and cooperation. Discussion of the person's responses should follow completion of the inventory to clarify the information provided.

Instructions 1: Review the following list of values. Place a checkmark by all of the values that are important to you. Then review the values that you have checked and list, in priority order, the three that are most important to you.

Instructions 2: Assume that you have $1,000 to spend at an auction of values. Review the following list and decide how you will allocate your money. Allocating too little to any one value may mean you will lose the auction for that value, but allocating too much to a value limits how much you can allocate to other values.

List of Values	
Achievement	Learning and Knowledge
Beauty	Love and Romance
Career Success	Nature/Outdoor Activities
Child Rearing	Order
Creativity	Possessions and Wealth
Fame	Power
Friendship	Prestige and Admiration
Health and Fitness	Security
Helping Others	Spirituality
Independence	Variety and Excitement

CASE ILLUSTRATION

The following dialog illustrates use of a Symbolic Growth Experience (SGE) with Edie. As you learned earlier in this chapter, processing an SGE entails four steps:

1. People are educated about the concept of the SGE.
2. They select an important past experience and explore its importance and symbolism in their lives.
3. They are helped to understand the meaning in the experience.
4. They develop a clearer sense of meaning and can repeat their use of these strategies to understand the significance of other experiences.

Assume that Edie has already been educated about the concept of the SGE. As you read this dialog, observe how exploration of the significance of past experiences helps her develop a greater sense of meaningfulness in her life as well as understanding of some of her emotions and choices. Also note the existential clinician's role.

Clinician: Edie, I see great sadness on your face today.

Edie: Yes, the weekend was tough. I told you that Roberto and I were planning to attend my 20th high school reunion. I bought a new dress, got my hair styled, picked out pictures of Ava to show off. I thought it would be wonderful, but it was horrible.

Clinician: How did something you were so looking forward to bring you so much pain?

Edie: You remember my telling you that when I was 10 years old, I was diagnosed with cancer. No one thought I would survive, except maybe my father. I had chemotherapy and lost all my hair. And I took steroids to help with the nausea and that made me gain weight. There I was, disgusting-looking, maybe dying . . . and I was supposed to go to school, if I could drag myself there. The other children would make fun of me, laugh at me, call me baldy. I know they didn't understand, but it was so awful.

Clinician: That must have been such a difficult time for you, not only coping with cancer but also with the teasing. How is the reunion connected with that?

Edie: I guess I wanted to show everyone that I had survived, that I was attractive now and had a family. But when I got to the reunion, all those feelings I had when I was 10 came back to me.

Clinician: So in your mind, the reunion was to be a life-affirming experience, but somehow it was just the opposite. What sense do you make of that?

Edie: I don't know.

Clinician: Edie, you have talked quite a bit about the impact cancer had on your life and your concern that it might recur despite the doctors' reassurances. Perhaps that strong fear of death has never left you and the reminder of the reunion intensified that fear.

Edie: That's true. You know, when I hit the 10th anniversary of my cancer diagnosis, the doctors said I was cured, but I never really believed it.

Clinician: And you're still living as though death is imminent.

Edie: Yes, I am. I felt like a fake at the reunion. How could I present myself as a woman who had survived when I knew inside that I was really dying?

Clinician: Most of us have anxiety about death, but for you, of course, it is particularly strong. How do you think this fear affects your life now?

Edie: I worry a lot about dying before Ava is grown. She needs me so much, and I don't want to abandon her. I try to do all I can for her while I still have time, but I never feel like I do enough. Roberto can't understand. He says I pamper her and I should stop, but she's my only child. I couldn't get pregnant again because of the cancer. It's a miracle I got pregnant with Ava. She's like a gift from God.

Clinician: I hear you saying so many important things. Ava's birth and your role as a mother have given meaning to your life, and you want to make the most of that. But I also hear a sense of urgency, a fear that time might run out for you before Ava is grown and that terrifies you.

Edie: Yes, I still feel like it's just a matter of time before the cancer catches up with me again. Why can't Roberto understand that?

Clinician: You feel very alone. I think one of the hardest things about being human is that no matter how much other people care about us, they can't really know what it is like to feel the way we feel. That can be very lonely.

Edie: That's true. I know Roberto loves me and Ava, but he never does seem to really understand me. Maybe I've been too hard on him and expected too much.

Clinician: What could you choose to do differently?

Edie: Instead of blowing up at him, I could remind myself that he hasn't been through what I have, that there's no way he could really understand, and that's all right. I have a better awareness of myself now that I understand why I treat Ava the way I do.

Clinician: How does that fit with the importance in your life of being a good mother?

Edie: I love Ava and do all I can for her. Roberto says it's not good for her, though—that she needs more independence and confidence in herself.

Clinician: I know your anxiety pushes you to do everything possible for Ava and to be a different parent to her than your parents were to you. Could it be that your anxiety makes it hard for you to see any value in what Roberto is saying?

Edie: You mean that I'm scared something bad will happen to Ava if I don't keep a close watch on her? Yes, I guess I can be overprotective. . . and I know that's not really good mothering. I want her to feel confident and good about herself, not the way I felt when I was growing up.

At this point, Edie has developed a clearer idea of the meaning, for her, of both her experience with cancer and the recent reunion. She is more aware of the impact that her fear of death and her sense of aloneness have on her. She has gained some clarification about the primary purpose of her life—to stay alive so that she can continue to be a good parent to Ava—and has begun to increase her awareness of both her own behavior and the possible validity of Roberto's words. She is now in a better position to make choices that will help her to move toward the meaning she has created in her life, to feel more actualized, and to improve her relationships with both Ava and Roberto.

EXERCISES

Large-Group Exercises

1. Discuss the differences and similarities between person-centered counseling and existential therapy. What differences do you note in the clients for whom each approach is suitable?

2. Conduct a values auction in class based on the list in the "Skill Development" section. Notice the items for which you bid, how much you wager to win values of importance to you, and how you feel when you win or lose values on which you have bid. Did any of your wagers or reactions surprise you? What have you learned from this exercise about your values?

3. Are clinicians who focus primarily on profound issues of the human condition doing people a great service, or are they doing them a disservice by de-emphasizing immediate problems and symptoms that led people to seek treatment? Create a debate in the classroom, with a group of people taking each side of this question.

4. Engage in a round-robin counseling dialog, with one person assuming the role of either Roberto or another hypothetical client and the class assuming the role of the clinician. Focus on helping the client increase the sense of meaning in his or her life.

Small-Group Exercises

1. Divide into your groups of four students. Each dyad should have an opportunity to assume clinician and client roles for a dialog of approximately 15 minutes in length. The client in each dialog should present an experience in his or her life that was

probably a Symbolic Growth Experience (SGE). The clinician should help the client explore the importance of that experience and the connection it has to the meaning the client has created in his or her life. Take particular note of themes and connections in the information presented by the client.

Feedback about the dialog should focus on the following:
- Ability to incorporate existential issues into the dialogue
- Clarification of the meaning of the SGE
- Use of empathy
- Use of questions
- Therapeutic alliance

2. Engage in another role-played counseling session following the format in Exercise 1. This time, focus on values clarification, exploring both expressed and manifest values. Questions listed in this chapter can be used to facilitate the discussion. Feedback on the dialog should address the list of focus points in Exercise 1.

Individual Exercises

1. Write a paragraph in your journal about the meaning or purpose you have created in your life. Then list three choices you have made recently. Write another paragraph, discussing whether those choices were congruent with the purpose of your life.
2. List your three greatest fears. Do they reflect the fears that are important in existential theory? Consider the impact your fears have on your life. Write down a change you might make to reduce their negative impact.

SUMMARY

Existential therapy grew out of a European society devastated by two great wars. It seeks to help people deal with the deep and powerful issues that affect everyone. More a philosophy than a system of treatment, the approach addresses troubling dimensions of the human condition such as the inevitability of death and loss, loneliness and alienation, meaninglessness, and guilt. Clinicians and their relationships with their clients are the primary instruments of change; establishment of a genuine, caring, supportive, and authentic client-clinician relationship is essential in this treatment model. Existential therapy enables people to become more actualized, aware, and connected to others, which can help them make wise and responsible choices and create meaning in their lives.

RECOMMENDED READINGS

Bauman, S., & Waldo, M. (1998). Existential theory and mental health counseling: If it were a snake, it would have bitten! *Journal of Mental Health Counseling, 20*(1), 13–27.

Bugental, J. F. T. (1987). *The art of the psychotherapist.* New York: Norton.

Bugental, J. F. T. (1990). *Intimate journeys.* San Francisco: Jossey-Bass.

Frankl, V. (1963). *Man's search for meaning.* Boston: Beacon.

May, R. (1969). *Love and will.* New York: Norton.

Yalom, I. D. (1980). *Existential psychotherapy.* New York: Basic Books.

Yalom, I. D. (1989). *Love's executioner and other tales of psychotherapy.* New York: Basic Books.

ADDITIONAL SOURCES OF INFORMATION

www.go.to/existentialanalysis—This is the website for the Society for Existential Analysis, a London-based membership organization that provides training, holds conferences, and publishes the *Journal of the Society for Existential Analysis*.

http://www.meaning.ca/links/humanistic_existential—This website for the International Network on Personal Meaning offers information on existential therapy and its developers as well as links to other relevant websites.

http://www.psychnet-uk.com/psychotherapy/psychotherapy_existential_therapyl.htm—This is a rich source of information on Viktor Frankl.

CHAPTER 12

Gestalt Therapy

Gestalt therapy encompasses many of the concepts of both existential therapy and person-centered counseling. It emphasizes the importance of the therapeutic alliance and is phenomenological, experiential, humanistic, and optimistic. Promoting awareness and responsibility are important in Gestalt therapy. The present receives more attention than the past, and exploring and experiencing emotions and sensations are integral to treatment.

What distinguishes this approach from others is its emphasis on the *Gestalt,* which Laura Perls (1992) defined as "a structured entity that is more than and different from its parts. It is the foreground figure that stands out from its ground, it 'exists' " (p. 52). According to Gestalt therapists, people experience psychological difficulties because they have become cut off from important parts of themselves such as their emotions, bodies, or contacts with others. The purpose of Gestalt therapy is to help people become aware of these neglected and disowned parts and restore wholeness, integration, and balance.

Gestalt therapy was developed primarily by Fritz Perls, with contributions from wife Laura Perls. Erving and Miriam Polster also made important enhancements to Gestalt therapy. Widely used during the 1960s and 1970s, it continues to have many followers and to influence other approaches to treatment.

THE PEOPLE WHO DEVELOPED GESTALT THERAPY

Frederick Perls, known as Fritz Perls, was born in 1893, the middle child and only son of a middle-class Jewish family living in Berlin, Germany. Although Perls was not always a motivated student, he succeeded in receiving an M.D. degree with a specialization in psychiatry (Perls, 1969b). Interested in becoming a practicing psychoanalyst, Perls moved to Vienna, home of Sigmund Freud, where he met many of the leaders in his field. Perls studied with Karen Horney and was psychoanalyzed by both Horney and Wilhelm Reich. Reich's emphasis on the use of facial, bodily, and linguistic cues to promote understanding and personal growth had a powerful influence on Perls and on the concepts and strategies of Gestalt therapy (Wulf, 1998).

Perls also was strongly influenced by several other experiences. During World War I, he served as a medical corpsman, a powerful personal experience. After the war, he worked with the neurologist Kurt Goldstein at the Frankfurt Neurological Institute, a treatment facility for people with brain injuries. Both experiences led Perls to reflect on the workings of the human mind, on Gestalt psychology, and on better ways to help people (Simkin, 1975; Wheeler, 1991). Even early in his career as a psychoanalyst, he was becoming disenchanted with that mode of treatment as well as with behaviorism.

The versatile and extroverted Perls also worked as an actor in the 1920s. He later reported that his experiences in the theater gave him an understanding of and appreciation for nonverbal communication, an essential aspect of Gestalt therapy. In 1930, Fritz Perls married Laura Posner, a concert pianist and dancer (Serlin, 1992). While Fritz Perls emphasized independence and confrontation, Laura Perls advocated support and connections. She studied existentialism with Martin Buber and Paul Tillich and drew on this background as she became involved in developing Gestalt therapy.

When Hitler came into power, the couple left Europe, relocating first in Holland and then in South Africa, where Fritz Perls served as a captain in the South African Medical Corps. During his years in South Africa, he outlined his theory of personality integration, which later became Gestalt therapy (Simkin, 1975). In 1946, the couple immigrated to the United States, where Fritz Perls published *Gestalt Therapy: Excitement and Growth in the Human Personality* (Perls, Hefferline, & Goodman, 1951). In 1952, he established the Gestalt Institute of America.

The most important impetus for the growth of Gestalt therapy was Fritz Perls's work between 1962 and 1969 at the Esalen Institute in Big Sur, California. He became best known there for his use of the "hot seat" in his workshops and soon was regarded as an innovative and charismatic advocate of the human potential movement.

Perls's personality enhanced the popularity and success of Gestalt therapy. An outspoken free spirit, unafraid to challenge and reject established traditions and procedures, both Perls and his work were in tune with the 1960s, when many people sought more fulfillment in their lives and new ways to live. As he stated, "The meaning of life is that it is to be lived; and it is not to be traded and conceptualized and squeezed into a pattern of systems. We realize that manipulation and control are not the ultimate job of life" (Perls, 1969a, p. 3).

Fritz Perls died in 1970, when the popularity of Gestalt therapy was at its height. Many clinicians abandoned traditional systems of treatment in favor of this exciting approach, while others incorporated elements of Gestalt therapy into already-established treatment approaches. After her husband's death, Laura Perls continued their work on Gestalt therapy until her death in 1990.

Others continue to develop and refine Gestalt therapy. Particularly important are Erving and Miriam Polster. Both served for many years as co-directors of the Gestalt Training Center in San Diego. The Polsters expanded on the ideas of Fritz and Laura Perls, emphasizing the importance of theory to increase the credibility of this treatment system (Polster & Polster, 1973). The Polsters saw Gestalt therapy as a major integrative force in society, ameliorating common human concerns and increasing meaning and creativity in our lives.

THE DEVELOPMENT OF GESTALT THERAPY

Like many other treatment approaches, Gestalt therapy has its roots in Europe. A group of Gestalt psychologists in Berlin, including Max Wertheimer, Kurt Koffka, and Wolfgang Köhler, laid the groundwork for Gestalt therapy with their studies of perception and integration of parts into perceptual wholes. These theorists believed that understanding knowledge in "units of wholes, Gestalten" is more useful to the expansion of knowledge than dissecting the parts (Wulf, 1998, p. 86). In other words, they believed that the whole is greater than the sum of the parts. They also viewed people as having a natural tendency toward closure and equilibrium, which leads to thinking in terms of wholes rather than parts.

Although Gestalt psychologists provided the name and a basic premise for Gestalt therapy, Perls drew on many sources of knowledge in developing his treatment system, including existentialism. The ideas of Sigmund Freud, Karen Horney, Wilhelm Reich, and Otto Rank also shaped Gestalt therapy.

In addition, Jacob Moreno's psychodrama, along with Perls's own experiences as an actor, influenced the development of Gestalt therapy. Psychodrama encourages people to work out personal difficulties by creating dramatizations of problematic situations such as a family fight. With the help of a therapist, members of the audience assume family and other roles and give the protagonist an opportunity to relive and change painful experiences. Feedback from observers both enhances the impact of the process and affords observers vicarious benefits. Perls's techniques, including the empty chair, role plays, group feedback, and perhaps even the hot seat, were influenced by Moreno's ideas, as was Perls's emphasis on spontaneity, creativity, and enactment (Wulf, 1998).

During Perls's lifetime, the highly charged techniques associated with his approach received attention because of their use at Esalen, their powerful impact, and their application to encounter groups, widely used during the 1960s and early 1970s. Since then, Gestalt therapy has become less sensational and more solid. The integration of Gestalt therapy and transactional analysis, discussed later in this chapter, also contributed to establishing Gestalt therapy as not just a collection of exciting and highly charged interventions but an approach with much to contribute to counseling and psychotherapy.

IMPORTANT THEORETICAL CONCEPTS

Although Perls often used distinctive terminology, his theoretical concepts are in many ways consistent with person-centered and existential approaches. However, Perls and his associates did add their own ideas, which distinguish Gestalt therapy from other treatment systems. In addition, the strategies used in Gestalt therapy represent a considerable departure from existential and person-centered treatment approaches which make minimal use of specific intervention strategies.

View of Humankind

Like other humanists, Perls had an optimistic and empowering view of people and placed great importance on actualization: "Every individual, every plant, every animal has only one inborn goal—to actualize itself as it is" (Perls, 1969a, p. 33). He believed that people were basically good and had the capacity to cope with their lives successfully, although he recognized they sometimes needed help. According to Perls, healthy people engaged productively in the tasks of survival and maintenance and intuitively moved toward self-preservation and growth. As Enright (1975) stated, "The basic assumption of this therapeutic approach is that people can deal adequately with their own life problems if they know what they are and can bring all their abilities into action to solve them" (p. 22). Gestalt therapy helps people develop awareness, inner strength, and self-sufficiency. These qualities enable them to recognize that the resources they need for positive growth and change are within themselves rather than in a partner, title, career, or clinician.

Wholeness, Integration, and Balance

As its name implies, Gestalt therapy emphasizes the importance of wholeness, integration, and balance in people's lives. According to Simkin (1975), "Man is a total organism functioning as a whole, rather than an entity split in dichotomies such as mind and body" (p. 4). Perls (1969a) said of the human organism, "We *have* not a liver or a heart. We *are* liver and heart and brain and yet, even this is wrong—we are *not* a summation of parts but a *coordination* of the whole. We do not have a body, we *are* a body, we *are* somebody" (p. 6).

Unfortunately, many personalities lack wholeness and are fragmented (Korb, Gorrell, & Van de Riet, 1989). People with such personality structures are aware only of some parts of themselves and deny or cut off other parts. For example, people who believe they must always be independent may deny the part of themselves that craves support and wants to express grief over a loss, while people who believe that their intellect is their greatest gift may cut themselves off from their emotions and sensations.

To some extent, this fragmentation and denial of parts of the self stem from a drive toward homeostasis. People have difficulty dealing with ambiguity or disequilibrium and prefer stability and cohesiveness. This may lead them to exclude from awareness the parts of themselves that seem incongruent or cause discomfort, in a misguided effort to force equilibrium. Some men, for example, deny the sensitive and aesthetic aspects of their personalities because they view them as conflicting with their image of themselves as strong and masculine.

Integrating Polarities   People's need for homeostasis also can lead them to view themselves and their world in terms of *polarities* or extremes. The world may seem easier to understand if we categorize people as either good or bad, lazy or productive. However, these polarities generally reflect internal or interpersonal conflicts. To truly achieve wholeness, people must become aware of and integrate their polarities, especially the polarities of the mind and the body. Unless we accomplish that, the neglected or rejected side of the polarity is likely to build barriers against our efforts toward growth.

Integrating Figure and Ground   Although people strive for homeostasis, our lives and our world are always in flux, always changing. People constantly experience disequilibrium and then try to restore balance. We are hungry, so we eat. We are tired, so we nap.

Perls used the concept of the *figure-ground* to clarify this constant flux. The world around us is the ground, or background, of our lives. We cannot possibly attend to every facet of our experience. Rather, certain elements come into the foreground, depending on our needs. These are the figures that emerge. In a simple example, when we go into the kitchen to get a drink, we focus on that need. The refrigerator, the container of milk, and a glass are the figures, or foreground that we notice. We barely see the vase on the counter or the cat on the floor. However, if the cat jumps up on the counter and knocks down the vase, the figure-ground changes; the glass of milk recedes into the ground, and the broken vase becomes the figure.

More significant figure-ground shifts lead to sudden and often important changes in our understanding of events and experiences. For example, after dating for 10 months, Joyce arrived about 45 minutes late to pick up her boyfriend Leo for a party at his supervisor's house. Before she could explain that an accident caused her delay, Leo became enraged and hit Joyce in the face. He had become angry with her before and had come close to hitting her, but Joyce had overlooked those signs of Leo's violent behavior; she had grown up in an environment in which anger and shouting were acceptable and even desirable expressions of feeling. However, when Leo actually hit her, she saw those early warning signs in a new light, integrating figure and ground. She recognized that Leo presented a danger to her and that they did not have a healthy relationship.

Ego Boundary   Just as the figure-ground relationship changes, so does the ego boundary. Perls (1969a) described the *ego boundary* as "the organism's definition in relation to its environment, . . . this relationship is experienced both by what is inside the skin and what is outside the skin, but it is not a fixed thing" (p. 7). The two processes of the fluid ego boundary are identification and alienation. Identification, as with our parents, our bodies, and our jobs, brings those aspects of our lives into our ego boundaries, while alienation, as from other people or parts of ourselves, leads us to put those aspects outside our ego boundaries. According to Perls (1969a), "So the whole idea of good and bad, right and wrong, is always a matter of boundary, of which side of the fence I am on" (p. 9).

Gestalt therapy, like the other approaches discussed in part 3, is *phenomenological:* It recognizes that people's perceptions of a situation can vary widely; that even within a person, perceptions can change; and that our perceptions greatly influence our thoughts, emotions, and behaviors. Perceptions play a major role in shaping our ego boundaries. For example, people with low self-esteem and a confused sense of self commonly have weak ego boundaries. They overidentify with other people in an effort to feel acceptable and accepted. However, they tend to have difficulty distinguishing their own needs and feelings from those of other people and may erroneously assume that others feel exactly as they do. On the other hand, people with rigid ego boundaries have difficulty bringing new experiences and relationships into their lives and may feel different and separate from other people. Inflexibility, particularly in response to change, is often a problem for them.

Homeostasis Versus Flux   Perls used a great many terms, including figure-ground, ego boundary, and polarities, to refer to the constant state of flux that people experience. These constructs all pose threats to our homeostasis. Clearly, people cannot achieve a state of fixed homeostasis and then freeze the action. Our lives are always changing. However, through awareness of and identification with all aspects of ourselves, we can deal successfully with flux and still have a sense of integration and wholeness. As Simkin (1975) stated, "Organismically balanced individuals have the capacity to experience intellectually, emotionally and sensorially" (p. 7).

Awareness

For Gestalt therapists, awareness is an essential element of emotional health: "Awareness per se—by and of itself—can be curative. Because with full awareness you become aware of this organismic self-regulation, you can let the organism take over without interfering, without interrupting; we can rely on the wisdom of the organism" (Perls, 1969a, p. 17). Awareness is both a hallmark of the healthy person and a goal of treatment.

Several possible causes have been identified for people's limited awareness. Preoccupation is one of the foremost. We may be so caught up with our pasts, our fantasies, our perceived flaws or strengths, that we lose sight of the whole picture and become unaware. Another reason for lack of awareness is low self-esteem: "The less confident we are in ourselves, the less we are in touch with ourselves and the world, the more we want to control" (Perls, 1969a, p. 21). Low self-esteem makes it difficult for people to trust themselves, to allow their natural health and strength to propel them toward growth and self-actualization. Rather, people with low self-esteem typically set out to control themselves and others in an effort to realize an idealized self-image rather than to truly become actualized. The result is often exactly the opposite of what is intended.

Environmental Contact to Promote Growth   People engage in many efforts to achieve awareness, and contact with the environment is one of the most important. Contact is made through seven functions: looking, listening, touching, talking, moving, smelling, and tasting (Polster & Polster, 1973, pp. 129–138). Contact is necessary for growth; when we make contact with other people or aspects of our world, we must react and change. The experience of contact teaches us about ourselves and our environment and helps us to feel a part of our world, while defining more clearly who we are. People who avoid closeness with others and live isolated and circumscribed lives may believe that they are protecting themselves, but, in reality they are preventing their growth and actualization.

Perls (1969a) identified five levels or stages of contact and growth:

1. *The phony layer.* People play games, assume roles, react in stereotyped and inauthentic ways, and are insincere.
2. *The phobic layer.* People avoid pain, hide their real selves to prevent rejection, act out of fear, and feel vulnerable and helpless.
3. *The impasse layer.* Having passed through the first two layers, people feel confused, stuck, and powerless; they seek help from others.
4. *The implosive layer.* People become aware that they have limited themselves and begin to experiment with change, to deal with unfinished business, to lower defenses, and to move toward greater integration. People connect with their possibilities and give up old layers. This implosion turns into an explosion in the fifth layer.

5. *The explosive layer.* People experience reintegration and wholeness, become their authentic selves, gain access to great energy, feel and express emotions, and become more actualized.

Treatment often involves helping people progress through the layers, peeling away each one like the skin of an onion to expose the next healthier layer of the adult personality. In this way, people truly become their authentic, actualized selves, capable of full contact with the environment, other people, and themselves (Korb et al., 1989).

Here and Now   Another way to increase awareness is to live in and be conscious of the present moment rather than remaining tied to the past or focusing on hope of a better future. According to Perls (1969a), "Nothing exists except the here and now. . . . The past is no more. The future is not yet. . . . You should live in the here and now" (p. 44). When we are centered in the present, we are more likely to be congruent—to have our minds, our bodies, and our emotions integrated. When we are not fully in the present, we may be fragmented. Our emotions may be stuck in past hurts and our thoughts may wander to future anticipations while we talk with people in the present. When we are not centered in the present, we give confusing messages to others, have a poorly integrated sense of ourselves, and have difficulty making contact because we are not fully present.

Responsibility   Like the other theorists discussed in part 3, Gestalt therapists place importance on accepting responsibility for our own lives rather than giving that power away or blaming and resenting others for our disappointments. Gestalt therapists believe that people must make their own choices rather than allowing others to choose for them.

Perls's focus, in keeping with the climate of the 1960s, was on the individual; but modern Gestalt therapists have modified the concept of responsibility. Now it refers not only to taking care of ourselves but also to recognizing that we are part of an interdependent society. Achieving a healthy balance between contact with others and self-sufficiency is essential to emotional health. To achieve that balance and act in responsible ways, we must have awareness, which is at the core of the healthy person.

The Nature of Growth Disorders

Of course, not all people are emotionally healthy. Although Perls sometimes used the term *neurosis* to describe emotional problems, he believed that these difficulties should more accurately be referred to as "growth disorders" (Perls, 1969a, p. 30). This term describes people who deny or reject aspects of themselves and their environment, are not living in the present, are not making fulfilling contact with others, lack awareness, and are not becoming actualized. They are stuck; the environment no longer gives them the support they need to grow and mature, but they do not yet have confidence in their own resources. They feel guilty and resentful and hold onto the past, blaming their parents and others for their failure to grow. Their ego boundaries are probably either diffuse or rigid.

Avoidance and resistance keep people trapped in this unhealthy state. They avoid dealing with uncomfortable feelings, remain unaware, and circumscribe their lives to minimize flux or change. They make extensive use of ego defenses such as projection of disowned aspects of themselves onto others, distraction, failure to set boundaries between themselves and others, and withdrawal from their surroundings. Wholeness, integrity, freedom of choice, and actualization are sacrificed to the illusion of safety and homeostasis. Such people do not allow themselves to be aware of, anticipate, and cope successfully and flexibly with the changes in their lives. Rather, they persist in unsuccessful defensive maneuvers to avoid change. Paradoxically, as Perls observed, people who operate in this way actually experience greater turmoil and discomfort than do those who are aware of the here and now and use their own powerful resources to manage their lives.

People who are not developing in healthy ways often have a great deal of unfinished business. According to Perls (1969a, p. 15), "our life is basically practically nothing but an infinite number of unfinished situations—incomplete Gestalts. No sooner have we finished one situation than another comes up." Most of us have our never-ending lists of tasks to be done; when one item is crossed off the list, another takes its place. Unfinished business is inevitable. Healthy people may be disconcerted by the constant unfinished business in their lives but learn to use their resources to deal with it effectively.

People with growth disorders, however, are overwhelmed by unfinished business, particularly resentments and unexpressed emotions. Because they are alienated from many aspects of their environments and themselves, they cannot deal effectively with the demands of their lives, and so they accumulate more and more unfinished business. Their energy is sapped by their unproductive efforts to cope, leaving them depleted of the resources they need to live their lives successfully. People who are overwhelmed by unfinished business typically feel stuck or blocked and may experience physical symptoms (Enright, 1975). Their current issues tend to mirror unresolved past issues and are never finished because they are not addressed in the here and now. One of the major goals of Gestalt therapy is to help people become aware of their backlog of unfinished business and bring it to closure—finish it so that they are able to live more fully in the present.

TREATMENT USING GESTALT THERAPY

Unlike person-centered counseling and existential therapy, Gestalt therapy includes a rich array of strategies that facilitate treatment. Many also can be incorporated into other treatment systems. These strategies have been developed to further what Perls, Hefferline, and Goodman (1951) identified as the four major emphases in Gestalt work:

1. To pay attention to experience and become aware of and concentrate on the actual present situation
2. To maintain and promote the integrity and interrelationships of social, cultural, historical, physical, emotional, and other important factors
3. To experiment
4. To encourage creativity

Goals

Many of the treatment objectives of Gestalt therapy are similar to those of person-centered and existential therapy. However, others are unique to this approach. The most important goals of Gestalt therapy are:

- Promoting attention, clarity, and *awareness*
- Helping people live in the *here and now*
- Improving people's sense of *wholeness, integration, and balance*

Additional goals of significance in this treatment system include:

- Enabling people to bring *closure* to their unfinished business
- Increasing people's appreciation of and *access to their own considerable resources*
- Promoting responsibility, appropriate choices, and *self-sufficiency.*
- Promoting self-esteem, self-acceptance, and *actualization*
- Facilitating people's efforts to have *meaningful contact* with all aspects of themselves, other people, and their environment
- Developing the skills people need to *manage their lives successfully* without harming others

According to Perls (1969a), "The difference between Gestalt therapy and most other types of psychotherapy is essentially that we do *not* analyze. We *integrate*" (p. 70). The ultimate aim of Gestalt therapy is to promote the natural growth of the human organism and enable people to live aware and actualized lives—not just to solve problems or promote adaptation but also to help clients feel more fulfilled and whole.

How People Change

Gestalt clinicians believe that awareness is the primary vehicle of change. If people can gain awareness of their unfinished business (the areas in which they are blocked and alienated) and their own strengths and resources, they can grow and become more actualized. Particularly important is awareness gained through the body since, according to Gestalt theory, most people over-emphasize intellectual awareness and ignore messages from the body and the senses.

Therapeutic Alliance

Like existential therapists, Gestalt therapists seek to create an I-thou relationship with clients in which both client and clinician are fully present in the here and now (Korb et al., 1989). Gestalt clinicians strive to be genuine and aware of their own feelings, experiences, and perceptions. They do not urge or persuade people to change or tell them how they should be. Rather, they establish a climate that promotes trust, awareness, and a willingness to experiment with new ways of thinking, feeling, and acting. Clinicians and clients enter into a partnership in which both are committed to and active in the treatment process. However, clients take responsibility for their own development and decide for themselves how they will use the information that emerges in their sessions.

As long as clients are fully present and aware in the sessions, clinicians do not interrupt people's efforts to deal with their concerns (Enright, 1975). However, when a clinician observes that a client's attention is wandering, that conflicts are emerging, or that a person seems fragmented or out of contact, the clinician calls attention to these phenomena. The clinician makes this observation without interpretation or judgment, but simply to provide information that is likely to refocus attention, create awareness of blocks, and help people maintain contact with their present activities and experiences. Instead of trying to figure out their clients, Gestalt therapists focus on listening and helping clients find their "own way through the pauses and blocks" (Enright, 1975, p. 22).

Experiments

One task of Gestalt therapists is suggesting experiments or learning experiences for their clients. These are individually tailored to each client in order to accomplish a purpose relevant to that person, usually to promote awareness and bring problems and unfinished business into the present where they can be resolved. These experiments should not be threatening or negative; instead, they should be positive and growth-promoting. Presentation of suggested experiments should always be respectful, inviting, and carefully timed. While confrontation may be used to encourage involvement, clients are never demeaned and can always choose whether or not to involve themselves in the experiments.

Experiments might take the form of enactments, role plays, homework, or activities for clients to accomplish between sessions (Polster & Polster, 1973). For example, a Gestalt therapist suggested to a withdrawn and guarded woman who wanted to have closer relationships with people that she tell a friend something about herself that would surprise and please the friend. Spending time thinking about what she would tell the friend promoted the woman's self-awareness, while the eventual sharing increased the closeness between the woman and her friend.

Use of Language

Language plays an important part in Gestalt therapy. By choosing their words carefully, clinicians create an environment that encourages change.

Emphasis on Statements   Although questions are part of Gestalt therapy, clinicians typically prefer statements. They are more likely to say, "I am experiencing a loss of contact between us," than "Where has your attention gone?" The immediacy and direct person-to-person contact of a statement promotes a collaborative client-clinician relationship. Questions, on the other hand, are reminiscent of a teacher-student relationship in which the power differential may undermine the process. Talking *with* someone rather than *at* someone is critical in building a connection.

"What" and "How" Questions   When Gestalt therapists do ask questions, they usually begin them with "what," "how," or sometimes "where," but rarely with "why." Questions such as "What are you experiencing when you stamp your foot?" and "How does it feel when you stamp your foot?" are more likely to keep the client in the present moment and promote integration than are questions such as "Why are you stamping your foot?" "Why" questions typically lead to a focus on past experiences, as well as blocks and manifestations of resistance.

I Statements   Gestalt therapists encourage people to own and focus on their own feelings and experiences rather than talk about other people (they) or events (it). Statements beginning with "I" such as "I feel angry" and "In the dream, I am lost" encourage ownership and responsibility as well as integration. Statements such as "My mother made me angry" and "My dream was about being lost" take the focus off the client and the present moment and promote fragmentation and externalizing of responsibility.

The Present Tense   Even when clients talk about past events, Gestalt clinicians encourage them to focus on their present experience of the events—to bring events into the room and into the moment. For example, rather than focusing on a client's perceptions of how his father abandoned him when he was a child, the therapist might suggest that the client describe how that early abandonment affects his feelings and behaviors in the therapy session. This fosters awareness as well as a true connection with the clients' experience of the events.

Encouraging Responsibility   Gestalt therapists encourage people to take responsibility for themselves, their words, their emotions, their thoughts, and their behaviors in order to facilitate integration. Language also can further that goal. For example, the clinician might suggest that people temporarily begin all their sentences with the phrase, "I take responsibility for . . . " to help them recognize and accept their feelings. They might also apply to themselves statements they have made about others to facilitate awareness of their projections. The woman who says, "My sister only thinks of herself," might be asked to say, "I think only of myself," and then talk about what feelings this brings up for her. Another way to encourage people to take responsibility for themselves is for clinicians to help them make the implicit explicit. For example, a woman assured her husband that she would be happy to accompany him to church as he requested. However, each Sunday she told him that she had work to do so she could not go to church. Her therapist encouraged her to make her feelings explicit by stating, "I really don't want to go to church with you; I feel uncomfortable and out of place there because it is not the religion I was brought up to believe."

Dreams

Dreams occupy an important place in Gestalt therapy. Perls viewed dreams as the royal road to integration rather than the royal road to the unconscious, as Freud had viewed them. Perls believed that the parts of a dream represent projections or aspects of the dreamer. Awareness comes from assuming the various roles or parts of the dream and enacting the dream as though it is happening in the present.

For example, a man had a dream about a rabbit, chased across a field by a fox, escaping into a burrow. Freud, of course, would focus on the unconscious meaning of the conflict between the fox and the rabbit and the possibly sexual significance of the burrow. Perls, on the other hand, would encourage the man to assume the roles of each of the salient parts of the dream. One at a time, the client would enact the roles of the frightened rabbit, the menacing fox, the open field, and the protective burrow, speaking the thoughts and feelings that arose for him in each role. For example, he might say, "I am that rabbit, running scared, afraid that I will be swallowed up. I am always running for cover, safe just in the nick of time, but knowing that I might not make it the next time."

This approach to understanding dreams puts the client in charge of the process. It also allows people to take responsibility for their dreams, see their dreams as part of themselves, increase integration, and become aware of thoughts and emotions reflected in the dream that they might otherwise disown.

Fantasy

Fantasies, like dreams, can help people become more self-aware. Clinicians might use guided imagery to take people on a journey into their imaginations. They might be encouraged to imagine themselves walking through a beautiful meadow with a ramshackle house, looking around to see who is with them, and deciding what to do in that situation. Clinicians might make the fantasy more productive by asking questions to promote exploration and suggesting actions the person might take in the fantasy.

As with dreams, Gestalt therapists assume that the parts of the fantasy represent projections or aspects of the person. When the fantasy is completed, clinicians encourage people to process the experience by becoming the parts of the fantasy, speaking as though they are each part. This technique, like exploration of dreams, often helps people become more aware of and in contact with their feelings and more able to express those emotions.

Fantasies also can be used to bring closure to unfinished business. For example, a woman who had undergone surgery was left with some angry feelings about her surgeon and the need to have her surgery redone. When she called to express her feelings to the physician, he failed to return her telephone calls. To help her reach closure, her clinician led her on a guided fantasy in which she expressed her feelings to the physician and affirmed her ability to take care of herself and have the unsatisfactory surgery corrected.

Role Play Using Empty Chair Methods

Role play, in various forms, is an essential tool of Gestalt therapists. Although Perls was influenced by Moreno's psychodrama, Gestalt therapy rarely uses other people to play roles, in part because that might encourage fragmentation. Rather, an empty chair is more often used to represent a role.

The Two-Chair Method for Addressing an Inner Conflict   This common type of role play is intended to help people become aware of and resolve inner conflicts, tension, and struggles (Strumpfel & Goldman, 2002). Two chairs are used, representing two parts of the person that are in conflict, perhaps the intellect and the body or love and anger. Resolving conflicts involving anger, accompanied by emotions such as shame, grief, and sadness, seems especially therapeutic. The client spends time sitting in each chair and talking from the perspective represented by that chair.

Underlying this exercise is the Gestalt concept of the top dog and the underdog. Perls believed that "we constantly harass ourselves with . . . the top dog/underdog game where part of ourselves attempts to lecture, urge, and threaten the other part into 'good behavior' " (Fagan & Shepherd, 1970, p. 4). The top dog, a sort of superego or conscience, makes judgments and tells the underdog how it should feel, think, or act. The underdog tends to be meek and apologetic but does not really try to change. Although the top dog may seem more powerful, the underdog really has control by refusing to change or cooperate despite feelings of guilt. In addition to having both top dog and underdog within them, people may cast another person into the role of top dog while they assume the role of the guilty but ineffectual underdog. Some clients seek such a relationship with their clinicians, creating a hierarchical and nonproductive relationship.

When the two-chair method is used to address an inner conflict or split, the dialog generally begins with the top dog or dominant part of the person expressing strong criticism of the other part which is likely to become defensive and vulnerable. As the dialog continues, the clinician encourages the critic to become even harsher while prompting the underdog to express its pain and sadness. Recollections, misunderstandings, and previously unspoken and unacknowledged feelings may surface at this point. This, in turn, creates what has been described as an "ah-ha" experience: the shock of recognition in which people gain new emotional awareness and understanding. The goal of this exercise is to avoid an impasse and enable the two parts to achieve resolution; the critic becomes more tolerant and accepting while the underdog gains self-confidence and direct means of self-expression. People become more able to own and integrate both parts of themselves. The case illustration in this chapter demonstrates the two-chair technique.

The Empty, Chair Method for Addressing Unfinished Business   According to Strumpfel and Goldman (2002, p. 196), ". . . significant unmet needs represent unclosed gestalts that have not fully receded from awareness." The empty chair dialog is a way of addressing and resolving in the imagination those unclosed gestalts. The empty chair might represent another person, a troubling and confusing part of a person's dream or fantasy, or a physical symptom the person is having such as a headache.

Clients visualize in the empty chair a person (or symptom or part of a dream) with whom they have important unfinished business. They then express their thoughts and feelings to that person, in an effort to complete a process that had been interrupted. The goal of this experience is a resolution in which clients develop greater understanding and acceptance of the other person or issue, as well as growth in their own self-confidence.

Sujata, a woman who was born in India, had unfinished business with her father. Constantly trying to earn his approval, she proudly called him with each professional and academic achievement. His usual response was to ignore her information or ask when she was going to produce another grandchild for him. When she finally earned her doctorate after many years of hard work and received the same reply from her father, she became discouraged and devalued her accomplishments. Through an empty chair dialog with her father, she came to understand the influence of his cultural background and the messages he had received from his parents. This led her to become more tolerant and accepting of his values while maintaining pride in her own accomplishments.

The Body as a Vehicle of Communication

Gestalt therapy seeks to give people a sense of wholeness, enabling them to access and be aware of their thoughts, emotions, and physical sensations. Many people have fairly good awareness of their thoughts and emotions. However, they ignore or cut themselves off from their bodily sensations. Consequently, Gestalt therapists pay particular attention to the messages of the body.

The following strategies are especially useful in focusing attention on the body:

- *Identification* —Clinicians remain alert to bodily messages. If they notice that a part of a person's body is in a reactive state, such as fingers tapping on a table or a leg strenuously swinging, they call attention to the movements and ask about their message. A clinician might say, "I notice that your leg began swinging when we started to talk about your relationship with your sister. What is your leg saying?" or "Become your leg and give your leg a voice. What is your leg feeling?"

- *Locating Emotions in the Body* —Another strategy is helping people locate their emotions in the body so that they can more fully experience their feelings. A clinician might say, "You have told me that you feel rage toward your sister. Show me where you are experiencing this rage?" Once the client locates the rage, perhaps in her stomach, the clinician can explore the client's physical sensations, enabling her to more fully connect with and express her feelings.

- *Repetition and Exaggeration* —When they observe body movements or symptoms, clinicians often encourage clients to repeat and exaggerate them. For example, a clinician might say, "I notice you are tapping your foot. I would like you to exaggerate the tapping, do it as hard as you can, and then talk about what feelings come up." The techniques of exaggeration or repetition also can be applied to a tone of voice or a meaningful phrase that the person uses. This intervention focuses attention on where energy is located and can succeed in releasing blocked awareness and energy.

THE USE OF GESTALT THERAPY IN GROUPS

Initially, Gestalt therapy usually took the form of individual therapy practiced in a group. Today, Gestalt therapy is practiced in both individual and group formats (Strumpfel & Goldman, 2002). Individual therapy is the primary mode of treatment, but use of this approach in a group setting offers many benefits. Gestalt therapy groups focus on both interpersonal dynamics and the dynamics of the group system. Feedback and support from both the clinician and the group members can accelerate the process of awareness and empowerment. Members also can learn vicariously from each other. The use of Gestalt therapy in a group setting has led to the development of several useful techniques.

The Hot Seat

Fritz Perls's work at the Esalen Institute emphasized the use of the hot seat in a group setting. This powerful technique brought him considerable attention, and it was widely adopted by encounter groups during the 1960s and 1970s. The hot seat is a chair, placed in the middle of the group, usually with a box of tissues nearby since sitting in the hot seat often evokes strong emotions. Group members volunteer to work, one at a time, spending 5–10 minutes in the hot seat and becoming the center of the group's attention. When people are in the hot seat, they are encouraged to express and stay with their feelings. Feedback from the group on their body language and verbal messages promotes their awareness of themselves and their feelings.

Making the Rounds

When making the rounds, people in the hot seat speak to each member of the group, perhaps identifying something they want from that person or something in him or her that reminds them of themselves. Alternatively, group members might take turns giving people in the hot seat feedback, perhaps on their strengths in an effort to empower them. Like many of the other experiments used in Gestalt therapy, this is a powerful technique that is likely to have an enduring impact on people.

GOULDINGS'S REDECISION THERAPY: GESTALT THERAPY AND TRANSACTIONAL ANALYSIS

Goulding and Goulding (Goulding, 1987; Goulding & Goulding, 1979) integrated Gestalt therapy and transactional analysis (TA) into what they called redecision therapy, modifying and broadening the use of the Gestalt approach. The basic premise of redecision therapy is that early life decisions are reversible if people re-experience them both intellectually and emotionally. Redecision therapy helps people re-experience their early life situations, have a corrective emotional experience, and emerge from that experience with new decisions about how they will lead their lives. Clients and clinicians then collaborate to implement those new decisions in the present. Key questions in redecision therapy are "What do you want to change today?" and "What are you going to do differently now?" (McClendon & Kadis, 1995). Primary goals of this approach include helping people gain more autonomy and zest for life.

Redecision therapy uses the concepts and terminology of TA but implements treatment in ways that reflect the Gestalt model (Gladfelter, 1992). For example, group therapy is the primary mode of treatment in redecision therapy. Although group members do not interrupt the treatment of any individual in the group, the process of learning from the work of another allows them to benefit too. In addition, clients are often asked to act as if they are important people in their lives in order to understand the transactions and strokes in those relationships. For example, a person may be asked to assume the role of one of his or her parents and to talk to the clinician about that person's life. This allows clients to get in touch with and better understand their own parent ego states.

Transactional analysis itself is not widely practiced today. However, it continues to have advocates who use this approach, either alone or in combination with Gestalt or other treatment systems. The following additional information on TA is provided for readers who want to learn more about this approach.

TRANSACTIONAL ANALYSIS

Developed by Eric Berne, TA has its roots in psychoanalysis but today is often combined with Gestalt therapy. TA de-emphasizes the unconscious and instead focuses on responsibility, emotional health, and social relationships (Clarkson, 1993). However, Berne also stressed the importance of early childhood development and of parental messages. Like Alfred Adler, Berne believed that people form life scripts in childhood that guide their lives.

The Person Who Developed Transactional Analysis

Eric Berne was born in 1910 in Montreal, Canada. He received a medical degree from McGill University and completed his psychiatric residency in the United States, training under Erik Erikson, discussed in chapter 4. Through TA, Berne sought to reduce the complexity and increase the relevance of psychoanalytic concepts. His book, *Transactional Analysis in Psychotherapy* (1961), was soon followed by *Games People Play* (1964), a bestseller that led to widespread interest in TA. Berne died in 1970, having published 8 books and 64 articles.

Theoretical Concepts and Development of Transactional Analysis

Rapid development of TA occurred during the last 15 years of Berne's life (Dusay & Dusay, 1989). Since his death, others, notably Thomas Harris and the Gouldings, have continued to develop TA. Probably the most important development since Berne's death is the integration of TA with both Gestalt therapy and psychodrama. Although TA is complex, the concepts are clear and understandable, providing us insight into our lives.

Human Development and Ego States   Berne suggested that people evolve through eight developmental stages (Poidevant & Lewis, 1995; Sapp, 1997). Although Erikson's influence is evident, Berne put his own stamp on the stages through his concept of the three ego states: parent, adult, and child.

- *Stage 1,* from birth to age one, is the time when the child ego state begins to evolve. The *child ego state* contains early experiences, emotions, intuitions, inquisitiveness, and the capacity for both joy and shame. The child ego state may talk in superlatives, focus on the self, and manifest such nonverbal behaviors as tears, whining, giggling, and squirming. All people are born with a *natural child* that is dependent, spontaneous, and lovable. During the first year, the three parts of the child ego state develop. The *adapted child* is inhibited, well-behaved, socialized, conforming, and sometimes self-critical. The *free child* encompasses the spontaneity and intuitiveness of the natural child and is playful, joyful, and exuberant. The *little professor* is a precursor of the adult ego state. It is curious and inquisitive, but also can be didactic and rigid.

- *Stage 2* extends from age 1 to age 3 and is characterized by development of the adult and parent ego states that continue to evolve until about 6 years of age. These two ego states are shaped primarily by social interactions, particularly injunctions and restrictions that are placed on children's behavior.

The *adult ego state* is like a computer; it is objective and rational, emphasizes logic over emotion, processes information, integrates messages from the other ego states, and solves problems. This ego state is straightforward, gives opinions, and asks questions. It cannot erase material in the parent or child ego states, but it can integrate or minimize the input from those states.

The *parent ego state* has two parts: the nurturing parent which provides support, affirmation, and caring but can be overprotective; and the critical parent, which makes judgments, disapproves and criticizes, and sets standards. The critical parent grows out of the rules, reprimands, praise and rewards that children receive from parents, teachers, and other authority figures and reflects their conceptions of right and wrong (Harris, 1967). The parent ego state tends to use words such as *always, never,* and *should* and focuses on *you* ("You need to clean your room" or "You aren't doing a good job"). Nonverbal signs include pointing, sighing, and a raised voice. The parent ego state may provide clear guidelines or give mixed messages.

- *Stage 3,* from ages 3 to 6, continues the development of the ego states. Messages from others as well as people's experiences continue to shape their ego states.

- *Stage 4* occurs at age 6. By now, the three major ego states (parent, adult, and child) are developed, although they will continue to evolve.

- *Stage 5* encompasses the period between ages 6 and 12. Educational and interpersonal experiences contribute to changes in the ego states. The adult ego state is particularly likely to grow during this stage.

- *Stage 6* includes ages 13 through 16, the years of puberty. The child ego state develops rapidly during this stage and may be manifested by rebellion and conflict between both the internal child and parent ego states and between children and their parents.

- *Stage 7,* late adolescence, is the time when, for most, the adult ego state becomes able to achieve balance among the three ego states. This promotes the person's maturation and need fulfillment.

- *Stage 8* is adulthood when, optimally, people have achieved psychological maturity. They function independently; make wise decisions; have purpose and direction; and have a healthy balance of parent, adult, and child ego states.

Ideally, the three major ego states (parent, adult, and child) are in balance in the personality. However, if a person relies too heavily on one or two of the ego states, or if one ego state contaminates or intrudes on another, the person is likely to develop difficulties, especially in relationships. For example, the person who has too little adult is likely to be illogical, while the person with too much adult will probably be uninteresting (Dusay, 1972; Dusay & Dusay, 1989). Similarly, the person with too little free child is likely to be constricted and rigid, while the person with too much free child may be irresponsible. A structural analysis can assess ego state balance.

Transactions   Transactions are the basic units of behavior. They involve an exchange of verbal or nonverbal messages between two people. TA describes three types of transactions characterized by the source of the transaction, its target, and the replying ego state:

1. *Complementary transaction.* The target and the replying ego states are the same, and the reply is directed to the source ego state. Complementary transactions are likely to lead to interactions and relationships that are clear, open, and rewarding. People say what they mean and can understand what other people are saying. Any disagreements are evident and can be addressed.

   Example A

   Parent (source ego state) to child (target ego state): Please pick up your toys.

   Child (replying ego state) to parent (target of reply): All right, I will.

2. *Crossed transaction.* The target ego state and the replying ego state differ. In crossed transactions, the responses people receive usually are different from what they anticipated, and they may feel ignored and misunderstood.

   Example B

   Adult to adult (target ego state): It's cold out. Do you want to get your coat?

   Child (replying ego state) to parent: Don't tell me what to do!

   Example C

   Parent to child (target ego state): Your desk is a mess. Aren't you ever going to clear off that junk pile?

   Adult (replying ego state) to adult: You know, I realized the other day that my desk really has become a mess. I'm planning to clear it off as soon as I finish this project.

3. *Ulterior transactions.* These transactions take place on two levels of communication simultaneously: an overt or social level and a covert or psychological level. They involve more than one ego state as a source or target of a communication. Ulterior transactions are the most problematic: the overt communication is incongruent with the covert communication, and neither person really knows what is in the mind of the other. A continuing pattern of ulterior transactions is likely to lead to a dysfunctional relationship or one that is terminated.

   Example D (Person 1 to Person 2, after Person 2 arrives home late)

   Adult to adult (overt message): Is it after 11 P.M. already? I don't know where the time went tonight.

   Parent to child (covert message): I want you to know I noticed that you came in after your curfew. Don't expect an extended curfew this weekend!

Example E (Person 2 to Person 1)

Adult to adult (overt message): Yes, it is after 11. Excuse me; I need to read my e-mail.

Child to parent (covert message): There she goes again, ready to give me a hard time because I came in a few minutes late. I'll go into my room so she won't bother me.

The overt transactions in these last examples appear to be complementary transactions from adult to adult. However, the covert transactions are actually from parent to child and from child back to parent, as the thoughts behind the words reflect.

Strokes and Injunctions   Children's emotional and ego state development are largely determined by the messages and responses they receive from their caregivers. Berne identified two types of messages. *Strokes* are positive messages and are best when they are unconditional, while *injunctions* (negative strokes) express disapproval and dislike and include criticisms and prohibitions. Positive and negative strokes may be verbal (such as words of praise and criticism) or nonverbal (such as a hug, a slap, or a lack of eye contact). According to Berne (1961), strokes are the basic motivation for human interaction; and even negative strokes are preferred to no strokes—that is, being ignored and discounted.

Children who are encouraged and receive many positive, unconditional, and affirming messages usually develop in healthy ways and have a sound balance among their ego states (Massey, 1995). Although some injunctions are necessary, children who receive an abundance of negative messages, are ignored, or receive many conditional strokes (e.g., "You are very pretty when you sit quietly") are unlikely to develop in positive ways. Particularly affected is their child ego state, which may become suppressed and inhibited or self-centered and out of control. People whose lives are ruled by a great many *shoulds* usually are people who heard many *don'ts* (injunctions) while they were children. Massey (1995) summed up the impact of strokes: "Permissions foster the differentiation of the real self whereas injunctions promote anxiety-ridden fusion or symbioses" (p. 278).

Basic Life Positions   According to Harris (1967), people develop basic life positions that reflect the value they perceive in themselves and others. These positions are revealed in people's thoughts, feelings, and behaviors (White, 1995). Harris (1967) described four possible life positions:

1. *I'm not OK; you're OK.* This position is appropriate for young children who perceive themselves as weak and helpless and seek strokes from others who appear powerful and in control. However, if this position persists, it can cause difficulties. In this position, people typically feel guilty, depressed, powerless, and inferior to others, although they long for acceptance and appreciation. They may have a constricted free child and a rigid adapted child, always following the rules in hope of acceptance. On the other hand, they may act out, viewing themselves as unworthy of positive strokes and preferring negative strokes to none.

2. *I'm OK; you're not OK.* This position also might characterize people who received few positive strokes. However, they survived through self-stroking. They grow up believing that they must rely totally on themselves. They treat others in angry and punitive ways and have a sense of entitlement and grandiosity. They blame others for their difficulties and have little empathy or caring for others. They may engage in criminal behavior or abuse of others.

3. *I'm not OK; you're not OK.* This is the most negative of the four positions. As children, people in this position typically were deprived of strokes. Consequently, they become hopeless and even suicidal, seeing no value in themselves or others.

4. *I'm OK; you're OK.* In this position, people feel good about themselves and others. While they need strokes, they can be caring and reciprocate those strokes. Harris viewed this as the healthiest of the four positions. These people focus on win-win situations and have a good balance among their ego states.

Scripts   According to TA, people develop scripts that guide them through life. These scripts are shaped primarily by the internalized strokes and injunctions that they received as children and reflect their life positions. Scripts lead people to envision life as a sort of ongoing drama in which the actors may change but the plot and the role of the person with the script does not change. Three common scripts or roles include persecutor, rescuer, and victim (Woollams and Brown, 1979).

Treatment Using Transactional Analysis

Although TA has psychoanalytic roots and relies heavily on analysis, its concepts and vocabulary are much easier to understand. Similarly, its goals and the nature of the client-clinician relationship differ from traditional psychoanalysis.

Goals   The goal of TA is not insight into the unconscious but autonomy. According to Berne (1964), this is comprised of awareness, spontaneity, and intimacy. In addition, TA helps people move into an "I'm OK; you're OK" position, achieve balance among their ego states, and make healthy use of their time.

Therapeutic Alliance   In TA, clinicians assume a flexible role, adapting to the needs of the clients and the treatment process (Clarkson, 1993). Collaboration between clients and clinicians is important. Both participate actively and share responsibility for the treatment. Clinicians provide education on the language and concepts of TA and guide the therapeutic process. Clients are expected to be open, responsible for themselves, and willing to take risks to make positive changes. Clinicians are alert to the possibility that the ways in which clients communicate with them may reflect childhood patterns. Carefully used reparenting is sometimes part of TA; clinicians take on a reparative role, providing strokes to compensate for a lack of strokes in the client's childhood.

Contracts   Contracts are an important component in TA (Dusay & Dusay, 1989). They clarify the nature of the treatment process and affirm the roles and responsibilities of clinicians and clients. TA was one of the first approaches to use such an agreement to establish a collaborative and effective clinician-client relationship.

How People Change   According to Harris (1967), people are prompted to change when they are hurting or bored or discover that they can change. Woollams and Brown (1979) identified seven stages of treatment in TA: motivation, awareness, the treatment contract, de-confusing the child, redecision, relearning, and termination. Treatment involves considerable information gathering, exploring with clients their early family background, the strokes they received, their intrapsychic processes, the important people and factors in their current lives, and their social and cultural context (Massey, 1995). The goal is to obtain a clear picture of the following in each client:

- The balance of the ego states forming the personality
- The nature of the person's transactions with others
- Their games and rackets (dysfunctional, manipulative roles and interactions)
- The person's basic position (e.g., "I'm not OK; you're OK")
- The person's life script

By analyzing and understanding this information, people become more aware of their patterns and why those patterns developed. This, in turn, frees people to modify patterns and choose healthier ways of relating to others. It enables them to form a more positive picture of themselves and of the people in their lives: "I'm OK; you're OK."

Application of Transactional Analysis

Although TA no longer is as popular as it was in the 1960s and 1970s, it still has a following. The International Transactional Analysis Association has more than 10,000 members (Sapp, 1997). The *Transactional Analysis Journal* contains information about the application of TA and its integration with other theoretical approaches. Many clinicians integrate its concepts and techniques into their work. The combination of TA and Gestalt therapy is particularly effective, with TA emphasizing the cognitive and analytical aspects of the person and Gestalt drawing in the affective parts.

The applications of TA are broad and varied. It is used in individual and group counseling, corporate settings (Dusay & Dusay, 1989), and family counseling. Massey (1995) believed that TA was useful for understanding family patterns and described a model for integrating TA and family systems counseling. Script analysis also helps people look at how they operate in a social context and the choices they make in their families. Harris (1967) believed that helping a couple understand their own and each other's balance of ego states could help them assess their compatibility and the strengths and weaknesses in their relationship. TA also has been used in educational and preventive ways, often along with books such as *Staying OK* (Harris & Harris, 1985), *TA for Kids,* and *TA for Tots* (Freed & Freed, 1974a, 1974b).

Another strength of TA is its emphasis on health and its belief that people want to have a zestful life, full of rewarding, open relationships. TA theorists attribute problems not to pathology but to lack of education and strokes and take the optimistic stance that people can find the tools they need to make and implement more fulfilling choices.

As with most approaches to treatment, research on the effectiveness of TA is limited. Miller and Capuzzi (1984) reviewed a substantial number of studies of TA that had been conducted in either clinical or educational settings. The studies showed that, in educational settings, TA improved self-esteem, social status, and internal locus of control in elementary-age students; behavior and attendance in high school students; and self-esteem and internal locus of control in college students. The results of studies of TA in clinical settings are less clear, in part because of methodological flaws. TA does seem beneficial in some cases, especially when combined with Gestalt and behavior counseling strategies and when the client-clinician match is a good one.

APPLICATION OF GESTALT THERAPY

Gestalt therapy seems to have broader application than TA. Gestalt therapy is a powerful, action-oriented approach. Its success depends largely on the establishment of a trusting and collaborative relationship between client and clinician and, correspondingly, the client's willingness to take risks and engage in experiments that may elicit strong emotions and new awareness. Because it is usually a forceful approach to treatment that can have a great impact, Gestalt therapy should be used with considerable thought and care. However, research suggests that it does have broad application, perhaps even broader than Fritz and Laura Perls originally anticipated.

Application to Diagnostic Groups

According to Laura Perls (1992), Gestalt therapy "is not useful in working with very disturbed people and not usable at all with the real schizophrenic or paranoid patient" (p. 51). For people to engage in the I-thou relationship and safely participate in highly charged and dynamic experiments of Gestalt therapy, they seem to need a good measure of emotional health. Consequently, Gestalt therapy historically has not been considered suitable for people in urgent crises, those who are out of touch with reality, those who are unable to make good contact with another person, those who are unwilling to take responsibility for themselves, those who attribute all their problems to others, and those who are very fragile. It also is not designed to help people who only want counseling for a specific problem such as an unrewarding job.

Surprisingly, research has, in fact, shown that Gestalt therapy can help people with severe mental disorders, including people with schizophrenia and those with serious personality disorders (Strumpfel & Goldman, 2002). Improvement was noted in such areas as self-image, interactions with others, and behavior.

Gestalt therapy seems particularly well suited for people who realize they are not living their lives fully, feel detached and uninvolved, or feel so caught up in the pressures of daily life that they no longer have a sense of joy. These people may have mood or anxiety disorders such as dysthymic disorder (a long-standing, moderately severe depression), generalized anxiety disorder (pervasive anxiety about many aspects of their lives), phobias, or mild dysfunctional personality patterns or traits.

With its emphasis on the integration of the emotional and the physical, Gestalt therapy also is well suited for people who channel emotional concerns into their bodies. Such people might be diagnosed with somatoform disorders (often called psychosomatic illnesses) in which they report physical complaints that have no medical basis. Several relatively large-scale research studies have been conducted, using Gestalt therapy with clients such as these. Results show reductions in both physical and psychosocial symptoms (Strumpfel & Goldman, 2002).

People with substance-use disorders also have benefitted from Gestalt therapy. Although this approach is not symptom-focused, outcome measures reflected a high (70–80%) abstinence rate, as well as improvement in mood and personality variables.

Gestalt therapy may be helpful to people with eating disorders including anorexia nervosa and bulimia nervosa. Angermann (1998) found that people with eating disorders tend to have distorted perceptions of their bodies; dichotomize themselves, perhaps separating mind and body; have problems with contact and boundaries in relationships; and have extensive unfinished business. Appropriate goals for Gestalt treatment of people with eating disorders might include increasing awareness of both physical and emotional states, promoting integration of the self and self-image, bringing closure to unfinished business that blocks growth, and reducing barriers to healthy contact with others, in addition to changing eating habits.

Application to Culturally Diverse Groups

Gestalt therapy seems well suited to a diverse range of clients. Groups particularly appropriate for treatment via this approach include people with chronic and life threatening illnesses, people with disabilities, and people in their later years.

Gestalt therapy is likely to help people who are dealing with issues of grief as well as of death and dying because of its emphasis on living life to its fullest in the present. For example, this approach has been used to treat homosexual men diagnosed with HIV/AIDS who were experiencing symptoms of depression (Mulder et al., 1994). Gestalt therapy also has been used to help people over 65 who have few social supports.

Livneh and Sherwood (1991) concluded that Gestalt therapy was a rich source of help for people with disabilities. It could promote their responsibility for themselves, their self-awareness, and the integration of their mind and body.

Enns (1987) suggested integrating Gestalt and feminist therapy (discussed in chapter 13), believing that the Gestalt approach could empower women, promote their self-awareness and establishment of healthy interpersonal boundaries, and facilitate their expression of denied or suppressed emotions. Gestalt therapy also seems likely to help men who are dealing with gender issues, feelings of powerlessness, and impaired awareness of themselves and their emotions.

At the same time, some people, particularly those from non-western cultures, may be uncomfortable with the sometimes confrontational nature of this approach as well as its attention to nonverbal aspects of communication. They also may be reluctant to engage in a collaborative relationship with the clinician, preferring to view that person as the expert. The Gestalt emphasis on dreams, fantasies, and symbols also may be foreign to some people and incompatible with their orientation to the world, although others may welcome the attention to these inner processes.

Application to Other Groups

Gestalt therapy has been used with many other client groups and problems. Alexander and Harman (1988) used this approach to help middle school students deal with the suicide of a classmate. This approach also has been used with low achieving high school students (Strumpfel & Goldman, 2002). It has been used to help pregnant women prepare for the birth of their children. Although Gestalt therapy usually is not used with people in crisis, Korb et al. (1989) found that a brief version of this approach, in conjunction with a contract that narrowed the focus of treatment, could be used to address urgent concerns. Gestalt therapy's present orientation, as well as its use of powerful exercises, can quickly bring all aspects of an issue into awareness and encourage closure as well as growth. Used skillfully, and adapted to the needs of a particular client or group, the range of this approach is almost unlimited.

CURRENT USE

Although Gestalt therapy is no longer as popular as it was in the 1960s and 1970s, it has firmly established its place among the important treatment systems of counseling and psychotherapy. It has influenced and is often integrated with a broad range of other treatment systems, especially transactional analysis (Polster & Polster, 1993). The empty chair and two-chair dialogs of Gestalt therapy as well as other strategies also have been integrated into a new experiential therapy called process-experiential therapy (Greenberg, Elliott, & Lietaer, 1994) which has demonstrated its effectiveness in several studies.

In addition, Gestalt therapy itself has changed in recent years. Jacobs (1989) reported that Gestalt therapists have become even more aware of the importance of the client-clinician relationship and strive to establish a true I-thou collaborative relationship rather than adopting the charismatic and powerful role modeled by Fritz Perls. At the same time, they have de-emphasized the importance of techniques, leading to the emergence of a gentler and less confrontation therapy. The Gestalt approach to dreamwork, as well as the use of role plays, continue to play a prominent part in treatment.

Gestalt therapy continues to develop in the work of many practitioners and at Gestalt Institutes in Cleveland, San Diego, Los Angeles, Israel, Canada, France, Chile, and other parts of the world. Although Fritz Perls was the embodiment of Gestalt therapy during his lifetime, his ideas have attracted many followers and live on.

EVALUATION OF GESTALT THERAPY

Like other treatment approaches, Gestalt therapy has both strengths and limitations. Because of its powerful nature, clinicians need to be particularly aware of its limitations and appropriate use.

Limitations

Saner (1989) believed that Gestalt therapy was not universally or cross-culturally valid and asked: "Is this focus on individual Gestalt formation an indication of theoretical choice or a general reflection of individualism so typical of white American middle class society?" (p. 58).

Polster and Polster (1993) addressed other possible shortcomings, expressing concern about the risk of oversimplification as well as of neglecting important past concerns in the service of promoting immediacy. They also speculated that some clinicians might be more concerned with replicating the charismatic style of Fritz Perls than finding their own way to use this approach and really understanding its underlying theory and philosophy. Gestalt therapy also runs the risk of overemphasizing emotions and ignoring cognitions, which most clinicians now view as important determinants of emotions and vehicles for modifying feelings.

In addition, Gestalt therapy tends to evoke strong emotional reactions. In one group therapy session, a woman in the hot seat became so anxious that she lost control of her bladder, which led her to experience shame and social withdrawal. Thus, just as this approach has the power to do good, it also has the power to do harm. Its strategies are appealing and may seem deceptively simple but in reality require a skilled and experienced clinician who can determine their appropriate use, guide people through the treatment process, and protect them. This is more likely to happen if clinicians do not take on the powerful role embodied by Fritz Perls but, instead, temper that role with support, education, exploration of cognitions, and recognition of the importance of culture and background. In addition, combining Gestalt strategies with those from other approaches, including feminist and cognitive-behavioral therapy, reduces the risk of overemphasizing emotions and creates a more supportive treatment environment.

Strengths

Despite these limitations, Gestalt therapy has many strengths. Over the past 25 years, more empirical research seems to have been conducted on the process and outcomes of Gestalt therapy than on most of the other approaches discussed thus far in this book. When research compares Gestalt therapy to cognitive-behavioral therapy, the two have comparable positive outcomes. In two large studies of Gestalt therapy, 73% of the clients showed "a strong to mid-range improvement in the symptoms and problems that led them to seek therapy; only 5% suffered a worsening in their symptoms . . . Ninety percent of all clients reported that they had learned strategies in Gestalt therapy with which to successfully combat any reappearing symptoms (Strumpfel & Goldman, 2002, p. 204). Studies on the impact of the empty chair and two-chair experiences have been particularly positive. In addition, research suggests that positive treatment results from Gestalt therapy are enduring.

The flexibility of Gestalt therapy is one of its strengths. It has been successfully combined with other treatment approaches including transactional analysis, cognitive-behavioral therapy, person-centered therapy, and brief therapy. A manualized approach to Gestalt therapy has been developed and is used for research as well as practice.

Gestalt therapy is a philosophy of life, growth, and change and also provides specific ways to help people realize that growth. It respects the individual and adapts treatment to the needs of each person. Its emphasis on process and the client-clinician relationship are consistent with current understanding of how counseling and psychotherapy effect change. Gestalt therapy is a compassionate approach that can empower people and enable them to have more joy and fulfillment in their lives.

Contributions

Gestalt therapy has made many contributions to counseling and psychotherapy. The concepts of immediacy and wholeness, as well as the importance of mind-body integration, are particularly important and have been assimilated into other theoretical systems (Polster & Polster, 1993). Similarly, many innovative strategies, including the empty chair, the emphasis on nonverbal messages, Perls's approach to processing dreams, and I statements, have achieved wide acceptance. The empty chair and two-chair exercises have been so well accepted that many forget their Gestalt origins. The Gestalt approach to dreamwork has become an often-used and powerful alternative to psychoanalytic dream interpretation. In addition, the work of Gestalt therapists, along with that of the person-centered and existential theorists, established the importance of phenomenological, experiential, and humanistic approaches to treatment as well as the realization that the therapeutic alliance is probably the most important tool for change.

SKILL DEVELOPMENT: GESTALT DREAMWORK

People often bring dreams into their treatment sessions. They believe that their dreams are important but do not know how to make sense or meaning out of them. Theorists have suggested several approaches to using dreams in treatment. Freud emphasized the importance of the dream as a reflection of unconscious wishes and conflicts that need to be brought into consciousness. Jung wrote about the importance of identifying and using archetypes and symbols in dreams (see chapter 6). Perls dealt with dreams in a present-oriented way, viewing them as projected aspects of the person.

Dreams are a powerful but complex vehicle of communication. They can be a fruitful source of information and can promote awareness, but dreamwork also can be harmful. Because dreams have a mystical quality, some people place too much emphasis on dreams and their interpretation. They may even believe that dreams are prophetic. Consequently, clinicians should exercise caution when helping people make sense of their dreams and be sure not to impose their own ideas or interpretations on the client.

The approach to dreamwork used by Gestalt therapists seems less likely to cause harm or impose ideas on people than more interpretative and analytical approaches. In Gestalt dreamwork, clinicians should be supportive and guide the client through the process, making sure that no unfinished business remains to trouble the person. Many examples of dreamwork are included in *Gestalt Therapy Verbatim* (Perls, 1969a). The following four steps reflect Gestalt dreamwork:

1. The person presents the dream, using the present tense in the narration. Recurrent or emotionally charged dreams are particularly fruitful sources of information.
2. The elements of the dream are identified. Gaps or omissions also are noted and may have meaning.
3. With the guidance of the clinician, the client assumes the roles of each element of the dream and speaks about the emotions and experiences of that element.
4. Clinician and client work together to make sense of the dream in light of what is already known about the person, integrating the messages of the dream into the person's self-image and seeking to increase self-awareness.

The following is an abbreviated illustration of the four steps of Gestalt dreamwork:

Step 1: Narration of dream
Client: I walk into my office, and I see that my desk is clear. All the papers are gone. And all the books on the shelf are different. Instead of my technical books, there are books on history and theater and art. I think that the housekeeper must have moved everything.

Step 2: Identification of elements of the dream
Clinician: What are the elements in this dream?

Client: I'm in the dream, as well as my office, my desk, and the new books.

Clinician: You also refer to your technical books, which are no longer in the office, and the housekeeper who you believe has made the change.

Step 3: Becoming the elements of the dream
Clinician: Be the desk.

Client: I am the desk. I am a beautiful antique wooden partner desk. Usually no one can see my beauty because I am covered with papers. Now I have no papers; I am empty.

Clinician: Empty?

Client: Yes, I know I am beautiful, but I feel exposed, unnatural. Somehow I like it better when I am covered with papers even though I look like a mess.

Clinician:	Describe the way the desk looks.
Client:	I have beautiful carvings. My finish is old but still shiny. I am wide and have space for two people even though only one person is using me now.
Clinician:	Now be the new books.
Client:	What are we doing here? We don't belong in this office. No one will ever read us here in this office. We have so much to offer, but we will never be appreciated.
Clinician:	Now be the old books that are no longer on the shelf.
Client:	We are tired and old and dog-eared. We have done our job well, but now we've just been stuffed away somewhere. No one will pay attention to us any more.
Clinician:	I'd like you to repeat what you just said but use "I" instead of "we."
Client:	I am tired and old and dog-eared. I have done my job well, but now I've just been stuffed away somewhere. No one will pay attention to me any more.

Step 4: Making sense of the dream

Clinician:	You are looking sad as you speak.
Client:	Yes, I feel like those old books. You know, I have started to think about retiring, and I wonder if my life will have meaning anymore. My whole life has been my work.
Clinician:	I'd like you to be the beauty of the desk now.
Client:	Yes, I am beautiful, but no one notices. I guess the housekeeper notices when she dusts. Maybe that's why she cleared me off. But I feel so exposed.
Clinician:	Repeat that.
Client:	I feel so exposed. I know that I have beauty; I have something to offer, but I have kept it hidden for so long. I am afraid to show who I am.
Clinician:	So someone else has to do it for you?
Client:	Yes, the housekeeper in the dream. But maybe I can do it for myself.

This dream seems to have brought into awareness polarities within this client, her identification with her intellectual side, and her alienation from her creative and physical aspects. She also has become aware of her reliance on others to bring out the neglected aspects of herself and begins to feel powerful enough to do that independently. Of course, this is just a beginning step in helping this person deal with her separation from important aspects of herself, but it is a powerful beginning that she seems to find useful.

CASE ILLUSTRATION

The following dialog illustrates the use of the two-chair technique with Roberto to address a split within him. This is one of the most powerful and widely used of the Gestalt strategies.

Clinician: Roberto, you have talked about feeling like there is a split within you between your tough side and your caring side and how hard it is for you to ex-press that caring side. I have set up two chairs here, one to represent your tough side and one to represent your caring side. I would like you to role-play each side of you while sitting in the chair that represents that side.

Roberto: All right. I'll start out with the tough side. That's the easy one. I was the biggest bully on the block.

Clinician: Would you talk in the present?

Roberto: Okay. I am the biggest bully on the block. No one messes with me. I have quite a reputation. My father is proud that I can take care of myself. I protect the younger kids.

Clinician: Now change seats.

Roberto: Well, here I am, in the caring seat. I'm not sure what to say. I do care deeply about my family, Edie and Ava. I make sure they are safe, that we have enough money, that Ava goes to a good school. But they say that's not enough. I feel invisible. No one seems to see me and all that I do.

Clinician: What do you look like?

Roberto: I am small and weak.

Clinician: Continue to be the caring side and talk to the tough side in the empty chair.

Roberto: I feel overshadowed by you. I try to let people know I'm here, but you're all they notice. I feel powerless and helpless.

Clinician: Now change chairs and have the tough side talk to the caring side.

Roberto: I know you're there, but I want to keep you hidden. What will it do to my reputation if people see you? They won't think I'm the tough guy anymore. You're not worth much to me.

Clinician: Change chairs and continue the conversation.

Roberto: Yes, I know your tough reputation is important to you. But I'm important too. Without me, you don't get along very well with people. Edie gets mad at you, and Ava goes off and cries. You need me even if you don't know it. I don't want to be as big as you, but maybe you could let me grow a little bigger.

Clinician: How could the caring side grow?

Roberto: It . . . I could exercise. That's how the tough side got so big. Practice. If I could just keep the tough guy from sitting on me every time I try to show my face . . .

Clinician: Can you tell him that?

Roberto: Yeah. Hey, tough guy, how about giving me a little space? I won't take over your turf. You don't have to be afraid of me ruining your reputation. I have respect for you. You worked hard to get where you are. Can you give a little guy a chance?

Clinician: Change chairs again and respond.

Roberto: Yeah, I guess I could do that. As long as we agree that I run the show, I'm in charge . . . at least for now.

Roberto has a top dog and an underdog as well as a split within himself. His tough side has served him well, and he identifies strongly with that aspect of his personality; but he has nearly cut himself off from his caring side. This dialog increased his awareness of these two sides of himself and the negative impact the neglect of his caring side has on his life. Although Roberto is still apprehensive about revealing his caring side, he has moved toward integrating the two sides and allowing them to coexist. He also has begun to recognize that he does not need to choose between the two.

EXERCISES

Large-Group Exercises

1. You now have had the opportunity to learn about three approaches to counseling and psychotherapy that emphasize the importance of emotions and sensations. Discuss and list the similarities and differences among person-centered counseling, existential therapy, and Gestalt therapy. Then discuss which approach is more appealing to you and the benefits each has to offer clients.

2. Review the illustration of the use of the two-chair experience with Roberto. Using this dialog as a starting point, discuss how a Gestalt therapist would continue to work with him. What blocks and impasses do you see in Roberto? From what you know about him, can you identify other splits that he might be struggling with in addition to the tough/caring one? What unfinished business do you think Roberto has? What do you imagine Roberto would look like if his body expressed his emotions? How would he sit? What would his eye contact be like? Would he have characteristic gestures? Plan experiments you might suggest to Roberto to promote his awareness and integration.

3. Look around you, at your clothes, your books and other possessions, and the contents of the room. Pick an object with which you identify. Write down the object as well as a few "I statements," speaking from the point of view of the object, such as "I am a chalkboard. I am blank and impressionable. I have little character but am here to reflect the ideas of others." Have volunteers share their objects and accompanying statements.

4. Ask for volunteers to lead a guided fantasy. Then divide the class into groups, with one volunteer for each group. Ideally, each group should have approximately six to eight participants. Allow approximately 15 minutes for the guided fantasy and another 15 minutes for participants to share and process their reactions to the experience.

Small-Group Exercises

1. Divide into your groups of four people in two dyads. Each dyad should have an opportunity to assume client and clinician roles and engage in a 10- to 15-minute exploration of a dream according to the four-step model in the "Skill Development" section above. The clinician should use interventions that are characteristic of Gestalt therapy. As always, clients should take care of themselves. Clinicians should not confront, interpret, or pressure clients.

Feedback following the role play should focus on the following areas:

- Clarification of the dream
- Use of questions and other interventions that reflect Gestalt therapy
- Nonverbal messages of both client and clinician
- Therapeutic alliance
- Strengths of the role play
- Ways in which the dialog might have been improved

2. Each dyad should engage in an exercise using the two-chair or empty chair technique. The person in the client role should identify an internal or external conflict that can be represented by two chairs. With the help of the person in the clinician role, the client should engage in a 10-minute dialog between the two people or aspects that represent the conflict. Be sure to bring closure to the experience.

Feedback following the exercise should focus on:

- The effectiveness of the exercise
- Use of questions and other interventions that reflect Gestalt therapy
- How Gestalt therapy might help the client deal with the split or conflict that has been presented
- Nonverbal messages of both client and clinician
- Therapeutic alliance
- Strengths of the role play
- Ways in which the dialog might have been improved

Individual Exercises

The individual exercises in this chapter are especially challenging. If you want to engage in these exercises but have difficulty doing so, you might seek help from your professor, a counselor, or someone else you trust.

1. Observe your own body language, your eye contact, the way you sit, the way you use your hands, and any other body movements you display. What messages do they seem to give? What can you learn about yourself from your body language? Did you notice any incongruities between your verbal and your nonverbal messages? Think about whether your body language reflects any internal splits or disowned parts of yourself. Write about this in your journal.

2. Write down a dream that you have had. Identify the parts of the dream. Write down what each element of the dream would say if it had a voice. What did you learn about yourself from this exercise?

3. Think about a criticism you recently made of someone else. Turn the statement around so that you apply it to yourself. For example, instead of saying, "My friend is an irresponsible person," say "I am an irresponsible person." Think about whether the new statement has any truth to it. Write about this in your journal.

SUMMARY

Fritz Perls, along with his wife Laura Perls, developed Gestalt therapy in the 1950s. This is a humanistic and phenomenological approach that pays particular attention to emotions and sensations. The concept of Gestalt implies that patterns and wholes are important to people. Gestalt therapists believe that we all have a natural drive toward integration, homeostasis, and actualization. However, people sometimes deny or become alienated from parts of themselves or their world. This can lead to fragmentation, an overload of unfinished business, and what Perls termed a growth disorder.

Gestalt therapy is an active approach that emphasizes the importance of a trusting, collaborative, I-thou relationship between client and clinician. The security of that relationship enables people to engage in growth-promoting experiments developed by the clinician to meet the needs of each client. Techniques such as dreamwork, the hot seat, the empty chair, the two-chair technique, the fantasy trip, the use of I statements, a focus on "what" and "how," and attention to nonverbal communication all help people reach the goals of Gestalt therapy, which include awareness, integration, and actualization.

RECOMMENDED READINGS

Gestalt Therapy

Korb, M. P., Gorrell, J., & Van de Riet, V. (1989). *Gestalt therapy: Practice and theory* (2nd ed.). New York: Pergamon.

Perls, F. (1969a). *Gestalt therapy verbatim*. Lafayette, CA: Real Person.

Perls, F. (1969b). *In and out of the garbage pail*. Lafayette, CA: Real Person.

Polster, E., & Polster, M. (1993). Fritz Perls: Legacy and invitation. *Gestalt Journal, 16*(2), 23–25.

Stephenson, F. D. (Ed.). (1975). *Gestalt therapy primer: Introductory readings in Gestalt therapy*. Springfield, IL: Thomas.

Strumpfel, U., & Goldman, R. (2002). Contacting Gestalt therapy. In D. J. Cain & J. Seeman (Eds.), *Humanistic psychotherapies: Handbook of research and practice* (pp. 189–219). Washington, DC: American Psychological Association.

Transactional Analysis

Berne, E. (1961). *Transactional analysis in psychotherapy*. New York: Grove.

Berne, E. (1964). *Games people play*. New York: Grove.

Goulding, M. (1987). Transactional analysis and redecision therapy. In J. L. Zeig (Ed.), *The evolution of psychotherapy* (pp. 285–299). New York: Brunner/Mazel.

Harris, T. A. (1967). *I'm OK—You're OK*. New York: Avon.

ADDITIONAL SOURCES OF INFORMATION

www.gestalt.org/igta.htm

The International Gestalt Therapy Association

P.O. Box 1045

Highland, New York 12528-1045

Site includes a bookstore, an international directory of Gestalt therapists, a bibliography of writings on Gestalt therapy, a news board, and articles relevant to this treatment approach.

www.http://www.gestalt.org

The Center for Gestalt Development, Inc.

P.O. Box 990

Highland, New York 12528-0990

(845) 691-7192

The Center publishes both a directory of Gestalt practitioners and the *Gestalt Journal*. It also is the headquarters of the Association for the Advancement of Gestalt Therapy, a membership organization for people interested in this approach to treatment.

www.aagt.org—Website of the Association for the Advancement of Gestalt Therapy.

www.behavior.net (go to Gestalt therapy)—Discussion board for issues related to Gestalt therapy.

www.newyorkgestalt.org—This site for the New York Institute for Gestalt Therapy offers suggested readings, a message board, articles, and training opportunities.

www.gestalttherapy.org—Website for the Pacific Gestalt Institute.

http://www.itaa-net.org—Website for the International Transactional Analysis Association includes information on events, products, training, certification, and members of the association. Website also provides links to regional branches of this organization.

CHAPTER 13

Emerging Approaches Emphasizing Emotions and Sensations

As in all dynamic fields, new theories and strategies of counseling and psychotherapy continually emerge, while established approaches undergo expansion and revision. This chapter, which concludes part 3, introduces four emerging approaches that emphasize emotions and sensations: narrative therapy, constructivist therapy, feminist therapy, and transpersonal therapy. At present, the literature does not provide much empirical evidence of their effectiveness. However, all four have much to offer when used either on their own or in combination with other approaches. In addition, they are changing the way many clinicians interact with clients and conceptualize clients' concerns.

The four approaches reviewed in this chapter have many similarities. All are:

- Holistic
- Consistent with postmodern thinking about counseling and psychotherapy
- Sensitive to issues of diversity, multiculturalism, individual differences, and people's multiple roles and perspectives
- Supportive of a clinician role that is more facilitator than expert
- Appreciative of the mutuality inherent in the treatment process, recognizing that both client and clinician are affected and changed by counseling and psychotherapy

More information is provided on hallmarks of these approaches in the discussion of each treatment system.

NARRATIVE THERAPY

Mascher's (2002, p. 58) description of narrative therapy emphasizes the close connection of this approach to others considered in this chapter: "Narrative therapy is a postmodern-feminist-constructivist approach that entails the co-construction of real, imagined, or possible stories of the past, present, or future." According to narrative therapy, people are interpretive beings who make meaning of themselves and their world through the language of stories that have become part of themselves, as well as their understanding of those stories (Gottlieb & Gottlieb, 1996). Narrative theorists believe that through exploration, deconstruction, and revision of problematic stories, people can shift their perceptions and create alternative scripts, leading to greater empowerment and the ability to more successfully manage their lives.

Narrative therapy views problems as manufactured in social, cultural, familial, political, and historical contexts, rather than being intrinsic to or inherent in the person (Monk, 1997). As Epston (1993, p. 161) stated, "The person isn't the problem; the problem is the problem." If people can externalize their concerns, they can give them new shapes and meanings that lead to healthier functioning. This is the essence of narrative therapy.

The Development of Narrative Therapy

Narrative therapy has its roots in Australia in the work of Michael White and David Epston (1990). However, clinicians and researchers worldwide have shown interest in its application and study. Important influences on narrative therapy include the ideas of Gregory Bateson and Michael Foucault.

Bateson suggested that, in order to detect and acquire new information, people must engage in a process of comparison in which they distinguish between one body of information and another (Monk, 1997). Building on this concept, White discovered that by drawing people's attention to subtle changes in their lives, he could foster new insights, promote empowerment, and help people develop better ways to resolve difficulties.

Foucault's writing on the equation of knowledge and power led White to address the damaging effects of encouraging people to adjust and comply with stereotyped standards of behavior that could undermine their efforts to lead a life of their own design (Monk, 1997; White & Epston, 1989). White believed that only through knowledge could people truly be the authors of their own lives.

In several important ways, narrative therapy represents a departure from conventional counseling and psychotherapy. White has been described as a "therapeutic anthropologist" (Lee, 1997, p. 5) and refers to himself as a consultant. He does not seek to heal or fix people but to learn about them, understand them, and provide a different and helpful perspective. Narrative therapy has been characterized as *postmodern* because it perceives people as having many selves and promotes their liberation from constricting definitions (Parry & Doan, 1994). Another new perspective is narrative therapy's *constructivist* nature, which emphasizes the concept that our personal realities and self-images are not absolute but are created and maintained by our societies and ourselves. Narrative therapy has taken the phenomenological emphasis of the other treatment systems discussed in part 3 one step further; not only do narrative therapists believe that people's perceptions determine their realities, but they believe that loosening and changing people's perceptions are the best routes to facilitating their positive development.

Theories and Strategies

Lee (1997) summarized this approach to treatment: "The narrative perspective attempts to address the human dilemma of existence in a postmodern world by focusing on the linguistic and discursive ways that people construct their lives. It assumes that humans are interpretive beings in the phenomenological sense, active in the interpretation of everyday life and in the attribution of meaning through stories or self-narratives" (pp. 5–6). In other words, narrative therapists believe that people's lives are created and interpreted through stories: the ones they hear, the ones they create in their own minds, and the ones they tell and retell. There are no essential truths; realities are constructed and maintained through language, social interactions, and story (Mascher, 2002).

Consider the following example. Suki, a young woman from an Asian background, sought counseling because of her difficulty trusting others, her inability to form close relationships, and what she termed her "self-hatred" that led her to cut herself repeatedly. Suki's mother had told her the following story many times since Suki was a young child: "When I became pregnant with you, I was living with your father. He was a terrible man. He beat me, he stayed with other women, and he took all the money I had. I wanted so badly to leave him. When I found out I was pregnant, I was devastated. I thought I would never be able to escape. So I went to a wise woman in the village and asked her to help me abort you. I did everything she told me, but it didn't work. I went back to her, and she told me other things to do. I did everything again, but it still didn't work. Then I decided that this baby was meant to be. I packed up everything I could carry and ran away. I found my way to the home of my aunt, who took me in and helped me until you were born."

Hearing this story again and again led Suki to adopt a negative view of herself and her world. She perceived herself as unwanted by both her father and her mother. She saw herself as a burden to her mother and viewed men as abusive and untrustworthy. She believed that she could only survive if she avoided closeness and intimacy with others; at the same time, she viewed herself as unworthy of survival and thought that everyone would have been happier if the abortion had been successful. Her self-injurious behavior and her inability to trust reflected views of herself and the world that grew out of the story her mother had told her. Although Suki's mother later married an American man who brought Suki and her mother to the United States and was a loving father to Suki, the story continued to have an impact. Stories give messages and can become the road maps of our lives. Narrative therapy helped Suki change those messages and improve her life.

The Therapeutic Alliance In narrative therapy, the clinician is a consultant in a partnership. Clients are the experts on themselves and their stories, while the clinician is the expert on narrative therapy. The two are co-authors and collaborators, sharing the responsibility for shaping the treatment process (Winslade, Crocket, & Monk, 1997).

Narrative therapists place great emphasis on being respectful and encouraging of clients' strengths and resources. Although clinicians do share their own perceptions and stories, including those about the clients, they assume a tentative stance, never prescribing or judging. Concepts such as resistance, denial, and mental disorders, which may give the clinician the upper hand, are not a part of narrative therapy. In fact, resistance is viewed as the client's effort to make the pace of treatment more comfortable for them.

According to Monk (1997), "This way of working requires therapists to squarely face the moral and ethical implications of what it is they create in their interactions with their clients. They can no longer hide behind a 'truth-based theory' in accounting for their ethical behaviors" (p. 26). In fact, they must be accountable and self-reflective, as they facilitate shifts and co-create new meaning in clients' stories.

Narrative clinicians encourage and facilitate rather than change people. They are inquiring rather than knowing, asking questions about the content and context of stories, as well as their meaning to the person. They are active, suggesting exercises, offering new viewpoints, and soliciting feedback (Richert, 2003). They help their clients appreciate themselves and enable them to play an important part in their treatment. Clinicians use careful listening, empathy, summarization, and paraphrasing to give people ownership over their right to create themselves and to listen to themselves in new ways that engender courage, hope, and resourcefulness (Winslade et al., 1997).

Typical of the treatment approaches discussed in this chapter, narrative clinicians remain aware of the part they play in clients' development and often discuss this with them. Unlike person-centered therapists, narrative therapists are "participatory witnesses" and "interpersonal relationship-based collaborators" (Mascher, 2002, p. 72). They do not simply reflect what clients present but, rather, engage in "interactive mirroring," which acknowledges that they are reflecting themselves as well as the client. More will be said on this mutuality in the discussion of feminist therapy later in this chapter.

Nature of the Stories People have a large repertoire of stories that they carry with them. All stories are accepted as legitimate and important in narrative therapy. However, stories tend to fall into several categories. Many people have a single dominant story that shapes who they are, as did Suki (Parry & Doan, 1994). A dominant story typically acts as a sort of tyrant that censors and changes a person's other stories and can send those stories into oblivion. What White (1986) called *specifications of personhood*—the information in the stories that tells people how to behave as individuals or family members—act as restraints and keep people stuck in and limited by their dominant stories.

Lost, unnoticed, or marginalized stories also need to be told and may serve people better than their dominant stories, particularly if the lost stories portray a life in which problems are either solved or absent. Suki's stepfather told her stories about how she used to make up poems when she was a child and how much he enjoyed reading her poems. However, as long as her single dominant story was in control, Suki paid little attention to her stepfather's stories, which reflected appreciation for her intelligence and creativity. Accessing those neglected stories and others helped Suki value herself and use her intelligence and creativity to relate more successfully to others.

Eliciting Stories   Most people produce stories spontaneously and typically enjoy telling stories. However, those stories that support the dominant theme are usually closest to the surface and most accessible. Narrative therapists have strategies to encourage people to tell a wider variety of stories (Carr, 1998):

- They may ask people to tell alternative stories about a single event or emotion.
- They may suggest that people create a story about themselves and their lives as if they were another person or assumed a different perspective.
- They may suggest that people extend their stories into the future.
- They may ask about neglected aspects of the stories.
- They may ask people to tell stories in which they are more powerful than their problems.

Deconstruction of Stories   Before stories can be changed, they must be taken apart, analyzed, and understood. Narrative therapists use several strategies to accomplish this, with their goals being to identify themes and metaphors that are prominent in the stories, enable people to recognize the influence the stories have had on them, and help people see that they did not totally create their stories themselves.

White (1992) speaks of landscapes of consciousness and landscapes of action. *Landscapes of consciousness* are the backdrops of values, feelings, motives, beliefs, and attitudes that recur in a person's stories. *Landscapes of action* are the sequences of behaviors related to events in people's lives that similarly pervade and recur in a person's stories. Questions help people identify, reflect on, determine the meaning of, and perhaps change these landscapes. In Suki's stories, the landscapes of consciousness generally reflected hopelessness, sorrow, and pain. People in her stories usually experienced rejection and loss. In the landscape of action, Suki usually was withdrawn and ineffectual.

Mapping is another approach to help people reflect on their stories. Clients' presenting problems are identified and linked to their stories, illustrating how their problems emerge and are handled in the stories. Similarly, people are encouraged to look at how their positive interpersonal experiences mesh with and potentially change their dominant stories and landscapes.

Externalizing is the process of creating a separation between people and their stories and problems. Problems are discussed as the problems; people are not viewed as problems. Instead of saying, "I am unable to have close relationships," a person might be encouraged to say, "Developing close relationships is a problem for me." Externalization is facilitated by helping people identify the threads connecting many stories and the assumptions the stories suggest about the self and the world. Once externalization occurs, access points for changing the story can be identified. Careful and deliberate use of language by the clinician facilitates externalization and can empower clients.

This process of externalization seems to conflict with the emphasis of Gestalt therapists on helping people own and take responsibility for their difficulties. However, narrative therapists believe that externalizing and objectifying problems reduces feelings of failure and guilt, decreases unproductive discussion about fault and blame, provides people new perspectives on their difficulties, reduces blocks to action and change, and opens the way for people to reclaim their lives from their problems (White, 1988–1989). Instead of believing they are the problem, people can mobilize their resources to combat the problem, now separate from who they are. They can establish new views of their problems and themselves, seeing themselves as competent and powerful people who have some problems that need attention rather than people who are problem-ridden and flawed.

Revisioning and Reauthoring   Once stories have been told and deconstruction has begun, the stories can be modified or revisioned. Only the clients have the right to make and accept changes to their stories, although clinicians often suggest alternative viewpoints and elicit stories of power and resourcefulness.

Revisioning entails both changing the story and changing people's visions of their lives. The two are inseparable; as people come to see more clearly the rules and meanings that govern the old stories, their vision changes, a new interpretation of their lives emerges, and the stories can be revisioned. As revisioning proceeds, it provides opportunities for further deconstruction, which in turn allows for more story revisioning. Gradually, alternative stories that offer exceptions to the dominant story emerge, and other perspectives become available for incorporation into the stories. White (1989) referred to this as the *insurrection of subjugated knowledge.*

Reauthoring now can take place. Possibilities for thoughts, actions, and emotions are expanded as therapists and clients share new descriptions of old stories (Gottleib & Gottleib, 1996). People have come to understand their meaning constructions and can move toward a more productive version of their self-narratives in terms of their feelings about themselves and their relationships with others (Lee, 1997).

Through revisioning and reauthoring, people develop alternative and preferred self-narratives extending into the future, in which the self is viewed as more powerful than the problem (Carr, 1998; White, 1995). People are now ready to solidify their gains and share them with others.

Therapeutic Documents   Therapeutic documents are materials, usually prepared by the clinician in collaboration with the client, to reinforce and provide evidence of accomplishments. Both client and clinician decide on the form for the documents, how they should be prepared, when and how they should be consulted, and with whom they should be shared (Carr, 1998). The documents may take the form of literary productions such as personal letters, lists, reports, certificates and awards, news releases, personal declarations, letters of reference, or manifestos that articulate people's problems, contradict the dominant plots of their lives, and suggest ways for them to deal with these problems (White & Epston, 1990). An exchange of letters between client and clinician is another form of documentation; these may be used to promote clients' reflection and to put their ideas and alternatives into a concrete form that can be kept as a resource.

Importance of the Social Network   Narrative therapists believe that stories have a cultural and interpersonal basis and that their meanings are generated in social interactions (Richert, 2003). Consequently, they maintain awareness of people's social and cultural contexts and incorporate them into treatment in several ways. Stories may be passed from one person to another, shaped along the way, and given to people as a legacy from their families. Clients are encouraged to recognize the family origins of some of their stories and to find people in their social and family networks who have similar experiences and problems. Drawing on those relationships, and learning about ways in which other people have addressed similar problems, can provide support, resources, and education about problem solving.

Because of the importance of people's social systems in creating and forming their stories, narrative therapists also use social systems to promote and solidify people's revisioned stories. Clients may be encouraged to tell their new stories to significant members of their social system who are chosen to hear and witness the new self-narrative (Carr, 1998). This public declaration helps solidify changes and puts others on notice to expect people to reauthor their lives.

Clinicians practicing narrative therapy also encourage people to share their learning with others. In what has been called the *bringing-it-back process,* people prepare a written account of their new knowledge and behaviors to share with future clients who have similar difficulties. The authors of the written accounts are then invited to share in person the narratives of how they solved their problems (Carr, 1998). These innovative procedures not only help new clients but also solidify and reinforce the gains of those who already have made progress through treatment.

Current Status

Narrative therapy views human problems as arising from and being maintained by oppressive stories that dominate people's lives. Therapists using this approach seek to develop a deep understanding of people through their stories and enable them to reauthor their stories as well as their lives. A collaborative client-clinician relationship, empowerment of the client, and use of the social network are essential in this approach.

Because the approach is not focused on specific types of problems and is deeply respectful of people's ownership of their own lives, it can be useful with a broad range of clients and concerns. For example, narrative therapy has been used successfully to treat delinquency, bullying, and other conduct problems in children; people coping with eating disorders; marital conflict; people who experienced childhood abuse; people coping with grief; and people diagnosed with schizophrenia (Carr, 1998).

A description of the use of narrative therapy with people who misuse alcohol makes clear its distinctive characteristics (Winslade & Smith, 1997). Rather than accept the stance of Alcoholics Anonymous that encourages people to internalize their problem ("I am an alcoholic"), clinicians help them to externalize the problem, give it a name (Al), and then divorce him. In this way, people separate themselves from a close identification with alcohol and are in a better position to combat its influence. In addition, rather than assuming the role of expert and teaching people skills to change their behaviors, clinicians help clients discover and use the knowledge they already have about ways to deal with the problems alcohol has brought into their lives. By using their own resources, creating new stories, and making better use of relationships, people can change and overcome problems.

Narrative therapy seems particularly well suited for the treatment of people who have been victimized and disenfranchised by others, such as women, the elderly, and those from some ethnic and cultural groups (Drauker, 1998; Kropf & Tandy, 1998; Lee, 1997). Drauker (1998), discussing the use of narrative therapy with abused women, wrote: "A therapy that challenges sociopolitical conditions that contribute to violence, highlights women's personal insurrections against these conditions, and supports the reauthoring of their life stories should be considered as a potentially useful approach for women who have been victimized throughout their lives" (p. 168). Similarly, when used with older people, narrative therapy can be positive and life-affirming, transforming stories that are based on loss and worthlessness into those that reflect a rich and full life. Narrative therapy also can provide a respectful way to understand people from diverse cultural backgrounds, giving them the opportunity to tell the stories of their lives and revision those stories in ways that give them greater power and control and also are consistent with the values and beliefs of their cultures.

Another strength of narrative therapy is the ease with which it can be combined with other compatible treatment approaches. For example, Richert (2003) described ways to integrate narrative and humanistic-experiential approaches and Mascher (2002) integrates narrative therapy with feminist and constructivist concepts. Incorporating people's stories and their revisions into treatment seems to be a useful strategy for many clinicians.

Although narrative therapy clearly has value for a broad range of people, clinicians still must take care when applying this approach. It may be unsuitable for people who cannot engage in a coherent conversation because of their poor contact with reality, for those who seek a quick solution to a specific problem or are in crisis, and for those who anticipate little benefit from treatment. In short, like all approaches to counseling and psychotherapy, narrative therapy has limitations but does offer a new perspective on the treatment process as well as considerable promise.

CONSTRUCTIVIST PSYCHOTHERAPY

Constructivist psychotherapy (or constructivism) and feminist therapy, discussed next, bear considerable similarity to narrative therapy. In fact, some theorists consider narrative therapy a form of constructivist therapy.

Although both constructivist therapy and feminist therapy attend to thoughts and behaviors as well as emotions, they are discussed in part 3 of this book because they are strongly phenomenological and experiential. Like narrative therapy, both constructive therapy and feminist therapy focus on people's perceptions of themselves and their worlds. These approaches adopt the postmodern assumption that there is no such thing as universal, objective knowledge and that our perceptions reflect the language, values, and beliefs of our particular community or social system. Both are holistic and seek to understand people fully and from many perspectives.

The Development of Constructivism

George Kelly (1955) was the first to write about the principles of constructivism (or constructive therapy as it also is called) in *The Psychology of Constructs*. He suggested that people have a system of constructs and symbols that reflect their views of themselves and their world. His book proposed ways to elicit and modify the content and structure of those constructs. Although Kelly's work emphasized cognitions, his ideas have influenced constructivist theory.

Today, Robert Neimeyer and Michael Mahoney are the names most strongly associated with constructivism. Both have contributed to the development of constructivist theory and its use as an approach to psychotherapy.

Theories and Strategies

According to Mahoney (1988a), "Constructivist theories recognize that psychological realities are inherently private, even when they are shared collectively, and that the forum of psychological change lies in the domain of those dynamic processes referred to as the self" (p. 9). He further stated, "Psychological construction refers to a family of theories that share the assertion that human knowledge and experience entail the (pro)active participation of the individual" (p. 2).

This is reminiscent of the classic tale of the blind men encountering an elephant. Each touched a different part of the elephant and so described the elephant in a different way. Their perceptions of the elephant were colored not only by their direct and limited contact with the elephant but by their own life experiences and interactions, which gave them the language and comparisons they used to understand what the elephant was like.

We, too, have a reciprocal relationship with our world. We bring our past perceptions and experiences with us as we encounter and assess new experiences; those assessments, in turn, affect the new experiences as well as our development and sense of self. A key concept in constructivism is that personal identity is socially constructed.

For example, Suki, discussed previously in this chapter, viewed people as untrustworthy and aloof and herself as having little to offer. This led her to avoid contact with others and, in turn, contributed to their lack of interest in her. When she began college, she felt out of place and excluded by the other students, not recognizing the part that her construction of the world played in determining her isolation.

Five Basic Themes of Constructivism   Mahoney (2003, p. 4) identified five basic themes that further clarify the nature of constructivism. These include:

1. *Active agency* —People are active participants in shaping their lives. Through choices, actions, and the focus of our attention, we continuously influence our experiences.
2. *Order* —People seek order and organization and to make meaning of their experiences. Too much order can lead to emotional overcontrol while too little order can lead to loss of balance and direction.
3. *Self and identity* —According to Mahoney (2003, p. 33), "Relationships with self are critical to life quality. These include self-concept, body image, self-esteem, and capacities for self-reflection and self-comfort." When our sense of self becomes inflexible or fragmented, we are likely to experience both intrapersonal and interpersonal difficulties.
4. *Social-symbolic processes* —Order, meaning, and identity stem largely from social interactions and symbolic processes (e.g., language, images, stories).
5. *Dynamic dialectical development* —People experience constant cycles of experience that can lead to organization or disorganization. We seek balance and may resist change in healthy and self-protecting ways. At the same time, some disorganization is necessary for reorganization.

Levels of Focus   Constructivist clinicians conceptualize treatment as encompassing at least three levels of focus: problems, patterns, and processes (Mahoney, 2003). *Problems* are a perceived discrepancy between people's current situation and they way they want or expect things to be. *Patterns* are composed of recurrent and related problems. *Process* underlies problems and patterns and includes reality (actual and perceived), values, the self, and power. Uri, for example, enters treatment because of a problem: he has lost his job. Discussion reveals a pattern. He has had a series of unsuccessful and unrewarding jobs over the past 10 years, with long periods of unemployment in between. A deeper exploration reflects a process: Uri has an unrealistic view of his abilities, values control rather than collaboration, is desperately trying to convince his parents that he is worthy of their love, but does not have effective ways to relate to them and to succeed in his work.

Therapeutic Alliance   The therapeutic alliance in constructivist treatment is a collaborative and nonauthoritarian one in which client and clinician co-create a connection. As Mahoney (1988b) stated, "Constructivist psychotherapy is a very intimate and personalized exchange between human beings" (p. 308). Client and clinician differ only in terms of roles and training. In treatment, both embark on an exploration. Clinicians do not direct the process or seek to persuade, analyze, or instruct. Rather, they use empathy, encouragement, affirmation, reflection, elaboration, and metaphor to advance the treatment. They provide clients a safe place, focus on clients' strengths and abilities, and are caring and compassionate. Clinicians help people "construct more coherent and comprehensive self-theories or, as coauthors, assist clients in the identification and revision of central themes in their personal narratives," but it is the clients who are the primary change agents (Neimeyer, 1993, p. 230).

Process of Treatment   Constructivism views people in positive and optimistic terms, seeing them as "pro-active, goal-directed, and purposive organisms" (Neimeyer, 1993, p. 223). People operate according to the knowledge they possess, reflecting their construction of their experiences and actions. Knowledge evolves and changes with new experiences and perceptions. A central goal of constructivist treatment is helping people develop possibilities and recognize that experiences have alternative meanings and interpretations. People's knowledge can then be assessed and either changed or validated, leading to knowledge that allows more satisfying ways of being.

Treatment initially begins with a focus on current problems and distress, then shifts to an exploration of patterns or recurrent difficulties, and finally moves to an understanding of underlying processes or constructions that perpetuate patterns. This can enable people to develop more rewarding ways of being and coping.

Constructivist approaches situate the self in the social context (Neimeyer, 1993) and suggest that people can best be understood and helped if attention is paid to that context. Constructivist clinicians pay considerably more attention to background than do other treatment approaches discussed in part 3 of this book and believe that early attachment plays an important part in shaping who we are. They also attend to thoughts, actions, and emotions to help people achieve a sense of integration (Mahoney, 1988a).

Constructivist therapists draw on a variety of perspectives and treatment systems in order to know and help their clients. Everything that people bring with them is construed as reflecting who they are and providing information on how they manage their lives. Both positive and negative emotions, for example, are viewed as people's efforts to make meaning out of their experiences and as something to work with rather than against. Resistance is similarly viewed as an understandable form of self-protection.

Although constructivist therapy is not associated with a specific group of techniques, some strategies are emphasized in this approach. Language is an important focus in constructivism; people make meaning through language. As Lynch (1997) stated, language not only labels human experience; it forms it. Deconstructing or loosening constructs is another frequently used strategy, as are co-creating new constructs, promoting empowerment, exploring themes and metaphors, expanding people's behavioral options, and helping people create support or referrent groups (Petersen & Benishek, 2001). Strategies that integrate mind, body, and spirit such as breathing exercises, meditation, and relaxation also are important in constructivist therapy (Mahoney, 2003).

Constructivist treatment seeks to help people change what Mahoney (2003) called their core ordering processes, which operate at primarily unconscious levels and shape people's emotions, perceptions, thoughts, and actions. However, because core ordering processes are difficult to access, the focus of treatment is on exploring people's subjective reconstructions of their lives.

Current Status

Constructivist therapy has captured the attention of many clinicians because of its compatibility with modern clinical thought. It appreciates the importance of the individual in society, diversity, and the client-clinician collaboration. It is holistic, integrative and flexible. It is respectful and optimistic, viewing people's efforts to cope as sources of knowledge that can promote positive change.

Although research is still limited on the effectiveness of this approach, constructivism is being applied to a wide range of concerns and settings. It is used in schools to promote active, social, and creative learning (Perkins, 1999). It has been adapted for use with couples and families (Neimeyer & Neimeyer, 1994). It has been used to treat a broad range of problems and mental disorders, including attention-deficit/hyperactivity disorder, posttraumatic stress disorder, and grief (Neimeyer & Stewart, 1996). The *Journal of Constructivist Psychology* promotes and disseminates the rapidly expanding research on this treatment approach. According to Mahoney (2003, p. 217), "One can find constructivist themes in contemporary work in neuroscience, human development, education, ethics, government, science, spirituality, and world peace. The expressions of constructivism in psychology and psychotherapy are only a part of the picture." Constructivist therapy has much to offer, and I anticipate it will grow in importance and influence in counseling and psychotherapy.

FEMINIST THERAPY

Feminist therapy was originally developed by Helene Deutsch, Karen Horney (discussed in chapter 7), and other psychodynamic and developmental theorists in reaction to what they perceived as Freud's lack of understanding of women. However, it has evolved and broadened greatly since that time.

Bruns and Trimble (2001) describe three waves of feminism. The first wave was represented by the suffrage movement, seeking voting rights for women. The second wave gained prominence in the 1970's with women's struggle for equal rights. These two waves were of greatest relevance to upper middle class educated white women. The third wave is coming to prominence in the 21st century and is reflected in Funderburk and Fukuyama's (2001, p. 4) definition of feminism as, "The belief that human beings are of equal worth and that the pervading patriarchal social structures which perpetuate a hierarchy of dominance, based upon gender, must be resisted and transformed toward more equitable systems." Postmodern feminist therapy is directed toward both women and men, toward people of all sexual orientations, races, classes, age groups, and cultures; it is designed to combat limiting and harmful influences and to empower all people so they can combat oppression while developing full and rewarding lives. Despite its misleading name, feminist therapy strives to help both men and women change themselves and their societies and act together to make a difference (Forcey & Nash, 1998). As you read this section, keep in mind this current and broad goal of feminist therapy.

Underlying Concepts

Feminist therapy has been shaped by several important tenets (Chrisler & Lamont, 2002; Sands, 1998):

- The personal is political.
- Egalitarian relationships are prized, both in and outside of therapy.
- Attention must be paid to understanding and addressing the impact of power and gender in social interactions and situations.
- The experiences and perceptions of all people must be heard and valued, whether they belong to powerful or marginalized groups.
- Group membership (e.g., gender, race, age) has a pervasive impact on our lives, affecting perceptions, emotions, conflicts, styles of relating, and more.

Feminist therapy has been strongly influenced by humanistic and phenomenological approaches as well as by cognitive therapy and existentialism. Like constructivism, it postulates that people's internal and external worlds, the subjective and objective, are interconnected and that both must be part of the therapeutic process (Day, 1992). Of particular concern to feminist therapists are cultural messages that limit and oppress.

Feminist Therapy and Women   Some feminist therapists view women as oppressed by their culture. They perceive cultures that are patriarchal in nature as associating masculinity with values such as individualism, self-sufficiency, and competition, while femininity is associated with caring, cooperation, and expression of emotions. Such cultures typically value masculine characteristics over feminine ones and view women as secondary to men.

Many of the emotional, cognitive, and behavioral difficulties experienced by girls and women can be directly linked to societal messages. For example, the recent great increase in eating disorders in females has been caused, at least in part, by messages equating beauty with thinness. Depression and anxiety, much more common in women than in men, probably have both biological and societal roots, with women experiencing these symptoms in response to feelings of powerlessness, loneliness, and role confusion.

Feminist therapy helps women value their traditional roles while deconstructing the discriminatory aspects of their societies and recognizing that they need not be limited to the roles of mother, wife, and caregiver or have an identity that is restricted to the spiritual, nurturing, and emotional (Lewis, 1992). Particular attention is paid to the unique roles of women such as motherhood and the mother-daughter bond in a way that recognizes their value and also gives women the message that biology need not be destiny, that they can be the architects of their lives (Lewis, 1992). This approach gives women a broad view of their options and a sense of community with other women while affording them greater power as well as new possibilities and ways of seeking knowledge.

Feminist Therapy and Men   Clients of feminist therapy may be men or women just as feminist therapists may be women or men. This treatment approach is particularly well suited to men who are dealing with masculine gender role strain. Recent research and writing suggest that men, like women, often develop difficulties as a result of conformity or nonconformity to traditional gender roles (Jakupcak, Lisak, & Roemer, 2002; Levant et al., 2003). Some men experience "discrepancy strain" when they perceive themselves as not conforming to traditional masculine norms. Others may feel conflicted and confined by their efforts to conform to masculine norms and suppress any feminine elements in themselves (dysfunction strain). A third type of gender role strain is trauma strain which can result when young boys are forced to conform to uncomfortable gender roles. Gender role strain is associated with higher levels of anger, aggression, anxiety, health-risk behavior, depression, and distress and with lower levels of self-esteem. (Of course, many men have flexible conceptions of the masculine role and do not experience gender role strain.)

Another perspective on the impact of gender role constriction was advanced by Mahalik, Good, and Englar-Carlson (2003) who suggested that many men adhere to masculine scripts such as strong-and-silent, playboy, winner, and homophobia. These scripts can act as barriers, curtail men's options, and prevent them from seeking help.

Feminist therapy might well be helpful to men experiencing gender role strain. Treatment would promote understanding of societal messages and their impact, flexibility in thinking, self-awareness and self-acceptance, gender role analysis, distress tolerance, and relaxation.

Role of the Clinician

Descriptions of feminist therapists resemble those of narrative and constructivist therapists. Clinicians are respectful, empathic, empowering, collaborative, and encouraging. They are authentic, enthusiastic, and open to new perceptions and experiences. Clinicians are resources and support systems rather than experts. They work with clients to establish goals and decide on pacing. They discredit traditional ideas of resistance, transference, and countertransference and, instead, view those processes as reflective of meanings and information that need attention. Countertransference, termed a "symbolic relationship" by feminist therapists, can be a particularly fruitful source of information (Brown, 2001).

Current feminist therapy also discusses the construct of relational power. One of the hallmarks of today's feminist therapy, relational power is the process in which both clinician and client are changed by the treatment process. Relational power reflects the egalitarian nature of feminist therapy as well as its prizing of all perspectives, its emphasis on the impact of social interaction, and the importance of clinician openness and genuineness. This construct is illustrated in the following example.

Example of Case Illustrating Relational Power   Angela, a married African American woman in her early 40s with two young children, sought counseling shortly after she was diagnosed with early-stage cancer. She deliberately sought help from a clinician about her own age who had cancer 8 years earlier. Her clinician Lesley was married, had one child, and was Caucasian. Angela's presenting concerns included dealing with her fear of not living long enough to see her children grow up and of wanting to clarify her priorities so that she lived a more fulfilling life.

Although Angela's concerns shaped the treatment, counseling involved considerable sharing between the two women and each learned from the other. Early in treatment, they discussed their common experiences (cancer, marriage, motherhood, age, education) as well as their differences (race) and the probable impact these would have on Angela's treatment. At Angela's suggestion, and with the counselor's encouragement, Angela provided considerable information on role expectations for African American women, the importance her mother and sisters had for her, the value she placed on her professional job, and the challenges she had encountered in finding a suitable partner, leading her to defer marriage until her mid-30s. Both women shared thoughts and feelings on the challenges of combining family and professional career, as well as on how race made that challenge somewhat different for each of them.

Angela realized that she had been devoting most of her attention to her well-established career and now wanted to reduce her work hours so she could spend more time with her children. Her increased acceptance of traditional female roles and her ability to reduce her unwarranted fear of living in poverty like her mother helped her make this change with comfort. She regained the powerfulness and hopefulness she had lost as a result of her medical diagnosis and coped effectively with changes in her body image resulting from her cancer treatment. She initiated an exercise program and formed a support group of other African American women dealing with cancer; these activities both reflected her sense of empowerment and further enhanced her powerfulness.

As a participant in this process, Lesley learned a great deal about the special role of the African American woman and also gained insight into her own rejection of some traditional female attitudes and behaviors, stemming from her need to carve out a different path for herself than that of her mother. In addition, Lesley saw more clearly the influence on her of growing up as a white middle-class woman, a condition of privilege. Although these insights were shared only briefly with Angela, Lesley did make clear that she, too, had learned and grown through the mutuality in the treatment process.

Strategies of Feminist Therapy

Feminist therapy emphasizes the here and now, the importance of self-actualization, and both individual and group empowerment. It promotes people's efforts to construct language, stories, and symbols drawn from their own experiences that strengthen and expand possibilities. It stresses the importance of relationships that respect diversity and that are nonhierarchical. Gender, race, and other contexts are explicitly discussed. Inclusiveness and plurality rather than discrimination are advocated. Narratives are elicited and viewed from individual and cultural perspectives. Analysis of gender roles and messages, power differentials in social interactions, and encouragement of clients to use and develop their self-awareness, strengths, and resources are important interventions.

Feminist therapy typically is integrated with other treatment systems and draws on a wide array of treatment strategies. However, this approach relies only minimally on techniques. Rather, it emphasizes the growth, learning, and empowerment that can result from an authentic connection of people, involving genuine interest and sharing.

Current Status

Feminist therapy is fast becoming an important perspective in counseling and psychotherapy. Many aspects of this approach are consistent with current trends in the field. It emphasizes human potential and people's ability and right to make choices that enable them to live their lives in rewarding ways. It is integrative and, according to Brown (2001, p. 1011), reflects "an ultimate feminist perspective; that mind and body and spirit must be addressed together in order to make therapy effective." It can, and usually is, combined with other approaches ranging from systemic to psychodynamic models. It can be used with individuals, families, and groups, and can be particularly helpful to couples who are struggling with gender role conflicts and confused and unmet expectations. It empasizes the importance of context and of social change, encouraging clinicians to focus their efforts at both individual and societal levels.

The recent literature on feminist therapy emphasizes the multicultural relevance of this approach. Funderburk and Fukuyama (2001), for example, described the convergence of feminism, multiculturalism, and spirituality: "Specifically, all three of these movements or forces place emphasis on consciousness, context, and connection in order to heighten awareness regarding suffering, liberation and enlightenment" (p. 6). All three "encourage the examination of socially, culturally, and cognitively constructed worldviews and beliefs" (p. 8) and "are interested in liberating the individual and transforming oppression and suffering in society and accomplish this, in part, by deconstructing 'social realities.' "

The literature reflects the application of this approach to multicultural groups including people coping with chronic and life-threatening illnesses, people with a homosexual orientation, African American and Chicana women, and adolescent girls. Like narrative therapy and constructivist therapy, feminist therapy has made an important contribution to our thinking and is expected to further advance our knowledge of human development, knowledge, and growth.

TRANSPERSONAL THERAPY

Transpersonal psychotherapy represents an effort to integrate western and eastern approaches to personal growth and change (Holden, 1993). Many see this approach as well suited to addressing today's problems of violence, addiction, and alienation, which may reflect spiritual impoverishment, lack of purpose and meaning, and a failure to recognize the interconnection of all living beings (Cowley, 1993). We consider transpersonal psychotherapy here because of its connection to humanism, its emphasis on experiences and sensations, and its phenomenological stance.

The People Who Developed Transpersonal Therapy

Many names are associated with the development of this approach. Carl Jung (discussed in chapter 6) has been called its philosophical parent, while Abraham Maslow is credited with originating transpersonal psychology in the United States (J. M. Holden, personal communication, October 22, 1999). Maslow (1971) hypothesized that people have a hierarchy of needs that include, in sequence, physiological needs, safety, belonging, self-esteem, self-actualization, and transcendent self-actualization. Lower-order needs must be met before people can direct their efforts toward achievement of higher-order needs. Maslow's work initially focused on helping people achieve self-actualization. However, he came to believe that a step beyond self-actualization existed: transcendent self-actualization. He also concluded that peak or transcendent experiences were instrumental in enabling people to move toward this state. A central goal of transpersonal psychotherapy is helping people achieve a higher state of consciousness which, for Maslow, was transcendent self-actualization.

Roberto Assagioli (1965, 1991), an Italian contemporary of Freud, was one of the early theoreticians in transpersonal psychology, which he called psychosynthesis. Assagioli believed that people have seven levels of consciousness beginning with the lower unconscious (including fundamental drives and urges as well as dreams and repressed material) and culminating in the collective unconscious, similar to that described by Jung.

Wilber (1996, 1999), an important modern theoretician in transpersonal psychology, believed that human development involved a progression through three successive stages toward increasing differentiation and transcendence:

1. The prepersonal or pre-egoic stage characterizes newborn and young children who are in the process of developing a sense of themselves. Adults still at the prepersonal

    level have not developed a strong sense of self. People diagnosed with borderline personality disorders are an example.

2. The personal or egoic stage characterizes the years from late childhood through adulthood and is as far as most people develop. The self is based in rationality and functions reasonably well in the world but does not achieve higher states of consciousness.

3. The transpersonal or transegoic stage, beyond the personal or the egoic, unfolds in later adulthood, if at all. It is characterized by expanded consciousness that includes the transpersonal experiential domain, which provides depth and richness to people's lives. People in this stage can make use of transrational processes involving intuition and mystical and paranormal experiences.

These stages are considered sequential; people cannot successfully skip a stage. In fact, if people immerse themselves in the transpersonal domain before having a well-developed ego, psychopathology results (J. M. Holden, personal communication, October 22, 1999).

Janice Miner Holden (1993, 1996) also has made an important contribution to transpersonal theory. Her work operationalizes transpersonal psychology and offers useful guidelines to clinicians using this theory.

Important Theoretical Concepts

According to Atwood and Maltin (1991), ". . . [transpersonal psychotherapy] creates psychological health, which is defined as the ability to live in harmony with oneself and nature, to understand one's relationship to the universe, to show tolerance and compassion to one's fellow human beings, to endure hardship and suffering without mental disintegration, to prize nonviolence, to care for the welfare of all sentient beings, and to see a meaning and purpose in one's life that allows one to enter old age or to face death with serenity and without fear" (p. 374). Transpersonal psychology assumes that all people have the potential to transcend the usual limitations of the ego and attain higher levels of consciousness that will give much greater meaning and fulfillment to their lives.

Assumptions   The following assumptions characterize transpersonal therapy (Tart, 1992):

- The universe has a purpose.
- People are more than their physical being.
- People are part of and interdependent with the rest of the world. All beings are interrelated.
- People have a function or purpose.
- People are here to understand and fulfill their place in the universe, not to make the universe fit them.
- People have the potential for higher levels of awareness but generally have not realized this potential.
- To grow, people must question and modify.
- Both rational and experiential knowledge are important.
- Intuition is a powerful cognitive faculty and can be developed.
- Spiritual growth is an essential need for everyone.

The Process of Change

Transpersonal theorists emphasize the value of integrating transpersonal concepts and approaches into more traditional treatment approaches, despite their apparent differences. For example, many conventional treatment systems encourage making the unconscious conscious, controlling our thoughts, strengthening the ego, and working toward clear goals. Transpersonal theorists, on the other hand, believe that, once realized, goals need to be transcended; that people first need to develop strong egos and then detach from them, thereby losing self-centeredness and connecting to the universe.

Transpersonal therapy does not challenge the assumptions of more traditional approaches. In fact, it embraces those assumptions as completely relevant at the pre-egoic and egoic levels. Rather than saying no to the pre-egoic and egoic domains, the transpersonal approach says, "yes, and there's more" (J. M. Holden, personal communication, October 22, 1999).

Transpersonal theory suggests shifts in orientation to facilitate movement toward higher levels of experience and functioning. In an apparent paradox, transpersonal theory holds that only by letting go of power and control and abandoning our driven and goal-directed ways can we achieve more responsibility for our lives as we move toward higher levels of consciousness and fulfillment. After reasonable success in achieving power, we need to be open to experience. After achieving the capacity for clear and logical thinking, we need to be open to intuition and spontaneity. After developing our capacity to modify and direct our feelings, we need to feel and experience them.

Feelings are viewed as important in transpersonal therapy, as they are in other humanistic theories. Transpersonal theorists believe that both positive and negative feelings are valuable and should be recognized and accepted (Atwood & Maltin, 1991). They also perceive people as responsible for both their behaviors and their emotions (J. M. Holden, personal communication, October 22, 1999).

Transpersonal Experiences　Learning and change come from present experiences. Of greatest importance are experiences of altered states of consciousness that involve a sense of transcending our usual boundaries. According to Holden (1996), "Transpersonal experience is a spontaneous, transient experience involving perception or action that *transcends* the ego boundaries of space and/or time, and which is, paradoxically, perceived as authentic or potentially authentic by the experiencer's ego with consensus reality intact" (p. 7).

For most people, transpersonal experiences are hard to explain and just seem to happen, although they can be facilitated by circumstances. Categories of transpersonal experience include *mystical experiences,* involving a sense of other-worldliness and higher consciousness; and *paranormal experiences*—meaningful, inexplicable experiences involving the everyday world, such as predicting events accurately and gaining information about people from objects (Holden, 1996).

Transpersonal experiences give people access to their higher selves and their deepest resources of creativity, as well as to reality that goes beyond human knowledge. Insight, intuition, and sudden awareness are important aspects of these experiences and often lead to a paradigm shift or a new way of viewing the world. Mystical experiences, for example, are typically characterized by such emotions as joy, love, and peace; a sense of unity and spirituality; and positive changes in attitude and self-image.

Blocks to Development　Holden (1993) identified four impediments to people's personal and transpersonal development that keep the higher self "repressed or undeveloped" and prevent people from having transcendent experiences (p. 8). She refers to these as the four I's:

1. Innate (genetic/physiological) factors
2. Cognitive immaturity
3. Inexperience limiting knowledge of options
4. Impotence (internal and external constraints on access to options)

The four *I*'s are reflected in a person's style of adaptation. They need to be assessed and addressed in treatment to alleviate blocks to growth. In addition, Holden recommends assessing people's physical, interpersonal, intrapersonal, and transpersonal realms. By *transpersonal,* she refers to people's sense of connectedness to a higher power either within themselves or outside themselves.

Treatment

Like existential therapy, transpersonal psychotherapy is more a philosophy than a set of interventions. However, writings since 1990 place greater emphasis on application and do provide useful guidelines.

Goals   Transpersonal therapy promotes people's spiritual development. According to Cowley (1993), "Prime concerns . . . are the search for ultimate values, peak or mystical experiences, and unitive consciousness and the legitimation of spiritual practices" (p. 527). Goals include increased feelings of self-worth, self-acceptance, spirituality and hope, appreciation of life and caring for others; a decrease in materialism; greater inner-directedness and a sense of meaning and freedom. People are helped to lose their self-centeredness and develop "global awareness, a knowledge of one's place in the universe" (Atwood & Maltin, 1991, p. 372), in order to develop the "ability to live in harmony with oneself and nature" (p. 374). People can resolve past pain, anger, and disappointment and replace them with peace and harmony. They can achieve spiritual awareness and enlightenment, a transcendence of the self, and an appreciation of the unity of all things.

Therapeutic Alliance   The process of change through transpersonal therapy can be disconcerting and even painful because it involves movement into new and unfamiliar areas (Holden, 1993). Consequently, the role of the clinician and the therapeutic alliance are very important.

The clinician should provide the core conditions of empathy, genuineness, respect, and caring (described in chapter 10) as well as a safe therapeutic environment. Collaboration between client and clinician is integral to treatment. Both are expected to learn and develop from this process. Clinicians are viewed as more advanced students of enlightenment—educating, facilitating, offering help, and guiding clients but never directing, forcing, or imposing. Clinicians facilitate transpersonal experiences and enhance their benefits. They are carriers and agents, not sources of enlightenment. Clinicians often share their own transpersonal experiences. However, whether or not to self-disclose is up to each clinician.

Clinicians should be experienced and have sound training in established approaches to treatment. In addition, they should have considerable personal and spiritual development (Holden, 1993). If possible, they should experience transpersonal techniques themselves before suggesting them to clients.

Interventions   According to Holden (1993), "Transcendence can occur through the sensory modality of new experience. . . . this results in disintegration of the old pattern and reintegration of a new, more inclusive and gratifying one" (p. 15). People in transpersonal therapy typically need "some sort of psychological or contemplative practice that will provide the practitioner with direct experience of transpersonal phenomena," an altered state of consciousness (Walsh, 1992, p. 41). Interventions also seek to develop qualities needed to deepen awareness, including patience, a nonjudgmental attitude, acceptance of things as they are, and comfort with ambiguity (Atwood & Maltin, 1991).

Holden (1996) described four broad approaches to transcendental treatment, which can help people address and stay in touch with spiritual material without being overwhelmed by it, so that they can experience and integrate its benefits.

1. *Grounding* is used if people's functioning is diminished because they are overwhelmed by their spiritual experiences. It narrows people's focus of attention to outer reality only. Grounding can be accomplished through physical exercise, problem solving, concentration on daily tasks and activities, and focusing (a strategy developed by Eugene Gendlin).

2. *Centering* helps people benefit from spiritual experiences. It brings attention to inner reality while maintaining outer awareness. Centering techniques include deep breathing, relaxation, quieting exercises, biofeedback, yoga, meditation, massage, and focusing.

3. *Opening* reduces concentration on both outer and inner reality to help people attend to spontaneous and emerging inner experiences—to facilitate a "passive surrender of deliberate thought" (Holden, 1996, p. 20). Techniques include trance induction, focusing, meditation, imagery, hypnosis, Reiki and other energy methods, and biofeedback.

4. *Processing* integrates both inner and outer spiritual experiences into the ego using focusing as well as therapeutic dialog.

Many other techniques also can be productively incorporated into transpersonal therapy. They include writing down dreams and transpersonal experiences, creating a spiritual autobiography, Rolfing and other forms of body work, and a day of silence.

Meditation   Meditation, the intervention most associated with transpersonal therapy, has received considerable attention and study. Meditation has been described as voluntary redirection and self-control of attention. It "may promote inner calm, loving kindness toward oneself and others, access to previously unconscious material, transformative insight into emotional conflicts, and changes in the experience of personal identity" and can enhance concentration, memory, and coping (Bogart, 1991, p. 383).

Meditation typically is preceded by 5–10 minutes of preparation that might include muscle relaxation, stretching, deep breathing, and scanning the body for strong sensations. Then "the instructions for meditation can be put very simply: Calmly attend to a simple stimulus. After every distraction, calmly return your attention—again and again and again" (Smith, 1986, p. 67). The stimulus might include a relaxing sound or word, a visual image such as a candle or a picture of a child, breathing deeply and slowly, or a repetitive movement such as walking.

Many types of meditation have been developed. Probably the best known is transcendental meditation (TM). Research has shown that TM can promote improvement in variables such as affective maturity, integrative perspective of self and world, resilient sense of self, and inner-directedness (Alexander, Rainforth, & Gelderloos, 1991, p. 191). Another type of meditation is mindful meditation, which involves being in the present moment as much as possible—concentrating one's full, undivided attention on the details of everyday life. In mindfulness, "attention is focused upon registering feelings, thoughts, and sensations exactly as they occur, without elaboration, preference, selection, comments, censorship, judgment, or interpretation" (Holden, 1993, p. 384).

Application

Research on the appropriate use of transpersonal therapy is still emerging. However, some tentative conclusions can be drawn.

Appropriate Clients   Transpersonal therapy is particularly well suited to people who present spiritual concerns or goals (Cowley, 1993). They might include people who lack direction or meaning in their lives, those whose current spiritual practices are unsatisfying, those who believe their lives will be enhanced by experiences that go beyond their awareness of reality, those who have had spontaneous transpersonal experiences that do not fit into their existing worldview, and those who feel that life must have more to offer them.

Because transpersonal therapy is a flexible approach that can be tailored to meet the needs of the individual and because transpersonal clinicians do not coerce people to change, this approach is suitable for a broad range of people. Its emphasis on the spiritual dimension may appeal to people from many cultural groups who may be uncomfortable with more traditional approaches to treatment that neglect the importance of spirituality.

At the same time, transpersonal therapy is a powerful approach that can create chaos in people's views of themselves and their world. It also can precipitate a spiritual crisis and can expose people to experiences that are confusing and disconcerting. Consequently, this approach should be used only with relatively healthy and well-functioning people who have strong egos and can tolerate ambiguity and address the profound questions and experiences that may arise. This treatment system does not seem appropriate for people who lack a sound grasp on reality, are looking for magical solutions to all their problems, or are very fragile or suicidal. Just as this approach seems more suited for use by advanced clinicians, so it seems best for clients who already have experienced considerable growth and development, are managing their lives relatively well, but are now ready to take the growth process to a higher level.

Current Status

Little empirical research has been conducted on transpersonal therapy. With the exception of transcendental meditation, most of the interventions have not yet proven their value. This is especially important because some of the interventions (e.g., past life regression) are controversial and can be used in harmful and misleading ways.

Perhaps more than any other approach discussed in this book, transpersonal therapy has the potential for misunderstanding and exploitation. Practitioners have been accused of both overemphasizing traditional religious beliefs and advocating practices that violate conventional religion. Used by well-trained and experienced clinicians, this approach allows people to develop their spirituality and simply guides and facilitates their growth. However, in the wrong hands, the approach may be dangerous. Before engaging in transpersonal therapy, training, or supervision, people should investigate the credentials of those with whom they will be working. They should also obtain enough information about these clinicians' treatment approaches to be sure that they are compatible with the professional literature on treatment as well as on ethical and legal practices.

Although relatively few clinicians identify themselves as transpersonal therapists, many more draw heavily on the interventions associated with this approach including meditation, yoga, and imagery. Although transpersonal therapy has not yet made a place for itself among the mainstream approaches to treatment, interest is growing, as is the integration of aspects of this approach with other systems of treatment.

Evaluation

Transpersonal therapy has many limitations, connected primarily to a lack of research on this approach and the powerful interventions it uses. Also, the literature on transpersonal therapy is often complex and laden with terminology that can seem unfamiliar and disconcerting.

On the other hand, transpersonal therapy has many strengths. It can give people a sense of meaning and purpose and an interconnection with the rest of the world. It advocates values such as altruism, peace, joy, and love that have the potential of ameliorating many problems in people's lives and in the world as a whole. This is an optimistic and empowering approach that emphasizes people's potential for higher levels of awareness and views our lives as unending growth processes. Its rich array of strategies can be incorporated into many other approaches. In addition, transpersonal therapy recognizes that spirituality, broadly defined, is an appropriate focus of attention in treatment and that ignoring or refusing to acknowledge its place in people's lives does them a disservice. In sum, while this approach is emerging and must prove itself, it has expanded people's thinking on psychotherapy and may make a considerable contribution.

SKILL DEVELOPMENT: GUIDED IMAGERY

Visualization or guided imagery is an important strategy in transpersonal therapy. It is also widely used in cognitive and behavior therapy (discussed later in this book) and can be productively incorporated into almost any treatment approach. Imagery can reduce anxiety and facilitate relaxation, promote feelings of empowerment and control, improve problem solving and decision making, ameliorate pain and other physical symptoms, and help people develop new perspectives on themselves and their lives.

Encouraging Cooperation with Visualization

Although most people are eager to try any treatment strategies that are likely to help them, some view guided imagery and other nontraditional techniques as silly, worthless, or even threatening. To encourage cooperation, clinicians should give people a rationale for using the strategy, along with encouragement to approach it with a playful, curious, open attitude. Clinicians might say something like, "I don't know whether guided imagery will be beneficial to you, but many people find it helpful and relaxing. I'd be curious to see how you react. How about if we try it? You can let me know if you want to stop at any point, but you may discover some new and interesting things about yourself." In addition, clients should have as much control over the process as possible. They may need help to recognize that imagery is not some mysterious process that is being done to them but, rather, their inner resources coming to the fore. Timing of the guided imagery and its duration and intensity should be carefully adapted to the needs of the individual. Imagery is especially likely to be well received if it appeals to a person's dominant sense (visual, auditory, tactile, gustatory, or olfactory) (Siegel, 1990).

Visualization is most powerful if it is practiced and used between sessions. Guided imagery sessions can be tape recorded so that clients can listen to them daily as well as before stressful events. Practicing as little as 3–5 minutes a day, in the same comfortable place, facilitates the process of visualization (Fanning, 1988). The best times to use visualization are upon waking and before falling asleep. Keeping an arm slightly raised can keep the person awake during the imagery if that is a concern.

The Process of Guided Imagery

The following steps are typical of a guided imagery session (Seligman, 1996b, pp. 88–95):[1]

1. The clinician promotes the client's relaxation via deep breathing, muscle tension and release, or other techniques.
2. The person imagines a peaceful, relaxing scene in which he or she feels secure, whole, and healthy. This can be a familiar place or an imaginary place.
3. The person is given the opportunity to find a wise inner guide; means are provided in the image for the guide to appear (e.g., on a path, from behind a rock, through a door). The guide offers a channel for clients to access their inner resources and unconscious. When a possible guide appears, the person should visualize greeting the visitor and asking whether it is the guide. If the answer is no, the person can ask for the guide to be sent.
4. The person presents a question or a task to the guide.
5. The guide assists the person with the task or question, usually either providing more information and ideas or facilitating a decision.
6. The person visualizes him or herself as empowered and successful at dealing with the task or question.
7. The person thanks the guide, says good-bye, and affirms that the guide can be summoned whenever that would be helpful. The guide departs.
8. The person gradually leaves the peaceful scene and returns to reality.

In the following example, a clinician leads a person through a second session of guided imagery, with an abbreviated introduction and relaxation. The guide and the images are based on information that arose for the client during the first imagery session.

Clinician: Now I would like you to relax your body and sink deeply into your chair. Uncross your arms and legs and gently let your eyelids close. Pay attention to your breathing. Breathe deeply and from your diaphragm, in and out, in and out, feeling your diaphragm rise and fall with each breath . . . Take full, deep, slow breaths and with each breath, you will feel all the tension, all the stress flowing away . . . feel all your muscles relax, your head, . . . your

---

[1] From Linda Seligman, *Promoting a Fighting Spirit.* Copyright © 1996, John Wiley & Sons, Inc. This material is used by permission of John Wiley & Sons, Inc.

face, . . . your shoulders, . . . your arms, . . . your hands. Feel the tension being released. Now relax your chest, . . . your lower body, . . . your legs, . . . and your feet. Feel the breath flowing through your body, relaxing all your muscles.

Now when you feel ready and relaxed, I'd like you to return to that special place, that beautiful lush forest where you feel as strong as the strongest tree. Look around you, and remember how happy you feel here, how calm and peaceful you are, surrounded by the tall, green trees and the tall mountains, how happy you are to be back here. Now as you look around, you will see your inner guide, the fox, coming out from behind the tree. He has been waiting for you to call on him, always ready to help you. I'd like you to greet your guide; and when the two of you are ready, you will once again go on a journey.

The question you have decided to work on with your guide is whether to end your marriage. Explain your question to your guide so that your guide can help you as much as possible. When you are ready, you and your guide may walk down the path you see before you, going toward the yellow house with three rooms that you visualized in our last session. Being in that house with your guide may give you information about the decision that is worrying you. As you approach the house, look at it carefully. Be on the alert for information and messages all along this journey.

When you approach the house, decide how you will enter the house and go into the first room you see. This is the room of problems in your marriage: the abuse, the untruthfulness, and the alcohol. Be aware of your feelings, both in your body and in your heart, as you look around this room. Look at the furniture, the walls, any windows you might see, any decorations in this room. Remember that your guide is there to help you. Take the time and really experience this room.

When you are ready to go to the next room, let me know by raising a finger. . . . Now you are entering the next room. This is the room of joys in your marriage: your children, your home, the close and intimate times you have with your husband, the security that is so important to you. Be aware of your feelings, both in your body and in your heart, as you look around this room. Look at the furniture, the walls, any windows you might see, any decorations in this room. Remember that your guide is there to help you. Take your time and really experience this room.

When you are ready to go to the next room, let me know by raising a finger. . . . Now you are entering the third room. This is the room of your life, the joys and the disappointments, the wholeness of your life. Again, look around the room. Be aware of your thoughts and feelings. Be open to any messages and information that come up while you are here. Even if it doesn't seem to make any sense, whatever comes up for you may be important and meaningful. You may see a container in this room; you can use that to bring back with you all the experiences, thoughts, emotions, and sensations you experience while you are in this house. Remember that your guide is there to help you.

When you are ready to leave the house, let me know by raising a finger. . . . Now you and your guide may leave the house, pausing outside the house to look back and reflect on all you learned, all you gained from this journey. . . . It's time to say good-bye to your guide for now, but you know that he is always there to help you. Every time you open the front door to your house, it will remind you of your guide, and you will know that he is always with you.

Now look around the forest once more. Think about all you have accomplished so far and all you are proud of: your children, your graduation from college, your furniture-making, and the person you are. Notice how capable and strong you feel, knowing that whatever steps you take, they will be the right ones for you. You will be able to take those steps with the assurance that you have explored all your choices and all the rooms of the house and have found the choice that is best for you . . . When you are ready, gradually come back to this room, slowly open your eyes, and remember where you are . . . Now I'd like you to draw a picture of the images you had, and then we can talk about what came up for you during this visualization.

This guided imagery was carefully planned to include 10 important elements:

1. Relaxation
2. Images that promote a sense of control, hope, competence, and empowerment
3. Reassurance, strength, and support provided by the clinician and the inner guide
4. Reminders of the guide's availability
5. Images that promote greater awareness (the house with three rooms)
6. Encouragement to notice emotions, sensations, and thoughts
7. An opportunity for synthesis, decision-making, and closure
8. Reminders of the person's previous successes and accomplishments
9. An image of the person as successfully resolving the concern
10. Processing and reinforcing of the guided imagery without judging the person, the images, or the person's success in creating images

Uses for Visualization

Following are some helpful ways to use visualization in treatment:

• The threat and discomfort presented by an aversive experience can be reduced by imagining the experience in a way that is ridiculous, desensitizes the person to the threat, or changes the threat into something positive. A child who was fearful about giving a talk to her class gained confidence by imagining the other students dressed as cheerleaders, applauding her performance.

• Imagery can provide a mental rehearsal for coping with challenging experiences. Meichenbaum (1985) suggested that such imagery should include the experience of stress as well as successful coping with the stressor; imagining only mastery or success without the stressor and the challenge of coping seems to provide a less realistic and less useful image. People can imagine a movie of themselves successfully performing feared acts, thereby identifying and reinforcing desired behaviors.

- Brigham (1994) suggested using a *transformational fantasy*. The clinician guides the client on a symbolic journey, typically walking down a strange road, seeing a house, and exploring the house. The person is encouraged to describe and explore reactions to the scene. Brigham believed that the scene symbolized the person's life and that the house and its features gave information about the person. She used this strategy successfully with people who were coping with cancer; it can be used productively with people coping with any significant life event or turning point.

- Imagery can provide positive distraction. Creation of an absorbing and readily accessed fantasy or series of images can decrease people's rumination and provide them with a tool for reducing anxious images and messages.

- Reliving a troubling or powerful experience through the imagination can help people retrieve their feelings and reassess their behaviors. This can help them understand the experience and view their reactions from a different perspective.

- Imagery, using the inner guide, can help people find answers to difficult questions. Fanning (1988) called this receptive visualization.

- McWilliams and McWilliams (1991) suggested having people imagine hosting a gratitude party in which all the people and events for which they can be grateful are reviewed. This technique can promote optimism and a positive outlook, as can an image that projects a person into a positive time in the future.

CASE ILLUSTRATION

This case illustrates the use of feminist therapy with Roberto. He addresses here issues similar to those he discussed in the illustration of Gestalt therapy (chapter 12). Notice similarities and differences in the two approaches. The clinician is male.

Clinician: I'd encourage you to reflect back on the years since you were a young boy and think about the messages you got about how men should be. Think about messages you received from your parents, male role models you had, messages you have gotten from Edie and Ava, and even messages from films and television and advertising.

Roberto: The first thing I thought of was my dad. He was really tough and strong. You didn't argue with him or you'd be sorry.

Clinician: Sounds like you really admired him.

Roberto: Yeah, he was my idol. I wanted to be just like him. Now I can see that his anger and drinking caused some problems but, as a kid, I didn't see any of that. I tried to talk like him, dress like him, do anything I could to be like him.

Clinician: How did that work for you?

Roberto: Great! Everyone looked up to me too.

Clinician: You know, I grew up with similar messages. I'm older than you, and the messages about men's roles, be-

ing like John Wayne, were pretty strong in my life too. How do those messages work for you now?

Roberto: Things used to be pretty clear; a man needed to support and protect his family and the woman kept house and took care of the kids. But here's Edie who has her own career and expects me to vacuum and set the table. I never thought I'd be doing things like that. And the problem is not just Edie; some of my own feelings are all mixed up too.

Clinician: Your own feelings?

Roberto: Yeah, like when Ava was born and they put her in my arms, I almost started to cry. I had to get out of the room quick so nobody would see. And sometimes when Edie and I are close, I want to do everything for her, even if I vacuum and set the table. But then when I do it, it feels like I'm selling out, and I get angry at her and myself.

Clinician: Are there parts of your life that keep that male image of your father alive for you and make it hard for you to see other options?

Roberto: Yeah, you still see that kind of man in the movies . . . Bruce Willis, Vin Diesel, all the rest. They don't cry over babies. And in a way, Edie makes it harder for me. Sometimes she calls me "macho man," real demeaning in a way. Like I don't have a brain in my head and am stuck in some stereotype. But instead of making me want to change, it's like a challenge. I just get more bull-headed, tell her off, and don't really think about what she's trying to get across. She could sure find a better way to say what's on her mind.

Clinician: So in a way she makes the problem worse and keeps you in that masculine role that your father represented to you.

Roberto: But I do admire my father. He's still tough, even at his age. What's wrong with being like that?

Clinician: You learned a lot from your father that you don't want to lose and you also want to be able to express other sides of you.

Roberto: How can I do that? I'm a man and that's who I want to be.

Clinician: I struggled with that too, and still do, but what I wanted as a man was respect and appreciation. I got even more of that from the people who mattered to me if I could be strong enough to be different sometimes and try out new feelings and actions that I wasn't used to and that my dad never did.

Roberto: Wait a minute . . . are you telling me I need to be strong to set the table?

Clinician: Pretty strange thought . . . but I guess I am. You know, when we have a model of how to be, we don't have any hard choices to make. We know what to do. But then when we try to add onto the model, it's confusing. We don't know what the rules are.

Roberto: So we're not just talking about setting the table . . . we're really talking about how to be a man. I never thought about that much. I thought I knew the answer, but maybe it's not so easy. I thought my dad was great. My mom didn't always think so, but she still acted like a woman is supposed to act. Edie doesn't do that.

Clinician: Sounds like maybe we should talk about this when Edie joins us next week.

Roberto: Yeah, that's a good idea. Tell her to lose the "macho man" stuff.

This exert of a feminist therapy session with Roberto helps him look at his conception of masculine and feminine roles, the sources of his restrictive and traditional ideas, and possible ways to increase flexibility in his thinking. He is experiencing discrepancy strain (discomfort with nonconformity to his view of the male gender role) as well as a "tough guy" masculine script. Self-disclosure on the part of the clinician facilitated exploration of Roberto's gender role stress.

EXERCISES

Large-Group Exercises

1. The approaches described in this chapter (narrative therapy, constructivism, feminist therapy, transpersonal therapy) may have elicited some strong reactions because of their innovative and nontraditional approaches to treatment. Each member of the class should take 5 minutes to write spontaneously about his or her reactions to these approaches. Read several of these aloud to the class and then discuss your reactions to the approaches. Listen to others' ideas, even if they conflict with yours.

2. This is an exercise in mindfulness. Give a cookie to each member of the class. Eat the cookie slowly. Try to be fully aware of the experience—noticing the textures, the smells, the tastes, and the way you approach the process of eating the cookie. Try to tune out all distractions, focusing only on the experience of savoring the cookie. Then discuss the experience.

3. Select someone to lead the class in a guided visualization. Begin the session with relaxing diaphragmatic breathing and then spend approximately 15 minutes in the visualization. The script may be similar to the one provided in this chapter, or an alternate script may be used. After the visualization, draw a picture of the image that was most powerful for you. Allow time for the class to discuss and process the experience.

Small-Group Exercises

1. One member of each dyad should lead his or her partner in a guided visualization. Spend 15 minutes in the relaxation and visualization phase and then allow 5–10 minutes for discussion. Process the experience so that client, clinician, and observers all have the opportunity to talk about what the visualization experience was like for them as well as its benefits and shortcomings.

2. Take about 10 minutes to write a brief story that is meaningful to you about the community in which you grew up. Share that story with the other three members of your group and discuss what picture emerges of your background and your experiences in this community.

Individual Exercises

1. Write your spiritual autobiography in your journal, describing important spiritual experiences that you have had in your life. If you feel comfortable doing so, share your writing with someone to whom you feel close.

2. Choose a word or image that is meaningful to you, ideally one that helps you to feel peaceful and optimistic. For 1 week, spend 15 minutes a day meditating on that word or image. If your mind wanders, simply bring it back to the image you have chosen. Think about this experience and write about it in your journal. You may want to use this as an opportunity to initiate regular meditation.

3. Write in your journal a story about yourself that family members often told you. Describe how you are portrayed in this story and the impact it might have had on you. If you believe the story had a negative impact on you, rewrite the story, portraying yourself in a more positive light.

SUMMARY

This chapter provided information on four approaches to counseling and psychotherapy: narrative therapy, constructivist therapy, feminist therapy, and transpersonal therapy:

- Narrative therapy suggests that people's conceptions of themselves and their lives come from the stories they have made a part of themselves. By helping people to explore, understand, and modify their stories, clinicians can enable them to revision and reauthor their lives.

- Constructivist psychotherapy and feminist psychotherapy have many similarities to narrative psychotherapy. All three are phenomenological approaches that focus on people's perceptions of themselves and their worlds. All are holistic, attending to background as well as emotions, thoughts, and actions. They view people in a social context and believe that each person has a subjective psychological reality that has grown out of his or her life experiences. Constructivism emphasizes the reciprocal relationships we have with our world. It helps people understand their underlying constructions and expand their interpretations and possibilities. Feminist therapy seeks to help both men and women overcome rigid gender and other roles. This approach encourages people to appreciate the special attributes of their gender while expanding their options and promoting empowerment and egalitarian relationships.

- Transpersonal therapy emphasizes the importance of spiritual growth, the interrelationship of all beings, and the potential of all people to achieve higher levels of awareness. By creating experiences and conditions that are likely to release intuition and creativity, clinicians help people move toward transcendent self-actualization and spiritual development.

All four approaches emphasize emotions and sensations, and all offer new and emerging ways for clinicians to treat their clients more effectively.

RECOMMENDED READINGS

Boorstein, S. (Ed.). (1996). *Transpersonal psychotherapy* (2nd ed.). Albany: State University of New York Press.

Bruns, C. M., & Trimble, C. (2001). Rising tide: Taking our place as young feminist psychologists. *Women & Therapy, 23,* 19–36.

Holden, J. M. (1993). Transpersonal counseling. *TCA Journal, 21*(1), 7–23.

Journal of Constructivist Psychology—all issues.

Mahalik, J. R., Good, G. E., & Englar-Carlson, M. (2003). Masculinity scripts, presenting concerns, and help seeking: Implications for practice and training. *Professional Psychology: Research and Practice, 34,* 123–131.

Mahoney, M. J. (1988b). Constructive metatheory. II: Implications for psychotherapy. *Journal of Consulting and Clinical Psychology, 61,* 299–315.

Mahoney, M. J. (2003). *Constructive psychotherapy.* New York: Guilford.

Tart, C. T. (1992). *Transpersonal psychologies.* San Francisco: HarperCollins.

Wellings, N., & McCormick, E. W. (2004). *Transpersonal psychotherapy.* Thousand Oaks, CA: Sage Publications.

White, M., & Epston, D. (1990). *Narrative means to therapeutic ends.* Adelaide, Australia: Dulwich Centre.

Worrell, J., & Remer, P. (2002). *Feminist perspectives in therapy: Empowering diverse women.* New York: Wiley.

ADDITIONAL SOURCES OF INFORMATION

http//www.massey.ac.nz—Website for the Dulwich Centre in New Zealand. Site provides information on narrative therapy, interviews with leaders in that treatment approach, and other resources.

http://www.atpweb.org—Website for The Association for Transpersonal Psychology, P.O. Box 50187, Palo Alto, CA 94303, (650) 424-8764. ATP is a membership organization that offers training, products, and other resources for people interested in transpersonal psychology. It publishes the *Journal of Transpersonal Psychology.*

http://www.itp.edu—Website for The Institute of Transpersonal Psychology, 1069 East Meadow Circle, Palo Alto, CA 94303, 650-493-4430. ITP offers online graduate coursework in transpersonal psychology as well as other training programs, a bulletin, and relevant products and resources.

www.feministtherapyinstitute.org—Website of the Feminist Therapy Institute, a membership organization that holds conferences and provides information for people interested in feminist therapy.

www.constructivism123.com—Website of the Society for Constructivism in the Human Sciences provides information about leaders and publications in constructivism.

Part Four

Treatment Systems Emphasizing Thoughts

CHAPTER 14

Overview of Thought-Focused Treatment Systems

Thoughts, like emotions and sensations, are our constant companions. We wake up thinking about our plans for the day, fall asleep reviewing the day's experiences, and have a myriad of thoughts in between. The term *stream of consciousness* has been applied to the constant flow of thoughts we all have.

Part 4 of this book focuses on approaches to counseling and psychotherapy that view thoughts and cognitions as the primary avenue to change—the third of the four elements in the BETA model (background, emotions, thoughts, actions). Cognitive clinicians believe that thoughts lead to emotions and behaviors and that, through awareness and modification of their thoughts, people can change their feelings and actions.

As an illustration, consider the examples of Paula and Carmen. Both are single women in their early 30s who graduated from college and have been employed in professional positions for the past 10 years. Both saved their money and recently achieved a longstanding goal of purchasing a town house. Both prepared to move into their new homes by spending a weekend painting and wallpapering. What distinguishes the two women in this example are their thoughts about the experience.

While she was painting, Paula thought, "Here I am, all alone, with no one to share my life. I will never find the sort of partner I am looking for. Buying this house and having to do all this work myself really confirms that I will spend the rest of my life all alone."

Carmen, on the other hand, thought, "It's hard to believe I did this all myself, bought the house I have been dreaming of for 10 years. No one thought I could accomplish this on my salary, but I did. And here I am painting and wallpapering. The house looks great! I can't wait to invite people to dinner in my new home."

Not surprisingly, Paula felt depressed after she moved into her new home. She rarely invited friends to visit, made little effort to meet her neighbors, and viewed her purchase as a sign of her unhappy future. Carmen, on the other hand, entertained friends and neighbors, felt proud of the purchase and decoration of her home, and became even more optimistic about achieving her next important goal—a graduate degree. The differences in the thoughts the two women had about their purchase of a home led to very different emotions and behaviors. If Paula were to seek counseling from a cognitive therapist, that clinician would help her express, reality-test, dispute, and modify her cognitions to effect changes in her emotions and actions.

Part 4 of this book presents two major approaches to cognitive treatment. Chapter 15 considers cognitive therapy, developed by Aaron Beck and his associates, which has attracted considerable attention since its development. Many concepts, procedures, and clinical tools are associated with this approach. For example, Beck developed the idea of cognitive distortions, discussed further in this chapter and in chapter 15. Research has demonstrated the value of cognitive therapy with a broad range of disorders and problems.

Albert Ellis's rational emotive behavior therapy (REBT), presented in chapter 16, was the first major treatment approach focused on thoughts. Ellis's pioneering efforts established a solid foundation for future theoreticians.

In chapter 17, we consider three emerging approaches that focus on changing thought patterns: eye movement desensitization and reprocessing (EMDR), neurolinguistic programming (NLP), and thought-field therapy (TFT). Their innovative techniques to disrupt and change thought patterns enhance the power of clinical work.

USE OF COGNITIONS IN COUNSELING AND PSYCHOTHERAPY

Either alone or in combination with other theoretical approaches, cognitive treatment systems are powerful and flexible approaches with broad application. Focusing treatment on thoughts has many strengths and benefits.

Beck and others have extensively researched cognitive approaches to treatment, and their effectiveness is well established. Martin Seligman (1995), for example, found that cognitive therapy was successful in treating depression as well as some types of eating and anxiety disorders. Francine Shapiro (1995, 2001) and her colleagues found that eye movement desensitization and reprocessing was effective in treating posttraumatic stress disorder.

Thoughts are readily accessible. When we attend to our thoughts about a subject, we typically have little difficulty becoming cognizant of them and articulating them.

Asking people about their thoughts is usually less threatening than asking them about their feelings. People are used to being asked questions such as, "Do you think it will rain today?"

"What do you think about the president's speech?" and "Who do you think will win the game?" Most people do not hesitate to respond to such questions and do not find them intrusive or inappropriate. On the other hand, asking questions about emotions, beyond the routine "How are you feeling today?" may seem like prying.

Cognitions seem more amenable to change and analysis than are feelings. Thoughts can be written down, their validity and helpfulness can be assessed, and, if appropriate, they can be disputed, and modified. For example, assume Pablo is at home reading a book when the doorbell rings. He thinks, "I bet that is my brother wanting to borrow some money." He feels unhappy and apprehensive. The reality of his thought can easily be tested; all he needs to do is answer the door. If it is not his brother, Pablo's thought will change, leading to a shift in his emotions. However, focusing directly on Pablo's emotions and trying to change his apprehensions probably will be a more complex process; emotions often feel amorphous, difficult to identify, and even harder to explain and analyze.

Changing thoughts can be relatively rapid. Experiencing positive gains early in treatment increases people's motivation and optimism, which can accelerate the course of treatment.

Learning to identify, dispute, and change thoughts can be empowering. Those skills can give people a greater sense of control over their lives and provide highly effective strategies for addressing problems.

Treatment that emphasizes thoughts is likely to be comfortable for and make sense to a wide range of people. Particularly important, a focus on thoughts can make the counseling process more acceptable to people who are not used to sharing their emotions, including some men, many older people, and people from Asian and other cultural backgrounds who view expression of emotions to a stranger as inappropriate, weak, or in conflict with their upbringing and self-images.

SKILL DEVELOPMENT: ANALYZING AND MODIFYING COGNITIONS

This Skill Development section focuses on analyzing and modifying cognitions. It draws heavily on Aaron Beck's work and provides a preview of cognitive therapy.

People have thoughts, emotions, and behaviors. When a person describes a problem or concern, one of these is likely to be more accessible or prominent than the other two. Harold was very upset about an interaction with his wife Carol which occurred when Harold's younger brother Louis was dying of cancer. Review the following three ways in which Harold might describe the interaction with his wife:

Description 1: We were supposed to take our vacation when I found out that Louis was dying. I talked to the doctors, who said he only had a few weeks to live. I tried to be there for Louis. I told Carol that I wanted to postpone the vacation, so we put it off for a month. Louis was failing but was still alive then, so I suggested we postpone the vacation again. Carol wouldn't consider it. So I went on the vacation even though it was not what I wanted to do. Louis died while we were in Spain. We flew right home for the funeral.

Description 2: We were supposed to take our vacation when I found out that Louis was dying. I was devastated when I found out. I couldn't bear the idea of going on a vacation while he was dying. I felt enraged when Carol refused to postpone our vacation a second time, but

I was afraid I would lose my marriage if I didn't comply with her wishes. Louis died while we were in Spain. I felt so guilty that I hadn't been there with him.

Description 3: We were supposed to take our vacation when I found out that Louis was dying. All I could think of was that I needed to be with him when he died. When Carol refused to postpone our vacation the second time, I thought she didn't care anything about me and only thought about her own needs. But I believed that it would hurt my marriage if I didn't go on the trip with her. Louis died while we were in Spain. I thought that I would never be able to forgive myself for not being with him.

Eliciting Actions, Emotions, and Thoughts

Each of these descriptions has a different focus. Description 1 focuses on actions, Description 2 on emotions, and Description 3 on thoughts. When eliciting and analyzing thoughts, obtain all three aspects of a person's reactions. Start with the most accessible of the three (thoughts, emotions, or actions) and then ask about the other two, writing them down concisely and checking with the client to make sure that important thoughts, feelings, and behaviors have been captured accurately.

Burns (1999) referred to this process as the triple column technique. This strategy involves eliciting people's actions, thoughts, and emotions in relation to a particular situation. A 0–100 rating scale is then used to assess the strength of people's emotions and the extent of their belief in their thoughts. This approach provides a baseline for use later in determining whether people's thoughts and feelings have changed.

For Harold, his description of his actions, thoughts, and emotions and the accompanying rating of his thoughts and emotions looked like this:

Identifying Actions
Clinician: Describe the actions you took in response to this situation.

Harold: I persuaded Carol to postpone our vacation once; but when I asked her to postpone the vacation a second time, she refused. I went to Spain with her.

Identifying and Rating Thoughts
Clinician: Identify the thoughts you had in response to this situation. Then, on a 0–100 rating scale, with 100 representing absolute belief and 0 reflecting no belief, indicate how much you believe your thoughts.

Harold: 1. I thought Carol didn't care about my feelings when she wouldn't postpone the vacation: 95.
            2. I believed it would cost me my marriage if I didn't go on a vacation with Carol: 90.
            3. I think I am a terrible person for abandoning my brother: 99.

Identifying and Rating Feelings
Clinician: Identify the emotions you had in response to this situation. Then, on a 0–100 rating scale, with 100 representing the strongest possible emotion, indicate how strongly you are experiencing the feelings you reported.

Harold: 1. Devastated by my brother's death: 99.
            2. Fearful of losing my marriage: 95.
            3. Guilty that I had left my brother: 92.

Assessing the Validity of the Cognitions

The next step is helping people determine whether their cognitions have validity and are healthy and helpful to them. The clinician's role is not to criticize or devalue the cognitions but to maintain an objective stance and help clients evaluate their cognitions. Below are examples of approaches to evaluating and modifying cognitions:

- *Reality testing.* Assess the accuracy of the thought, using past experiences, research, logic, experiments, and other sources of information. Harold might consider whether his wife's past behavior supports his cognition that she doesn't care about his feelings. He also might talk with his wife about his interpretation of her insistence on their taking a vacation while his brother was dying (Moorey & Greer, 1989).

- *Seeking alternative explanations.* Clinician and client brainstorm other possible and usually more positive explanations. For example, Harold considered the possibility that his wife felt a strong need for a vacation and was afraid to travel without him, as well as the possibility that she believed a vacation would help him deal with his brother's dying.

- *Decatastrophizing.* This involves identifying the most negative possible outcome or interpretation of a cognition and then assessing its likelihood, probable impact, and possible solutions. For Harold, this would be the thought that his wife no longer loved him and that their marriage was over. Articulating the thought allowed him to see that he could survive the end of his marriage although it would be difficult for him.

- *Reattribution.* Reattribution helps people recognize that factors outside of themselves might be the cause of their difficulties, thereby reducing their self-blame. Harold was a spiritual man with great faith in God and the human spirit. He came to believe that perhaps the timing of his brother's death had a purpose or meaning. He considered the possibility that his brother chose to die when Harold was away to spare Harold the pain of seeing his brother die.

Beck and Emery (1985) suggested a five-step process called A-FROG to determine if one is thinking in rational and healthy ways. This involves assessing thoughts according to the following criteria:

> A: Does it keep me *alive?*
>
> F: Do I *feel* better as a result of this thought?
>
> R: Is the thought based on *reality?*
>
> O: Does it help me in my relationships with *others?*
>
> G: Does it help me achieve my *goals?*

If "yes" is not the answer to all of these questions about a given thought, that thought may be unhealthy, unhelpful, and distorted.

Harold found the process of reattribution helpful. In addition, he decided to engage in some reality testing. Although Carol sometimes seemed insensitive to his needs, when he pointed them out to her, she usually showed concern for his feelings. Viewing her as indifferent to his feelings, then, was not consistent with their history. Assisted by the clinician, he planned a conversation with Carol to seek a better understanding of her insistence on a vacation and her perception of their marriage. Carol told Harold that she had been concerned about his health and believed that Louis would survive for at least another month. She thought that Harold, who had been with his brother night and day during his illness, needed to get away. When Louis died while they were on vacation, Carol realized that she had made a mistake but thought that she would only make matters worse if she told Harold that. She reassured him that, although they did have some difficulties in their marriage, she was not considering a divorce and was willing to seek help for their marriage.

Identifying a Core Cognition

A core cognition often underlies specific thoughts. This cognition is a general statement that serves as a sort of screen for how people view their world and themselves. Identifying core cognitions can help people apply their learning and see that their specific, automatic cognitions may not be valid.

One of Harold's core cognitions was "I must please other people or they will reject me, since I don't have much to offer them." After identifying this cognition, he could see that his inability to assert himself with his wife was related to his low self-esteem. He recognized how this core cognition colored many aspects of his life and often led him to make choices that he later regretted. It also prevented him from letting other people get to know him and curtailed the closeness and intimacy in his relationships.

Categorizing the Cognitive Distortions

Dysfunctional or distorted cognitions are, in some way, inconsistent with objective reality. Usually these are negative thoughts about the self, reflecting guilt and low self-esteem, or negative thoughts about people's relationships and context that exaggerate the likelihood of undesirable events and behaviors. Such thoughts typically lead to unhealthy emotions and unhelpful actions.

Distorted cognitions can be categorized (Beck, 1995; Burns, 1999). Following is a list of types of cognitive distortions, illustrated by statements that Harold might make:

- *All-or-nothing thinking:* If I don't do everything in my power to please my wife, she will leave me.
- *Overgeneralization:* Relationships just don't work out for me. My high school sweetheart dumped me. My first wife was unfaithful. My marriage to Carol is doomed too.
- *Mental filter:* I know that Carol said she wanted to work on our marriage and said that she loved me, but my first wife said those things too. I don't think I can trust Carol.
- *Disqualifying the positive:* Yes, it's true that I spent every day for a month with Louis when he was dying. I made sure he had good care; I brought hospice in to help him; I even got a lawyer to come to the hospital so he could have a will prepared. I know I made a difference for him. But the bottom line is I wasn't there when he died. What good is all the rest if I wasn't there when he needed me most?
- *Jumping to conclusions:* Carol and I had a big fight this morning, and now she's over an hour late coming home from work. I think she's left me.
- *Magnification/minimization:* Carol told me that she wanted diamond earrings for her birthday, but I forgot. Instead, I got her some pearls. She was really disappointed. How could I have forgotten something that was so important to my wife? Why would she want to stay married to me?
- *Emotional reasoning:* My sister told me she made sure Louis was comfortable when he was dying, and she was with him until he died. She said Louis understood why I left.

But I still feel awful. We were so close; it must have been harder for him without me there. No matter what my family says to me, I still feel guilty for leaving Louis.

- *"Should" and "must" statements:* A good husband should do everything he can to please his wife. I must be exactly the sort of husband that Carol wants.
- *Labeling and mislabeling:* I'm a loser. Nothing I do works out. No matter how hard I try, I'm just a failure.
- *Personalization:* Maybe Louis would have lived longer if I had been there. I think I gave him a reason to go on. He had already lived longer than the doctors expected, and who knows how long he could have kept going. It's my fault that he died when he did.
- *Catastrophizing:* If Carol leaves me, my life is not worth living. I couldn't go on.
- *Mind reading:* I know Carol doesn't understand my concern for my family. She probably just thinks I can't stand up for myself.
- *Tunnel vision:* I can't do anything to please Carol.

Becoming familiar with these categories of cognitive distortions can help people identify, understand, and dispute their own cognitive distortions. In addition, reviewing this list can reassure clients that having cognitive distortions is common and that dysfunctional thinking can be changed. This reassurance can reduce self-blame and facilitate their efforts to formulate healthier and more valid cognitions.

Harold's original cognitive distortions can be categorized as follows:

1. I thought Carol didn't care about my feelings when she wouldn't postpone the vacation: *Jumping to conclusions.*
2. I believed it would cost me my marriage if I didn't go on a vacation with Carol: *All-or-nothing thinking.*
3. I am a terrible person for abandoning my brother: *Mislabeling and magnification.*

Disputing and Replacing Cognitions

Once the distorted cognitions have been identified, examined, and categorized, they can be disputed. Client and clinician collaborate in finding alternate cognitions that have more validity and are likely to be more helpful to the client. These are written down as replacements for the original cognitions. Harold's revised thoughts follow, along with the ratings of his belief in these new thoughts:

1. "I thought Carol didn't care about my feelings when she wouldn't postpone the vacation" was replaced with "Although I felt hurt when Carol refused to postpone our vacation, I can see that she was doing what she thought was best for both of us."—65
2. "I believed it would cost me my marriage if I didn't go on a vacation with Carol" was replaced with "Although I believed that I had to go on a vacation with Carol to save my marriage, my marriage is stronger than I thought. We do have problems but we are committed to our marriage and willing to work on the problems."—80
3. "I am a terrible person for abandoning my brother" was replaced with "I still regret deeply that I was not there when my brother died, but I can see that I did a great deal for him throughout his life, especially after he got sick. I had no way of knowing that he would die while we were away. If I had known that, I would not have left him."—95

Rerating Thoughts and Feelings and Modifying Actions

The final steps include:

- Rerating the original thoughts
- Rerating the original emotions
- Identifying and rating new emotions
- Revising actions

Harold's Reratings of His Original Thoughts

1. I thought Carol didn't care about my feelings when she wouldn't postpone the vacation: 30.
2. I believed it would cost me my marriage if I didn't go on a vacation with Carol: 15.
3. I am a terrible person for abandoning my brother: 45.

Harold's Reratings of His Original Feelings

1. Devastated by my brother's death: 75.
2. Fearful of losing my marriage: 40.
3. Guilty that I left my brother: 50.

Harold's Ratings of His New Feelings

1. Sad about the loss of my brother: 100
2. Hopeful about the future of my marriage: 65
3. Regretful that I wasn't with my brother when he died: 90

Harold's New Actions

1. Carol and I have agreed to enter marital counseling.
2. My brother had been on the police force and volunteered considerable time to help children whose parents had been on the force and were killed in the line of duty. I will continue his work in honor of his memory.

Harold has experienced considerable change. Although he is, of course, still grieving the death of his brother and regrets that he was not present when Louis died, he is beginning to forgive himself and to come to terms with his brother's death. Significant change is evident in his perceptions of both his wife's feelings and the stability of his marriage. Success in collaborating with his wife to improve their marriage should help him feel even more secure in his marriage and more positively about himself and his relationship with his wife. The volunteer work he plans to undertake is a meaningful way to honor his brother's values and advance his brother's goals; it also should bring personal rewards to Harold.

Review of Steps in Analyzing and Modifying Cognitions

1. Elicit and write down actions, emotions, and thoughts related to a troubling experience.
2. Rate the belief in the thoughts and the intensity of the emotions on a 0–100 scale.
3. Assess the validity of the cognitions.

4. Identify any accessible core cognitions.
5. Categorize the cognitive distortions.
6. Dispute and replace dysfunctional cognitions with healthier and more valid cognitions.
7. Rate the revised cognitions.
8. Rerate the intensity of original thoughts and emotions.
9. Identify and rate new emotions.
10. Identify new actions.

CASE ILLUSTRATION

The case of Harold has already illustrated the process of eliciting, identifying, assessing, disputing, and modifying cognitive distortions. Consequently, what we consider here is only the first part of a case illustration; the exercises that follow will enable you to complete the picture.

This dialog with Edie is designed to elicit cognitive distortions. Look for them as you read.

Edie: I'm really glad we had an appointment today. I've been so worried. I think Roberto may be involved with another woman.

Clinician: What led you to think that?

Edie: He always has his cell phone on. But yesterday I tried to call him for hours, and it was turned off. And then he put on a sports jacket and tie today when he left for work. He never dresses up like that. I started to think that maybe he's trying to impress someone.

Clinician: Those thoughts must have been upsetting. What other thoughts did you have about this?

Edie: You know that my father was unfaithful to my mother. I thought, here we go again. It's happening to me now. I'm just like my mother. I can't make my marriage work.

Clinician: So it seemed like the past was repeating itself. How have you and Roberto been getting along lately?

Edie: Actually, pretty well, but that makes me suspicious too. He gave me a beautiful gift for Mother's Day. He's probably just feeling guilty. But who would want to stay married to me? All I do is complain. I'm not much of a wife. And forget about sex. . . .

Clinician: What feelings do all these thoughts bring up for you?

Edie: I feel pretty discouraged. Here we've been seeing you for months, and I thought there was some hope of keeping our family together, but it doesn't look that way. I feel scared. How will I manage without Roberto?

Clinician: This situation must be very frightening. What actions are you going to take?

Edie: What can I do? If I ask Roberto about it, it might just bring the situation to a head and he'll decide to leave. Maybe if I just pretend I don't notice what's going on, he'll stay married to me . . . until the next woman comes along.

Clinician: Do you know for sure of extramarital relationships that Roberto has had?

Edie: No, he must hide them pretty well.

EXERCISES

Large-Group Exercises

Using the dialog with Edie, go through the following steps of cognitive therapy:

1. List Edie's prominent thoughts, emotions, and planned actions. Try to hone in on her central thoughts, summarizing them in 3–5 cognitions.
2. From what you know about Edie, rate the probable belief in her thoughts and the intensity of her feelings on the 0–100 scale.

3. Using the list of cognitive distortions presented in the "Skill Development" section, identify the nature of each of the distorted cognitions you identified.
4. Develop a plan to help Edie assess the validity of her cognitions. Draw on the suggestions presented previously in this chapter as well as your own ideas.
5. Assume that your work with Edie has been successful. Write rational responses or restatements to replace each of the cognitive distortions you identified. Be sure to use language that is likely to be acceptable to Edie.
6. Identify new emotions and actions that might characterize Edie's responses after you have helped her replace her distorted cognitions with healthy thoughts.

Small-Group Exercises

1. Identify the type (or types) of cognitive distortion reflected in each of the following examples. As a group, discuss ways you would help each of the following people assess the validity of his or her statement:

Person A: My physician didn't call to tell me the test results. She probably has bad news and doesn't want to tell me.

Person B: My agency didn't get the grant we had applied for. My colleagues did such a good job writing the proposal. It was probably the budget I prepared that ruined it for them. I thought I was asking for too much money, but I wanted to be sure the project would succeed.

Person C: I was doing great on my diet, but then I went to Gary's wedding and made a pig of myself. I just know I'll gain back all the weight I lost. It's hopeless for me to even try to get myself in shape.

Person D: I really should visit my mother every day. It's hard for me because she has dementia and doesn't recognize me, but a daughter should see her mother as often as she possibly can, no matter what.

Person E: I was having a great time on my date with Nur until I made a fool of myself. We were at an amusement park, and she wanted to go on this ride that went up and down and around and around. I didn't really want to, but I thought, "If she wants to go, I should go too." I started to feel sick on the ride; and as soon as we got off, I had to run for the bathroom. You can imagine the rest. I was so humiliated. She'll never go out with me again. She's probably telling everyone what a jerk I am.

Person F: The other girls avoid me because they know that my mother works in the school cafeteria. I know she needs a job and wanted one that would let her be home with me when I'm not at school, but she's ruining my life. I'll never be popular or have lots of friends like Jessica. Her mother doesn't have to work at all and drives a Mercedes when she picks her up after school.

Individual Exercises

1. Select a recent experience during which you had strong emotions. Identify at least three emotions, one action, and two thoughts that accompanied the experience. Try to identify at least one cognitive distortion that you had in relation to the experience. Write down the distortion in your journal. Then, in writing, go through the steps of

rating, assessing, classifying, disputing, replacing, and rerating your cognition(s). What new emotions and actions now seem available to you?

2. We all have thoughts, emotions, and actions. Observe yourself as you go through the day. Which of these categories is most accessible to you? Are you most likely to discuss thoughts, feelings, or actions with other people? Which of the three is most likely to worry you and stay in your mind? Write out your answers in your journal.

SUMMARY

This chapter reviewed the importance of thoughts in understanding and counseling people. It also provided guidelines, examples, and exercises to teach you how to help people assess and, if indicated, modify thoughts, as well as their accompanying emotions and actions. The skills you have learned in this chapter provide a foundation on which to develop your understanding of cognitive approaches to treatment as presented in the remaining chapters of part 4.

CHAPTER 15

Aaron Beck and Cognitive Therapy

Cognitive therapy has grown rapidly in importance over the past 25 years and is now recognized as one of the major approaches to counseling and psychotherapy. Albert Ellis (discussed in chapter 16) established the foundations of cognitive therapy. However, the work of Aaron T. Beck and his colleagues fueled the growth of this approach. We discuss their treatment aproach first because it is better structured and organized than Ellis's, providing a clear introduction to cognitive therapy.

Cognitive therapy is a phenomenological model as are person-centered counseling, existential therapy, Gestalt therapy, and other approaches discussed in part 3. However, cognitive therapy focuses on the meaning that people give to experiences through the way they think about them, rather than how they feel about them. Although cognitive therapy recognizes that background, emotions, and behavior are important and worthy of attention in treatment, it views thoughts as the primary determinant of both emotions and behaviors, as well as of mental disorders and psychological health. Cognitive therapists believe that the basic material of treatment is people's transient automatic thoughts and their deeply ingrained and fundamental assumptions and schemas. Once these have been identified, clinicians draw on a variety of interventions to help people test and modify their cognitions. Replacing dysfunctional cognitions with ones that are more accurate, helpful, and healthy enables people to deal more successfully with their immediate difficulties and lead more rewarding lives. Inventories, suggested tasks, development of life skills, and other strategies are used to advance the goals of cognitive therapy. This is a well-organized, powerful, usually short-term approach that has proven its effectiveness through many research studies.

AARON BECK

Aaron T. Beck, the man behind the development of cognitive therapy, was born in New England in 1921. He was the fifth and youngest child of Harry Beck and Elizabeth Temkin Beck, Russian Jewish immigrants to the United States (Weishaar, 1993). Two of the five children born to this family died in infancy, apparently contributing to emotional problems in Beck's mother. He perceived her as depressed, unpredictable, and overprotective—very different from his calm father.

Beck himself had many difficulties during childhood. He was often ill, missing many days of school. As a result, he had to repeat a grade, leading him to develop negative views of his intellectual abilities. In addition, his illnesses left him with many apprehensions, including a blood/injury phobia and fears of public speaking and of suffocation. Beck used reasoning to alleviate his anxieties and apparently was successful since he studied surgery as part of his medical training and gave many presentations throughout his life. A connection seems probable between his early experiences with anxiety and depression and his subsequent work, focused on treating those symptoms.

Beck graduated from Brown University and Yale Medical School, where he studied psychiatry. Although he was trained in psychoanalysis, he had little faith in that approach, even early in his career. At the University of Pennsylvania Medical School, Beck, an assistant professor of psychiatry, engaged in research designed to substantiate psychoanalytic principles. Instead, his work led him to develop cognitive therapy, which has since been the focus of his teaching, research, writing, and clinical work. He has spent most of his professional career at the University of Pennsylvania, where he established the Beck Institute for Cognitive Therapy and Research.

THE DEVELOPMENT OF COGNITIVE THERAPY

According to Moss (1992), the roots of cognitive therapy lie in the ideas of the Stoic philosophers of ancient Greece and Rome. Epictetus's belief that people are disturbed not by things but by the view they take of them is particularly relevant. George Kelly's (1955) personal constructs psychology is a modern precursor of cognitive therapy. Kelly was one of the first theorists to recognize the role of beliefs in controlling and changing thoughts, emotions, and actions. He suggested that people each have a set of personal constructs that enable them to make sense of and categorize people and experiences. These constructs operate like scientific hypotheses, paving the way for people to make predictions about reality. When their predictions are not borne out or when people recognize that their personal constructs are harmful, they may seek alternative constructs (Hergenhahn, 1994).

Like Beck, Albert Ellis also was trained in psychoanalysis. He, too, became disappointed with that approach and began focusing on cognitions. Ellis was the first clinician to become well known for his belief that thoughts were the route to changing emotions and behaviors. Rational emotive therapy (RET), which he developed in the 1950s, quickly became an important alternative to Freudian psychoanalysis and Rogers's person-centered counseling. While Ellis's dynamic and sometimes abrasive style brought attention to RET, it became associated with Ellis's personal style. For some people, the sound theory and interventions of RET were overshadowed by Ellis's personality, probably limiting RET's popularity.

Aaron Beck's carefully designed research and professional writing led to the current widespread use of cognitive therapy. Beck drew on the ideas of George Kelly, Alfred Adler, and Karen Horney as he sought efficient and effective ways to help people. Working at the University of Pennsylvania in the 1960s, Beck and his colleagues initially sought to develop a structured, short-term, present-oriented, problem-solving approach to the treatment of depression (Beck, 1995). *Cognitive Therapy of Depression* (Beck, Rush, Shaw, & Emery, 1979), describing the results of this work, had a powerful impact on the field of psychotherapy. It offered a clear and structured approach to the treatment of depression, the symptom clinicians most often see in both inpatient and outpatient mental health settings. Beck and his colleagues provided evidence that cognitive therapy was more effective in treating depression than the antidepressant medications of that time.

Beck has acknowledged a strong debt to Albert Ellis's work (Weishaar, 1993). At the same time, Beck's personal style, as well as the development of his theory, differ from Ellis's. Beck enhanced the importance of his system of cognitive therapy through research, clinical application, and writing. In demonstrations and videotapes, he appears reserved and thoughtful, a researcher at least as much as a clinician. His books and articles, such as *Anxiety Disorders and Phobias* (Beck & Emery, 1985) and *Cognitive Therapy of Personality Disorders* (Beck, Freeman, & Associates, 1990), continue to expand the application of cognitive therapy and validate its effectiveness.

Two other names should be mentioned for their contributions to cognitive therapy. Aaron Beck's daughter, Judith S. Beck, has been collaborating with him for many years. Now director of the Beck Institute for Cognitive Therapy and Research and professor at the University of Pennsylvania, she continues the development of cognitive therapy (Beck, 1995). In addition, David Burns's writings, primarily *The Feeling Good Handbook*, first published in 1989, a self-help book based on cognitive therapy, have increased awareness of this approach and provided inventories and interventions that enhance its usefulness.

IMPORTANT THEORETICAL CONCEPTS

Judith Beck (1995) has summarized cognitive therapy: "In a nutshell, the *cognitive model* proposes that distorted or dysfunctional thinking (which influences the patient's mood and behavior) is common to all psychological disturbances. Realistic evaluation and modification of thinking produces an improvement in mood and behavior" (p. 1). The purpose of cognitive therapy is to teach people to identify, evaluate, and modify their own dysfunctional thoughts and beliefs.

Development of Cognitive Distortions

Cognitive therapists believe that many factors contribute to the development of dysfunctional cognitions, including people's biology and genetic predispositions, life experiences, and their accumulation of knowledge and learning. According to Beck et al. (1990), "We speculate that these dysfunctional beliefs have originated as the result of the interaction between the individual's genetic predisposition and exposure to undesirable influences from other people and traumatic events" (p. 23). Distorted cognitions begin to take shape in childhood and are reflected in people's fundamental beliefs; this makes people more susceptible to problems that "impinge on their cognitive vulnerability" (p. 23). Although cognitive therapy focuses on the present, an extensive intake interview is used to give clinicians a good understanding of their clients' history, development, and background (Beck, 1995).

Unlike many theorists who focus on emotions, cognitive theorists value the importance of making an accurate diagnosis of any mental disorders that are present in their clients. Using the guidelines in the *Diagnostic and Statistical Manual of Mental Disorders* (DSM) (American Psychiatric Association, 2000), clinicians determine whether a client's symptoms meet the criteria for a mood disorder, an anxiety disorder, a personality disorder, or another mental disorder.

Cognitive theory suggests that each mental disorder is characterized by relatively predictable types of underlying cognitive distortions. For example, feelings of depression typically stem from thoughts of loss. An accurate diagnosis can therefore facilitate identification of those distortions and ways to change them. It also can guide clinicians' information gathering so that they can better understand their clients. For example, discussion of childhood experiences probably is important in treatment of people with personality disorders, while discussion of traumatic experiences is essential for people diagnosed with posttraumatic stress disorder. However, discussion of past experiences is less likely to be important in the treatment of people with disorders that are mild, brief, transient, and recent, such as adjustment disorders.

Although cognitive theorists focus primarily on thoughts, they take a holistic view of people and believe that learning about and understanding their feelings and behaviors also is important (Beck et al., 1990). According to cognitive theory, the three areas are largely interdependent, with problems or change in one area spilling over and affecting the other two (Persons, 1989). Particularly important, and related to positive outcome, is understanding the emotional responses people have to their faulty cognitions and the impact of those cognitions on mood (Coombs, Coleman, & Jones, 2002). Having a comprehensive understanding of people is particularly useful in helping clinicians develop interventions that target all three areas of functioning: thinking, feeling, and acting.

According to cognitive theory, psychologically healthy people are aware of their cognitions. They can systematically test their own hypotheses and, if they find they have dysfunctional and unwarranted assumptions, can replace them with healthier, more accurate, and more helpful beliefs that lead to more positive emotions and behaviors.

Principles of Cognitive Therapy

The following important principles characterize the practice of cognitive therapy (Beck, 1995; Beck & Emery, 1985; Beck et al., 1990):

- Cognitive therapy is based on the finding that changes in thinking lead to changes in feeling and acting.
- Treatment requires a sound and collaborative therapeutic alliance.
- Treatment is generally short-term, problem-focused, and goal-oriented.
- Cognitive therapy is an active and structured approach to treatment.
- It focuses on the present, although attention is paid to the past when indicated.
- Careful assessment, diagnosis, and treatment planning are essential.
- Cognitive therapy uses a broad range of strategies and interventions to help people evaluate and change their cognitions.
- Inductive reasoning and Socratic questioning are particularly important strategies.
- This is a psychoeducational model that promotes emotional health and prevents relapse by teaching people to identify, evaluate, and modify their own cognitions.
- Task assignments, follow-up, and client feedback are important in ensuring the success of this approach.

Levels of Cognitions

Cognitions can be categorized according to four levels: automatic thoughts, intermediate beliefs, core beliefs, and schemas. In cognitive therapy, treatment typically begins with automatic thoughts and then proceeds to identification, evaluation, and modification of intermediate and core beliefs and finally to revision of schemas.

Automatic thoughts are the stream of cognitions that constantly flow through our minds. As we go through our day, situation-specific thoughts spontaneously arise in reaction to our experiences: "I don't think I'll ever be able to get all that work done; I think I'll eat a healthy lunch today; I don't think I should call my father yet; I'm going to help Bill with his homework tonight; that man makes me think of my brother;" and on and on. When people pay attention to their thoughts, they become more accessible and people can articulate and evaluate them.

Automatic thoughts mediate between a situation and an emotion. Consider the following example:

Situation: Michael learns that his sister has been in town but did not call him.

Michael's Automatic thought: She finds me unlikable and doesn't want to be with me.

Michael's Emotion: Sadness.

What caused the emotion, sadness, was not the situation itself but the man's automatic cognition, reflecting the meaning he made of the situation. Understanding people's automatic thoughts is important in helping them change their emotions.

Intermediate beliefs often reflect extreme and absolute rules and attitudes that shape people's automatic thoughts. In the previous example, Michael's intermediate beliefs might include "A sister should call her family when she is in town" and "Being ignored by your sister is a terrible thing."

Core beliefs are central ideas about ourselves that underlie many of our automatic cognitions and usually are reflected in our intermediate beliefs. Core beliefs can be described as "global, overgeneralized, and absolute" (Beck, 1995, p. 167). They typically stem from childhood experiences, are not necessarily true, and can be identified and modified. Core beliefs reflect our views of the world, other people, ourselves, and the future. They may be positive and helpful such as "I am likable," "I am a capable person," and "The world is full of interesting and exciting opportunities and people." However, they also can be negative, such as "People only care about themselves," "The world is a dangerous place," and "I make a mess of everything." Most negative core beliefs can be categorized as *helpless core beliefs* such as "I am weak" and "I am a failure" or as *unlovable core beliefs* such as "I am not good enough" and "I am bound to be abandoned" (Beck, 1995, p. 169). Michael seems to have unlovable core beliefs.

As clinicians get to know and understand their clients and hear a series of automatic thoughts, the clinicians can formulate hypotheses about a client's core beliefs. At an appropriate time, clinicians can share this hypothesis with the client for confirmation or disconfirmation, along with information on the nature and development of core beliefs. Clients are encouraged to view their core beliefs as ideas rather than truths and to collaborate with the clinician to evaluate and, if indicated, change their core beliefs.

Schemas have been defined as "cognitive structures within the mind" that encompass the core beliefs (Beck, 1995, p. 166). They go beyond core beliefs, in breadth and depth, and include thoughts, emotions, and actions. Schemas have content as well as structural qualities such as breadth, flexibility, and prominence.

Beck viewed schemas as "specific rules that govern information processing and behavior" (Beck et al., 1990, p. 8). Schemas lead us to have expectations about experiences, events, and roles and to amplify those with information contained in our schemas. Schemas can act as mental filters, affecting the way we perceive reality. Schemas are idiosyncratic and habitual ways of viewing what Moss (1992) termed *the cognitive triad:* ourselves, the world, and the future. Schemas can be personal, familial, cultural, religious, gender, and occupational in origin and application (Beck et al., 1990). Examples of maladaptive schemas include dependence/incompetence and deprivation.

Schemas may be activated by a particular stimulus or lie dormant until triggered ("Controversies," 1993). For example, a person may have a danger schema that gives the message, "The world is a dangerous place. Avoid any possible danger." This schema is usually latent but can be activated by threats to that person's safety.

When a schema has been activated, it readily incorporates any confirming information and tends to neglect contradictory information. For example, when people view themselves as incompetent, they accept negative information they receive about themselves and overlook or dispute anything positive. Tuckey and Brewer (2003) found that schemas influence retention and distortion of memories. We are more likely to recall observations that are consistent or inconsistent with our schemas, compared to observations that are irrelevant to our schemas; inaccuracies in recollections are particularly likely to be schema-consistent.

The distinctions among automatic cognitions, intermediate beliefs, core beliefs, and schemas can be confusing. Consider the following example, illustrating each of these. After several disappointing relationships, Joshua has developed a rewarding relationship with Sharon; after dating for 2 years, Sharon suggests marriage and Joshua agrees. He has the following thoughts:

- *Automatic thoughts*—I can't be the sort of husband Sharon wants and our marriage will end.
- *Intermediate beliefs*—A good husband must be willing to sacrifice his own needs for those of his wife and children. Marriage is a difficult endeavor at which few succeed.
- *Core belief*—I am not able to love another person and have little to offer in my relationships.

- *Schema*—I am inadequate and am destined to fail, no matter how hard I try. This makes me feel discouraged about my upcoming marriage; I feel disaster and shame hanging over my head. What's the point of trying if I know I will fail at whatever I do.

Because of this maladaptive schema, Joshua will probably focus on information that confirms his beliefs and ignore or explain away disconfirming information. He will enter marriage with a negative attitude, accompanied by ineffective behaviors that will contribute to the destruction of his marriage and the substantiation of his beliefs.

Schemas become amenable to analysis and modification after people have experienced some change as a result of assessing and altering their automatic thoughts, intermediate beliefs, and core beliefs. Beck viewed schema work as the heart of the therapeutic process (Beck et al., 1990).

Cognitive therapy operates at several levels, seeking to elicit and change people's symptoms as well as their automatic thoughts, intermediate beliefs, core cognitions, and underlying schemas. Once healthy thinking has been restored, clinicians help people to develop the skills they need to monitor, assess, and respond to their own cognitions as well as lead their lives more successfully.

TREATMENT USING COGNITIVE THERAPY

Treatment via cognitive therapy usually is time-limited, 4–14 sessions long for relatively straightforward problems (Beck, 1995). Sessions are carefully planned and structured to maximize their impact and efficiency. People complete inventories and intake questionnaires before beginning treatment. Clinicians review these before the first session in order to be well prepared.

Each session has clear goals and an agenda. Judith Beck (1995, pp. 26–27) recommends the following 10 procedures for an initial session:

1. Establish an agenda that is meaningful to the client.
2. Determine and measure the intensity of the person's mood.
3. Identify and review presenting problems.
4. Elicit the person's expectations for treatment.
5. Educate the person about cognitive therapy and the role of the client.
6. Provide information about the person's difficulties and diagnosis.
7. Establish goals.
8. Recommend tasks and homework between sessions.
9. Summarize the session.
10. Obtain the client's feedback on the session.

Throughout the session, clinicians promote development of the therapeutic alliance and build trust, rapport, and collaboration while encouraging realistic hope and optimism.

Subsequent sessions follow a similar structure. They typically begin with an assessment of the person's mood, focusing particularly on changes. Next, the foundation for the session is established by making a transition from the previous session to the current one; clinicians ask about clients' learning from and reactions to the previous session and obtain an overview of the clients' week, highlighting any important happenings. This facilitates establishment of an agenda for the session, which always includes reviewing homework. The central part of the session addresses items on that agenda, with clinicians eliciting and assessing thoughts as well as emotions and actions related to the identified issues. Each session concludes with new homework, a summary of the session, and feedback from clients on the session and the process of treatment. Ending the session on a positive note promotes optimism and motivation.

Cognitive therapists make sure to explain to clients the nature and purpose of the sessions's structure. Clients generally find that structure reassuring. They know what to expect and are optimistic that this plan will help them as it has helped others. Of course, an agenda may be modified if needed, perhaps if a crisis has occurred; but any changes are planned when the agenda is determined at the outset of each session.

Goals

Cognitive therapists carefully specify goals for their treatment, and they draw on a rich array of interventions to achieve them. The overall goal of cognitive therapy is to help people recognize and correct errors in their information-processing systems. To accomplish this, clinicians help people identify both their immediate (automatic) and underlying (intermediate, core, schema) thoughts and beliefs as well as associated emotions and behaviors; evaluate the validity of these thoughts; and modify them if indicated. Throughout treatment, people learn to use this process independently and also to develop skills and attitudes they need to think more realistically and lead more rewarding lives.

Clinicians and clients collaborate on determining specific goals. Once identified, goals are written down, with copies made for both client and clinician. Goals are referred to regularly to assess progress. Having clear, specific, and measurable goals is an important component of cognitive therapy and increases the likelihood that clients and clinicians will collaborate to achieve a shared objective.

Therapeutic Alliance

Cognitive therapists value a trusting and collaborative client-clinician partnership (Beck et al., 1990). Although cognitive therapy does not focus primarily on feelings, an essential role of the clinician is communicating support, empathy, caring, warmth, interest, optimism, and the other core conditions that promote a successful therapeutic alliance. Cognitive clinicians make great efforts to really know and understand their clients and welcome the opportunity to serve as their role models. Coombs, Coleman, and Jones (2002) concluded that a collaborative emotional exploration between clinician and client is related to positive outcomes in cognitive, as well as other, treatment approaches.

Cognitive therapists strive to be nonjudgmental; they do not tell people that their thinking is irrational or argue with them about the merits of their thoughts. Rather, clinicians help clients to develop the skills they need to make their own judgments and choices. To accomplish this, clinicians take on the roles of teacher, scientist, joint empirical investigator, and truth seeker, encouraging people to search for accurate and realistic information (Moss, 1992). Clinicians also are responsible for orienting clients to treatment and helping them develop realistic treatment expectations and goals. Clinicians focus on and reinforce successes and attribute progress to clients' efforts and growth.

Unlike psychodynamic therapists, cognitive therapists do not try to elicit or provoke transference reactions. However, if clients do manifest transference, clinicians address it to more fully understand and help the clients. Role flexibility characterizes cognitive therapists.

Persons (1989) found that technical interventions and relationship factors both made "independent contributions" to the success of cognitive therapy (p. 160). Although a positive client-therapist relationship alone was not sufficient to help people reach their goals, it was a necessary ingredient in the treatment system.

Cognitive Distortions in Clinicians

Persons (1989) advises clinicians to be alert to the possibility that they may have their own distorted cognitions related to their role as clinicians. Common examples include "If the therapy fails, this means I'm an incompetent therapist" (p. 209); "The patient won't be able to cope with this failure" (p. 210); and "If I terminate the treatment, the patient will feel rejected or abandoned" (p. 211). Clinicians as well as clients are prone to dysfunctional thinking and should monitor the nature and accuracy of their thoughts.

Case Formulation

Before cognitive therapists move forward with interventions designed to modify cognitions, they take the time to develop a case formulation, reflecting in-depth understanding of the client. According to Persons (1989), a complete case formulation includes six elements:

1. List of problems and concerns
2. Hypothesis about the underlying mechanism (core belief or schema)
3. Relationship of this belief to current problems
4. Precipitants of current problems
5. Understanding of background relevant to development of underlying beliefs
6. Anticipated obstacles to treatment

A thorough case formulation enables clinicians to develop treatment plans that are likely to be successful. When planning treatment, cognitive clinicians identify the best points for initial intervention, treatment strategies that are likely to be helpful, and ways to reduce anxiety and other obstacles to progress. Treatment usually focuses first on overt automatic cognitions related to clients' presenting problems and, as progress is made, shifts to identification and assessment of underlying core beliefs and schemas.

Eliciting and Rating Cognitions

The "Skill Development" section of chapter 14 described ways for clinicians to help clients identify and evaluate their cognitions. Although we review these procedures here, readers should refer back to chapter 14 for additional information.

Judith Beck (1995) suggests a basic question to elicit people's thoughts: "What was going through your mind just then?" (p. 81). Once one thought is presented, it often leads to production of other thoughts. Especially important are thoughts that appear repeatedly in conjunction with a variety of experiences and have a negative impact on the person. Beck uses what she calls a dysfunctional thought record to facilitate identification and modification of such thoughts (p. 126). This record includes six items:

1. The situation that elicited the thoughts and its accompanying physical responses
2. Date and time of the situation

3. Automatic thoughts and extent of belief in those thoughts rated on 0–100% scale
4. Emotions and their intensity, rated on 0–100% scale
5. Nature of distortion and ways of modifying the thoughts
6. Outcome, including revised beliefs, ratings of automatic and revised thoughts, current emotions and intensity ratings, and new actions

The first four items are completed initially, as in the following example:

1. The school called to tell me that my son had been seen breaking into the school over the weekend. He was accused of vandalizing the computer room. I felt a knot in my stomach; I felt lightheaded and tense all over.
2. This happened on Monday morning about 8:30 a.m.
3. I am a failure as a parent: 95% belief rating. My son is a hopeless criminal, and it's my fault: 90% belief rating.
4. Anxious: 95% intensity; sad: 85% intensity.

Determining the Validity of Cognitions

Once the cognitions have been elicited and placed in context, people can assess their validity. Several approaches to accomplishing this are presented in chapter 14. Especially important is clinicians' use of guided discovery via skillful questioning and experiments to help people test the reality of their thoughts. These are powerful techniques that must be used with care. Therapists should never act as though they know better than the client, should not debate or argue with clients, and should remain neutral on whether a thought is distorted. The clinician's role is to help clients find the truth.

The following dialog illustrates the use of questioning to help the client in the previous example assess the logic and validity of her thoughts:

Clinician: One thought you had was that your son was a hopeless criminal. What led you to have that thought?

Client: Well, it sounds like he committed a crime.

Clinician: Yes, he may have. Does he have a history of criminal behavior?

Client: No, not at all. He's always been very well-behaved.

Clinician: So this is the first time he has been suspected of breaking the law?

Client: Yes.

Clinician: And what is your definition of a hopeless criminal?

Client: I guess it's someone who repeatedly breaks the law, who can't be rehabilitated.

Clinician: And does that sound like your son?

Client: No. I guess I overreacted when I said he was a hopeless criminal.

Clinician: And what about your thought that you are to blame for his behavior. What led you to think that?

Client: I'm his parent. Aren't I the biggest influence in his life?

Clinician: Yes, your role is certainly an important one. How might you have encouraged him to become a criminal?

Client: I don't know what you mean.

Clinician: I wonder if you have engaged in criminal behavior yourself.

Client: No, of course not.
Clinician: Perhaps you condoned criminal behavior or didn't try to teach him the difference between right and wrong?
Client: No, just the opposite. I have very strong values, and I always tried to transmit them to my son. When he misbehaved, I would talk to him about what was wrong with his behavior and teach him how to act differently.
Clinician: I'm confused then, about how you might have caused his criminal behavior.
Client: I guess I was just feeling bad and wanted to find an explanation. But I can see that I certainly never taught him to break the law.

Experiments designed to test hypotheses stemming from faulty thinking are another important approach to helping people evaluate the reality of their cognitions. In the previous example, the client might use her statements "My son is a hopeless criminal" and "I am to blame for my son's criminal behavior" as hypotheses. Clinician and client then develop experiments or ways to test these hypotheses. The client might talk with her son about the reasons for his behavior, confer with school personnel about this incident as well as about her son's usual behavior at school, and read about criminal behavior.

A third approach to assessing cognitions is seeking alternative explanations. For example, the boy might have been erroneously accused of breaking into the school. Even if he had committed the crime, mitigating factors might have played a part, such as his being forced or coerced to engage in the break-in.

Following are additional approaches that cognitive therapists use to help people evaluate the validity of their cognitions:

- Asking clients how another person whom they respect would think about the situation
- Asking them what they would say if their child or friend had the thoughts they have
- Using humor or exaggeration to take an idea to its extreme
- Helping people see that they are catastrophizing to counter their tendency to anticipate the worst
- Encouraging people to imagine their worst fears and then think of ways to deal with them so the fears have less power over them
- Suggesting alternate explanations for a situation
- Helping people find a middle ground to counteract extreme ways of thinking
- Redefining or reconceptualizing a problem so that it is more amenable to change
- Decentering, or helping people see they are not the cause of the problem or the center of attention

Labeling the Distortion

Evaluation of distorted cognitions can be facilitated by categorizing and labeling the distortions. This helps people see more clearly the nature of their unrealistic thinking, reminds them that other people have had similar distorted cognitions, and gives them a tool for assessing subsequent thoughts. Categories of distorted cognitions are presented in chapter 14 (Beck, 1995; Beck & Weishaar, 1995; Burns, 1999). Here these categories are illustrated with statements made by the previous client:

- *All-or-nothing or polarized thinking:* Viewing a situation in terms of extremes rather than on a continuum. "Either my son is innocent, or he is a hopeless criminal."

- *Overgeneralization:* Drawing sweeping conclusions that are not justified by the evidence. "I am a failure as a parent because my son was arrested."
- *Mental filter (selective abstraction):* Focusing selectively on negative details and failing to see the broad picture. "I know my son has been a good student and has not caused any problems in the past, but all I can think about is that he broke the law."
- *Disqualifying the positive:* Paying attention only to negative information. "What good are all my efforts to be a good mother if this is the result?"
- *Jumping to conclusions (arbitrary inferences):* Drawing hasty and unwarranted conclusions. "My son must be guilty. Someone saw him hanging around the school late that night."
- *Magnification/minimization:* Making too much of the negative, devaluing positive information. "My son stole a candy bar from another child when he was four. He was destined to become a criminal."
- *Emotional reasoning:* Believing that something is true because it feels that way; paying no attention to contradictory evidence. "I just feel like this is my fault, and no one can convince me it isn't."
- *"Should" and "must" statements:* Having definite and inflexible ideas about how we and others should behave and how life should be. "I should never have let Kevin get his driver's license. I should have made sure I met all his friends. I should have been a better mother to him."
- *Labeling and mislabeling:* Attaching an extreme, broad, and unjustified label to someone. "Kevin is a hopeless criminal."
- *Personalization:* Assuming inordinate responsibility for events or others' behaviors. "My son and I had an argument about his curfew three days before the school break-in. If I hadn't yelled at him, this probably never would have happened."
- *Catastrophizing:* Predicting a negative outcome without considering other possibilities. "I just know Kevin will be sent to prison for this."
- *Mind reading:* Attributing negative thoughts and reactions to others without checking if they are present. "My husband will never forgive Kevin for this. He'll disown him."
- *Tunnel vision:* Focusing only on the negative aspects of a situation. "I can't do anything right as a parent. There I was, eating dinner, while my son was breaking into the school. How could I not have known what was going on?"

Assessment of Mood

Assessing mood is an important part of cognitive therapy for many reasons. Troubling emotions are often the reason people seek treatment. Upsetting emotions are likely to be close to the surface and presented early in treatment. Those feelings can point the way to distorted cognitions. In addition, monitoring the nature and intensity ratings of people's emotions can provide evidence of progress, while improvement in mood can enhance clients' motivation and optimism. Cognitive therapy was initially developed for the treatment of depression and anxiety and considerable research demonstrates the effectiveness of this approach in treating those emotional symptoms.

Cognitive therapists use structured approaches to assess emotions, as they do to assess thoughts. One of Aaron Beck's major contributions to psychotherapy is the development of brief, concise inventories that provide a quick measure of the nature and intensity of emotions that are most likely to be troubling to people. These inventories include the Beck Depression Inventory (BDI), the Beck Anxiety Inventory (BAI), the Beck Hopelessness Inventory, and the Beck Scale for

Suicidal Ideation. Published by Psychological Corporation, these inventories each take only a few minutes to complete. Any or all of these might be administered before a person begins treatment to obtain a sort of emotional baseline. If elevated scores are obtained on an inventory, administration of that inventory every few sessions enables client and clinician to track and quantify changes in emotions. An even more rapid assessment of emotion can be obtained using an informal 0–100 scale of severity or intensity of a specific mood such as anger, jealousy, or sadness. Clients can rate themselves on these scales at the beginning of each session.

Changing Cognitions

The last two steps in Judith Beck's (1995) dysfunctional thought record include

- Helping people to formulate new cognitions that are more realistic and adaptive
- Evaluating treatment outcome by asking people to rate their belief in the new cognitions, identify and rate their emotions, and determine actions that will be taken in light of their altered thinking

Clinicians work closely with clients to restructure their cognitions and help them find words to express their new cognitions accurately, realistically, and in ways that are compatible with their emotions. This process involves helping people deepen their beliefs in their revised cognitions and make those cognitions part of themselves.

Once again, cognitive therapists draw on a wealth of strategies to accomplish these goals. While many of these techniques are primarily cognitive in nature, others are behavioral and will be addressed further in part 5. Following are some of the strategies that enhance the work of cognitive therapists (Seligman, 1996a; Seligman, 2004b):

- *Activity scheduling* encourages people to plan and try out new behaviors and ways of thinking as well as to remain active despite feelings of sadness or apprehension. Particularly helpful are experiences that bring people feelings of both pleasure and mastery (Burns, 1999). Learning a new and interesting skill and having a good time can contribute to improved moods and clearer thinking.

- *Mental and emotional imagery* (discussed in chapter 13) helps people envision and try on new ways of thinking and feeling. They might imagine themselves coping successfully, changing parts of an image, or repeating an image to reduce its emotional impact. A man who thought of himself as uninteresting, for example, might imagine himself telling fascinating stories to an admiring audience.

- *Cognitive and covert modeling* is a strategy in which people mentally rehearse a new behavior and then create a cognitive model of themselves successfully performing that behavior. Some athletes use this technique to improve their skills in their sport. A woman married to a verbally abusive husband used this approach to rehearse asserting herself to her husband, making it easier for her to stand up to him when he spoke to her in a demeaning way. A variation is for people to imagine themselves as someone they admire and then tackle a challenging situation as if they were that person.

- *Thought stopping* can be useful when people have difficulty ridding themselves of persistent harmful thoughts. Thought stopping involves saying, "Stop!" either aloud or subvocally each time the unwanted thought recurs and replacing it with a more positive thought. Over time, the harmful thought is likely to diminish in frequency and intensity.

- *Diversions or distractions* also can help people reduce their negative thinking. A woman who was diagnosed with a life-threatening illness had a good prognosis but still experienced constant thoughts of death. To distract herself from these troubling thoughts, she mentally catalogued each item in her extensive wardrobe, beginning the mental list anew each time the negative thoughts returned.

- *Self-talk* is a technique in which people repeat to themselves many times a day positive and encouraging phrases that they have identified as helpful, such as "Don't let fear control you. You can do it." In essence, they are giving themselves a pep talk.

- *Affirmations* are closely related to self-talk. An affirmation is a sort of slogan that is positive and reinforcing. People can post these in prominent places such as the refrigerator or the mirror where they will see them frequently and be reminded to shift their thinking. An adolescent girl chose as her affirmation "Someday you will realize your great potential." Keeping those words in mind helped her deal effectively with challenges.

- *Diaries* of events, realistic and distorted cognitions, emotions, and efforts to make positive changes can increase people's awareness of their inner and outer experiences. These written records can provide important material for discussion in sessions and serve as a way to track both progress and difficulties.

- *Letter writing* provides another avenue for exploring and expressing thoughts and feelings. The woman whose son was accused of breaking into his school (discussed previously) might benefit from drafting a letter to her son expressing her reactions to his behavior. The letters need not be mailed but can be used as the focus of a session.

- *Systematic assessment of alternatives* (cost-benefit analysis) is an approach that can help people make wise decisions or choices. They first list their options, along with the pros and cons of each one. Then they assign numbers on a 1–10 scale, showing the importance of each advantage and disadvantage. Finally, they total the numbers assigned to the pros and cons of each option. A man considering a career change used this approach to help him decide whether to remain in his secure, well-paying position in computer technology or pursue his lifelong goal of becoming a counselor; the numerical totals strongly reflected a preference for becoming a counselor while the list of cons pointed out obstacles to this goal.

- *Relabeling or reframing* experiences or perceptions can help people think differently about them. For example, a woman who had few dating experiences at age 35 stopped thinking of herself as a failure and instead viewed herself as a late bloomer.

- *Role playing* can enable people to actualize some of the new thoughts they have about themselves. For example, a man who had developed a more positive view of his abilities role-played sharing his accomplishments with his friends, asking his supervisor for a raise, and inviting a colleague to join him for lunch.

- In *rational emotive role play,* clients play the emotional part of the mind while clinicians play the rational part; the two then engage in a dialog (Beck, 1995).

- When *role-playing a dialog between old and new thoughts,* clients use two chairs (as described in chapter 12) to represent both their old and their new thoughts. Moving from one chair to another, they engage in a dialog between the two groups of thoughts. This can help people clarify changes in their thinking and solidify their rational thoughts.

• *Distancing* involves projecting into the future to put a problem in perspective and diminish its importance. A woman realized that getting a *B* in a college course would mean little to her in 10 years.

• *Bibliotherapy,* reading about other people who have coped well with experiences similar to the client's, can help a person modify his or her thinking.

• *Graded task assignments* are activities that clients complete between sessions. Starting with easy assignments that guarantee success, clinicians gradually increase the difficulty of the tasks, so that people continue to learn from them and feel a sense of mastery and accomplishment. You will learn more about graded tasks later in this chapter.

Termination and Relapse Prevention

Like the other phases of cognitive therapy, the concluding phase is carefully planned and structured to help people successfully apply what they have learned through treatment. Sessions are scheduled less frequently, typically shifting to every other week, then to once a month, then to every three months for at least a year (Beck, 1995). This gives people the opportunity to test their skills and cope with almost inevitable setbacks while maintaining contact with their clinicians.

Normalizing setbacks and stressing the importance of ongoing learning can enable people to cope with future disappointments successfully. Life skills such as assertiveness, decision making, coping strategies, and communication skills, which have probably been taught throughout the treatment process, are reviewed and solidified. Progress also is reviewed, with every effort made to help clients accept credit for and take pride in their accomplishments. Clinicians address any concerns that clients have about termination and elicit feedback about the treatment process. Finally, clients and clinicians collaborate in developing goals and plans for clients to continue their progress on their own.

APPLICATION OF COGNITIVE THERAPY

Cognitive therapy has established itself as a major treatment approach. Because Aaron Beck and his colleagues, as well as other cognitive therapists, encourage and engage in extensive research on the impact of this approach, its effectiveness has been more clearly demonstrated than that of most other treatment systems.

Application to Diagnostic Groups

Research during the past 20 years has established the effectiveness of cognitive therapy in treating a broad range of mental disorders. One of the first important indications of the power of this approach came from Smith, Glass, and Miller's (1980) meta-analysis of over 400 studies on psychotherapy outcome. They concluded that cognitive therapy had a broad range of effectiveness and a particularly strong impact on the treatment of fear and anxiety, specific phobias, and problems in overall adjustment.

Treatment of Depression   Extensive research documents the effectiveness of cognitive therapy in the treatment of depression. Probably the most compelling is a study by the NIMH Treatment of

Depression Collaborative Research Program (Elkin et al., 1989), which found that, for treatment of moderately severe depression, cognitive therapy was somewhat better than interpersonal therapy (discussed in chapter 8) and much better than medication alone. Dobson (1989) reviewed 27 studies using cognitive therapy to treat depression and concluded that cognitive therapy is significantly better than psychodynamic therapy, person-centered therapy, behavior therapy, or medication. Research by Hollon and Najavits (1988) found that the relapse rate for people treated for depression by cognitive therapy was 30% compared with 60% for people treated via medication.

The book *Cognitive Therapy of Depression* (Beck, Rush, Shaw, & Emery, 1979) describes how this approach is used to treat people with depression. Assessment, prior to initiation of treatment, determines whether people are good candidates for this approach and provides baseline measures of symptoms and functioning on the Beck Depression Inventory and other inventories. At the outset of treatment, people are given a rationale for cognitive therapy: Thoughts are the primary determinant of emotions and actions, dysfunctional thoughts lead to depression and other symptoms, and substituting helpful and reality-based thoughts for those that are distorted can alleviate symptoms and improve functioning. Readings such as *Coping with Depression* (Beck & Greenberg, 1995) help people understand cognitive therapy. Clinicians then teach clients to recognize and record their negative thoughts on the Daily Record of Dysfunctional Thoughts and to use "logical and empirical investigation" (p. 4) to assess their thoughts for "logic, validity, adaptiveness, and enhancement of positive behavior versus maintenance of pathology." Positive and valid thoughts are developed to replace dysfunctional ones. Behavioral change strategies such as schedules of activities, especially those that bring mastery and pleasure, and increasingly challenging task assignments enhance and accelerate treatment effectiveness. Treatment consists of approximately 20 weekly sessions, followed by more widely spaced follow-up or booster sessions.

This format, developed over 25 years ago, still serves as the basis for cognitive therapy of depression. However, modifications, such as Judith Beck's use of rating scales and attention to core cognitions and schemas, have given greater structure, depth, and power to the treatment of depression via cognitive therapy. In addition, a manual for using cognitive therapy has been developed to increase uniformity of treatment. Recent research, using this manual to treat people diagnosed with major depressive disorder, concluded that cognitive therapy was "effective in reducing self-reported depressive symptoms and in increasing global functioning" (Merrill, Tolbert, & Wade, 2003, p. 406).

Treatment of Other Mental Disorders   Cognitive therapy also has proven effective in treating many other disorders:

• Gottlieb (2004) reported that this approach was helpful to people diagnosed with hypochondriasis, a challenging disorder to treat. In six 90-minute group sessions, people learned to modify their beliefs about the causes of their physical symptoms and about their moods. At 12-month follow-up, people in the treatment group had significantly lower hypochondriasis scores than those in the control group.

• A study of 125 women who had been physically abused and who manifested symptoms of posttraumatic stress disorder (PTSD) concluded, "There is considerable evidence that cognitions play an important role in the maintenance or chronicity of posttraumatic stress" (Kubany, Owens, McCaig, Hill, Iannuce-Spencer, & Tremayne, 2004, p. 4). PTSD remitted in 87% of the women, with large reductions noted in depression and guilt, as well as increases in self-esteem.

• Dattilio and Freeman (1992) found that cognitive therapy could successfully alleviate chronic pain, adjustment disorders, social fears, and performance anxiety.

• Arntz and Van Den Hout (1996) reviewed multiple studies of the treatment of panic disorder via cognitive therapy and found that it had a strong positive impact on both the frequency of attacks and the fear of future attacks; 75–90% of people treated for panic disorder with cognitive therapy were panic-free after treatment.

• Some research suggests that cognitive therapy can effectively treat personality disorders. Beck et al. (1990) advanced a model for using cognitive therapy to treat these disorders. Linehan and Kehrer (1993) report success in using dialectical behavior therapy, a cognitive-behavioral approach, in treatment of people with borderline personality disorders. Although research is still limited on the use of cognitive therapy with personality disorders, distorted thinking is characteristic of people with these disorders, suggesting that cognitive treatment may well be effective.

• Many other disorders also are likely to respond to treatment via cognitive therapy, although further research is needed. Eating disorders, including anorexia nervosa and bulimia nervosa, often involve underlying depression and a distorted self-image, symptoms which typically respond well to cognitive treatment. Judith Beck (1995) reported that, in combination with medication, cognitive therapy was successful in treating people with schizophrenia and bipolar disorders. She also obtained good results using cognitive therapy to treat people with posttraumatic stress disorder, obsessive-compulsive disorder, or substance use disorders.

Application to Multicultural Groups

Because cognitive therapy is respectful, addresses present concerns, and does not require disclosure of emotions and experiences that may feel very personal, this approach appeals to people from a wide variety of ages and backgrounds. It is especially useful in treating people for whom sharing thoughts is more comfortable and acceptable than sharing emotions.

Logic, as well as empirical research, suggests the value of using cognitive therapy with people from diverse cultures. The respectful stance of the cognitive clinician, as well as the emphasis on thoughts inherent in this approach, seems well-suited for people from Asian backgrounds who often are reluctant to share deeply personal experiences and emotions with people who are not close family or friends. Thomas (1992) found that cognitive therapy was useful in exploring negative cognitions and engendering hope in African American clients. This approach, combined with outreach interventions such as child care and transportation, also proved effective in reducing depression in low-income Latina and African American women, although medication did have a more robust outcome (Miranda, et al., 2003). Kubany et al. (2004, p. 3) found that, in an adapted version of cognitive therapy used to treat "battered women" with PTSD, "white and ethnic minority women benefited equally" from treatment.

Cognitive therapy has been used with children and adolescents as well as adults. It has successfully improved the social skills of children with attention deficit/hyperactivity disorder (Cousins & Weiss, 1993; Rapport, 1995). It also has helped young people with disruptive behavior disorders to manage their anger (Lochman, White, & Wayland, 1991) and improve their problem-solving skills (Kazdin, 1997). Cognitive interventions demonstrated effectiveness in treating middle-school students who had witnessed traumatic and violent events and who manifested symptoms of PTSD (Stein et al., 2003).

CURRENT USE OF COGNITIVE THERAPY

Although the fundamentals of cognitive therapy have changed little in the past 25–30 years since it first gained attention, elaborations on this approach have given it greater depth, consistency, and usefulness. Grounded in a logical and tested premise, cognitive therapy continues to expand in relevance and application.

Core Cognitions and Schemas

One of the most important changes in this approach is the recognition that automatic thoughts stem from underlying core cognitions and schemas, discussed earlier. These constructs have deepened cognitive therapy and facilitated its use with recurrent and severe disorders such as major depressive disorder, personality disorders, and other disorders that typically are linked to long-standing underlying dysfunction. An offshoot of Beck's cognitive therapy, schema-focused cognitive therapy developed by Jeffrey Young and his associates, focuses on identification and modification of schemas.

Integration with Other Treatment Approaches

Cognitive therapy has increasingly been combined with other approaches, to make a powerful integrated treatment system. The most common combination is cognitive-behavioral therapy (CBT), discussed further in the next section of this book. Behavioral change strategies, combined with cognitive interventions, are especially effective in changing actions as well as emotions and thoughts.

Clinicians currently practicing cognitive therapy also seem more attuned to the importance of addressing emotions (Coombs, Coleman, & Jones, 2002). Again, the combination of cognitive and affective exploration is associated with positive outcomes.

Group, Family, and Psychoeducational Cognitive Therapy

Increasing use has been made of cognitive therapy in group and family treatment and as part of psychoeducation. These modalities enable cognitive therapists to reach more people and to use cognitive therapy to prevent difficulties as well as to treat them.

Stein et al. (2003, p. 605) provide a useful model for cognitive group therapy in their study of a 10-session CBT group intervention used for middle-school students with symptoms of PTSD. The following summarizes the treatment, session by session: (1) introductions, explanation of treatment using stories, information on types of stress and trauma; (2) education on responses to stress and trauma, relaxation training; (3) introduction to cognitive therapy, the connection between thoughts and feelings, measuring fear, fighting off negative thoughts; (4) more on fighting off negative thoughts; (5) coping strategies, construction of a fear hierarchy; (6) and (7) exposure to troubling memories via the imagination, drawing, writing; (8) social problem solving; (9) practice using social problem solving via the hot seat; (10) relapse prevention, "graduation."

A study by Pavuluri et al. (2003) illustrates the delivery of cognitive therapy in a family environment; the integration of cognitive therapy, behavior therapy, and family-focused therapy (FFT); and the use of cognitive therapy in psychoeducation. Thirty-four children diagnosed with bipolar disorders were treated with a combination of medication, CBT, and FFT. Interventions focused on increasing coping skills and empathy in family members; decreasing stress and expression of negative emotions; and improving family problem solving and communication. Treatment also included collaboration with the children's teachers and psychoeducation on bipolar disorders. Outcome measures found significant reductions in symptoms such as attention difficulties, aggression, mania, psychosis, depression, and sleep disturbance, along with improved overall functioning.

Psychoeducation, based on cognitive therapy, can be conducted with people experiencing problems or mental disorders, with people at risk, and with a general population. Cognitive psychoeducation presents the concept that thoughts underlie feelings and actions and describes strategies that people can use to monitor, assess, dispute, and modify their thoughts. Information on behavioral strategies further enhances the process.

EVALUATION OF COGNITIVE THERAPY

Although cognitive therapy has a great deal to offer, it also has limitations. Keeping these in mind can help clinicians maximize the effectiveness of this approach.

Limitations

Cognitive therapy is, of course, not for everyone. It is a structured approach that requires people to assume an active and collaborative role in their treatment and to complete suggested tasks between sessions. In addition, cognitive therapy stresses present-oriented, relatively brief treatment. The goal of cognitive therapy is improved ability to think clearly and cope with life's challenges.

People seeking unstructured, long-term treatment that focuses on development of insight and exploration of background may view this therapy as ill-suited to their needs. In addition, people who are reluctant to participate fully in their own treatment, are intellectually limited, or are unmotivated to make changes may not be good candidates. At the same time, high intelligence or motivation is not required for this approach; adaptations may lead to successful treatment (Haaga, DeRubeis, Stewart, & Beck, 1991). Careful screening of clients as well as discussion about the nature of cognitive therapy can help clinicians determine if a client is an appropriate candidate for treatment.

Cognitive therapy also is demanding of clinicians. Clinicians must be organized, comfortable with structure, and willing to use inventories and forms to elicit and assess clients' concerns and progress. They must be knowledgeable about human development, learning theory, behavior therapy, and diagnosis, and be able to skillfully use a broad range of interventions. Planning and effort are integral to the success of cognitive therapy. Both clients and clinicians should be aware of the commitment required by this approach.

Other potential limitations can result from therapist shortcomings. At its inception, some clinicians erroneously viewed cognitive therapy as a rapid solution to immediate concerns; they neglected to develop a strong therapeutic alliance, downplayed the importance of empathy, and even became critical and judgmental of what the clinicians perceived as people's dysfunctional thoughts. These views reflect a misunderstanding of cognitive therapy and would not be reflected in effective treatment. Readers should keep in mind that cognitive therapy has more depth and complexity than may be evident initially and care should be taken to fully understand this powerful approach.

Strengths and Contributions

According to Aaron Beck (1993), by the mid-1980s cognitive therapy had achieved the status of a system of psychotherapy. It had a theory of personality and psychopathology, a teachable and testable treatment model with strategies to implement the theory, and a body of research documenting its effectiveness. Its efficacy has been supported with a broad range of populations; in both inpatient and outpatient settings; and in individual, couples, family, and group therapy formats. Cognitive therapy has been used with all ages, from preschool children to the elderly (Beck, 1995). Its use has been refined and expanded, and its effectiveness continues to grow.

Cognitive therapy has many strengths. Because this approach is effective at ameliorating the most common concerns presented for treatment—depression and anxiety—it is useful with a broad range of disorders and clients. It is well-received by most people because it is clear and logical and is not intrusive. Cognitive therapy does not require people to share intimate details of their past, focus extensively on their emotions, or engage in analysis of dreams or other activities that may be uncomfortable. It is an empowering and nonthreatening approach. In addition, cognitive therapy draws on a broad array of interventions and can be integrated with many other treatment approaches.

The clear and carefully planned structure of cognitive therapy facilitates both teaching and research on this treatment system. It is a versatile approach that can be modified and adapted to address a broad range of people and disorders. Its time-limited nature makes it efficient and appealing, while its use of long-term follow-up provides a safeguard against relapse. Its emphasis on building a collaborative client-clinician alliance, providing assignments between sessions, giving the client credit for progress, reinforcing positive changes, and teaching skills is empowering. This approach is designed not just to resolve immediate problems but to enable people to manage their lives successfully.

Although mastery of cognitive therapy is not as simple as it seems, with training and experience most clinicians can easily learn and use it effectively. All clinicians should be familiar with the powerful and important concepts of cognitive therapy.

Contributions   Cognitive therapy has made important contributions to counseling and psychotherapy. Aaron Beck's work, in particular, has emphasized the importance of research and evidence of effectiveness. This has led to increased research throughout the helping professions as well as development of treatment manuals designed to provide some uniformity to treatment and facilitate assessment of efficacy. Cognitive therapy's use of case formulations and treatment planning is compatible with today's emphasis on goal setting and accountability in treatment and has established a standard that other treatment systems are expected to follow. The wealth of techniques and interventions that have grown out of cognitive therapy provide useful ideas for all clinicians. Cognitive therapy has promoted the development and use of many helpful inventories including the Beck Depression Inventory, the Beck Anxiety Inventory, and the Young Schema Questionnaire (Lee, Taylor, & Dunn, 1999). Its emphasis on the therapeutic alliance has helped to dispel the myth that cognitive and behavioral therapists are indifferent to the nature of their relationships with their clients. On the contrary, they recognize that a positive and collaborative therapeutic relationship is essential. Perhaps the most important contribution of cognitive therapy is the message that analysis and modification of distorted cognitions are important ways to help people change. While emotions, actions, and background should never be ignored in treatment, helping people develop more realistic cognitions is an effective and efficient way to help them reach their goals.

SKILL DEVELOPMENT: PLANNING AND PROCESSING HOMEWORK

The mere mention of homework as an integral part of treatment can bring up negative images for both clinicians and clients—memories of deadlines, failures, and blame for poor performance. However, homework, or what Aaron Beck called task assignments, also can be an asset to treatment; it can help people feel empowered, encourage them to take credit for their gains, and accelerate treatment. According to Judith Beck (1995), "Cognitive therapy patients who carry out homework assignments progress better in therapy than those who do not" (p. 248). The guidelines that follow can help make homework a positive experience for both clients and clinicians.

Terminology

For some people, the words *homework* and *assignment* have negative connotations. Those words also imply that the clinician/teacher is telling the client/student to complete a requirement. This can create a hierarchy rather than a collaboration, which is undesirable in cognitive therapy. Finding more acceptable language can help. Terms such as *tasks, between-session projects,* and *suggested activities* may be more acceptable. Clinicians should use language that will elicit a positive response from clients.

Determining the Assignment

Collaboration. Clients and clinicians should collaborate in determining assignments. Although initially suggestions may come primarily from clinicians, clients should have the opportunity to shape the tasks in ways that make them meaningful. They also should have the right to accept or reject any assignments. As clients progress and become familiar with cognitive therapy, clinicians can encourage them to suggest tasks they find meaningful.

Relating Assignments to Sessions. Clinicians should clarify for clients the rationale behind each assignment. The assignments should continue progress or address issues that arose during the current session. For example, a woman who expressed thoughts of self-blame related to the abuse she and her younger sister received from their mother was urged to draft a letter to her mother, expressing her thoughts and feelings about the abuse of her sister. The woman could think more clearly about the abuse of her sister than about her own abuse. The letter-writing assignment helped her become more aware of those thoughts so she could eventually believe similar thoughts about her own abuse. This letter was not actually mailed but served as a learning experience.

Making Assignments Specific. Assignments should be specific so that people know exactly when and how to complete them. This reduces resistance and barriers to the assignment. Rather than suggesting that a client "have more contact with friends," the assignment might involve "having telephone conversations of at least 5 minutes with two friends on Wednesday evening and inviting at least one of them to lunch."

Ease of Accomplishment. Assignments should be fairly easy to accomplish. This, too, reduces resistance and makes it more likely that people will complete the tasks. In addition, success in accomplishing tasks can help them feel empowered and optimistic about their treatment. Graded task assignments, which gradually increase in difficulty, are particularly useful in helping people build on past successes and confront increasing challenges. Again, clinicians should plan carefully when making tasks more difficult, always seeking success. Assigning tasks that are too hard for clients or that bring up strong negative feelings are likely to undermine treatment and increase clients' self-doubts.

Practicing Tasks in the Session. Clinicians can increase the likelihood of clients' completing suggested tasks by starting or practicing a task in the session before asking people to complete tasks on their own. For example, a person who wanted to stop thinking negative thoughts about his failure to graduate from college with honors was encouraged to deliberately think the negative thoughts in the session and then practice thought stopping followed by an affirmation to curtail his negative ruminating. Coaching and encouraging him through this process in the session increased his motivation to use these skills outside of the session.

Addressing Possible Barriers. Clinicians should address possible barriers to accomplishment of assignments, as well as potential negative outcomes, to prevent them from interfering with treatment. Elinor, a woman who had been adopted as an infant, had successfully modified cognitions about her unlovableness. Her newfound confidence led her to decide to contact her biological mother. She and her counselor spent time talking about the possible responses of her biological mother to prepare Elinor to handle any outcome. In addition, the clinician helped Elinor focus on the personal achievements that enabled her to take this step, rather than the outcome of her interactions with her mother, to determine whether this experience was a success or a failure. Role plays and cognitive rehearsal are useful strategies for helping prepare people for challenging tasks.

Minimizing Excuses. Clinicians also should plan assignments so that they minimize the likelihood of excuses. For example, "If I go out to dinner with my mother and if she orders a glass of wine, I will tell her my thoughts about her excessive use of alcohol" is a weak assignment. It has too many ifs and possible pitfalls. Create assignments that depend on the client rather than on other people or external circumstances.

Addressing Clients' Reactions. Clinicians should address clients' reactions to the concept of homework assignments. Some people have a strong need for perfection, may fear failure or judgment, or may be very eager to please the clinician (Persons, 1989). Clinicians should explore clients' feelings about completing task assignments, making sure that people understand the reason for the homework and know that the clinician will not judge them. Keeping clients' reactions to homework in mind when suggesting or processing tasks should increase the likelihood that they will enhance treatment.

Offering Options. For people who are beginning treatment or who may be apprehensive about completing assignments, offering options can be helpful. For example, identifying three tasks but encouraging a client to complete only two of them gives the person some control as well as the message that this is not school where all assignments must be done.

Writing Down Assignments. Task assignments should be written down, by either the client or the clinician, in a place where the client can easily locate them. Some clinicians have space on the back of their appointment cards for assignments, some give clients a form at the end of each session that lists their suggested tasks, and others have clients bring a notebook or date book to each session to record their homework for the week. Clinicians also should note the homework in their own records so that they can follow up appropriately in the next session.

Processing Homework

Clinicians should be sure to discuss and process homework in the session following the one in which it was suggested. Most clients invest considerable effort into their tasks and want to share their accomplishments with their clinicians. Processing homework is likely to improve clients' self-esteem and cooperation with the completion of future tasks, and also helps identify and reinforce the learning that has come from the task.

Of course, clients will not always complete homework, and their experiences with assignments may not always be rewarding. Even under these circumstances, homework can be viewed as a learning experience so that something positive always emerges from that process. For example, in an effort to develop her social skills and relationships, Mary joined a cooking class. Unfortunately, traffic problems delayed her arrival at the class. When she got there and saw that the class was already in progress, she became anxious and left the class. Although this disappointed her, she could take credit for making an effort to attend the class and learned that she needed to plan her next social experience more carefully to maximize her comfort level. The experience also gave Mary an opportunity to identify an automatic thought, "I am a failure at whatever I undertake," and replace it with "I was wise to know that coming into the class late was too much for me. I can learn from this and be more successful next time."

Homework can be a rewarding and reinforcing experience for clients and provide an opportunity for clinicians to use their creativity and understanding of clients to craft meaningful, interesting, and growth-promoting tasks. One clinician who made regular use of homework reported that many of her clients kept a file of their assignments over the course of treatment and viewed them as a reflection of how much they had accomplished.

CASE ILLUSTRATION

This case illustrates the application of many strategies of cognitive therapy to Edie, who came to a session upset because she had not received a promotion at work. Assume that she and her clinician have already used cognitive therapy in their sessions so that Edie is familiar with this mode of treatment.

Edie: I had really been hoping to get promoted when the position as assistant director of the library opened up. I should have known they wouldn't hire me.

Clinician: I can hear that this is very upsetting to you. Let's take a close look at this situation and some of your reactions. When did this happen?

Edie: Just yesterday, February 23rd.

Clinician: Fill me in on the situation.

Edie: The assistant director of our library resigned, and the position was announced. I put in my application, really hoping for the job and the promotion. But they hired someone from outside our library system.

Clinician: That must have been a real disappointment for you. What physical sensations did you have when you heard the news?

Edie: I felt like I was going to cry, but I didn't want to do that in the middle of the library.

Clinician: What thoughts went through your mind when this happened?

Edie: I'm really a loser. No matter how hard I try, I fail. Everybody must be laughing at me behind my back.

Clinician: On a 0–100% scale, how much do you believe each of those thoughts?

Edie: I'm really a loser: 90%. No matter how hard I try, I fail: 95%. Everybody must be laughing at me behind my back: 80%.

Clinician: So you have a pretty strong belief in all of them. Tell me what emotions you had when you learned you would not receive the promotion and what the intensity rating of those emotions would be on the 0–100% scale.

Edie: I felt disappointment and sadness: 99%; and hopelessness: 95%.

Clinician: Now let's take a closer look at these beliefs. How about starting with the last one, "Everyone must be laughing at me behind my back," which you gave the lowest rating. How did people react to you when the new assistant director was named?

Edie: I only told two people that I was applying for the job in case I didn't get it. One of them came right over to me and she said, "You should have gotten that job. Nobody knows this library better than you. They just hired that other person because she has a doctorate and they thought she was a big deal."

Clinician: When you think about what was said to you, what thoughts come up for you?

Edie: Well, I guess I was exaggerating when I said everyone was laughing at me. Most people didn't even know I wanted that job. I just felt so embarrassed that I didn't get the job. And, my friend could be right. I don't have a doctorate, and the advertisement did say doctorate preferred.

Clinician: What about your statement that you fail at everything you do? Let's evaluate that statement.

Edie: I guess that one is an exaggeration too. I did feel like a failure though.

Clinician: Let's look at the other side of the coin. Tell me some things at which you succeed.

Edie: I generally do a good job as a mother. I know I do well at the library; I even got an award from the county.

Clinician: Anything else?

Edie: I'm a pretty good ice skater. And I write pretty well. I managed to learn the computer system at the library. That wasn't easy.

Clinician: So there are many aspects of your life where you are successful. If you were to say what percentage of the things you do are successful, what would you say?

Edie: I guess at least 75%.

Clinician: So you succeed at most of what you do.

Edie: Yes, that does seem true.

Clinician: Let's go back to your original beliefs. How would you rate them now on the 0–100% scale?

Edie: I'm really a loser: 40%. No matter how hard I try, I fail: 30%. Everybody must be laughing at me behind my back: 20%.

Clinician: So there's been a big change. From this list of types of cognitive distortions, what distortions are reflected by your statements?

Edie: I can see emotional reasoning: feeling like people were laughing at me just because I felt so embarrassed. And overgeneralization: calling myself a failure and a loser because I had this one disappointment. I also was discounting the positive: ignoring all the things I do well.

Clinician: How would you respond to those initial beliefs now?

Edie: I don't think many people are laughing at me. If they are, well, they'll be sorry I didn't get the job. No one does know the library as well as I do. And I'm not a loser. I don't succeed at everything I try, but I have a pretty good track record; 75% isn't bad.

Clinician: What emotions are you feeling now?

Edie: Disappointment, about 75%; but sadness and hopelessness are way down to about 50% and 20%. In fact, I heard about a job at another library that I think I'll look into.

Clinician: Let's come up with some homework to help solidify the work you've done today. Any ideas on what might be useful?

Edie: Yes, if I do start to feel like a failure, I can use that thought-stopping technique you taught me. Maybe an affirmation would help too.

Clinician: What would be a good one?

Edie: How about "I succeed at least 75% of the time"?

Clinician: Is that positive enough for you?

Edie: If it were too positive, I wouldn't believe it. This works for me.

Clinician: All right. How can you remind yourself of that affirmation?

Edie: I'll write it down and put it in my date book so I'll see it every time I look at my calendar, which I do often.

Clinician: How about writing it down now, and let's both make note of the homework you agreed to do this week.

Edie: Sure. And I'll also make a note to myself to get some information about that other job opening.

EXERCISES

Large-Group Exercises

1. Review the list of types of cognitive distortions (pp. 293–294). Then, focusing on Roberto or another hypothetical client, generate one example of each type of distortion that might reflect the client's thinking.

2. Select at least three of those distorted cognitions. Identify strategies you would use to enable the person to evaluate each of those thoughts.

3. For each of the following cognitive distortions, come up with at least two alternative interpretations or attributions that might be used to raise questions about the validity of the belief.

Person A: Susan told me she would call me on Sunday morning to arrange to meet for brunch. Now it's the afternoon. I guess she didn't really want to spend time with me but was just afraid to tell me. I'll never be able to make a good friend. I'm so unlikable.

Person B: When the principal announced that I had won the math award, my teacher gave me a really funny look. She probably wanted Nancy to win. Nancy does get better grades than I do. It's just a fluke that I won that award.

Person C: I had a business trip to the town where my nephew goes to college and called him to see if we could get together. He told me he was too busy right now and couldn't get off the phone fast enough. I know the family has felt differently about me since I let them know I was gay. My brother probably told him not to have anything to do with me. My nephew and I used to be close, but I guess he can't deal with my being gay. He did call me back later and apologized for being abrupt, but I know what he was really feeling.

Small-Group Exercises

1. Form into your small groups of four people in two dyads. Each dyad should have an opportunity to role-play both client and clinician. Allow 15–20 minutes for each role play. The client should open the session by describing an upsetting experience. The task of the clinician is to guide the client through the following process:

- Identify date, time, situation, and accompanying sensations.
- Identify two automatic thoughts, write them down, and rate the belief in each on the 0–100% scale.
- Identify the accompanying emotions and rate their intensity on the same scale.
- Identify actions taken in response to the experience.
- Use strategies from this chapter to help the client evaluate the cognitions.
- Replace any distorted cognitions with more adaptive responses, and rate how much each of those is believed.
- Rerate the belief in the original cognitions.
- Identify and rate the intensity of the current emotions.
- Identify any new actions to be taken.
- Decide on a homework task to solidify the learning in the session.

Allow time for group members to share feedback after each role play has finished. Feedback should look at both general counseling skills and the process of taking the client through the previous steps and should focus on both strengths and suggestions for improvement.

2. After all the role plays are completed, list the distorted cognitions that were identified in the role plays. Then review the types of distorted cognitions and categorize each distorted cognition on the list.
3. As a group, develop an appropriate affirmation for each of the clients in the previous role plays.

Individual Exercises

1. Becoming your own therapist is an important aspect of cognitive therapy. Writing your responses in your journal, identify, evaluate, and if appropriate modify your thoughts, emotions, and actions after an upsetting experience. Follow the format in Small-Group Exercise 1.
2. Develop, write down, and use an affirmation that feels right to you and will help you meet your goals.
3. Identify an upcoming experience that presents difficulty for you—perhaps public speaking, meeting new people at a business or social gathering, or making a request of someone. Use cognitive rehearsal to imagine yourself successfully handling the experience. Rehearse the experience in your mind at least three times. Write about your reactions to this exercise.

SUMMARY

Cognitive therapists believe that the most effective way to help people make positive changes is by enabling them to identify, evaluate, and, if indicated, modify their thoughts. While attention is also paid to emotions and actions, distorted thoughts are the target of treatment. Developed by Aaron Beck and his associates, cognitive therapy is a relatively brief, structured approach that offers specific plans for change, gives people clear explanations of all steps in the treatment process, and teaches skills that empower people and promote their emotional well-being. Clients and clinicians work collaboratively, with clinicians drawing on an extensive array of creative interventions to promote and reinforce positive change. Task assignments and inventories are used and contribute to the clarity and impact of cognitive therapy. Research has proven the effectiveness of cognitive therapy with a broad range of mental disorders and clients. It is especially effective in treating depression and anxiety.

RECOMMENDED READINGS

Beck, A., Freeman, A., & Associates. (1990). *Cognitive therapy of personality disorders.* New York: Guilford.

Beck, J. S. (1995). *Cognitive therapy: Basics and beyond.* New York: Guilford.

Bricker, D. C., & Young, J. E. (1993). *A client's guide to schema-focused cognitive therapy.* NY: Cognitive Therapy Center of New York.

Dattilio, F. M., & Freeman, A. (Eds.). (1992). *Comprehensive casebook of cognitive therapy.* New York: Plenum.

Merrill, K. A., Tolbert, V. E., & Wade, W. A. (2003). Effectiveness of cognitive therapy for depression in a community mental health center: A benchmarking study. *Journal of Consulting and Clinical Psychology, 71,* 404–409.

ADDITIONAL SOURCES OF INFORMATION

Although many journals in psychology and counseling include articles on cognitive therapy, two focus specifically on treatment via this approach: the *Journal of Cognitive Psychotherapy* and the *International Cognitive Therapy Newsletter.*

Training in and information on cognitive therapy is widely available. The following is a good place to begin gathering additional information on education and resources:

www.beckinstitute.org—This is the website for the Beck Institute for Cognitive Therapy and Research (GSB Building, City Line and Belmont Avenues, Suite 700, Bala Cynwyd, PA 19004-1610, (610) 664-3020).

The Beck Institute offers weekend and weeklong training opportunities as well as extended training, videoconferences, distance learning, recommended readings, and books and inventories.

Information also can be obtained from:

www.cognitivetherapynyc.com—This website is for The American Institute for Cognitive Therapy (136 East 57th Street, Suite 101, New York, NY 10022).

This organization of researchers and psychotherapists provides cognitive-behavioral treatment as well as informa-

tion. The affiliated Foundation of the Advancement of Cognitive Therapy (FACT) conducts research and provides training on CBT.

www.academyofct.org—The Academy of Cognitive Therapy, founded in 1999, is an organization of clinicians, educators, and researchers in cognitive therapy. The Academy supports continuing education and research and also serves as a certifying organization for CBT. In addition, the website provides information to help people locate certified cognitive therapists.

www.cognitive-behavioral-therapy-ny.com/schema—This is the website of an organization that provides information on schema-focused cognitive therapy, developed by Jeffrey Young who has worked closely with Aaron Beck.

Inventories developed by Aaron Beck and others and used in cognitive therapy can be ordered from:

The Psychological Corporation
555 Academic Court
San Antonio, TX 78204
(800) 211-8378

CHAPTER 16

Albert Ellis and Rational Emotive Behavior Therapy

R ational emotive behavior therapy (REBT), like cognitive therapy, emphasizes thoughts. REBT initially was developed by Albert Ellis in the 1950s. Ellis continues to be the primary advocate and spokesperson for this approach, although many other clinicians practice REBT. This treatment approach assumes that people's cognitions are the primary source of their difficulties. Although, like Aaron Beck, rational emotive behavior therapists believe that thoughts, emotions, and behaviors are interrelated (Bond & Dryden, 1996), they view helping people think more rationally as the most effective route to improving all three areas of functioning. In particular, REBT hones in on "self-defeating absolutistic beliefs" (Nielson & Ellis, 1994, p. 327).

Cognitive therapy and REBT have much in common in terms of their theories of human development, concepts of effecting change, and strategies used. Both treatment approaches are structured and active, while emphasizing the human element in treatment. As Ellis (1992) stated, REBT "tries to combine a tough-minded scientific attitude with a down-to-earth humanistic approach to psychotherapy" (p. 357).

However, the two approaches also have differences. REBT has its own approach to disputing and modifying distorted cognitions. Persuasion and teaching, along with gathering evidence, are important strategies for rational emotive behavior therapists. In addition, REBT addresses change on two levels: General REBT focuses on resolving immediate and practical concerns, while elegant REBT "helps people achieve an intensive, profoundly philosophical and emotional change" (Ellis, 1995a, p. 1). We discuss these two types of REBT later in this chapter.

ALBERT ELLIS

Albert Ellis, the originator of REBT, was born in 1913 in Pittsburgh. He moved to New York as a young child and has lived there for most of his life. Ellis's family of origin included an independent mother, a father who cared about the family but was often absent, and a younger brother (Weinrach, 1980). Ellis was apparently the family favorite. He got along well with the others in his family, although in many ways he had a difficult childhood. At an early age, he perceived his family as "pretty crazy" and stated that he basically raised himself from the age of 7 (p. 159). In addition, Ellis, like Beck, was sickly as a child and was often hospitalized, usually for nephritis. To overcome these difficulties, Ellis decided not to be miserable about his circumstances and maintained strong positive thoughts about his competence and worth (Ellis, 1997). Thus, at an early age he learned that the way people think can enable them to overcome adversity.

In the 1940s, Ellis received M.A. and Ph.D. degrees in clinical psychology from Columbia University and began practicing as a marriage, family, and sex therapist. Seeking to help people achieve profound change, he obtained training as a psychoanalyst with an emphasis on the work of Karen Horney (Ellis & Dryden, 1997). However, his dissatisfaction with the inefficiency of psychoanalysis as well as his readings in Greek and Asian philosophy led him to develop a way to treat people that focused on their thoughts.

Ellis began practicing what he initially called rational therapy in 1955, founded the still-active Institute for Rational Emotive Therapy (now the Albert Ellis Institute) in 1959 to offer both treatment and training in this approach, and published the first of his many works on REBT in 1962. Since then, he has had an illustrious career advancing his treatment system. A prolific writer, Ellis has authored over 700 papers and 55 books and monographs. He has received many awards, including the Distinguished Professional Psychologist Award in 1974 and the Distinguished Professional Contributions Award in 1985, both from the American Psychological Association. In a 1991 survey, Canadian clinical psychologists chose Ellis as the most influential psychologist (Ellis, 1997). American clinical psychologists and counselors ranked him second, after Carl Rogers but before Sigmund Freud.

Ellis is open about his personal life and often uses himself as a role model in his work. A classic story he has told about himself is that, as a young man, he was apprehensive about asking women for dates. To overcome his fears, he forced himself to approach 100 women and invite them out. Although all refused, this experience of forcing himself to do repeatedly what he feared most enabled him to overcome his anxieties. Ellis's shame-attacking exercises (discussed later in this chapter) recall this experience. Ellis has had two brief marriages; both ended in divorce. For more than 30 years he has lived with Janet Wolfe, a psychotherapist who also writes about and practices REBT.

Now in his 90s, Ellis is "partially disabled with diabetes, tired eyes, deficient hearing" and other disabilities (Ellis, 1997, p. 17). He uses REBT to cope with these difficulties, and continues to write, lecture, and practice. A typical work day extends from 9:30 a.m. to 11:00 p.m. In a week, he might see 80 people for individual counseling and another 40 for group therapy at the Psychological Clinic of the Albert Ellis Institute. Ellis also gives many talks about his work. Ellis's recent writings reflect continuing changes in his thinking, largely reflecting increased flexibility and sensitivity to diversity (Ellis, 2003).

Ellis is a man with a strong personality. Windy Dryden, another leading proponent of REBT, described Ellis as abrasive, humorous, and flamboyant. Ellis's direct manner and his use of colorful language always make an impact; many people are impressed, while others are offended. In studying REBT, keep in mind that one need not emulate Ellis's style to practice successfully the important treatment system he has developed.

THE DEVELOPMENT OF RATIONAL EMOTIVE BEHAVIOR THERAPY

Now about 50 years old, rational emotive behavior therapy has evolved considerably, although its basic premise—that emotions and behavior can best be modified by changing thinking—has not changed. Early influences on REBT include Buddhist and Taoist philosophy and writings on happiness, secular humanism, and behaviorism. Alfred Adler's emphasis on the social system, the importance of goals and purpose, and use of live demonstrations also are apparent in REBT. In addition, Karen Horney's concepts, especially about the power of *shoulds* in our lives, are evident in REBT.

Ellis has changed the name of his theory twice. In 1961, rational therapy became rational *emotive* therapy (RET), reflicting the attention this approach paid to feelings. This modification may, at least in part, have been a response to the popularity of Carl Rogers's ideas, which emphasized the importance of emotions. RET became rational emotive *behavior* therapy in 1993, reflecting its increased emphasis on behavior, especially as a vehicle for reinforcing and implementing changes in thinking (Ellis, 1995b). As practiced today, REBT emphasizes thoughts, but views emotions, behaviors, and thoughts as intertwined and inseparable. To maximize success, treatment must attend to all three.

Although many ideas and strategies associated with REBT have been modified over the years, one of the greatest changes is the conception of REBT as two-tiered. *General REBT* is used with all clients to target immediate presenting concerns. *Preferential* or *elegant REBT,* on the other hand, seeks deep philosophical changes and is used only with people who seem able to benefit from it. According to Ellis and Dryden (1997), general REBT is comparable to cognitive therapy, while preferential REBT goes beyond it, seeking to help people effect long-lasting and profound change.

Since its initial development, the theories, structure, and strategies of REBT have become less absolute and more compatible with postmodern treatment approaches, including narrative therapy, constructivist therapy, and existential therapy. Ellis's emphasis on people's perceptions of the world have led some to view him as constructivist in his outlook (Weinrach & Ellis, 1995). Interventions used in REBT have become more varied and eclectic. In addition, REBT now pays greater attention to understanding the background and viewpoints of each client and is more accepting of people's religious and other beliefs, as long as they are not rigid and harmful.

IMPORTANT THEORETICAL CONCEPTS

Like cognitive therapy, REBT focuses on helping people identify, evaluate, and modify dysfunctional cognitions. However, rational emotive behavior therapists differ from cognitive therapists following Beck's approach in terms of the strategies they use and their conception of healthy development.

Human Development and Emotional Health

According to REBT, dimensions of psychological health include the following (Ellis, 1995a; Ellis & Dryden, 1997, pp. 18–19):

- Awareness, acceptance, and appreciation of oneself and others
- Social interest: recognition that contributing to the world enhances our own happiness
- Self-direction and personally meaningful goals
- Involvement in long-range absorbing creative pursuits; commitment to something outside oneself
- Long-range hedonism; the ability to enjoy the present as well as the discipline to defer immediate gratification and seek pleasure in the future
- Acceptance of uncertainty and ambiguity
- Flexibility, ability to adapt to change
- High frustration tolerance so we are not devastated by disappointments
- Ability to think in a clear, logical, scientific, and rational way
- Willingness to take sensible risks, experiment, and be reasonably adventurous
- Recognition that we cannot always be totally happy and that life will not always go exactly as we hope
- Acceptance of responsibility for our own emotional difficulties

Self-Acceptance   Self-acceptance is an important concept in REBT. This approach suggests that emotional difficulties often are found in people with conditional self-acceptance; they value themselves because of their accomplishments rather than because of their basic worth as a person. When they experience failures or disappointments, their self-esteem plummets. They cannot separate "performance from personhood" (Barrish, 1997, p. 73), and believe "I am what I do" and "If I fail, I am a bad, worthless person." According to Ellis, people should have a realistic sense of their strengths and weaknesses and take pride in their achievements. At the same time, they will feel happier and more stable if they accept, value, and believe in themselves even when they are disappointed in their behaviors or experiences. REBT teaches people to assess their thoughts and behaviors, not themselves.

Barrish (1997) extended this concept to child-rearing practices and emphasized the importance of parents' contributions to children's self-esteem. Consistent with REBT, Barrish suggested that parents give their children messages such as "I value you even when I don't agree with you or am disappointed with your performance" and "I am proud of what you did," praising the act rather than judging the intrinsic value of the person. By recognizing that people are fallible and not equating the worth of the child with the child's accomplishments, parents can help their children value themselves unconditionally.

Origins of Emotional Disturbance   REBT suggests that, because irrational thinking is so widespread, people must have a strong biological tendency to think dysfunctionally and believe that life should go their way. However, people do vary in their propensity to think irrationally. REBT recognizes that childhood difficulties and traumas may contribute to a person's tendency to think and act in unhealthy ways. Emotional disturbance, then, results from a combination of an innate predisposition toward irrational thinking and life experiences.

According to REBT, emotional disturbance usually is characterized by underlying anxiety. Ellis (1991) described two levels of anxiety. *Discomfort anxiety* is linked to situational problems such as recent losses, while *ego anxiety*, which includes strong feelings of guilt and inadequacy, results when people's sense of self is threatened. These two levels of anxiety seem to parallel the two levels of REBT, with general REBT being sufficient to treat discomfort anxiety but preferential REBT needed for ego anxiety.

Despite its recognition of the impact of biological, social, and other forces on human development, REBT maintains an optimistic view of human nature. It emphasizes will and choice and perceives people as having inborn drives toward actualization as well as irrational thinking (Bernard, 1995). REBT perceives people as able to exercise choice, see that their thoughts are responsible for disturbing them, and actively and continually work toward positive change and fulfillment (Ellis & Dryden, 1997).

Secular Humanism

With its focus on the perceptions and responsibility of the individual, REBT is rooted in secular humanism. According to Ellis (1992), "Secular humanism is relativist, skeptical, and nondogmatic and emphasizes the best and most practical aspects of the scientific method together with human choice and meaningfulness" (p. 349). Secular humanists view people as unique individuals who usually value and choose to live in interdependent social groups. They see people as neither good nor bad but simply human; only people's acts are evaluated. People who adopt a philosophy of secular humanism typically are concerned with social systems and advocate peace, fairness, and democracy. They seek possibilities and alternatives rather than absolute truths.

REBT and Religion   Because of his criticism of certain types of religious beliefs, Ellis and REBT have sometimes been seen as opposed to conventional religion. This reflects a misunderstanding of Ellis's viewpoint. Ellis and Dryden (1997) describe REBT as compatible with a Christian viewpoint in that it "condemns the sin but not the sinner" (p. 3).

Ellis and REBT recognize that belief in a higher power and involvement with a religious community can help people find a personally meaningful direction. REBT suggests that clinicians should explore and encourage the benefits of people's religious and spiritual beliefs, be aware of and express their own beliefs, use spiritual resources and rituals in treatment, and establish treatment plans and goals that are compatible with clients' beliefs (Johnson, Ridley, & Nielsen, 2000).

REBT clinicians are only opposed to religious and other beliefs that they perceive as irrational and harmful belief systems: those that are absolutist rather than probabilistic and are dogmatic, rigid, and antihumanistic (Weinrach, 1980). Rather than uncritically accepting people's religious beliefs "for the sake of embracing diversity," clinicians practicing REBT ask: "Do the client's beliefs provide a way to avoid reality and responsibility? Do the client's beliefs create false expectations of God? Do the client's beliefs lead to self-destructive behavior? If the answer to any of these questions is 'yes', the client may harbor distorted and destructive beliefs that warrant revision" (Johnson, Ridley, & Nielsen, 2000, p. 16).

Thoughts as the Route to Change

According to REBT, people need to recognize and accept that they are largely responsible for creating their own emotional problems (Ellis, 1988). Regardless of when and how the problems began, REBT maintains that emotional problems stem primarily from irrational beliefs. As Shakespeare wrote, "Things are neither good nor bad but thinking makes them so" (DiGiuseppe, 1996). Rational emotive behavior therapists have found that, through hard work and practice, people can change their absolute and irrational beliefs and correspondingly alleviate their emotional difficulties.

Focus on Present Thoughts   REBT focuses on present thoughts rather than past events. Although clinicians recognize the significance of the past, they discourage lengthy, in-depth exploration of people's backgrounds and the origins of their thoughts (Ellis, 1995a). Instead, they believe that a present-oriented focus is more meaningful to people, more likely to enhance rapport, and in keeping with the idea that people's current thoughts and behaviors maintain their self-defeating thoughts, whatever the origins of those thoughts.

Of course, REBT recognizes that traumatic and other painful past experiences can have a profound impact on people. Even for people who have been traumatized, the focus of REBT is on present thoughts—on gently helping people accept their experiences, stop blaming themselves, and focus on the present and the future.

REBT also recognizes the role of early experience in human development. However, this approach does not focus extensively on the roots of people's difficulties. Instead, emphasis is on people's current beliefs and related actions that keep their disturbances alive (Bernard, 1995). Clinicians use forceful and creative strategies to help people identify and dispute their irrational beliefs; REBT asserts that positive results are obtained when people gain awareness of their irrational beliefs and take effective action to change them. Like other cognitive therapists, clinicians practicing REBT provide people the skills they need to become their own therapists—to enable them to use the methods of REBT throughout their lives to identify and change their self-destructive thoughts.

REBT's View of Insight   Helping people gain insight into the origins of their problems and emotional disturbances is not an essential part of REBT. Not only is insight viewed as insufficient for change, but it is seen as potentially harmful, leading to self-blame and immobilization. However, gaining insight into the principles of REBT is important. Ellis (1988) described three levels of insight, which he views as necessary for people to make positive changes:

1. The insight to see that we choose to upset ourselves
2. The insight to see that we acquired our irrational beliefs and to see how we continue to maintain them
3. The insight to see that we need to work hard to change

REBT's View of Emotions   Clinicians using REBT do not spend a great deal of time exploring emotions and do not seek to change them directly. However, clinicians recognize that if people can become aware of their emotions and their impact, this can facilitate their efforts to identify and change their irrational beliefs.

Ellis (1986) distinguished between inappropriate/self-destructive emotions and appropriate/nondefeating emotions. *Self-destructive emotions* are enduring, immobilizing, and nonproductive; reflect overreactions to stimuli; and lead to negative self-images and actions. Examples include rage, shame, jealousy, hatred, self-criticism, anxiety, and depression. On the other hand, *appropriate emotions* are transient, manageable, in proportion to the stimulus, and enhancing of self-acceptance. They include both positive emotions such as joy, satisfaction, and peacefulness and negative emotions such as annoyance, regret, and sadness. Of course, we all have negative reactions when we experience losses and disappointments. However, our thoughts about those disappointments determine whether we develop emotions that are inappropriate and self-destructive or appropriate and nondefeating.

REBT's View of Behavior   Although the word *behavior* has recently been added to its name, REBT always paid attention to people's behaviors (Ellis, 1995b). However, like emotions, behaviors are a secondary focus of treatment. They provide a measure of progress, are used to modify and reinforce thoughts, and are a prime target of homework assignments. Although REBT views behaviors, emotions, and thoughts as having a reciprocal relationship, thoughts are the primary route to change. Changing thoughts and accompanying self-statements leads to changes in both actions and emotion.

Irrational Beliefs

Ellis and Dryden (1997) identified six types of beliefs. These include the following, along with definitions and examples:

1. *Nonevaluative observations* reflect perceptions and are neutral rather than judgmental: A person is running toward a bus that is pulling away from the curb.
2. *Nonevaluative inferences* draw conclusions based on observations and, similarly, are neutral rather than judgmental: The person is probably trying to catch a bus.
3. *Positive preferential evaluations* draw tentative, rewarding conclusions: My friend smiles and pats my hand as we talk, so I presume she is enjoying my company.
4. *Positive musturbatory evaluations* draw absolute, rewarding conclusions: I am always an entertaining conversationalist, so I am a wonderful person.

5. *Negative preferential evaluations* draw tentative, distressing conclusions: Because my friend keeps fidgeting and looking at her watch, I presume that she is bored by my company.
6. *Negative musturbatory evaluations* draw absolute, distressing conclusions: Because I am not holding my friend's interest, I am a boring failure. That is unbearable.

Ellis (1984) referred to nonevaluative observations and inferences as cold cognitions. Positive and negative preferential evaluations are warm cognitions. They may or may not be accurate, but they are grounded in reality, reflect preferences rather than convictions, and are not absolute or exaggerated. Consequently, they can be viewed as rational beliefs. However, positive and negative musturbatory evaluations are hot cognitions that involve overgeneralization, judgments of self and others, and inflexibility. Negative musturbatory evaluations also are characterized by what Ellis and Dryden (1997) called "awfulizing" and "I-can't-stand-it-itis" as well as by shoulds, oughts, and condemnation of self and others (p. 12). These lead to disturbances, problems, and emotional difficulties.

The three major musturbating belief systems that follow reflect thoughts and demands about the self, others, and the world (Ellis, 1984, p. x; Ellis; 2003, p. 236–7).

1. I must act perfectly and be achieving and lovable at all times. If I do not, I am incompetent and worthless. (This belief usually leads to feelings of anxiety, depression, and low self-esteem.)
2. Other people must always treat me kindly and fairly or I can't stand it and they are terrible, evil people who should be punished for mistreating me. (This belief typically leads to rage and vindictiveness.)
3. Life must go the way I want it to go and must never be too difficult or frustrating. Otherwise, life is terrible and I cannot bear it. (This belief often results in inaction, low frustration tolerance, self-pity, anger, and depression.)

Irrational beliefs usually are characterized by at least one of the following themes: awfulizing, global evaluations of human worth and self-criticism, demandingness, justice, and frustration intolerance (Bernard, 1995; DiGiuseppe, 1996).

REBT, then, identifies thoughts as either rational beliefs (rB) or irrational beliefs (iB). Irrational beliefs, usually hot cognitions, often include words such as *should, ought,* and *must* and may include immediate demands. Irrational beliefs are typically absolutes about oneself, other people, or one's circumstances. They tend to be evaluative and judgmental, viewing life in extremes. They are logically incorrect, inconsistent with empirical reality, and prevent people from attaining their goals (Maultsby, 1984).

Common types of irrational beliefs identified by clinicians practicing REBT are similar to those described on pages 293–294 in chapter 15 (Ellis & Dryden, 1997). Examples of iBs include thoughts such as these:

Vince: I must have a date for New Year's Eve by tomorrow, or I will be the laughing stock of my fraternity.
Martin: My supervisor should praise me and is a jerk for not seeing how hard I work.
Natasha: I ought to spend every evening with my family. I am a terrible mother if I don't do that.

Here are rational versions of the same beliefs:

Vince: I would like to have a date for New Year's Eve so that I can join my friends in that celebration.

Martin: I believe that my supervisor is not really familiar with my work and so is not giving me the praise I would like.

Natasha: My family and I enjoy spending time together and I believe that is helpful to my children, but I can take some time for myself and still be a good mother.

The previous irrational beliefs are extreme statements that promote negative emotions and difficulties in relationships. They do not facilitate problem solving or constructive action because they view success or failure in extreme terms, are demanding and inflexible, and blame people rather than assess a situation clearly. The rational beliefs, on the other hand, reflect preferences, hopes, and wishes. They do not judge but look at possibilities. Problem solving and constructive action are facilitated because, without extremist thinking, many options and solutions are available. Vince can take steps to find a last-minute date but still may be able to celebrate the holiday with his friends even if he doesn't have a date. Martin can plan to acquaint his supervisor with the quality of his work. Natasha can build in more time with her family while not demanding perfection from herself. Ellis (1995b) defined a rational belief as a "cognition that is effective or self-helping" as well as "empirically or logically valid" (p. 85).

THE FORMAT OF SESSIONS

Sessions in REBT tend to follow a relatively predictable pattern. A typical session includes 10 steps similar to those used in Beck's cognitive therapy (Walen, DiGiuseppe, & Dryden, 1992, p. 65):

1. Review old business from the previous session
2. Check up on mood, behavior, thoughts, symptoms, and medication
3. Elicit new business, especially any major life changes
4. Follow up on homework
5. Establish the agenda for the sessions
6. Do the work according to the *ABCDEF* format (discussed later in this chapter)
7. Summarize the work that has been done
8. Assign new homework
9. Obtain feedback on the session
10. Close the session

Inclusion of additional steps at the beginning and end of the treatment process is invaluable in maximizing the success of REBT. Clinicians typically begin by explaining the theory of REBT and familiarizing clients with its procedures and with what is expected from them as clients. Although clinicians who practice REBT are less likely to use a formal assessment process incorporating many inventories than are other cognitive therapists, they, too, engage in assessment during the first few sessions of treatment, exploring clients' history and background, thoughts, emotions, behaviors, and symptoms. Once that has been accomplished, focus shifts to helping clients recognize that they largely create their own disturbance, understand that psychological difficulties typically stem from irrational beliefs, and see that they can change their beliefs and alleviate their difficulties.

By the end of treatment, clients should have learned to evaluate and dispute their own beliefs using a variety of strategies, and be prepared to continue that process throughout their lives (Ellis, 1995a). Follow-up sessions facilitate people's efforts to continue REBT on their own. Relapse prevention is especially important for people who have made significant philosophical changes through elegant REBT and may need help in continuing to maintain those changes.

While REBT is often a relatively brief process, clinicians generally do not predetermine the number of sessions. Rather, treatment lasts as long as necessary to help people accomplish their goals. Efficiency rather than brevity is valued.

General Versus Elegant REBT

For many years, REBT focused primarily on immediate, presenting concerns, probably at least in part to distinguish this approach from psychoanalysis that Ellis had rejected. However, over the past decade, Ellis and his colleagues have taken a broader and deeper look at people and how to help them and have distinguished between general and elegant REBT. According to Ellis (2003, p. 231), REBT "now is more interested in the explicit and implicit *meanings* and *philosophies* that people use to upset themselves." These core philosophies and basic meanings are reflected in people's self-talk, their images and fantasies, their interactions with others, and in many other ways. While general REBT focuses primarily on immediate concerns, elegant REBT seeks profound philosophical change in people that will affect all aspects of their lives.

TREATMENT USING RATIONAL EMOTIVE BEHAVIOR THERAPY

Clinicians who practice REBT foster the therapeutic alliance and use a wide range of strategies, particularly the ABCDEF approach to modifying irrational beliefs. Many of these are described here.

Goals

REBT is a goal-oriented treatment system that focuses on outcomes such as changes in beliefs and reduction in symptoms. It de-emphasizes processes such as exploration of early development and insight into the impact of the past on the present. Although REBT helps people to become more aware of their thoughts, emotions, and behaviors, this approach is primarily concerned with enabling people to learn cognitive skills that promote rational thinking and lead to greater happiness and self-acceptance (Ellis, 1995a). REBT seeks to help people "make themselves elegantly effective, including less *disturbable*" (Ellis, 1995a, p. 3).

Therapeutic Alliance

Clients and clinicians have a collaborative relationship in REBT. Clients assume some responsibility for planning and implementing their treatment, just as they are encouraged to take considerable responsibility for their difficulties. Clinicians teach clients about rational and irrational thinking; help people identify, dispute, and modify their irrational beliefs; and facilitate their efforts to develop a more rational philosophy of life. Although problem solving is part of treatment, REBT clinicians go beyond problem solving and enable people to establish more balanced, logical, and rewarding lives.

The roles of clinicians in REBT are somewhat different from their roles in cognitive therapy, perhaps because of the model reflected by Albert Ellis. Rational emotive behavior therapists are more of a presence in the treatment process, often using their influence on clients to effect change, whereas cognitive therapists tend to assume a more neutral role. Clinicians in REBT do not hesitate to use persuasion, praise, exaggeration, instruction, humorous songs, and anecdotes from their own lives to help people think more rationally and make positive changes. According to Ellis (1992), clinicians should not be blank screens; they should be highly active, genuine, and directive, revealing their own thoughts and experiences, but always maintaining a professional relationship with clients.

Ellis and Dryden (1997, p. 29) suggest that clinicians practicing REBT be:

- Structured but flexible
- Intellectually, cognitively, and philosophically inclined
- Active and directive in their style
- Comfortable using behavioral instruction and teaching
- Untroubled by fear of failure and willing to take thoughtful risks
- Emotionally healthy, accepting of themselves and others as fallible
- Practical and scientific rather than mystical and magical
- Comfortable with a variety of interventions

Clinicians practicing REBT assume many roles. They are teachers, role models, confidence builders, cheerleaders, and motivators. They strive to communicate acceptance and caring to their clients, helping them to both overcome problems and lead happier lives.

Establishment of mutual liking and rapport is less important in REBT than it is in many other approaches to treatment (Ellis, 1995a). While clinicians do not judge their clients, they may judge their behaviors. Ellis has often told clients he dislikes some of their behaviors and would not want to befriend them in social situations—certainly a powerful message.

Ellis cautions against clinicians becoming gurus and creating a situation in which clients change to please the clinician rather than themselves. In REBT, self-acceptance is paramount.

Most clinicians practicing REBT do not seem to emulate Ellis. According to Walen et al. (1992), "RET therapists have many different yet effective styles" and do not need to replicate Ellis's (p. 42). Walen et al. found that rapport and empathy are compatible with an active and directive treatment stance and view rapport as important in REBT, developing over time as clients and clinicians work together. Adapting REBT to the needs of a particular client is essential to effective treatment (Weinrach, 1995).

Identifying, Disputing, and Modifying Irrational Beliefs

Like Beck's cognitive therapy, REBT uses a structured format for identifying, assessing, disputing, and modifying beliefs—a six-step plan represented by the letters *ABCDEF* (Ellis, 1995a, 1995c). The REBT Self-Help Form or the Attitudes and Beliefs Inventory (Lega & Ellis, 2001) are sometimes used to help people identify their beliefs (Bs). To illustrate the *ABCDEF* model, we consider Martin's beliefs about his supervisor (presented earlier in this chapter).

A, the first step, is identification and description of the *activating event*. This is the external and objective source of discomfort, the experience that initiates the process of irrational thinking and precipitates the negative thoughts, emotions, and behaviors.

Martin A: "My supervisor gave me an average rating on my evaluation."

B is the person's *belief* about the activating event, evaluating that stimulus as positive, negative, or neutral. The belief may be rational or irrational. REBT holds that people may not have a choice about experiences or activating events but do have a choice about their beliefs related to those activating events.

Martin B: "My supervisor should praise me more and is a jerk for not seeing how hard I work. It is awful that I work so hard and am not valued as I ought to be."

C stands for the *consequences* of the belief. Of course, the activating event itself can produce negative consequences; but according to REBT, beliefs mediate between events and consequences, with beliefs being a major determinant of most consequences. By assessing the nature and consequences of a belief, clinicians can determine whether the belief is a cool, warm, or hot cognition and whether it is irrational and harmful to the client or rational and either neutral or helpful. If the belief is irrational, consequences are likely to be unhealthy and harmful and might include inappropriate and self-destructive emotions (e.g., rage, anxiety, depression) and inappropriate and self-destructive behaviors (e.g., excessive use of alcohol, blaming self and others, withdrawal). Rational beliefs usually lead to healthier and more constructive consequences such as appropriate emotions (e.g., disappointment, annoyance) and appropriate behaviors (e.g., taking effective steps to change the situation or distracting oneself with exercise or a creative pursuit).

Initial consequences of a belief can lead to subsequent reinforcing consequences that themselves become activating events. For example, if Martin expressed his anger toward his supervisor in loud and attacking ways and the supervisor reacted with further disapproval, Martin's irrational beliefs and negative emotions probably would be reinforced (Wessler, 1986).

Martin C: Martin experienced anger, shame, and anxiety about losing his job. His behaviors included berating his supervisor.

D, dispute (also referred to as debate), is the next step in the process. Exploration of beliefs and their consequences determine whether they are rational or irrational. In general, clinicians begin by focusing on irrational beliefs about immediate situations and then move to more generalized and abstract irrational beliefs, comparable to Beck's core beliefs and schemas.

Gandy (1995, p. 39) suggested the following four questions to determine whether a belief is irrational:

1. Logic—"Where is the logic that this should not have happened to me?"
2. Empirical evidence—"Where is the evidence that this condition should not have happened to me?"
3. Pragmatic/functional—"How will holding this belief help me achieve my goals?"
4. Constructing an alternative rational belief—"What is an alternative belief that would better help me achieve my goals?"

Later in the chapter, we will talk more about the many strategies available to help people contest their irrational beliefs. Some are similar to strategies discussed in chapter 15. However, in REBT, clinicians rely more on persuasion, teaching, and techniques that elicit strong emotions than do other cognitive therapists, who rely more on logic. Ellis, for example, is well known for his powerful statements and humorous songs, intended to help people see the irrational nature of their thoughts.

Martin D: Strategies to dispute irrational beliefs include cognitive, behavioral, and emotional approaches to change. For Martin, all three are relevant. Cognitive approaches might involve examining the logic of his belief, including the adequacy of the supervisor's information on Martin's performance and whether receiving an average evaluation was truly awful or simply undesirable. Ellis would probably also use emotional methods, pointing out Martin's awfulizing, his tendency to catastrophize, and his musturbating: his need to have his life be exactly as he wishes. Ellis might encourage Martin to feel appropriate and nondestructive emotions such as annoyance and disappointment, which contribute to rational thinking, rather than shame and anger, which are self-destructive and inappropriate emotions. Martin might also benefit from behavioral strategies, such as meeting with his supervisor, providing her additional information about his work, and planning an outing or creative project to help him focus on rewarding aspects of his life.

E, the fifth step, stands for *effective,* describing the desired outcome of the disputation. The outcome of REBT is likely to include both effective rational beliefs and an effective new philosophy.

Martin E: After disputing his beliefs, Martin developed more rational beliefs such as: "Although I am disappointed that my evaluation was average, it is not the end of the world. I will take steps to familiarize my supervisor with my work and hopefully obtain a more positive evaluation next time."

F, the last step in the process, represents the *new feelings and behaviors* that result from the effective rational beliefs. Again, interventions are used to promote change.

Martin F: Martin reported the following emotions and behaviors: "I do still feel disappointed with the evaluation, but I am no longer devastated or depressed. I am optimistic that my next evaluation will be better. I will meet with my supervisor and provide her with information so that is likely to happen."

Although the *ABCDEF* process may seem simple and straightforward, changing irrational beliefs to rational ones is a challenging and complex process. It requires effort and practice on the part of the client, as well as well-chosen and skillfully used interventions on the part of the clinician. The process can be complicated by the tendency of many people to have second-order disturbances: to feel bad about feeling bad. This creates several layers of irrational beliefs that need attention. In addition, people sometimes prefer their familiar discomfort to the risk of the unknown discomfort of change (Ellis & Dryden, 1997). They also may value the sympathy, attention, and other secondary gains they receive as a result of their problems.

Approaches to Disputing Irrational Beliefs

Even if people can intellectually grasp the *ABCDEF* model and the message that our beliefs, rather than activating events, are the primary source of our disturbance, people often have difficulty modifying their thoughts. Ellis (2003, p. 241) explains this by saying, ". . . they tend to *keep* holding these irrational beliefs and upsetting themselves by them, not because they held them in the past but because they are still actively, though unconsciously, reaffirming them and acting as if they are still valid." "Work and practice" are the ways to address these entrenched beliefs (Ellis, 2003, p. 242). Using a combination of cognitive, emotive, and behavioral interventions in a forceful and persistent way, REBT clinicians actively work with clients to identify their irrational beliefs, dispute them, and replace absolutist and irrational beliefs with flexible preferences.

Beal, Kopec, and DiGiuseppe (1996) described four *strategies of disputation:*

1. *Logical disputes* identify magical thinking and leaps in logic. Example: "Just because your sister seemed quiet and distracted when she visited you on her birthday, it doesn't logically follow that she is rejecting a close relationship with you."
2. *Empirical disputes* focus on an accumulation of evidence. Example: "You told me that after her visit, your sister called to tell you what a good time she had and suggested you visit her soon. You also told me that your sister is a quiet person. When we examine this evidence, there is little reason to believe that your sister is withdrawing from you. In fact, the evidence suggests just the opposite."
3. *Functional disputing strategies* focus on the practical consequences of people's beliefs, looking at whether their beliefs get them what they want. Example: "Believing that your sister is withdrawing leads you to withdraw from her and brings up memories of past wrongs you believe she has done to you. This belief isn't helping you rebuild your relationship with your sister, as you want to do."
4. *Rational alternative beliefs* offer a viable alternative belief. Example: "I know your sister is going through a difficult divorce. I wonder if another possible explanation for her quietness could be that she felt sad because she wasn't with her husband on her birthday."

Beal et al. (1996) also describe *four disputing styles:*

1. A *didactic style* is explanatory, educational, and efficient but involves giving information rather than using dialog. Example: "Marnie, I think you may be jumping to unwarranted conclusions about the significance of your sister's behavior. Keep in mind that she is still recovering from her divorce and that may be affecting her mood."
2. A *Socratic style* involves using questions to promote client reasoning. This is the most common REBT technique. Example: "What do you make of your sister's call and invitation to visit? Do those behaviors suggest she is withdrawing from your relationship?"
3. A *metaphorical style* uses analogies, especially from the client's own experience, to dispute beliefs. Example: "Your reaction to your sister's visit reminds me of the time you believed your supervisor was dissatisfied with your work because she did not offer you a ride to a conference. Then later you learned that she had to leave the meeting early because of a medical appointment and so could not give you a ride. I think that was the same month you received a top evaluation from your supervisor."
4. A *humorous style* disputes the belief in a lighthearted way. Clinicians should be sure never to make fun of people, only of their thoughts and behaviors. Example: "So let's see. . . . It sounds like you are equating the number of words a person speaks to you with how much they like you. How about for the next day you count how many words each person you encounter says to you. Then we can determine which one likes you best."

The four strategies of disputation and four disputing styles can be combined to form 16 different ways in which clinicians can approach the process of disputing beliefs. This great variety of strategies allows clinicians to adapt their approaches to disputing beliefs to the needs of a particular client as well as to the clinician's own personality.

Other Intervention Strategies

REBT incorporates a wide range of interventions and strategies to help people change. Although some of these strategies are strongly associated with REBT, most are similar to those used by other cognitive therapists. Ellis (1995a) believes that active, directive, and vigorous strategies lead to more rapid change. Strategies commonly used by clinicians practicing REBT can be categorized according to whether their focus is primarily cognitive, behavioral, or affective, although cognitive techniques are almost always combined with behavioral or emotive ones (Ellis, 1995a, 1996; Ellis & Dryden, 1997). The following list organizes many of these interventions according to whether they target thoughts, behaviors, or emotions:

Cognitive Strategies

- Detecting, evaluating, disputing, and modifying irrational cognitions
- Writing to express and explore thoughts and feelings
- Teaching the difference between rational and irrational beliefs
- Confronting irrational beliefs
- Identifying disadvantages of particular thoughts, actions, and feelings
- Socratic questioning
- Reducing thinking to absurdity
- Identifying and changing self-talk
- Reframing a situation by changing labels and language
- Promoting tolerance to counteract I-can't-stand-it-itis
- Listing ways to cope with the worst that might happen
- Rating experiences on a continuum to counteract awfulizing
- Generating alternatives
- Distracting oneself
- Using visualization and imagery
- Rating degree of conviction in beliefs and then rerating after change
- Formulating, writing down, and repeating rational coping statements
- Problem solving
- Decision making
- Hypnotherapy
- Being persistent; accepting no denials or excuses
- Projecting into the future to gain perspective
- Encouraging acceptance of oneself and others as fallible human beings
- Promoting a focus on happiness

Behavioral Strategies

- Using relaxation strategies
- Staying with uncomfortable activities until the discomfort diminishes
- Desensitizing or reducing anxiety via graduated exposure to feared situations
- Engaging in shame-attacking exercises (potentially embarrassing experiences such as singing loudly on a bus to insulate oneself against feelings of shame)
- Creating challenging situations and then coping with them
- Role playing

- Reversing roles; clinician takes on client's irrational beliefs, and client talks clinician out of those beliefs
- Using two chairs to represent a rational and an irrational belief, person enacts a dialog between the two beliefs, moving from one chair to another
- Acting as if a person is someone else; stepping out of character
- Reading self-help books and listening to tapes (especially those by Albert Ellis) intended to effect change
- Training in skills such as assertiveness and effective communication
- Taking reasonable risks
- Teaching REBT to others
- Rewarding or penalizing oneself
- Socializing
- Planning pleasurable activities and involvement in an absorbing interest or long-range pursuit

Affective Strategies

- Flooding or inundating a person with a particular feared or overvalued stimulus until it loses its power (this should be used cautiously!)
- Imagining the worst that might happen
- Providing emotionally powerful stories, metaphors, and parables
- Using emotionally charged language
- Persuading
- Eliciting inappropriate emotions via imagery and then practicing changing them
- Singing rational humorous songs such as Ellis's "I'm Just Wild About Worry" to elicit and change emotions
- Using humor
- Encouraging willpower and determination to change
- Promoting unconditional clinician- and self-acceptance

Strategies such as these may be incorporated into homework or used within sessions. As in cognitive therapy, use of task assignments is viewed as an essential part of treatment and is planned collaboratively. This promotes client responsibility, builds optimism, and facilitates progress.

Although the previous array of strategies is very comprehensive, certain strategies are discouraged in REBT (Ellis & Dryden, 1997):

- Strategies that create dependency (e.g., excessive therapist warmth, analysis of transference)
- Those that do not promote rational thinking, such as unrealistic positive thinking
- Those that are inefficient, such as lengthy exploration of a client's history and activating events
- Those that promote only immediate improvement, such as catharsis or encouragement to discharge anger
- Prolonged use of strategies that deflect people from working on their underlying difficulties, such as overreliance on distraction and relaxation
- Unscientific techniques, such as faith healing and mysticism
- Strategies that focus on changing activating events rather than beliefs
- Strategies that have not received adequate empirical support

APPLICATION OF RATIONAL EMOTIVE BEHAVIOR THERAPY

REBT is a well-established and widely used approach to treatment. It is appropriate for a broad range of people, problems, and settings, although not everyone is a suitable candidate.

Application to Groups, Families, and Psychoeducation

REBT is a flexible approach. It is appropriate for use in both group and family counseling as well as psychoeducation. Because it emphasizes teaching and is a fairly straightforward approach that can be readily learned and applied, REBT has been widely used for psychoeducation with client groups, as well as for "large groups, classroom courses, workshops and seminars, intensives, and other mass applications" (Dryden & Ellis, 2001, p. 339). Many video and audiotapes, pamphlets, self-help books, and other resources are available to facilitate instruction on REBT.

Ellis and Dryden (1997) described the use of rational emotive behavior couples therapy, focused on common irrational beliefs about relationships such as "My partner should know intuitively what I want" and "Romantic love will always endure." Treatment goals include modifying cognitions, resolving disturbances, and increasing relationship satisfaction.

REBT is particularly useful in helping family members realize they have little power to change others but need to take responsibility for themselves. It is recommended for people dealing with a severely disturbed family member; treatment encourages the family to accept that person as a fallible human being and enables them to increase happiness in the family.

REBT also is well-suited for group counseling, offering participants an opportunity to observe and try out behaviors and to share feedback and reactions. Group members are encouraged to take responsibility for helping each other as well as themselves. Ellis and Dryden (1997) recommend a group of 8–10 participants, meeting weekly for 2¼ hours for at least six months. However, groups as large as 20 or 30 people also can be successful. People who are reasonably well functioning can begin treatment in a group setting, whereas 5–15 sessions of individual REBT are recommended first for people who are shy or have other significant interpersonal difficulties. REBT also is used for time-limited groups focusing on the development of communication and other specific skills.

Marathon group REBT sessions of 9 or more hours, often with a 4-hour follow-up in 6–10 weeks, have also been conducted (Ellis & Dryden, 1997). These groups make extensive use of experiential exercises to promote rapid self-disclosure and accompanying changes in cognitions, behaviors, and emotions.

For many years, Ellis conducted Friday-evening demonstrations of his work at his Institute in New York City. Sometimes attended by more than 200 people, these presentations contributed to the popularity of REBT.

Application to Diagnostic Groups

REBT is appropriate for treatment of many mild to moderately severe mental disorders, including depressive disorders, anxiety disorders, and adjustment disorders. In addition, symptoms that often respond well to REBT include anger and aggression, obsessiveness, sexual difficulties, unassertiveness, withdrawal, and low frustration tolerance (Weinrach & Ellis, 1995). The literature suggests that REBT also can be effective with problems of drug and alcohol misuse. In fact, a self-help group called SMART (Self-Management and Recovery Training), based on REBT, is available, primarily for people with difficulties related to substance use. In addition, elegant REBT seems likely to help people diagnosed with the milder personality disorders (e.g., avoidant and dependent personality disorders).

Despite its broad application, REBT, with its forceful and directive nature and its emphasis on client responsibility, should be avoided or used with extreme care in treatment of people with some mental disorders. REBT does not seem appropriate for people with psychotic disorders, dangerous impulse control disorders, or other severe mental disorders or for people who are highly suicidal or very fragile. In addition, REBT should be used with great caution, if at all, for people who have had traumatic childhood experiences (Ellis & Dryden, 1997). Misapplication of REBT may lead inexperienced clinicians to ask those who have survived traumas whether their experiences were "really so awful" or whether they "really can't stand the feelings and flashbacks." Questions such as these may re-traumatize or otherwise harm such clients. People who are unwilling to complete homework, manifest narcissistic or histrionic symptoms or rebellious behavior, have severe intellectual limitations, or have a very low frustration tolerance also do not seem to be good candidates for REBT. However, careful integration of some of the concepts and strategies of REBT with those of other treatment approaches may extend the application of REBT to some of the severe mental disorders. Ellis's recent recognition of the contributions of medication to treatment also broadens the use of REBT (Ellis, 2003).

Application to Multicultural Groups

Researchers and clinicians interested in REBT lately have paid considerable attention to the multicultural applications of this approach. Theory as well as empirical studies suggest that REBT can be used with a diverse client population.

Janet Wolfe (1995), Albert Ellis's partner, has found REBT useful in counseling women. She conducted a 20-year review of REBT-based women's groups and concluded that REBT "helps women deal with the shoulds, self-rating, and love-slobbism inherent in female sex role messages" and enables them to "take steps to increase their social, economic, and political power" (pp. 161–162). She found that REBT couples therapy could help men as well as women negotiate new gender roles.

Ellis's use of REBT to address his reactions to his own disabilities, as well as the efforts of REBT to help people stop dwelling on their difficulties and make the most of their strengths, suggest that this approach is well suited to treatment of people with disabilities (Ellis, 1997). Its emphasis on unconditional self-acceptance also seems useful with this population.

REBT has been used successfully with children and adolescents as well as adults for both therapeutic and educational purposes (Ellis, 2003). Manuals are available for using REBT preventively with young people in school settings and for teaching their parents how to incorporate the principles of REBT into their interactions with their children (Vernon, 1989a, 1989b). Stories, fables, plays, films, and other resources have been developed to teach the elements of REBT in simplified ways. These resources probably also can be used with people who have mild impairment in intelligence.

Ellis and his associates have begun to research the use of REBT with people from various cultures and for people with medical concerns. One notable study by Lega and Ellis (2001) reports the outcome of studies of irrational beliefs in five countries, with college students and their parents, with men and women, and with people coping with medical conditions. The authors conclude that, although irrational beliefs, *musts,* and demandingness appeared in all groups, the groups manifested significant differences in the content, process, and degree of their irrational beliefs and the impact of REBT.

Ellis and other proponents of REBT acknowledge the importance of the social system and people's cultural backgrounds but have not written much about how to adapt this approach to the needs of a culturally diverse client group (Weinrach, 1996). Clinicians should exercise care in using REBT with people from non-western backgrounds, especially those whose cultures stress interdependence, privacy, and respect; those who may not have the background needed to appreciate the humor and linguistic subtleties of REBT; and those whose strong or mystical spiritual beliefs may conflict with REBT's pragmatic stance. Nielsen and Ellis (1994) caution clinicians not to attack beliefs that are strongly anchored in people's ethnic, religious, and cultural backgrounds unless they are clearly self-defeating. Ellis and Nielsen also state that, of course, people should never be humiliated or demeaned during treatment.

Just as clinicians vary in their comfort with the active and directive stance of REBT, so do clients vary in their reactions. People who are highly motivated, fairly resilient, pragmatic, logical, and tough-minded are most likely to enjoy this energetic and interactive approach and appreciate the characteristic directness and humor of the REBT clinician. Garfield (1995) suggested that REBT is particularly likely to be well received by people who are externally oriented, intelligent, well-educated, and articulate. Solomon and Haaga (1995) also viewed this approach as successful with people who intellectualize.

CURRENT USE

Weinrach (1995, 1996), a leading spokesperson for REBT, suggested that this approach has not received the professional acceptance that it deserves. In part, he attributed this to misconceptions that REBT ignores emotions, advocates harsh confrontation, lacks depth, overemphasizes hedonism, and neglects rapport in the therapeutic relationship. Some of these misconceptions can be explained by REBT's strong association with the personality of Albert Ellis. While Ellis's style initially contributed to REBT's popularity, that association now may deter some from practicing or seeking treatment via REBT. This does a disservice to REBT, which has many strengths and can be adapted to both the style of the clinician and the needs of the client.

The misconceptions about REBT have become particularly invalid over the past decade, as Ellis and his associates have moved rapidly toward making REBT more flexible and inclusive. Examples of this include Ellis's recognition of the benefits of medication, the religion-sensitive application of REBT, the increased attention REBT pays to understanding people's backgrounds, and the development of elegant REBT.

EVALUATION OF REBT

Like other cognitive approaches to treatment, REBT has many strengths and has proven its value through empirical and theoretical research. Of course, it also has limitations.

Limitations

Despite the increasing practice of clinicians studying REBT via empirical research, more research is needed in particular areas. The use of REBT with specific diagnostic groups and with people from diverse cultural, religious, and ethnic backgrounds needs more study. Additional tools to facilitate analysis and modification of cognitions would be useful (Bernard, 1995). Ziegler (1999, p. 19) and others have emphasized the need for REBT to have "a more comprehensive and detailed theory of personality at its base". REBT sometimes pays too little attention to clients' history and moves too rapidly toward promoting change; clinicians should be sure to allow adequate time to assess and understand people before moving forward.

Neenan and Dryden (1996) identified the following six common errors or pitfalls for clinicians who practice REBT:

1. Skimming the surface and moving too quickly to dispute beliefs
2. Focusing on beliefs other than those held by the client
3. Failing to obtain enough information about the client's emotions
4. Not paying attention to clues that provide important information
5. Automatically moving through the *ABCDEF* process without sufficiently addressing the needs of a particular person
6. Not giving enough depth to each part of the process, especially exploration of the activating event and the beliefs

The strong personality of Albert Ellis might be considered both a limitation and a strength of REBT. Ellis, more than anyone, has created awareness of the power and effectiveness of cognitive treatment approaches. At the same time, Ellis can be abrasive and is not always an appealing spokesperson for REBT. In addition, clinicians who mistakenly view it as desirable to emulate Ellis's style run the risk of harming their clients and violating their rights and individuality. REBT probably is best served, at present, by honoring Ellis for his important contributions but separating the man from the theory.

Strengths and Contributions

REBT has many strengths. An efficient and positive approach, it can lead to rapid reduction in symptoms as well as philosophical change. It teaches and empowers people to help themselves after treatment has ended. Its theory is relatively straightforward and clear. Because it draws on a broad range of interventions, REBT can be adapted to a wide variety of people and problems and used for prevention and psychoeducation as well as treatment.

REBT is compatible with and can be integrated into many other treatment approaches, although it seems most easily combined with existential and humanistic approaches. The importance that clinicians practicing REBT place on the intrinsic value of each individual is similar to Rogers's unconditional positive regard. The importance they attribute to each person's finding a personally meaningful and rewarding direction is consistent with existential therapy. A phenomenological approach, REBT maintains that people's views of reality are the source of their disturbance; this is compatible with narrative therapy and constructivism. Of course, great overlap exists between Beck's cognitive therapy and Ellis's REBT. However, Ellis has been critical of transpersonal approaches to treatment, viewing them as antihumanist because of their mystical and unscientific aspects (Ellis, 1992).

Many inventories have grown out of REBT, including the Attitudes and Beliefs Inventory and the Jones Irrational Beliefs Test. Most help identify irrational beliefs. According to Dryden and Ellis (2001, p. 337), "The tests have been shown to distinguish reliably between various kinds of disturbed individuals and control groups."

Although much of the writing on REBT is theoretical and clinical, many empirical studies of its impact have been conducted. DiGiuseppe (1996) reported that more than 240 studies of REBT were conducted before 1995, and many have been conducted since. (Of course, many more studies have been conducted on cognitive therapy that has much in common with REBT.) A review of 31 outcome studies using controls found significant improvement immediately after treatment with REBT compared to no treatment (Solomon & Haaga, 1995). These conclusions are typical of research on the impact of REBT. Lyons and Woods (1991) concluded, "The results demonstrated that [REBT] is an effective form of therapy. The efficacy was most clearly demonstrated when [REBT] was compared to baseline and other forms of controls. The differences among comparisons of [REBT] to CBM (Cognitive Behavior Modification) and Behavior Therapy were not significant" (pp. 367–368). Although REBT cannot be viewed as superior to other cognitive and behavioral approaches to treatment, it has clearly demonstrated its effectiveness.

Probably REBT's most important contribution is raising awareness of the importance of thinking in people's lives and the need to attend to and change thinking in treatment. Information on the differences between rational and irrational thinking, the *ABCDEF* model, and the many interventions associated with REBT have shaped psychotherapy and counseling, leading to the development of Beck's cognitive therapy as well as other approaches that focus on cognitions.

SMART Recovery, a self-help group grounded in REBT for people with substance use problems, is another outgrowth of this theory. An alternative to Alcoholics Anonymous (AA) and other 12-step programs, SMART Recovery diverges from AA in its belief that people are not always in the process of recovering but can actually recover from drug and alcohol problems. In addition, unlike AA, which emphasizes the importance of a higher power, SMART Recovery focuses on personal responsibility for effecting change.

In 1998, nine members of REBT's International Training Standards and Review Committee made predictions about REBT's future 25–50 years after Albert Ellis's death. (He was 85 years old at the time of the meeting.) Most believed that REBT would continue to have a great impact. However, several, including Wolfe and Weinrach, whose writings we have discussed in this chapter, anticipated that REBT would eventually become integrated into a more general theory of cognitive-behavioral therapy.

Whether or not this integration occurs, REBT is currently a widely used and important treatment approach. REBT centers are located in 10 countries throughout the world (Ellis & Dryden, 1997); and Albert Ellis continues to practice, write, and spearhead its development.

SKILL DEVELOPMENT: RATIONAL EMOTIVE IMAGERY

Ellis and Maultsby developed the technique of rational emotive imagery (REI) to help people practice changing their unhealthy and inappropriate negative emotions into healthy and appropriate ones (Ellis & Dryden, 1997). Clinicians teach clients the steps in this exercise during a session in which they can learn and practice REI. Then clinicians encourage clients to spend at least 10 minutes a day practicing REI on their own.

REI includes the following steps (Thompson, 1996):

1. *Visualize an unpleasant activating event.* "Picture yourself or fantasize, as vividly and intensely as you can, the details of some unpleasant activating experience (A) that has happened to you or will likely occur in the future" (Thompson, 1996, p. 115).

Example

"I met a man over the Internet; Gary was his name. We exchanged e-mails and IMs for a month and then decided to meet. We agreed that, no matter what, we would have a pleasant time—just have dinner together and get better acquainted. I was very apprehensive. I hadn't had a date in 12 years, since I married my ex-husband. I can visualize myself standing in front of the museum, waiting for Gary to show up. I was cold but I didn't want to put my coat on because I wanted him to see my pretty dress. I think being anxious made me feel even colder. So there I was, shivering, feeling like I could hardly breathe. Then this man walks by real close to me, looks me up and down, and keeps walking. I knew it was Gary because he told me what he looked like."

2. *Experience the unhealthy negative emotions.* As you vividly imagine the experience, let yourself feel any strong emotions that come up for you—the *C,* or emotional consequence of this experience. Really feel those feelings, get in touch with them, and for a few minutes fully experience them. Don't try to avoid the feelings or change them; just face them and feel them.

Example:

"I felt sick to my stomach. I felt disgusted with myself. I just wanted to disappear into a hole in the ground. I felt so repulsive. I felt overwhelming shame. And then I felt rage at Gary. How could he have made me feel so bad?"

3. *Changing the emotions.* After you have allowed yourself to feel these disturbing emotions for a few minutes, push yourself to change those feelings so that you feel different inside. Change them so that instead of feeling unhealthy and inappropriate emotions such as rage, shame, and depression, you feel emotions such as disappointment or annoyance. You can do this. Keep pushing yourself and working at it until you start to experience a shift in your feelings, a new emotional consequence.

Example:

"This is hard, but I'm sort of doing it. I do feel annoyed; I got this new dress and took time off work so I could get ready, and then this guy doesn't even speak to me. I feel disappointed too. He seemed so nice over the Internet. I thought maybe this would turn into a special relationship."

4. *Examine the process.* You are succeeding in changing your emotions from the self-destructive ones of shame and rage to new and appropriate feelings of disappointment and annoyance. When we look at how you made that happen, we will see that you have changed your belief system (*B*), which mediates between the activating event (*A*) and the emotional consequence (*C*). Let's identify the old and the new beliefs.

Example:

"At first I was thinking, 'You really are a hopeless failure. It's unbearable that I was stood up like that—so humiliating.' And I felt so angry with Gary. We had an understanding, and he should not have treated me so badly. But then I started to think about it differently. Nobody but me knew what was going on. It wasn't a public humiliation. And I sure learned something about Gary fast. It's a good thing I didn't really get interested in him and then discover what a rat he was. I do still feel annoyed that I wasted all that time and effort, and I'm disappointed that things didn't work out. But I guess I just got carried away with my romantic fantasies. I think I'll find other ways to meet people besides the Internet."

5. *Repetition and practice.* Keep repeating the process. Imagine the scene, bring up the disturbing feelings, and then deliberately push yourself to change your feelings so that you feel displeased and disappointed but not disturbed. I encourage you to practice this exercise at least 10 minutes a day until you can easily bring up the activating event and the disturbing feelings and then, just as easily, change those into feelings that are not harmful to you.

6. *Reinforcing the goal.* It may take a few weeks, but before too long you will find that, when you bring up the activating event, you will automatically and easily experience the feelings of displeasure and disappointment rather than rage and shame.

7. *Generalization of skills.* Then you can use this same technique for other situations. If you find that an activating event brings up strong and disturbing emotions, imagine the event and then push yourself to change those feelings to ones that reflect displeasure rather than disturbance. Once you have done this, identify both the disturbing irrational belief and the rational belief that enabled you to change your emotions.

CASE ILLUSTRATION

In this case illustration, the clinician uses the *ABCDEF* model with Ava who expresses upsetting feelings about an interaction she recently had with her parents.

Clinician: Ava, tell me about the situation or activating event [A] that led you to feel so disturbed.

Ava: This awful thing happened to me at school. I had P.E. class, and I was in such a hurry to get dressed and catch the bus that I forgot to zip up my skirt. I went out in the hall like that! Some kids were looking at me, but I did not know what was wrong. One boy started to sing, "Zip-a-dee-do-da." Then I got it. I was so ashamed. All I wanted to do was go home and tell my mother. But when I got home, she was on the phone with my grandmother and couldn't be bothered with me. "I'm busy now," she said. "Go out and play with your friends." That was the last thing I wanted to do. So I took the dog and went up to my room. I wanted to die so that I wouldn't ever have to go back to school.

Clinician: Tell me some more about the feelings [emotional consequences/C] you had when all this happened.

Ava: Well, I told you I felt ashamed, like I was the big joke of the school. I bet all the kids will be talking about me tomorrow. It was so awful! And then when I got home, even my mother didn't care. I felt horrible, like nobody loved me, like I was just a hopeless mess.

Clinician: You had some strong negative emotions, feeling ashamed and rejected and unlovable, that were really disturbing you. Ava, remember we talked about irrational beliefs last week. Let's take out that list I showed you of common irrational beliefs [B] and figure out if any of them reflect the thoughts you had in reaction to this incident.

Ava: I certainly had this thought: "I am a bad or worthless person when I act weakly or stupidly." And then when my mom was too busy to talk to me, I thought this one: "I need to be loved by someone who matters to me a lot," and this one: "I am a bad, unlovable person if I get rejected." I thought this one too: "It's awful or horrible when major things don't go my way." I also thought, "My mom doesn't really love or care about me."

Clinician: Many of the thoughts on the list really hit home for you. It seems like you had two groups of thoughts: one about not being loved by your mother and another about feeling worthless and devastated when the kids teased you.

Ava: Yes, that's right.

Clinician: Let's start with the first group, thoughts about your mom not loving you and your feeling unlovable. Have there been other times when you needed to talk to your mom and she *was* there for you?

Ava: Yes, lots of times.

Clinician: Then just because your mom was in a phone conversation and couldn't talk to you this one time, does it logically follow that she doesn't love you [logical dispute]?

Ava: She should have known I really needed to talk to her!

Clinician: How should she have known that [empirical dispute]?

Ava: I don't know. I guess I didn't really tell her that.

Clinician: Then does it logically follow that if she didn't want to talk to you at that time, that she doesn't love you?

Ava: No, I know she loves me. I was just disappointed that she wasn't there for me. It made me *feel* like she didn't love me.

Clinician: Does the thought that she doesn't love you help you or hurt you [functional dispute]?

Ava: Well, it's making me feel pretty bad, and it kept me from talking to her when she finally got off the phone, so I guess it's hurting me.

Clinician: Could there be other explanations for her not wanting to talk to you at that time [rational alternative]?

Ava: Yes, she was on the phone with her mother. It sounded like Grandma's husband had wrecked her car. I guess my mom needed to help her.

Clinician: So can you tell me a thought that seems to be a more accurate reflection of your interaction with your mother?

Ava: Yes. My mom loves me, but I can't expect her to read my mind or be there for me every minute. She does her best to help me when I'm upset, but Grandma needed her then [effective rational belief].

Clinician: And how are you feeling now?

Ava: I still feel disappointed that my mom was on the phone when I needed to talk to her. I felt so hurt that I never did tell her what happened.

Clinician: What can you do about that now?

Ava: I guess I could go home and tell her about it. I think that would help me to feel better [new feelings and behaviors].

This process helped Ava change her beliefs about the activating events, resulting in changes in her feelings and behaviors. Her level of disturbance and the absolute nature of her thoughts both have changed, and she is no longer devastated by her interaction with her mother. This allows her to take constructive action to communicate her concerns to her mother. Ava's second group of irrational thoughts are addressed in the exercises.

EXERCISES

Large-Group Exercises

1. Review Ava's second group of irrational beliefs, including "I am a bad or worthless person when I act weakly and stupidly" and "It's awful or horrible when things don't go my way." Use the four strategies (logical, empirical, and functional disputes and rational alternative) to dispute her beliefs. Then formulate effective rational beliefs that might replace Ava's irrational ones and identify new feelings and behaviors that are likely to result from her new beliefs. Suggest homework that Ava might do to help reinforce these positive changes.

2. Ellis views REBT as incompatible with transpersonal therapy (discussed in chapter 13). Based on what you have learned about both approaches, discuss their differences and similarities and whether the two really do conflict. Can you think of ways to resolve that conflict and integrate the two approaches?

3. Considerable overlap exists between REBT and Beck's version of cognitive therapy. Discuss the similarities and differences between those two approaches. Assess whether the two are distinct theories or whether the differences are minor and semantic.

4. Drawing on your knowledge of diverse groups, discuss which cultural groups are likely to be favorably disposed to REBT and which are likely to be uncomfortable receiving treatment via this approach. What sort of screening would you do to determine people's suitability for treatment with REBT?

Small-Group Exercises

1. Form into your groups of four people in two dyads. If possible, each participant should have an opportunity to assume both the role of the clinician and the role of the client. Each dyad should engage in a role play in which the client begins by describing a disturbing experience. The clinician should then follow the *ABCDEF* model in counseling the client. Allow approximately 15 minutes for each role play, followed by 5–10 minutes of feedback from the observing dyad. Feedback should focus on the use of the *ABCDEF* format as well as the nature of the therapeutic alliance.
2. Using dyads as described in Exercise 1, engage in role plays using rational emotive imagery (illustrated in the Skill Development section) to practice changing emotions.

Individual Exercises

1. Write briefly in your journal about a time during the past week when you felt very upset or disturbed. Identify and dispute your irrational thoughts using the *ABCDEF* format. Write your responses to each step in the process.
2. Identify a personal goal you have for yourself this week. Drawing on the strategies used in REBT, assign yourself two or three homework tasks to help you reach your goal.

SUMMARY

Rational emotive behavior therapy, formerly known as rational emotive therapy, was developed by Albert Ellis about 50 years ago. REBT takes the position that people disturb themselves by their irrational beliefs and that changing those beliefs to rational ones will reduce people's levels of disturbance and lead to positive changes in emotions and behaviors. General REBT emphasizes problem solving, while elegant or preferential REBT goes beyond problem solving and aims toward deep philosophical change. Sessions typically focus on a six-step process to modify cognitions: identifying the activating event (*A*), identifying irrational beliefs (*B*), looking at the negative consequences (*C*) of those beliefs, disputing (*D*) the beliefs, replacing them with effective rational beliefs (*E*), leading to changes in feelings (*F*) and behaviors. Clinicians practicing REBT typically adopt an active, directive, and vigorous style and make use of a broad range of strategies to effect rapid change.

RECOMMENDED READINGS

Bernard, M. E. (1995). It's prime time for rational emotive behavior therapy: Current theory and practice, research, recommendations, and predictions. *Journal of Rational-Emotive & Cognitive-Behavior Therapy, 13,* 9–27.

Ellis, A. (1995). *Better, deeper, and more enduring brief therapy.* New York: Brunner/Mazel.

Ellis, A. (2001). *Overcoming destructive beliefs, feelings, and behaviors: New directions for rational emotive behavior therapy.* Amherst, MA: Prometheus Books.

Ellis, A. (2003). Early theories and practices of rational emotive behavior therapy and how they have been augmented and revised during the last three decades. *Journal of Rational-Emotive & Cognitive-Behavior Therapy, 21,* 219–243.

Ellis, A., & Dryden, W. (1997). *The practice of rational emotive behavior therapy* (2nd ed.). New York: Springer.

ADDITIONAL SOURCES OF INFORMATION

www.rebt.org—Website of The Albert Ellis Institute, 45 East 65th Street, New York, New York 10021-6593, (212) 535-0822 or (800) 323-4738.

Information on REBT, training on this approach, Friday evening workshops, as well as relevant publications and other resources can be obtained here.

www.rational.org.nz—This is the website for the New Zealand Centre for Rational Emotive Behaviour Therapy. It offers articles, resources, self-help information, training opportunities, and links to many REBT sites around the world.

CHAPTER 17

Emerging Approaches Emphasizing Thoughts

Clinical experience and research have led to the appreciation of the importance of thinking in human development and functioning. This chapter focuses primarily on three innovative treatment approaches emphasizing thoughts: eye movement desensitization and reprocessing (EMDR), neuro-linguistic programming (NLP), and thought field therapy (TFT). Other approaches also will be mentioned briefly. With the exception of EMDR, these have not yet, and may never, become fully developed treatment systems. However, they go beyond techniques and reflect new perspectives and strategies.

The current status of the treatment approaches discussed in this chapter vary considerably. Although attention to thought field therapy (TFT) has increased in recent years, that approach has not yet been well described or substantiated in the literature. Neuro-linguistic programming (NLP) has been used for many years and continues to have its advocates; however, it, too, has not yet been well supported by research. Eye movement desensitization and reprocessing (EMDR) is a relatively recent addition; while controversial, it has received empirical support and has become an important clinical tool. These approaches all require specialized training that goes beyond the scope of this book. Thus, descriptions are relatively brief in comparison to descriptions of the more established treatment approaches presented in this book. The goal of this chapter is to introduce readers to some ground-breaking approaches and excite interest and curiosity, with the hope of prompting readers to investigate and perhaps study these innovative approaches further.

EYE MOVEMENT DESENSITIZATION AND REPROCESSING

Eye movement desensitization and reprocessing (EMDR) has received considerable attention in recent years. EMDR uses directed bilateral eye movements, tones, and taps to accelerate people's processing of negative information and enable them to deal with that information in new ways that promote their emotional health.

The Development of EMDR

EMDR was discovered in 1987 by Francine Shapiro (1995), a senior research fellow at the Mental Research Institute in Palo Alto, California. As she was walking in the park, Shapiro noticed that her disturbing thoughts became less upsetting. She attributed this to her spontaneous eye movements and began to investigate whether those movements could help people process troubling memories and thoughts more effectively.

Shapiro originally called her approach *eye movement desensitization* (EMD) and focused her attention on people who had traumatic experiences. Her first study (Shapiro, 1989) included a group of 22 people between the ages of 11 and 53, all of whom had traumatic memories such as rape, molestation, and war experiences, as well as pronounced symptoms such as flashbacks, sleep disturbances, and relationship difficulties that had lasted at least 1 year. All were treated with EMD. Following procedural guidelines, people focused on their upsetting memories and moved their eyes rapidly back and forth 25–30 times, following the movements of the clinician's hand. This series of movements was repeated again and again over a 15–90 minute session, while brief dialogue between client and clinician between each series enabled the clinician to monitor clients' progress and guide their attention. Outcome measures indicated that, after only a single session of treatment, people reported less anxiety, more positive beliefs about themselves, and a reduction in symptoms.

Since that time, EMDR, as it was renamed in 1990, has been greatly refined and its use expanded. Extensive research has led to changes in the timing and administration of the procedure, protocols for treating a variety of symptoms and mental disorders, additional strategies that are integrated into the basic protocols, and the development of structured formats for evaluation of progress (Shapiro, 2001). In addition, EMDR has demonstrated effectiveness not just for treatment of posttraumatic stress disorder but for a wide range of disorders and concerns. Other bidirectional techniques, including tones in alternate ears, lights flashing on alternating sides of a bar, and tapping on alternating hands, have been found as effective as the original eye movements.

Important Theoretical Concepts

EMDR holds the optimistic view that people have an innate system that enables them to process information to a healthy resolution. However, sometimes this system becomes unbalanced or blocked, and negative memories are held in the nervous system in harmful ways. EMDR is a complex approach that uses bidirectional stimulation and other interventions to facilitate processing of troubling memories, transformation and integration of the negative emotions linked to the memories, and the modification of self-destructive cognitions. Learning, as well as new positive cognitions and behaviors, result from this process and are available for future use (Shapiro, 1995).

The exact mechanism that underlies the impact of bilateral stimulation is unclear. The bidirectional eye movements have been compared to rapid eye movements during sleep as well as to the rhythmical eye movements that often accompany periods of deep concentration and problem solving (Shapiro & Forrest, 1997). In all of these, eye movements seem to be linked to cognitive processing and integration of the functioning of the two hemispheres of the brain. By artificially producing bilateral stimulation and linking that to disturbing memories, EMDR may, in effect, speed up the derailed information-processing system and allow a memory to progress rapidly and positively through the neural networks.

EMDR is based on an information-processing model and can be a powerful element in a treatment plan. It is generally integrated with and draws on a wide range of approaches to treatment. EMDR has its roots in cognitive therapy with its stress on information processing and modification of beliefs. It encompasses principles of desensitization, in which strong negative reactions to certain stimuli or recollections gradually diminish via exposure to those stimuli or recollections, in a controlled and supportive context. In its use of desensitization, EMDR reflects the constructs of behaviorism and classical conditioning. In addition, EMDR includes psychodynamic strategies including free association and catharsis. Shapiro (1995) views EMDR as also being person-centered because, during treatment, the clinician assumes a relatively neutral role and, other than directing the bilateral stimulation, lets the client guide the process.

Strategies of EMDR

Developing client-clinician rapport and a collaborative, trusting, and empowering treatment alliance is essential in EMDR. The directed eye movements seem strange, questionable, and even threatening to some clients. Their willingness to participate in this treatment and their ability to benefit from EMDR is, in large measure, connected to the trust they have in their clinicians. In addition, EMDR can lead troubling and traumatic memories to surface, risking the retraumatization of people in treatment. Strong clinical skills as well as a positive therapeutic alliance are needed to address these possibilities.

The Eight Phases of EMDR   The process of EMDR includes eight phases (Dworkin, 2003; Shapiro, 2001):

1. *Establishing the foundation.* From the outset, clinicians promote development of rapport, creating a supportive environment and making sure that the client is a suitable candidate for EMDR. Clinicians take a client history, explore presenting problems and symptoms as well as coping skills, and assess client's readiness and suitability for treatment. EMDR is not appropriate for everyone; use of this approach can be dangerous and harmful to people who are highly dissociative, in poor contact with reality, suicidal, violent, very fragile, or in crisis.

2. *Client preparation.* The clinician explains the nature, theory, and goals of EMDR to the client. Often, all three approaches to bilateral stimulation (eye movements, alternating sounds, and tapping) are demonstrated briefly and the client selects one or more of

these for use in treatment. Clients learn to use a "stop" hand signal and create an image of a safe place for use as resources if their treatment becomes too disturbing. Clients' expectations and fears are elicited and addressed if needed.

3. *Assessment.* The clinician obtains the following information from the client in preparation for treatment:
   - Identification of a presenting issue or troubling memory
   - A visual image or picture that represents the worst part of the memory or issue
   - A negative cognition or self-statement that the client currently holds about the self that goes along with the picture and incident. These are similar to the irrational beliefs addressed in rational emotive behavior therapy such as "I cannot stand it," "I am stupid," "I am not lovable," and "I am a bad person"
   - A positive cognition or self-statement that captures what the person would like to believe about the self when the picture or incident is recalled (e.g., "I can handle it," "I deserve love," and "I am a good person")
   - Rating of the validity of the positive cognition (VoC), reflecting how true that statement feels to the person, on a 1–7 scale, with 1 representing completely untrue and 7 completely true
   - The person's rating of his or her level of disturbance on a 0–10 subjective units of distress (SUDS) scale, with 0 reflecting no disturbance and 10 the highest disturbance
   - Emotions associated with the incident or picture
   - The location in the body of these emotions and sensations

4. *Desensitization.* The client brings up the disturbing picture while many sets of directed eye movements or other bidirectional stimuli help the person process the troubling issue or recollection. The clinician checks in with the client briefly between sets of about 30 movements to determine what is coming up for the person, as well as the person's SUDS level. The clinician is reinforcing, caring, and encouraging during this phase but maintains a detached stance, usually intervening little during desensitization so that the client's own brain can produce the associations necessary for resolution. Desensitization may be accomplished in one session, but usually extends over a series of sessions.

5. *Installation.* When the SUDS rating is low (ideally 0 or 1) and the validity rating of the positive cognition is high (ideally 6 or 7), the installation phase is used to reinforce the results. (If the bilateral stimulation needs to be stopped, due to time or other factors, before these ideal levels are reached, relaxation and other procedures are used to tide the person over until the next session.) During the installation, the positive cognition is linked to the initial memory during additional bilateral stimulation.

6. *Body scan.* The person scans his or her body, while keeping in mind the target memory and the positive cognition. Any residual discomfort that may need to be reprocessed is identified and addressed via bilateral stimulation.

7. *Closure.* Debriefing is the focus of this phase, with client and clinician reviewing and processing the experience. Exercises such as visualization of a healing light stream may be used to promote a state of equilibrium in the client. Clinicians also might teach self-control techniques to empower clients and help them maintain their positive feelings and perceptions. Clinicians also encourage clients to keep a log of any relevant memories, thoughts, or experiences that arise between sessions.

8. *Reevaluation.* Reevaluation occurs at the beginning of each subsequent session. The client's log, as well as any changes associated with the EMDR treatment, is processed. The reevaluation phase helps clinicians determine whether they should further address the previous target memory or issue, progress to additional EMDR protocols, use other procedures, or move toward closure.

The Cognitive Interweave   The cognitive interweave is one of the most powerful techniques used in EMDR to facilitate information processing and reinforce new learning. It helps people to process information differently and to see new possibilities and viewpoints. The cognitive interweave is a clinician statement made between sets of bilateral stimulation. It directs clients' attention in ways that facilitate information processing and desensitization and accelerate treatment. It is intended to "weave together the appropriate neural networks and associations" (Shapiro, 1995, p. 244). Cognitive interweaves are most often used when the bilateral stimulation alone does not "shift the client's brain into a more functional way of processing dysfunctionally stored information" (Dworkin, 2003, p. 178). The following dialogs present examples of cognitive interweaves:

Example 1: A man who was sexually abused as a young boy had the negative cognition "I'm spoiled goods." To help increase the validity of his positive cognition ("I'm okay as I am"), the clinician suggested he imagine that his son had been abused at that same age and to consider whether he would view the son as spoiled goods (Shapiro, 1994, p. 22).

Example 2: A young woman with an eating disorder was having difficulty believing that she could overcome her disorder. During EMDR, she spoke of how well her recently deceased grandmother had known her and the faith her grandmother had in her. To increase the validity of the woman's belief in her positive cognition ("I am a worthwhile person and can make healthy choices"), the clinician asked, "What would your grandmother who knew you so well have to say about you and your ability to make better choices for yourself?"

The Importance of Training   Although this process may seem simple, EMDR is a complex and powerful tool. No clinician should use it without adequate training. The EMDR Institute offers a basic two-part training. Each training program is about 20 hours long and includes lectures, demonstrations, and supervised practice. Additional training and supervision is required for certification in EMDR.

Evaluation and Application

Francine Shapiro, who continues to spearhead the development of EMDR, strongly encourages research on EMDR. Consequently, many relevant empirical studies have been done. EMDR has an impressive success record. Its effectiveness as part of treatment for people with posttraumatic stress disorder (PTSD) is well established (Wilson, Becker, & Tinker, 1995). A meta-analysis of all psychological and drug treatments for PTSD found that EMDR was not only effective in treating this disorder but was more efficient than other treatments (Van Etten & Taylor, 1998). Division 12 (Clinical Psychology) of the American Psychological Association recently added EMDR to a list of empirically supported treatments for PTSD (Chambless et al., 1998), and the International Society for Traumatic Stress Studies also declared it effective for treating PTSD (Foa, Keane, &

Friedman, 2000). In addition, EMDR shows promise in the treatment of many other disorders, including depression, anxiety, substance use, sexual dysfunction, somatoform disorder, panic disorder, and specific phobias (Davidson & Parker, 2001; Manfield, 1998). It also is used to help people deal with their emotional reactions to life-threatening illnesses such as cancer and AIDS (Shapiro & Forrest, 1997). EMDR has been used successfully with children as well as adults (Tinker & Wilson, 1999) and may well be effective in enhancing performance and improving overall functioning in emotionally healthy people.

At the same time, some question the efficacy of EMDR's procedures while others speculate that EMDR may not be more effective than standard exposure therapy (Taylor et al., 2003). One important question is whether the bilateral stimulation is a necessary ingredient of treatment. Davidson and Parker (2001, p. 310), for example, while recognizing the effectiveness of EMDR, found "no significant incremental benefit because of eye movements" or other alternating movements.

Whether EMDR is as powerful as its proponents believe and whether bilateral stimulation is needed are, as yet, unanswered questions. Nevertheless, the effectiveness of EMDR has been clearly established through extensive empirical research and carefully designed meta-analyses, although clinicians should not think that bilateral stimulation alone is sufficient for change. Instead, we need to recognize that therapist skill, a sound and empathic therapeutic alliance, helpful use of cognitive interweaves, and wise integration of EMDR into other therapeutic approaches are essential to its effective use (Dworkin, 2003; Shapiro, 2002; Taylor et al., 2003).

As Dworkin concluded (2003, p. 172), "The time is right for mental health professionals to end the bitter feuding that has characterized some of the discourse surrounding EMDR . . . and to continue to develop and improve on new technologies that synthesize useful ideas for the betterment of the mental health field." According to the EMDR Institute, well over 40,000 clinicians have been trained in this approach, and further growth in the use and application of EMDR is anticipated. Research also is expected on the integration of EMDR with other approaches to treatment.

Information on EMDR can be obtained from the EMDR Institute, Inc. (P.O. Box 51010, Pacific Grove, CA 93950, (831) 372-3900, http://www.emdr.com) and the EMDR International Association (EMDRIA) (P.O. Box 141925, Austin, TX 78714-1925, (512) 451-5200, http://www.emdria.org).

NEURO-LINGUISTIC PROGRAMMING

Neuro-linguistic programming (NLP) was initially developed in the 1970s by John Grinder, a linguist, and Richard Bandler, a mathematician and student of psychology, (Kamp, 1996). According to de Luynes (1995), "NLP embraces an attitude based upon a curiosity about people and how they do the things they do, supported by a methodology—a way of thinking about people and the process of communication—and a technology, to obtain well-defined and ecological results" (p. 34). NLP theorists believe that people's internal representations (thoughts and images) determine their repertoire of choices and behaviors. Identifying patterns in those internal representations and consciously changing or manipulating them can lead to desired behavioral outcomes.

The Development of NLP

Grinder and Bandler believed that psychotherapy overemphasized pathology and neglected what enabled people to function well (Kamp, 1996). Focusing on excellence and seeking to learn more about effective treatment, they studied three outstanding clinicians: Virginia Satir, Fritz Perls, and Milton Erickson. Grinder and Bandler found that the styles of these clinicians had commonalities. All three were gifted with intuition (a great ability to read their clients) as well as intervention and response skills that made a difference.

Drawing on many disciplines including cybernetics, linguistics, behaviorism, family and systems theory, personality theory, and communication, Bandler and Grinder sought ways to replicate the skills of the master therapists. Their findings highlighted:

- Methods for operationalizing the intuitive skills of excellent therapists
- The discovery that people who function well pay much more attention to their desired outcomes than they do to their problems; once the problem has been clarified, they put their energy into defining in detail an ideal resolution

Bandler and Grinder's first book, *The Structure of Magic* (1975), presents these results.

Important Theoretical Concepts

The name of this approach, neuro-linguistic programming, reflects three essential concepts in this model (de Luynes, 1995, p. 34):

1. *Neuro.* All behavior is the result of neurological processes.
2. *Linguistic.* Neural processes are represented, ordered, and sequenced into models and strategies through language and communication systems.
3. *Programming.* The components of a system are organized or programmed to achieve specific outcomes.

According to NLP (Kamp, 1996), people learn and develop automatic patterns or *programmes* in both their neural system and their language. These programmes constitute most of people's daily responses to themselves, others, and their environment and form the personality. When these programmes were originally put into place, they worked more successfully than any other approach in a person's repertoire. Over time, however, these automatic responses become deeply entrenched. People generally do not evaluate or change them unless they conclude that the responses are causing them difficulties.

The primary goal of NLP is helping people become conscious of their internal representations of reality and the ways in which those representations are reflected in their linguistic patterns (Sterman, 1990). According to NLP, people experience internal and external events through sensory modes including visual, auditory, kinesthetic (touch), olfactory (smell), and gustatory (taste) modes. Change is made primarily through these sensory modes, leading to modification of linguistic patterns.

NLP is a phenomenological approach; it suggests that people respond to their maps or pictures of reality, not to reality itself (de Luynes, 1995). Consequently, the meaning of a communication may be different for the sender and the receiver, with the receiver determining the meaning and impact of the message.

For example, Anita suggested to her friend Jennifer, recently diagnosed with cancer, that Jennifer should lose weight and eat more healthfully to improve her immune system. Anita intended to be helpful and caring; however, Jennifer experienced her message as hurtful and intrusive; she responded by avoiding Anita. Regardless of Anita's good intentions, Jennifer's response to the message determined its meaning.

According to NLP, people are responsible for the responses they receive to a communication. Although Anita did not desire Jennifer's response, Anita's message was the cause of the response. Anita operated according to deeply ingrained internal representations of friendship, illness, and helping, which led her to communicate, both verbally and nonverbally, in ways that Jennifer saw as belittling and hurtful. Clinicians using NLP with Anita might help her become more aware of her internal representations and how they contribute to the responses she receives. Then, by identifying the responses and outcomes she desires, they would help Anita modify her internal representations as well as the nature of her communication.

Assumptions   NLP is an encouraging and optimistic approach that assumes a positive view of people and the world. The following are some of its basic assumptions (de Luynes, 1995; Isaacson, 1990; Sterman, 1990):

- People always make the best choice available to them at the time.
- All behavior serves a purpose, but that purpose may be unconscious.
- No one is wrong or broken; by finding out how a person functions now, change can be facilitated.
- There is no such thing as failure, only feedback; all responses can be used.
- An organism naturally moves toward well-being.
- Mind and body are integrated; changing one can change the other.
- Anything can be accomplished by breaking tasks into small-enough chunks.
- The world is a place of abundance that provides resources and opportunities for continued growth and development.
- People already have all the resources they need in their lifetimes; they just need help in accessing those internal resources.

The Process of Facilitating Change

Isaacson (1990) described NLP as a systems model that changes behavior by identifying conscious and unconscious internal representations and patterns and intervening, both verbally and nonverbally, through the sensory modes. By increasing and expanding people's internal representations, NLP enables them to construct a repertoire of internally generated choices that are effective in eliciting desired outcomes in a wide variety of life situations.

NLP believes that people can increase their effectiveness by using all aspects of themselves, including the rational mind, intuition, the emotions, and the body. This enables people to consider situations from different perspectives and develop multiple descriptions that increase their appreciation of other people's interpretations and responses.

Bandler and Grinder (1975) described a six-step process of change via NLP, illustrated here with the example of Anita, introduced previously:

1. Identify the pattern to be changed.
    Anita grew up in a family that expressed little empathy but overemphasized advice and viewed illness as a weakness. Anita internalized these views and applied them to her friends.

2. Establish communication with the part of the person responsible for the pattern. Then use sensory systems and internal and external representations to initiate change.

Anita accessed and explored her internal representations of illness, herself as a friend, her auditory and visual processing of information, and her linguistic style.

3. Determine the positive function of the pattern and separate the pattern from that function since all behaviors serve some positive function.

In Anita's family, giving advice was one of the few acceptable ways to connect with and show concern for another person. However, Anita separated pattern from function by recognizing that her behavior no longer accomplished those goals.

4. Access a creative part of the person to generate new behaviors that accomplish the positive function.

Using her creative strengths, Anita developed some skill at empathy and communication of warmth and concern, which she perceived as more likely to accomplish her goal of connecting with and expressing caring and support for her friends.

5. Connect the new response with the relevant context for change, using all representational sensory modes to reinforce the change. Ask the creative part of the self if it is willing to take responsibility for using the new alternative behaviors when appropriate.

Techniques including reframing and anchoring (discussed later in this chapter) helped Anita link her new response to the context for change. Reframing allowed her to view her new behaviors as meeting her friends' needs rather than communicating pity, which was how she initially and negatively viewed empathy. Drawing on multiple sensory modalities, she visualized herself looking directly at Jennifer, listening to her concerns, touching Jennifer's shoulder, and communicating heartfelt caring. An anchor, clasping her hands, helped Anita easily retrieve this scenario and the good feelings it brought her.

6. Do an ecological check, asking whether any part of the person objects to using the new behaviors. If the answer is yes, return to Step 4 for revision of the behaviors.

Anita reported that the new behaviors were appealing to her and she was eager to try them out in context.

These six steps reflect a simplified and streamlined version of NLP. This is a complex approach that draws heavily on a broad range of theories. Readers are encouraged to study this approach more fully to appreciate its depth and richness.

Strategies for Change

NLP uses an extensive array of strategies to promote change. Many of these strategies have a neurological basis and so differ from those used by most treatment systems. Although a detailed discussion of the interventions associated with NLP is beyond the scope of this book, a brief overview of the most important ones introduces readers to NLP practice.

- *Rapport* between client and clinician is essential.
- Clinicians enhance rapport by *sharing the client's view of the world,* emphasizing language and sensory modalities that reflect the client's preferences (Lankton, 1980). A clinician might say to a client who relies heavily on the visual modality, "Can you see the benefit of that?" and "Can you visualize yourself engaged in the new behavior?" To a client who

emphasizes the auditory modality, the clinician might say, "I hear what you are saying," and "Listen carefully to your description of the behavior."

- *Feedback* and monitoring help people become aware of slight changes in their physiological and mental reactions and fine-tune their actions and reactions (Kamp, 1996).
- *Leading* people from one sensory channel to another can promote awareness and provide new experiences and useful tools. For example, a clinician may shift a client from a kinesthetic to a visual channel by remarking, "I know how you feel about being unable to get a handle on things (kinesthetic), but has there been a time when you had a different perspective and were able to see things clearly (visual)?" (Lankton, 1980, pp. 62–63)
- *Calibrating* links a person's internal state with his or her external behavior and makes sure that the two are consistent. Close attention to language and sensory channels is important in helping people align verbal and nonverbal messages.
- Calibrating enhances *reframing,* the process of creating "a framework in which all parts of the system are aligned toward achieving the desired outcome" (Dilts, 1983, p. 32). Reframing gives people a different and typically more integrated perspective. For example, the clinician might view a situation as a learning opportunity rather than a failure.
- *Anchoring* associates a stimulus with a particular experience and can facilitate access to resources. For Anita, the stimulus of clasping her hands was linked to the experience of communicating concern and caring to her friends. When she clasped her hands (the anchor), the learning that she had acquired about better ways to communicate became accessible to her because of the link between those skills and the anchor.
- *Eye movements* reflect how people process data. NLP theory suggests that, for most people, upward eye movements reflect visual processing, lateral eye movements reflect auditory processing, and downward movements represent either kinesthetic processing or an internal dialog in the client. For most right-handed people, an eye movement up and to the left reflects an effort to access a visual or auditory memory. Movement up and to the right usually indicates that the person is creating a new visual or auditory image. NLP therapists pay close attention to people's eye movements. This information helps clinicians identify the sensory channels that people are using, facilitates clinicians' efforts to match their clients' sensory modalities, and enhances the process of calibration.

Application, Evaluation, and Current Use

The literature provides examples of the application of NLP to a wide variety of people and groups. NLP has been used to treat substance use disorders (Sterman, 1990), to help people deal effectively with traumatic experiences (Lankton, 1980), and to improve family functioning. Although NLP has been available to clinicians for more than 25 years, it has not yet received strong empirical support and should be viewed as an interesting concept with useful techniques rather than a theory or complete approach to treatment. In recent years, interest in NLP has increased, perhaps as a result of its connection in people's minds to EMDR, discussed in this chapter, and to brief solution-focused therapy, discussed in chapter 21. The concepts and tools of NLP are compelling and may enhance treatment, but research is needed to establish the value of this approach.

THOUGHT FIELD THERAPY

Thought field therapy (TFT) is a new, innovative, and controversial approach. TFT is designed to change disturbing and intrusive thoughts and has been described as an energy-oriented approach to treatment and a power therapy. Roger Callahan (2001, p. 1154), a clinical psychologist, developed TFT and wrote of this approach, "TFT is a very rapid method of treating psychological problems typically requiring a matter of minutes to effect change, which usually endures . . . The TFT treatment consists of stimulation (usually by tapping) of a precise sequence of meridian points on the body, which are the points of what are more commonly known as the acupuncture meridians."

According to TFT, people have many thought fields, each comprised of a focused and circumscribed group of thoughts (Callahan & Callahan, 1997). Thought fields may be intrusive and present themselves frequently and automatically, or they may appear only when a person is reminded of a disturbing situation linked to that thought field. According to TFT, negative emotions are elicited when perturbations or instability occur in a disturbing thought field. The goal of TFT is to quiet the perturbations so that the body's nervous system no longer is activated by the disturbing thought field.

Callahan and Callahan (1997) stated, "The precise explanation for why TFT works is still under development" (p. 261). However, they believe that TFT causes slight modifications in the body's neurotransmitter systems that result in changes in the body's bioenergy system, leading to transformation of negative emotions.

TFT begins by having people think about an unpleasant thought and rate their emotional state on the subject units of distress (SUDS) scale. This provides a baseline rating. Clinicians then direct people to tap a specific sequence of acupressure points (meridians) on the body such as the eyebrow, the cheek, or the collar bone while focusing on their upsetting thoughts and painful issues. Other activities such as humming, directed eye movements, and verbalizations such as "I accept myself even though I still have some of this problem" may accompany the tapping. TFT uses different treatment algorithms for different problems. The SUDS rating is checked periodically to assess progress and the TFT process is repeated if necessary to lower the rating until the SUDS is down to 1.

Current Use and Evaluation

Proponents of thought field therapy report rapid success in treating problems such as PTSD, phobias, depression, guilt, grief, addictions, anxiety, extreme fatigue, anger, arthritis, and many other psychological and physical concerns. However, the American Psychological Association has been critical of TFT, leading to considerable conflict between that association and practitioners of TFT. In an effort to resolve this impasse, the *Journal of Clinical Psychology* (McNally, 2001) offered to serve as a professional forum for dialog on TFT. In its October 2001 issue, that journal published both articles advocating TFT and peer critiques of those articles.

An article by Callahan (2001, p. 1155) in that journal presented information on 20 people treated with TFT. Although no control group was used, Callahan reported that TFT had a positive impact on heart rate variability (HRV), the "length in the intervals between heartbeats." Responses to the article questioned both the meaningfulness of HRV as a measure of treatment outcome and the overall effectiveness of TFT. In a critique of Callahan's article, McNally (2001, p. 1173) concluded that TFT lacked "any credible theory or convincing data."

At present, TFT must be considered a highly experimental procedure. Research has not substantiated its value, nor has clear information yet emerged on its appropriate use. However, we consider TFT here because of recent attention to this and other energy-related interventions. They are innovative and potentially fruitful approaches to effecting change and may eventually prove to have value. Information on thought field therapy can be obtained from Callahan Techniques, Ltd. (78-816 Via Carmel, La Quinta, CA 92253, (760) 564-1008, http://www.tftrx.com) and from the Association for Thought Field Therapy (ATFT) (47-159 Youngs Lane, Indio, CA 92201).

OTHER EMERGING APPROACHES EMPHASIZING THOUGHTS

EMDR, NLP, and TFT are the most widely used and studied of the so-called energy or power therapies that emphasize changing thoughts. However, others are being developed, some of which we briefly describe here.

Cognitive Therapy of Evaluation

Derived from a general semantics theory developed by Alfred Korzybski, cognitive therapy of evaluation (CTE) focuses primarily on how language affects perceptions and how changes in language can correspondingly change beliefs and emotions. Influences on this approach include strategic family therapy, Fritz Perls's Gestalt therapy, Aaron Beck's cognitive therapy, and Albert Ellis's rational emotive behavior therapy.

CTE takes the position that most emotional problems are due to "wrong or inappropriate evaluations": People make judgments before obtaining the facts and then react to their words or judgments as though they were facts (Caro, 1991, p. 192). Three premises reflect the theory of CTE:

1. Perceptions do not equal reality.
2. Interpretations depend on cognitive processes that are fallible.
3. Beliefs and cognitions are only hypotheses that need to be tested and perhaps modified.

CTE clinicians encourage clients to assume the role of scientist, search for facts before making judgments, and use language that is concrete and descriptive rather than emotional and evaluative. For example, a person is encouraged to say, "I am not doing as well as I would like in school," rather than, "How could I have gotten a C? I'm so stupid!"

Researchers at the University of Valencia in Spain initially developed CTE. Preliminary results suggest that 15–20 sessions may be effective in treating generalized anxiety disorder, panic disorder, and mood disorders. However, CTE has not yet been widely used nor has it proven its effectiveness. CTE should be viewed as a new and emerging approach that merits study, rather than one to be adopted.

Emotional Freedom Techniques

Like TFT, Emotional Freedom Techniques (EFT) are meridian-based and energy-based. EFT, too, involves stimulating a person's acupuncture points or other energy systems via tapping while that person imagines troubling emotions or experiences. Used primarily to treat anxiety disorders, proponents of EFT report positive results with most people in two–four sessions.

Theoretically, EFT procedures remove emotional blocks and restore balance of both body and mind. Preliminary research conducted in South America over a 14-year period suggests this approach has potential (Andrade & Feinstein, in press). Information on EFT can be obtained from Gary H. Craig (P.O. Box 398, The Sea Ranch, CA 95497, (707) 785-2848, http://www.net-energy.com and http://emofree.com).

SKILL DEVELOPMENT: ANCHORING

Although many of the interventions associated with the approaches presented in this chapter require special training, some can be readily used and easily incorporated into other treatment systems. One such technique is anchoring, associated with neuro-linguistic programming. An *anchor* is defined as any trigger or stimulus that evokes a consistent response pattern from a given person. An example of a common anchor is the smell of fresh-baked cookies. For some, this scent evokes positive memories of childhood experiences, while for others it evokes feelings of sadness, loss, and longing. The anchor itself is neutral; only the associated cognitions and emotions give the anchor meaning.

Anchors can occur in any of the sensory channels. The following are examples of sensory anchors that are likely to evoke emotional responses:

- *Visual (sight):* A stranger who resembles a loved one; photographs; pictures of familiar places; places where very good or very bad experiences occurred
- *Auditory (hearing):* Music, particularly songs that marked special occasions; the sound of someone's voice; the screech of car brakes that are reminiscent of an accident
- *Kinesthetic (touch, feeling):* Touching clothing worn on a special occasion; holding a child; being touched in ways that are reminiscent of particularly good or bad experiences
- *Olfactory (smell):* A perfume worn by a loved one; the aroma of a particular food or flower; smells associated with meaningful places
- *Gustatory (taste):* Eating food associated with important memories; smoking a cigarette after a good meal or a sexual experience; the first cup of coffee in the morning

Anchors can be internal or external or can be combined in a sort of chain reaction. For one woman, the song "Autumn Leaves" (an external anchor) made her think of her father, who had appreciated that song, and initially brought up positive feelings. However, when images of him came into her mind, she was reminded of his painful death and how much she missed him (an internal anchor), which led to feelings of sadness.

Anchors can be positive or negative. William, who was undergoing chemotherapy for cancer, associated the smell of the heating unit in the doctor's office with his treatment. Whenever he was exposed to a similar smell, he became anxious and nauseated. However, he created a positive anchor to help himself. He always brought pictures of family vacations to his treatment; the positive feelings and thoughts associated with the photographs helped reduce his discomfort and anxiety during chemotherapy.

Anchors can be spontaneous or planned. People are constantly exposed to unanticipated anchors throughout the day—stimuli that consistently elicit certain emotional responses. Anchors also can be planned and constructed like William's use of photographs in the previous example so that they help people reach their goals. Both spontaneous and planned anchors can be important elements in treatment.

Although emotions sometimes seem to arise without cause or explanation, a trigger for the emotions can usually be identified. Clinicians can help people to identify those triggers and then use that information to help them deal with the emotions more successfully. For example, William became anxious every time he went to the airport because the smell reminded him of his difficult medical treatment. Once he became aware of this association, his trips to the airport became less disturbing, and his negative feelings even diminished over successive visits to the airport. Had the feelings continued to be painful for him, he could have chosen to avoid the airport or offset those negative feelings with some planned and positive anchors. Knowledge of the link between triggers and the emotions and thoughts they evoke gives people options and control.

Positive anchors can be planned to reinforce learning and growth. For example, William used visualization to help him relax, become more optimistic, and cope with his disease and its treatment. When he achieved a peaceful and hopeful state through his visualization, he anchored those feelings by clasping his hands in a prayerlike gesture. After practicing this connection many times, William found he could bring up peaceful and hopeful feelings just by clasping his hands. At stressful times such as when he received chemotherapy, he could clasp his hands and immediately experience positive feelings.

Anchoring has many possibilities as a useful adjunct to any form of treatment. Most people find it an easy and appealing tool to use and benefit from understanding and developing ways to help themselves via anchoring.

CASE ILLUSTRATION

Presented here is a brief segment of a session in which eye movement desensitization and reprocessing (EMDR) is used with Edie to help her deal with troubling memories of being abused by her grandfather. The first and second phases of the EMDR treatment—planning the treatment and client preparation—have already been completed. Edie and the clinician have had five previous sessions; they have developed some rapport and discussed Edie's history. After determining that Edie is ready for EMDR, the clinician explained and demonstrated EMDR to Edie, made sure her expectations were realistic, and taught her how to stop the process and imagine a safe place if her memories became too disturbing. The dialog begins with the third phase of EMDR, assessment.

Clinician: Edie, we decided that you will be working on images and memories of times when you were abused by your grandfather. Can you describe a visual image or picture that represents the worst part of the memory?

Edie: Yes. I must have been about seven years old. I was in bed at my grandparents' house. My grandfather came in and lay down on the bed. Then he started touching me.

He had locked my grandmother out of the house. I heard her outside, yelling and banging on the door, but she couldn't get in to help me.

Clinician: What is a negative self-statement that you have now about yourself that goes along with that memory?

Edie: I feel so dirty, so bad about myself because of what happened. I guess the statement would be "I am worthless."

Clinician: And what is a positive statement that reflects what you would like to believe about yourself when you remember that incident?

Edie: That I am a worthwhile person.

Clinician: On the 1–7 validity scale, with 1 representing completely false and 7 completely true, how true does the statement "I am a worthwhile person" feel now?

Edie: I guess about a 2.

Clinician: What emotions do you associate with the memory you described to me?

Edie: Disgust, depression, hatred of myself.

Clinician: How do you rate your level of disturbance on a 0–10 scale, with 0 reflecting no disturbance and 10 the highest possible disturbance?

Edie: A 7; no, maybe 8.

Clinician: And where in your body do you experience that disturbance?

Edie: Mainly in my stomach. It feels queasy. And my chest feels tight.

Phase 4, desensitization, begins.

A series of eye movements occurs after each brief client-counselor dialog.

Clinician: (after the first series of eye movements) What comes up for you now?

Edie: I can see myself lying on the bed and my grandfather coming into the room. I can hear my grandmother outside. It's awful. (eye movements)

Clinician: How about now?

Edie: The picture is getting less distinct, sort of fuzzy. (eye movements)

Clinician: And now?

Edie: Still fuzzier. (eye movements)

Clinician: What comes up for you now?

Edie: This is strange. It's like I'm up on the ceiling looking down on myself in the bed, and the image of the bed is getting smaller. (eye movements)

Clinician: How about now?

Edie: The girl on the bed, me, is getting up off the bed. She's going out the bedroom door. (eye movements)

Clinician: And now?

Edie: My grandfather is still there on the bed, but I've left the room and I'm about to walk out the front door. (eye movements)

Clinician: What do you see now?

Edie: She . . . I've walked out the front door, and I'm out there with my grandmother. The two of us are getting into the car and driving away. (eye movements)

Clinician: How would you rate your level of disturbance now on the 0–10 SUDS scale?

Edie: Wow, it's really changed. I'd say it's down to a 4.

Clinician: And how about the rating of your self-statement "I am a worthwhile person"? On the 1–7 validity scale, how true does that statement feel now?

Edie: That's gone up. I'd say it's a 5.

Edie is making progress in reprocessing and desensitizing herself to the traumatic memory, as reflected by both the SUDS rating and the VoC rating. EMDR would continue at this point, perhaps for multiple sessions, seeking to reduce the SUDS score further and increase the validity (VoC) of the positive cognition. Once the SUDS score is a 0 or 1 and the VoC score is a 6 or 7, EMDR will be used to install and reinforce those results (Phase 5). A body scan would follow, to make sure that the unpleasant feelings Edie is experiencing in her stomach and chest have been alleviated (Phase 6). The session would close with a review of the EMDR process (Phase 7). Edie would keep a log of her reactions and experiences between this session and the next, and the log would be used as part of the reevaluation process (Phase 8) in the next session.

EXERCISES

Because of the innovative and powerful nature of the approaches in this section and the need for specialized training before people can practice most of them, this chapter includes only large-group exercises.

Large-Group Exercises/Discussion Questions

1. EMDR, NLP, and TFT all involve procedures that have not yet been fully explained. Discuss how you feel about using approaches that are not well understood. What information would help you feel more comfortable about using these approaches? How could that information be obtained? How do you feel about using tools such as tapping and directed eye movements as part of the treatment process?

2. EMDR and NLP have been referred to as power therapies because of the great impact they can have on people. Although both approaches emphasize the importance of the client-clinician relationship, that relationship is primarily a context for the use of the interventions. This contrasts with approaches such as person-centered counseling and

existential therapy, which emphasize the healing power of the therapeutic alliance. Which conception of the therapeutic relationship is more comfortable for you and why? Which is more compatible with your view of the role of the clinician?

3. NLP and TFT have not yet been well researched. Develop a research study that would help determine the value of one of these approaches. This can help you reflect on how clinicians and researchers go about assessing the effectiveness of a treatment system.

SUMMARY

This chapter focused primarily on three emerging approaches that emphasize the importance of thoughts: eye movement desensitization and reprocessing, neuro-linguistic programming, and thought field therapy. (It also mentions several other approaches that are less well developed.) Of those three approaches, only EMDR has thus far been well supported by empirical research. However, all of the approaches, with their innovative use of language and interventions such as directed eye movements and tapping, have the potential of becoming useful additions to the clinician's repertoire of skills.

RECOMMENDED READINGS

Bandler, R., & Grinder, J. (1975). *The structure of magic.* Palo Alto, CA: Science and Behavior Books.

Callahan, R. J., & Callahan, J. (1997). Thought field therapy: Aiding the bereavement process. In C. R. Figley, B. E. Bride, & N. Mazza (Eds.), *Death and trauma* (pp. 249–267). Washington, DC: Taylor & Francis.

Caro, I. (1991). An introduction to the cognitive therapy of evaluation. *Counselling Psychology Quarterly, 4,* 191–206.

de Luynes, M. (1995). Neuro-linguistic programming. *Educational and Child Psychology, 12,* 34–47.

Journal of Clinical Psychology, 2001, 57 (entire issues).

Manfield, P. (Ed.) (1998). *Extending EMDR.* New York: Norton Professional Books.

Shapiro, F. (2001). *Eye movement desensitization and reprocessing: Basic principles, protocols and procedures* (2nd ed.) New York: Guilford.

Shapiro, F., & Forrest, M. (1997). *EMDR: The breakthrough therapy for overcoming anxiety, stress and trauma.* New York: Basic Books.

Part Five

Treatment Systems Emphasizing Actions

Overview of Action-Focused Treatment Systems

Actions, the fourth component in the BETA model (background, emotions, thoughts, actions) are the focus of part 5 of this book. Throughout the book, the terms "actions" and "behaviors" are used interchangably. Actions are usually overt, observable, and measurable. Actions affect and are intertwined with our thoughts and emotions. Treatment focused on modifying behaviors often leads to clear and rapid changes.

Actions or behaviors shape our lives, as history and literature have shown. In "The Road Not Taken," poet Robert Frost (1962, p. 223) described a man standing where two roads diverge. After choosing to follow one path, the man reflected on his actions:

> "Oh, I kept the first for another day!
> Yet knowing how way leads on to way,
> I doubted if I should ever come back."

Each of us may be the only one who is aware of our feelings and thoughts; they can be kept private, and any given thought or emotion may not have an impact on our lives. That is not the case with behaviors. Once we take action—choose which road to travel—we make an irrevocable move in a certain direction. In addition, the potentially public and observable nature of behaviors intensifies their impact. Although background, emotions, and thoughts may underlie our behaviors, the actions we take are most likely to determine the direction of our lives as well as our relationships with others and their perceptions of us. Even a small act such as leaving for work early has a profound impact if it enables a person to avoid an accident, meet a new friend in the cafeteria, and make a positive impression on a supervisor.

Sometimes people feel overwhelmed and immobilized when they consider the possible impact of their behaviors and so avoid making choices and taking action. However, inaction is an action in itself and does have consequences.

Part 5 of this book focuses primarily on treatment systems designed to modify behaviors and actions. However, because behavioral approaches to counseling and psychotherapy are typically integrated with cognitive approaches, we also pay attention to the integration of behavioral and cognitive approaches to change. Chapter 19 reviews the theory and strategies of behavioral and cognitive-behavioral counseling and psychotherapy, paying particular attention to Donald Meichenbaum's approach to cognitive-behavioral therapy. Chapter 20 focuses on reality therapy, developed by William Glasser, which is particularly useful in settings such as schools, correctional institutions, and substance use treatment programs that emphasize changing behavior. Finally, chapter 21 reviews solution-focused brief therapy, an efficient and widely used approach that helps people build on strengths and successes to effect change in their lives.

THE IMPORTANCE OF ACTIONS IN COUNSELING AND PSYCHOTHERAPY

Focusing on behavior change has many advantages in treatment, most of which are similar to the advantages of focusing on cognitions. However, an emphasis on actions has additional advantages as well as some drawbacks.

The Advantages of Focusing on Actions

Most clinicians recognize that emotions, thoughts, and actions have reciprocal relationships. Whether or not clinicians focus primarily on behaviors, they should be aware of the potential benefits of paying attention to clients' actions.

Behaviors as Presenting Problems   Clients' presenting problems often focus on behaviors. People rarely seek treatment because of dysfunctional thoughts, although they do sometimes seek help for negative emotions such as depression and anxiety. Usually, however, what impels them to seek help is an upsetting behavior, either their own or someone else's. Common behavioral concerns include overeating, unhealthy use of drugs or alcohol, poor impulse control, difficulty finding a rewarding job, and problems in developing rewarding relationships. Because behaviors often prompt treatment, people are more likely to feel heard and to believe that treatment will be helpful if, at least initially, it addresses those concerns.

Attending to unrewarding or self-destructive behavior is particularly important in treatment of people who are not self-referred for help. For example, people who are court-mandated to treatment, encouraged to meet with an employee-assistance counselor at work, or brought for help by a concerned parent or dissatisfied partner usually are in treatment because their behaviors have violated the law or been unsatisfactory or troubling to others.

The Accessibility of Behaviors   Behaviors usually are more accessible than either thoughts or emotions. Think back to yesterday at this same time. You may have difficulty recalling your thoughts and feelings, but you can probably remember where you were and what you were doing. You may have been listening to a lecture, driving home from work, or taking a nap. Because behaviors are linked to the structure of our days, we can usually remember them, whereas thoughts and emotions are more difficult to recall.

Comfort in Discussion of Behaviors   Discussion of people's behaviors is likely to be less threatening than discussion of their early childhood experiences or their troubling emotions and somewhat less uncomfortable than discussion of their cognitions. People are used to talking about their activities with others but are less likely to talk with others about thoughts and emotions.

In addition, most actions are overt and observable, whereas thoughts and emotions are covert and often not obvious. Thus, questions about behaviors seem less intrusive than questions about emotions and cognitions. Few people, for example, would be uncomfortable with questions such as "What time did you get up this morning?" and "What did you say to your child when you learned he lied to you?" although they might experience discomfort in response to questions such as "What thoughts led you to stay in bed all day?" and "How did you feel when your child lied to you?"

Accuracy of Information   Discussion of actions is socially acceptable, even among casual acquaintances, and people seem more able to present accurate information about their behaviors than about their emotions and cognitions. Having clear and valid information, especially at the beginning of treatment, is essential in formulating realistic goals and a viable treatment plan, as well as in developing a positive therapeutic alliance. (Of course, keep in mind that some people will deliberately present inaccurate information about their behaviors, especially those that are socially and legally unacceptable such as excessive use of drugs or aggressive expressions of anger.)

Ease of Measurement   Actions are amenable to measurement. People can determine the baseline frequency of a behavior and then assess change in such variables as how many beers they drink each day, how often they exercise, how many hours they devote to work, and how much time they spend with friends. Because even small changes can readily be identified, people trying to modify their actions often have rapid evidence of improvement. This can be empowering and promote motivation, optimism, and further change.

At the same time, if an incorrect diagnosis, case formulation, or treatment plan has been made, that probably will be reflected in a lack of behavior change in response to treatment. This alerts the clinician to the need for a revised and more effective treatment approach.

The Availability of Behavior Change Strategies   A broad range of behavior change strategies has been developed. This enables clinicians to individualize treatment plans, bring creativity to their work, and maximize the likelihood of success by tailoring treatment to a particular person and behavior.

Extensive Research Support   Because the impact of behavior change strategies usually is easy to assess and because most behaviorally oriented clinicians are favorably disposed toward empirical research, an extensive body of literature describes and affirms the effectiveness of behavior and cognitive-behavioral therapy. These treatment approaches have received more support than other approaches, not necessarily because behavior and cognitive-behavioral therapy are superior, but because of the extensive research conducted on these approaches.

In 1995, a task force of the Division of Clinical Psychology of the American Psychological Association conducted a thorough review of the literature to identify treatment approaches that had been empirically supported (Division 12 Task Force, 1996). They identified 22 well-established treatments and 7 treatments that were probably effective; as a group, these treatments were viewed as appropriate for use with 21 different mental disorders listed in the *Diagnostic and Statistical Manual of Mental Disorders* (DSM) (American Psychiatric Association, 2000). Nearly all of these were behavioral or cognitive-behavioral in nature. Another 8 well-established treatments and 19 probably effective treatments were added to the list in 1996; 12 of these were behavioral or cognitive-behavioral in nature. Clearly, behavior therapy and cognitive-behavioral therapy have proven their value in treating a broad range of disorders and symptoms.

No Symptom Substitution   In the past, some clinicians expressed concern that effective treatment of one troubling behavior would simply change the nature of the problem, leading to the emergence of other undesirable behaviors. However, research has demonstrated that symptom substitution is not usually a concern (Myers & Thyer, 1994). In fact, generalizability operates in a positive way; once people learn to modify one behavior, they have strategies they can use to change other unwanted behaviors.

The Limitations of Focusing on Actions

Although treatment systems that focus on behavior change have many advantages, they also have some shortcomings. An exclusive focus on actions can lead clinicians and clients to ignore thoughts and feelings that need attention and are important in solidifying change. This can lead to superficial treatment and limited results.

For example, Mimi sought counseling for help with time management; she expressed a wish to have more involvement with her husband and children. Underlying her presenting problem were feelings of self-doubt and low self-esteem, disappointment with her marriage, and fear that her husband was having an affair. Mimi's marital concerns were exacerbated by feelings of betrayal stemming from childhood sexual abuse by her father. Neglect of Mimi's thoughts, emotions, and background would have done her a disservice and probably led to treatment that at best would have had limited success.

Several safeguards can reduce the possibility that clinicians focusing on actions will miss important underlying concerns. First, they should conduct a comprehensive assessment of their clients via a thorough intake interview and appropriate inventories. This helps provide a full picture of clients and facilitates development of a treatment plan that is broad enough to address both presenting problems and relevant underlying concerns. Second, clinicians should closely monitor the progress of treatment; if rapid change is not evident, clinicians may not have accurately conceptualized a case and may need additional information and a revised treatment plan. Third, behavior counseling should usually not be used alone. Combining behavior treatment strategies with cognitive approaches, in particular, enhances the power of behavior therapy and enables clinicians to successfully address a broad range of concerns.

SKILL DEVELOPMENT: PLANNING AND IMPLEMENTING BEHAVIOR CHANGE

Helping people change behaviors involves a series of steps that can, of course, be adapted to meet the needs of a particular person or problem. We review these steps here, illustrating them with the example of Ernest, whose supervisor reprimanded him for getting to work late. By learning and reviewing these steps, readers can both incorporate them into their work and apply them to themselves. These steps facilitate change in a variety of undesirable behaviors, including overeating, substance misuse, poor time management, unsatisfactory performance at work or school, inappropriate expressions of anger, children's misbehavior, insufficient exercise, smoking, unwanted personal habits such as nail biting, and deficiencies in social skills.

1. Describing the Behavior

The first step in changing actions is describing the target behavior in specific and measurable terms. Both the undesirable behavior and the desirable change should be specified.

Ernest's presenting concern was arriving late to work. First the undesirable behavior was explored in detail. Ernest worked full time and had a wife and three children. His days were full and demanding. Because he had little time to unwind, Ernest would stay up until about 2:00 a.m. watching television so that he could have some time to himself. In the morning, he was tired and had difficulty rising early enough to help his wife get the children ready for school. As a result, mornings were usually very hectic. The children sometimes missed the school bus, requiring Ernest to drive them to school. Even when the children caught the bus, Ernest was usually at least 30 minutes late to work. Obtaining a full description of the undesirable behaviors made it clear that Ernest's lateness was a complicated situation with many contributing factors.

Ernest excused his lateness by explaining that he often worked through his lunch hour and stayed late at work. However, he recognized that his job description stated his working hours as 9:00 a.m. to 5:30 p.m. and that he was not adhering to those hours. The desirable change he sought was clear: arriving at work on time on a regular basis. Ernest also hoped to better manage the needs of his family while having more time for himself.

2. Establishing a Baseline

Once the problem behaviors have been clearly described, a baseline can be obtained, reflecting the severity and frequency of the behaviors at the inception of treatment. To determine the baseline, client and clinician must agree on the following:

- *Ways to measure the behavior.* The two most common dimensions for measuring behavior are *frequency* (e.g., how many glasses of wine does a person drink daily?, how many times in one hour did a child get out of his seat at school?, how many times a week does a man yell at his wife?) and *severity* (e.g., how late was the homework assignment?, how much damage was caused by the nail biting? how much clutter has resulted from a person's hoarding behavior?). Describing the behavior in clear and specific terms facilitates its measurement. For example, the problem of a messy house is difficult to assess unless it is described as including a floor piled with clothes, six boxes that remain unpacked, and a mildewed shower.

- *Ways to record the measurement.* People in treatment generally keep a record of their behaviors. They can use a checklist, a diary, or another written record of desirable and undesirable behaviors. Ernest used his date book to record his schedule for 5 days. He listed the times when the alarm went off, when he got out of bed, when he arrived at work, when he left work, and when he went to bed. For each day, he also wrote a brief description of what he did between rising and arriving at work.

In his next session, Ernest reviewed his records with the clinician. Ernest set his alarm for 6:00 a.m. each morning, but he rarely arose before 6:30. He was 30–45 minutes late to work each day—twice because he had to drive his children to school, once because he was delayed by his daughter who had misplaced her homework, once because the dog required attention, and once because Ernest slept until 7:00 a.m. He left work between 6:00 and 6:30 p.m. Four out of five nights he watched television until nearly 2:00 a.m.

3. Determining Goals

Goals should be meaningful, clear, specific, measurable, and achievable. They should be logical outgrowths of the baseline information. Both clinician and client should understand and have a record of the goals, and both should agree that the client could accomplish the goals without extreme difficulty. Success in reaching goals is reinforcing and encourages people to tackle more challenging goals, but failure to achieve goals can be discouraging, leading people to doubt themselves and their abilities. Consequently, goals should be designed to facilitate accomplishment rather than frustration. (Chapter 21 includes more information on goal setting.)

Although Ernest was eager to make changes so that he could get to work on time each day, the complexity of the problem as well as its severity, as reflected by the baseline, suggested that goals should be approached gradually and incrementally. Ernest established an initial goal of getting to work by 9:00 a.m. at least once during the next week and getting to bed by 1:00 a.m. at least three times during the week.

4. Developing Strategies

The next step in the process of changing behavior is identifying strategies to help people achieve their goals. Because chapter 19 reviews many specific strategies, we will not repeat them here. However, clinicians should consider several categories of strategies when helping people move toward their goals.

Skill Development and Education   People often need to develop new skills and learn new information to help them change problem behaviors. These might include assertiveness and communication skills, parenting skills, time management, decision-making, and others.

Impulse Control   Problems with impulse control are often a key element in undesirable behaviors. Ernest, for example, described himself as "addicted to late-night television" and had difficulty curtailing that behavior. Teaching people impulse-control strategies such as relaxation, distraction, and avoidance of triggers, can facilitate change.

Reinforcement   Rewards can motivate people to achieve their goals, help them take pride in their accomplishments, and encourage them to take on more challenging goals. Rewards can be *social,* such as encouragement and compliments from friends and family; *intrinsic,* such as the good feelings and improved health benefits a person experiences after losing weight or giving up smoking; or *extrinsic,* such as going out to dinner to celebrate purchasing a desired object. Extrinsic rewards can most easily be planned and controlled; they are most likely to be motivating if they are identified in advance and made contingent on the person's performance. As with goal setting, plans should be formulated so that the person is likely to receive a reward.

Reinforcements can be delivered regularly (each time the desired behavior is emitted) or intermittently. Lundin (1977) described four schedules of reinforcement:

1. *Fixed-interval reinforcement* occurs on a regular schedule, such as a weekly paycheck or quarterly report card.
2. *Variable-interval reinforcement* occurs at irregular intervals that average out to a specified time. For example, a pet receives five treats in 75 minutes or an average of one every 15 minutes, but the intervals between the treats vary from 5–30 minutes.
3. *Fixed-ratio reinforcements* are provided at a specified rate that depends on the number of responses made. People working on an assembly line may be paid for the number of parts they put together rather than for the hours they work.
4. *Variable-ratio reinforcements* usually seem random and unpredictable to the recipient, although they are controlled or planned by the provider. Winning at slot machines is an example. Variable-ratio reinforcements are powerful in encouraging responses because each response holds the promise of a reward.

Although penalties or punishments are sometimes used instead of rewards to shape behavior, rewards are generally more effective. They make the process of change a positive and empowering experience and promote motivation. In addition, if other people are dispensing the consequences, they are likely to be perceived positively if they are giving rewards but viewed negatively if they are providing punishments.

However, punishments can give a powerful and immediate message and do have a place in behavior change. Arrest of people guilty of domestic abuse, for example, can break through their denial, leading them to enter treatment and make positive changes.

Reasonable (or natural) consequences (discussed further in chapter 20) avoid some of the potentially harmful consequences of other types of punishment but still give a strong message. Reasonable consequences are designed to grow logically out of the undesirable behavior; for example, a boy who neglects his homework is required to keep a notebook in which his teachers write down daily homework assignments for parent follow-up. The girl who uses six towels each time she bathes is made responsible for doing the laundry.

Planning   Planning is almost always an essential element of behavioral change. Planning enables people to specify exactly how and when they will modify their behaviors and can help them anticipate and overcome obstacles to their efforts.

Commitment   Clinicians should help their clients invest themselves in the process of change and give it their best effort. Making a commitment to change, as well as a public declaration of the intent to change, encourages people to follow through on their plans. Their resolve can be further solidified through a written contract with the clinician and by talking about their goals and plans with friends or family members who can give them support and encouragement. Having a partner in a behavior change program, perhaps a friend who also wants to stop smoking or exercise regularly, can be reinforcing.

Ernest's Strategies   Ernest and his counselor identified the following helpful strategies:

1. *Skill development.* Ernest had little knowledge of time management. Before he began his program of change, his counselor reviewed principles of time management with him and suggested a book he might read on the subject. Ernest also received information on the cumulative effects of inadequate sleep so that he could realize the part that fatigue played in his difficulties.

2. *Impulse control.* Ernest needed help in controlling his impulse to watch television. He reported that he typically drowsed in front of the television and lost track of time. He decided to set a timer to go off at 12:30 a.m., reminding him that it was time to shut off the television and get ready for bed.

3. *Planning.* Planning was important in helping Ernest change his behavior. Ernest determined that he needed to rise by 6:15 a.m. to get to work on time. He set two alarms, one next to the bed for 6:00 a.m. and one across the room for 6:15 a.m. This allowed him a few welcome minutes to gradually awaken but made it likely that he would get out of bed at 6:15 a.m. to shut off the second alarm.

   Although some of the morning crises at Ernest's house were unavoidable, some could be averted by careful planning. Ernest and his wife agreed that, before their children went to bed, they would organize their clothes, books, homework, and lunch money to streamline the morning routine. The two older children were asked to assume responsibility for setting the table and putting out the breakfast food.

   To help Ernest shift some of his relaxation time to an earlier hour, he and his wife agreed that they would alternate taking responsibility for the children each evening. While one person was in charge of baths and homework, the other had an hour of quiet time to relax, read, or watch television.

4. *Reinforcement.* Ernest expected to receive some automatic reinforcement for his behavioral change. He anticipated getting better evaluations from his supervisor, feeling more relaxed, and having a less harried home environment. In addition, Ernest decided that, once during each week in which he achieved his goals, he and his wife would hire a sitter so they could go out to dinner. This extrinsic reinforcer enhanced Ernest's sense of relaxation and positive feelings about his family.

5. *Commitment.* Ernest and his counselor wrote up a contract, including goals and strategies. Ernest shared this with his wife and asked her to help with his change efforts.

5. Implementation

Once goals have been established and strategies determined, the plans for behavior change are implemented. People should keep a record of their progress as they did when determining the baseline of their undesirable behaviors. They also should make notes about anything that facilitates or hinders the implementation.

Ernest found that he did well with the parts of his plan that were under his control but had difficulty persuading his children to help out in the morning and prepare for school the night before. He planned to ask the counselor for some help with this situation.

6. Assessment

At regular intervals, clients and clinician monitor progress to maintain and reinforce successes and address difficulties in the plan. Prolonged experiences of failure should be avoided. When discussing the outcome of clients' behavior change plans, clinicians should be encouraging and optimistic but not judgmental, critical, or blaming. People often do not fully achieve their goals. This should be viewed as an opportunity for learning and for refining the plan rather than as a failure. Rather than focusing on excuses and disappointments, clinicians should help clients congratulate themselves on their efforts and any successes they had.

The initial assessment of Ernest's efforts indicated that Ernest got to work on time two days out of five and was less than 30 minutes late on other days. He arose by 6:15 a.m. every day and went to bed by 1:00 a.m. on four out of five nights; he felt that he could get to bed even earlier in the future without much difficulty. Ernest had enjoyed the hour of quiet time in the evening, even though he and his wife implemented that change on only two evenings. The children made progress in organizing themselves but were reluctant to accept new responsibilities.

7. Reinforcement

Assuming rewards have been built into the change plan and some success has been achieved, people can now reward themselves. Clinicians also can cautiously provide some social reinforcement, congratulating clients on their efforts and helping them to take pride in their accomplishments. However, clinicians should place more emphasis on encouraging clients to praise themselves. Clinicians who make positive as well as negative judgments of their clients risk imposing their values on clients and can detract from clients' self-direction and self-esteem.

Ernest experienced both intrinsic and extrinsic rewards for his efforts. He felt proud of his success and also felt less fatigued. In addition, his wife had complimented him for reducing some of the morning chaos. Ernest hired a sitter and made dinner reservations so he and his wife could celebrate his success.

8. Continuing the Process

This last stage of a behavioral change plan takes one of three directions:

1. If the plan had some shortcomings and clients did not reach their goals, client and clinician consider what revisions in goals and strategies are likely to lead to greater success. Considerable attention may be paid to the strengths and weaknesses of the original plan to determine how it needs to be improved.
2. If the plan had been successful but the client has additional goals or wants to build on the accomplishments of the initial plan, client and clinician agree on new objectives and develop strategies to facilitate their accomplishment.

3. If clients are satisfied with their accomplishments, they work with their clinicians to solidify those gains and prevent relapse. Strategies such as involvement in a peer support group, ongoing self-monitoring, stress management, and periodic follow-up sessions are common elements in a relapse-prevention plan.

Ernest thought he had made a good start toward accomplishing his goals but recognized that he had only begun to make a significant change in his behaviors. He and his counselor developed additional goals and strategies to help him continue his efforts. In addition, the counselor suggested strategies Ernest could use to facilitate change in his children's behavior such as modeling, using praise and reinforcement, letting them choose their chores from a list, and reframing their new responsibilities as reflecting their maturity.

CASE ILLUSTRATION

As part of improving his health, Roberto asked his clinician to help him include more exercise in his life. Roberto reported that he was so busy at work that he had no time for physical activities, although the family did belong to a health club. The following dialog illustrates the use of a behavior change plan with Roberto.

Clinician: Roberto, let's begin by getting a clear picture of the situation [description of behavior]. Here's an outline of a behavioral change plan that might help us. You can use this form to write down your plans as we figure them out. The first step is describing the behavior you want to change.

Roberto: All right. I know I need more exercise to keep my weight down and improve my overall health. My father was very overweight, and he had a heart attack when he was just a few years older than I am, so I know I need to make a change. I just can't seem to do it. I work long hours and I travel a lot for work. At the health club, they told me I should get there at least three times a week, but that seems impossible.

Clinician: How much exercise do you get now [establishing baseline]?

Roberto: About all I do is get to the health club once a week on Fridays after work.

Clinician: Do you get any informal exercise like sports with the family or just walking?

Roberto: Not really. Once a week at the health club is about it. I don't see any way you can get me there three times a week.

Clinician: Perhaps we need to define our goals differently. What I'm hearing is that your goal is to get sufficient exercise, not necessarily get to the health club [establishing goals].

Roberto: Yes, that's right.

Clinician: Perhaps we can find more realistic ways to help you get that exercise. Exercise can be thought of in terms of frequency and duration. Using those terms, what would you see as an acceptable amount of exercise, not necessarily ideal?

Roberto: At the health club, they say you should get at least 20–30 minutes of exercise a day for at least three days a week.

Clinician: How does that sound as an initial goal?

Roberto: It's a place to start, although I'd really like to exercise more than that.

Clinician: We can increase the goal later, but it sounds like you would feel all right about an initial goal of exercising at least 20 minutes at least three days a week. How about writing that down on your plan?

Roberto: Sure, that sounds like a reasonable goal.

Clinician: Did you know that you don't need to do that 20–30 minutes of exercise all at once? You can break that into segments of 10 minutes or so and achieve the same results. That might sound more manageable.

Roberto: Yes, it does. Ten minutes doesn't sound like much.

Clinician: I wonder if you can build one or two 10-minute walks into your day?

Roberto: Yes, I could do that. If I park my car over at the picnic area sometimes instead of by the entrance to my office, that would give me a 10-minute walk at each end of the day. I could even take a 10-minute walk after lunch. That would be 30 minutes a day.

Clinician: I can hear that you're starting to generate some ideas. Remember that, at least at the beginning, we want to make this change fairly easy for you.

Roberto: Okay, I can make that lunch walk optional and only walk at lunch on days when I don't have too much work.

Clinician: Making the plan as specific as possible might help you to follow the plan. How about choosing the specific days when you will park your car by the picnic area?

Roberto: I could do Mondays and Wednesdays. Those days tend to be less busy; no regular meetings on those days.

Clinician: So you have identified two possible days to walk each week. Let's look at some possible obstacles. What if the weather is bad on those days?

Roberto: I guess if it's really bad, I could shift to the next day; but I can walk even if it's cold or raining.

Clinician: It sounds like you are determined to do this!

Roberto: Yes, I know I have to.

Clinician: I wonder if you can build in some exercise with your family for the weekend?

Roberto: That's a good idea. Before Ava was born, Edie and I used to take bike rides together. I wonder if I could talk her into that again. If not, I bet Ava would come with me, especially if I bought her a new bike.

Clinician: That idea really appeals to you. When could you fit biking into your schedule?

Roberto: Either Saturday or Sunday afternoon would work.

Clinician: If you continue going to the health club on Fridays, park by the picnic area twice a week, and go biking on the weekend, then we have four days planned when you will exercise. Because of your travel and work schedule, it might make sense to include those four opportunities in the plan in case you have to miss one. Then you can still reach your goal of exercising three days a week.

Roberto: That sounds good, and some weeks I might even hit four. I'll write that down.

Clinician: Let's come up with some strategies to help you [development of strategies].

Roberto: All right.

Clinician: Having even more information about exercise and its benefits might be useful to you. That could motivate you and help you plan your exercise better.

Roberto: The health club has lectures on that, but I've never gone. I think they have the lectures on tape. I could borrow them.

Clinician: That sounds like a way to get some information. Let's write that down on our plan. Sometimes people have great intentions about exercise, but other things get in the way. How can we try to prevent that from happening?

Roberto: I'll make copies of the plan we're writing down, and I'll post it at home and work. I can tell Ava and Edie what I'm doing and ask them to help. If one of them went biking with me, I'd really enjoy it.

Clinician: Sharing your plan with people you're close to, and having someone with whom you can exercise, can be helpful. Another useful strategy is building in a reward for yourself if you accomplish your goal. Would you like to make that part of your plan?

Roberto: How about two pieces of apple pie each day that I exercise?

Clinician: Will that help you reach your goal?

Roberto: Just joking! Let's see . . . I could use a new bike, but that's big bucks.

Clinician: What about putting aside a certain amount of money each week that you succeed in reaching your goal?

Roberto: That should work. I could put away $10 a week. By the end of the year, I'll have that bike.

Clinician: Let's review the whole plan now to make sure it's clear and that you are comfortable moving ahead. As we go over the plan, let me know if you see any more obstacles that might get in the way of your following the plan. We can think of ways to prevent them from keeping you from your goals. I also suggest that you keep a record of your exercise for the next week as well as notes on any factors that helped or hurt your efforts to exercise as you have planned. We'll use that information next week when we assess how things went to see if we need to change the plan in any way.

Roberto: Sounds good to me. I have a calendar set up on my computer and when I do my last e-mail check of the day, I can list my exercise for that day, along with any problems I ran into in following the plan [assessment].

EXERCISES

Large-Group Exercises

1. Develop a plan for changing each of the following behaviors:
   - Smoking
   - Procrastination
   - Children's tantrums
   - Overeating

Your plan should include the following five elements from the eight-step format presented in this chapter:

- Describing the behavior
- Obtaining a baseline
- Establishing goals
- Developing behavior change strategies
- Assessment

2. This book includes chapters on treatment approaches that emphasize background, those that focus on emotions, those that emphasize thoughts, and those that attend primarily to actions. Discuss which group of theories is most appealing to you and why.
3. Behavior change strategies can be used to shape the behavior of another person. Discuss how clinicians can help parents use behavior change strategies with their children.

Small-Group Exercises

1. Divide into your groups of four, composed of two dyads. Each dyad should engage in a 15-minute dialog in which the person playing the client presents a behavior that he or she actually wants to change. The person in the clinician role should take the client through the five steps listed in large-group Exercise 1 to formulate a behavior change plan. The process should culminate with a written contract. Record and play back the recorded interview after it is completed so that the group can identify each of the five steps and provide feedback to clinician and client.
2. Each dyad should role-play another interview, remaining in the same roles, with the person in the client role presenting the same behavioral concern. However, this time, the clinician should emphasize exploration of emotions and thoughts related to the behavior and make little use of behavior change strategies. Discuss the two interviews. How did the participants feel about their roles? Which interview was more challenging and why? Which interview was more successful and why? What was the impact of each interview on the therapeutic alliance? What other important differences did you notice between the two interviews? What did you learn from this exercise?
3. After the role plays have been completed, list the behaviors that group members wanted to change. Discuss them one at a time, identifying at least three strategies that might facilitate change in each of the behaviors. Then discuss and address obstacles that might arise when efforts are made to change each behavior.

Individual Exercises

1. Nearly everyone has behaviors that he or she would like to change. Identify one of your behaviors that you view as undesirable. Be your own behavioral counselor and develop a plan to change that behavior. Your plan should include the following elements:

- Describing the behavior
- Obtaining a baseline

- Establishing goals
- Developing behavior change strategies
- Assessment

2. Now implement the plan you have developed. Review your efforts to change your behavior. Reward yourself for any successes and think about how you might change your plan if it is not as successful as you had hoped. Write about this in your journal.
3. Think about a time when you tried to change your behavior. Perhaps you tried to stop smoking, or set out to take a more active part in discussions at work or school. Identify the strategies you used to change your behavior. Then assess the outcome. What factors were important in determining the outcome of your efforts? Now that you have learned about strategies to facilitate behavior change, what, if anything, would you have done differently? Write about this in your journal.

SUMMARY

This chapter discussed the importance of focusing on behaviors in counseling and psychotherapy as well as some of the advantages and disadvantages of emphasizing actions in treatment. The chapter also outlined a process for planning and implementing behavior change: describing the behavior, establishing a baseline, setting clear and realistic goals, developing helpful strategies, implementing the plan, assessing the outcome, and reinforcing and maintaining progress.

CHAPTER 19

Behavior Therapy and Cognitive-Behavioral Therapy

By the 1970s, behavior therapy, initiated during the 1950s and 1960s, presented a powerful challenge to the principles of psychoanalysis. Behavior therapy's focus on the present rather than the past; on observable behaviors rather than the unconscious; and on short-term treatment, clear goals, and rapid change had considerable appeal.

Behavior therapy continues to play an important role in counseling and psychology. It offers clinicians a wealth of helpful strategies and is useful in a broad range of settings and with a diverse clientele. Behavior therapy usually is integrated with cognitive therapy and other treatment approaches.

This chapter introduces the principles of behavior therapy and describes many of its useful strategies. In addition, we review cognitive-behavioral therapy (CBT) and present information on its application and effectiveness. We pay particular attention to cognitive behavior modification and stress inoculation training developed by Donald Meichenbaum, which integrate cognitive and behavioral approaches. Readers should keep in mind that the demarcation between cognitive and behavioral approaches is not clear and that the cognitive approaches of Beck, Ellis, and others also pay attention to behaviors.

The differences among cognitive therapy, behavior therapy, and cognitive-behavioral treatment are primarily those of emphasis. Cognitive approaches focus on changing thoughts; behavioral approaches concentrate on modifying actions; and cognitive-behavioral approaches attend to both thoughts and actions.

THE DEVELOPMENT AND DEVELOPERS OF BEHAVIOR THERAPY

Unlike many of the theories discussed in this book, behavior therapy is not strongly associated with one or two names. Instead, many people contributed to the evolution of this approach. Some, like Eysenck, Lazarus, Wolpe, Dollard and Miller, Krumboltz, and Bandura, applied behavior therapy and learning theory to people. Others, including Skinner, Harlow, and Pavlov, used principles of behavior change to shape the actions and reactions of animals. All of these contributed to the development of behavior therapy.

B. F. Skinner

B. F. Skinner, an experimental psychologist, may be the best-known behavioral theorist. Skinner received many awards for his contributions to psychology from the 1950s until his death. He emphasized the orderliness of behavior and sought principles to describe and predict behavioral patterns as well as ways to modify behavior. His ideas, known as *operant reinforcement theory* (Skinner, 1969), postulate that how often a behavior will be emitted is largely determined by the events that follow that behavior. Drawing on the principles of *operant conditioning* in one of his studies, Skinner used rewards to gradually shape pigeons' naturally emitted behaviors until the pigeons learned to peck at a red disc. Similarly, children's behavior can be shaped through parental reinforcement; for example, parents who attend primarily to children's misbehavior inadvertently reinforce that behavior.

Ivan Pavlov

In the early 1900s, Ivan Pavlov (1927), a Russian physiologist, identified and described a type of learning that now is known as *classical conditioning*. His study of conditioning dogs' responses is well known. Pavlov demonstrated that, by simultaneously presenting an unconditioned stimulus (meat paste) and a conditioned stimulus (the sound of a tuning fork), researchers could elicit the dogs' salivation using only the conditioned stimulus (the sound) because the dogs learned to associate the sound with the meat.

Pavlov also studied the process of *extinction*. For a while, the dogs in his study salivated to the sound of the tuning fork, even when the sound was no longer accompanied by the meat. However, over time, the salivating response diminished and eventually disappeared in response to the tuning fork alone.

John W. Watson

John W. Watson, an American psychologist, used Pavlov's principles of classical conditioning and *stimulus generalization,* along with concepts of learning theory, to change human behavior. Rejecting psychoanalysis, then the prevailing treatment approach, Watson (1925) proposed what he called *behaviorism.* Watson demonstrated that an unconditioned stimulus (a loud bell), paired with a conditioned stimulus (a white rat), could lead a child to emit a conditioned response (startle) in reaction not only to a white rat but also to white cotton and Watson's white hair.

John Dollard and Neal Miller

Subsequent work by John Dollard and Neal Miller (1950) contributed greatly to understanding of learning theory and paved the way for behaviorists to move into the arena of psychotherapy. Dollard and Miller identified four important elements in behavior: drive, cue, response, and reinforcement. In *Social Learning and Imitation* (Miller & Dollard, 1941), they wrote:

> What, then, is learning theory? In its simplest form, it is the study of the circumstances under which a response and a cue stimulus become connected. After learning has been completed, response and cue are bound together in such a way that the appearance of the cue evokes the response . . . The connection between a cue and a response can be strengthened under certain conditions. The learner must be driven to make the response and rewarded for having responded in the presence of the cue. (p. 1)

The more frequently a stimulus and a response coincide, with the response being rewarded, the stronger is the tendency to emit the response when that stimulus occurs, leading to the development of a habit or habitual response. This is the essence of the *stimulus-response (S-R) concept,* which, according to behavior theorists, determines the behaviors that people learn.

For example, Jamila was the third child in a family of seven children. Both parents worked outside of the home and had little time for positive interactions with their children. Whenever one of the children was sick, however, the parents gave them extra time and attention. Jamila learned that illness was the best way to elicit her parents attention and so exaggerated even minor physical symptoms for the nurturance that would bring her. She continued this behavior into adulthood, even though it had a deleterious effect on her relationships, her employment, and eventually on her marriage.

Dollard and Miller found that *counterconditioning* could reverse habits. This involves pairing the behavior to be changed with a strong incompatible response to the same cue. For example, Jamila's behavior gradually changed as her employer, friends, and partner became annoyed with her frequent complaints of physical discomfort and withdrew from her when she reported feeling ill.

Joseph Wolpe

Joseph Wolpe (1969) described a similar process, *reciprocal inhibition,* in which eliciting a novel response brings about a decrease in the strength of a concurrent habitual response. A parent who makes a silly face to cheer up a child who is crying after a minor fall is a simple example; the silly face elicits amusement, which automatically reduces the sad emotions associated with the fall. Wolpe's ideas led to the development of *systematic desensitization,* a powerful tool that pairs relaxation with controlled exposure to a feared stimulus such as heights or dogs. This technique still is widely used, especially in treatment of phobias, and is discussed in detail later in this chapter. Wolpe also developed strategies to promote assertive behavior.

Wolpe's work reflects the concept of *stimulus generalization*. When people learn to respond in a particular way to one stimulus, they often behave in that same way when presented with similar cues. For example, a child who is taught to be respectful of teachers is likely to behave respectfully toward other authority figures. Sometimes behavior is overgeneralized and becomes inappropriate or unhealthy. Then people need to learn *stimulus discrimination*—the ability to distinguish among similar cues. For example, most of us have learned to confide in a small number of close friends but recognize that it is inappropriate to share many details of our personal lives at work (stimulus discrimination). However, some people share intimate details of their lives not only with close friends but with casual associates, perhaps reflecting inappropriate stimulus generalization.

Albert Bandura

Albert Bandura (1969) played an important role in the development of behavior therapy through his application of principles of both classical and operant conditioning to social learning. He found that learning and subsequent behavior change could occur vicariously through observation of other people's behaviors. This process, which Bandura called *modeling,* can elicit both positive and negative behaviors.

Modeling often has a beneficial impact. Observing someone we admire undertake a challenging task can reduce our fears and facilitate our efforts to perform the task. On the other hand, Bandura's experiments suggested that children who observed adults acting aggressively were more likely to manifest aggressive behavior than children who had not been exposed to such models. These findings have implications for understanding the apparent increase in violent behaviors in young people.

Current Development

By the 1980s, behavior therapy had established its place in psychotherapy, and its effectiveness was well substantiated by research. However, many clinicians were dissatisfied with traditional behavior therapy which de-emphasized the therapeutic alliance, viewed the clinician as the authority, and sometimes seemed dehumanizing. As a result, the shape of behavior therapy has evolved over the past 25 years. A positive and collaborative treatment alliance is now an essential element of treatment. The move to integrate behavior therapy and cognitive therapy (reflected in the work of Meichenbaum, Lazarus, Ellis, Beck, and others) has broadened the application of this approach and made it less mechanical and more sensitive to individual needs.

IMPORTANT THEORETICAL CONCEPTS

The application of behavior therapy varies, depending on clinician, client, concern, and setting. Most approaches to behavior therapy can be described by one or more of the following five models (Wilson, 1995):

1. *Applied behavioral analysis.* Derived from Skinner's theory of operant conditioning, this approach looks at the impact of environmental events on behavior. It takes a scientific approach and focuses on observable, measurable behavior.

2. *Neo-behaviorism.* Drawing on Pavlov's classical conditioning as well as stimulus-response theories, this focuses on the process of conditioning or learning responses.

3. *Social learning theory.* Based on the research of Bandura, this approach seeks to understand the interaction of cognitive, behavioral, and environmental factors in shaping behavior. Many strategies that clinicians use to enhance self-efficacy and reduce learned helplessness reflect understanding of social learning (Seligman, 1990).

4. *Cognitive-behavioral therapy.* Reflected in the work of Meichenbaum, Ellis, and Beck, this approach looks at how cognitions shape behaviors and emotions. This treatment system makes use of both cognitive and behavioral strategies to effect change.

5. *Multimodal therapy.* Multimodal therapy (discussed in part 6), developed by Arnold Lazarus, is based on principles of behavior therapy. More a holistic approach to assessment and treatment planning than a type of behavior therapy, it systematically integrates strategies from a wide range of approaches.

Principles of Behavior Therapy

Regardless of their specific approach to behavior therapy, behavior therapists generally subscribe to the following principles (Myers & Thyer, 1994; Stuart, 1998):

- Although genetics play a role, individual differences are derived primarily from different experiences.
- Behavior is learned and acquired largely through modeling, conditioning, and reinforcement.
- Behavior has a purpose.
- Behavior is the major determinant of habits, thoughts, emotions, and other aspects of personality.
- Behavior therapy seeks to understand and change behavior.
- Therapy should be based on the scientific method and be systematic, empirical, and experimental. Goals should be stated in behavioral, specific, and measurable terms, with progress assessed regularly.
- The focus of treatment should generally be on the present. Even if behaviors are long-standing, they are maintained by factors in the current environment.
- However, behaviors must be viewed in context, and some exploration of the past is appropriate to provide that context and help people feel understood.
- Education, promoting new learning and transfer of learning, is an important aspect of behavior therapy.
- Strategies of behavior therapy need to be individualized to the particular person and problem.
- People need to take an active part in their treatment to successfully change their behaviors. Clients have primary responsibility for defining their goals and completing homework tasks. The treatment plan is formulated collaboratively, with both client and clinician participating actively in that process.

Some people think of behavior therapy as narrow, directive, and deterministic. However, Myers and Thyer (1994) and Stuart (1998) dispute those misconceptions, asserting that modern behavior therapy has both depth and breadth as reflected in the following concepts and practices:

- Although behavior therapists may focus on observable behavior, they interpret behavior broadly as anything an organism does, including thinking and feeling, and are interested in the total person.
- Behavior therapists recognize the importance of a collaborative and positive therapeutic relationship and the communication of encouragement as important in promoting learning and motivation.
- Although objectivity and the scientific method are valued, behavior therapists also recognize the importance of understanding and respecting individual differences.

The Development of Personality

According to behaviorists, when children are born, they have three basic building blocks of personality:

1. Primary drives, such as those toward food and warmth
2. Specific reflexes, such as sucking and blinking
3. Innate responses to particular stimuli, such as escape or crying in reaction to pain

Many behavior therapists also acknowledge that some temperaments have a hereditary basis. Beyond that, behavior therapists believe that personality is shaped primarily through learning and maturation. New behaviors may be emitted accidentally, acquired after observation of others, or be the product of thought. Whether these new behaviors continue to be emitted frequently and become a habit or are rarely if ever produced depends largely on the conditions accompanying or following the behavior. Both maladaptive and healthy behaviors are learned because they have yielded positive reinforcement or led to a decrease in an aversive stimulus. In other words, both internal reinforcements, such as good or bad feelings, and external reinforcements, such as praise or punishment, are the primary determinants of the development of a behavior.

UNDERSTANDING TERMINOLOGY

Terminology of behavior therapy can be confusing. However, becoming familiar with terminology facilitates understanding of this approach as well as of personality development. Following is a review of important terms, illustrated by the experiences of Theresa, a 33-year-old woman receiving chemotherapy for breast cancer. Although we discussed some of these terms previously, we review them here for clarification.

Theresa presented many issues related to her diagnosis of cancer. She had always been fearful of injections and found blood tests and intravenous chemotherapy difficult. She had anticipatory nausea associated with her chemotherapy, becoming queasy when driving into the parking lot of the clinic where she received treatment, whether or not she was scheduled for chemotherapy. In addition, although her prognosis was encouraging, Theresa constantly ruminated about the likelihood of her death.

Theresa's anticipatory nausea can be explained by *classical conditioning*. The *unconditioned stimulus*, the chemotherapy, elicited the *response* of nausea. Because that stimulus was paired with the *conditioned stimulus* of driving to the clinic, entering the parking lot became a stimulus that also elicited the response of nausea whether or not the chemotherapy also was present.

Theresa, like all of us, had an innate *drive* to avoid pain. When she received inoculations as a child, her parents reinforced her fears by paying special attention to her when she became fearful. As a result of this *operant conditioning,* her fear of injections became *habitual* and evolved into a *phobia.* In fact, through the process of *stimulus generalization,* Theresa experienced inordinate anxiety in reaction to any medical appointment, whether or not it necessitated an injection. Her *learned behavior* reflected a *stimulus-response model;* because her fearful behavior was rewarded in childhood, Theresa demonstrated fear and avoidance (response) to the stimulus of any medical visit.

Her therapist used several behavioral approaches to modify Theresa's responses. *Systematic desensitization* was used in the hope of *extinguishing* Theresa's excessive fear of medical visits and inoculations. An *anxiety hierarchy* was created, listing her fears in ascending order from the mildest fear (a visit to a dermatologist that would not involve any physical discomfort) to the most frightening (a visit to the oncologist for chemotherapy). Beginning with the mildest fear, the therapist helped Theresa to relax and feel empowered while visualizing the frightening stimulus. This process of *reciprocal inhibition* paired relaxation and positive feelings with an *aversive stimulus* (a frightening image) to decrease the strength of the fear response. Theresa also learned to use both relaxation and *stimulus discrimination* to reduce her fears; she learned to relax when approaching medical visits and driving into the parking lot at the oncology clinic and reminded herself that not all medical appointments involved discomfort.

Counterconditioning was used to help Theresa further reduce her fears; when she began to ruminate or felt anxious, she visualized herself triumphantly completing her chemotherapy and setting off on a trip to Bali that she was planning. The feelings of pride and optimism elicited by that image counteracted and reduced her apprehension. To make sure she could readily access this positive image, the therapist led Theresa through a process of *covert modeling* in which she mentally rehearsed dealing effectively with her fears about chemotherapy. Joining a support group of other women diagnosed with breast cancer also provided Theresa with an experience in *social learning and reinforcement* and gave her additional *role models.*

STEPS IN TREATMENT

Chapter 18 discussed the steps in a plan to effect behavior change. Although we review them here, readers will find more detailed information in that chapter. Once behavior therapists believe they have obtained enough information to have at least a basic understanding of their clients and to put their concerns in context, clinicians and clients collaborate to develop a plan, generally characterized by the following eight steps:

1. Describe the problem.
   - Review the nature of the problem and its history.
   - Explore the context of the target (unwanted) behaviors.
2. Establish a baseline, reflecting the current frequency, duration, and severity of the target behaviors.
3. Determine goals.
   - Make sure that goals are realistic, clear, specific, and measurable.
   - Make sure that goals are meaningful to the client.
   - State goals positively. "Arrive at work on time at least twice this week" is a more appealing goal than "Avoid being late to work at least twice this week."

4. Develop strategies to facilitate change.
   - Change precipitating conditions that trigger undesirable behaviors.
   - Teach skills and provide information that contribute to the desired change.
   - Review and enhance impulse-control strategies.
   - Use additional strategies such as modeling, rehearsal, and systematic desensitization to facilitate positive change.
   - Formulate appropriate reinforcement contingencies and, if indicated, meaningful consequences.
   - Carefully plan implementation of the change process as well as ways to monitor and record the outcomes of that process.
   - Client and clinician make a written contract; clinician encourages the client to share the commitment to change with others.
5. Implement the plan.
6. Assess progress and evaluate the success of the plan.
   - Monitor and review the results of the implementation.
   - Emphasize successes.
   - Identify and address any obstacles to change.
   - If necessary, revise the plan.
7. Reinforce successes to promote empowerment, continue progress and positive changes.
8. Continue the process by making plans to promote maintenance of gains and prevent relapse.

COGNITIVE-BEHAVIORAL THERAPY

Behavior therapy is often integrated with cognitive therapy to create a powerful treatment approach known as cognitive-behavioral therapy (CBT). (This is also referred to as cognitive behavior therapy.) The National Association of Cognitive-Behavioral Therapists (NACBT) views Ellis's rational emotive behavior therapy and Beck's cognitive therapy (discussed in part 4 of this book) as examples of CBT, along with Meichenbaum's and Linehan's treatment approaches, discussed later in this chapter. In effect, any treatment approach that emphasizes thoughts as well as behaviors, and pays only secondary attention to background and emotions, can be viewed as CBT.

CBT evolved from cognitive therapy through incorporation of components of behavior therapy (Parker, Roy, & Eyers, 2003). Descriptions of CBT emphasize cognitions over behaviors, but do integrate guidelines and strategies for the two approaches in a synergistic way. According to NACBT, cognitive-behavioral therapy is based on the principle that thoughts, rather than external circumstances, cause feelings and behaviors. Treatment generally focuses most on a cognitive event, in which a stimulus activates a dysfunctional thought process, leading to an erroneous and harmful thought which, in turn, promotes dysfunctional behaviors. This pattern usually is linked to underlying or core cognitions, discussed in part 4. NACBT further describes CBT as a brief and time-limited approach that recognizes the importance of a sound and collaborative therapeutic alliance. CBT is structured and directive, relying heavily on education, questions, and the inductive method. These strategies are not intended to tell people how to think, act, or feel, but rather to help them test their hypotheses and think, act, and feel in ways that are helpful to them and consistent with reality. Homework is an essential ingredient of CBT, and is used to help people make progress between sessions and apply what they have learned.

Meichenbaum's Cognitive Behavior Modification

Probably the best-known treatment approach that bills itself as a form of CBT is Donald Meichenbaum's cognitive behavior modification. That approach is discussed here to illustrate CBT.

Meichenbaum (1993) developed cognitive behavior modification (CBM) in an effort to integrate psychodynamic and cognitive treatment systems with the "technology of behavior therapists" (p. 202). He believed that no one of these treatment systems alone was sufficient to explain psychopathology and promote behavior change but that the combination could accomplish both goals.

Three assumptions of CBM clarify how Meichenbaum (1993) integrates cognitive and behavior theory:

1. *Constructive narrative.* People actively construct their own reality; "reality is a product of personal meanings" (p. 203).
2. *Information processing.* As previously described, an activating event taps into a person's core cognitions, leading to an unhelpful, inaccurate, and distorted thought. People experience negative emotions and engage in unwise and harmful behaviors because they distort reality as a result of cognitive errors and misperceptions.
3. *Conditioning.* Cognitions are viewed as covert behaviors that have been conditioned. Correspondingly, they can be deconditioned and modified through both external and internal contingencies (rewards or negative consequences), thereby strengthening new and healthier cognitions. Modeling, mental rehearsal, and other strategies are important in effecting cognitive change.

The Role of the Clinician   According to Meichenbaum (1993), the role of a cognitive-behavioral therapist is that of co-constructivist: helping people alter their stories and cognitions so they can build "new assumptive worlds" (p. 203). To accomplish this, treatment via CBM entails the use of cognitive interventions, such as Socratic dialog (questions designed to promote clearer perceptions and thoughts) and reframing (changing terminology in an effort to change perceptions).

To illustrate these strategies, let's consider Telly who believed that, following an argument, his daughter was enraged with him because she had not returned his telephone calls. The clinician might ask the following Socratic questions, of course pausing for responses between questions, "What leads you to assume that her silence reflects rage? Is she prone to react with rage? Is it possible that she is hurt or needs time to sort out her reactions to the argument? How can you determine what she is really feeling?" Using reframing, the clinician might refer to the daughter's decision to "take a break" or "take some time to cool off," rather than using Telly's language that describes her as "ending their relationship."

Although clinicians practicing CBM draw on a broad range of treatment strategies, they generally believe that treatment should be demystified and techniques de-emphasized. Learning and self-help are encouraged, and feedback from the client is welcomed. Clients become active, knowledgeable, and responsible partners in their own treatment.

Stress Inoculation Training

Meichenbaum (1985) developed stress inoculation training (SIT), a useful and effective cognitive-behavioral treatment procedure. People typically experience stress because of a perception that their life circumstances exceed their capacity to cope, to effectively use "behavioral and cognitive efforts to master, reduce, or tolerate the internal and/or external demands that are created by stressful transactions" (p. 3). SIT is an approach to reducing stress. It assumes that if people can successfully cope with relatively mild stressors, they will be able to tolerate and successfully cope with more severe ones. In other words, as its name implies, SIT seeks to immunize people against the adverse impact of stress by helping them successfully handle increasing levels of stress. SIT usually consists of 12–15 weekly sessions plus additional follow-up sessions over 6–12 months.

SIT has three phases (Meichenbaum, 1985):

1. *Conceptualization.* Clients and clinicians develop a collaborative relationship. People are taught about stress; the relationship between stress and coping; and the roles that thoughts, actions, and emotions play in engendering and maintaining stress. Once people have an understanding of stress and factors that promote it, their stressful thoughts and experiences (as well as the antecedents and consequences of those thoughts and experiences) are explored. Particular attention is paid to stress-inducing and stress-reducing self-statements and self-talk. Initial goals of treatment include translating stress into specific fears and problems that are amenable to solution and helping people achieve some control over their lives.
2. *Skills acquisition and rehearsal phase.* Treatment during this phase teaches people to cope effectively with mild stressors by gathering information, using coping self-statements, learning relaxation strategies, changing their behaviors, or using other strategies to reduce those fears. In addition, people learn to apply problem solving to their fears according to the following five steps:
   • Problem identification
   • Goal selection, focusing on small manageable units of stress
   • Development of alternatives
   • Evaluation of each possible solution and its probable consequences
   • Decision making and rehearsal of coping strategies
3. *Application and follow-through.* In phase 3, people implement their plans to solve problems and reduce stress. Increasingly distressing stressors are tackled as people become able to modify their dysfunctional thoughts, effectively use coping skills, and apply what they learned in phase 2. For example, a person might initially use self-talk to address a minor stressor such as being kept waiting for an appointment and gradually work up to addressing major stressors such as a verbally abusive partner. Like Beck's cognitive therapy, SIT uses the 0–100 subjective units of distress (SUDS) scale to identify the impact of stressors and then track clients' progress in coping with them.

Treatment includes continuous reinforcement and assessment of people's efforts and accomplishments. Strategies such as coping imagery and cognitive rehearsal are used to solidify gains, generalize learning to more significant fears, and help people to prevent or cope with relapses. Learning ways to reduce their fears, along with increased confidence from initial successes in managing stress, facilitates people's efforts to address other fears and problems successfully. Taking one step at a time and building on successes can make challenging situations manageable and foster self-esteem and more desirable cognitions and behaviors. In addition, encouraging people to have a sense of responsibility for their futures rather than their pasts during this phase of treatment can be very empowering.

TREATMENT USING BEHAVIOR THERAPY AND COGNITIVE-BEHAVIORAL THERAPY

Behavior therapy and CBT make substantial use of specific strategies and interventions. Although these are important treatment ingredients, they should not overshadow the broad goals of treatment and the importance of the therapeutic alliance.

Goals

Behavior therapy, as its name implies, seeks to extinguish maladaptive behaviors and help people learn new adaptive ones. The following is a partial list of goals that can be achieved through behavior therapy:

- Reduction in use, or abstinence, from drugs and alcohol
- Reduction of undesirable habits such as nail biting and pulling out one's own hair
- Improvement in social skills such as assertiveness and conversation
- Amelioration of fears and phobias such as fear of flying, apprehension about public speaking, and excessive fear of snakes
- Improvement in concentration and organization
- Reduction in undesirable behaviors in children such as tantrums, disobedience, acting out, aggressiveness, and difficulty going to bed
- Improvement in health and fitness habits such as more nutritious eating, increased exercise, and more regular sleep patterns

In addition to specific goals such as these, behavior therapists also have the general goal of teaching people skills that will help them improve their lives. Skills such as decision-making, problem analysis and resolution, time management, assertiveness, and relaxation often are incorporated into behavior therapy.

CBT encompasses similar goals, but also entails additional goals related to modification of thoughts. These might include enabling people to recognize, assess, and modify their dysfunctional cognitions; changing persistent underlying cognitions such as "I must be perfect" and "I am unlovable;" and helping people make positive changes in their self-talk and sense of empowerment.

In CBT, cognitive goals and behavioral goals are usually complimentary and often intertwined. For example, Megan has been unable to locate employment because of a combination of her self-defeating thoughts (e.g., I can't do anything right; no one would want to hire me) and impairment in her skills (e.g., writing a resume, presenting herself well in an interview, initiating conversations, time management). Although Megan's primary goal is to locate rewarding employment, many small goals along the way would focus on changing both thoughts and behaviors to help her achieve that goal.

Therapeutic Alliance

Modern behavior and cognitive-behavioral therapists believe that establishment of a positive and collaborative therapeutic alliance is essential. In fact, some studies have found that cognitive-behavioral and behavior therapists outperformed psychodynamic/interpersonal therapists in terms of their ability to establish highly effective working alliances with their clients (Myers & Thyer, 1994; Raue, Goldfried, & Barkham, 1997).

Clinicians practicing CBT assume many roles: teacher, consultant, advisor, devil's advocate, supporter, role model, encourager, and facilitator. Active listening, understanding, caring, respect, and concern all are part of the therapist's repertoire as is helping clients to understand and make use of the principles of CBT. Although therapists encourage and reinforce positive change, they also value genuineness and professionalism. According to Jacobson (1989), "The therapist who offers unsolicited reassurance, arbitrary reinforcement, or deceptive acceptance will be acting in a self-defeating manner" (p. 93). Clinicians practicing CBT are cautious about giving advice and praise. They want clients to take credit for their positive changes rather than attribute them to the therapists. Symbolic of the caring that behavior therapists have toward their clients was the American Humanist Association's 1972 selection of B. F. Skinner as Humanist of the Year.

Clients are expected to participate fully in the process of behavior or cognitive-behavioral therapy and take responsibility for presenting their concerns, identifying their goals, and implementing plans for change. Clinicians typically encourage clients to try out new behaviors, complete tasks between sessions, self-monitor, and provide feedback to the clinicians. CBT and behavior therapy today are shared endeavors.

Strategies and Interventions

Behavior and cognitive-behavioral therapists use a broad range of specific change strategies. These strategies also can be useful to clinicians using other treatment approaches.

Cognitive techniques have been discussed in earlier chapters of this book. However, to facilitate their integration into behavior therapy and CBT, they are listed here followed by the chapter number in which they are described in more detail. Behavior change strategies are also listed here, with an accompanying description.

Cognitive Strategies

Strategies to improve thinking

- Ellis's *ABCDEF* model (16)
- Self-talk (15)
- Development and assessment of alternatives (15)
- Relabeling and reframing (15)
- Projecting into the future/distancing (15)
- Systematic decision making (16)
- Problem solving (16)

Strategies to curtail ruminating and repetitive self-destructive thoughts

- Distraction (16)
- Thought stopping (16)

- Writing out thoughts, letter writing (16, 17)
- Flooding (17)

Strategies to improve coping skills

- Cognitive and covert modeling (16)
- Visual imagery (14, 16)
- Graded task assignments (16)
- Bibliotherapy (16)
- Role playing (16)

Strategies to reinforce positive change

- Affirmations (16)
- Focusing on the positive (17)
- Cueing, anchoring (18)

Behavioral Strategies

Acting as if. This strategy was first developed by Alfred Adler (discussed in chapter 5), whose ideas can be viewed as an early version of CBT. When confronting a challenging situation, people "act as if" they are someone whom they view as capable of handling the situation effectively. Children undergoing medical treatments, for example, have coped more successfully when they pretended to be their favorite superhero. Adults, too, can benefit from this empowering approach by acting as if they are an admired friend or colleague.

Activity scheduling. Planning activities that are rewarding and provide a sense of accomplishment can help people in many ways. Having a schedule provides focus and direction, which can counteract inertia, confusion, and problems in decision making. It can limit excessive sleeping or television watching and prevent isolation. It increases optimism and reduces depression by helping people realize that they can enjoy their lives and have successes.

Activities designed to accomplish treatment goals are particularly valuable. For example, the person who is overwhelmed by a recent job loss can benefit from preparing a realistic schedule of activities to find another job. The schedule should list the activities, when they will be performed, and how much time will be spent on each task.

Exercise and other forms of physical activity also can be very helpful. Research has shown that physical exercise can reduce depression and increase the secretion of endorphins that improve feelings of well-being (Locke & Colligan, 1987).

Aversion therapy. Rewards rather than punishments or negative consequences are usually favored in therapy because they enhance self-esteem, optimism, and relationships. However, sometimes linking undesirable behaviors with negative experiences motivates change. Readers should bear in mind that aversion therapy is a risky intervention. Care must be exercised in planning and implementing aversion therapy to be sure it does not have a negative emotional or physical impact and is respectful of people's rights and choices. Done poorly, aversion therapy can cause people to leave therapy prematurely, to feel exploited and traumatized, and to develop even more severe symptoms.

Antabuse, an emetic used to discourage people from consuming alcohol, is an example of aversion therapy. Time-outs, used to modify children's behavior, are another form of aversion therapy, although their primary purpose is to give a child an opportunity to calm down and reflect.

Visual imagery sometimes entails aversion therapy. For example, a woman who wants to stop smoking might imagine herself having severe difficulty breathing or coping with a smoking-related disease. A young man who is contemplating suicide so that his girlfriend will feel guilty about ending their relationship may change his mind after imagining himself lying in his grave while she goes on to have a full and rewarding life.

Satiation—giving people excessive exposure to a negative stimulus or behavior—is a type of aversion therapy (see chapter 16). For example, the woman who wants to stop smoking might smoke a large number of cigarettes in rapid succession until she feels ill.

Behavioral rehearsal. This strategy gives people an opportunity to practice a challenging task. The rehearsal might involve a role play with the clinician or a practice session with a friend. Tape-recording the rehearsal or observing oneself in the mirror while practicing the desired behavior offers opportunities for feedback and improvement.

Behavioral rehearsal can be used for a wide variety of experiences. Making or refusing requests and sharing positive and negative feelings with others lend themselves particularly well to behavioral rehearsal. Behavioral rehearsal also can help people improve their social skills—for example, by practicing ways to initiate and maintain conversations or invite other people to join them in social activities.

Biofeedback. Biofeedback involves the use of instruments that monitor bodily functions such as heart rate, sweat gland activity, skin temperature, and pulse rate and give people feedback on those functions via a tone or light. Biofeedback can promote reductions in tension and anxiety and increased relaxation. It also can have physical and medical benefits such as lowering blood pressure and improving pain control.

Contracting. Establishing a clear agreement between client and clinician about the goals of treatment and the roles of both participants is an important component of CBT and behavior therapy. Contracting is usually done early in the treatment process. However, each time a new problem area is targeted for change, client and clinician can expand their contract to include additional objectives and procedures. This provides direction and motivation and can increase client cooperation with the treatment process.

Diaphragmatic breathing. Taking slow, deep breaths and focusing on breathing can be calming and even induce sleep. This sort of breathing supplies the body with more oxygen, focuses concentration, and increases self-control and mindfulness. Abdominal, or diaphragmatic, breathing is particularly helpful; people breath in through the nose, expanding the diaphragm, and then expel the air through the mouth. Counting to eight with each breath creates a slow and relaxed pace (Golden, Gersh, & Robbins, 1992).

Expressive and creative activities. Although art therapy, dance therapy, and music therapy are professions in their own right, clinicians with other areas of specialization sometimes incorporate these and other forms of creative self-expression into their work. This can enable people to become more aware of and give form to their emotions. Expressive techniques can be particularly successful with people who have difficulty verbalizing their feelings and concerns or who may feel stuck or blocked. These approaches can be freeing and empowering and are useful with both adults and children. Of course, they should be used cautiously by clinicians who do not have specialized training in therapeutic use of the arts.

Extinction. Extinction involves withdrawing the payoff of an undesirable behavior in hopes of reducing or eliminating it. For example, parents who give their children extra attention whenever they misbehave may be inadvertently reinforcing the undesirable behavior. Coaching the parents to pay attention to positive behavior and ignore misbehavior as much as possible is likely to reduce negative behavior.

Flooding. Flooding, like aversion therapy, is a high-risk intervention that must be used with caution, and only by clinicians who are well versed in the appropriate use of this strategy. In flooding, people are exposed to high doses of a feared stimulus in the expectation that this will desensitize them to the feared stimulus. An example is putting a person with a fear of balloons in a room full of balloons. The person must remain in the feared situation long enough for the fear to peak and then diminish. If the person leaves the situation prematurely, the fear may worsen and the person may learn to fear those who staged the flooding. In addition, the fear may lead the person to act in unsafe ways.

Some people believe that pushing a child into a swimming pool is a way to cure a fear of water. This misguided belief can endanger the child's life, create a traumatic experience, and impair the child's trust in others. Flooding should rarely be used, and then only after the client is fully informed about the procedure and consents to the procedure.

Modeling. By observing models and identifying the ingredients that make their behaviors successful, people can expand their repertoire of positive behaviors. People are most likely to be influenced by models who are similar to them in terms of gender, age, race, and beliefs; perceived as attractive and admirable in realistic ways; and viewed as competent and warm (Bandura, 1969). Clients can observe others engaged in behaviors or activities that they would like to emulate, such as public speaking, conversing at social gatherings, or offering suggestions at a meeting. Clinicians can serve as models, demonstrating target behaviors. Clients also can serve as their own models by making audio or video recordings of themselves engaged in positive and desired behaviors.

Reasonable (natural) consequences. Discussed further in chapter 20, reasonable consequences are the logical, and usually unpleasant, outcomes of undesirable behavior. For example, the child who does not pick up her toys before dinner is required to clean her room after dinner instead of watching her favorite television program. Getting fired for repeatedly coming to work late is another example of such a consequence. Although reasonable consequences can be viewed as punishment, they are preferable to arbitrary and contrived punishments because they have a logical connection to the undesirable behavior and give people a strong message about the implications of their behavior.

Reinforcements. Reinforcements and rewards encourage behavior change, enhance learning, and solidify gains. Reinforcements should be carefully selected and planned; they should be meaningful and worthwhile to the person so that they are motivating and should be realistic and reasonable. For example, giving a child a video game for cleaning his room once is not realistic, but setting aside $3 toward the purchase of a video game each week the child cleans his room five out of seven days probably is.

Adults can create their own reinforcement plans. One woman who had difficulty paying bills on time set aside 1 hour twice a week for organizing her finances. Each time she completed the hour of financial planning, she rewarded herself by going to the bookstore to buy a new mystery and spending the rest of the evening reading her book.

Rewards need not be material. Social reinforcement, such as parental approval, a positive rating at work, and admiration from friends can be at least as powerful. In addition, clients can reward themselves through positive affirmations and reminders of their success such as the declining balance on their credit bill and their improved grades. Reinforcements usually are most powerful if they are provided shortly after the success and are clearly linked to the accomplishment. Such reinforcers are particularly likely to solidify the desired change in behavior and contribute to either further change or maintenance of goal achievement.

Relaxation. Relaxation is often combined with other techniques such as systematic desensitization, abdominal breathing, hypnosis, and visual imagery. Teaching relaxation strategies in a treatment session and encouraging practice between sessions can facilitate people's efforts to reduce stress and anxiety and make behavioral changes. Several well-established relaxation strategies are available, including progressive muscle relaxation (sequentially tensing and relaxing each muscle group in the body); a body scan (each part of the body is systematically assessed and relaxed); and simple exercises such as head rolls, shoulder shrugs, and shaking one's body until it feels loose and relaxed.

Shaping. This technique is used to effect a gradual change in behaviors. People make successive approximations of desired behaviors, eventually leading to new patterns of behavior. For example, the following steps might help people with social anxiety to improve their interactions with others:

- Spend 5–10 minutes at a social gathering. Do not initiate any conversations.
- Spend 5–10 minutes at a social gathering and greet at least two people.
- Spend 15–20 minutes at a social gathering, greet at least two people, introduce yourself to at least one person, and ask a question of one other person.
- Follow the previous step and, in addition, have a brief conversation about the weather and compliment the host on the food.

Skill training. An important component of promoting positive change is teaching people the skills they need to effect that change. Clinicians can teach clients both general skills (e.g., assertiveness training, decision making, problem solving, communication skills) and those serving the needs of a particular person (e.g., interviewing, anger management). Parents often benefit from learning to use behavior change strategies with their children. Bibliotherapy, or relevant readings, can supplement clinicians' efforts to teach new skills. Many books are available, for example, on assertiveness, time management, parenting, and other positive behaviors.

Systematic desensitization. Systematic desensitization, a powerful behavior change strategy, is useful in reducing fears, phobias, obsessions and compulsions, and anxiety. Systematic desensitization can be conducted in the imagination (imaginal desensitization) or in context (*in vivo* desensitization).

Initial fears often are worsened when the person avoids the feared stimulus and the avoidance is reinforced by the good feelings that ensue. For example, Dwanna feared interacting with strangers. As a result, she remained in her home, venturing out only with her husband. She was relieved not to struggle with her fear of people, but her avoidance kept her a prisoner and contributed to her dissatisfaction with herself and her life. Systematic desensitization is designed to reverse this process by gradually exposing a person to the disturbing stimulus in ways that reduce rather than increase fear.

The first step is the construction of an anxiety hierarchy: a list of frightening or disturbing stimuli ranked from the mildest to the most severe. Clients then learn relaxation and cognitive coping strategies to help them handle exposure to the disturbing stimuli and counteract any fears that might arise. Desensitization begins when the clinician suggests that the person focus on the mildest fear (for Dwanna, this might be standing alone in front of her open front door), pairing exposure to the stimulus with relaxation. This is repeated until the person develops comfort with a given stimulus. Then the clinician moves onto the next troubling stimulus on the list until even the greatest fears have been reduced to manageable levels. Continuing desensitization until a fear has subsided is imperative; stopping the process while a fear still is great can be iatrogenic, increasing rather than decreasing apprehension. Practicing desensitization between sessions enhances progress.

Token economies. Particularly useful in group settings such as schools, day treatment programs, hospitals, prisons, and even families, token economies are an effective and efficient way to change a broad range of behaviors in a group of people. Behavioral rules or guidelines first must be established and then understood and learned by all participants. These guidelines are generally written out and posted to maintain awareness. Then a system of rapidly identifying and recording each person's performance of the desired behaviors is developed. Staff members in a group home, for example, might place stars or marks on a chart or distribute a poker chip as soon as possible after a desired behavior is emitted.

Finally, a system of rewards is developed. The rewards should be clear, realistic, and meaningful to the participants and be given in ways that are fair and consistent. In a typical token economy, the stars, points, or poker chips are used like trading stamps to earn privileges. For example, 2 points might be exchanged for television time or a telephone call, 5 points might merit a trip to the movies, and 15 points might be exchanged for a new CD. Opportunities should be provided for frequent redemption of rewards to provide reinforcement. In addition, social reinforcement (praise, appropriate physical affection) should be paired with the material rewards to develop intrinsic motivation and internalization of the desired behaviors. Generalization of the behaviors outside of the therapeutic setting promotes their establishment.

APPLICATION OF BEHAVIOR THERAPY AND COGNITIVE-BEHAVIORAL THERAPY

Behavior therapy and cognitive-behavioral therapy have a broad range of applications. Used either alone or in combination with other treatment systems, their principles and strategies can be applied in almost any treatment setting and with almost any client or problem.

Application to Diagnostic Groups

Many empirical studies support the use of CBT with the most prevalent mental disorders. These include mood disorders, anxiety disorders, some personality disorders, eating disorders, substance use disorders, and others. In addition, CBT can relieve both emotional and physical symptoms associated with medical conditions.

Mood Disorders   Cognitive-behavioral therapy has demonstrated strong effectiveness in the treatment of mood disorders (Sexton, 1995a). Cognitive interventions can modify dysfunctional thoughts that maintain depression, hopelessness, and low self-esteem. Similarly, behavior change strategies such as activity scheduling and systematic decision making can reduce the severity of depression, counteract the inertia and confusion often associated with depression, and promote feelings of mastery and competence. The collaborative nature of CBT, as well as its clear rationale and its use of structure and achievable goals, also enhances its effect in treating depression.

Parker, Roy and Eyers (2003) conducted a meta-analysis of the efficacy of CBT in treating depression. They concluded that this approach was most effective with mild or moderate depression and that the combination of CBT and medication was more effective in treating depression than either alone.

Anxiety Disorders   Behavior therapy and CBT also are effective in treating many types of anxiety disorders. Systematic desensitization is a powerful tool in the treatment of agoraphobia and specific phobias such as fear of flying, fear of heights, and fear of snakes. People diagnosed with social phobia often benefit from training in social skills involving instruction in assertiveness and communication, modeling, role playing, and practice. Reduction in level of self-criticism via CBT also can enhance treatment of people with social phobias. Thought stopping, distraction, and substitution of positive activities for negative ones can help people cope with obsessive-compulsive disorder (OCD). In addition, aversion therapy, satiation, and flooding, used with great care, also can be useful in treatment of OCD.

Trauma-based concerns, including acute stress disorder and posttraumatic stress disorder, also respond well to CBT. Jaycox, Zoellner, and Foa (2002), for example, studied the use of CBT with women who had been sexually assaulted. They concluded that strategies such as education about PTSD, cognitive restructuring, breathing retraining, imaginal desensitization, and confrontation of feared situations gave people a greater sense of control and alleviated symptoms. Although exposure-based treatments such as systematic desensitization must be used cautiously with people who have experienced traumas, the authors found that few of those in their study experienced symptom exacerbation.

Borderline Personality Disorders   Borderline personality disorder is reflected in six behavioral patterns: emotional vulnerability, self-invalidation, constant crises, restricted emotions, learned helplessness, and impaired competence (Smith & Peck, 2004, pp. 29–30). Many people with this disorder have multiple symptoms (e.g., depression, substance misuse, impulsivity), are chronically suicidal, and have impaired functioning.

Marcia Linehan (1993) and her colleagues developed Dialectical Behavior Therapy (DBT), a form of CBT, primarily to treat people with borderline personality disorders. DBT is guided by seven assumptions (Smith & Peck, 2004, pp. 30–31):

1. Clients are doing the best they can.
2. They want to improve.
3. They must learn their new behaviors in each and all relevant contexts.
4. Clients cannot fail in DBT; any effort is progress.
5. Clients may not have caused all of their problems, but they have to solve them anyway.
6. Clients need to do better, try harder, or be more motivated to change.
7. Their lives are currently unbearable as they are being lived.

Although based on CBT, DBT also incorporates insight-oriented therapy and considerable support into the treatment package. Clients receive at least 1 year of 1-hour weekly individual therapy sessions and 2-hour weekly group therapy, emphasizing skill training and problem solving.

Available in a manualized version, DBT is characterized by four stages:

1. Clinicians help people make a commitment to treatment and facilitate their attainment of basic competencies such as keeping themselves safe, reducing self-destructive behaviors (e.g., drug and alcohol use, unwise sexual activity, self-injury), and teaching relevant skills such as interpersonal effectiveness, self-care, and emotional regulation.

2. Desensitization and other strategies help people deal with traumatic experiences and the impact of past messages and events.
3. Self-respect, problems of living, and individual goals are the focus of this stage, as clients begin to look to the future and apply what they are learning.
4. This stage promotes synthesis and generalization of gains; integration of past, present, and future; development of spirituality; acceptance of self and reality; increased self-respect; achievement of individual goals; better coping skills; and a greater capacity for happiness.

Empirical research, focused primarily on the first stage of DBT, yielded positive results. People treated with at least one year of DBT achieved considerable reductions in suicidal ideation, hospitalization, anxiety, and anger and increases in occupational and social adjustment (Linehan & Kehrer, 1993). Treatment of suicidal adolescents via DBT for one year led to significant reductions in behavioral problems, suicidal ideation, and depression (Katz, Cox, Gunasekara, & Miller, 2004). These and other studies also indicated that common symptoms accompanying borderline personality disorder, including substance misuse and dysfunctional eating, were alleviated.

Other Mental Disorders   Cognitive-behavioral therapy and behavior therapy also have demonstrated effectiveness with many other mental disorders and problems. Token economies and reasonable consequences have been used successfully to treat children and adolescents diagnosed with conduct disorders. Relaxation, activity scheduling, and time management all can be helpful to people with attention-deficit disorders. Behavior therapy has demonstrated effectiveness in helping people diagnosed with mental retardation, impulse-control disorders, sexual dysfunctions, sleep disorders, and paraphilias. Behavior therapy plays a major role in the treatment of eating disorders, including bulimia nervosa and anorexia nervosa (Pike, Walsh, Vitousek, Wilson, & Bauer 2003), as well as disorders that involve unhealthy use of drugs or alcohol. Research also supports the use of behavior therapy and CBT in the treatment of people with suicidal ideation (Carney & Hazler, 1998) and assaultive behavior (Lanza et al., 2002). CBT has facilitated improved grade-point averages, attendance, and self-concepts in academically at-risk students (Sapp, 1994).

Application to Multicultural Groups

Although research is limited on the use of behavior therapy and CBT with people from diverse backgrounds, these approaches seem well suited to treatment of a multicultural population. Behavior therapy and CBT have wide appeal. These approaches are easily understood and logical, respect individual differences, and can be adapted to a broad range of people and problems. Behavior therapy and CBT offer a large repertoire of interventions to address almost any concern. These approaches are not intrusive; they do not emphasize the unconscious, the early years of development, or the covert meanings of dreams and body language. Behavior therapy and CBT encourage people to play an active and informed role in their treatment, promote learning and competence, and can produce rapid and positive results that are reinforcing. These approaches are particularly appropriate for people from cultures that do not emphasize personal growth, insight, and self-expression. As Stuart (1998) stated of behavior therapy, "Individual differences must be understood and respected. People want to be accepted for who they are, not only for who they could be" (p. 8).

Several studies affirm the use of CBT with multicultural clients. Miranda et al. (2003), for example, found that CBT, along with medication, reduced depression in low-income young African American and Latina women. Treatment was enhanced by being combined with encouragement, intensive outreach, and direct services such as child care and transportation. Butcher and Manning (2001/2002) illustrated the application of Skinner's behavioral approaches, as well as those of other theorists, to classroom management in middle schools. Use of CBT also has shown benefits for people with medical conditions, including those experiencing chronic pain, chronic fatigue, or depression following a heart attack. In addition, CBT, along with medication, effectively reduced symptoms in Cambodian refugees experiencing posttraumatic stress disorder.

Current Use

Behavior therapy and CBT have been used in a wide variety of settings (Kazdin, 1994) and with a wide variety of people. Their use extends far beyond treatment of individuals with mental disorders. Relaxation, hypnosis, and visual imagery have been used in behavioral medicine to reduce pain and help people cope with cancer, heart disease, and other chronic and life-threatening illnesses. Schools and correctional institutions, as well as day treatment and inpatient treatment programs, rely heavily on behavior therapy to teach and establish positive behaviors.

In addition, behavior therapy and CBT can be used in family and group counseling, as well as individual therapy. The reinforcement and modeling provided by the other group members make the group setting especially well suited for CBT. Cognitive-behavioral group counseling enables people to learn and experiment with new behaviors, while receiving information and feedback from multiple sources. Hearing other people's thoughts also can help people to broaden their perspectives, identify and modify their own dysfunctional thoughts, and solidify their valid and reasonable thoughts and feelings.

Parents can benefit from learning behavior change strategies and using those to shape their children's behavior. Such common parental interventions as time-out's, rewards, consequences, and limit setting reflect behavior therapy.

Most of us use behavior change strategies in our everyday lives. When we reward ourselves with a snack after finishing a difficult chore, give a chronically late friend a message by deciding not to wait more than five minutes, buy a kitten for a child who is afraid of animals, or embark on a plan to improve our nutrition and exercise, we are using behavior change strategies. These approaches, then, have a great deal to offer a broad and diverse range of people.

Behavior therapy, as well as CBT, generally are combined with a broad range of other approaches, including psychodynamic therapy, Gestalt therapy, and person-centered counseling. Such combinations can deepen the impact of treatment and ensure that resulting changes are meaningful and enduring.

EVALUATION OF BEHAVIOR THERAPY AND COGNITIVE-BEHAVIORAL THERAPY

Extensive research has been conducted on behavior therapy and CBT. The literature suggests that treatment focused on cognitions and behavior can be very powerful and effective. Of course, it also has limitations.

Limitations

Most of the criticisms of behavior therapy and CBT focus on the possibility that they will accomplish only superficial and temporary gains. Emotions and insight may not receive the attention they merit in treatment. Clinicians may hone in too quickly on behaviors, without sufficiently exploring their underlying antecedents and dynamics. For example, a clinician may emphasize development of social skills in a woman who is fearful of dating and neglect her history of abuse.

In addition, clinicians may become so caught up in the power of CBT that they fail to help clients take adequate responsibility for their treatment and progress. As a result, people may feel manipulated and powerless rather than experience the growth in self-worth and competence that should result from treatment.

These potential limitations usually can be avoided by skilled clinicians who take a holistic view of their clients, understand behavior in context, and remember the importance of empowering people. At the same time, treatment limited to CBT is not the ideal approach for all clients. An initial focus on cognitions and behavior can promote change and enhance motivation. However, for people with longstanding and deep-seated problems, perhaps stemming from an early history of abuse and inadequate parenting, psychodynamic and other approaches should probably be combined with behavior therapy and CBT. This combination can help clients develop insight and allow them to work through past concerns, while also helping them make cognitive and behavioral changes. In addition, although CBT can help people with psychotic and other severe disorders, medication and other interventions also are needed. Behavior therapy and CBT are useful with almost all clients but often need to be combined with other treatment modalities to maximize their effectiveness.

Strengths and Contributions

Behavior therapy and CBT have many strengths. They offer a straightforward approach to treatment that has both face and empirical validity. They are flexible and broad treatment modalities, encompassing many useful interventions that facilitate their application to a wide range of people and problems. These approaches emphasize goal setting, accountability, and results. They are respectful and collaborative, encouraging people to take responsibility for themselves. Although improved behaviors and thinking are the targets, treatment also seeks to improve emotional health.

Early versions of behavior therapy and CBT downplayed the importance of background, individual differences, and the therapeutic alliance, and sometimes seemed too directive and contrived. However, modern versions address these shortcomings. Today, clinicians practicing behavior therapy and CBT recognize that problems must be viewed in context. Clinicians explore the historical roots and antecedents of people's concerns, are sensitive to individual differences, develop positive and collaborative therapeutic alliances, and seek to know and understand their clients as individuals. Clinicians practicing behavior therapy and CBT help to empower clients so that they can not only deal with immediate presenting concerns but also develop skills and strategies they can use in the future to lead healthier and more rewarding lives.

Some clinicians dismissed behavior therapy, and even CBT, when they were first developed, viewing them as superficial and likely to worsen or shift symptoms from one problem area to another (symptom substitution). However, extensive research has dispelled these concerns. The positive outcomes of behavior therapy and CBT tend to be enduring. Rather than leading to symptom substitution, these approaches often lead to a generalization of positive change in which people spontaneously apply the skills they have learned to many areas of concern. As Jacobson (1989) concluded of CBT, there is "no doubt that the treatment is a powerful one" (p. 87).

Behavior therapy and CBT have made important contributions to counseling and psychotherapy. Behavior therapy, more than any other treatment system, has emphasized the importance of research on treatment effectiveness. Through research, behavior and cognitive-behavioral therapists have demonstrated the success of their work. Their emphasis on goal setting, accountability, and outcome is very much in keeping with modern conceptions of counseling and psychotherapy. The requirements of managed care for treatment plans and progress reports, as well as clients' demands for efficient and effective treatment, can readily be met through behavior therapy and CBT. In addition, these approaches paved the way for other treatment systems to research their effectiveness, establish clear goals and interventions, and assess their impact.

Behavior therapy and CBT also have provided a foundation for the development of several other approaches—for example, reality therapy and solution-focused brief therapy (discussed in chapters 20 and 21) as well as multimodal therapy (discussed in part 6). The practice of behavior and cognitive-behavioral therapy is widespread, and articles on these approaches to treatment appear regularly in most psychotherapy and counseling journals.

CBT is well positioned to provide the basis for new treatment approaches that incorporate emerging learning on cognitive processes and to remain a leading and innovative treatment approach. Research on brain functioning has expanded greatly in recent years. CBT already has focused attention on thinking processes in determining emotions and actions and should continue to lead the way in incorporating this research into approaches to counseling and psychotherapy.

SKILL DEVELOPMENT: SYSTEMATIC DESENSITIZATION

Systematic desensitization is one of the most powerful interventions in behavior therapy and CBT. It is particularly important in the treatment of phobias and excessive fears of certain situations such as socializing, flying, and public speaking. It also is useful in addressing other apprehensions and anxieties. For example, it can reduce fear of surgery and chemotherapy in people who have been diagnosed with cancer.

Systematic desensitization involves gradually exposing people to the object of their fears while helping them relax. Relaxation and fear are incompatible responses; as a result, fear of a stimulus typically diminishes if relaxation can be achieved and maintained during exposure to that stimulus. However, this treatment can have a reverse effect if not well planned; premature exposure to frightening stimuli or exposure that is aborted while the fear is still high can increase terror of the stimulus. Consequently, careful pacing is essential to successful treatment using systematic desensitization.

Exposure to the frightening stimulus may occur in the imagination (imaginal desensitization) or the real world (*in vivo* desensitization). One is not clearly more effective than the other. The choice of whether to use imaginal desensitization, *in vivo* desensitization, or a combination of the two is determined primarily by the nature of the feared stimulus and the ease of creating a situation of controlled exposure to that stimulus. For example, imaginal desensitization, perhaps enhanced by pictures and films, would be used to treat someone with a fear of hurricanes, while *in vivo* desensitization could help someone overcome an inordinate fear of dogs or balloons. A combination of imaginal and *in vivo* desensitization would probably work best for someone coping with a fear of flying or of heights.

Systematic desensitization typically follows a series of steps, after one or more sessions have been spent on developing the therapeutic alliance, exploring the antecedents and symptoms of the fear, and discussing the person's history and present life situation so that the symptoms can be viewed in context. These steps are illustrated by the case of Makita, a young girl who was frightened by balloons bursting at a party and has since developed a phobia of balloons that prevents her from attending any parties or social gatherings where balloons might be present.

1. *Teach an effective relaxation strategy.* Makita was taught to relax by shifting her breathing to a pattern of slow diaphragmatic breaths while focusing on her breathing. She also was taught to progressively relax her body, gradually moving her attention down from her head to her toes, until her entire body felt relaxed.

2. *Establish an anxiety hierarchy.* A list of fear-provoking stimuli is developed and ranked according to the amount of fear each elicits. A 0–100 SUDS (subjective units of distress) scale is used to obtain an initial rating of the fear associated with each item on the list and to facilitate ordering the list. Here is Makita's list:

Stimulus	SUDS Rating
Picture of a balloon	55
One small deflated balloon	60
A bunch of larger deflated balloons	67
One small inflated balloon	74
Several medium-sized inflated balloons	80
Several large inflated balloons	84
Gradually deflating a balloon	88
Bursting one small balloon	95
Bursting a group of large balloons	99

3. *Provide controlled exposure.* Makita's counselor used *in vivo* desensitization to help Makita overcome her fear because the object of her fears, balloons, could easily be brought into the treatment room. After helping Makita relax as fully as possible, her counselor brought out a picture of a balloon as she and Makita had agreed. With guidance from Makita, the picture was gradually moved closer to her and finally handed to her. The counselor encouraged Makita to hold the picture and look at it until she felt her fear subside significantly. The SUDS scale was used to track the fear level. This experience was repeated as often as necessary, perhaps over several sessions, until Makita and her counselor decided she was ready to move to the next item on the list. The exposure and desensitization process must be carefully planned so that it does not raise anxiety but promotes feelings of self-confidence, optimism, and control.

Continuing the desensitization between sessions, with the help of a friend or a family member who has been coached by the clinician, can accelerate progress. Makita's parents helped her continue her treatment at home, never exposing her to more than she had successfully handled in her counseling sessions.

Approximately five sessions were required to complete the desensitization process and reduce Makita's fears to a manageable level. Although she was able to deal with some of the fears on her list rapidly, several sessions were necessary to help Makita feel comfortable with the actual bursting of a balloon. However, Makita and her family were able to celebrate her success by having a family party, complete with balloons.

CASE ILLUSTRATION

As treatment of Edie, Roberto, and Ava Diaz progressed, the clinician realized that Edie's self-consciousness, her apprehensions about socialization, and her weak interpersonal skills had an impact not only on Edie but on the rest of the family. Because of her social discomfort, Edie avoided talking to Ava's teachers and the parents of Ava's friends and was reluctant to accompany Roberto to office parties or on business trips. Her avoidance of these and similar situations had relieved Edie of considerable stress and anxiety; however, negative reinforcement had occurred. The rewards she experienced from social avoidance had further entrenched this behavior, so that Edie's apprehension about and avoidance of interpersonal contact had worsened over the years.

Edie and her therapist decided to use Meichenbaum's (1985) stress inoculation training (SIT) to address her social difficulties. This approach integrates both cognitive and behavior change strategies. The process of using SIT with Edie had three phases.

1. *Conceptualization* First, the clinician explained SIT to Edie, reviewing the interventions that would probably be used and describing how SIT was likely to help her. Once Edie's questions and concerns were discussed, she felt ready to cooperate with the process and was optimistic that it might alleviate her longstanding social discomfort.

   Edie and her therapist then clarified the nature of the problem and established realistic goals. Edie believed that people generally found her unappealing and uninteresting. She feared that if she risked exposure to social situations, she would experience painful rejection and humiliation. Using the SUDS scale, the extent of Edie's fears were assessed. Specific goals were identified, focused on reducing her fears of rejection and humiliation in social situations and increasing her participation in social conversations and activities.

2. *Skills Acquisition and Rehearsal* Several techniques were used to help Edie overcome her fears:
   - At work, where Edie felt competent and her professional role was clear, she experienced little social anxiety and interacted well with others. Edie identified communication skills that served her well in her role as librarian and identified ways to transfer them to other interpersonal arenas.
   - The therapist helped Edie dispute her belief that she would certainly be rejected and humiliated in social situations. This had not happened to her since adolescence, and she could report only two instances of ever having seen other people rejected and embarrassed in a social setting.
   - Edie further developed her social skills. Her therapist provided readings and exercises on assertiveness and communication and helped Edie to identify and practice skills that seemed useful to her. She and the therapist paid particular attention to role-playing ways to initiate and develop conversations.
   - Because she enjoyed reading, Edie sought out literature on shyness, as well as biographies of people who viewed themselves as having had social difficulties, so that she could learn more about ways to cope with her social discomfort.
   - Edie identified a co-worker whose social skills she admired. She observed that person in order to identify her social strengths and use her as a role model. In addition, Edie tried to act as if she were that person when she role-played conversations in her treatment sessions.

3. *Application and Follow-Through* Edie and her clinician generated some small steps for Edie to take in order to apply her developing social skills and increased self-confidence. Edie considered volunteering at Ava's school, accompanying Roberto on a business trip, and throwing a small party. Although she anticipated engaging in all these activities eventually, she decided to begin by inviting the mother of one of Ava's friends to have tea with her after they dropped their daughters off at ballet class. Edie felt relatively safe with this woman and believed that meeting one person at a time with readily available topics of discussion (tea, the bal-

let class, their daughters) would provide a successful experience. A role play of social conversation over tea helped Edie feel well prepared for this venture.

After the tea, Edie processed the experience with her therapist, focusing on what she did well and identifying a few ways in which she might have improved on the experience. For example, she had gotten flustered when it was time to pay the check and saw that she needed to develop more comfortable strategies for dealing with that. Edie rewarded herself for her efforts, as well as for her success, and began to plan the next steps to improve her social skills.

EXERCISES

Large-Group Exercises

1. Although the value of CBT has clearly been substantiated by research, some clinicians view it as less powerful than psychodynamic therapy. Discuss what thoughts and feelings might underlie this perception and then discuss your reactions to and perceptions of CBT.
2. Using your class as the target group, plan implementation of a token economy that might be useful in promoting learning in the class. Identify the behavioral goals, the system for tracking and recording performance, and the rewards for positive behavior.
3. Ava was troubled by fears of the dark and of being alone. Plan her treatment, using behavioral strategies. Be sure to view her presenting problems in the context of what you already know about Ava and her family. The treatment plan should include, but not necessarily be limited to, determining how to establish a baseline, setting specific goals, identifying treatment strategies, establishing rewards or reinforcements, and specifying ways to track progress. In addition, consider whether to integrate other approaches with the behavioral interventions.

Small-Group Exercises

1. Divide into your groups of four participants. Identify one person to lead the group in a relaxation exercise, beginning with diaphragmatic breathing, continuing to progressive muscle relaxation, and ending with an anchoring of the feelings of relaxation. (The skill of anchoring was presented in chapter 17.)
2. Following the guidelines presented in Large-Group Exercise 3, plan treatment for the following behavioral difficulties:
   - A 4-year-old refuses to go to bed on time and delays his bedtime by several hours each evening with requests for stories, drinks of water, and other attention.
   - A 33-year-old man reports family conflict as a result of his nightly consumption of 8–10 cans of beer.
   - A 42-year-old man describes himself as "addicted to sex." Although he is married and has a sexual relationship with his wife, he has had many extramarital affairs. His wife has warned him that she will end their marriage if this continues. He wants to continue his marriage but feels unable to control his sexual impulses.
3. Divide into your groups of four, composed of two dyads. Each dyad should engage in a 15-minute role-played counseling interview in which the person playing the client talks about a behavior he or she would like to change while the person in the clinician role gathers information on the nature of the concern; its context; and its

frequency or severity. If you have time, begin to identify realistic goals and procedures to effect behavioral change. Spend 10 minutes processing each role play after it is completed, providing feedback to both client and clinician on strengths and areas needing improvement.

Individual Exercises

1. Identify a fear or source of apprehension in your life. Following the guidelines presented in the Skill Development section of this chapter, develop a plan to use systematic desensitization to help yourself reduce this fear. Write down the plan in your journal and then try to implement it.

2. Consider a behavior that you would like to increase, decrease, or change. Develop a written treatment plan to help yourself make that change. The treatment plan should include, but not necessarily be limited to, determining how to establish a baseline, setting specific goals, identifying treatment strategies, establishing rewards or reinforcements, and specifying ways to track progress. Continue your learning by actually implementing the plan you have developed. Write in your journal about the successes and challenges you experience as you try to implement this plan.

3. Most of us automatically use behavior change strategies on ourselves and others without being aware of what we are doing. Monitor yourself for the next 2 days and list in your journal any behavior change strategies you used such as rewarding yourself for completing a difficult task, using a time-out with a child, or applying consequences when you are treated badly.

SUMMARY

Behavior therapy evolved during the twentieth century from the research of B. F. Skinner, Ivan Pavlov, John W. Watson, Joseph Wolpe, and others. This treatment approach takes the stance that behavior is learned and consequently can be unlearned. Behavior therapists are concerned about results; so they take the time to establish a baseline, develop interventions that facilitate behavioral change, use reinforcements to solidify gains, carefully plan implementation, and monitor progress.

Today, behavior therapy and cognitive therapy, are more likely to be combined rather than used alone. Their merger into cognitive-behavioral ther-

apy, promoted by Donald Meichenbaum and others, expanded the application of cognitive and behavioral strategies and created a powerful treatment approach. Although practitioners of CBT focus on improving thoughts and behaviors, they also pay attention to the whole person; recognize the importance of history, background, and context; explore emotions; and take steps to develop a positive and collaborative therapeutic alliance. Behavior therapy and CBT have demonstrated strong effectiveness with a wide range of people and problems; their concepts and interventions should be incorporated into the work of all clinicians.

RECOMMENDED READINGS

Meichenbaum, D. (1985). *Stress inoculation training.* Elmsford, NY: Pergamon.

Smith, L. D., & Peck, P. L. (2004). Dialectical behavior therapy: A review and call to research. *Journal of Mental Health Counseling, 26,* 25–39.

Stuart, R. B. (1998). Updating behavior therapy with couples. *Family Journal, 6*(1), 6–12.

Thorpe, G. L., & Olson, S. L. (1997). *Behavior therapy.* Needham Heights, MA: Allyn & Bacon.

Numerous journals focus on CBT and behavior therapy, including *Behavior Therapy, Cognitive and Behavioral Practice, Advances in Behaviour Research and Therapy, Child and Family Behavior Therapy, Cognitive Therapy and Research,* and *Journal of Behavior Therapy and Experimental Psychiatry.*

ADDITIONAL SOURCES OF INFORMATION

http://www.aabt.org—Website of The Association for Advancement of Behavior Therapy (AABT) (305 Seventh Avenue, 16th floor, New York, New York 10001, 800-685-AABT).

AABT focuses its training and publications primarily on analysis and assessment of behavior and the use of behavior therapy and CBT. AABT publishes two journals, *Behavior Therapy* and *Cognitive and Behavioral Practice,* as well as directories of internships and training opportunities. It holds an annual convention and offers continuing education and other learning resources. Student, associate, and full memberships are available.

www.nacbt.org—Website for The National Association of Cognitive-Behavioral Therapists. This association is dedicated to the teaching and practice of CBT. It offers seminars and other educational opportunities, literature on CBT, and certification for practitioners.

http://www.cognitivetherapy.com—Website for the New York Institute for Cognitive and Behavioral Therapies.

http://drugabuse.gov/TXManuals/CBT/CBT1—Website for the National Institute on Drug Abuse of the National Institutes of Health website, focusing on the use of CBT with people who abuse substances.

CHAPTER 20

Reality Therapy

Reality therapy, initially developed by William Glasser in the 1960s, is solidly grounded in cognitive and behavioral theory and interventions. Like other cognitive-behavioral approaches to treatment, reality therapy focuses on the present and helps people change their thoughts and actions so they can lead more rewarding lives.

However, reality therapy is more philosophical than other cognitive-behavioral approaches and emphasizes self-determination and process more than results. This no-excuses approach encourages people to take responsibility for both their difficulties and their joys, rather than blaming their history, heredity, or society (Wubbolding, 1988). As Glasser (1998) stated, "We choose *everything* we do, including the misery we feel" (p. 3). Helping people make choices that increase their happiness and meet their needs without harming others is the essence of reality therapy.

Drawing heavily on cognitive and behavioral strategies, reality therapists guide people through a process of change that helps them become aware of their needs; recognize the ingredients of a rewarding life; and establish goals and procedures to improve their lives. Through this process, people gain more control over their lives and assume responsible and rewarding roles in society.

Reality therapy has been used in many mental health settings. Schools and substance abuse treatment programs are particularly suited to this approach. According to Glasser, reality therapy can be effective with almost anyone, regardless of diagnosis or background. Although not all clinicians agree, reality therapy does have much to offer.

WILLIAM GLASSER

William Glasser was born in 1925 and grew up in Ohio. His early years were difficult; Glasser (1998) reports that his father was occasionally violent, while his mother was overly controlling. Even as a child, he recognized the incompatibility in his parents' relationship. This history is telling in light of Glasser's later emphasis on personal responsibility, not harming others, and the marital or partner relationship.

Glasser became a chemical engineer but later changed his career goals and entered medical school. He received his medical degree from Case Western Reserve University in 1953 and then trained to become a psychiatrist.

Between 1956 and 1967, Glasser was a psychiatrist for the Ventura School for Girls, a prison school operated by the California Youth Authority, housing 400 delinquent adolescents. This experience had a profound impact on Glasser's views of mental health and psychotherapy. He concluded that traditional psychoanalysis offered little to help the young women at the Ventura School and began to develop what would be reality therapy.

Glasser concluded that many of the difficulties of the adolescents at the Ventura School stemmed from their failure to take responsibility for themselves and their lives and to act in ways that truly met their needs. Although they might have believed that they were seeking to meet their needs, the result—their involuntary stay at the Ventura School—was not their desired outcome. By helping the girls think more clearly about their present needs, holding them responsible for their behavior, and playing an active and involved role in treatment, Glasser became much more effective. Implementation of his ideas for change resulted in an 80% success rate.

Glasser's first book, *Mental Health or Mental Illness?* (1961), laid the groundwork for reality therapy. *Reality Therapy* (1965) spelled out the principles that continue to be fundamental to this approach: that people who take responsibility for themselves and their behaviors and are aware of and able to meet their basic needs without harming others are likely to lead happy and fulfilling lives. Glasser's work emphasizes the importance of relationships as well as responsibility. He believes that a warm, accepting clinician is essential to the success of treatment, just as he believes that close and positive relationships are essential to mental health and happiness.

Relationships have been important in Glasser's own life. His first wife, Naomi Glasser, shared in the development of reality therapy. That marriage ended with his wife's death. Glasser said he married his present wife after they checked their needs to ensure they were compatible. Glasser's three children also play a significant role in his life.

Since the 1960s, Glasser has developed and expanded the scope of reality therapy. Focusing his writings and lectures on the application of reality therapy in treatment as well as its use in school and business settings, he has succeeded in establishing its importance. Currently based at the William Glasser Institute in Chatsworth, California, Glasser continues to play an active role in the development of reality therapy.

ROBERT WUBBOLDING

Reality therapy found another important spokesperson in Robert E. Wubbolding, director of the Center for Reality Therapy in Cincinnati, Ohio; training director at the William Glasser Institute; and faculty member at Xavier University in Cincinnati. Wubbolding has played an important role in the development and promotion of reality therapy. He is a prolific writer whose books include *Reality Therapy for the 21st Century* (2000), *Understanding Reality Therapy* (1991), and *Expanding Reality Therapy: Group Counseling and Multicultural Dimensions* (1990), among others. His writings facilitate implementation of reality therapy through case studies, exercises, and treatment protocols.

THE DEVELOPMENT OF REALITY THERAPY

Reality therapy began in the 1960s with three relatively straightforward concepts that Glasser (1965) labeled *reality, responsibility,* and *right and wrong.* He believed that all people have two basic and intertwined human needs: relatedness (to love and be loved) and respect (to feel worthwhile to oneself and others). Behavior that shows appreciation for our own needs and those of others leads to feelings of self-worth and to rewarding relationships, thereby meeting the two basic needs. Desirable behavior also reflects awareness of reality, responsibility for oneself, and understanding of right and wrong.

Some aspects of Glasser's initial ideas have stayed the same while others have changed. His early writings placed considerable emphasis on ethical issues and de-emphasized individual differences. However, recent writings sound less judgmental and imply, rather than insist, on the importance of right and wrong in the therapeutic process. In addition, his writings now convey greater appreciation of individual differences, although reality therapy generalizes about the causes and appropriate treatment of emotional difficulties.

Early writings identified eight steps for clinicians to follow in using reality therapy (Evans, 1982). These include (1) Build rapport with clients, (2) Ask "What are *you* doing?," (3) Collaborate with clients in evaluating their behavior, (4) Help people make a plan to do better, (5) Help clients commit to the plan, (6) Do not accept excuses, (7) Do not interfere with reasonable consequences, and (8) Do not give up! Although current writing rarely includes these steps, they still are relevant to reality therapy.

In addition, Glasser's list of basic needs has expanded, as have treatment procedures. (We discuss these points later in this chapter.) Glasser's emphasis on responsibility, relationships, and making choices and taking action that fulfills our needs has changed little. These concepts form the foundation of reality therapy.

Control Theory

In the 1970s, Glasser discovered the writings of Powers (1973) and others on control theory or control system theory. Glasser incorporated concepts of control theory into reality therapy. He conceptualized people as driven by inner control systems in the brain that guide behaviors and emotions so that they are instrumental, moving people in directions that seem likely to fulfill their needs. According to Glasser (1984), "A control system acts upon the world and itself as part of the world to attempt to get the picture that it wants" (p. 39). Unfortunately, people's control systems sometimes cause difficulties by misdirecting their efforts and leading them to try to control others.

For Glasser, awareness and assessment are the keys to modifying our control systems and improving our lives. He believed that the first step is to become cognizant of the pictures in our heads that reflect our needs and wants. We then can become aware of what we are doing to reach our goals. By assessing the impact and success of our behaviors, we can determine whether change is warranted and, if so, use creative strategies to modify our thoughts, emotions, and behaviors. Although Glasser (1984) recognizes that immediate, intense, short-term feelings can emerge spontaneously at times of frustration or satisfaction, he is convinced that people can choose and control their long-term feelings.

Choice Theory

For many years, this treatment system was known as reality therapy/control theory. However, in 1996, Glasser determined that underlying reality therapy was choice theory rather than control theory. Choice theory postulates that people's choices of thoughts, feelings, and actions largely determine the quality of their lives. Glasser's view of the brain as a control system "aligning the external world to what we want as well as closing the gap between what we want and what we have" continues to be part of reality therapy (Wubbolding, 2000, p. xiii). However, choice theory, underlying reality therapy, is more important in helping people improve their lives (Glasser, 1998).

IMPORTANT THEORETICAL CONCEPTS

Reality therapy has evolved considerably over the years and has expanded its applications (Wubbolding, 1995b). At present, it is a well-developed treatment system that is used successfully in a broad range of settings.

Human Development

According to Glasser (1998), problems originate during early childhood when we encounter people who believe they know what is right for us. Because of our youth, inexperience, and self-doubts, we accept this external control and come to believe that others make us feel or act as we do. However, "external control harms everyone, both the controllers and the controlled" (p. 7).

Instead, according to reality therapy, the way to rear emotionally healthy children is to surround them with loving and supportive people who enable them to experience freedom, power, and fun in responsible ways. Children's belief in themselves as well as their ability to identify and meet their needs in positive ways should be fostered, instilling attitudes and behaviors that will serve them well as they mature.

Despite this emphasis on childhood development, reality therapy views people as basically self-determining and able to overcome their early difficulties. According to Glasser (1998), "We are rarely the victims of what happened to us in the past" (p. 3). However, if people have not learned to satisfy their needs during the early years, they may require help in developing new ways of feeling, thinking, and behaving.

Reality therapists pay little attention to the past. Instead, they believe that past issues are expressed in present unsatisfying relationships and behaviors. Treatment is most likely to succeed by focusing on those present manifestations. According to Wubbolding (1991), "People are motivated to fulfill a current force inside of them. . . . early childhood conflicts, unconscious reasons, and external stimuli do not cause present behavior" (p. 21).

Five Basic Needs

Reality therapy holds that all people are born with the following five basic needs that are fixed at birth (Glasser, 1998). The relative strengths of these five needs give people their different personalities (Wubbolding, 1991):

1. *Belonging:* Loving and being loved; having contact, connections, interactions, and relationships with people
2. *Power/achievement:* Feelings of accomplishment and competence, self-esteem, success, and control over one's own life
3. *Fun/enjoyment:* Pleasure; the ability to laugh, play, and appreciate being human
4. *Freedom/independence:* The ability to make choices; to live without excessive and unnecessary limits or constraints
5. *Survival:* The essentials of life, including good health, food, air, shelter, safety, security, and physical comfort

Because these needs overlap, fulfillment of one may speed fulfillment of others. For example, people with positive relationships probably have greater enjoyment of life. However, these needs also can conflict. People who channel great effort into achieving power or independence may have difficulty forming rewarding relationships.

Reality therapy takes the position that all human behavior is purposeful and directed at meeting one or more of the fundamental needs (Wubbolding, 1988). Although the five needs are universal, the specific wants that people pursue in an effort to meet their needs are particular to the individual. For example, having a family may be a want that satisfies one person's need for belonging, while another person may satisfy that need with an involvement in team sports. People are motivated to bridge the gaps between what they have and what they want to meet their needs. However, feelings such as loneliness and deprivation can limit people's motivation. Reality therapists seek to change those feelings, not by directly addressing emotions, but by changing thoughts about wants and needs as well as corresponding purposeful behaviors.

Concept of Mental Illness

Mental illness, according to reality therapy, is actually people's failure to meet their five needs in responsible and effective ways—overemphasizing some needs while neglecting others. According to Glasser (1998), people engaged in antisocial behavior, for example, generally focus on their needs for power and freedom and do not satisfactorily address their needs for love and enjoyment. Conventional diagnostic terminology is not central to reality therapy; instead, mental illness is conceptualized as problems in choices, need satisfaction, and responsibility. Common symptoms of emotional difficulties include loneliness (rather than belonging); loss of control (rather than empowerment); boredom and depression (rather than fun); frustration, inhibition, or rebelliousness (rather than freedom); and illness or deprivation (rather than safety and security).

Concept of Mental Health

Reality therapy has a clear vision of emotionally healthy people: those who are successful in meeting their five basic needs. Emotionally healthy people choose thoughts, feelings, and behaviors wisely and responsibly. Their choices help them meet their needs while respecting the rights of other people to fulfill their own needs. Furthermore, emotionally healthy people not only seek to improve their own lives but take steps to help others and to make the world a better place (Wubbolding, 1991). Such people have a success identity rather than a failure identity (Glasser & Wubbolding, 1995). They have a clear and positive sense of themselves that reflects their own internal frames of reference; they do not derive their sense of themselves from the perceptions of others.

Total Behavior and Motivation

As Glasser (1998) observed, all people can do at birth is behave. All aspects of functioning are linked to behavior. He calls people's overall functioning *total behavior,* which is composed of four inseparable components: acting, thinking, feeling, and physiology. Reality therapists believe that all behavior is chosen, that people can directly control the acting and thinking components and thereby gain indirect control over feelings and physiology. Glasser compared the four elements in total behavior to the four wheels of a car, with acting and thinking represented by the front wheels. This emphasis on thoughts and behaviors is what makes reality therapy a cognitive-behavioral approach to treatment.

Quality Worlds

According to Glasser (1998), people have quality worlds formed of pictures or images of the sort of life they would like to have, the people they want to be with, the possessions or experiences they would like to have, and the ideas and beliefs they value. These pictures guide people's efforts to satisfy their needs and are linked to the success they have in meeting those needs. For example, if a woman with good work skills puts a promotion into her quality world, representing a way for her to meet her need for achievement, she has made responsible picture choices, and her related behaviors will probably be successful. However, if her way to satisfy her need for love is represented in her quality world by a picture of her best friend's husband, she is not making responsible choices and is unlikely to meet her needs.

Reality therapists believe that people can choose the pictures they put in their quality worlds. If they choose pictures that are unattainable or unlikely to meet their needs, they probably will experience frustration and disappointment. By becoming aware of their needs, as well as the pictures in their quality world, people can make better, wiser, and more realistic choices; have greater control over their lives; and fulfill their needs.

WDEP System

The procedures involved in reality therapy are represented by the acronym WDEP, which includes four main elements: wants, direction and doing, evaluation, and planning. These can be applied in whatever order seems most likely to be helpful.

W: *Wants*   Reality therapists explore clients' wants and the pictures in their quality world, focusing on what they want that they *are* getting, what they want that they *are not* getting, and what they are getting that they *do not want* (Wubbolding, 1995b). Keeping in mind that wants are linked to needs, clinicians also encourage clients to look at that connection by asking questions such as "How do you perceive your wanting to drop out of high school as meeting your needs?"

Reality therapy, a phenomenological approach, recognizes the role that perceptions have in behavior. It helps people become aware of their perceptions so that they can modify them if appropriate. According to Wubbolding (1991, 1995a), perceptions pass through two filters. The lower-level filter, called the *total knowledge filter,* recognizes and labels perceptions, while the upper-level filter, *the valuing filter,* evaluates perceptions. Reality therapists facilitate this evaluation by suggesting that people distinguish among positive or need-satisfying perceptions, negative perceptions, and neutral perceptions. For example, "That is an attractive piece of jewelry" is a neutral perception; "I deserve that diamond more than she does" is a negative perception which can lead to relationship difficulties; while "I share my friend's happiness about receiving a beautiful engagement ring" is a positive perception because it enhances feelings of love and belonging. Becoming aware of and evaluating their perceptions can help people meet their needs.

An aspect of the *W* in WDEP is helping people choose to make positive changes. Wubbolding (1995b, p. 408) identified five levels of client commitment to change:

1. I don't want to be here.
2. I want the outcome but not the effort.
3. I'll try; I might.
4. I will do my best.
5. I will do whatever it takes.

If people begin treatment at the first or second level, an important goal of treatment is to help them see how they can benefit from changing their choices so that they move on to higher levels of commitment.

D: *Direction and Doing*   Reality therapists devote considerable attention to exploring people's total behavior, including actions, thoughts, emotions, and physiology. Helping people describe their total behavior as specifically as possible, as well as the goals and impact of those behaviors, is integral to treatment. The focus of reality therapy is on what people are doing, not *why* they are acting in certain ways.

E: *Evaluation*   Clinicians encourage clients to evaluate their goals, their actions, their perceptions, and the consequences of all these. Evaluation does not involve a judgment about the goodness or badness of these dimensions. Instead, evaluation is based on whether behaviors and perceptions are realistic and helpful to clients as well as to others. Clinicians might facilitate the process by asking thought-provoking questions such as "How realistic is it to expect that your daughter will never misbehave?" and "What success have you had in using drugs to build relationships?"

Both the discussion of doing and the evaluation process focus primarily on the present and emphasize positive and successful aspects of people's lives. The past is discussed only in terms of its impact on the present. According to Wubbolding (1988), "We talk little about the past—we can't undo anything that has already occurred" (p. 41).

P: Planning   Reality therapists view planning as essential and encourage people to have long-range plans and goals that are subdivided into a series of short-term, realistic plans. As Wubbolding (1991) put it, "To fail to plan is to plan to fail" (p. 95). Plans should evolve from self-evaluation and reflect desired changes in wants and total behavior. Wubbolding (1995b, p. 411) listed the following eight qualities of viable plans, represented by the acronym SAMI2C3. Plans should be:

- *Simple,* clear, and understandable.
- *Attainable,* able to be accomplished by the client
- *Measurable* via inventories, diaries, and other methods of recording progress
- *Immediate;* implementation can start right away
- *Involving* the clinician in appropriate ways such as giving feedback, serving as a sounding board
- Under the *control* of the client rather than someone else
- In keeping with the client's *commitment* to change and recognition that this change is important
- Reflecting *consistent* and repeated changes in behavior

Usually, planning focuses on modifying and improving actions because that is the aspect of total behavior over which people have the greatest control. However, focusing on thoughts may provide a point of entry, enabling people to believe that choosing different actions will be beneficial. According to reality therapy, feelings do not need to be addressed directly, although they can be important sources of information on wants and perceptions; if actions change, emotions will correspondingly change.

Planning and choice go hand in hand. The primary goals of planning are to help people make better choices and take more control of their lives. According to Glasser (1998), if people can make bad choices, they can make better ones.

Unlike some other approaches to cognitive and behavior therapy, reality therapy focuses more on process than outcome, more on the behaviors that are used to achieve desired results than on the achievement of the results themselves. This perspective offers two advantages: It encourages people to develop behaviors they can generalize to other situations and reduces the risk that people will view themselves as failures if they make better choices in their behaviors but do not immediately obtain their desired outcomes.

Importance of Relationships

Since its inception, reality therapy viewed relationships as key to both development of difficulties and achievement of a more rewarding life. According to Glasser (1998), "People who have no close relationships are almost always lonely and feel bad" (p. 30).

Glasser (1998) is particularly interested in the partner relationship and suggests that the best marriages are between people with similar personalities. In addition, he believes that marriages are most likely to be successful if both people are low in power and freedom needs and high in their needs for fun, love, and belonging.

Parenting is, of course, another important role in relationships. Glasser advocates loving children no matter what, but suggests that parents may dislike how children behave and can let them know that some behaviors make loving them difficult. He cautions parents to avoid being punitive and judgmental, although he believes they do need to establish guidelines, rules, and limits for their children. Encouragement and praise are seen as far more helpful than censure. Like Adlerian therapists, reality therapists maintain that an essential element in good parenting is helping children learn from their mistakes, thereby turning disappointments into successes rather than promoting feelings of failure.

TREATMENT USING REALITY THERAPY

As a cognitive-behavioral approach, reality therapy uses many of the same strategies that have been discussed in parts 4 and 5 of this book. However, reality therapy also is characterized by its own set of goals, relationships, and strategies.

Goals

The fundamental goal of reality therapy is enabling people to have greater control over their lives by making better choices. Wise choices are perceived as those that meet the following three criteria:

1. They help people meet their innate needs and their specific wants, reflected by the pictures in their quality world.
2. The choices are responsible; they not only help the person making the choices but also respect the rights of other people and contribute to their efforts to make wise choices.
3. The choices are realistic and are likely to be attained through sound planning.

The following goals are also important:

- People form and sustain positive, mutually rewarding, respectful relationships.
- They develop a success identity rather than a failure identity.
- They have a consistent repertoire of healthy actions that enhances their total behavior by helping them think clearly, experience happiness and other positive emotions, and take steps to maintain their physical health.

Therapeutic Alliance

Reality therapists view a positive client-clinician relationship as essential to treatment. As Glasser (1975) stated, "The ability of the therapist to get involved is the major skill of doing reality therapy" (p. 22). Bassin (1993) echoed those sentiments by stating that involvement with the client is the "most important and most difficult assignment in conducting reality therapy" (p. 4).

Reality therapists are very much human beings in the treatment process. They share their perceptions and experiences and frequently ask for feedback. They pay little attention to transference and countertransference. Instead, they present themselves as people with skills and information they can use responsibly to help others. They are warm, friendly, caring, respectful, optimistic, attentive, and authentic with clients. Although reality therapists maintain ethical and professional behavior, they may talk about a sports event or give a person advice about what to wear to a meeting if such interactions promote rapport and help people achieve their goals.

Clients and clinicians form a team to help clients explore, evaluate, and revise their choices. Clinicians do not assume responsibility for telling clients what choices to make or for evaluating clients' behaviors. However, they do take considerable responsibility for the direction and success of treatment. They promote motivation and commitment, provide support and encouragement, guide the WDEP process, teach planning and other skills, and use creativity and imagination to motivate clients and provide new perspectives.

Clinicians help people formulate realistic and viable plans. As part of this process, they negotiate clear commitments and contracts with their clients. They avoid wasting time on excuses and strive to move forward rather than backward. Reality therapists are firm and determined to help people. They never give up.

Language is important in this approach. Reality therapists consciously use active verbs such as *angering* and *depressing* to help people take responsibility for their emotions and behaviors. Reality therapists make extensive use of the first-person pronouns *I* and *we* to emphasize the collaborative nature of the treatment process. Clinicians focus on the present and on behaviors rather than on emotions. They ask *what* rather than *why* questions. Clinician self-disclosure sometimes facilitates involvement. Clinicians use caring confrontation, usually via thought-provoking questions. They also represent the voice of society, reminding people of the reality of moral, legal, and ethical standards.

Strategies

Reality therapists value creativity as well as understanding, appreciating, and motivating each person. As a result, they draw on a broad range of interventions to promote clients' involvement in treatment and bring energy and interest into the sessions. Included in reality therapists' repertoire are a broad range of cognitive and behavioral interventions, particularly the following:

Metaphors   Reality therapists use metaphors, similes, images, analogies, and anecdotes to give clients a powerful message in a creative way (Wubbolding, 1991). Clinicians also listen for and use metaphors and themes that clients present. For example, a therapist told a client whose hobby was fishing that his efforts to meet his goals seemed like fishing without bait in a lake with few fish.

Relationships   Reality therapists view relationships as essential to a rewarding life. They encourage clients to form relationships and coach them on ways to make them rewarding. According to Wubbolding (1991, pp. 55–57), the foundation of a strong relationship is time spent together with the following characteristics: it is effortful, valued by each person, enjoyable, focused on the positive, noncritical and nonargumentative, promoting awareness of each other, regular and repetitive, but time-limited. As an example, he suggests taking frequent and regular walks with a friend as a way to build closeness.

Questions   Although reality therapists advocate evaluation of total behavior, they want that assessment to come from the clients. Reality therapists avoid telling people what is not working for them or how they should change. Rather, they use carefully structured questions to help people take a close look at their lives and determine what does and does not need change (Wubbolding, 1991, p. 90). Examples of such questions include "Is what you are doing helping you?" "Is the plan you have made the most effective plan you are capable of formulating?" and "Is your present commitment to change the best or highest that you are willing to make?"

WDEP and SAMI2C3   As we have discussed, the concepts represented by these acronyms play an important part in keeping both clients and treatment focused and productive. WDEP reflects the process of moving toward change by *evaluating wants* and *direction* and formulating *plans*. SAMI2C3 represents the elements that maximize the success of plans: simple, attainable, measurable, immediate, involving, controlled, consistent, and committed.

Positive Addictions   According to Glasser (1976), negative addictions or repetitive self-destructive behaviors such as misuse of substances, acting out, and depressing oneself reflect giving up. Such behaviors characterize people who either have never learned to meet their needs in effective and responsible ways or have lost that ability.

Glasser suggests that people can reduce negative behaviors by developing positive addictions. These are behaviors that provide mental strength and alertness, creativity, energy, confidence, and focus, but do not dominate or control people's lives. Examples include regular exercise, journal writing, playing music, yoga, and meditation. Acquiring a positive addiction generally takes 6 months to 2 years of regular practice, usually 45–60 minutes at a time. Glasser suggests the following guidelines for choosing and nurturing positive behavioral patterns:

- The behavior should be noncompetitive and capable of being done alone.
- The behavior can be accomplished without inordinate mental or physical effort.
- The behavior should have value to you.
- The behavior should be one that you believe will lead you to improve in some way if you persist in it.
- The behavior should be one that you can perform without criticizing yourself.

Using Verbs and "ing" Words   Because reality therapists want people to realize that they have considerable control over their lives and can choose their total behavior, clinicians deliberately make extensive use of active verbs and "ing" words. Rather than describing people as angry, depressed, phobic, or anxious, they describe them as angering, depressing, phobicking, or anxietying. This implies that these emotions are not fixed states but instead are actions that can be changed.

Reasonable Consequences   Reality therapists believe that people should be responsible and therefore should experience the consequences of their behaviors. For example, the adolescent who returns home after curfew may have to be grounded for the next weekend, and the woman who is never ready when her carpool arrives may need to be dropped from the carpool. Reality therapists do not advocate making excuses or special exceptions. At the same time, they are not punitive; rather than focusing on what people did wrong, they focus on what people can choose to do differently so that they do not suffer the negative consequences of irresponsible and unrealistic behaviors.

Renegotiation   Client progress in counseling and psychotherapy is rarely smooth; occasional lapses or backsliding are the norm. When this occurs in reality therapy, clinicians use renegotiation to help people do something different. Emphasis is on developing new or revised plans with a high likelihood of success and identifying and rehearsing ways to cope with temptations to diverge from agreed-on plans and goals.

Paradoxical Interventions   Reality therapists use paradoxical interventions, initially developed by Viktor Frankl, an existential therapist discussed in chapter 11. These creative interventions encourage people to take responsibility for themselves. Paradoxical interventions typically take two forms (Wubbolding, 1988):

1. They *relabel or reframe* to promote choice and control. People might be viewed as lacking in skills rather than psychotic. Disappointments might be referred to as learning experiences rather than failures.
2. They involve *paradoxical prescriptions*. Reality therapists might encourage people to imagine the worst that could happen and find ways to cope with that; to choose their symptoms rather than fight them; to do the opposite of what is not working; or to schedule a relapse. Of course, suggestions always reflect accepted ethical standards.

Skill Development   Education is an important aspect of reality therapy. Clinicians help people develop skills to help them fulfill their needs and wants in responsible ways. Reality therapists might teach people assertiveness, rational thinking, development of positive addictions, planning, and other skills that promote growth and responsibility.

APPLICATION OF REALITY THERAPY

Reality therapy is a flexible approach that has been used for individual, group, and family therapy and for a great variety of people and problems. It is widely used in schools, correctional institutions, and rehabilitation programs and probably is the most popular approach to treating problems of drug and alcohol use. Reality therapy also has been used in both inpatient and outpatient mental health settings (Wubbolding, 1995b).

Application to Diagnostic Groups

The literature suggests that reality therapists view their approach as useful with almost everyone, regardless of the nature of their backgrounds, problems, or mental health. Although this perspective is questionable, assessing the effectiveness of reality therapy with particular diagnostic groups is difficult. Reality therapists avoid using common diagnostic nomenclature and view the concept of mental illness as invalid and harmful. Instead, reality therapists view people with mental disorders as lacking the skills necessary to meet their needs.

As a result of this stance, few empirical studies describe the use of reality therapy with people diagnosed with specific mental disorders. Glasser (1998), Wubbolding (2000), and others (Carey, 2003; Howatt, 2003; Mottern, 2002) do present case studies of people presenting concerns that suggest the presence of mental disorders. For example, Wubbolding (2000) describes the successful use of reality therapy with adults and adolescents who are incarcerated, with people who misuse substances, and with those experiencing depression and low self-esteem. He also provides examples of the effective use of reality therapy with people who experience bullying, domestic violence, and family conflict.

Although reality therapy may well be effective in treating many mental disorders, the limited empirical research on the use of reality therapy with people diagnosed with mental disorders is a concern. The nature of reality therapy suggests that it is best suited for treatment of people with mild to moderately severe mental disorders, including adjustment disorders, anxiety disorders, mood disorders, impulse control disorders, substance use disorders, and conduct disorders. With severe disorders such as bipolar and psychotic disorders, as well as with long-standing disorders such as personality disorders, reality therapy should be used with caution and will probably need to be combined with medication and other treatment approaches.

Application to Multicultural Groups

Reality therapy seems well suited to a diverse and multicultural population. Reality therapy is phenomenological and is interested in getting to know people and understanding their worldviews and quality world. It helps people identify their wants, evaluate them, and develop responsible plans to achieve their wants. It is a respectful and humanistic approach. It advocates treating each person as an individual, recognizes the importance of relationships, and encourages people to help each other. Although reality therapy promotes self-evaluation, therapists do not make judgments or impose their values on others. The positive and action-oriented nature of reality therapy makes it especially appropriate for people who might find a psychodynamic approach to be intrusive and inappropriate.

The reality therapy literature since 2000, particularly the *International Journal of Reality Therapy,* has focused heavily on the use of this approach with multicultural clients. Wubbolding (1990) taught reality therapy in Asia, Europe, and the Middle East and has described ways to adapt this treatment system to other cultures. For example, he emphasizes the importance of looking at the particular balance of basic needs in each culture and suggests that "I'll try" should be viewed as a firm commitment for people from Asian cultures. Many articles, both theoretical and applied, describe the multicultural use of reality therapy. Cheong (2001), for example, discussed the use of this approach in Korea and Li (1998) described the use of reality therapy to help Chinese Americans cope with acculturation differences in families.

Sanchez and Garriga (1996), however, raised concerns about the application of reality therapy to some cultural groups. They point out, for example, that fatalism (the idea that some things are meant to happen regardless of what people do) is an important belief in Hispanic culture. Clinicians should exercise particular caution and sensitivity when using reality therapy with people whose belief system emphasizes a higher power, predestination and predetermination, and the value of an external locus of control. Sanchez and Garriga suggest speaking of a dual control framework with such clients, sharing action and responsibility with a higher power but still striving for an improved quality world and better need satisfaction.

Livneh and Sherwood (1991) suggest that reality therapy may be helpful to people coping with physical disabilities. Its encouragement of a success identity and emphasis on responsibility, autonomy, and self-efficacy are likely to be empowering. Other studies support this conclusion. Kelsch (2002), for example, used choice theory to help people with multiple sclerosis to gain more control of their illness.

Application to Schools

In light of reality therapy's origins in a correctional school, it is not surprising that Glasser (1969) has maintained a strong interest in the use of reality therapy in schools. He has sought to replace the punitive and judgmental atmosphere of many schools with an environment that is encouraging and reinforcing: "A good school could be defined as a place where almost all students believe that if they do some work, they will be able to satisfy their needs enough so that it makes sense to keep working" (Glasser, 1986, p. 15).

Glasser has suggested several approaches to effecting positive change in schools:

• *Learning teams.* Groups of two to five students of varying ability levels study and learn cooperatively, motivated by feelings of belonging in the group. Their goals include both learning new material and convincing their teachers that they have mastered the material. Teams are changed regularly to promote interaction.

• *Quality School Model.* This model reconceptualizations the school environment to eliminate coercion and promote cooperation, safety, and consideration (Schatz, 1995). Teachers strive to make coursework useful and meaningful and to teach in a way that meets students' basic needs and contributes to their sense of fulfillment. Features of this model include year-round education to promote continuity, parent action teams to increase involvement, teachers and students sharing lunch and other activities, partnerships with businesses, elimination of bells to signal times, elimination of grading, peer tutoring in multi-age learning groups, open classrooms, computer-aided learning, student portfolios, student-led conferences and businesses, and daily self-evaluations for staff and students. The model recognizes the importance of both psychological and academic growth and emphasizes a win-win perspective.

Although a relatively small number of schools have fully implemented the Quality School Model, many have incorporated facets of reality therapy into their teaching and counseling programs. Murphy (1997) reviewed six studies of reality therapy used with varied student populations, including students with learning disabilities, students at risk, and Mexican American students. Programs were 4–12 weeks long. All studies yielded some positive results. However, the diversity of the studies and the weak design of some studies led Murphy to conclude that, although reality therapy seems to enhance behavior and interest in school, more research is needed before firm conclusions can be drawn.

Stehno (1995) suggested ways for school counselors and other clinicians to apply reality therapy to the classroom. Rather than assuming the role of expert or diagnostician, counselors engage in process or collaborative consultation with teachers, forming a partnership to identify and resolve problems. This sort of consultation is characterized by five steps: (1) Becoming involved, (2) Identifying wants, (3) Identifying and evaluating the success of current behaviors, (4) Making a plan, and (5) Following up.

Application to Business and Industry

Glasser (1998) has applied principles of reality therapy to management in business and industry. He distinguishes between *boss management,* which is authoritarian, judgmental, and punitive, and more effective *lead management,* which uses praise and encouragement and seeks to make work meaningful and rewarding to employees. Glasser's philosophy of leadership emphasizes collaboration, self-evaluation, choices, and competencies rather than rote learning. He suggests, in both school and work settings, that tests should not be given once to determine passing or failing but should be given repeatedly until people develop the skills they need to pass the tests.

CURRENT USE OF REALITY THERAPY

Reality therapy continues to have a strong following among mental health professionals. Glasser, Wubbolding, and others continue to lecture and write in support of their approach. In addition to its well-established use in schools and substance use treatment programs, reality therapy also is used in a broad range of other settings.

Particularly important in recent years are efforts to combine reality therapy with other approaches that will broaden and deepen its use. Examples include Fulkerson's (2003) integration of transactional analysis, psychoanalysis, and reality therapy to help families become aware of and change dysfunctional patterns; Pierce's (2003) development of mindfulness-based reality therapy which integrates Buddhist philosophy and interventions such as relaxation and meditation with reality therapy; and Mottern's (2003) effort to combine choice therapy with a multicultural perspective based on Native American stories and viewpoints.

EVALUATION OF REALITY THERAPY

Like the other cognitive-behavioral approaches to treatment, reality therapy has a great deal to offer clients and clinicians. However, it also has limitations.

Limitations

Reality therapy has some important shortcomings that clinicians should bear in mind. It pays only limited attention to helping people understand and deal with their environments and minimizes the importance of the past in people's development and difficulties. As a result, reality therapists may overlook some of the barriers and experiences that limit people's choices, and they may focus too much on symptoms.

In addition, reality therapists' disregard of the importance of diagnosis is inconsistent with current professional guidelines. Equating mental illness with lack of knowledge about responsible ways to meet one's needs is highly questionable and may lead to inadequate treatment and neglect of important areas of concern. Many clinicians also disagree with Glasser's (1998) doubts about the existence of repressed memories and the diagnosis of posttraumatic stress disorder.

In addition, Glasser (1998, p. 88) minimizes the value of psychotropic medication, stating: "Good psychotherapy precludes the need for [brain] drugs." Glasser believes that medication is dangerous to people's health and undermines their ability to help themselves (Lennon, 2003). This lack of recognition that some disorders have a biological component and benefit from medication is worrisome, especially since we do not have adequate research to substantiate the value of reality therapy in treating severe mental disorders.

Finally, reality therapy has not paid sufficient attention to individualizing application of this approach in terms of people's gender, age, ethnic and cultural background, and level of functioning. All of these shortcomings may cause both clinicians and clients to have an unrealistically optimistic view of what can be accomplished by reality therapy alone and can lead to feelings of disappointment and failure if those expectations are not realized.

Strengths and Contributions

Nevertheless, reality therapy has many strengths. It is a clear, straightforward approach to treatment that makes sense to most people. It is respectful, empowering, and encouraging and addresses fundamental issues in people's lives such as motivation, need satisfaction, and control. Reality therapists become involved with their clients in appropriate professional ways. Reality therapy's emphasis on the importance of both relationships and responsibility in people's lives is relevant and timely in light of prevalent problems of violence and family disruption. Also relevant is its emphasis on choice at a time when many people feel overcommitted and overprogrammed. In addition, reality therapy has a strong preventive component and offers sound and hopeful ideas for changes in schools and other institutions.

Research documents positive outcomes for reality therapy, particularly in schools and therapeutic communities (Wubbolding, 1995b). In addition, many published case studies describe the successful use of reality therapy with a variety of clients (Wubbolding, 2000). However, continued research is needed on the application of reality therapy to specific client groups so that clinicians have a clearer idea of its appropriate use.

Reality therapy has made important contributions to counseling and psychotherapy. It provides a clear and structured approach to treatment that is widely used in schools and rehabilitation programs. It emphasizes the importance of values in treatment and reminds clinicians not to neglect relationships and responsibility. Its appreciation and description of the collaborative therapeutic relationship has broadened the appropriate role of the clinician. Finally, it focuses attention on the need to help people engage in honest self-evaluation and make wise and responsible choices and plans.

SKILL DEVELOPMENT: CARING CONFRONTATION

Confrontation is a highly charged word that may seem incompatible with the supportive and encouraging role of the clinician. However, when done with caring and sensitivity, confrontations can help people more honestly and accurately evaluate their behaviors, acquire a better grasp of reality, and act in more responsible ways.

Confrontation can be defined as the process of noting discrepancies, usually in a person's words and behaviors, and reflecting those discrepancies back to the person. Confrontation should never involve shaming, belittling, or attacking, and should not precipitate a debate between client and clinician about who is right.

A confrontation typically has three parts:

1. An introduction that identifies the client statements, actions, or thoughts that prompted the intervention.
2. The body of the confrontation that points out the issues or discrepancies. In keeping with reality therapy, this statement should be tentative, gentle, and respectful.
3. Invitation for the client to respond. Questions such as "What do you make of that?" and "Would you be willing to explore that with me?" usually are used. They prompt people to reflect and self-evaluate and are unlikely to lead them to feel judged. Questions also offer people the opportunity to choose not to discuss the confrontation or to disagree with the clinician. These responses suggest that the clinician probably should not pursue the topic at present. However, it has been mentioned and is likely to arise again.

Consider the following example of a caring confrontation:

Clinician: Ronnie, several weeks ago, you told me that you and your fiancé are on a limited budget and are saving to buy a house. Today, you told me that you are buying a wedding gown that costs $3,000. I wonder if buying the wedding gown will help you meet your need for your own home. Would you be willing to take a look at that with me?

The clinician has identified a discrepancy in the information that Ronnie has presented. This is reflected back to her in an unemotional and nonjudgmental way, with an invitation for Ronnie to explore this discrepancy.

Ronnie may respond in a variety of ways. She may have information that resolves the discrepancy: "I didn't tell you that my aunt gave me $3,000 specifically to buy a wedding dress." She may open the door to further clarification of her values and choices: "This is the most important event in my life, and I want it to be as special as possible." Or she may reflect on her choices and make a self-evaluation: "I never put those two pieces together. Maybe it isn't a good idea for me to spend so much on a dress. That's only important for one day, but the house will mean something to us for years." Whether or not Ronnie sees the situation as her clinician does is not important; what does matter is that she has an opportunity to reflect on, clarify, evaluate, and possibly change her choices so that they better meet her needs. The exercises later in this chapter will give you an opportunity to develop some caring confrontations.

CASE ILLUSTRATION

Roberto consulted his therapist a few weeks before Thanksgiving because of family difficulties over the previous year's Thanksgiving. His therapist applied the WDEP and SAMI2C3 formats in the context of reality therapy to help Roberto plan to make the holiday more rewarding this year.

Roberto: Thanksgiving last year was a disaster. I don't want a repeat of that.
Clinician: What did you do?

Roberto: Well, I came home early on the day before Thanksgiving to have some extra time with Edie and Ava. I did have to bring some work home, and I wanted to get that done first, so I just said hello and headed over to the room where we have the computer. Before I know it, Edie flings the door open and is in my face about how I never help and am not really part of the family. I could not calm her down, so I just picked up my stuff and went back to the office. Who needs that! Of course, this spoiled Thanksgiving Day; Edie and I just glared at each other for most of the day.

Clinician: So even though you came home early and were thinking of your family, somehow your actions backfired and wound up not meeting either your needs or your family's. When you think about the five basic needs that we have discussed, how do you evaluate your efforts?

Roberto: You know, I can see that my thoughts and actions were at cross-purposes. In coming home early, I was focused on my needs for love and fun; I really wanted to have a close, enjoyable time with my family. But I did not give them that message. When I went right to the computer, all Edie saw was me trying to meet my need for achievement. She didn't know I just had a little work to do and then was going to spend time with the family. I guess I really didn't try to see things from her perspective.

Clinician: So you have some new thoughts about what happened last year. What are the needs you want to focus on this Thanksgiving?

Roberto: Definitely fun and love and belonging.

Clinician: And what pictures do you have in your head about what that would look like?

Roberto: We would all get along. We'd all pitch in to cook dinner. We'd have some good food and good conversation. I'd make a fire in the fireplace. Then maybe we could do something fun like taking a walk or going to a movie.

Clinician: Let's develop a plan to help you make those pictures real. We've reviewed the eight steps in the SAMI2C3 model for making successful plans: simple, attainable, measurable, immediate, involving, controlled, consistent, and committed. What plan comes into your mind?

Roberto: I could come home early again on the day before Thanksgiving but not bring any work home. I could ask Edie if she needs any help. And I could suggest something fun to do after Thanksgiving dinner.

Clinician: How does that plan fit the criteria?

Roberto: It seems simple and attainable. I guess it's measurable; I can tell if I'm doing what I planned or not. I'm certainly committed to changing our holiday experience. But I'm not sure the plan is immediate; and I don't know how I could make it more involving, controlled by me, or consistent.

Clinician: So you've made a start at planning, but how could you modify the plan so that it meets more of the criteria?

Roberto: I could make it immediate by starting right now. I'll write down the plan and tell Edie about it when I get home. I could even ask her now if there are ways I could help, like shopping or cleaning the house. If I offer specific ways to help, I have more control over the plan, and I'm taking more initiative. Edie complains that I leave everything at home up to her, so taking initiative seems like a good idea.

Clinician: So you see ways to make the plan more immediate and consistent as well as more under your control. Are there ways I could be involved in helping you?

Roberto: Maybe you could touch base with me sometime during the week to help me stay on track. I really want to, but sometimes I get so caught up with work. . . .

Clinician: How about if I telephone you on Tuesday to see how things are going?

Roberto: That would be great.

Clinician: Now let's look at the plan again to evaluate how well it promises to fulfill your needs and wants in realistic and responsible ways. Then you can write down the specifics.

EXERCISES

Large-Group Exercises

1. Although reality therapy has many strengths, it also presents some potential pitfalls, notably the risks that clinicians will ignore important diagnostic information and will fail to refer clients for medication when research suggests that is necessary to treat their difficulties. Discuss the potential negative impact of these risks on the treatment process and then develop ways to minimize those risks while practicing reality therapy.

2. Glasser's Quality School Model suggests many innovative ways to improve education. Discuss ways in which that model could be applied successfully to your college or university. How would that improve the educational experience for you?

3. Reality therapy takes the stance that nearly all aspects of people's lives are under their control. Discuss whether this belief is realistic and responsible, especially as applied to people in groups that often have experienced discrimination such as African Americans, people with visible disabilities, and people who are homosexual? In what ways is this stance likely to be helpful to people? Hurtful to them?

4. Review the "Case Illustration" in this chapter. Identify in the dialog the elements of the WDEP and SAMI2C3 formats.

Small-Group Exercises

1. Divide into your groups of four, composed of two dyads. Each dyad should engage in a 15-minute, role-played counseling interview in which the person playing the client presents a behavior he or she would like to change and the person in the clinician role uses the SAMI2C3 format to facilitate development of a plan to effect change. Feedback should focus on the use of the SAMI2C3 format as well as overall strengths and areas needing improvement in the role play.

2. Divide into your groups of four, composed of two dyads. Each dyad should engage in a 15-minute, role-played counseling interview in which the person in the clinician role helps the client discuss the balance of his or her five basic needs and identify at least one important way in which he or she is fulfilling each of the five needs. Feedback should focus on how well the clinician helped the client to explore balance and implementation of the five basic needs as well as overall strengths and areas needing improvement in the role play.

3. In your small groups, develop caring confrontations in response to the following client statements. Your statements should reflect the format for caring confrontations presented in the Skill Development section. Each group member should write out his or her responses individually before discussing and refining them in the group. Evaluate the responses in terms of whether they are likely to facilitate client awareness and self-evaluation without sounding judgmental or negative.

Client A: My co-workers have been giving me grief because I get to work late. They say they need my input on our project each morning. They don't understand that I'm a night person. I like to stay up late, and it's hard for me to get up in the morning. My job is important to me, but I don't think it should matter so much when I get there.

Client B: My mother is just impossible. You know, she's nearly 80 years old and really can't live alone anymore. I offered to come up and help her move into one of those continuing care places. I suppose they're all awful, smelly and depressing. . . I've never been inside one. . . but what choice does she have? So, no, she doesn't want to do that. She didn't say it, but I bet she wants to move in with me.

Client C: I can't believe what my stepfather did. When I was out, he went through my backpack and found some drugs I had in there. I told him I was just keeping the stuff for a friend; but of course, he didn't buy that. Now he's saying I need to go into a drug rehab program. What does he think I am. . . a drug addict? I just smoke some marijuana once in a while. At least I don't go nosing around in people's personal possessions.

Client D: My supervisor said some things that upset me. She said that people who get welfare payments are "ripping off the government" and "taking advantage of the middle class" and "getting a free ride." She doesn't know that I had to go on welfare when my husband left me with three young children. She's so wrong about what it's like to be on welfare. I wish I could straighten her out; but if I tell her about my background, she'll just write me off as one of those "welfare cheats." She's usually caring and understanding, so I know she didn't mean to hurt me. I'll just keep quiet about my reaction.

Individual Exercises

1. Identify a positive addiction that you would like to make part of your life. Write out a plan, following the SAMI2C3 format, to establish that positive behavior in your life.
2. Reality therapy stresses the key role that relationships play in both people's happiness and their misery. Write one or two pages in your journal about ways in which relationships have had an impact on your feelings of well-being. Then identify two small and specific changes you would like to make in the way you relate to others. Write them down and consider making a commitment to implementing those changes.
3. Draw a picture of the images in your quality world. Write a paragraph about what your drawing represents and means to you.

SUMMARY

Reality therapy, initiated by William Glasser in the 1960s and developed primarily by Glasser and Robert Wubbolding, is an optimistic and encouraging treatment approach. It focuses on present thoughts and behaviors and helps people meet their basic needs more successfully by making better choices. Responsibility (fulfilling one's own needs in ways that respect other people's rights to meet their needs) is key to this approach as are positive relationships. Clinicians play an active and involved role, promoting client self-evaluation and realistic and viable planning. Katz (1991) captured the essence of reality therapy: "When you behave the way you want to be, then you will be that way" (p. 65).

RECOMMENDED READINGS

Glasser, W. (1965). *Reality therapy.* New York: Harper & Row.

Glasser, W. (1986). *Control theory in the classroom.* New York: Harper & Row.

Glasser, W. (2000). *Counseling with choice theory.* New York: HarperCollins.

Wubbolding, R. E. (1990). *Expanding reality therapy: Group counseling and multicultural dimensions.* Cincinnati: Real World.

Wubbolding, R. E. (1991). *Understanding reality therapy.* New York: HarperCollins.

Wubbolding, R. E. (2000). *Reality therapy for the 21st century.* Briston, PA: Accelerated Development.

ADDITIONAL SOURCES OF INFORMATION

The William Glasser Institute, founded in 1967, offers training, certification, and resources on reality therapy, as well as information and consultation on the Quality School Program. Contact the Institute at 22024 Lassen Street, Suite 118, Chatsworth, CA 91311, 800-899-0688 and 818-700-8000, http://www.wglasser.com

ROGHA (an Irish-Gaelic word meaning choice) is a website that contains articles on reality therapy. It also offers an e-mail discussion list for those interested in reality therapy and can be contacted at http://www.angelfire.com/ab/brightminds/

Reality Therapy UK provides information on reality therapy, choice theory, and quality management. It promotes knowledge and practice of reality therapy. Website is http://www.realitytherapy.co.uk/

Information on the *International Journal of Reality Therapy* can be found at http://www.journalofrealitytherapy.com

The website for Robert Wubbolding is http://www.realitytherapywub.com

CHAPTER 21

Solution-Focused Brief Therapy

Solution-focused brief therapy has become an important treatment system in recent years. This approach seeks solutions, rather than attacking problems (O'Hanlon & Weiner-Davis, 1989). Treatment is usually brief, although progress is measured by results, not by number of sessions.

This treatment system is known by various names, including solution-oriented therapy, solution-focused therapy, problem-focused brief therapy, solution-focused brief therapy, and simply brief therapy. Although each name is associated with particular strategies and theorists, these models have much in common. We will pay some attention to their distinctions but will focus primarily on their shared characteristics. We will refer to this group of treatment systems as solution-focused brief therapy (SFBT).

Solution-focused brief therapy is, in many ways, similar to reality therapy and behavior therapy (Greenwalt, 1995). All three emphasize behavior change as the most effective and efficient way to help people improve their lives. All three value planning, focus on wants and goals, and build on successes. They de-emphasize the past but place importance on the clinician's role in promoting positive change. However, SFBT has historical influences, concepts, and strategies that set it apart from other cognitive and behavioral treatment approaches and enhance its power and appeal.

Clinicians today experience considerable pressure from managed care, schools and agencies, clients, and themselves to be accountable and demonstrate results. Solution-focused brief therapy accomplishes these goals. As a result, it has grown rapidly in popularity and is widely recognized as an effective treatment approach for certain types of problems and clients.

THE DEVELOPMENT OF SOLUTION-FOCUSED BRIEF THERAPY

No one name is associated with the development of SFBT, as Glasser is with reality therapy or Rogers with person-centered counseling. Rather, many ideas and people played important roles in the evolution of this approach since it first appeared in the professional literature in the 1970s. However, Steve de Shazer, Bill O'Hanlon, Michele Weiner-Davis, and Insoo Kim Berg probably have made the greatest contributions to solution-focused brief therapy as it is currently practiced.

Early writings on brief therapy in the 1970s and early 1980s include important contributions from Richard Fisch, John Weakland, Paul Watzlawick, and Gregory Bateson, among others, who were affiliated with the Mental Research Institute in Palo Alto, California (Fisch, Weakland, & Segal, 1982). Their vision of treatment is reflected in the following statement: "We try to base our conceptions and our interventions on direct observation in the treatment situation of *what* is going on in systems of human interaction, *how* they continue to function in such ways, and *how* they may be altered most effectively" (Weakland, Fisch, Watzlawick, & Bodin, 1974, p. 150). Initially, treatment was generally limited to 10 sessions. Typical interventions encouraged people to reverse or alter what they were doing, not just do more of the same (O'Hanlon & Weiner-Davis, 1989).

Milton Erickson, another innovative thinker at the Mental Research Institute, also contributed to SFBT (Gilligan, 1997). Erickson, who practiced from the 1920s to the 1970s, realized how important it is for people to have an open and receptive attitude toward change and new possibilities; he sought to induce a trance-like state in his clients that would increase their responsiveness to treatment (Stalker, Levene, and Coady, 1999). Erickson also recognized that people were more likely to benefit from treatment if clinicians accepted and used whatever clients presented and focused on current and observable behavioral interactions (Weakland et al., 1974). Solution-focused brief therapy (like neuro-linguistic programming discussed in chapter 17) reflects Erickson's concepts.

Brief psychodynamic psychotherapy (discussed in chapter 8) also contributed to the early development of SFBT. Brief psychodynamic therapists value efficient and results-oriented treatment. They advocate identifying a focal concern to narrow and streamline the therapeutic process. These strategies have become part of solution-focused brief therapy, although unlike brief psychodynamic psychotherapy, SFBT usually pays little attention to clients' past history.

Behavioral and cognitive-behavioral treatment approaches provide the underpinnings of SFBT. Those approaches demonstrated that changing current actions and thoughts could have a profound impact on people's lives and that resulting changes were typically enduring and generalizable. Cognitive and behavioral approaches to treatment also provide solution-focused therapists with an extensive repertoire of interventions that can be used both within and between sessions to promote change.

Systems family therapy is another approach that contributed to solution-focused brief therapy. The writings of Salvador Minuchin (Minuchin & Fishman, 1981) and other family therapists brought home the importance of reciprocal relationships between client and environment and client and others. SFBT emphasizes appreciation of circular or reciprocal relationships as well as of linear relationships. SFBT pays considerable attention to people's social systems, including the therapeutic alliance, the family, the community, and the cultural group.

In the 1980s and 1990s, Steve de Shazer (1985, 1988), Insoo Kim Berg (DeJong & Berg, 2002), Bill O'Hanlon, and Michele Weiner-Davis (O'Hanlon & Weiner-Davis, 1989; Weiner-Davis, 1992) all made important contributions to SFBT. Steve de Shazer and Insoo Kim Berg, co-founders of the Brief Family Therapy Center in Milwaukee, developed what they called *solution-focused brief therapy*. De Shazer probably is best known for his use of the miracle question (discussed later in this chapter). However, his contributions to brief therapy go far beyond that. De Shazer, Berg, and their colleagues used a decision tree to determine which interventions to use with a client. They generally began treatment with a standard task such as suggesting that clients observe and describe what was happening in their lives that they wanted to continue to happen. If clients completed such a straightforward task, treatment continued in a fairly traditional way. However, if people failed to complete suggested tasks, indirect treatment strategies were tried, such as the use of metaphors or paradoxical interventions. De Shazer, Berg, and their colleagues are known for creative use of clues or suggested tasks to help people find solutions to their problems. They also sometimes use a reflecting team that observes treatment sessions and interrupts with suggestions or ideas.

O'Hanlon and Weiner-Davis were influenced by the work of de Shazer and Berg but also made their own contributions through what they called *solution-oriented brief therapy*. Their treatment approach helps people focus on future goals and determine the steps they can take to reach them. O'Hanlon and Weiner-Davis are unconcerned with how problems arose or how they are maintained but only with how they will be solved. By creating images of what might be and raising awareness of potentials, they seek to change clients' viewpoints and actions so they can find solutions. O'Hanlon and Weiner-Davis view small changes as stepping-stones to larger ones, and suggest that understanding follows rather than precedes behavior change.

Talmon's *Single Session Therapy* (1990), with its compelling title, brought further attention to brief therapy. Talmon does not actually encourage limiting treatment to only one session; rather, his book is a reminder that effective interventions can begin in the first moment of contact with a client and that brief treatment, building on natural, spontaneous, and ongoing changes in people, can be very powerful. Talmon (1990) initiates treatment in his first telephone conversation with a client, saying, "Between now and our first session, I want you to notice the things that happen to you that you would like to keep happening in the future. In this way, you will help me find out more about your goals and what you are up to" (p. 19). This powerful intervention changes people's focus from what is wrong to what is right and initiates the work of building on strengths.

This overview of important contributors to solution-focused brief therapy is by no means exhaustive. Because this new approach is still evolving rapidly, the array of contributors will continue to grow and expand.

IMPORTANT THEORETICAL CONCEPTS

Solution-focused brief therapy lacks many of the features associated with a well-developed treatment approach. Its literature does not offer a detailed understanding of human development, nor does it address at length the impact of past experiences on present difficulties. Neither does it elaborate on mental disorders it can treat successfully.

These omissions might be interpreted to mean that SFBT is an emerging approach rather than a full-fledged treatment system. However, these omissions are consistent with the nature of the approach, which pays little attention to the origins of people's difficulties and touches lightly, if at all, on their histories. Adopting an idea suggested by Albert Einstein, this treatment system maintains that a problem cannot be solved at the same level it was created. Therefore, SFBT focuses on the present and the future rather than on the past and emphasizes even small glimmers of health and positive change rather than past pathology (de Shazer, 1985). It is included in this book because of its widespread use, its impact on counseling and psychology, and its internal coherence and consistency, even though it lacks some elements that might be viewed as essential in a fully developed treatment system.

Underlying Assumptions

Solution-focused therapists assume that people's complaints involve behavior that stems from their view of the world. These behaviors are maintained when people do more of the same in the belief that there is only one right and logical thing to do. Clinicians base their ideas and suggestions for change on clients' conception of their lives without their symptoms. Suggesting a new possibility or frame of reference often is enough to prompt people to take effective action. Brief therapists believe that even minimal changes can effect progress since changes tend to have a self-perpetuating ripple effect. Once behavior is changed, the whole system is different.

Solution-focused brief therapy assumes that people have the ability to resolve their difficulties successfully but that they have temporarily lost confidence, direction, or awareness of resources. Clinicians believe they usually need only limited information about a complaint to resolve it and do not seek to discover the cause or purpose of a complaint. SFBT spends little time helping people figure out why they have been unable to resolve their problems and carefully avoids giving people the message that they have been deficient in their efforts to help themselves. Instead, it assumes that people are doing the best they can at any given time. The thrust of treatment is to increase people's hope and optimism by creating expectancy for change, no matter how small. In this way, people become more aware of what is working rather than what is not. As they become cognizant of the possibilities for positive change, their empowerment and motivation increase correspondingly, creating a beneficial circle; positive change fuels people's belief that change can happen, which enhances their motivation and efforts to change, which in turn leads to more positive changes.

Solution-focused therapists believe that change is constant, that things cannot *not* change. Often, all that is needed to help people is to enable them to notice and build on positive changes that are already happening.

According to SFBT, reality is not fixed or static, and there is no one right way to view things. By helping people "negotiate a solvable problem" (O'Hanlon & Weiner-Davis, 1989, p. 56) or even "dissolve the idea that there is a problem" (p. 58), clinicians can enable people to set meaningful and viable goals and achieve rapid resolution of their complaints. Establishment of concrete goals, as well as changes in behavior and perception, promote progress.

SFBT assumes that exceptions to the problem, times when the problem is absent, give clues to effective solutions. Identifying these exceptions and building on the ingredients that created them provide further impetus to change.

Finally, clinicians practicing SFBT believe that solutions may not directly relate to the problems. Rather, clinicians often suggest "skeleton keys" that help people transform a variety of problems into solutions.

Stages in Treatment

SFBT typically proceeds according to seven stages (de Shazer, 1985):

1. *Identifying a solvable complaint* is an essential first step in treatment. Not only does it facilitate development of goals and interventions, but it promotes change. Client and clinician collaborate to create images of the complaints that place their solutions in the client's hands. For example, "making my spouse stop his abuse" probably is out of the client's hands and is not a readily solvable complaint. However, "remaining strong and taking care of myself when my spouse is abusive" is within the client's control.

   Clinicians phrase questions so that they communicate optimism and expectancy for change and empower and encourage. People's difficulties are viewed as normal and able to be changed. Clinicians might ask, "What led you to make an appointment *now?*" rather than "What problems are bothering you?" or ask, "What do you want to change?" rather than "How can I help you?"

   Clinicians use empathy, summarization, paraphrase, open questions, and other active listening skills to understand the client's situation in clear and specific terms. They might ask, "How do you do anxiety?" "What would help me to really understand this situation?" and "How does this create a problem for you?"

   In SFBT, presenting complaints are not viewed as symptoms or evidence of pathology. Rather, they are seen as a function of unsuccessful interactions with others or the mishandling of everyday experiences. People often believe that what they are doing is the only right way and keep doing more of the same, even though they are unsuccessful. As a result, "the solution becomes the problem" (Weakland et al., 1974, p. 31). People may fail to take necessary action, take action when none is indicated, or take action in the wrong way. SFBT assumes that if people's actions and interactions change, their complaints can be alleviated (Fisch et al., 1982).

   Like other behaviorally-oriented clinicians, solution-focused therapists often use scaling questions to establish a baseline and facilitate identification of possibilities and progress. The clinician might ask, "Let's say 1 stands for how bad you felt when you first came to see me with this concern and 10 stands for how your life will be when you don't need to see me anymore. On a scale between 1 and 10, where would you put yourself today?" (Berg & Miller, 1992a, p. 362). This scale also can be used to assess specific areas of focus, including symptoms and relationships.

2. *Establishing goals* continues the treatment process. Clinicians collaborate with clients to determine goals that are specific, observable, measurable, and concrete. Goals typically take one of three forms: *changing the doing* of the problematic situation; *changing the viewing* of the situation or the frame of reference; and *accessing resources, solutions,* and strengths (O'Hanlon & Weiner-Davis, 1989). Again, questions presuppose success: "What will be the first sign of change?", How will you know when this treatment has been helpful to you?", How will I be able to tell?" Detailed discussion of positive change is encouraged to obtain a clear view of what solutions look like to the client. (The "Skill Development" section of this chapter offers more information on goal setting.)

   One of the most useful ways for solution-focused clinicians to establish treatment goals is to use the *miracle question* (de Shazer, 1991, p. 113): "Suppose that one night there is a miracle and while you were sleeping the problem that brought you to therapy is solved. How would you know? What would be different? What will you notice different the next morning that will tell you that there has been a miracle? What will your spouse notice?" This question enables people to imagine that their problems are solved, instills hope, and facilitates discussion of how to make the miracle a reality. People's responses to the miracle question usually provide clinicians with potential solutions to clients' concerns.

Delivery of the miracle question is important to its success. Clinicians typically speak slowly, using an almost hypnotic tone of voice, when presenting this question. This engages clients and evokes openness and responsiveness. The miracle question can be adapted to be compatible with the client's concept of the divine. Berg and Miller (1992a), for example, suggest that the miracle might be presented as a magic pill, divine intervention, a silver bullet, or a magic wand, depending on the client's beliefs.

Solution-focused therapists accept and use whatever clients present (Gilligan, 1997). For example, when asked the miracle question, one woman replied, "The first thing I will notice is that my husband has brushed his teeth before returning to bed for some romance." She had tried to tell her husband that his morning breath bothered her, but increasing nagging yielded no results. After determining that the woman and her husband were playful, the clinician suggested that the woman hide a toothbrush and toothpaste under her pillow and whip it out to brush her husband's teeth the next morning. She felt empowered by having something to do other than complain, and tried this suggestion. This conveyed her message to her husband and also introduced humor into their interaction.

3. When *designing an intervention,* clinicians draw on both their understanding of their clients and their creative use of treatment strategies to encourage change, no matter how small. Typical questions during this stage include "What changes have already occurred?", "What worked in the past when you dealt with similar situations?", "How did you make that happen?", and "What would you need to do to have that happen again?"

4. *Strategic tasks* then promote change. These are generally written down so that clients can understand and agree to them. Tasks are carefully planned to maximize client cooperation and success. People are praised for their efforts and successes and for the strengths they draw on in completing tasks.

   Careful assessment of the client is essential in determining an appropriate task. De Shazer (1988) identified three types of tasks, each linked to the level of client motivation:

   • If people are *visitors or window shoppers* who have not presented clear complaints or expectations of change, clinicians should only give compliments. Suggesting tasks prematurely is likely to lead to failure that can jeopardize the treatment process.

   • If people are *complainants* who have concerns and expect change, but generally in others rather than in themselves, clinicians should suggest observation tasks. This helps people become more aware of themselves and their situations and more able to describe their wants. The clinician might suggest, "Between now and our next appointment, I would like you to notice things that are happening in your life that you want to continue." Observation tasks require little client effort or motivation and, once suggested, usually are done almost automatically.

   • Finally, if clients are *customers* who want to take steps to find solutions to their concerns, clinicians can suggest action tasks with the expectation that they will be completed. Tasks should both empower clients and effect a change in their complaints. For example, Neva had many fears, including learning to drive a car and initiating conversations. Her counselor suggested she ask at least two people to tell her how they learned to drive. Neva found that people enjoyed talking about this topic. She not only gained useful information on driving but initiated several conversations.

5. *Positive new behaviors and changes are identified and emphasized* when clients return after they have been given a task. Questions focus on change, progress, and possibilities and might include "How did you make that happen?", "Who noticed the changes?", and "How did things go differently when you did that?" The problem is viewed as "it" or "that" and as external to the client; this helps people view their concerns as amenable to change, not as an integral part of themselves.

   Particularly during this stage of treatment, solution-focused clinicians serve as a sort of cheering squad for their clients. They provide compliments and highlight areas of strength and competence.

6. *Stabilization* is essential in helping people consolidate their gains and gradually shift their perspectives in more effective and hopeful directions. During this stage, clinicians might actually restrain progress and predict some backsliding. This gives people time to adjust to their changes, promotes further success, and prevents them from becoming discouraged if change does not happen as rapidly as they would like.

7. Finally, *termination* of treatment occurs, often initiated by the clients who have now accomplished their goals. Because SFBT focuses on presenting complaints rather than resolution of childhood issues or significant personality change, it recognizes that people may return for additional treatment, and clients are reminded of that option. At the same time, SFBT is not just seeking to help people resolve immediate concerns. Through the process of developing confidence, feeling heard and praised rather than blamed, and finding their strengths and resources, people treated via SFBT can become more self-reliant and capable of resolving future difficulties on their own.

Timing

Most therapy or counseling relationships are relatively brief, whether or not that is planned and regardless of treatment approach. Budman and Gurman (1988) found that the mean number of sessions is six to eight, with 80% of clients concluding treatment by the 20th session and most of their positive changes occurring by the 8th session.

SFBT capitalizes on this pattern, and both clinician and client are aware from the outset that treatment is likely to be short. Because SFBT emphasizes present-oriented efficient treatment that seeks solutions to specific concerns, treatment usually requires fewer than 10 sessions with an average treatment length of about 5 sessions (Stalker et al., 1999). However, duration is not determined by an artificial conception of how long therapy is supposed to be; rather, treatment is as long as it needs to be to help people meet their goals and resolve their complaints. Clinicians do not hesitate to extend treatment as long as positive change and forward movement are evident.

Solution-focused therapists tend to be flexible in scheduling appointments. Breaks within sessions allow clinicians the opportunity to develop clues, sometimes in consultation with a reflecting team (Stalker et al., 1999). Clinicians might plan treatment intervals of one or more months to give clients time to implement suggested strategies and allow changes to evolve. Clinicians also use extended follow-up if people need continued reinforcement. Adapting treatment to the individual is essential.

Finding Solutions

Finding solutions or clues to resolve complaints is an essential component of SFBT. Clinicians put considerable thought into identifying strategies that are likely to succeed and avoiding those that are discouraging or likely to fail. The following guidelines can help clinicians find effective and empowering solutions:

- View clients as experts on their complaints as well as on what solutions will work.
- Assume they have the strengths and resources they need to change.
- Focus on natural and spontaneous changes that are already in progress.
- Expand and build on positive exceptions.
- Interrupt and change repetitive and nonproductive sequences of behavior.
- Provide a rationale to explain how tasks can be helpful, to increase clients' motivation to perform the tasks. If people are skeptical, tasks might be presented as an experiment that they can stop at any point.
- Make interventions congruent with people's worldviews (de Shazer, 1982).
- Learn from past solutions in formulating future solutions. For example, if people respond to direct suggestions, keep providing them; but if they do the opposite of what is suggested, create paradoxical interventions in which doing the opposite is desirable.
- Embed compliments in suggestions to promote optimism and encourage follow-through on tasks.
- Encourage new behaviors rather than simply cessation of old and ineffective ones.
- Create an expectancy for change and a context in which people can think and behave differently.
- Make solutions practical and specific.

TREATMENT USING SOLUTION-FOCUSED BRIEF THERAPY

Although the process of solution-focused therapy is important, the outcome determines whether treatment has been successful. SFBT helps people use the strengths and resources they already possess to effect positive change in their lives. Initial goals include creating an atmosphere that is conducive to change and development of multiple perspectives and possibilities, thereby enabling people to do something different. Eventual goals entail helping people lead more balanced lives and become more resourceful in thinking about resolving future concerns.

Therapeutic Alliance

The client-clinician relationship is an important element in solution-focused brief therapy. Some early practitioners of this approach, including Milton Erickson, viewed the therapist as being in charge of treatment. However, most clinicians now advocate a collaborative therapeutic alliance and maximize client involvement to empower people and enhance their commitment to treatment (Gilligan, 1997). Although clinicians have primary responsibility for creating and suggesting solutions and presenting them in ways that promote action, they view clients as collaborators and talk about how clients can help the clinician and the treatment process.

Clinicians use a wide variety of interventions. Active listening, empathy, open questions, explanation, reassurance, and suggestion all are important, while interpretation and confrontation are rarely used. Clinicians engage actively with their clients, communicating acceptance, promoting cooperation, serving as role models, telling metaphorical stories, and suggesting actions to effect change. Because they recognize the importance of people's social systems, clinicians may use resources in the environment and involve clients' significant others in the therapeutic process to further the goals of treatment. Osborn (1999, p. 176) suggests the following helpful guidelines for clinicians: "listen, do not label; investigate, do not interrogate; level, do not lecture; cooperate, do not convince; clarify, do not confront; solicit solutions, do not prescribe them; consult, do not cure; commend, do not condemn; explore, do not explain; be directive, not dictatorial." Clinicians maintain a positive, respectful, and health-oriented focus and assume that every session is important, that change is inevitable, and that it will have a ripple effect on many aspects of a client's life (Budman & Gurman, 1988).

Specific Interventions

Solution-focused brief therapy uses a broad range of strategies and interventions. Although most have been discussed in previous chapters on cognitive and behavioral treatment systems, some are particular to SFBT. We have already discussed the miracle question, the use of scaling to measure change, and the use of suggested solutions. The following are other interventions often used in SFBT (Campbell & Elder, 1999):

Clinicians *create an environment that is conducive to change.* Tone of voice, metaphorical stories, and suggestions embedded in discussions promote such a state. This enables people to become more open to new possibilities and interpretations, more creative, more amenable to changing the ways they have always behaved, and more able to access neglected or overlooked alternatives.

Identifying exceptions to people's problematic patterns can lead to solutions to their complaints. Although people commonly come into treatment with a desire to vent and process their difficulties, solution-focused therapists believe that a negative focus stabilizes the system and makes change difficult. They believe that a positive focus is far more likely to lead to beneficial transformations. As a result, solution-focused clinicians encourage people to examine times when their difficulties were absent, as sources of information about ways to effect desired change.

For example, Fredda, in her first job as a teacher, sought help with anxiety that she experienced nearly every morning before beginning to teach. Rather than focusing on her unpleasant feelings, the clinician asked whether she could remember a morning when she did not experience anxiety. Fredda described one morning when she got to school early, organized her materials for the day, and then had tea with another teacher who gave Fredda some good ideas about managing a difficult student. This exception suggested several routes to alleviating Fredda's symptoms: arriving early, being well prepared, relaxing before class, and seeking advice from more experienced teachers. By building these behaviors into her routine, Fredda gained control over her anxiety and also began to form friendships at work.

If clients cannot readily recall exceptions to their difficulties, clinicians can take an active role in promoting exceptions. They might suggest a strategic change in behavior. They might predict an exception if one seems likely to occur. They also might encourage clients to search for exceptions, a strategy that is likely to be fruitful if exceptions seem to go unnoticed. Questions such as "What is different about the times when the difficulty does not happen?", "When is the problem less severe?", "How does your day go differently without the problem?", "How is that different from the way you handled the situation the last time it occurred?", "How did you resolve this concern before?", and "What would you need to do to have that happen again?" focus attention on exceptions.

Solution talk is an important tool in SFBT. Clinicians choose their words carefully so that they increase clients' hope and optimism, their sense of control, and their openness to possibilities and change. The focus is on solutions, not problems. Some examples of how language can be used to enhance treatment follow:

- Emphasize *open questions.*
- Use *presuppositional language* that assumes that problems are temporary and that positive change will occur. For example, clinicians speak of *when,* not *if,* the problem is solved: "When this problem is solved, what will you be doing?" Clinicians may emphasize the temporary nature of problems: "Up to now, this has been difficult for you" or "You have not yet found a solution to this problem."
- *Externalize the problem.* For example, clinicians discuss ways people can solve problems rather than ways they can work through their emotional barriers.
- *Normalizing people's problems* provides reassurance and can reduce feelings of inadequacy. A clinician might say to a parent, coping with a child's drug use, "Your son seems to be engaging in some risky behaviors and it makes sense that you are worried."
- *Focus on coping behavior* via questions such as "What has kept you from harming yourself?" and "How do you manage to keep going?"
- *Reinforce and notice strengths and successes.* Congratulate and compliment people for their improvements and efforts; avoid emphasizing problems and failures. Affirmations developed in collaboration with clients can help them focus on their achievements.
- *Create hypothetical solutions* such as "If you weren't feeling afraid, what might you be feeling and doing instead?" This expands possibilities and encourages change.
- *Concentrate on describing and changing behaviors* rather than thoughts or emotions.
- *Use rituals, metaphors, stories, and symbols* to convey indirect messages that can promote change. For example, Mary envisioned a formidable brick wall standing between her and the sort of life she wanted. Her counselor suggested that she remove one brick, leaving it up to Mary to determine how she would complete this task. She responded by changing several behavioral patterns and reported that she had made a hole in the wall big enough for her to crawl through.
- Make frequent use of words such as *change, different, possibility, what,* and *how* that suggest change.
- Use *inclusive language such as "and"* that allows potentially incompatible outcomes to coexist. Rather than saying, "You can feel like you can't do it, but you can do it," the clinician might say, "You can feel like you can't do it, *and* you can do it."
- *Use reframing and relabeling* to offer different perspectives. For example, an event might be viewed as an opportunity for learning rather than a disappointment, and a person might be depicted as "taking the time to sort out options" rather than "stuck" or "paralyzed by fear."

- *Match clients' vocabulary or style of talking* to promote a collaborative therapeutic alliance. Then change the language to encourage change in clients' perspectives.

Make suggestions.

- Recognize that *indirectness and implied suggestions* are sometimes more powerful than direct suggestions and advice.
- At the same time, *homework tasks and suggestions* are part of SFBT. These are typically presented in such a way as to afford people options and increase awareness of possibilities. For example, Gretchen felt overwhelmed by her unrewarding and stressful career and viewed her life as "unending misery." Her therapist suggested that she notice what kept her going from one day to the next.
- *Solution prescriptions,* a common form of suggestion in SFBT, are tasks designed to help people discover ways to resolve their concerns. These may be designed to fit a particular person or situation or may be a standard prescription in the clinician's repertoire. Commonly used prescriptions include "Do something to surprise yourself or someone else," "Keep track of what helps you," and "Notice what happens that you want to continue to happen" (O'Hanlon & Weiner-Davis, 1989).

Complaint pattern intervention.

- O'Hanlon and Weiner-Davis (1989) suggest many approaches to helping people get "unstuck," modify unhelpful patterns, and move forward, including changing the frequency or rate of an undesired behavior, changing its duration, changing the timing, changing the location, changing the sequence, and adding or subtracting at least one element in a sequence of behaviors.

For example, Matthias's girlfriend recently broke their engagement and moved away. Night after night, he came home from work, sat in front of the television, and cried for approximately 2 hours before calling his girlfriend and pleading with her to reconsider her decision. His behavior might be changed in the following ways:

- He might cry for one hour and then take a walk before crying for the second hour.
- He might call his girlfriend before crying.
- He might cry in another room.
- He might cry in the morning.

None of these interventions tells Matthias not to cry or feel bad; however, by changing his behavior, his thoughts and feelings are likely to change as well.

- *Videotalk* involves encouraging people to describe their concerns in action terms, as though they are viewing themselves in a film. They might even imagine themselves in a theater, watching the action related to their problem on the screen, and holding a remote control which can change the volume, stop the action, modify the size and intensity of the picture, and even shut off the film. Once the action has been described, clinicians can suggest alterations in the action that are likely to effect positive change. Videotalk gives people a new perspective on their problems, helps them distance themselves from their problems, and allows them to view the problems more objectively. This can help them discover and change repetitive patterns, increase their control over those problems, and reduce self-blame (O'Hanlon & Bertolino, 1998).

APPLICATION OF SOLUTION-FOCUSED BRIEF THERAPY

Because solution-focused brief therapy is a relatively new approach, information on its appropriate use is still limited. However, indications are that this approach is useful with a broad range of concerns and in a wide variety of settings.

Particularly good candidates for SFBT are people who are motivated to face their difficulties and change, have a history of good relationships, can be flexible and creative, succeeded in finding solutions to past problems, and have a support network that encourages and reinforces change (Thompson, 1996). Solution-focused treatment also is likely to help people who are stuck in their efforts to resolve a specific problem or complaint (Talmon, 1990).

The scope of solution-focused therapy has expanded beyond treating people with mild or moderately severe problems to successfully treating people with a history of serious difficulties such as sexual abuse. In their work with people who have been abused, O'Hanlon and Bertolino (1998) help people see that they are more than their symptoms and experiences. They use trances, stories, and solution talk to validate what people have invalidated in themselves and invite them to consider new possibilities. Promoting clients' recognition of appropriate boundaries, as well as their ability to maintain those boundaries, is another important aspect of treatment. In addition, rituals are beneficial in providing stability and continuity as well as facilitating transitions. They also can promote connection with other people, memories, resources, and one's history and culture.

Application to Diagnostic Groups

Like other cognitive and behavioral approaches to treatment, SFBT is well suited to treatment of mood and anxiety disorders, as well as adjustment disorders accompanied by symptoms of anxiety and depression. Some of the concepts and strategies associated with SFBT—notably attention to motivation, emphasis on small successes, and efforts to find exceptions—are likely to enhance treatment for people with personality disorders, somatoform disorders, impulse control disorders, and substance use disorders. Osborn (1999), for example, describes the use of solution-focused strategies to increase the cooperation and collaboration of "involuntary" clients seen in school, mental health, and substance abuse treatment programs. However, treatment of disorders such as these probably will not be brief and will need to integrate additional treatment approaches.

Solution-focused brief treatment should be used with great caution, if at all, with people who are actively suicidal or dangerous, are suffering from psychosis or dissociative identity disorder, have severe eating disorders, or have difficulties that necessitate medication (Talmon, 1990). Such people usually need a more intensive form of treatment, although elements of SFBT may be beneficially integrated into those approaches or even be effective as a primary mode of treatment. For example, Rowen and O'Hanlon (1999) describe the successful use of SFBT with people diagnosed with chronic and severe mental illness, helping them reclaim their lives and change ideas of impossibility, blame, nonaccountability, and disempowerment. Similarly, Sharry, Darmody, and Madden (2002) discuss the use of solution-focused approaches with people who are suicidal; they recommend combining this approach with more traditional approaches to establish safety and assess risk. SFBT may be particularly useful in treating severe mental disorders once improvement has been achieved via medication or other forms of psychotherapy.

Application to Multicultural Groups

Research is limited on the use of solution-focused therapy with multicultural groups and writers have conflicting perspectives on the appropriateness of using SFBT with people from culturally diverse backgrounds. DeJong and Berg (2002) see much in SFBT to give this approach multicultural relevance including its flexibility and its emphasis on health, resources, strengths, client dignity, collaboration, empowerment, and self-determination. In addition, SFBT's respect for people's views of the world, its recognition of the importance of people's connections with their environment and with others, and this treatment approach's brief and nonintrusive nature all seem to make it suitable for use with a broad range of people. In addition, solution-focused therapists' recognition of the importance of client motivation and efforts to promote clients' involvement in treatment make SFBT useful with people who are resistant to or leery about treatment.

According to Berg and Miller (1992a), SFBT "has been used successfully with various ethnic populations at the Brief Family Therapy Center in Milwaukee, Wisconsin" (p. 357). In describing their use of SFBT with Asian American clients, they report that the questions used by clinicians practicing this approach "suggest curiosity and respect for the client's view without pressuring the client to change" (p. 362).

Research reported by DeJong and Berg (2002) reflects little difference among racial groups or between genders in intermediate and final outcomes of solution-focused therapy. However, sample sizes in that research are small.

On the other hand, Stalker, Levene, and Coady (1999) express concern about broad and multicultural applications of SFBT. They fault this approach for neglecting client history, downplaying multicultural factors, disregarding the impact on people of large systems such as extended families, and placing more emphasis on theory and technique than on the therapeutic alliance.

A close reading of these sources suggests that these two perspectives can be reconciled. According to DeJong and Berg (2002)

> Certainly, it is important for practitioners to learn about the worldviews and preferred lifestyles of different groups, and all practitioners need to become more aware of their own attitudes regarding diversity. However, our preference for a solution-building paradigm makes us uneasy with attempts to address diversity within the context of professional assessments and interventions. Instead, we regard cultural diversity as one aspect of the enormous differences among people and as further confirmation of the need to take a posture of not knowing when interviewing clients. (p. 257)

In other words, while multicultural sensitivity is prized in SFBT, clinicians apparently do not place great weight on the importance of cultural factors. Some readers will be comfortable with this stance while others will not.

Application to Other Groups

Solution-focused therapy seems useful with children and adolescents as well as with adults, although it might need to be modified for treatment of children. Littrell, Malia, and Vanderwood (1995) studied the impact of single-session brief counseling with high school students and concluded that the approach worked well in treating developmental, behavioral, and interpersonal problems. On the other hand, they discouraged its use for crises and severe emotional difficulties, noting that a brief approach might miss important underlying issues.

Corcoran and Stephenson (2000) found that treatment via solution-focused therapy yielded significant improvement when used with children presenting behavior problems in their schools. Positive changes were reflected in the Conners' Parent Rating Scales assessing conduct, learning, and psychosomatic problems, as well as impulsivity and hyperactivity.

Although most of the literature on SFBT focuses on its use with individuals, it has recently been adapted for use with families, couples and groups. Metcalf's (1998) writings are especially helpful for clinicians who want to use this approach with groups in both school and mental health settings.

In addition, O'Connell (1998) recommends the use of solution-focused therapy in a broad range of settings. These include work environments, employee assistance programs, schools and colleges, corrections, and medical settings.

CURRENT USE

Interest in and use of SFBT are growing rapidly, and many schools, agencies and clinicians now emphasize this approach in their work. The rapid acceptance of SFBT is due, in part, to its efficiency and effectiveness. However, it also has been well received because it advocates goal setting, measurement of progress, empowerment of clients, a collaborative therapeutic alliance, and brief treatment that characterize much of psychotherapy at the beginning of the 21st century.

Because SFBT encourages thoughtful use of interventions and homework tasks, it lends itself well to integration with other treatment approaches, particularly those that take a phenomenological perspective and focus on behavior change. Although the current literature offers only limited guidance on integrating SFBT with other approaches, future writing is expected to clarify this process further.

EVALUATION OF SOLUTION-FOCUSED BRIEF THERAPY

Although most of the literature on solution-focused treatment consists of case studies and descriptions of treatment strategies, the value of SFBT seems clear. Additional empirical research is expected to enhance the reputation of this powerful approach.

Limitations

Solution-focused brief therapy has limitations, which many of its practitioners seem to realize. Unless clients and clinicians carefully co-create problem definitions, the approach can cause clinicians to focus prematurely on a presenting problem and thereby miss an issue of greater importance. Solution-focused treatment is not usually appropriate as the primary or only treatment for severe or urgent emotional difficulties. In addition, its implementation appears easier than it is. In reality, this approach requires well-trained clinicians who are skilled and experienced in assessment, goal setting, treatment planning, and effective use of a range of creative and powerful interventions.

Another drawback to SFBT is the misapprehension among some clinicians and clients, as well as some managed care organizations, that brief treatment is all that is ever needed to treat clients successfully. This is, of course, a dangerous overgeneralization, with the result that people may fail to receive the intensive treatment they need. Clinicians should exercise caution when using SFBT to be sure that this approach is adequate to meet their clients' needs.

Strengths and Contributions

SFBT has many strengths. It is effective and efficient with a broad range of problems, is generally well received by clients, is encouraging and empowering, and offers new ways of thinking about helping people. It addresses immediate problems while enabling people to make better use of their strengths and resources in addressing future difficulties.

Research on the outcomes of treatment via SFBT has been published and continues. Gingerich and Eisengart (2000) reviewed 15 controlled outcome studies of SFBT. Although all studies yielded positive results, the authors viewed 10 of the studies as not well-controlled. Gingerich and Eisengart (2000, p. 477) concluded, ". . . the 15 studies provide preliminary support for the efficacy of SFBT but do not permit a definitive conclusion." This article and others (DeJong & Berg, 2002) suggest that SFBT is effective, but we cannot conclude that it is superior to other treatment approaches that also have demonstrated their value.

Solution-focused brief therapy has made important contributions to counseling and psychotherapy. Many clinicians and clients now believe that treatment need not be prolonged and costly to be effective. SFBT also has provided clinicians with powerful new interventions. Its use of the miracle question, its emphasis on exceptions and possibilities, its use of presuppositional and other solution-focused language, and its emphasis on small behavioral changes are innovative concepts that are changing the way many clinicians think about and provide treatment. The miracle question, in particular, has gained widespread acceptance as a useful tool to facilitate information gathering and goal setting.

SKILL DEVELOPMENT: GOAL SETTING

Goal setting is an essential component of treatment, not only in solution-focused brief therapy where it receives particular attention, but in nearly all approaches to counseling and psychotherapy. Goals give both clients and clinicians a sense of purpose and direction. Having goals in sight helps people feel optimistic about their treatment and facilitates change in behaviors, thoughts, and emotions. Goals guide the treatment process and help clinicians choose effective strategies. Finally, a clear statement of goals enables clients and clinicians to assess progress and, if necessary, make changes in a treatment plan that is not advancing people's efforts to reach their goals.

Formulating goals should be a collaborative process involving both client and clinician. As much as possible, clients should take the initiative in identifying their goals. However, clinicians can help them to describe goals in clear, specific, measurable, and achievable terms. For example, Agnes sought help in changing the attitudes and behaviors of her students. However, exploration of the problem led client and clinician to co-create a goal of helping Agnes find successful ways of acting toward and talking to her students.

Clinicians sometimes need to suggest goals to clients that are essential in helping them resolve their difficulties. For example, a man who is having marital difficulties because his wife is bothered by his frequent intoxication is unlikely to benefit from treatment aimed at improving his communication with his wife unless he also establishes the goal of reducing or eliminating his use of alcohol.

Goals should be written down, and both client and clinician should have a copy of the goals. This can help them keep the goals in mind and identify interventions and changes that seem likely to lead to goal attainment. In addition, having clear written goals paves the way for assessing whether people are moving toward achievement of their goals and allows the goals to be changed or expanded if necessary.

Sound treatment goals are (Berg & Miller, 1992a, 1992b; de Shazer, 1991):

- Meaningful and important to clients
- Small and within easy reach
- Realistic and achievable
- Within clients' control
- Perceived by clients as involving their hard work and effort
- Described in specific, concrete behavioral terms
- Measurable
- Presented in positive language, stating what clients will do rather than what they will not do
- Viewed as a beginning or a first step rather than the end or final product
- Reflected in new behaviors or changes

Consider the following examples of goals formulated by Lucy, a shy, self-effacing woman reporting low self-esteem and depression:

1. Lucy will tell another person about the sale of her first painting within the next 48 hours and will write down her statement, the person to whom she spoke, and that person's response.
2. Lucy will not denigrate her accomplishments but will tell others about them.

The first goal is a sound one because it is small, realistic, within the client's control, specific and behavioral, stated in positive language, and a first step toward developing new behaviors. The second goal, however, has many shortcomings; it is vague and general, difficult to measure, stated in negative language, and probably unrealistic and too ambitious. It is likely to lead to disappointment and frustration, whereas the first statement is likely to promote effort, motivation, success, and a sense of accomplishment. The exercises later in this chapter will give you further opportunities for formulating and analyzing goal statements.

CASE ILLUSTRATION

The following dialog illustrates the use of the miracle question with Edie, who is having difficulty managing stress and fulfilling all her responsibilities.

Edie: I don't know how I can get everything done by the holidays. It's all I can do to take care of the family and the house. I don't know when I'll ever find time to buy presents, write cards, bake cookies, and make special meals. I've been getting up early and staying up late to get it all done, but it's not working. I feel overwhelmed!

Clinician: You have a great many responsibilities, and I know you can find a way to make them manageable. Edie, let's suppose that one night there is a miracle and, while you are sleeping, this problem you are describing is solved. What will you notice the next morning that will tell you there has been a miracle?

Edie: I will be able to sleep until at least 7 a.m. When I wake up, the house will be clean and orderly but not because I stayed up late to clean it. I'll still have things to do, but they'll be the fun parts of the holiday, like baking cookies. I'll still have a list, but I'll know that I can accomplish the items on the list and still have time to read or take a hot bath.

Clinician: How will Roberto know that the miracle has occurred?

Edie: I won't be grumpy in the morning. I'll be smiling and looking forward to the day. Maybe I'll even make him pancakes, which he loves.

Clinician: You have a clear picture of how things will be when you figure out a strategy to solve the problem. I think your answer to the miracle question has raised some possibilities. What seems important to you?

Edie: Just imagining that it could be different made it seem possible. If I could get help with some of the holiday preparations, especially the ones I don't like such as cleaning the house and writing the holiday letter, then maybe I could really enjoy the other parts.

Clinician: So you're starting to figure out a way to make some changes. I wonder if you can recall other times when you felt stressed and overwhelmed by all you had to do and handled the situation pretty well.

Edie: Yes, I was eight months' pregnant with Ava, and we were moving out of our apartment into a new house. As if that weren't enough, my mother fell and broke her leg and really needed help.

Clinician: What worked for you then?

Edie: I guess because I was pregnant and, of course, did not want anything to go wrong, I wasn't as hard on myself and was able to set priorities and get some help. Once I made sure my mother's medical needs were taken care of, I got her a housekeeper to help out. I had the movers pack and unpack, and I asked Roberto to oversee that. He's good at taking charge of things, which is hard for me. I focused my attention on what was important to me: having a healthy baby and making sure we had our finances under control so we could pay for all this.

Clinician: So you were very resourceful then, and you did not expect to do everything yourself. You figured out your priorities and what you could do best and then hired help and asked Roberto to assist with other tasks.

Edie: Yes, that did work out well. I can see that maybe I do need to make some changes so this holiday won't turn into a disaster and me into a wreck.

Clinician: How would you do that?

Edie: I could ask Roberto to do the holiday letter on the computer; he'd do a great job at that. I could splurge and hire someone to clean the house; I have been working overtime, so we can afford that this year. I could even get Ava to help me wrap packages and my mother to help with some of the cooking for the holiday dinner.

Clinician: Sounds like you're being very resourceful again. We still have four weeks until the holidays. What would be the first small step you could take, beginning this week, to get the control of your life that you want?

Edie: I could have a family meeting with Roberto and Ava and maybe also my mother to decide what we need to do, set priorities, and figure out how to work together to get things done. That would give me a chance to enlist their help, bring up the possibility of a cleaning woman, and start things off on the right track.

Edie has now taken the first steps toward changing her behavior at holiday time. She saw the possibility that she might not have to do all the preparations herself and is moving forward to get the help she needs and gain desired control over her life. By encouraging her to focus on only one step, the clinician maximizes the chances that Edie's initial efforts at change will be successful and will have a ripple effect, enabling her to effectively manage other aspects of the holiday as well as future stressful times in her life.

EXERCISES

Large-Group Exercises

1. Reality therapy and solution-focused brief therapy have much in common as well as some important differences in both theory and application. Discuss these similarities and differences. Which approach appeals to you more? Why?

2. Formulate hypothetical goals for the following people. Keep in mind the importance of helping clients figure out what they want and of having the client and clinician co-create goals. Be sure that your goals meet the criteria discussed in the Skill Development section of this chapter.

   - Danielle, age 27, wants to get along better with her father. She perceives him as judgmental and cold toward her and, whenever she is around him, she feels uncomfortable and apprehensive and has little to say to him.

   - Jonathan, age 11, has been misbehaving at school. According to his teacher, he is disruptive in class, bullies younger children, and rarely completes his homework. Jonathan complains that the children in his class make fun of him because he is overweight. He wants this to stop. He would like to develop friendships and feel more important at school.

   - Angela has recently had heart surgery. Although she has recovered physically and has an excellent prognosis, she fears that she will have a heart attack. She has avoided sexual relations with her husband and reports that she can hardly stand to look at the scars left by her surgery. Angela wants to stop feeling like her medical condition has taken over her life, be more comfortable with her body, and resume sexual relations.

3. Some people believe that brief therapy cannot possibly be as effective as intensive, long-term treatment, while others believe it can be as good if not better than long-term treatment. Discuss these two positions, considering the evidence for each side, and try to arrive at a conclusion that most of the class can accept.

Small-Group Exercises

1. Divide into your groups of four, composed of two dyads. Each dyad should engage in a 15-minute, role-played counseling interview in which the person in the client role presents a problem and the person in the clinician role uses the miracle question to help the client see other possibilities and find solutions. Feedback following the role play should focus on use of the miracle question as well as the client-clinician interaction.

2. Each dyad should role-play another interview while remaining in the same roles. This time the interviewer should not seek solutions or offer suggestions but, instead, should use solution-oriented, presuppositional language as described in this chapter. Record this interview so that you can listen to it again and identify examples of solution-focused language. Compare the interviews. Which was more challenging and why? Which was more rewarding and why? Which seemed more helpful to the client? What was the impact of each on the therapeutic alliance? What other differences did you notice?

3. Consider the following interventions. Identify their shortcomings from the perspective of a solution-focused therapist. Then the small group should collaborate in rewriting each intervention so that it is more helpful and consistent with this approach.
   - You have come for counseling to improve your relationship with your son. What kind of relationship did you have with your father when you were your son's age?
   - Why do you think you will feel guilty if you end your friendship with Howard?
   - I can see you didn't have much success with your homework task.
   - I know you do not feel optimistic that treatment will work; but if you complete the homework tasks I am suggesting, I think you will really see a difference.

Individual Exercises

1. Identify a problem or concern you are currently experiencing. Then find at least one exception to the problem or a time when you handled a similar problem successfully. Plan a small change based on this information. Write about this in your journal.
2. Write down at least three goals that you hope to achieve within the next month. Be sure that your goal statements meet the criteria discussed in this chapter.
3. Apply the process of scaling to the goals you have identified above. On a 0–10 scale, with 10 representing complete success in achieving the goal and 0 representing no progress toward meeting the goal, indicate where you are now in terms of your achievement of each of the three goals. Write down these ratings and use the scale to rate your progress each week over the next month.

SUMMARY

Solution-focused brief therapy, developed by Milton Erickson, Bill O'Hanlon, Michele Weiner-Davis, Insoo Kim Berg, Steve de Shazer, and others, is an optimistic and empowering treatment approach that focuses on possibilities and helps people make small behavioral changes that lead to solutions to their concerns. Collaboration of client and clinician is essential. Client and clinician co-create clear, specific, meaningful, and realistic goals that guide the treatment. This approach focuses primarily on the present and on clients' strengths and successes. Strategies such as the miracle question, use of exceptions, suggested tasks, and solution-focused language enhance the impact of this approach.

Berg and Miller (1992b) summarized solution-focused brief therapy succinctly:

If it ain't broke, don't fix it!

Once you know what works, do more of it!

If it doesn't work, then don't do it again. Do something different! (p. 17)

RECOMMENDED READINGS

De Jong, P., & Berg, I. K. (2002). *Interviewing for solutions (2nd edition)*. Pacific Grove, CA: Brooks/Cole.

de Shazer, S. (1988). *Clues: Investigating solutions in brief therapy*. New York: Norton.

de Shazer, S. (1991). *Putting difference to work*. New York: Norton.

Matthews, W. J., & Edgette, J. H. (1997). *Current thinking and research in brief therapy*. New York: Brunner/Mazel.

Metcalf, L. (1998). *Solution focused group therapy: Ideas for groups in private practice, schools, agencies, and treatment programs*. New York: Free Press.

Miller, S., Hubble, M., & Duncan, B. (1996). *Handbook of solution-focused brief therapy*. San Francisco: Jossey-Bass.

ADDITIONAL SOURCES OF INFORMATION

The Brief Family Therapy Center (P.O. Box 13736, Milwaukee, WI 53213, http://www.brief-therapy.org), is home to Steve de Shazer, Insoo Kim Berg, and other innovators in SFBT. Website provides information on the history of SFBT, the Center, online and face-to-face training opportunities, and articles and resources.

http://www.brieftherapy.com—This is the website of Bill O'Hanlon, one of the developers of brief therapy. Site provides information on O'Hanlon and training opportunities he provides as well as lists of books, tapes, and videos on what O'Hanlon calls solution-oriented/possibility therapy.

http://thesolutionsfocus.com—Based in England, the site, The Solutions Focus, offers practical ideas for using a solutions-oriented approach in nonclinical ways such as leadership, coaching and consulting.

Part Six

Integrated and Eclectic Treatment Systems

CHAPTER 22

Overview of Integrated and Eclectic Treatment Systems

Parts 2 through 5 of this book focused on theories of counseling and psychotherapy reflecting four major emphases—background, emotions, thoughts, and actions—and reviewed treatment strategies and skills associated with each. Knowledge of an array of theoretical approaches is necessary so that clinicians can determine which treatment approach is best for them and for each of their clients and to afford clinicians an array of useful interventions.

Although this knowledge is integral to the professional development of every effective clinician, many counselors and psychologists today do not align themselves strongly with one particular approach. Instead, they draw on a variety of theories and interventions in developing a treatment plan that seems likely to help a given person. In fact, nearly 30% of psychologists, 34% of social workers, and 37% of counselors describe their primary theoretical orientation as eclectic or integrative (or integrated) (Prochaska & Norcross, 2003). This percentage has been increasing over the years, and the trend seems likely to continue. Even clinicians who adhere to one theoretical orientation commonly incorporate into their work interventions from other treatment approaches.

REASONS FOR THE GROWTH OF ECLECTIC AND INTEGRATED APPROACHES

Many factors account for this trend toward integrative and eclectic treatment. As Thompson (1996) stated, "Essentially, no single theory can account fully for the myriad of [phenomena] that characterize the full range and life span of human experiences. Further, adhering to exclusive models of counseling and psychotherapy could be perceived as limiting therapeutic options when working with clients" (p. xxi). Thompson's points seem valid in light of the diversity of people seeking treatment who vary according to many dimensions including culture, ethnicity, gender, sexual orientation, intelligence, abilities, interpersonal skills, life experiences, self-awareness, support systems, and symptoms.

In addition, no one theoretical model has proven itself superior to the rest despite efforts to identify such a theory. Luborsky, Singer, and Luborsky (1975) reviewed the comparative literature on psychotherapy and concluded that the result was a dodo bird verdict. (The dodo bird, in *Alice's Adventures in Wonderland,* stated that since everyone had won the race, all must have prizes.) Despite extensive research since 1975, the dodo bird verdict still stands. According to Hansen (2002, p. 315), ". . . meta-analysis of counseling outcome studies clearly shows that no one approach has emerged as the correct or most helpful . . . it seems that all well-established approaches promote healing." In fact, research suggests that treatment systems have more commonalities than differences.

At the same time, research has demonstrated that some treatment approaches are more effective than others with particular problems, diagnoses, or types of people. For example, cognitive therapy and interpersonal psychotherapy are particularly powerful in the treatment of major depressive disorder (Elkin et al., 1989) while reality therapy has been widely used in treating conduct disorders.

The following 12 factors have combined during the past 20–25 years to move clinicians in the direction of preferring integrative and eclectic approaches over adherence to one specific treatment system (Prochaska & Norcross, 2003):

1. The large and growing number of approaches to treatment; more than 400 treatment systems have been identified
2. The increasing diversity and complexity of clients and their concerns
3. The inability of any one treatment system to successfully address all clients and all problems
4. The growing importance of solution-focused brief approaches that encourage clinicians to draw on and combine interventions from various systems of therapy to find the most effective and efficient strategy for each treatment situation
5. The availability of training opportunities, as well as case studies and other informative literature, that give clinicians the opportunity to study, observe, and gain experience in a wide variety of treatment approaches
6. The requirement of some state and national credentialing bodies that clinicians obtain postgraduate continuing education units; this encourages continued professional growth and development of new skills and ideas
7. Increasing pressure from managed care organizations, governmental agencies, consumers, and others for clinicians to determine the most effective and efficient treatment approach for each client, to plan and document their work, and to maintain accountability

8. The growing body of compelling research demonstrating which treatment approaches are most likely to be successful in the treatment of particular people, disorders, or problems (Seligman, 1998)

9. The increasing availability of manuals, providing detailed and empirically validated treatment plans for specific mental disorders

10. The development of organizations such as the Society for the Exploration of Psychotherapy Integration that focus on studying and promoting treatment integration

11. The emergence of models providing blueprints or guidelines for logical and therapeutically sound integration of treatment approaches

12. Clinicians' increasing awareness that common factors among treatment approaches, such as the nature of the therapeutic alliance, are at least as important in determining treatment success as are specific strategies

This array of factors nudges many clinicians toward an eclectic or integrative model as their preferred orientation toward treatment.

THE CHALLENGES OF ECLECTIC AND INTEGRATED APPROACHES

Choosing to adopt an eclectic or integrated theoretical orientation is a challenging choice that probably demands more of clinicians than does adherence to one specific theory. If clinicians decide, for example, that they will specialize in cognitive therapy, they should develop expertise in that approach and know when it is and is not likely to be helpful so that they can refer to others those clients who are unlikely to benefit from cognitive therapy. Because they have limited the scope of their work, these clinicians do not have to develop expertise in other treatment approaches, although they should be familiar with other approaches.

However, clinicians who view their primary theoretical orientation as eclectic or integrated need expertise in a range of treatment systems so they can draw on those approaches in creating effective treatment plans. Of course, clinicians who have an eclectic or integrated orientation also set limits on the scope of their practice; no clinician could have sufficient knowledge and expertise in the entire range of therapeutic approaches to treat all clients and all problems. Clinicians should define the scope of their practice according to the nature of their clientele, the problems or mental disorders they treat, and the strategies they employ. Nevertheless, clinicians who prefer eclectic or integrated treatment approaches still have a professional role that is more comprehensive and challenging than that of clinicians with a specific theoretical orientation.

In addition, clinicians advocating an eclectic or integrated treatment approach must carefully think through their treatment of each client to ensure that the disparate parts of treatment comprise a seamless whole in which each intervention is chosen deliberately to accomplish a purpose. Treatment must not just be an amalgam of "tricks of the trade" but rather should reflect coherence, relevance, and planning and be solidly grounded in both theory and empirical research. As Schwartz and Waldo (2003) stated, "The danger of creating a 'hodge-podge' of apples and oranges can be avoided if the theories are compatible, carefully integrated, and if they reflect the basic characteristics of mental health counseling" (pp. 101–102).

BENEFITS OF ECLECTIC AND INTEGRATED APPROACHES

Integrated and eclectic theoretical approaches have benefits as well as challenges. They bring flexibility to the treatment process, enabling clinicians to tailor their work to specific clients and concerns in an effort to find a good fit between treatment and client.

This is especially important when clinicians treat people from diverse cultural backgrounds who may respond better to modified or integrated approaches than they do to standardized ones. For example, people from Asian backgrounds may respond best to treatment approaches that are structured in nature but that also recognize the importance of the family and society. Clinicians can demonstrate multicultural competence by creating integrated treatment plans that reflect sensitivity to clients' culture and context.

Because they have greater flexibility in their work, clinicians espousing an integrated or eclectic approach probably can work with a broader range of people and problems than those who affiliate themselves with a single treatment system. Of course, all clinicians must practice within their areas of expertise or obtain supervision or training to expand their skills.

In addition, integrated and eclectic approaches allow clinicians to adapt standard treatment approaches to their own beliefs about human growth and development as well as to their natural style and personality. In my own work, for example, I emphasize cognitive and behavioral interventions but usually temper the structured nature of those approaches with a heavy dose of empathy and support, reflecting the influence of person-centered therapy. Because I believe that our family backgrounds provide us with templates for future relationships, I spend more time than most cognitive-behavioral therapists looking at the connections between people's early relationships and their current ones. In addition, I frequently work with people who are coping with chronic and life-threatening illnesses. With those clients, I usually integrate some existential concepts into the treatment I provide.

Finally, integrated and eclectic approaches facilitate clinician efforts to assume a scientist-practitioner role and to combine theoretical information, empirical research, and practical experience in their work. Basing their work on treatment approaches that have proven their value through research, clinicians can expand on that foundation by incorporating into their work ideas that have face validity as well as strategies that they have used successfully with other clients.

THE NATURE OF ECLECTIC AND INTEGRATED APPROACHES

When clinicians began to describe their theoretical orientations as *eclectic,* the term lacked a clear meaning; it simply suggested that clinicians drew on more than one approach to treatment. Although some clinicians who characterized their work as eclectic were gifted therapists and astute theoreticians with a clear rationale for combining interventions in their work, others lacked a thoughtful and systematic approach to treatment. Eysenck (1970) denounced what he referred to as "lazy eclecticism," the use of a grab bag of interventions, combined without an overriding logic (p. 140). Without a logic or structure, eclecticism can lead to treatment that is haphazard and inconsistent, lacking in direction and coherence. This has been referred to as *syncretism.* Such an approach reflects a lack of knowledge and professionalism and is incompatible with current emphases on accountability and treatment planning in counseling and psychotherapy.

Types of Eclectic and Integrated Approaches

Four types of eclecticism have been identified:

1. *Atheoretical eclecticism* is characterized by combining interventions without an overriding theory of change or development. Unless an intuitive or underlying logic prevails, clinicians whose work reflects atheoretical eclecticism run the risk of syncretism—providing treatment that is without direction, including elements that are disparate and perhaps incompatible. Such an approach probably will be confusing to clients, may lead them to question the clinician's competence (as well as their own), can interfere with client cooperation and motivation, and may well lead to treatment failure.

2. *Common factors eclecticism* hypothesizes that certain elements of treatment, notably a therapeutic alliance that communicates support, empathy, and positive regard, are primarily responsible for promoting client growth and change (Hansen, 2002). Specific interventions are linked to these common factors rather than to a specific theory. In part 1 you learned about commonalities in successful treatment.

3. *Technical eclecticism* provides a framework for combining interventions from different treatment systems without necessarily subscribing to the theories or philosophies associated with those interventions. According to Hansen (2002), "Counselors who practice technical eclecticism endeavor to use the most effective techniques available for client problems, without regard for the various theories that gave rise to the techniques. Therefore, like common factors eclecticism, technical eclecticism is process or technique focused and places little or no emphasis on underlying theories of counseling" (p. 316). Technical eclecticism can be thought of as an organized collection of interventions, rather than an integration of ideas. It may have an actuarial or empirical basis, reflecting research on the effectiveness of various interventions in successfully addressing clients' concerns. However, it lacks a coherent model for human development and growth. Lazarus's multimodal therapy exemplifies this type of eclecticism.

4. *Theoretical integration* offers conceptual guidelines for combining two or more treatment approaches to provide a clearer understanding of clients and more effective ways to help them. A theoretical integration usually provides clinicians with a framework for understanding how people grow and change and guidelines for developing treatment plans that reflect that understanding. Integrated treatment approaches often include a multistage, systematic approach to treatment as well as information on assessing client strengths and difficulties and matching treatment to client. Clinicians have guidelines to help them answer the question, "*What* treatment, by *whom,* is the most effective for *this* individual with *that* specific problem, and under what set of circumstances" (Paul, 1967, p. 109). In a true theoretical integration, the whole is greater than the sum of its parts. The combination of approaches blends well and forms a new theory or treatment system that builds and improves on each of the individual approaches to form a better product. Treatment is theory-focused rather than techniques-driven. Developmental counseling and therapy (DCT), discussed in chapter 23, is an example of theoretical integration.

Chapter 23 provides information about important and emerging approaches to eclectic and integrated treatment. Included is information on multimodal therapy developed by Arnold Lazarus, a structured and comprehensive approach to treatment planning that facilitates clinicians' efforts to match intervention to problem. Also reviewed is developmental counseling and therapy (DCT) developed by Allen Ivey, Sandra Rigazio-DiGilio, and others. Additional eclectic approaches considered in chapter 23 include Prochaska and Norcross's transtheoretical model of change, the adaptive counseling and therapy/readiness model (ACT), the TFA (thinking-feeling-acting) model, Hill and O'Brien's three-stage integrated model, Wachtel's integrative psychodynamic-behavior therapy, and common factors models.

INTEGRATING TREATMENT SYSTEMS

Although most clinicians do not adhere to a systematic approach to theoretical integration such as DCT, they probably have formulated their own logic for combining compatible theories. The most common combinations of theories, in descending order of frequency, include (1) cognitive and behavioral treatment systems, (2) humanistic and cognitive approaches, and (3) psychoanalytic and cognitive approaches (Prochaska & Norcross, 2003). The presence of cognitive therapy in all three combinations is noteworthy, suggesting the flexibility of that approach and its importance in treatment.

Characteristics of Sound Eclectic and Integrated Approaches

Certain hallmarks distinguish conceptually sound integrated and eclectic approaches from eclecticism that is haphazard and ill-conceived. Sound eclecticism has the following characteristics:

- Evidence of building on the strengths of existing theories
- A coherent combination of theories that create a unified whole
- An underlying theory of human behavior and development
- A philosophy or theory of change
- Logic, guidelines, and procedures for adapting the approach to a particular person or problem
- Strategies and interventions, related to the underlying theories, that facilitate change
- Inclusion of the commonalities of effective treatment, such as support, positive regard, empathy, and client-clinician collaboration

FORMULATING AN ECLECTIC/INTEGRATED TREATMENT SYSTEM

When clinicians formulate an integrated or eclectic treatment system, they must address many questions, including the following:

1. What model of human development underlies the theory?
2. How does this treatment approach suggest that change is best facilitated?
3. What information should be obtained in an intake interview?
4. What conception does this approach have of the influence of the past on the present, and how should past experiences and difficulties be addressed in treatment?
5. How important is insight in promoting change, and how much attention should be paid in treatment to improving insight?
6. How important is exploration of emotions in promoting change, and how much attention should be paid in treatment to helping people identify, express, and modify their emotions?

7. How important is identification and modification of dysfunctional cognitions in promoting change, and how much attention should be paid in treatment to helping people alter their cognitions?
8. How important is identification and modification of self-destructive and unhelpful behaviors in promoting change, and how much attention should be paid in treatment to helping people alter their behaviors?
9. What sorts of people and problems are likely to respond well to this approach?
10. In what treatment settings and contexts is this approach likely to be successful?
11. How well does this approach address issues of diversity, and what is the appropriate use of this approach with people from multicultural backgrounds?
12. What is the place of diagnosis and treatment planning in this approach?
13. What are the overall goals of treatment?
14. What types of therapeutic alliances and client-clinician interactions are most likely to be productive?
15. What clinical skills are especially important for those who adopt this approach?
16. What interventions and strategies are compatible with this treatment system?
17. How should this approach be adapted for use with individuals? Families? Groups?
18. How long is treatment likely to last?
19. How is effectiveness measured, and what determines when treatment is finished?
20. Has this treatment system been adequately substantiated by empirical research? If not, what information is needed to support the value of this approach?

SKILL DEVELOPMENT: TREATMENT PLANNING

Treatment planning is rapidly becoming one of the most important skills of today's clinicians. Treatment plans provide a road map for both clinicians and clients, indicating how they will proceed from their starting point (the client's presenting concerns, underlying difficulties, strengths and limitations) to their destination, reduction in painful and unhelpful symptoms and patterns and establishment of better coping skills, improved self-esteem, and a more rewarding lifestyle.

Treatment planning serves the following four purposes (Seligman, 2004a):

1. A carefully developed plan, grounded in research on treatment effectiveness, provides assurance that counseling or psychotherapy is likely to succeed.
2. A treatment plan specifying goals and strategies helps clinicians and clients to track progress, determine whether goals are being met, and, if not, revise and improve the plan.
3. Treatment plans provide structure and direction to the therapeutic process. They help clinicians and clients to develop shared and realistic expectations for treatment and promote optimism that treatment will be helpful.
4. Treatment plans, in conjunction with post-treatment evaluations, allow clinicians to determine and demonstrate their effectiveness. This assists clinicians in obtaining funding for programs and in receiving third party payments for their services. Treatment plans also can provide a sound defense in the event of allegations of malpractice.

Treatment planning is essential, regardless of what concerns clients present or what theoretical orientation clinicians adopt. Treatment planning is particularly important for clinicians who follow integrated or eclectic approaches to treatment. A treatment plan can organize the disparate elements of various theories into a cohesive whole, clarify the sequence of interventions, and help ensure that treatment strategies address the entire range of clients' concerns.

Exactly when treatment planning occurs varies, depending on the client and the nature of that person's concerns, motivation, and self-awareness. Some people are immediately ready to discuss their goals and to collaborate with their clinicians in formulating a treatment plan while others may need three or four or more sessions before a viable treatment plan can be developed. Clinicians should explore clients' difficulties and symptoms; gain some understanding of their strengths, weaknesses, and context; and develop at least a preliminary connection with clients before moving into treatment planning. In addition, the treatment plan should be viewed as a work in progress; as clients develop hope that treatment can help them, as they share more of themselves in their sessions, and as they make progress, the treatment plan may need to be changed. Adhering doggedly to an outdated and inappropriate treatment plan can lead to ineffective treatment and can damage the therapeutic alliance. Instead, good clinicians regularly review and update treatment plans to reflect new information and their assessment of client's progress.

Although many agencies and managed care organizations have their own guidelines and formats for treatment plans, few widely accepted models for treatment planning are available. However, many clinicians have adopted my DO A CLIENT MAP model (Seligman, 1998, 2004a). The first letters of the 12 steps in this model spell out DO A CLIENT MAP and so serve as a mnemonic device. The purpose of the plan is, of course, to map out the treatment process for a given client. The 12 steps in this comprehensive treatment process include

1. Diagnosis
2. Objectives of treatment
3. Assessments
4. Clinician
5. Location of treatment
6. Interventions
7. Emphasis
8. Number of people seen in treatment
9. Timing
10. Medication
11. Adjunct services
12. Prognosis

The rest of this section provides additional information on these steps, and the following case illustration presents a treatment plan based on the DO A CLIENT MAP format.

1. *Diagnosis.* The first step in treatment planning is making an accurate diagnosis of a person's difficulties using the multiaxial assessment format and diagnostic terminology of the *Diagnostic and Statistical Manual of Mental Disorders* (American Psychiatric Association, 2000). The rest of the treatment plan should grow logically out of that diagnosis and be linked to the client's presenting concerns.

2. *Objectives of treatment.* Once problems and symptoms have been explored and a diagnosis formulated, client and clinician collaborate in establishing written objectives for treatment that address the diagnoses and problems presented by the client. (See chapter 21 for detailed information on establishing goals or objectives.) Ideally, objectives should be specific, measurable, realistic, and meaningful. Such objectives are likely to promote client motivation and facilitate assessment of progress.

3. *Assessments.* Clinicians often use assessment tools to enhance their efforts to make accurate diagnoses, establish worthwhile and viable objectives, and measure progress. Included in this section of the treatment plan are assessments administered by the clinician (e.g., measures of symptoms, personality, interests, abilities) as well as assessments to be conducted by others such as psychiatrists, neurologists, other physicians, and school psychologists.

4. *Clinician.* Variables that characterize the sort of clinician likely to work well with a given client are specified in this section of the treatment plan. Included might be information about the desired training and expertise of the clinician as well as information on the preferred clinician's gender, age range, ethnicity, cultural and religious background, and other relevant characteristics.

5. *Location.* This item specifies whether treatment should be inpatient, outpatient, or an alternative such as a day treatment program and might suggest a specific agency or treatment facility.

6. *Interventions.* This part of the plan provides two important pieces of information. First, the treatment approach is specified (e.g., cognitive therapy, solution-focused brief therapy, Gestalt therapy). If an integrated model is used, the treatment plan should indicate the specific theories that will be combined in treatment and how they will be integrated. Second, the specific strategies or interventions chosen to achieve the objectives are listed. This includes interventions such as systematic desensitization, modification of distorted cognitions, and teaching relaxation. Objectives and interventions should be linked, with each intervention designed to contribute to the accomplishment of one or more objectives.

7. *Emphasis.* Although many clinicians share a particular theoretical orientation, no clinician ever does exactly the same thing as another clinician, nor does a given clinician practice in exactly the same way with each client. This section of the plan outlines how the theoretical approach identified in the interventions section will be adapted to meet the needs of a particular person. For example, the clinician may decide that a client needs considerable support or would benefit from a great deal of structure and direction during treatment.

8. *Number of people.* This section of the treatment plan specifies whether individual, family, or group therapy will be the primary mode of intervention. Individual therapy is usually the treatment of choice, especially at the outset. However, people with concerns such as relationship issues, impulse control disorders, chronic and life-threatening illnesses, eating disorders, and substance misuse often benefit from family counseling because of the impact of these difficulties on the whole family and their connection to family dynamics. Similarly, people with concerns such as posttraumatic stress disorder, physical and sexual abuse, eating disorders, substance misuse, and anger management typically respond well to group therapy because of the feedback, support, reinforcement, and role models provided by the group.

Treatment sometimes involves a combination of individual, family, and group therapy; if so, this should be specified in the plan. For example, treatment of an adolescent boy with behavioral, interpersonal, family, and self-esteem concerns might begin with a combination of individual and family therapy. Once the boy has made some progress, group therapy might replace individual treatment so that he has the opportunity to try out new social skills in context, benefit from peer role models, and receive feedback and encouragement from the group members.

9. *Timing.* This part of the plan encompasses four scheduling aspects of the therapeutic process: the length of each session, the frequency of sessions, the duration of treatment, and the pacing of the treatment process. Traditionally, treatment occurs once a week in sessions of 45–50 minutes. However, sometimes treatment is more effective if that pattern is changed. Longer sessions are often used for group therapy and sometimes for family therapy, while school counselors typically have sessions of 30 minutes or less. Altering frequency also can enhance treatment. People in crisis might benefit from more than one session a week, while people who have met most of their treatment goals might be seen only for monthly follow-up sessions. Although the exact duration of treatment is usually difficult to determine at the outset, clinicians should anticipate whether short-, medium-, or long-term treatment is required for a particular person. The pacing of the session is another timing variable. Pacing is likely to be rapid for relatively healthy and motivated clients as well as for those in crisis, while treatment will probably move more slowly for people who are fragile or have long-standing and deeply entrenched concerns.

10. *Medication.* Psychologists, counselors, and social workers often collaborate with psychiatrists in treating clients who require medication. The combination of psychotherapy and medication can be powerful in alleviating some symptoms and mental disorders. Although psychologists, counselors, and social workers generally are not qualified to prescribe medication, they should know which symptoms and disorders respond well to medication and the benefits and possible side effects of common medications. Clinicians should refer clients to a psychiatrist for an evaluation if clients exhibit loss of contact with reality, mania, severe depression, disorientation and memory loss, and excessive sleepiness. Other symptoms such as dysfunctional eating, attentional problems, obsessions and compulsions, and panic attacks also often benefit from medication. A sound collaboration with a psychiatrist can enhance the work of the nonmedical clinician.

11. *Adjunct services.* Most clients benefit from adjunct services. These sources of help, support, and information contribute to the effectiveness of treatment and help people progress toward their goals.

Examples of useful adjunct services include skill development (e.g., study skills, parenting), peer support groups, legal and medical services, weight-control and exercise programs, cultural and religious organizations, clubs and classes for social and leisure activities (e.g., Parents Without Partners, bridge clubs, hiking groups), and governmental services (e.g., aid to dependent children, subsidized housing). Twelve-step programs such as Alcoholics Anonymous, Gamblers Anonymous, and Overeaters Anonymous can be particularly helpful to clients when relevant to their concerns.

12. *Prognosis.* This last step specifies the likelihood of clients achieving the specified objectives according to the treatment plan. Of course, a prognosis that is excellent,

very good, or good is desired. If the prognosis is less optimistic, clinicians might revise their objectives or interventions to increase the likelihood of a successful outcome.

CASE ILLUSTRATION

The following treatment plan for Ava illustrates the DO A CLIENT MAP format:

1. *Diagnosis.*
   Axis I: 313.81 Oppositional Defiant Disorder, Moderate
   309.0 Adjustment Disorder with Depressed Mood
   Axis II: V71.09 No diagnosis on axis II.
   Axis III: Client reports she is farsighted and wears corrective lenses.
   Axis IV: Psychosocial stressors: Parental conflict.
   Axis V: Global assessment of functioning score: 62.

2. *Objectives.* Short-term objectives include
   a. Reduce level of depression by at least 3 points on a children's depression inventory
   b. Decrease frequency of acting-out behaviors from more than 5 per week to no more than 3 per week, as measured by teacher's report
   c. Increase number of days of completed homework from 0 or 1 per week to at least 3 per week, as measured by teacher's report
   d. Increase Ava's self-rating of her happiness in her family from the current rating of 2 to at least 4, as measured by an informal 0–10 rating scale

   Medium-term objectives include
   e. Bring mood level into the normal range on a children's depression inventory
   f. Reduce frequency of acting-out behavior further to no more than 1 per week, as measured by teacher's report
   g. Increase number of days of completed homework to at least 4 per week, as measured by teacher's report
   h. Increase Ava's self-rating of her happiness in her family from the current rating of 2 to at least 7
   i. Increase the amount of pleasurable time that Ava reports spending with her family from an average of less than 15 minutes per day to at least 4 hours per week
   j. Increase Ava's rating of her self-esteem from the current rating of 3 to at least 7 on a 0–10 rating scale

3. *Assessments.* Children's depression inventory, informal rating scales of self-esteem and family happiness, teacher reports of Ava's behavior and homework completion.

4. *Clinician.* Ava is likely to benefit from a clinician who has experience in treating both children and families, works collaboratively with teachers and school counselors, and is both supportive and able to set appropriate limits. Ava expressed a preference for a female therapist, and this request should be honored. A clinician with sensitivity to the religious and cultural backgrounds and differences in Ava's parents also is recommended.

5. *Location.* Outpatient comprehensive private practice or community mental health center offering treatment for children, adults, and families

6. *Interventions.* Primary theoretical orientations will be cognitive-behavioral therapy and reality therapy. Ava's dysfunctional thinking contributes to her depression and leads to her acting-out and uncooperative behavior at school. The following specific strategies will be used initially, with the letters after each intervention specifying the objectives it is designed to accomplish:

   - Identifying and modifying dysfunctional thoughts (a, e, j)
   - Teaching communication and assertiveness skills (b, d, f, h)
   - Teaching strategies for anger management (b, f)
   - Establishing a weekly family council and family outings (a, d, e, h, i)
   - Helping Ava plan and schedule her homework, with encouragement from and monitoring by her parents (c, g, j)
   - Planning and contracting for behavioral change (b, c, f, g), with impulse-control and additional treatment strategies probably included later

7. *Emphasis.* Ava is likely to benefit from structured treatment that helps her take responsibility for herself and change her unrewarding thoughts and actions. She

also needs considerable support, empathy, and understanding to enable her to deal effectively with the conflicts between her parents.

8. *Numbers.* Initially, treatment will include both individual and family sessions. Once Ava has made some progress, group therapy will replace the individual sessions to allow Ava the opportunity to practice and improve her new communication skills and develop her relationship skills.

9. *Timing.* Forty-five minute sessions will be held weekly. Pacing can be rapid because Ava functions fairly well and has support from her family. Approximately 10 sessions each of individual and family treatment are anticipated, followed by group counseling.

10. *Medication.* The nature of Ava's problems does not suggest a need for medication.

11. *Adjunct services.* Ava would probably benefit from involvement in an activity that gives her contact with other children as well as the opportunity to learn a skill that might enhance her self-esteem. She expressed an interest in learning ballet, and her parents have agreed to enroll her in an appropriate ballet class.

12. *Prognosis.* Ava's difficulties are relatively mild and brief and are largely in reaction to the conflict between her parents. She is motivated to engage in treatment and has the support of her parents. Consequently, the prognosis for achieving the specified objectives according to this treatment plan is very good.

EXERCISES

Large-Group Exercises

1. Integrating disparate treatment approaches can be challenging; some theories mesh well, while others seem incompatible. Discuss whether and how the following combinations could be successfully integrated:
   - Person-centered and psychodynamic approaches
   - Reality therapy and Adler's individual psychology
   - Existentialism and cognitive psychotherapy
   - Gestalt therapy and behavior therapy
2. Develop treatment plans, following the DO A CLIENT MAP format, for Edie and Roberto based on what you already have learned about them. Feel free to add information to fill out your knowledge of these clients.
3. No one theory has emerged as clearly superior to the rest. How do you explain that? Discuss whether you believe that research and practice will ever identify an ideal or universal approach to treatment and why that does or does not seem likely.

Small-Group Exercises

1. Divide into your groups of four, composed of two dyads. Each dyad should engage in a 10–15 minute, role-played counseling interview in which the person playing the client talks about a concern and the person in the clinician role deliberately integrates two or more approaches to treatment when responding. Record the interview. Play back the interview after it is completed so that the group can identify which theories were used by the clinician, the successful aspects of the integration, and ways in which the role play might have been even more successful.
2. Clinicians typically have mixed reactions to the process of treatment planning. In your small groups, discuss the benefits and drawbacks to treatment planning as well as some ways to overcome the drawbacks and maximize the benefits.

Individual Exercises

1. If you have had the experience of being a client, think about the treatment approch used by your clinician, identifying the theory or theories reflected in the treatment you received. Write about this in your journal, describing the most helpful and least helpful elements of your treatment.
2. Whether or not you have had previous experience as a client, write a paragraph discussing whether and why you would prefer to be treated by a clinician who follows an integrated approach or one who adheres to a single treatment system.
3. Identify a problem you have had that might have benefited from psychotherapy or counseling. Develop a written treatment plan for your own concern following the DO A CLIENT MAP format.

SUMMARY

This chapter provided an overview of integrated and eclectic approaches to treatment. As many as 50% of clinicians describe their primary theoretical orientation as eclectic. Eclectic and integrated approaches offer many advantages, including the flexibility of drawing concepts and interventions from a range of treatment systems, thereby enabling clinicians to tailor treatment to a particular client or concern. However, use of integrated approaches to treatment can be challenging, requiring clinicians to familiarize themselves with many theories and strategies. In addition, if approaches are not wisely and thoughtfully integrated, treatment can be random, haphazard, and unsuccessful.

RECOMMENDED READINGS

Seligman, L. (1998). *Selecting effective treatments* (2nd ed.). San Francisco: Jossey-Bass.

Seligman, L. (2004a). *Diagnosis and treatment planning in counseling* (3rd ed.). New York: Plenum.

CHAPTER 23

Theories of Integrated and Eclectic Treatment

Chapter 22 provided an overview of eclectic and integrated approaches to counseling and psychotherapy. The primary theoretical affiliation of many clinicians, these treatment approaches have both strengths and weaknesses. Some of their shortcomings can be overcome by adopting a sound and systematic rationale for developing treatment plans. As Lazarus and Beutler (1993) stated, "Procedures are not selected haphazardly, but their selection is specifically dependent on a logical decisional process that takes into account the client, setting, problem, and the nature of the counselor's skills" (p. 384).

This chapter reviews some established or promising approaches that demonstrate ways to provide eclectic and integrated treatment by design rather than default. Two models receive particular attention: multimodal therapy developed by Arnold Lazarus and developmental counseling and therapy developed by Allen Ivey, Sandra Rigazio-DiGilio, and others. These two differ considerably, although both are well-developed treatment systems with demonstrated success. We also give some attention to other integrated and eclectic treatment systems, including the transtheoretical model developed by Prochaska and his colleagues, adaptive counseling and therapy developed by Nance and Myers, the three dimensional model of multicultural counseling, the thinking-feeling-acting (TFA) model, Hill and O'Brien's three-stage integrated model of helping, Wachtel's integrative psychodynamic-behavior therapy, and common factors models.

MULTIMODAL THERAPY

An example of technical eclecticism, multimodal therapy was developed primarily by Arnold Lazarus. He provided the groundwork for this approach in *Multimodal Behavior Therapy* (1976) and *The Practice of Multimodal Therapy* (1981) and continues to develop this treatment system.

Arnold Lazarus

Arnold Lazarus was born in Johannesburg, South Africa in 1932, the youngest of four children. He received a Ph.D. in clinical psychology in 1960 from the University of the Witwaterstrand in Johannesburg. At the invitation of Albert Bandura, a well-known social learning theorist, Lazarus, accompanied by his wife and two children, joined the faculty at Stanford University in 1963. He also studied with Joseph Wolpe, another pioneer in behavior therapy. (The contributions of Wolpe and Bandura are discussed in chapter 19.)

Although Lazarus's early work reflected his training in behavior therapy, he soon recognized the limitations of that approach and began to incorporate cognitive and other strategies into his work. Suggesting that clinicians take a broad view of people and ways to help, Lazarus advocates technical eclecticism which draws on many theories and strategies to match treatment to client and problem.

Lazarus's contribution to eclectic therapy is only one of many ways in which he has broken new ground. He recently challenged traditional client-clinician boundaries by suggesting that clinicians can be more helpful to some clients if they modify those boundaries, perhaps by playing tennis or having lunch with clients. A former boxer, Lazarus's feisty spirit and outspoken behavior are reflected in his innovative ideas.

Lazarus served on the faculties of Stanford University, Temple University Medical School, and Yale University and now is a Distinguished Professor Emeritus at Rutgers University (Lazarus, 1997). He has written more than 200 articles and 16 books, most on multimodal therapy. Lazarus has received many awards, including the Distinguished Psychologist Award from the American Psychological Association. He is widely recognized as the leading proponent of technical eclecticism.

Theory and Practice of Multimodal Therapy

According to Lazarus (1985), "Human disquietude is multileveled and multilayered. . . . few, if any, problems have a single cause or unitary 'cure'" (p. 2). Consequently, treatment needs to be flexible and versatile, drawing on a variety of approaches. For Lazarus, technical eclecticism is the ideal way to plan such a treatment.

In describing technical eclecticism, Lazarus and Beutler (1993) wrote, "Technical eclectics select procedures from different sources without necessarily subscribing to the theories that spawned them; they work within a preferred theory but recognize that few techniques are inevitably wedded to any theory. Hence, they borrow techniques from other orientations based on the proven worth of these procedures" (p. 384). The ability to address client concerns from multiple vantage points simultaneously gives multimodal therapists considerable power and leverage.

Treatment that reflects technical eclecticism, as described by Lazarus, is

1. Grounded in a theory of the clinician's choice
2. Enhanced by interventions associated with compatible approaches to treatment
3. Focused on interventions that have had their value substantiated by research

Selection of specific treatment strategies is guided by a systematic framework for matching intervention to client, problem, and situation (Lazarus, 1981).

Multimodal therapy is a system for integrating theories and interventions, rather than a self-contained treatment approach. Grounded in behaviorism and emphasizing outcomes, multimodal therapy also draws heavily on cognitive therapy as well as social learning theory. In addition, multimodal therapy has a humanistic component and values the uniqueness and self-determination of each individual (Sherwood-Hawes, 1995). This approach also pays attention to context, looking at the individual as well as that person's culture, society, politics, and environment (Lazarus, 1981).

BASIC I.D.   In multimodal therapy, a careful assessment of clients and their concerns is an essential precursor of treatment planning. Lazarus (1981) developed a model to assess what he viewed as the seven basic categories of functioning, represented by the acronym BASIC I.D.:

1. *Behavior:* Observable actions and habits
2. *Affect:* Moods and emotions
3. *Sensations:* Physical concerns, sensory experiences (touch, taste, smell, sight, hearing)
4. *Images:* Fantasies, dreams, memories, mental pictures, and people's views of themselves, their lives, and their futures
5. *Cognitions:* Thoughts, beliefs, philosophies, values, plans, opinions, insights, self-talk
6. *Interpersonal relations:* Friendships and intimate relationships, interactions with others
7. *Drugs, biology:* Broadly defined as biological functioning, including overall health, nutrition, exercise, self-care

Assessment Instruments   Treatment via multimodal therapy typically begins with a comprehensive assessment of these seven areas, using questions and scales to identify both strengths and problem areas. This helps clinicians identify interventions that might be helpful in each of the seven areas. *The Multimodal Life History,* developed by Arnold Lazarus (1997) and his son Clifford Lazarus and published by Research Press, facilitates the assessment process. This is an extensive written questionnaire that asks about people's backgrounds, their personal and social histories, their presenting problems, and the seven areas of functioning.

Lazarus (1997) found that each person favors some BASIC I.D. modalities over others. For example, a person might be characterized as a sensory reactor, an affective reactor, or an imagery reactor depending on which modality is preferred. The *Structural Profile Inventory* helps identify a person's preferred modalities. This form asks people to indicate on a 1–7 scale how important each of the seven areas of functioning is in their lives. Listing the seven areas in descending order of a person's ratings yields a structural profile for that person. Constructing a diagram or bar graph of the relative strengths of a person's seven areas of functioning is useful in clarifying patterns (Lazarus, 1976).

People seem to respond best to interventions that target their preferred modalities. For example, a person who emphasizes imagery is likely to benefit from visualization, while a person who focuses on thinking and analyzing probably will respond well to identification and modification of cognitive distortions.

Structural profiles are useful in couples counseling as well as individual therapy. Comparing two people's structural profiles can shed light on their similarities and differences and help to explain and normalize some of their conflicts.

Analyzing the BASIC I.D.   The BASIC I.D. is a rich source of information about a person and can be processed in several ways. In addition to rating and rank-ordering the seven modalities, clients can identify changes they would like to make in each modality. Lazarus (1976) refers to this process as a second-order analysis of the BASIC I.D. A second-order analysis also can focus on identifying symptoms in each of the seven areas. Lazarus (1985) has found this a useful step to relieve a treatment impasse.

As an example of a Structural Profile, we present Edie's profile that includes a rank-ordered list of the seven modalities, with the score each received when Edie's profile was developed.

- Interpersonal relations: 7
- Affect: 7
- Cognitions: 6
- Behavior: 5 1/2
- Sensations: 4 1/2
- Images: 3 1/2
- Drugs, biology: 2

Completing this profile helped Edie realize that she sometimes lets her strong emotions and need for approval and closeness cloud her judgment so that her feelings control her decisions. Changes she saw as desirable included moderating these two areas and improving her self-care and health habits.

Another way to use the BASIC I.D. is to look at a person's modality firing order. Lazarus suggests that each person has a characteristic sequence of reactions to stressors and that this sequence usually mirrors that person's structural profile. For example, when Edie was under stress, she usually first felt rejected and unloved (interpersonal relations) while becoming angry and scared (affect). Then she began a dialog with herself, focused on how unlovable she felt and how many mistakes she had made in her relationships. This often caused her difficulty because she would erroneously accuse others of not caring about her, would overreact with anger and fear, and would then blame herself for the conflict. None of these reactions afforded her a way to discuss and dispel conflict with others. Consciously making some changes—in particular, moderating her emotions, considering new cognitions, and developing behaviors that promoted dialog and resolution—helped Edie handle stress more effectively.

Bridging and Tracking   Bridging and tracking are two useful techniques associated with multimodal therapy. In bridging, clinicians initially relate to clients through the clients' dominant modality to build connection and rapport and then branch off into other dimensions that are likely to promote new skills and ways of responding. Tracking is the process of using interventions in the same sequence as a person's preferred firing order. This seems to maximize receptivity to the interventions.

Therapeutic Alliance   Although collaboration between clients and clinicians is valued in multi-modal therapy, clinicians assume the primary role in assessment and treatment planning and remain active and in charge of treatment throughout the process. The multimodal therapist should constantly ask, "What works, for whom, and under which particular circumstances?" in an effort to determine the type of interventions that are most likely to be helpful (Lazarus, 1985, p. viii).

Application and Current Status   The importance of assessment in multimodal therapy requires that clients have some self-awareness; be motivated and reasonably reliable informants; and be capable of at least a moderate level of planning, organizing, and self-monitoring. Despite these constraints, multimodal therapy is a flexible and adaptable approach that can be used with a broad range of people and problems. It can be combined with medication for people who would benefit from drugs, integrate several treatment systems that are likely to be helpful, and be adapted to the needs of people from diverse cultural backgrounds. People who present a combination of different concerns (e.g., anxiety, time management, and poor social skills) might be particularly responsive to multimodal therapy. Interventions can be developed in each relevant modality, providing a systematic approach to both addressing specific concerns and relieving feelings of being overwhelmed and discouraged, common in multiproblem clients (Seligman, 1996a).

Recognizing the current trend toward brief therapy, Lazarus (1997) has described ways to adapt multimodal therapy to a brief framework. He suggests a four-step process:

1. Use the BASIC I.D. format to screen for presence of significant problems.
2. In collaboration with the client, identify three or four focal concerns.
3. If indicated, refer for a medication evaluation as well as a physical examination.
4. Use empirically validated treatment modalities and interventions to address the client's focal concerns.

Case studies in the literature illustrate the application of multimodal therapy to a broad range of problems and disorders, including agoraphobia, depression, obesity, posttraumatic stress disorder, eating disorders, somatization (Lazarus, 1985), anxiety, sexual dysfunction, and substance misuse (Lazarus, 1997), among others. Multimodal therapy has been used successfully with children as well as adults.

Evaluation   Multimodal therapy has some shortcomings and limitations. Some clinicians are concerned about the lack of a cohesive theory to unify this model. Despite the BASIC I.D. framework and other helpful tools associated with this approach, multimodal therapy, in the hands of an unskilled clinician, could become a poorly organized array of techniques not much different from syncretism (discussed in chapter 22). Multimodal therapy also lacks some of the strengths of a sound treatment system, including a concept of human development, a theory of change, and an explanation of why people develop problems. Another shortcoming is the inherent need for organization, structure, detail, and planning, as well as the demands the approach places on clinicians who must be familiar with and skilled in a broad array of theoretical approaches and interventions.

Nevertheless, multimodal therapy has many strengths, the most important of which is flexibility. It also can be powerful, systematically addressing client concerns on many fronts, using interventions that make a difference. In addition, the BASIC I.D. framework provides a useful and accessible way to gather client information and is interesting and appealing to most people. The Multimodal Life History questionnaire and the Structural Profile facilitate both assessment and treatment planning. Multimodal therapy is holistic and comprehensive, individualized and goal-directed. It offers structure and a clear direction to treatment, which can reassure clients and help make problems manageable.

Lazarus and other multimodal therapists advocate research to demonstrate the value of their treatment approach. Lazarus (1976) reported, for example, that 75% of people treated via multimodal therapy achieved major treatment goals. At the same time, the significance of research on multimodal therapy is unclear because each person is treated differently, prohibiting replication. In addition, research on this approach remains inadequate to truly demonstrate its effectiveness.

Multimodal therapy is not yet widely used, perhaps because of its complexity and structure, as well as its strong behavioral emphasis. However, the importance of this approach seems likely to increase for several reasons. It facilitates treatment planning, an essential tool for providing effective treatment and also for demonstrating accountability and meeting the requirements of third-party payers. *Brief but Comprehensive Therapy the Multimodal Way* (Lazarus, 1997) describes how multimodal therapy can be compatible with a short-term treatment model and consequently with much of the treatment that is provided today. Despite its shortcomings, multimodal therapy has a great deal to offer clinicians. Lazarus and Beutler (1993) wrote, "It is our view that a systematic, prescriptive, technically eclectic orientation will continue to become even more popular and may represent the psychotherapeutic Zeitgeist well into the twenty-first century" (p. 384). The use of multimodal therapy does seem likely to expand during this century. However, more time and research is needed to fully document its value.

DEVELOPMENTAL COUNSELING AND THERAPY

Developmental counseling and therapy (DCT), along with systemic cognitive developmental therapy (SCDT) for families, was developed by Allen Ivey, Sandra Rigazio-DiGilio, and their associates. Like multimodal therapy, DCT draws on a broad range of treatment systems and interventions and advocates the use of careful assessment to facilitate matching treatment to individual. However, DCT goes beyond technical eclecticism and is more accurately viewed as an integrated theory because it does have its own theoretical framework.

According to Rigazio-Digilio, Ivey, Ivey, and Simek-Morgan (1997), DCT is ". . . an integrated theory of assessment and treatment that is representative of postmodern thought" (p. 90). It is "based on three central constructs—(1) the co-constructive nature of relationships and knowledge, (2) a reformulation of Piagetian cognitive stages for use in the immediacy of psychotherapy sessions, and (3) a spherical metaframework that integrates multiple voices of therapy" (p. 94). Like narrative therapy (discussed in chapter 13), DCT views people as having multiple perspectives that continuously evolve. With Piaget's theories of cognitive development providing a basis for understanding people, DCT promotes change and growth by matching treatment strategies to each client's cognitive developmental orientation and perspectives.

The People Who Developed DCT

Allen Ivey has been a leader in counseling and psychotherapy since the 1970s and has been developing and writing about DCT since the publication of *Developmental Therapy: Theory into Practice* (1986). Ivey initially became known for his work on microcounseling and his training programs designed to teach basic attending and influencing skills. His research and writing currently focus on DCT and on counseling in a multicultural society. The importance of intentional counseling—using interventions in a thoughtful and deliberate way—has always been an underlying theme of Ivey's work.

Ivey received his doctorate from Harvard University and has spent most of his professional career at the University of Massachusetts at Amherst, where he is a Distinguished University Professor. He has received many awards, including the Professional Development Award from the American Counseling Association. Ivey was president of the American Psychological Association's Division of Counseling Psychology and has written over 25 books and 200 chapters and articles (Ivey, Ivey, & Simek-Morgan, 1997).

Sandra Rigazio-Digilio collaborated with Allen Ivey in the development of DCT and has applied DCT to families through an approach called systematic cognitive developmental therapy (SCDT). She also has formulated a model of supervision linked to DCT. Rigazio-Digilio received her doctorate from the University of Massachusetts at Amherst and is a faculty member at the University of Connecticut at Storrs. She has been associate editor of the *Journal of Mental Health Counseling* and in 1994 received the American Association of Marriage and Family Therapy Divisional Contribution Award.

Research on and development of DCT involves a group of people. Others who have made important contributions include Mary Bradford Ivey and Lynn Simek-Morgan.

Theory and Practice

According to Allen Ivey (1989),

> Mental health counseling is a profession which conducts its developmental practice with both the severely distressed and those facing normal developmental tasks. This developmental practice exists within a multicultural awareness and seeks to address clients and the systems within which they live. A developmental practice focuses on counseling and development, actualizing the potential of individuals and the systems—families, groups, and organizations. Mental health counselors are able to intervene at the individual or systemic level to produce positive change. Distinctions between pathology and normality become irrelevant within this model as the goal is to reintroduce growth regardless of the level of personal disturbance presented by the individual or system. (pp. 28–29)

This description of mental health counseling captures many aspects of DCT. It emphasizes both the person and the system; views development as occurring within a social and cultural context; attends to multiple perspectives; redefines pathology as developmental blocks or delays; and promotes growth and change by providing education and facilitating development (Ivey & Rigazio-DiGilio, 1991; Rigazio-DiGilio, 1994).

Underlying Theories   DCT is grounded in both philosophy and psychology. Ivey and his associates have borrowed from the ideas of Plato and Hegel and take the phenomenological perspective that the ways in which people understand and operate in the world can be both helped and hindered by their levels of cognitive development and the social units and systems in which they are involved (Rigazio-Digilio, Goncalves, & Ivey, 1995). According to DCT, understanding people from multiple perspectives is integral to the development of individualized and culturally sensitive treatment plans that are likely to be successful.

The research of Piaget, which focused on people's stages of cognitive development, is the framework used in DCT to determine people's levels of cognitive functioning. DCT postulates that cognitive functioning can be categorized and described according to four cognitive developmental orientations (Rigazio-Digilio et al., 1997):

1. *Sensorimotor.* In this orientation, people focus on acting and feeling in the present moment and rely on sensory input for information about their world. Emotions may overshadow cognitions and be overwhelming, or they may be split off and go unrecognized. Introspection is difficult in this modality.
2. *Concrete.* People using this orientation have more objectivity; they focus on actions and observable events, can describe experiences in great detail, and can name their emotions but have difficulty with reflection and cause-and-effect thinking. Particularly challenging is linking their emotional responses to their experiences.
3. *Formal operational.* People operating in this modality have a strong ability to be analytical and think about their thoughts, feelings, behaviors, and patterns in their lives. They have a capacity for abstraction and objectivity but may have difficulty experiencing their emotions directly and in the present.
4. *Dialectic/systemic.* In the fourth orientation, people can engage in metacognitions; they can reflect on their reflections and think about the ways in which they process information. They can assume multiple viewpoints and understand the impact their families, cultural groups, and other social units have on them. They are aware of the complexity and multidimensional nature of emotions and can identify not only straightforward emotions but also feelings that are complex, conflicted, or ambivalent. However, they may have difficulty experiencing feelings directly and can become so caught up with intellectual processing that they become detached from their emotions.

Ivey and his colleagues do not view any one of these four cognitive developmental orientations as better or more desirable than the others. Rather, healthy development is conceptualized as continuous mastery of life tasks, which promotes competency in all four of these orientations. Ideally, people should have access to a variety of well-integrated cognitive structures and be flexible and adaptable enough to shift into whichever cognitive structure is likely to work best under a given set of circumstances.

Of course, people do not always function optimally; instead, their cognitive organization may be rigid, and they may rely mainly on one orientation, have diffuse and underdeveloped cognitive structures, or have developmental blocks, leading to highly reactive, chaotic, and ineffective operations (Myers, Shoffner, & Briggs, 2002).

Goals   According to DCT, at any given time, people have a predominant cognitive developmental orientation in operation. An initial step in DCT is assessment of a person's cognitive orientations and patterns (discussed further later in this chapter). Once that has been accomplished, treatment focuses on three general goals (Rigazio-Digilio et al., 1995):

1. Helping people gain more integration, organization, flexibility, and range in their cognitive developmental structures
2. Enabling them to use these structures to acquire multiple perspectives of their lives and concerns, to see new possibilities
3. Collaborating with clients to develop solutions that are relevant to their developmental and environmental needs

Change and Development   Cognitive developmental structures evolve in two ways. Horizontal development, which enriches a particular cognitive developmental orientation, enables people to expand and solidify their use of that modality. For example, people with a strong formal-operational orientation may work on deepening their capacity for analysis and abstraction. Vertical development, on the other hand, helps people draw on multiple cognitive orientations to facilitate their use of varied perspectives and alternative ways of thinking, feeling, and acting. For people with a strong formal-operational orientation, vertical development might promote their objectivity, associated with the concrete orientation.

Clinicians practicing DCT promote change and growth in three ways:

1. Exploring and assessing people's worldviews, operations in the world, areas of strength and difficulty, and cognitive developmental orientations
2. Using this knowledge to select and craft appropriate interventions
3. Constructing with the client expanded (horizontal) and alternative (vertical) perspectives to remove blocks and encourage positive adaptive functioning

Assessment   Although assessment of a person's cognitive developmental orientations often can be accomplished by careful listening to informal conversation, a Developmental Assessment Interview also can be used in which clients discuss current issues from the perspective of each of the four developmental modalities (Myers, Shoffner, & Briggs, 2002; Rigazio-Digilio et al., 1997). This interview uses a series of sequential, open-ended questions, supported by encouraging and summarizing clinician interventions, to assess a person's access to the four cognitive developmental orientations and to identify that person's primary and secondary orientations. The assessment typically consists of five components:

1. *Preliminary assessment* involves open-ended discussion of a broad topic (such as the person's family of origin) to introduce the clinician to the client's developmental orientations.
2. *Sensorimotor (elemental) exploration* emphasizes questions about sensory experiences (seeing, hearing, feeling, touching, tasting) and the client's current situation.
3. *Concrete-operational (situational) exploration* uses questions that ask for linear descriptions of actions and experiences.
4. *Formal-operational (reflective) exploration* emphasizes questions that encourage reflection about patterns, roles, and relationships.
5. *Dialectic/systemic exploration* relies on questions that elicit analysis, integration, multiple perspectives, and examples of change and constructive action.

Planning Interventions   When clinicians have a good sense of a client's cognitive developmental orientations and have identified that person's primary and secondary orientations, they are ready to plan the treatment. Initially, clinicians probably will use interventions that fit the person's predominant orientations to promote horizontal development and deepen the therapeutic alliance. However, they will eventually encourage vertical development by mismatching—gradually introducing interventions that focus on less preferred and less accessible orientations.

In treatment planning, DCT addresses three levels of objectives and interventions: basic, intermediate, and deep levels. Basic interventions focus on symptom relief and developing coping skills. Intermediate interventions continue the development of effective problem-solving and interpersonal skills and promote awareness of patterns. Deep-level interventions aim toward integration, synthesis, and acquisition of new perspectives.

The following list provides information on the nature of the treatment, typical interventions, and goals associated with each cognitive developmental orientation (Ivey & Ivey, 1998; Myers, Shoffner, & Briggs, 2002; Rigazio-DiGilio & Ivey, 1991; Rigazio-DiGilio et al., 1997):

Sensorimotor Environmental Structuring

- *Goals:* Provide direction, promote awareness and direct experience, focus attention on the here and now, minimize denial and splitting
- *Associated interventions:* Gestalt empty chair, body work (e.g., yoga, massage), relaxation, imagery, modeling, medication, environmental change, music therapy, play therapy (for children)

Concrete Operational Coaching

- *Goals:* Encourage cause-and-effect thinking, develop skills, promote constructive action, foster multiple and alternate perspectives, improve self-esteem
- *Associated interventions:* Skills training (e.g., problem solving, assertiveness, communication), rational emotive behavior therapy, systematic desensitization, role playing, enactments, thought stopping, solution-focused therapy, identification of connections and patterns, empathy, strength identification, narrative and constructivist therapy addressing multicultural perspectives

Formal Operational Consultation

- *Goals:* Promote analysis, reflection, insight, and recognition of patterns and cycles; improve choices and decisions
- *Associated interventions:* Person-centered treatment, psychodynamic therapy, interpretation, cognitive restructuring, dream analysis, Adlerian early recollection analysis, reframing, life history, analysis of patterns, psychoeducation to develop self-awareness and self-esteem

Dialectic/Systemic Collaboration

- *Goals:* Facilitate integration and thinking that generates multiple perspectives, increase awareness of self in relation to others and one's systems (e.g., family, ethnic group), bring underlying issues to the surface, promote new constructs of self and reality
- *Associated interventions:* Consciousness raising, trauma work (e.g., eye movement desensitization and reprocessing), analysis of culture and context and of intergenerational patterns in families, family therapy, feminist therapy, exploration of the connections between the external world and internal experiences, examination of countertransference and projective identification, use of traditional healers, community action

Therapeutic Alliance   The role of clinicians practicing DCT is challenging and demanding. They need to be skilled in assessment of cognitive developmental orientations and be able to function in all four orientations. They need to be accomplished in a broad range of treatment systems and strategies so they can intentionally craft a treatment plan that is compatible with a particular person's cognitive developmental functioning and promotes that person's change and growth (Ivey

& Ivey, 1999). Clinicians need to be attuned to the developmental and sociocultural perspectives of clients while engaging with them in constructing alternative perspectives. Clinicians need to match their role to the cognitive developmental orientation they are seeking to develop in clients and thus need the ability to function in a variety of therapeutic roles (e.g., as coach, consultant, and collaborator).

Although clinicians practicing DCT have an important role in treatment, so do the clients. They are expected to engage fully in the treatment process; talk about their issues, their lives, and the groups to which they belong; and collaborate with clinicians as much as possible in developing new constructions or ways of viewing the world.

Application

Some treatment approaches pay little attention to the diagnosis of mental disorders. This omission complicates clinicians' efforts to develop a treatment plan that tailors treatment to problems and client. DCT, however, acknowledges the importance of both diagnosis and development and concludes that there is "no necessary conflict between a developmental and pathological view" (Ivey & Ivey, 1998, p. 334). In keeping with its emphasis on family, culture, environment, and biology, DCT views mental disorders and client distress as "logical responses to developmental history" (p. 334).

DCT proposes the following pattern to explain the etiology of symptoms and mental disorders, linked to the multiaxial structure of the *Diagnostic and Statistical Manual of Mental Disorders* (American Psychiatric Association, 2000):

- Environmental or biological insult (may lead to)
- Stress and physical/emotional pain, which is a threat to attachment and safety (this, in turn, may lead to)
- Sadness/depression (which may lead to)
- Defense against the pain and, in severe cases, Axis II personality styles (which may lead to)
- Axis I defensive structures (Ivey & Ivey, 1998, p. 339)

According to DCT, personality disorders (long-standing, pervasive dysfunctional patterns) are developmental blocks that have a positive, survival function that clinicians should respect and honor. Similarly, other mental disorders can be viewed as forms of self-protection and ways of coping with stress and trauma. These views are congruent with DCT's emphasis on constructing positive meanings. DCT minimizes stigma and pathology, empowers clients, and paves the way for them to develop more helpful ways of coping.

DCT can be used with a broad range of clients. This approach has had positive outcomes with people experiencing transitions, survivors of accidents, men who physically abuse their partners, students entering the work force, and children who have been abused (Rigazio-DiGilio et al., 1995). In addition, the approach has been successfully used to treat anxiety disorders and mood disorders. Myers, Shoffner, and Briggs (2002) suggest that school counselors incorporate DCT into their work in order to promote development while maintaining sensitivity to multicultural issues. Crespi and Generali (1995) endorse the use of DCT with adolescents. Rigazio-DiGilio's

(1994) adaptation of DCT to families—systemic cognitive developmental therapy—contributes to the wide application of this approach.

Inherent in DCT is a strong emphasis on understanding the person in context and adapting treatment to that individual. This makes DCT well suited for use with people from diverse and multicultural backgrounds.

Despite its considerable potential, DCT has received only limited attention except from Ivey, Rigazio-DiGilio, and their associates. This may be due to several factors. DCT is a complex approach that demands considerable clinician expertise, and training is not yet widely available. Although tools exist to facilitate assessment of cognitive developmental orientations, they have not been well researched. Additional tools are needed to help clinicians establish appropriate objectives and identify relevant interventions. In addition, the terminology associated with DCT, as well as its philosophy, may seem too esoteric to some clinicians.

Ivey, Rigazio-DiGilio, and others are actively conducting research to refine DCT and substantiate its value. The future of this promising but complex approach depends on the success they have in empirically validating the constructs and strategies of the approach, facilitating its application, and making training more available and accessible.

Evaluation

DCT has several shortcomings. The approach has not yet fully evolved and relies heavily on complex terminology and concepts. Unlike approaches such as cognitive therapy and behavior therapy, the concepts of DCT are not easy to convey to clients and may be confusing to clinicians. Also, DCT conflicts in some respects with Piaget's ideas. Piaget conceptualized cognitive developmental stages as largely linear and hierarchical, while DCT does not make value judgments of the stages and advocates that all people should develop facility with all four cognitive modalities. This can confuse clinicians who may view it as desirable for clients to be propelled toward the dialectic stage.

At the same time, DCT is probably the best developed and most promising of the integrated approaches to treatment. Both case studies and empirical research support its value. Research has validated the existence of the four cognitive developmental orientations. Empirical findings indicate high inter-rater reliability in determining an individual's predominant cognitive developmental orientation. In addition, DCT has been shown to increase the range of people's cognitive developmental functioning.

DCT reflects many of the hallmarks of sound treatment systems: it has a theoretical foundation, is holistic and comprehensive, can be adapted and individualized to meet the needs of particular clients, offers guidelines for assessment, and suggests systematic ways to develop effective treatment plans. According to Myers, Shoffner, and Briggs (2002, p. 196), "The DCT model provides a useful paradigm for planning and implementing appropriate interventions to facilitate change."

DCT is a promising and innovative approach that provides a useful prototype for integrated treatment. One of its important contributions is in demonstrating that such an approach can be described and tested. DCT may pave the way for the development of other integrated treatment systems that reflect the same careful thought and structuring. In addition, further empirical research on the effectiveness of DCT, as well as the addition of accessible training material and tools to facilitate its application, may enhance its appeal and acceptance.

EMERGING INTEGRATED AND ECLECTIC TREATMENT SYSTEMS

Integrated and eclectic approaches to counseling and psychotherapy are a rich area of inquiry and study. Most clinicians probably would benefit from having a framework or theory to guide them in organizing and applying a diverse array of treatment strategies, so that they can successfully treat a broad range of clients and concerns. Not only is this desirable from a clinical point of view, but a systematic approach to eclecticism would facilitate clinicians' efforts to demonstrate accountability and present treatment plans to third-party payers and clients in persuasive and powerful ways.

Clinicians and theoreticians today have developed an array of approaches to eclectic and integrated treatment. These can be categorized as follows:

- *Approaches that match treatment to client level of readiness for change and/or client personal characteristics*—DCT, multimodal therapy, transtheoretical model, adaptive counseling and therapy, thinking-feeling-acting model, three dimensional model of multicultural counseling
- *Approaches that feature a planned integration of specific theories*—Hill and O'Brien's three stage integrated model of helping, Wachtel's psychodynamic-behavioral therapy
- *Common factors models*—REPLAN

We have already reviewed multimodal therapy and DCT. We briefly review some of the emerging integrated or eclectic approaches here, touching on the more important of these at greater length than on those with less development, application, or use. Readers are encouraged to read further about these approaches, most of which are in a relatively early stage of development.

Transtheoretical Model of Change

The *transtheoretical model* (TTM), developed by Prochaska and others (Prochaska & DiClemente, 1986; Prochaska & Norcross, 2003), has received considerable attention. Also known as the stage-of-change model, TTM reflects the scientist-practitioner approach to developing theories and is based on both empirical research and practice. It is a stage model which links interventions (*processes of change*) and the target of change efforts (*levels of change*) to the person's *stage of change*. Assessment and matching are essential ingredients in this approach, as they are in many eclectic and integrated treatment models.

TTM provides an organized and methodical approach to planning and integrating treatment strategies based on the following:

- *Five stages of change*—TTM assumes that clients go through predictable stages as they engage in treatment and that treatment must be matched to a person's level of readiness for change. Although progression through these phases may be direct and linear, it is more likely to reflect a spiral, with relapses and other factors causing people to cycle back through previous phases in the change process. The five stages include (Petrocelli, 2002):
  - *Precontemplation*—People in this stage see no need to change. They may be involuntary clients, seeking help because of a court order or family pressure.
  - *Contemplation*—People in this stage recognize that they have difficulties but have not made a commitment to take action needed for change.

- *Preparation*—At this stage, people have decided to change and have even taken some small steps toward change.
- *Action*—Now people are motivated and committed to make changes. They exert effort over time to accomplish those changes.
- *Maintenance*—People act in ways that are likely to maintain and continue their positive changes and avoid relapse.
- *Ten processes of change*—Determination of a person's stage of change is used to identify strategies and interventions that are likely to be successful and to help that person progress to the next stage of change. The developers of TTM identified 10 change processes that demonstrated their value in both research and practice. These include: consciousness raising, catharsis/dramatic relief, self-reevaluation, environmental reevaluation, self-liberation, social liberation, counterconditioning, stimulus control, contingency management, and helping relationships (Prochaska & Norcross, 2003, pp. 516–517). Strategies that promote awareness such as consciousness raising and evaluation of self and environment are particularly helpful and well-received during the early precontemplation and contemplation stages, while action-oriented interventions such as contingency management and conditioning are more useful in the later action and maintenance stages.
- *Five levels of change*—This is a hierarchical organization of "five distinct but interrelated levels of psychological problems that can be addressed in psychotherapy" (Prochaska & Norcross, 2003, p. 528). The five levels include:
  1. Symptom/situational problems
  2. Maladaptive cognitions
  3. Current interpersonal conflicts
  4. Family/systems conflicts
  5. Intrapersonal conflicts

TTM recognizes the importance of the therapeutic alliance, which Prochaska and Norcross (2003) view as the most robust common factor in therapy. They also see the value of a healing setting and a confiding relationship. The clinician is viewed as an expert on change who has the task of tailoring the therapeutic relationship, as well as the treatment plan, to each client's stage of change.

TTM shows considerable promise. It provides a conceptual scheme to explain how people change and how to facilitate that change. It generalizes to a broad range of problems, it encourages innovation, and advocates both empirical research and experience to determine the value of this approach. Research has supported the stages of change framework but has not yet demonstrated the worth of the entire model. However, this stage model, providing guidance on the HOW (process), the WHEN (stages), and the WHAT (levels of intervention) of therapy, has much to offer clinicians.

Other Stages of Change and Matching Models

TTM probably is the best developed of the stages of change and matching models. Others are briefly reviewed here.

The Adaptive Counseling and Therapy/Readiness Model   The adaptive counseling and therapy/readiness model (ACT) is another treatment system that matches clinical approach to client needs, concerns, and readiness for treatment (Nance & Myers, 1991). The ACT model describes clinician style in terms of two dimensions: support and direction. Combinations of low and high levels of each of these dimensions result in four counseling orientations:

1. Approaches that are low in directiveness and high in support emphasize encouragement
2. Approaches that are high in both directiveness and support emphasize teaching
3. Approaches that are low in support and high in directiveness stress telling
4. Approaches that are low in both directiveness and support emphasize delegating

The Three-Dimensional Model of Multicultural Counseling   In a similar model, Atkinson, Kim, and Caldwell (1998) suggest adapting treatment to the special needs of multicultural clients by looking at three dimensions:

1. *Level of acculturation:* High or low
2. *Location of problem:* Internal or external
3. *Intervention needed:* Remediation or prevention

Once a client has been described according to these three dimensions, the approach suggests clinician roles and strategies that are likely to be helpful. For example, people with a low level of acculturation and internal problems needing remediation would probably benefit from healers from their own culture. On the other hand, people who are high in acculturation, focused on external concerns requiring prevention, are more likely to benefit from a helper in a consultant role.

The Thinking-Feeling-Acting Model   David Hutchins (1979) developed the thinking-feeling-acting (TFA) model. Identifying thinking, feeling, and acting as the three fundamental operations in human functioning, TFA is useful in "a) conceptually integrating thinking, feeling, and acting domains of behavior; b) assessing the interaction of TFA behavior dimensions in specific problem situations; and c) designing procedures and techniques that capitalize on client strengths and supplement limitations" (Mueller, Dupuy, & Hutchins, 1994, p. 576).

Assessment of a person's TFA orientation, often via the Hutchins Behavior Inventory, is a cornerstone of this approach (Hutchins & Mueller, 1992). Once the clinician has determined the relative strengths of thinking, feeling, and acting in determining a person's behavior, appropriate interventions are developed to both access that person's primary orientation and develop the less-preferred orientations.

Hill and O'Brien's Three-Stage Integrated Model

Hill and O'Brien's (1999) three-stage integrated model is solidly grounded in the work of a diverse group of important theorists: Freud, Rogers, Erikson, Mahler, Skinner, Ellis, Beck, and others. This approach takes the position that early experiences, especially those that are integral to the development of attachment and self-esteem, lay the groundwork for personality development and must be explored and understood in order for people to make positive changes.

This approach includes the following three stages:

1. *Exploration*—With Rogers's person-centered approach as the foundation, clinicians build rapport and a positive therapeutic alliance while exploring clients' thoughts, feelings, and actions. As clients tell their stories, clinicians develop hypotheses to facilitate understanding and also examine their own reactions to the clients.

2. *Insight and understanding*—With psychoanalysis and the ideas of Freud, Erikson, Mahler (individuation), and Bowlby (attachment) as the underlying theoretical framework in this stage, clinicians and clients seek insight and understanding into clients' thoughts, feelings, and actions. Strategies such as challenge, interpretation, self-disclosure, and immediacy help people see themselves in new ways and make sense of their lives. Clinicians also attend to conflicts and attachments in the therapeutic relationship.

3. *Action*—Based on what they have learned through the exploration and insight stages, clients now take constructive action including learning new skills, addressing barriers to growth, and experimenting with and evaluating changes in thoughts, feelings, and actions. Cognitive and behavioral theories are the basis for this stage. Important interventions include information giving, feedback, and direct guidance. Empathy, support, and other listening skills are part of treatment throughout the process.

Integrative Psychodynamic-Behavior Therapy

Developed by Paul Wachtel, integrative psychodynamic-behavior therapy, as its name implies, is another approach that meshes treatment systems. In this approach, also known as cyclical psychodynamics, Wachtel seeks to broaden the application of psychoanalysis and increase its relevance to the disenfranchised in society by integrating psychodynamic therapy and behavior therapy (Wachtel, 1977, 1987, 1990, 2002). His approach emphasizes the need to adapt treatment to the client's worldview, to consider both social and psychological dimensions, and to empower the client.

Wachtel suggests that early experiences trigger cycles or inclinations that are maintained by present attitudes and behaviors. He believes that an integration of psychodynamic and behavioral approaches provides more powerful treatment than either alone. For example, his treatment of anxiety, encouraging both insight and action, gradually exposes people to their frightening images and fantasies so that they can learn to cope with them more effectively. In a departure from the usual stance of the psychoanalyst, Wachtel encourages clinicians to assume an active and affirming role.

Common Factors Models

Some approaches to eclectic treatment have, as their unifying basis, a grounding in the common factors that make treatment effective (discussed in chapter 2). These approaches reflect the finding that, overall, "despite the theoretical and technical diversity among models of therapy, they share important similarities that are responsible for the equivalent therapeutic outcomes" (Lampropoulos, 2000, p. 416). These similarities are known by many terms including common change elements, universal healing factors, shared therapeutic components, therapeutic common factors, and others.

An example of a common factors treatment approach is REPLAN, developed by Young (1992). The name REPLAN (relationship, efficacy, practicing, lowering, activating, new) is an acronym representing six common and overriding factors in successful treatment:

1. Developing a positive therapeutic *relationship*
2. Increasing a client's *efficacy* and self-esteem

3. Teaching and encouraging client *practice* of new behaviors
4. *Lowering* or raising the client's emotional arousal
5. *Activating* the client's motivation and expectations for positive change
6. Providing the client with *new* learning experiences and perceptions

Building on this foundation, clinician and client collaborate in establishing goals and developing a treatment plan that targets the person's specific concerns.

Another example of a common factors model is *systematic eclectic psychotherapy,* developed by Beutler and Consoli (1993). In planning treatment, they suggest that clinicians look at four variables: client characteristics, treatment context, client-clinician relationship variables, and specific strategies and techniques. Beutler and Consoli assume that certain universal clinician qualities, including respect, a receptive attitude, and flexibility, are associated with positive outcomes and suggest that these traits should underlie all treatment. Beyond that, systematic eclectic psychotherapy provides guidelines for fitting the treatment approach to the person. Clinicians pay particular attention to the client's level of motivation and coping styles when determining the treatment plan.

Clearly, development and study of integrated and eclectic treatment approaches is a rich and fruitful area of inquiry and growth in counseling and psychotherapy. I encourage clinicians to use terms such as "eclectic" and "integrated" carefully and to have a clear treatment framework in mind if they describe themselves with these terms.

SKILL DEVELOPMENT: TERMINATION OF TREATMENT

The final skill presented in this book is the process of terminating psychotherapy or counseling with a client. Done well, that process can solidify gains, promote further growth, leave clients with positive feelings about their efforts and successes, and give clinicians a sense of pride and accomplishment. On the other hand, negative terminations can leave both clients and clinicians with unanswered questions and unfinished business, as well as feelings of anger, frustration, and disappointment.

Termination typically occurs in one of three ways:

1. *Clinician's choice.* Clinicians may be leaving the agency, retiring from practice, or making other changes that necessitate ending treatment with their clients.
2. *Client's choice.* Clients, too, may be relocating and so must end treatment. They may also decide to leave treatment because of its cost or because they do not view the process as beneficial. They may discuss their intent to end treatment with the clinician or may simply cancel an appointment and decide not to reply to telephone messages from the clinician.
3. *Mutual agreement.* Usually, termination by mutual agreement occurs when clients and clinicians both believe that the client has made good progress toward his or her goals and is ready to stop treatment, at least temporarily. Occasionally, clients and clinicians agree that treatment is not working and that the client would benefit more from another clinician or approach to treatment.

When treatment occurs before clients have made satisfactory progress toward their goals, termination may be difficult for both client and clinician. The following guidelines can facilitate the process of premature termination:

• If possible, *allow time to process the termination of treatment.* How much time is needed depends on many factors including the duration of the treatment thus far, the clinician's theoretical orientation, the nature of the client's concerns, and the client's strengths and resilience. As a general guideline, clinicians who are ending treatment should allow their clients a minimum of three sessions to talk about their reactions to termination. Clients who unilaterally stop treatment may be reluctant to return for additional sessions but often are willing to come in for one wrap-up session. If that cannot be arranged, they should have an opportunity to discuss their decision over the telephone.

• *Expect a variety of surprising client reactions.* Clients often show little emotion when initially informed that a clinician must end treatment. Over time, however, anger at the clinician may emerge as well as feelings of sadness and loss, perhaps accompanied by relief that they can avoid addressing their concerns further. Clients who initiate termination early may feel disappointed and angry because they perceive the treatment as a failure. However, sometimes they are contented with what they have gained from treatment and simply do not realize that a planned and gradual termination can be beneficial. Clinicians should allow space and time for clients to talk about their reactions to ending treatment, perhaps mentioning common reactions if clients have difficulty expressing or identifying their feelings.

• *Expect a variety of surprising clinician reactions.* Clinicians are human and may feel annoyed or angry with clients who terminate treatment suddenly and without explanation. Clinicians also may feel sad at the end of treatment, regret not being able to continue helping their clients, or feel sorry at the end of contact with people with whom they have developed a rewarding therapeutic alliance. Clinicians may feel guilty about leaving their clients or failing to meet the needs of clients who have ended treatment prematurely. Clinicians also may feel relief that they will no longer have to work with particularly contentious and difficult clients. Clinicians need time to become aware of their own feelings about termination, perhaps discussing them with a colleague or supervisor, and trying to use them as a learning experience. Of course, expression of these feelings to clients should be done with care and thought, if at all.

• *Ask clients for feedback about their treatment,* especially if they have initiated the termination. Many clients have difficulty criticizing their therapists, so clinicians may have to work hard to obtain meaningful suggestions for change. Sometimes asking clients to identify both the most beneficial aspect of treatment and one change they would have made in the treatment can help them overcome their reluctance to express any reservations. Clinicians should try to keep an open mind, listening for suggestions that may be helpful to future clients, but also not overreacting to the complaints of one unhappy client.

• *Leave clients with positive feelings about the treatment process and themselves.* Review their accomplishments with clients, being sure to underscore gains and help clients take credit for those gains. Remind them that although they might currently feel finished with treatment, you and your agency are available to help in the future. Offer referrals if clients need other sources of help.

Many of these guidelines also are relevant for mutually agreed-on terminations, although some changes and additions are likely. Pay attention to both clients' and clinicians' reactions to the end of treatment; again, expect surprises. Clients sometimes feel angry or abandoned as may clinicians, even though both agree that treatment has been beneficial and the time has come to end treatment.

Clinicians should request feedback, eliciting clients' thoughts about both the strengths and weaknesses of treatment. Identifying and solidifying gains that clients have made in treatment can be particularly rewarding for both clients and clinicians. Writing down clients' accomplishments is reinforcing and provides them with a record of their successes. Clients should direct the process of listing achievements as much as possible. The clinician might write down the items on the list as the client mentions them. Clinicians also can help clients identify their gains by reminding them of their initial treatment goals and facilitating clients' efforts to describe their successes in specific terms.

Clients rarely recall or think of all the successes they have had in treatment; so once they have run out of items to add to the list, clinicians can suggest other gains that they believe clients have made. Before writing down an item, the clinician should be sure the client does perceive it as a gain and that it is presented in language that is meaningful to the client.

Clinicians also might help clients formulate a list of goals they have for themselves now that treatment has ended. Identifying initial steps toward accomplishing those goals can help clients maintain the forward momentum they have developed through treatment.

CASE ILLUSTRATION

This is the concluding case study in this book. It illustrates termination with Edie.

Clinician: Edie, we agreed that next week would be our last session, although, of course, you can contact me in the future if you believe that some additional sessions might be useful to you.

Edie: I'm glad to know that; but as we discussed, I feel I have really made progress through my work with you, and I am ready to be launched . . . to try to put into practice all I have learned here.

Clinician: I agree that you have made good progress. Last week I suggested that we spend this session listing the accomplishments you have made through treatment. I encouraged you to think about what you might put on that list. How did that go?

Edie: I didn't actually write anything down, but I have been thinking about it. The more I think, the more I come up with for the list.

Clinician: How about if I write them down while you tell me what you've come up with?

Edie: Fine. My mood is certainly much better. We saw the numbers come down on that depression inventory you gave me, and I can tell the difference. I feel more cheerful and optimistic, I certainly don't have thoughts of suicide, I'm sleeping better, and I don't feel so guilty about any little thing that I don't do perfectly.

Clinician: Sounds like you are seeing many signs of the change in your mood.

Edie: Yes, it feels great! You know, sometimes I got so bogged down in depression, I didn't even know I was depressed; but I can really tell the difference now. Another important change is in my relationship with Roberto. I see lots of improvement.

Clinician: What are the signs of improvement?

Edie: I look forward to seeing him, we go out together and enjoy ourselves, . . . we've even resumed a sexual relationship. I used to blow up at him all the time. I can't say he never ticks me off, but now I can just tell him and he seems to listen to me and be concerned. And Ava and I are doing better too.

Clinician: What are you doing to make that happen?

Edie: Before, I was always after her about something. . . . Remember to do your homework; don't forget your lunch money; be sure to get home for dinner. What I thought was expressing my love was really driving her away and giving her the message that I didn't have any confidence in her. Now I can see that she's pretty responsible. Of course, she still needs my help; but now, instead of nagging, I can put some of that energy into doing something fun with her. Last week she and I went to a place where you paint unfinished pottery; together we painted a coffee cup and a snack plate for Roberto's birthday. We both enjoyed making a special gift for him.

Clinician: So things at home are better in many ways. How about the way you relate to your mother and stepfather?

Edie: Some changes there too. Now I usually can tell my mother what's on my mind in a way that she can hear without getting angry. We don't see eye to eye about my stepfather, but at least we can listen to each other and agree to disagree. Mom is spending more time with Ava, taking her out for lunch or ice cream, and that seems good for both of them.

Clinician: Let's look back at our initial goals to see if that reminds you of any other gains. One of your goals was to blame yourself less for the abuse you experienced and to distance yourself more from that experience. You rated your level of self-blame as an 8 out of 10. Any changes in this area?

Edie: Yes. I didn't remember that I had rated that so high. I still have twinges of guilt about the abuse, but I'd say the rating is down to 3 or 4. I can see that it wasn't my fault, I did the best I could.

Clinician: So you've made real progress there. How about in distancing yourself from the abuse?

Edie: That eye movement work we did seemed to make a difference. I remember what happened to me, and I'll never forget it; but it doesn't seem like a raw wound anymore . . .

Clinician: So your perceptions of that experience have really changed, and it does seem more distant for you. Are there other changes you can think of?

Edie: My reactions to having been diagnosed with cancer also have changed. I know I had cancer and it was awful; but it seems like a long time ago. I don't worry much about a recurrence, at least not like I used to, and I don't worry so much that every little thing I do is going to cause the cancer to return. Another area that's better is work. I'm managing work better, feeling less overwhelmed; but I still don't have as much balance in my life as I would like.

Clinician: How about starting another list. This one would include goals that you would like to work on after we finish our sessions?

Edie: Yes, that sounds good. More balance is one.

Clinician: How would you start to work toward that goal?

Edie: I bring work home too often. And I don't allow enough time for exercise. Those are two changes I could make.

Clinician: I'll jot those down for you. You might think about other future goals, and we can talk further about those in our last session, which will be next week. Let's take another look at your current list of achievements. One possible accomplishment I've heard you talk about is developing friendships. I remember you talking

about feeling very isolated and lonely when you began treatment, and now you have two women friends you really like. What do you think about adding that to the list of accomplishments?

Edie: Yes, definitely. I forgot about that. I'll never be the life of the party, but I do feel better about my social skills; and I have been spending time with Bettie and Sandy, who both seem to enjoy my company.

Clinician: So that is another area of accomplishment. I'll give you a copy of this list so you can review it and make any other additions you might think about. Before we wrap up for today, I wanted to ask you for some feedback about our work together. What has been helpful?

Edie: I don't know. It's all been useful.

Clinician: Can you pinpoint a few aspects of our work that stand out in your mind?

Edie: Teaching me how to change my thoughts when they didn't make any sense was helpful. I use that a lot. And the work on developing my social skills. Also the Myers-Briggs helped me understand myself and Roberto better and be more accepting of our differences. Also I felt you never gave up on me; you always had a plan to help me, and you really seemed to care about me.

Clinician: I'm glad to hear that so many aspects of our work together were helpful. I would also like to hear about any weaknesses. Perhaps you can identify one or two ways in which our work could have been improved.

Edie: I didn't like that book you gave me to read on assertiveness. It made me feel that I should turn into some other person. It's just not who I am.

Clinician: So that book wasn't right for you. I'm glad you could tell me that. What other changes would you suggest?

Edie: Once I called you when I was very upset. I guess I didn't tell you how upset I was when I left a message, but it took you three hours to return my call. I felt angry about that.

This session illustrates three of the important procedures in the termination process: listing and reinforcing the client's accomplishments during treatment, identifying future goals and initial steps toward them, and eliciting both positive and negative feedback on the treatment process. Although the clinician gives direction and structure to the process, the client takes an active role as she prepares to leave treatment. As this dialog shows, termination is an important part of the treatment process. It can be rewarding to both client and clinician and continues the process of positive change.

EXERCISES

Large-Group Exercises

1. Discuss and list the benefits and shortcomings of eclectic and integrated approaches to treatment. Discuss and list the benefits and shortcomings of adhering to a single treatment approach. Which would you prefer at this stage in your career? Which do you think will be right for you after you have 10 more years of experience as a clinician?

2. Using the BASIC I.D. format, develop a hypothetical structural profile for Roberto, as well as appropriate goals and interventions for helping Roberto in each area.

3. This chapter introduced you to many integrated and eclectic treatment approaches. Discuss the common elements found in all or most of these approaches. Then discuss what makes each approach unique. Although your understanding of these approaches is limited, discuss which treatment approaches seem most likely to make an important contribution and why.

4. Review the skill development section on termination and the accompanying illustration of terminating the treatment process with Edie. What do you see as useful in that process? What additions or changes would you make to the suggestions for termination that might further improve that process?

Small-Group Exercises

1. Divide into your groups of four, composed of two dyads. Each dyad should engage in a 15-minute, role-played interview in which the clinician helps the client develop his or her structural profile using the BASIC I.D. format as was done with Edie earlier in this chapter. Briefly discuss the person's strengths and desired changes in each of the seven areas. Focus feedback following the role play on the process of developing the profile, considering both strengths and areas needing improvement.

2. Each dyad should role-play another interview, approximately 10 minutes long, focused on exploring the most important function in the client's structural profile. Clinicians should try to be intentional and deliberate in their interventions, having a purpose in mind each time they speak. Record the interview and then play it back, stopping at each intervention to discuss the clinician's goal and whether it was accomplished.

3. Assume that your small group is going to develop an integrated approach to treatment. List the choices and decisions you need to make in developing your approach. Then make some of these choices and decisions as a group.

Individual Exercises

1. Using the BASIC I.D. format of multimodal therapy, develop your own structural profile. Rate the importance in your life of each of the seven areas. List those ratings in your journal, along with a list of your strengths and any changes you would like to make in each of the seven areas.

2. Identify the firing order of your first three preferred reactions to stressors. How well does that pattern of responses work for you? Do your characteristic responses to stress mirror your structural profile? Consider what changes, if any, you would like to make in the pattern of your responses to stress. Write about this in your journal.

3. According to developmental counseling and therapy, people can be described in terms of four cognitive developmental orientations: sensorimotor, concrete-operational/situational, formal-operational/reflective, and dialectic/systemic. Write about your own cognitive developmental orientations, responding to the following questions:
   - Which of these orientations best characterizes your current primary mode of functioning?
   - Identify a time in your life when another orientation was primary for you. What was that orientation?
   - How much flexibility do you have in your ability to move from one orientation to another?
   - Which orientation is most difficult for you to access?
   - Do you rely too heavily on one or two orientations?
   - Do your responses to these questions suggest any desirable changes?

SUMMARY

Many clinicians report that their primary theoretical orientation is an eclectic or integrated one. Integrated approaches are grounded in theory and seek to combine and blend multiple treatment strategies into a unique whole that is more than the sum of its parts. Eclecticism, on the other hand, lacks a unifying theory but is practical, providing a prototype or structure for selecting and applying interventions drawn from many approaches to counseling and psychotherapy.

This chapter described multimodal therapy, an eclectic approach to treatment developed by Arnold Lazarus, and developmental counseling and therapy, an integrated treatment system developed by Allen Ivey, Sandra Rigazio-DiGilio, and others. It also introduced you to some emerging eclectic and integrated treatment approaches. In the 21st century, we expect to witness the development of new and better-refined integrated and eclectic approaches to treatment.

RECOMMENDED READINGS

Hill, C. E., & O'Brien, K. M. (1999). *Helping skills: Facilitating exploration, insight, and action.* Washington, DC: American Psychological Association.

Ivey, A. E., & Ivey, M. B. (1998). Reframing the *DSM-IV*: Positive strategies from developmental counseling and therapy. *Journal of Counseling & Development, 76,* 334–350.

Lampropoulos, G. K. (2000). Definitional and research issues in the common factors approach to psychotherapy integration: Misconceptions, clarifications, and proposals. *Journal of Psychotherapy Integration, 10*(4), 415–438.

Lazarus, A. A. (1989). *The practice of multimodal therapy (update).* Baltimore: Johns Hopkins University Press.

Lazarus, A. A. (1997). *Brief but comprehensive psychotherapy.* New York: Springer.

Myers, J. E., Shoffner, M. F., & Briggs, M. K. (2002). Developmental counseling and therapy: An effective approach to understanding and counseling children. *Professional School Counseling, 5*(3), 194–202.

Rigazio-DiGilio, S. A., Ivey, A. E., Ivey, M. B., & Simek-Morgan, L. (1997). Developmental counseling and therapy: Individual and family therapy. In A. E. Ivey, M. B. Ivey, & L. Simek-Morgan (Eds.), *Counseling and psychotherapy: A multicultural perspective* (pp. 89–129). Needham Heights, MA: Allyn & Bacon.

Also recommended is the *Journal of Psychotherapy Integration.*

ADDITIONAL SOURCES OF INFORMATION

Institute for Integrative Psychotherapy (http://integrativetherapy.com)—Formed in 1976, this institute is dedicated to promoting unified approaches to therapy. The multilingual website offers articles (which can be downloaded), books, and workshops related to integrative psychotherapy. Definitions and information also are provided.

New Therapist (www.newtherapist.com/integrative)—Website provides articles and information on integrative and eclectic therapy.

International Network on Personal Meaning (www.meaning.ca/articles/integrative)—This website describes an integrative model of Meaning-Centered Counseling which draws heavily on Alfred Adler's ideas, existential therapy, and cognitive-behavioral therapy, and also incorporates ideas from other treatment approaches.

CHAPTER 24

Solidifying Understanding of Treatment Systems

Finally! You have reached the concluding chapter in this book and probably the end of a course or training program. Your mind is full of theories and theorists, strategies and skills. While you may be eager to apply what you have learned, you may also feel overwhelmed by all this information. This chapter should help. It provides a structured review of the important treatment approaches we have considered, organizing information on each one into categories to facilitate your understanding of major concepts as well as of differences and similarities.

In addition, this chapter will help you choose a treatment approach that reflects your strengths and beliefs as a clinician and is likely to be effective with your clients. Combining this information with what you already have learned about systems, strategies, and skills of counseling and psychotherapy should help you answer Paul's (1967) critical question: "*What* treatment, by *whom,* is most effective for *this* individual with *that* specific problem under *which* set of circumstances?" (p. 111).

An additional section on future directions in counseling and psychotherapy brings closure to this chapter and this book. Anticipating changes in our field can help you meet your professional goals, provide effective treatment, and contribute to your profession.

COMMON FACTORS IN EFFECTIVE TREATMENT

A great deal of attention has been paid during the past 15 years to identifying important commonalities in successful treatment. Research and clinical experience increasingly confirm the existence of common factors in counseling and psychotherapy, overriding characteristics associated with successful treatment, regardless of clinician's theoretical orientation. Chapter 2 considered desirable characteristics of the clinician and the client, as well as of the treatment context. Now that you know about a broad range of treatment systems and strategies, you probably have realized that beneficial commonalities in treatment approaches also play an important part in determining treatment outcome.

In a study of the ingredients of psychotherapeutic change, Hanna and Ritchie (1995) found that treatment is likely to be effective if it helps people to:

1. Acquire insight and new understanding
2. Face up to and confront problems
3. Develop new perceptions or views of their stressors and problems

Treatment is further enhanced if it helps people to exert effort and persistence in addressing difficulties, believe that change is needed, and accept some discomfort to achieve eventual treatment benefits.

The research and thinking of Lambert (1992) and Lambert and Bergin (1994) on common factors accounting for client improvement yielded three common factors:

1. *Support factors,* including a positive, reassuring, and trusting therapeutic alliance and a clinician who communicates warmth, respect, empathy, genuineness, and acceptance
2. *Learning factors,* including changes in clients' thinking and perceptions, receiving advice, acquisition of insight, corrective emotional experiences, and increased self-acceptance and expectations for personal effectiveness
3. *Action factors,* including an expectation for positive change, improved behavioral regulation, reality testing, modeling, practicing, completing homework tasks, receiving suggestions, confronting fears and problems, processing, working through, and having success experiences

In Lambert and Bergin's framework, as in Hanna and Ritchie's, emotions, thoughts, and actions all play essential roles in the process of successful treatment.

Frank and Frank (1991, pp. 42–44) suggested that common factors in effective treatment include:

- An emotionally involving, confiding relationship with a helping person
- A healing setting that provides safety
- A rationale that provides a plausible explanation for the client's problems
- A ritual or procedure for change that requires the active participation of both client and clinician

Kleinke (1994, p. viii) offered yet another perspective, suggesting that treatment encompasses five common therapeutic goals:

1. Overcoming demoralization and gaining hope
2. Enhancing mastery and self-efficacy
3. Overcoming avoidance
4. Accepting life's realities
5. Achieving insight

Grencavage and Norcross (1990) conducted a thorough study that proposed a total of 89 commonalities. Their analysis of many publications revealed that the most consensual commonalities were clients' positive expectations for treatment and a facilitative therapeutic relationship.

Another useful resource is Norcross's (2002) book *Psychotherapy Relationships that Work,* an edited book that reflects multiple viewpoints on commonalities of effective treatment. This book is linked to research conducted by an American Psychological Association task force on empirically supported therapy relationships.

In sum, many writers have succinctly synthesized the research on commonalities in treatment. Clinicians now can have a clear vision of the kind of therapeutic contexts, relationships, and processes that are most likely to lead to a positive outcome.

OVERVIEW OF TREATMENT SYSTEMS

Although the literature gives some guidance on the treatment interventions most likely to be facilitative (for example, those that encourage people to confront difficulties and increase their empowerment), it has not yet identified the specific strategies or treatment systems most likely to succeed. Clinicians still have the challenging task of identifying which treatment approaches are most compatible with their own conceptions of effective treatment and most appropriate for use with their clients. The following sections of this chapter are designed to help clinicians make those choices.

Hundreds of approaches to counseling and psychotherapy have been identified. Of course, this book has not tried to review all of them. Rather, it has focused primarily on treatment systems that meet all or most of the following 10 criteria of sound theories:

1. The theories are clear, coherent, and easily communicated.
2. They are compatible with or can be adapted to include the therapeutic commonalities just discussed.
3. They encompass a concept of positive emotional development and health that can be used in setting goals and assessing progress.

4. They help clinicians organize and make sense of information.
5. They are comprehensive, explaining and addressing a broad range of concerns and disorders.
6. They give clinicians direction, steps, and guidelines for facilitating positive change.
7. They encompass strategies and interventions that grow out of and are consistent with the underlying theory.
8. They provide clinicians with a common language that facilitates treatment and collaboration.
9. They are widely used in practice and generate research. Even if these approaches have not been conclusively validated by empirical research, the research is promising and their widespread use or growing popularity suggests that clinicians find these approaches beneficial to their clients.
10. They focus on individual counseling and psychotherapy. (Many of the approaches discussed in this book also are used for treatment of groups and families; however, this book primarily addresses treatment of individuals.)

The following four sections summarize the major treatment systems covered in this book. They can help readers learn more about these approaches, review their important concepts as needed, clarify their understanding of differences and similarities among approaches, and develop useful treatment plans. Emerging, eclectic, and integrated approaches are not included here because they are not yet comprehensive and well-developed treatment systems.

TREATMENT SYSTEMS EMPHASIZING BACKGROUND

Psychoanalysis

Founder/major contributor: Sigmund Freud.

Area of focus: Background.

Underlying theory/view of change: Biology, drives, and early childhood experiences largely determine development. Making the unconscious conscious through analysis and interpretation promotes insight, reduces the influence of the past, lessens internal conflict, and facilitates healthier choices.

Other important concepts:
- Id, ego, and superego comprise the personality.
- Psychosexual stages characterize development: oral, anal, phallic, latency, genital.
- Three levels of consciousness exist: conscious, preconscious, unconscious.
- Dreams, mistakes, and symptoms reflect unconscious wishes.
- Defense mechanisms are important in understanding personality.

Treatment of background: Understanding the first five years of life is essential.

Treatment of emotions and sensations: Affect must accompany recall of unconscious material. Abreaction is important in effecting change.

Treatment of thoughts: The ego is the thinking part of people and is important in the process of working through issues.

Treatment of actions and behavior: Actions are important largely as reflections of the unconscious.

Important strategies, techniques: Analysis and interpretation, transference, free association, working through.

Therapeutic alliance: Therapist remains relatively anonymous. Transference is encouraged and is integral to treatment.

Level of directiveness: Direction comes largely from the client, although the clinician keeps sessions on track.

Growth- versus problem-focused: Treatment of problems is the focus, but successful treatment leads to growth.

Client profile: Approach is primarily for people with "neurotic" disorders, not in crisis.

Attention to environment, diversity: Approach pays some attention to context but little attention to diversity.

Emphasis on goals, treatment planning: Overall goal is improving ego functioning. Little attention is paid to goal setting and treatment planning.

Duration: Very lengthy.

Use of homework, tasks between sessions: Not important.

Extent of research validation: Limited.

Individual Psychology

Founder/major contributors: Alfred Adler, Rudolf Dreikurs.

Area of focus: Background.

Underlying theory/view of change: Heredity and upbringing are important, but people's own efforts to find meaning and success can be more powerful.

Other important concepts: Social interest is an essential part of healthy development.

Treatment of background: Treatment involves extensive analysis of early recollections, family constellation, birth order, roles in family, childhood experiences.

Treatment of emotions and sensations: Particular attention is paid to feelings of encouragement/discouragement, competence/inferiority.

Treatment of thoughts: Individual perceptions and private logic are important.

Treatment of actions and behavior: Behavior is viewed as purposeful, reflecting goals and lifestyle.

Important strategies, techniques: Education; encouragement; discussion and analysis of dreams, early recollections, family constellation, and lifestyle; acting as if, interpretation and use of hunches to promote insight.

Therapeutic alliance: Clinicians are educators and role models as well as therapists; they encourage cooperation, mutual trust, and respect.

Level of directiveness: Collaboration with client is important.

Growth- versus problem-focused: Can be both, but Adler emphasized growth.

Client profile: Appropriate for a broad range of clients, including children, adults, couples and people with most of the common mental disorders.

Attention to environment, diversity: Social interest and social context receive considerable attention, as do people with disabilities.

Emphasis on goals, treatment planning: Shared goal setting is important.

Duration: Traditionally lengthy but flexible.

Use of homework, tasks between sessions: Important for learning.

Extent of research validation: Limited, more needed.

Analytical Psychology

Founder/major contributor: Carl Jung.

Area of focus: Background.

Underlying theory/view of change: Development is determined not only by our early experiences, but also by innate unconscious archetypes. Through analysis of dreams, symbols, and other material, as well as through regression, the unconscious can be brought into the conscious to promote balance, growth, and integration.

Other important concepts:
- The unconscious is a source of creativity and emotional growth as well as of psychological difficulties.
- The elements of the psyche, including the persona, ego, anima/animus, archetypes, shadow, and personal and collective unconscious, are important.

Treatment of background: Individual background, as well as archetypes and ancestral background, are very important.

Treatment of emotions and sensations: Catharsis is encouraged, especially early in the treatment process.

Treatment of thoughts: Thoughts receive attention, and education is an important treatment component.

Treatment of actions and behavior: Actions receive attention when they reflect imbalance and lack of integration.

Important strategies, techniques: Catharsis, clarification of meaning of symptoms and symbols, associations, analysis of dreams, education, use of myths and fairy tales.

Therapeutic alliance: Support, encouragement, and establishment of a collaborative therapeutic alliance are essential. Transference and countertransference are inevitable and should be used therapeutically.

Level of directiveness: The clinician is active and provides education and information, but collaboration is emphasized.

Growth- versus problem-focused: Growth-oriented.

Client profile: People experiencing an imbalance in their functioning, spiritual concerns, or lack of integration. This approach is largely directed toward people not in crisis who have mild to moderate concerns and a great interest in personal growth.

Attention to environment, diversity: Social values and relationships are important. Little attention is paid to diversity, but emphasis on spirituality facilitates individuation of approach.

Emphasis on goals, treatment planning: Not important.

Duration: Lengthy.

Use of homework, tasks between sessions: Dreams and other material should be brought to sessions. Otherwise, not specified.

Extent of research validation: Very limited.

Other important information: Jung viewed the second half of life as a time of particular growth and creativity.

Developmental/Psychodynamic Psychotherapy (Freudian Revisionists)

Founder/major contributors: Helene Deutsch, Karen Horney, Harry Stack Sullivan, Anna Freud, object relations theorists, Heinz Kohut.

Area of focus: Background.

Underlying theory/view of change: Early relationships are more important than drives; they provide the foundation for current relationships. Analysis and interpretation, linking past relationships to present ones, facilitate essential change and development of the ego.

Other important concepts:
- Internalization of an image of the childhood caregiver influences the self-image.
- The ego, as well as relationships throughout life, is important in development.
- Developmental patterns and defense mechanisms receive considerable attention.
- Several of these approaches provide new perspectives on women's development.

Treatment of background: Relationships and interactions during the very early years play a key role in development.

Treatment of emotions and sensations: Feelings about the self are important. Particular attention is paid to symptoms of depression and anxiety.

Treatment of thoughts: Some theorists are phenomenological, stressing the importance of people's ideas and perceptions.

Treatment of actions and behavior: Focus on behavior is limited, although some attention is paid to styles of relating to others.

Important strategies, techniques: Analysis and interpretation are paramount.

Therapeutic alliance: Transference is emphasized, but so is collaboration. Clinicians strive to communicate acceptance, support, and empathy.

Level of directiveness: Client and clinician collaborate whenever possible, although the clinician guides the sessions.

Growth- versus problem-focused: Concerned with both alleviation of symptoms and personal and interpersonal growth.

Client profile: People with mood, anxiety, and personality disorders seem well suited for these approaches. Motivation, commitment, and psychological-mindedness are likely to facilitate treatment.

Attention to environment, diversity: Approach pays little attention to diversity, but family and society are viewed as important.

Emphasis on goals, treatment planning: Overriding goals include building ego strength, self-concept, and sound interpersonal relationships.

Duration: Lengthy.

Use of homework, tasks between sessions: Little specific mention, but not excluded.

Extent of research validation: Research on attachment theory has lent some support to this treatment system but otherwise relevant research is limited.

Brief Psychodynamic Psychotherapy

Founder/major contributors: Alexander and French, Davanloo, Klerman, Levenson, Malan, Mann, Sifneos, Strupp.

Area of focus: Background.

Underlying theory/view of change: Problems stem from inability of the ego to suppress or moderate drives of the id. Change comes from awareness of the connection of the past to present patterns.

Other important concepts: Careful screening and selection of clients is essential.

Treatment of background: The past is important, especially attachment to and separation from primary caregivers.

Treatment of emotions and sensations: Emotional release is important in treatment.

Treatment of thoughts: Some attention is paid to thoughts that are related to the focal concern.

Treatment of actions and behavior: Behaviors are believed to reflect underlying conflicts.

Important strategies, techniques: Identification of a focal concern, strengthening the ego, making the unconscious conscious, promoting awareness and insight, resolving conflicts, providing education on skill development.

Therapeutic alliance: Treatment should provide a corrective emotional experience. Some attention is paid to transference. Collaboration, support, and empathy are valued.

Level of directiveness: Relatively directive.

Growth– versus problem-focused: Both are emphasized.

Client profile: Relatively healthy and well-functioning people with focal relationship conflicts. Especially useful in treating depression.

Attention to environment, diversity: Limited. May not be appropriate for many people from nonwestern cultures.

Emphasis on goals, treatment planning: Identification of focal concern and written statement of goals is essential. Overall goals include understanding and changing inner experience as well as developing improved relationships.

Duration: Medium length, usually three to six months.

Use of homework, tasks between sessions: Not essential.

Extent of research validation: Some strong evidence of effectiveness, especially the use of interpersonal psychotherapy (IPT) in treatment of depression.

TREATMENT SYSTEMS EMPHASIZING EMOTIONS AND SENSATIONS

Person-Centered Counseling

Founder/major contributor: Carl Rogers.

Area of focus: Emotions.

Underlying theory/view of change: A climate of acceptance and unconditional positive regard promotes self-esteem and facilitates growth.

Other important concepts: Theory is phenomenological and humanistic.

Treatment of background: Approach recognizes that childhood messages shape attitudes, emotions, and behavior but believes that the negative impact of those messages can be overcome through the therapeutic alliance and growth in self-esteem.

Treatment of emotions and sensations: Great importance is placed on eliciting and exploring emotions as well as communicating empathy.

Treatment of thoughts: Thoughts are viewed as resulting from past experiences and perceptions.

Treatment of actions and behavior: Behaviors are viewed as resulting from past experiences and perceptions.

Important strategies, techniques: Techniques are de-emphasized, but the approach does make considerable use of acceptance, reflection, and empathy.

Therapeutic alliance: Clinicians should communicate genuineness, congruence, acceptance, caring, and empathy to establish treatment conditions that facilitate growth.

Level of directiveness: Low; client direction of sessions is encouraged as long as that is therapeutically sound.

Growth- versus problem-focused: Growth-oriented.

Client profile: Ideal candidates are relatively healthy people not in crisis who have difficulties in fulfillment, self-esteem, actualization, and relationships.

Attention to environment, diversity: Approach emphasizes people's differences and commonalities, as well as the importance of respecting their perceptions and values.

Emphasis on goals, treatment planning: Overriding goals include promoting feelings of power and competence, encouraging people to become fully functioning and actualized, respect themselves and others. Treatment planning is de-emphasized.

Duration: Flexible, depending on the needs of the client. Typically medium length.

Use of homework, tasks between sessions: Rarely used.

Extent of research validation: Core conditions of the therapeutic alliance have received considerable support, but minimal empirical support is available for the overall approach.

Existential Therapy

Founder/major contributors: Viktor Frankl, Rollo May, Irvin Yalom, Abraham Maslow, and others.

Area of focus: Emotions.

Underlying theory/view of change: Through treatment and a positive therapeutic alliance, clinicians help people to face the uncertainties of life, gain awareness, and make responsible choices that create meaning and fulfillment in their lives.

Other important concepts:
- People always have choices.
- People need to face the inherent meaninglessness of life, the inevitability of death, and existential aloneness.

Treatment of background: The early years are recognized as formative and usually are discussed, but in relation to existential concerns.

Treatment of emotions and sensations: Depression, as well as existential guilt and anxiety, are common symptoms addressed through this approach.

Treatment of thoughts: Thoughts about meaning and values are explored.

Treatment of actions and behavior: Behaviors are looked at in relation to the meaning in people's lives to determine whether the behavior is helping or hindering people's efforts to find fulfillment.

Important strategies, techniques: Symbolic growth experiences, paradoxical intention, dereflection, discussion are designed to promote awareness.

Therapeutic alliance: This is an essential ingredient of this approach, which is viewed as a collaborative journey. Clinicians play an active role in sharing themselves and encouraging clients to value freedom, responsibility, authenticity, positive relationships, and actualization.

Level of directiveness: Collaboration is advocated, but clinicians do take a stance about what values are important.

Growth- versus problem-focused: Strongly growth-oriented.

Client profile: Suitable for people who are open to new ideas and seeking greater meaning in their lives. This approach is especially appropriate for people at a crossroads; who are dealing with losses, life-threatening illnesses, and limitations and disabilities; or who have long-standing underlying depression or anxiety.

Attention to environment, diversity: Social responsibility and the importance of the individual are emphasized.

Emphasis on goals, treatment planning: Goals include becoming actualized, clarifying values and meaning, and establishing a deep connection with other people and the world. Treatment planning is not important.

Duration: Varies but often lengthy.

Use of homework, tasks between sessions: Not specifically addressed; up to the client.

Extent of research validation: Some research suggests the value of this model in helping people clarify their values and deal with adversity.

Gestalt Therapy

Founder/major contributors: Frederick (Fritz) Perls, Laura Perls.

Area of focus: Emotions and sensations.

Underlying theory/view of change: People need awareness and an inner sense of balance and wholeness to deal with the constant flux around them. Treatment enables them to bring needed closure, integrate polarities, and function more fully. The whole is greater than the sum of its parts.

Other important concepts:
- Figure-ground
- Ego boundary
- Unity of the mind and the body

Treatment of background: Little attention is paid to background; here-and-now is emphasized. Past issues are brought into the present to effect change.

Treatment of emotions and sensations: Emotions and sensations are the focus of treatment, especially bodily sensations.

Treatment of thoughts: Little attention is paid to cognitions, although the importance of awareness of all aspects of the self is stressed.

Treatment of actions and behavior: Awareness of and taking responsibility for one's actions are important.

Important strategies, techniques: Promoting awareness and balance, use of language, experiments, dream work, integration of polarities, role play, empty chair, hot seat, fantasy trip.

Therapeutic alliance: Clinician creates a climate conducive to hope, trust, and awareness. Treatment alliance is a partnership in which client takes the lead.

Level of directiveness: This varies; clinician doesn't interrupt as long as client is aware and fully present. Clinician may become directive when client is not working productively.

Growth- versus problem-focused: Both important, although growth is emphasized.

Client profile: Not for people who are severely disturbed. Suitable for people with depression and anxiety, somatoform disorders, eating disorders, mild personality disorders and traits, physical disabilities.

Attention to environment, diversity: Interdependence and connection of people and environment are important. Individualizing the treatment to the person is emphasized.

Emphasis on goals, treatment planning: Goals include helping people to live in the present, use their resources, bring closure to unfinished business, achieve integration and wholeness, develop self-esteem, become more actualized, and achieve meaningful contact with self and others. Experiments (exercises or strategies) are developed for each person.

Duration: Varies, usually medium length.

Use of homework, tasks between sessions: Essential component of treatment.

Extent of research validation: Limited.

Other important information: Treatment system is humanistic and phenomenological and is useful in group therapy.

TREATMENT SYSTEMS EMPHASIZING THOUGHTS

Cognitive Therapy

Founder/major contributor: Aaron Beck.

Area of focus: Thoughts.

Underlying theory/view of change: Distorted thinking causes people's difficulties. Analysis and modification of dysfunctional cognitions leads to changes in emotions and behavior.

Other important concepts: People have levels of distorted cognitions, including automatic thoughts, intermediate beliefs, core beliefs, and schemas.

Treatment of background: Attention is paid as needed, especially in people with longstanding disorders. Enough information is gathered to make an accurate diagnosis.

Treatment of emotions and sensations: Emotions and sensations are explored and their intensity, rated. However, they are considered primarily in relation to thoughts.

Treatment of thoughts: Thoughts are the focus and the vehicle for effecting change.

Treatment of actions and behavior: Some attention is paid to behaviors to understand clients fully. However, behaviors are considered primarily in relation to thoughts.

Important strategies, techniques: This treatment system includes a wide variety of useful strategies including questioning, identification and reality-testing of thoughts, categorization of distorted cognitions, modification of thoughts, guided discovery, experiments, affirmations, cognitive rehearsal, thought stopping, and others.

Therapeutic alliance: A collaborative therapeutic alliance is essential to treatment, with clinicians providing the core conditions, including empathy, concern, and congruence.

Level of directiveness: This is a structured approach; clinicians take an active role in planning and implementing treatment.

Growth- versus problem-focused: Treatment of symptoms is emphasized, but growth is also important and stems from learning skills that people can use after treatment.

Client profile: Suitable for a broad range of clients, particularly people coping with depression and anxiety.

Attention to environment, diversity: Little specific attention to environment and diversity, but the respectful nature of this approach makes it suitable for a wide range of clients.

Emphasis on goals, treatment planning: Both are viewed as important. The overriding goals are helping people think clearly and cope effectively with their lives.

Duration: Short, usually 4–14 sessions, with extended follow-up.

Use of homework, tasks between sessions: Task assignments are essential.

Extent of research validation: Extensive validation is available, especially on the approach's effectiveness in treating depression.

Rational Emotive Behavior Therapy (REBT)

Founder/major contributor: Albert Ellis.

Area of focus: Thoughts.

Underlying theory/view of change: Irrational beliefs are the source of people's disturbances. Changing those thoughts to rational beliefs effects positive changes in emotions and behaviors.

Other important concepts:
- People have inborn drives toward both actualization and irrational thinking.
- Helping people take responsibility for their thoughts is important in treatment.

Treatment of background: Although life experiences are believed to combine with innate predispositions to determine how people think and act, treatment generally pays little attention to a client's history.

Treatment of emotions and sensations: Awareness of emotions, especially the underlying anxiety that usually accompanies disturbances, is important. However, emotions are believed to result from thoughts, viewed as the route to changing emotions.

Treatment of thoughts: Thoughts are the focus of treatment.

Treatment of actions and behavior: Actions are a secondary focus. They are used as targets of change and task assignments. They provide a useful gauge of progress.

Important strategies, techniques: ABCDEF model for identifying, disputing, and modifying irrational beliefs; strategies for disputing beliefs; wide variety of other cognitive, behavioral, and affective strategies.

Therapeutic alliance: Collaboration and client responsibility are emphasized.

Level of directiveness: Clinicians are relatively directive and use persuasion, self-disclosure, and humor to facilitate client change.

Growth- versus problem-focused: General REBT seeks to alleviate symptoms, while elegant or preferential REBT aims toward growth.

Client profile: People who are intelligent, articulate, pragmatic, logical, and tough-minded are likely to respond well to REBT. This approach probably is useful in treating people with disabilities and those with a range of mild to moderately severe mental disorders.

Attention to environment, diversity: Social interest is viewed as an important aspect of mental health. However, caution should be exercised in using this sometimes forceful approach with people from culturally diverse backgrounds, especially those from nonwestern countries.

Emphasis on goals, treatment planning: Overall goals include helping people think rationally, become more actualized, and enjoy their lives. Attention to treatment planning and establishment of specific goals is limited.

Duration: Relatively brief but flexible. Extended follow-up often used.

Use of homework, tasks between sessions: Task assignments are essential.

Extent of research validation: Considerable research validation demonstrates that, in general, REBT is superior to no treatment.

Other important information: Useful in individual, group, and family counseling; with children and adults; and for psychoeducation as well as treatment.

TREATMENT SYSTEMS EMPHASIZING ACTIONS

Behavior Therapy and Cognitive-Behavioral Therapy

Founder/major contributors: Early contributors include Pavlov, Skinner, Watson, Wolpe, Dollard and Miller, Bandura, and others. Donald Meichenbaum developed cognitive-behavior modification.

Area of focus: Actions in behavior therapy; actions and thoughts in cognitive-behavioral therapy.

Underlying theory/view of change: All behavior is learned. Negative behaviors therefore can be unlearned, while new and more effective behaviors can be learned. Thoughts and behaviors are intertwined; focusing on both can enhance the impact of treatment.

Other important concepts: Thoughts and emotions stem primarily from behaviors.

Treatment of background: Actions should be viewed in context. Consequently, some exploration of background is important.

Treatment of emotions and sensations: Depression and anxiety are common targets of behavior therapy and cognitive-behavioral therapy. Assessment of subjective units of distress is important in measuring progress.

Treatment of thoughts: In cognitive-behavioral therapy, thoughts receive considerable attention. They are less important in behavior therapy.

Treatment of actions: Actions are a major focus of treatment. Identification, assessment, and modification of dysfunctional behaviors, as well as the learning of new behaviors and skills, are the essence of these treatment systems.

Important strategies, techniques: A broad range of strategies is used, including education, skill development, systematic desensitization, activity scheduling, relaxation, modeling, hypnosis, acting as if, and reinforcement, as well as many others.

Therapeutic alliance: Collaboration and active involvement of both client and clinician are essential.

Level of directiveness: The clinician suggests tasks and interventions, but the client has primary responsibility.

Growth- versus problem-focused: Primarily problem-focused; but education and skill development, as well as generalization of learning, contribute to growth.

Client profile: Useful in treating almost any person or problem, although the approach may need to be combined with medication or another treatment system. These approaches are especially useful for people presenting problems of depression, anxiety, and dysfunctional behaviors.

Attention to environment, diversity: Behavior therapy and cognitive-behavioral therapy recognize the importance of context but pay little specific attention to client diversity. However, these treatment approaches usually are not intrusive or threatening, so they may be good choices for people from a wide variety of backgrounds.

Emphasis on goals, treatment planning: Establishing specific and measurable goals and a clear treatment plan are integral parts of these approaches.

Duration: Usually relatively brief (12–15 sessions), although extended follow-up is common and treatment length is flexible.

Use of homework, tasks between sessions: Homework and practice of new skills are important elements in treatment.

Extent of research validation: Extensive research validation is available, demonstrating a wide variety of positive benefits. Symptom substitution is uncommon.

Other important information: These treatment systems are effective with children, adolescents, and adults and can be used in group and family settings.

Reality Therapy

Founder/major contributors: William Glasser, Robert Wubbolding.

Area of focus: Actions.

Underlying theory/view of change: People are self-determining and choose their thoughts, actions, and emotions. Treatment helps people make responsible and realistic choices and responses that are likely to meet their basic needs.

Other important concepts:
- Five basic needs (belonging, power/achievement, fun/enjoyment, freedom/independence, survival)
- Quality world
- No excuses
- Total behavior
- Importance of awareness
- Emphasis on respecting the rights of other people to pursue fulfillment of their needs

Treatment of background: Problems are believed to originate in childhood but are best resolved by focusing on the present.

Treatment of emotions and sensations: Emotions are not targeted directly. Change in emotions results from changes in thoughts and actions.

Treatment of thoughts: This approach is phenomenological; people's beliefs, perceptions, and ideas are important and are considered in treatment.

Treatment of actions and behavior: Behaviors are usually the focus of treatment and are perceived as more amenable to change than are thoughts and emotions.

Important strategies, techniques: WDEP, SAMI2C3, paradoxical intention, positive addiction, questions, metaphors, caring confrontation, natural consequences, evaluation of own total behavior, other creative interventions.

Therapeutic alliance: Establishing a collaborative alliance is very important. Clinicians are encouraged to get involved with clients, become their ally, and never give up.

Level of directiveness: Clinician has considerable responsibility for the direction and success of the treatment.

Growth- versus problem-focused: Growth and process are more important than remediation and results, although all receive attention.

Client profile: This approach is useful for people with mild to moderate concerns, especially conduct disorders, oppositional defiant disorders, substance use disorders, and mood and anxiety disorders. It also is likely to help people coping with physical disabilities and those from nonwestern cultural backgrounds.

Attention to environment, diversity: Treatment system emphasizes the importance of people having a role in society. Clinicians seek to understand people's worldviews and adapt treatment to the individual.

Emphasis on goals, treatment planning: Identification of goals is important in treatment planning. However, process is more important than product.

Duration: Flexible, typically medium length.

Use of homework, tasks between sessions: Homework is an important component.

Extent of research validation: A substantial body of research supporting reality therapy is accumulating. Its use in school settings is particularly well substantiated.

Other important information: Useful for individual, group, and family treatment.

Solution-Focused Brief Therapy

Founder/major contributors: Insoo Kim Berg, Steve de Shazer, Bill O'Hanlon, Michele Weiner-Davis.

Area of focus: Actions.

Underlying theory/view of change: Small behavioral changes lead to larger changes that have ripple effects on the whole system.

Other important concepts:
- People's worldviews lead to their problems.
- People have the resources they need to solve their problems.

Treatment of background: Generally, little attention is paid to background and history.

Treatment of emotions and sensations: Actions are the route to changing emotions. Little direct attention is paid to emotions.

Treatment of thoughts: This approach is phenomenological, giving thoughts and perceptions some importance in the treatment process.

Treatment of actions and behavior: Behaviors are the focus of treatment. Changes in actions lead to changes in thinking, understanding, and emotions.

Important strategies, techniques: Scaling questions, exceptions, the miracle question, presuppositional and other solution-focused language, reinforcement, viewing problems as outside the person.

Therapeutic alliance: Collaboration is essential.

Level of directiveness: Clinician is responsible for suggesting tasks and determining interventions as well as for providing support and encouragement and maximizing client involvement in the treatment process.

Growth- versus problem-focused: Both are important. The focus is on current problems, but treatment helps people become more confident and capable of solving future problems.

Client profile: This approach is ideal for people who are motivated, have solved past problems, and have some supportive relationships. It is best for treatment of mild to moderately severe disorders and problems, but success also has been reported in treatment of abuse and chronic and severe mental disorders.

Attention to environment, diversity: Clients' social systems are viewed as important. Although approach does not specifically address client diversity, it is respectful, nonintrusive, and empowering.

Emphasis on goals, treatment planning: Co-constructing specific, realistic, and measurable goals is important. Careful selection of interventions also is essential.

Duration: Usually fewer than 10 sessions but takes as long as needed for people to reach their goals. Schedule is flexible, often including long intervals between sessions, as well as extended follow-up.

Use of homework, tasks between sessions: Tasks are important and are carefully planned and geared to client's level of motivation and readiness for change.

Extent of research validation: More case studies and descriptions of application are available than empirical research, but strong support for this treatment system is emerging.

TREATMENT EFFICACY

The American Psychological Association, the American Psychiatric Association, and the American Counseling Association all promote research to determine which treatments succeed in ameliorating the symptoms of which mental disorders. An important effort toward identifying evidence-based treatments has been conducted by the Task Force on Promotion and Dissemination of Psychological Procedures of the Division of Clinical Psychology of the American Psychological Association (Division 12 Task Force, 1996). An extensive review of the literature led the task force to identify 18 treatments whose efficacy had been well established and another 7 that were probably efficacious.

Treatments viewed as particularly effective include the following:

- Interpersonal therapy for treating depression and bulimia
- Cognitive-behavioral therapy for treating chronic pain, panic disorder, generalized anxiety disorder, and social phobia
- Beck's cognitive therapy for treating depression
- Behavior modification or therapy for treating developmental disabilities, enuresis and encopresis, headaches, irritable bowel syndrome, female orgasmic dysfunction, male erectile dysfunction, and marital difficulties
- Exposure treatment for phobias and obsessive-compulsive disorders
- Family education programs to help people diagnosed with schizophrenia
- Parent training to effect positive change in children with oppositional behavior
- Systematic desensitization for treating specific phobias
- Token economy programs for treating a wide variety of undesirable behaviors

Many treatment systems, including person-centered therapy, psychoanalysis, and existential therapy, do not appear on this list. This does not mean that they are ineffective. Rather, because their application varies so widely, making replication difficult, and because they use few specific intervention strategies, conducting research on their effectiveness is extremely difficult.

These findings about treatment efficacy have made an important contribution to counseling and psychotherapy, not only in identifying successful treatment approaches but in clarifying how little clinicians know with any certainty. Both novice and experienced clinicians are encouraged to keep up to date on the rapidly growing body of literature on treatment effectiveness to maximize quality of their work.

FINDING YOUR PREFERRED CLINICAL STYLE

Readers who are relatively new to counseling and psychotherapy may view it as presumptuous or unrealistic to consider which clinical approach is best for them. However, choosing and emulating a style of the masters is a good way to learn almost any skill. Even Picasso, generally regarded as one of the most creative and innovative artists of the 20th century, began his career as a representational artist, painting in the traditional styles of the masters and only moving on to seek his own style after he had developed skill in established approaches to painting. In counseling and psychotherapy, acquiring expertise in treatment systems that have established their value can provide a solid foundation for eventually developing your own eclectic or integrated approach or deciding to specialize in one or two established treatment systems.

Determinants of Theoretical Orientation

Although surveys suggest that as many as half of all clinicians align themselves primarily with eclectic or integrated approaches to treatment, the other half are affiliated with specific treatment systems. Many determinants, including the five factors that follow, contribute to clinicians' choice of theoretical orientation:

1. Clinicians who are encouraged, through course work and professional experiences, to adopt a particular approach to treatment are more likely to embrace a specific treatment system than an integrated or eclectic approach (Robertson, 1979). This is especially true if they are exposed to a charismatic proponent of that theory.
2. Beginning clinicians are more likely to embrace a specific theoretical approach. They have not yet determined which treatment system best fits them and their clients, nor have most beginning clinicians acquired enough understanding of the entire spectrum of treatment approaches to allow thoughtful integration of a variety of approaches. In addition, adherence to a single theory can provide new clinicians with reassuring structure and guidelines.
3. Similarly, length of clinical experience bears a positive relationship to the likelihood that a clinician will have adopted an integrated or eclectic orientation (Norcross & Goldfried, 1992). Exposure to a diverse and complex array of clients and concerns, as well as to clinicians who practice a range of treatment approaches, leads many counselors and psychologists to conclude that any one theory is too limited to meet their needs. Even theories that seem comprehensive and well supported in the literature may have gaps and shortcomings in practice.
4. Clinicians' perceptions of their work are another relevant factor. Robertson (1979) suggested that clinicians who view their work as a reflection of their philosophy of life are more likely to assume an integrated or eclectic stance than are clinicians who view their work in practical terms, seeing it primarily as a way to earn a living.
5. Clinicians' personalities and worldviews are other important factors. Finding a theoretical approach that is compatible with who they are and how they conceive of the process of helping people seems likely to enhance clinicians' effectiveness as well as their enjoyment of their work.

For many clinicians, their early years in their profession give them the opportunity to experiment with many approaches; determine what is and is not successful for them; and find a treatment system that is compatible with their professional roles, their self-images, their personalities, and their worldviews. Robertson (1979), for example, found that people who were skeptical and innovative were more likely to gravitate toward developing their own integrated approaches; this probably contributed to their feelings of ownership, genuineness, and congruence in their work. On the other hand, people who craved security, order, and structure were more likely to embrace a specific theoretical model. Most clinicians find that their professional interests and ideas evolve with experience, enabling them to refine their treatment approaches as they hone their skills.

Development of the Author's Style

My own development as a clinician has reflected the influence of many factors. My initial training at Columbia University in the 1970s emphasized Carl Rogers's person-centered counseling. I quickly developed some skill in this approach, found it compatible with my interest in helping people reach their potential, and began to view myself as a person-centered clinician. However, this approach often was not appropriate for the clients I encountered in my internships at inpatient and outpatient mental health treatment programs under the auspices of the Veterans Administration.

Many of my clients had experienced war-related traumas and had severe mental disorders, including schizophrenia, posttraumatic stress disorder, alcohol dependence, and major depressive disorder. My supervisor advocated the use of psychodynamic approaches with these clients and modeled skills in psychodynamic treatment. Although I was glad to have the fundamental skills of person-centered treatment, I next sought to develop my skills as a psychodynamic therapist.

My clinical experience since that time has included university counseling centers, substance abuse treatment programs, corrections, a treatment program for children and adolescents, and currently private practice. Exposure to a broad range of clients and treatment settings has given me the opportunity to find and develop the approach to treatment that works best for me. Although psychodynamic thinking and person-centered attitudes and relationship skills continue to be important tools in my repertoire, my work has increasingly emphasized cognitive and behavioral approaches, reflecting my interest in offering treatment that is both efficient and empowering. In the past few years, I have incorporated into my work eye movement desensitization and reprocessing as well as narrative therapy and solution-focused brief treatment. I anticipate that the evolution of my clinical style will continue throughout my career.

QUESTIONS TO HELP YOU IDENTIFY YOUR TREATMENT STYLE

Having studied many systems of counseling and psychotherapy, you may already have a preferred approach in mind. On the other hand, you may feel overwhelmed by the vast array of appealing choices. Responding to the following questions will help you determine the theoretical approach that currently seems right for you.

Background Questions

1. What theoretical approaches have been emphasized in your training and modeled by your professors?
2. If you have been employed as a clinician, what treatment approaches were advocated at your place(s) of employment? Which ones seemed most effective and compatible with your personal style?
3. If you received counseling or psychotherapy yourself, what approaches did your clinician emphasize? How successful were those approaches in helping you?

Multiple-Choice Questions

The following questions are linked to the previous comparative analysis of the major treatment approaches reviewed in this book. For each item, circle all responses that are compatible with your beliefs. Do not think of this as a test but rather as a way to explore and better understand your thoughts and preferences about counseling and psychotherapy.

1. Positive change can best be facilitated by
   a. Promoting insight, making the unconscious conscious
   b. Promoting awareness and expression of emotions
   c. Eliciting and modifying dysfunctional cognitions
   d. Facilitating change in self-destructive behaviors
2. The following strategies are very likely to make a difference in treatment:
   a. Analysis of transference, interpretation of dreams
   b. Reflection of feelings, focusing on sensations
   c. *ABCDEF* technique of rational emotive behavior therapy, visual imagery
   d. Systematic desensitization, reinforcement
3. Clinicians should
   a. Be relatively anonymous to facilitate transference
   b. Be genuine, warm, caring, and empathic, letting clients take the lead
   c. Build a positive therapeutic alliance, but take an active role in structuring sessions, planning treatment, and identifying dysfunctional thoughts
   d. Build a positive therapeutic alliance, but set clear goals and limits, use caring confrontations, and point out consequences
4. Direction of treatment sessions
   a. Is unpredictable and determined largely by important unconscious factors
   b. Should be primarily up to the clients
   c. Should follow a clear plan for eliciting and modifying thoughts
   d. Should be determined by the establishment of clear, specific, and measurable goals
5. The primary goal(s) of treatment should be
   a. Eliciting unconscious material, promoting the working through of past experiences, and developing insight
   b. Promoting expression of feelings and building self-awareness, self-confidence, and self-actualization
   c. Replacing dysfunctional thoughts and attitudes with ones that are more realistic and empowering of the self
   d. Replacing dysfunctional actions with new and healthier behaviors and skills
6. Problems and disorders I am most interested in treating include
   a. Long-standing, underlying depression and anxiety, the milder personality disorders
   b. Low self-esteem, confusion about goals and direction, lack of meaning in life
   c. Depression and anxiety, pessimism and hopelessness
   d. Drug and alcohol problems, eating disorders, conduct disorders, other problems of impulse control
7. The clinical setting(s) where I am most interested in working include
   a. Private practice, psychoanalytic training programs
   b. Programs designed to promote personal growth and self-esteem
   c. Mental health centers, private practice
   d. Drug and alcohol rehabilitation programs, schools

8. Understanding and addressing a person's environment and socioeconomic, ethnic, and cultural background are
   a. Not essential for successful treatment
   b. Important if they are important to the client
   c. Important in order to understand a person's worldview
   d. Important in understanding behavioral reinforcers and ways to effect change
9. Development of specific goals and treatment plans are
   a. Only important in short-term focused treatment
   b. Up to the client
   c. Essential for giving direction to treatment and empowering the client
   d. Essential for tracking progress and determining whether treatment is effective
10. Duration of treatment should be
    a. Lengthy in most cases to facilitate exploration of the past
    b. As long as needed to provide holistic treatment
    c. Relatively brief, but depends on diagnosis
    d. Relatively brief, with booster sessions used to prevent relapse
11. Use of homework assignments and between-session tasks is
    a. Not generally part of treatment
    b. Largely left up to the client
    c. Essential; treatment is unlikely to succeed unless people are willing to formulate plans and help themselves
    d. Very important and likely to enhance treatment
12. I view empirical research validating any treatment approaches I use as
    a. a/b. Not as important as case studies and my own experiences
    b. c/d. Essential

Evaluating the Questionnaire

Now that you have completed this questionnaire, go back and add up the numbers of *a*'s, *b*'s, *c*'s, and *d*'s you selected. As you probably have realized, the letters are associated with the four groups of treatment systems presented in this book:

a's: theories emphasizing background (psychodynamic approaches)

b's: theories emphasizing emotions and sensation (person-centered, existential, and Gestalt approaches)

c's: theories emphasizing thoughts (cognitive therapy, rational emotive behavior therapy)

d's: theories emphasizing actions (behavior, cognitive-behavioral, reality and solution-focused therapy)

If your choices reflect a clear preference for one letter and one treatment system, especially if that preference is compatible with your responses to the background questions, you should pay particular attention to the theories in that section of the book as you continue your training and professional experience. You probably will find your preferred theoretical orientation there.

If no clear pattern emerges from your responses to the questionnaire or the background questions, you still may be sorting out your perceptions of yourself as a clinician and your beliefs about how to provide effective treatment. On the other hand, your preferred style might be an eclectic or integrated one that combines two or more treatment approaches. Asking people who have observed you in the clinician role which theory they think best characterizes your style might be a place to start finding your way as a clinician. Additional reading, especially case studies reflecting the application of a variety of treatment approaches, also might be helpful.

Clinical Orientation and Clinician Personality

Whether or not you have honed in on your current theory of choice, be sure to pay attention to the influence of your personality. Clinicians tend to prefer approaches that are compatible with their personality styles. Erickson (1993), for example, studied the relationship between clinicians' preferred theoretical orientations and their personality types as reflected on the Myers-Briggs Type Indicator (MBTI). Findings suggested that "thinking types are disproportionately likely to choose predominately cognitive techniques (Adlerian, behavioral, rational-emotive, and reality therapy), whereas feeling types are likelier to choose predominantly affective approaches (Gestalt and client-centered therapy)" (p. 39).

Using your self-knowledge, feedback you have received from others, and the results of the MBTI or any personality inventories you might have taken, think about your personality and the treatment systems with which it seems most compatible. Again, further reading on and exposure to those treatment approaches might help you choose a theoretical approach that is best for you at this point in your career. Keep in mind that you are not making an irrevocable commitment but only choosing a starting point that will help you continue the development of your clinical skills in a comfortable and focused way. With experience, you will become increasingly clear about the best approach for you and your clients, and you will find your treatment style changing, evolving, and improving.

FUTURE DIRECTIONS IN COUNSELING AND PSYCHOTHERAPY

The following trends and issues are expected to have an impact on the direction of systems and strategies of counseling and psychotherapy in the 21st century (Prochaska & Norcross, 2003; Seligman, 2004a):

- The rapid growth of managed care is expected to level off. Managed care will continue to exert a considerable influence over psychotherapy by overseeing and limiting treatment although it is likely to become more user-friendly. This should afford clinicians more flexibility in the treatment they provide.
- Empirical research on what treatments are effective in ameliorating which disorders will increase, leading to greater emphasis on practice guidelines, prescriptive matching of diagnosis to treatment, treatment manuals, and evidence-based and standardized treatments that have proven their value.
- Research will continue to focus on and clarify the common elements across treatment approaches that are linked to treatment success. A positive and collaborative therapeutic alliance will continue to be one of the most important of these commonalities.
- New models of eclectic and integrated treatment systems will be developed and the existing models will be further refined.

- Solution-focused treatment, crisis intervention, and other models of brief therapy will grow in importance and use.
- Cognitive and behavioral treatment systems and strategies will also gain in importance as will eye movement desensitization and reprocessing and related approaches.
- The use and importance of psychodynamic treatment approaches will probably remain stable. Short-term psychodynamic therapy will be especially influential in directing clincal attention to understanding and resolving internal conflicts.
- Narrative, constructivist, feminist, and male-oriented treatment approaches will continue to influence conceptions of counseling and psychotherapy and are increasingly likely to be integrated into other treatment systems.
- Transpersonal and other spiritual approaches to treatment will continue to receive attention and exert influence but will not replace more traditional models of treatment.
- The use of self-help groups and homework tasks as adjuncts to treatment will increase because of the contributions they make to outcome.
- Clinicians will increasingly need to attend to client diversity, background, worldview, and philosophy. They will need to use their knowledge of diagnosis, culture and ethnicity, and individual differences to tailor treatment to each person.
- Attention to the contributions of biology and neurophysiology to emotional health and development will increase as they are better researched and understood. This may lead to increased use of medications, as well as new and more effective medications.
- New treatment approaches will be developed, with many reflecting the importance of biochemistry, but these approaches will be solidly grounded in the commonalities of effective treatment.
- Technology will have an increasing impact on counseling and psychotherapy. Widespread use of computers and the Internet will increase the use of telepsychotherapy—treatment provided through e-mail or other electronic means. Legal and ethical guidelines will continue to be developed to regulate this high-risk area.
- Goal setting and treatment planning will become accepted practice in nearly all treatment approaches and settings.
- Assessment will play an increasing role in treatment because of its contributions to diagnosis, clarification of the nature and severity of problems, goal setting, and monitoring of treatment effectiveness.
- Prevention will continue to be viewed as valuable in promoting mental health, but financial constraints will continue to limit its availability.
- Scheduling of treatment sessions is likely to become more flexible, as reflected by fewer weekly sessions with additional follow-up sessions designed to maintain progress and prevent relapse.
- Treatment will increasingly be used to help people deal with chronic and life-threatening illnesses and chronic pain.
- Collaborations between school counselors and mental health clinicians will increase in an effort to address problems of school violence, and outreach programs will make treatment more available to traditionally underserved groups such as the elderly and people from nonwestern cultural backgrounds.
- Counseling and psychotherapy will continue to be important in helping people cope with problems and emotional difficulties, in part because the value of mental health treatment has been so well established and in part because research and holistic thinking will extend the breadth of its reach.

EXERCISES

Large-Group Exercises

1. Review the tables in this chapter that summarize the highlights of the major treatment approaches. Look particularly at the information about the therapeutic alliance advocated by each approach. Discuss differences and similarities in the ways in which the various approaches view the therapeutic alliance. Do you see more similarities or more differences? What differences seem particularly important? Do the older theories reflect a different conception of the therapeutic alliance than do the newer theories?

2. Discuss the following questions in relation to the following four cases:
   - What treatment systems and strategies seem most likely to be effective in treating each person? Why?
   - What treatment systems and strategies seem least likely to be effective in treating each person? Why?
   - What sort of therapeutic alliance would be best for each client?
   - What possible obstacles to successful treatment are presented by each person? What interventions or approaches might you use to overcome these obstacles?

   Case A. Seneesha, age 15, was brought to counseling by her mother. Seneesha's mother is African American; her father is white. Six months ago, her father left the family to move in with a woman with whom he had been having a long affair. Since then, Seneesha has seemed very sad, lost weight, and has been sleeping at least 10 hours a day. She has withdrawn from most of her friends, especially her white friends, and has been talking about how different she feels from her friends. She blames herself for her father's departure and stated that if she were prettier or smarter, he might not have left. She has avoided contact with her father and has little interest in her schoolwork.

   Case B. Brian, age 33, has been married for nine years and has two children, ages seven and five. He sought treatment reluctantly at the urging of his wife. According to Brian, his wife believes his use of drugs and alcohol is a problem. Brian stated that he does consume 8–12 cans of beer each night and smokes marijuana on the weekends, but also runs a successful business, earns a good income, and "doesn't run around." He agrees that maybe he should spend some more time with the children when he comes home from work but otherwise sees no need for change.

   Case C. Lea, age 42 and single, was recently diagnosed with breast cancer. With treatment, her prognosis is excellent. However, she is terrified of surgery and is endangering her life by postponing her treatment. She explains her reactions by stating that she feels all alone with no one to help her and doesn't know how she can handle her recovery from surgery and her subsequent chemotherapy. Throughout the session, Lea makes poor eye contact, speaks in a low voice, and appears very shy and fearful. She tells you that she is lesbian but has not dated since a long-term relationship ended six years ago.

   Case D. Carmen, age 25 and recently married, sought treatment after one of the teachers in the elementary school where she is employed was found guilty of child abuse. This brought back to Carmen vivid memories of her own childhood sexual abuse by her brother. These memories have made it difficult for her to be intimate with her husband and led her to feel considerable discomfort at work.

3. Review the section on future directions in counseling and psychotherapy. Discuss whether you agree that each of these trends is likely and provide a rationale for your response. What future directions would you add to this list? What trends seem unlikely to happen but would be helpful to the mental health fields?

Small-Group Exercises

1. If you have not already completed and assessed your responses to the questionnaire included in this chapter, do so now. Then share your results with the other members of your group, discussing what those results mean to you. Drawing on what you know about the personalities and clinical style of the group members, give each person in the group feedback about what treatment system might be best as his or her preferred approach. Be sure to discuss the rationale behind your recommendations.

2. Each member of the group should serve as an advocate of one of the four categories of treatment systems (background, emotions, thoughts, actions) discussed in this book. Then discuss the following questions, with each spokesperson presenting an informed view of his or her chosen group of treatment approaches:
   • Which treatment system best addresses issues of culture and diversity?
   • Which can be used with the broadest range of clients and problems?
   • Which is most likely to grow in use and importance in the 21st century?

3. Form into your groups of four participants. You have probably been working together for many weeks and have learned a great deal about each other. Collaborate in developing a list of at least three clinical strengths for each member of the group. To make the feedback particularly meaningful, identify experiences in your group in which each of those strengths was evident.

4. In your small groups, each participant should describe to the group two ways in which he or she could develop better clinical skills. Supportive suggestions can be offered by the group members, but remember to emphasize strengths as the group moves toward closure.

Individual Exercises

1. By now, you probably have learned a great deal about yourself as a clinician. In your journal, list three clinical strengths that you believe you have. List three areas in which you think you need to improve your clinical skills. List three topics in this book that you would like to study further. Identify the first steps you could take in improving your skills and continuing your learning.

2. Identify the exercise or learning experience in this book that has been most interesting or enlightening for you. Write briefly in your journal about what made that experience so meaningful.

SUMMARY

This chapter synthesized information about a broad range of approaches to counseling and psychotherapy, summarizing them in the tables in this chapter. This chapter also reviewed trends expected to have an impact on counseling and psychotherapy in the future. The questionnaire in this chapter can help clinicians identify their preferred approaches to mental health treatment, as can the exercises designed to facilitate professional growth.

Counseling and psychotherapy are vital and exciting professions that help many people and provide a rewarding career to many clinicians. My hope is that this book has helped you to learn many important treatment approaches, skills, and strategies you can use to help others. However, like any book on theories and strategies of counseling and psychotherapy, it can give you only an introduction to these approaches. Our field is constantly changing and I strongly encourage you to continue to study and practice these treatment approaches through additional reading, continuing education, supervised experience, peer feedback, and research on your own practice.

As clinicians, we do very important work, work that can make a great difference in the lives of individuals, groups, families, and even societies. I hope you will treasure and honor the trust that people put in you and will do your best to use your skills to do good for others. I also hope that this book will help you to keep the energy and spirit of the mental health professions alive in your work.

References

Abdel-Tawab, N., & Roter, D. (2002). The relevance of client-centered communication to family planning settings in developing countries: Lessons from the Egyptian experience. *Social Science and Medicine, 54,* 1357–1368.

Acosta, F. X., Yamamoto, J., Evans, L. A., & Skilbeck, W. M. (1983). Preparing low-income Hispanic, black, and white patients for psychotherapy: Evaluation of a new orientation program. *Journal of Clinical Psychology, 39,* 872–877.

Adler, A. (1931). *What life should mean to you.* Boston: Little, Brown.

Adler, A. (1956). (1) The neurotic disposition; (2) Psychology of use; (3) Social interest. In H. L. Ansbacher & R. R. Ansbacher (Eds.), *The individual psychology of Alfred Adler* (pp. 126–162, 205–262). New York: Basic Books.

Adler, A. (1963a). *The practice and theory of individual psychology.* Paterson, NJ: Littlefield, Adams.

Adler, A. (1963b). *The problem child.* New York: Putnam.

Adler, A. (1979). *Superiority and social interest.* New York: Norton.

Ainsworth, M. D. S., Blehar, M. C., Waters, E., & Walls, S. (1978). *Patterns of attachment: A psychological study of the strange situation.* Hillsdale, NJ: Erlbaum.

Alexander, C. N., Rainforth, M. V., & Gelderloos, P. (1991). Transcendental meditation, self-actualization, and psychological health. *Journal of Social Behavior and Personality, 6*(5), 189–247.

Alexander, J., & Harman, R. (1988). One counselor's intervention in the aftermath of a middle school student's suicide: A case study. *Journal of Counseling and Development, 66,* 283–285.

Al-Krenawi, A. (1999). An overview of rituals in western therapies and intervention: Argument for their use in cross-cultural therapy. *International Journal for the Advancement of Counseling, 21,* 3–17.

Allan, J. A., & Lawton-Speert, S. (1993). Play psychotherapy of a profoundly incest abused boy: A Jungian approach. *International Journal of Play Therapy, 2,* 33–48.

Altman, M. L. (2003). Diversity and direction in psychoanalytic technique. *Psychoanalytic Review, 90,* 265–267.

American Counseling Association. (1995). *ACA code of ethics and standards of practice.* Alexandria, VA: Author.

American Psychiatric Association. (2000). *The diagnostic and statistical manual of mental disorders* (4th ed., text revision). Washington, DC: American Psychiatric Press.

Andrade, J., & Feinstein, D. (in press). Preliminary report of the first large-scale study of energy psychology. D. Feinstein (Ed.) *Energy psychology interactive: An integrated book and CD program for learning the fundamentals of energy psychology.* Ashland, OR: Norton Professional Books.

Angermann, D. (1998). Gestalt therapy for eating disorders: An illustration. *Gestalt Journal, 21,* 19–47.

Ansbacher, H. L., & Ansbacher, R. R. (Eds.) (1956). *The individual psychology of Alfred Adler: A systematic presentation in selections from his writings:* NY: Basic Books.

Apter, A., Gothelf, D., Offer, R., Ratzoni, G., Orback, I., Tyano, S., & Pfeffer, C. R. (1997). Suicidal adolescents and ego defense mechanisms. *Journal of the American Academy of Child & Adolescent Psychiatry, 36,* 1520–1527.

Arntz, A., & Van Den Hout, M. (1996). Psychological treatments of panic disorders without agoraphobia: Cognitive therapy versus applied relaxation. *Behavior Research and Therapy, 34*(2), 113–122.

Asay, T. P., & Lambert, M. J. (1999). The empirical case for the common factors in therapy: Quantitative findings. In M. A. Hubble, B. L. Duncan, & S. D. Miller (Eds.), *The heart and soul of change: What works in therapy* (pp. 33–55). Washington, DC: American Psychological Association.

Aspy, D. N., Aspy, C. B., Russel, G., & Wedel, M. (2000). Carkhuff's human technology: A verification and extension of Kelly's (1997) suggestion to integrate the humanistic and technical components of counseling. *Journal of Counseling and Development, 78,* 29–37.

Assagioli, R. (1965). *Psychosynthesis.* New York: Viking.

Assagioli, R. (1991). *Transpersonal development: The dimension beyond psychosynthesis.* San Francisco: HarperCollins.

Atkinson, D. R., Kim, B. S. K., & Caldwell, R. (1998). Ratings of helper roles by multicultural psychologists and Asian American students: Initial support for the three-dimensional models of multicultural counseling. *Journal of Counseling Psychology, 25*(4), 414–423.

Atwood, J. D., & Maltin, L. (1991). Putting eastern philosophies into western psychotherapies. *American Journal of Psychotherapy, 45,* 368–381.

Bachar, E. (1998). The contributions of self psychology to the treatment of anorexia and bulimia. *American Journal of Psychotherapy, 52,* 147–165.

Bachelor, A., & Horvath, A. (1999). The therapeutic relationship. In M. A. Hubble, B. L. Duncan, & S. D. Miller (Eds.), *The heart and soul of change: What works in therapy* (pp. 133–178). Washington, DC: American Psychological Association.

Baker, E. L. (1985). Psychoanalysis and psychoanalytic psychotherapy. In S. J. Lynn & J. P. Garske (Eds.), *Contemporary psychotherapies: Models and methods* (pp. 19–68). Upper Saddle River, NJ: Merrill/Prentice Hall.

Bandler, R., & Grinder, J. (1975). *The structure of magic.* Palo Alto, CA: Science and Behavior Books.

Bandura, A. (1969). *Principles of behavior modification.* New York: Holt, Rinehart, & Winston.

Barrish, I. J. (1997). Teaching children how to feel good without rating themselves. *Journal of Rational-Emotive & Cognitive-Behavior Therapy, 15*(1), 71–79.

Barton, A. (1992). Humanistic contributions to the field of psychotherapy: Appreciating the human and liberating the therapist. *Humanist Psychologist, 20,* 332–348.

Bassin, A. (1993). The reality therapy paradigm. *Journal of Reality Therapy, 12*(2), 3–13.

Bauman, S., & Waldo, M. (1998). Existential theory and mental health counseling: If it were a snake, it would have bitten! *Journal of Mental Health Counseling, 20,* 13–27.

Beal, D., Kopec, A. M., & DiGiuseppe, R. (1996). Disputing clients' irrational beliefs. *Journal of Rational-Emotive & Cognitive-Behavior Therapy, 14*(4), 215–229.

Beck, A. T. (1993). Cognitive therapy: Past, present, and future. *Journal of Consulting and Clinical Psychology, 61*(2), 194–198.

Beck, A. T., & Emery, G. (1985). *Anxiety disorders and phobias: A cognitive perspective.* New York: Basic Books.

Beck, A. T., Freeman, A., & Associates. (1990). *Cognitive therapy of personality disorders.* New York: Guilford.

Beck, A. T., & Greenberg, R. L. (1995). *Coping with depression.* Bala Cynwyd, PA: The Beck Institute.

Beck, A. T., Rush, A. J., Shaw, B. F., & Emery, G. (1979). *Cognitive therapy of depression.* New York: Guilford.

Beck, A. T., & Weishaar, M. E. (1995). In R. J. Corsini & D. Wedding (Eds.), *Current psychotherapies* (5th ed., pp. 229–261). Itasca, IL: Peacock.

Beck, D. F. (1988). *Counselor characteristics: How they affect outcomes.* Milwaukee: Family Service America.

Beck, J. S. (1995). *Cognitive therapy: Basics and beyond.* New York: Guilford.

Beecher, W., & Beecher, M. (1973). Memorial to Dr. Alfred Adler. In H. H. Mosak (Ed.), *Alfred Adler: His influence on psychology today* (pp. 1–5). Park Ridge, NJ: Noyes.

Berg, I. K., & Miller, S. D. (1992a). Working with Asian American clients one person at a time. *Families in Society: The Journal of Contemporary Human Services, 73,* pp. 356–363.

Berg, I. K., & Miller, S. D. (1992b). *Working with the problem drinker: A solution-focused approach.* New York: Norton.

Bernard, M. E. (1995). It's prime time for rational emotive behavior therapy: Current theory and practice, research recommendations, and predictions. *Journal of Rational-Emotive & Cognitive-Behavior Therapy, 13*(1), 9–27.

Berne, E. (1961). *Transactional analysis in psychotherapy.* New York: Grove.

Berne, E. (1964). *Games people play.* New York: Grove.

Bernier, A., & Dozier, M. (2002). The client counselor match and the corrective emotional experience: Evidence from interpersonal and attachment research. *Psychotherapy: Theory, Research, Practice, Training, 39,* 32–43.

Beutler, L. E., & Consoli, A. J. (1993). Matching the therapist's interpersonal stance to the clients' characteristics: Contributions from systematic eclectic psychotherapy. *Psychotherapy, 30*(3), 417–422.

Beutler, L. E., Machado, P. P. M., & Neufeldt, S. A. (1994). Therapist variables. In B. A. Garfield & S. L. Garfield (Eds.), *Handbook of psychotherapy and behavior change* (pp. 229–269). New York: Wiley.

Bogart, G. (1991). The use of meditation in psychotherapy: A review of the literature. *American Journal of Psychotherapy, 45*(3), 383–412.

Bond, F. W., & Dryden, W. (1996). Why two central REBT hypotheses appear untestable. *Journal of Rational-Emotive & Cognitive-Behavior Therapy, 14*(1), 29–40.

Bowlby, J. (1978). Attachment theory and its therapeutic implications. *Adolescent Psychiatry, 6,* 5–33.

Bowlby, J. (1988). *A secure base: Parent-child attachment and healthy human development.* New York: Basic Books.

Bozarth, J. D., & Brodley, B. T. (1991). Actualization: A functional concept in client-centered therapy. *Journal of Social Behavior and Personality, 6,* 45–59.

Bricker, D. C., & Young, J. E. (1993). *A client's guide to schema-focused cognitive therapy.* NY: Cognitive Therapy Center of New York.

Brigham, D. D. (1994). *Imagery for getting well.* New York: Norton.

Brown, L. S. (2001). Feelings in context: Countertransference and the real world in feminist therapy. *Journal of Clinical Psychology, 57,* 1005–1012.

Brunner, J. (1998). Oedipus politicus. In M. S. Roth (Ed.). *Freud: Conflict and culture* (pp. 80–93). New York: Knopf.

Bruns, C. M., & Trimble, C. (2001). Rising tide: Taking our place as young feminist psychologists. *Women & Therapy, 23,* 19–36.

Buber, M. (1970). *I and thou.* New York: Scribner.

Budman, S. H., & Gurman, A. S. (1988). *Theory and practice of brief therapy.* New York: Guilford.

Bugental, J. F. T. (1965). *The search for authenticity.* New York: Holt, Rinehart, & Winston.

Bugental, J. F. T. (1978). *Psychotherapy and process: The fundamentals of an existential humanistic approach.* Reading, MA: Addison-Wesley.

Bugental, J. F. T. (1987). *The art of the psychotherapist.* New York: Norton.

Bugental, J. F. T. (1990). *Intimate journeys.* San Francisco: Jossey-Bass.

Bugental, J. F. T. (1996). Rollo May (1909–1994). *American Psychologist, 51,* 418–419.

Buhle, M. J. (1998). *Feminism and its discontents: A century of struggle with psychoanalysis.* Harvard, MA: Harvard University Press.

Burns, D. D. (1999). *The feeling good handbook.* San Francisco: HarperCollins.

Butcher, K. T., & Manning, M. L. (Winter 2001/2002). Exploring the foundations of middle school classroom management. *Childhood Education,* 84–90.

Cain, D. J. (1987). Carl R. Rogers: The man, his vision, his impact. *Person-Centered Review, 2,* 283–288.

Callahan, R. J. (2001). The impact of thought field therapy on heart rate variability. *Journal of Clinical Psychology, 57,* 1153–1170.

Callahan, R. J., & Callahan, J. (1997). Thought field therapy: Aiding the bereavement process. In C. R. Figley, B. E. Bride, & N. Massa (Eds.), *Death and trauma* (pp. 249–267). Washington, DC: Taylor & Francis.

Campbell, J., & Elder, J. (1999). Crafting the "tap on the shoulder:" A compliment template for solution-focused therapy. *American Journal of Family Therapy, 27*(1), 35–48.

Carey, T. A. (2003). Improving the success of anti-bullying intervention programs: A tool for matching programs with purposes. *International Journal of Reality Therapy, 22*(2), 16–24.

Carkhuff, R. R. (2000). *The art of helping in the 21st century.* Amherst, MA: Human Resource Development Press, Inc.

Carlson, J., & Dinkmeyer, D. (2002). *Time for a better marriage.* Circle Pines, MN: Impact Publishers.

Carney, J. V., & Hazler, R. J. (1998). Suicide and cognitive-behavioral counseling: Implications for mental health counselors. *Journal of Mental Health Counseling, 20*(1), 28–41.

Caro, I. (1991). An introduction to the cognitive therapy of evaluation. *Counseling Psychology Quarterly, 4*(2/3), 191–206.

Carr, A. (1998). Michael White's narrative therapy. *Contemporary Family Therapy, 20,* 485–503.

Carroll, J. (1999). Compatibility of Adlerian theory and practice with the philosophy and practices of Alcoholics Anonymous. *Journal of Addictions & Offender Counseling, 19*(2), 50–61.

Cashdan, S. (1988). *Object relations therapy: Using the relationship.* New York: Norton.

Chambless, D. L., Baker, M. J., Baucom, D. H., Beutler, L. E., Calhoun, K. S., Crits-Cristoph, P., et al. (1998). Update on empirically validated therapies, II. *Clinical Psychologist, 51,* 3–16.

Chang, R. & Page, R. C. (1991). Characteristics of the self-actualized person: Visions from the east and west. *Counseling and Values, 36,* 2–11.

Chapman, A. H. (1978). *The treatment techniques of Harry Stack Sullivan.* New York: Brunner/Mazel.

Charles, S. T., Mather, M., & Carstensen, L. L. (2003). Aging and emotional memory: The forgettable nature of negative images of older adults. *Journal of Experimental Psychology: General, 132,* 310–324.

Cheong, E. S. (2001). A theoretical study on the application of choice theory and reality therapy in Korea. *International Journal of Reality Therapy, 20*(2), 8–11.

Chodrow, N. J. (1989). *Feminism and psychoanalytic theory.* New Haven, CT: Yale University Press.

Chrisler, J. C., & Lamont, J. M. (2002). Can exercise contribute to the goals of feminist therapy? *Women & Therapy, 25,* 9–22.

Christopher, E., & Solomon, H. M. (Eds.). (2003). *Contemporary Jungian clinical practice.* London: Karnac Books.

Clarkson, P. (1990). A multiplicity of psychotherapeutic relationships. *British Journal of Psychotherapy, 7*(2), 148–161.

Clarkson, P. (1993). Transactional analysis as a humanistic therapy. *Transactional Analysis Journal, 23*(1), 36–41.

Cocks, G. (Ed.). (1994). *The curve of life: Correspondence of Heinz Kohut.* Chicago: University of Chicago Press.

Coleman, H. K. L., Wampold, B. E., & Casali, S. L. (1995). Ethnic minorities' ratings of ethnically similar and European American counselors: A meta-analysis. *Journal of Counseling Psychology, 42,* 55–64.

Controversies in cognitive therapy: A dialogue with Aaron T. Beck and Steve Hollon. (1993). *Journal of Cognitive Psychotherapy, 7*(2), 79–93.

Coombs, M. M., Coleman, D., & Jones, E. E. (2002). Working with feelings: The importance of emotion in both cognitive-behavioral and interpersonal therapy in the NIMH treatment of depression collaborative research program. *Psychotherapy: Theory, Research, Practice, Training, 39*, 233–244.

Corcoran, J., & Stephenson, M. (2000). The effectiveness of solution-focused therapy with child behavior problems: A preliminary report. *Families in Society: The Journal of Contemporary Human Services, 81*(5), 548–562.

Corsini, R. J., & Wedding, D. (1995). *Current psychotherapies.* Itasca, IL: Peacock.

Cousins, L., & Weiss, G. (1993). Parent training and social skills training for children with attention-deficit hyperactivity disorder: How can they be combined for greater effectiveness? *Canadian Journal of Psychiatry—Revue Canadienne de Psychiatrie, 38*(6), 449–457.

Cowley, A. A. (1993). Transpersonal social work: A theory for the 1990s. *Social Work, 38*, 527–534.

Crain, W. (1992). *Theories of development: Concepts and application* (3rd ed.). Upper Saddle River, NJ: Prentice Hall.

Crespi, T. D., & Generali, M. M. (1995). Constructivist developmental theory and therapy: Implications for counseling adolescents. *Adolescence, 30*, 735–743.

Crits-Cristoph, P. (1992). The efficacy of brief dynamic psychotherapy: A meta-analysis. *American Journal of Psychiatry, 149*(2), 151–158.

Crits-Cristoph, P., Baranackie, K., Kurcias, J. S., Beck, A., Carroll, K., Perry, K., et al. (1991). Meta-analysis of therapist effects in psychotherapy outcome studies. *Psychotherapy Research, 1*(2), 81–91.

Dattilio, F. M., & Freeman, A. (Eds.). (1992). *Comprehensive casebook of cognitive therapy.* New York: Plenum.

Davanloo, H. (1979). Techniques of short-term psychotherapy. *Psychiatric Clinics of North America, 2*, 11–22.

Davanloo, H. (1980). A method of short-term dynamic psychotherapy. In H. Davanloo (Ed.), *Short-term dynamic psychotherapy.* Northvale, NJ: Aronson.

Davidson, P. R., & Parker, K. C. H. (2001). Eye movement desensitization and reprocessing (EMDR): A meta-analysis. *Journal of Consulting and Clinical Psychology, 69*, 305–316.

Day, B., & Mathes, W. (1992). A comparison of Jungian, person-centered, and Gestalt approaches to personal growth groups. *Journal for Specialists in Group Work, 17*, 105–115.

Day, G. L. (1992). Counseling for women: The contribution of feminist theory and practice. *Counseling Psychology Quarterly, 5*, 373–384.

Decker, H. S. (1998). Freud's "Dora" case. In M. S. Roth (Ed.), *Freud: Conflict and culture* (pp. 105–114). New York: Knopf.

Dehing, J. (1992). The therapist's interventions in Jungian analysis. *Journal of Analytical Psychology, 37*, 29–47.

De Jong, P., & Berg, I. K. (2002). *Interviewing for solutions* (2nd ed.). Pacific Grove, CA: Brooks/Cole.

de Luynes, M. (1995). Neuro-linguistic programming. *Educational and Child Psychology, 12*, 34–47.

Demos, V. C., & Prout, M. F. (1993). A comparison of seven approaches to brief psychotherapy. *International Journal of Short-Term Psychotherapy, 8*, 3–22.

de Shazer, S. (1982). *Patterns of brief family therapy: An ecosystemic approach.* New York: Guilford.

de Shazer, S. (1985). *Keys to solutions in brief therapy.* New York: Norton.

de Shazer, S. (1988). *Clues: Investigating solutions in brief therapy.* New York: Norton.

de Shazer, S. (1991). *Putting difference to work.* New York: Norton.

Deutsch, H. (1944). *The psychology of women.* New York: Grune & Stratton.

Deutsch, H. (1973). *Confrontations with myself: An epilogue.* New York: Norton.

Devine, D. A., & Fernald, P. S. (1973). Outcome effects of receiving a preferred, randomly assigned or nonpreferred therapy. *Journal of Consulting and Clinical Psychology, 41*, 104–107.

DiGiuseppe, R. (1996). The nature of irrational and rational beliefs: Progress in rational emotive behavior therapy. *Journal of Rational-Emotive & Cognitive-Behavior Therapy, 14*(1), 5–28.

Dilts, R. B. (1983). Part I: *Roots of neuro-linguistic programming.* Cupertino, CA: Mesa.

Dinkmeyer, D. C. (1982). *Developing understanding of self and others.* Circle Pines, MN: American Guidance Service.

Dinkmeyer, D. C., Dinkmeyer, D. C. Jr., & Sperry, L. (1987). *Adlerian counseling and psychotherapy* (2nd ed.). Upper Saddle River, NJ: Merrill/Prentice Hall.

Dinkmeyer, D. C., & McKay, K. (1997). *Systematic training for effective parenting.* Circle Pines, MN: American Guidance Services.

Division 12 Task Force. (1996). An update on empirically validated therapies. *Clinical Psychologist, 49*, 5–18.

Dobson, K. (1989). A meta-analysis of the efficacy of cognitive therapy for depression. *Journal of Consulting and Clinical Psychology, 57*, 414–419.

Dollard, J., & Miller, N. E. (1950). *Personality and psychotherapy: An analysis in terms of learning, thinking and culture.* New York: McGraw-Hill.

Dolliver, R. H. (1995). Carl Rogers's emphasis on his own direct experience. *Journal of Humanistic Psychology, 35,* 129–139.

Donner, S. (1991). The treatment process. In H. Jackson (Ed.), *Using self psychology in psychotherapy* (pp. 51–72). Northvale, NJ: Aronson.

Draucker, C. B. (1998). Narrative therapy for women who have lived with violence. *Archives of Psychiatric Nursing, 7,* 162–168.

Dreikurs, R. (1973). Private logic. In H. H. Mosak (Ed.), *Alfred Adler: His influence on psychology today* (pp. 19–32). Park Ridge, NJ: Noyes.

Dreikurs, R., & Cassel, P. (1972). *Discipline without tears.* New York: Hawthorn.

Dreikurs, R., & Stoltz, V. (1964). *Children: The challenge.* New York: Meredith.

Dryden, W., & Ellis, A. (2001). Rational emotive behavior therapy. In K. S. Dobson (Ed.), *Handbook of cognitive-behavioral therapy* (pp. 295–348). New York: Guilford Press.

Dusay, J. M. (1972). Egograms and the "constancy hypothesis." *Transactional Analysis Journal, 2*(3), 133–137.

Dusay, J. M., & Dusay, K. M. (1989). Transactional analysis. In R. J. Corsini & R. D. Wedding (Eds.), *Current psychotherapies* (4th ed., pp. 405–453). Itasca, IL: Peacock.

Dworkin, M. (2003). Integrative approaches to EMDR: Empathy, the intersubjective, and the cognitive interweave. *Journal of Psychotherapy Integration, 13,* 171–187.

Eckardt, M. H. (1984). Karen Horney: Her life and contribution. *American Journal of Psychoanalysis, 44,* 236–241.

Eckardt, M. H. (1991). Feminine psychology revisited: A historical perspective. *American Journal of Psychoanalysis, 51,* 235–243.

Edelson, M. (1985). *Hypothesis and evidence in psychoanalysis.* Chicago: University of Chicago Press.

Edgcumbe, R. (1985). Anna Freud's contribution to technique and clinical understanding in child psychoanalysis. *Bulletin of the Anna Freud Centre, 8,* 155–168.

Edmunds, P., Martinson, S. A., & Goldberg, P. F. (1990). *Demographics and cultural diversity in the 1990's: Implications for services to young children with special needs.* Washington, DC: U.S. Department of Education, Office of Special Education Programs.

Eisenberg, M. (1989). Exposing prisoners to logotherapy. *International Forum for Logotherapy, 12,* 89–94.

Elkin, I., Shea, T., Watkins, J. T., Imber, S. D., Sotsky, S. M., Collins, J. F., et al. (1989). National Institutes of Mental Health Treatment of Depression Collaborative Research Program. *Archives of General Psychiatry, 46,* 971–982.

Ellenberger, H. F. (1970). *The discovery of the unconscious: The history and evolution of dynamic psychiatry.* New York: Basic Books.

Elliott, T. R., Uswatte, G., Lewis, L., & Palmatier, A. (2000). Goal instability and adjustment to physical disability. *Journal of Counseling Psychology, 47,* 251–265.

Ellis, A. E. (1984). Foreward. In W. Dryden, *Rational-emotive therapy: Fundamentals and innovations* (pp. i–xv). London: Croom Helm.

Ellis, A. E. (1986). An emotional control card for inappropriate and appropriate emotions using rational-emotive imagery. *Journal of Counseling and Development, 65,* 205–206.

Ellis, A. E. (1988). *How to stubbornly refuse to make yourself miserable about anything—Yes, anything!* Secaucus, NJ: Lyle Stuart.

Ellis, A. E. (1991). The philosophical basis of rational-emotive therapy. *Psychotherapy in Private Practice, 8,* 97–106.

Ellis, A. E. (1992). Secular humanism and rational-emotive therapy. *Humanistic Psychologist, 20*(2/3), 349–358.

Ellis, A. E. (1995a). *Better, deeper, and more enduring brief therapy.* New York: Brunner/Mazel.

Ellis, A. E. (1995b). Changing rational-emotive therapy (RET) to rational emotive behavior therapy (REBT). *Journal of Rational-Emotive & Cognitive-Behavior Therapy, 13*(2), 85–89.

Ellis, A. E. (1995c). Rational emotive behavior therapy. In R. J. Corsini & D. Wedding (Eds.), *Current psychotherapies* (5th ed., pp. 162–196). Itasca, IL: Peacock.

Ellis, A. E. (1996). The treatment of morbid jealousy: A rational emotive behavior approach. *Journal of Cognitive Psychotherapy, 10*(1), 23–33.

Ellis, A. E. (1997). Using rational emotive behavior therapy techniques to cope with disability. *Professional Psychology: Research and Practice, 28,* 17–22.

Ellis, A. E. (2001). *Overcoming destructive beliefs, feelings, and behaviors: New directions for rational emotive behavior therapy.* New York: Brunner/Mazel.

Ellis, A. E. (2003). Early theories and practices of rational emotive behavior therapy and how they have been augmented and revised during the last three decades. *Journal of Rational-Emotive & Cognitive-Behavior Therapy, 21,* 219–243.

Ellis, A. E., & Dryden, W. (1997). *The practice of rational emotive behavior therapy* (2nd ed.). New York: Springer.

Ellwood, R. (1999). *The politics of myth: A study of C. G. Jung, Mircea Eliade, and Joseph Campbell.* New York: State University of New York Press.

Enns, C. (1987). Gestalt therapy and feminist therapy: A proposed integration. *Journal of Counseling and Development, 66,* 93–95.

Enns, C. Z. (1993). Twenty years of feminist counseling and psychotherapy: From naming biases to implementing multifaceted practice. *The Counseling Psychologist, 21,* 3–87.

Enright, J. B. (1975). An introduction to Gestalt therapy. In F. D. Stephenson (Ed.), *Gestalt therapy primer: Introductory readings in Gestalt therapy* (pp. 13–33). Springfield, IL: C. C. Thomas.

Epp, L. R. (1998). The courage to be an existential counselor: An interview of Clemmont E. Vontress. *Journal of Mental Health Counseling, 20,* 1–12.

Epston, D. (1993). Internalizing discourses versus externalizing discourses. In S. Gilligan & R. Price (Eds.), *Therapeutic conversations* (pp. 161–177). New York: Norton.

Erickson, D. B. (1993). The relationship between personality types and preferred counseling model. *Journal of Psychological Type, 27,* 39–41.

Erikson, E. H. (1963). *Childhood and society.* New York: Norton.

Estes, C. P. (1992). *Women who run with the wolves: Myths and stories of the wild woman archetype.* New York: Ballantine.

Evans, D. B. (1982). What are you doing? An interview with William Glasser. *Personnel and Guidance Journal, 60*(8), 460–466.

Ewen, R. B. (1993). *An introduction to theories of personality* (4th ed.). Hillsdale, NJ: Erlbaum.

Eysenck, H. J. (1970). A mish-mash of theories. *International Journal of Psychiatry, 9,* 140–146.

Fagan, J., & Shepherd, I. L. (1970). *Gestalt therapy now.* New York: Harper & Row.

Fanning, P. (1988). *Visualization for change.* Oakland, CA: New Harbinger.

Ferguson, E. D. (2000). Individual psychology is ahead of its time. *Journal of Individual Psychology, 56,* 14–20.

Ferguson, E. D. (2003). Social processes, personal goals, and their intertwining: Their importance in Adlerian theory and practice. *Journal of Individual Psychology, 59,* 136–144.

Fernald, P. S. (2000). Carl Rogers: Body-centered counselor. *Journal of Counseling and Development, 78,* 172–180.

Fisch, R., Weakland, J., & Segal, L. (1982). *The tactics of change.* San Francisco: Jossey-Bass.

Foa, E. B., Keane, T. M., & Friedman, M. J. (2000). *Effective treatments of PTSD: Guidelines from the International Society for Traumatic Stress Studies.* New York: Guilford.

Fonagy, P. (1999, May). Transgenerational consistencies of attachment: A new theory. *Paper to the Developmental and Psychoanalytic Discussion Group, American Psychoanalytic Association Meeting,* Washington, DC. Retrieved February 5, 2004, from http://www.psychematters.com/papers/fonagy2.htm.

Forcey, L. R., & Nash, M. (1998). Rethinking feminist theory and social work therapy. *Women and Therapy, 21,* 85–99.

Foreman, S. A., & Marmar, C. R. (1985). Therapist actions that address initially poor therapeutic alliances in psychotherapy. *American Journal of Psychiatry, 142,* 922–926.

Fox, H. (1996). *Projective identification.* Retrieved March 15, 2004, from http://object-relations.com.

Frank, J. D., & Frank, J. B. (1991). *Persuasion and healing* (3rd ed.). Baltimore: Johns Hopkins University Press.

Frank, M. L. (1995). Existential theory. In D. Capuzzi & D. R. Gross (Eds.), *Counseling and psychotherapy: Theories and interventions* (pp. 207–235). Upper Saddle River, NJ: Merrill/Prentice Hall.

Frankl, V. E. (1963). *Man's search for meaning.* Boston: Beacon.

Frankl, V. E. (1978). *The unheard cry for meaning.* New York: Simon & Schuster.

Frankl, V. E. (1987). On the meaning of love. *International Forum for Logotherapy, 10,* 5–8.

Frankl, V. E. (1992). Meaning in industrial society. *International Forum for Logotherapy, 15,* 66–70.

Freed, A., & Freed, M. (1974a). *TA for kids.* Sacramento: Freed.

Freed, A., & Freed, M. (1974b). *TA for tots.* Sacramento: Freed.

Freeman, S. (1993). Client-centered therapy with diverse populations: The universal within the specific. *Journal of Multicultural Counseling and Development, 21,* 248–254.

Freud, A. (1946). *The ego and the mechanisms of defense.* New York: International Universities Press.

Freud, A. (1965). *Normality and pathology in childhood.* New York: International Universities Press.

Freud, A. (1983). Excerpts from seminars and meetings. *Bulletin of the Hampstead Clinic, 6,* 115–128.

Freud, A., & Burlingham, D. T. (1943). *War and children.* New York: Medical War Books, International Universities Press.

Freud, A., & Burlingham, D. T. (1944). *Infants without families: The case for and against residential nurseries.* New York: Medical War Books, International Universities Press.

Freud, S. (1936). *The problem of anxiety* (H. A. Bunker, Trans.). New York: Norton.

Freud, S. (1938). *The basic writings of Sigmund Freud* (A. A. Brill, Trans.). New York: Modern Library.

Frick, W. B. (1987). The symbolic growth experience and creation of meaning. *International Forum for Logotherapy, 10,* 35–41.

Frost, R. (1962). *Robert Frost's poems.* New York: Washington Square Press.

Fulkerson, M. (2003). Integrating the Karpman drama triangle with choice theory and reality therapy. *International Journal of Reality Therapy, 23*(1), 17–20.

Funderburk, J. R., & Fukuyama, M. A. (2001). Feminism, multiculturalism, and spirituality: Convergent and divergent forces in psychotherapy. *Women & Therapy, 24,* 1–18.

Gabbard, G. O. (1990). *Psychodynamic psychiatry in clinical practice.* Washington, DC: American Psychiatric Press.

Gabbard, G. O., & Lazar, S. G. (1997). Efficacy and cost effectiveness of psychotherapy. Washington, DC: American Psychoanalytic Association. Retrieved January 23, 2004, from http://apsa.org/pubinfo/efficacy.htm.

Gandy, G. L. (1995). Disputing irrational beliefs in rehabilitation counseling. *Journal of Applied Rehabilitation Counseling, 26*(1), 36–40.

Garfield, S. L. (1995). The client-therapist relationship in rational-emotive therapy. *Journal of Rational-Emotive & Cognitive-Behavior Therapy, 13*(2), 101–116.

Garrow, S., & Walker, J. A. (2001). Existential group therapy and death anxiety. *Adultspan Journal, 3,* 77–87.

Gelso, C. J., & Carter, J. A. (1985). The relationship in counseling and psychotherapy: Components, consequences, and theoretical antecedents. *Counseling Psychologist, 13,* 155–243.

George, C., Kaplan, N., & Main, M. (1996). *Adult Attachment Interview.* Berkeley: University of California-Berkeley.

Gibbs, J. T., & Huang, L. N. (1989). *Children of color: Psychological interventions with minority youths.* San Francisco: Jossey-Bass.

Gilligan, C. (1993). *In a different voice: Psychological theory and women's development.* Cambridge, MA: Harvard University Press.

Gilligan, S. (1997). Living in a post-Ericksonian world. In W. J. Matthews & J. H. Edgette (Eds.), *Current thinking and research in brief therapy: Solutions, strategies, narratives* (vol. 1, pp. 1–23). New York: Brunner/Mazel.

Gingerich, W. J., & Eisengart, S. (2000). Solution-focused brief therapy: A review of the outcome research. *Family Process, 39,* 477–498.

Gladfelter, J. (1992). Redecision therapy. *International Journal of Group Psychotherapy, 42*(3), 319–334.

Glasser, W. (1961). *Mental health or mental illness?* New York: Harper & Row.

Glasser, W. (1965). *Reality therapy: A new approach to psychiatry.* New York: Harper & Row.

Glasser, W. (1969). *Schools without failure.* New York: Harper & Row.

Glasser, W. (1975). *Reality therapy.* New York: Harper & Row.

Glasser, W. (1976). *Positive addiction.* New York: Harper & Row.

Glasser, W. (1984). *Control theory.* New York: Harper & Row.

Glasser, W. (1986). *Control theory in the classroom.* New York: Harper & Row.

Glasser, W. (1998). *Choice theory.* New York: HarperCollins.

Glasser, W. (2000). *Counseling with choice theory.* New York: HarperCollins.

Glasser, W., & Wubbolding, R. E. (1995). Reality therapy. In R. J. Corsini & D. Wedding (Eds.), *Current psychotherapies* (5th ed., pp. 293–321). Itasca, IL: Peacock.

Glauser, A. S., & Bozarth, J. D. (2001). Person-centered counseling: The culture within. *Journal of Counseling and Development, 79,* 142–147.

Golden, W. L., Gersh, W. D., & Robbins, D. M. (1992). *Psychological treatment of cancer patients.* Needham Heights, MA: Allyn & Bacon.

Goldstein, J., Freud, A., & Solnit, A. J. (1973). *Beyond the best interests of the child.* New York: Free Press.

Goldstein, J., Freud, A., & Solnit, A. J. (1979). *Before the best interests of the child.* New York: Free Press.

Gordon, T. (1970). *Parent effectiveness training: The no-lose program for raising responsible children.* New York: Wyden.

Gordon, T. (1983). *Leader effectiveness training, L.E.T.: The no-lose way to release the productive potential of people.* New York: Putnam.

Gordon, T., & Burch, N. (1974). *T.E.T., teacher effectiveness training.* New York: Wyden.

Gottlieb, D. T., & Gottlieb, C. D. (1996). The narrative/collaborative process in couples therapy: A postmodern perspective. *Women and Therapy, 19,* 37–47.

Gottleib, S. (2004). Cognitive behavior therapy can reduce hypochondriasis. *British Medical Journal, 328,* 735.

Goulding, M. (1987). Transactional analysis and redecision therapy. In J. L. Zeig (Ed.), *The evolution of psychotherapy* (pp. 285–299). New York: Brunner/Mazel.

Goulding, M., & Goulding, R. (1979). *Changing lives through redecision therapy.* New York: Brunner/Mazel.

Grant, B. (1990). Principled and instrumental nondirectiveness in person-centered therapy and client-centered therapy. *Person-Centered Review, 5,* 77–88.

Green, R. & Herget, M. (1991). Outcomes of systemic/strategic team consultation. III: The importance of therapist warmth and active structuring. *Family Process, 30,* 321–336.

Greenberg, J. R., & Mitchell, S. A. (1983). *Object relations in psychoanalytic therapy.* Cambridge, MA: Harvard University Press.

Greenberg, L., Elliott, R., & Lietaer, G. (1994). Research on experiential psychotherapies. In A. E. Bergin & S. L. Garfield (Eds.), *Handbook of psychotherapy and behavior change* (4th ed., pp. 509–539). New York: Wiley.

Greenwalt, B. C. (1995). A comparative analysis of reality therapy and solution-focused brief therapy. *Journal of Reality Therapy, 15*(1), 56–65.

Grencavage, L. M., & Norcross, J. C. (1990). Where are the commonalities among the therapeutic common factors? *Professional Psychology: Research and Practice, 21,* 372–378.

Grey, A. L. (1988). Sullivan's contribution to psychoanalysis: An overview. *Contemporary Psychoanalysis, 24,* 548–576.

Grey, L. (1998). *Alfred Adler, forgotten prophet: A vision for the 21st century.* Westport, CT: Praeger.

Haaga, D. A. F., DeRubeis, R. J., Stewart, B. L., & Beck, A. T. (1991). Relationship of intelligence with cognitive therapy outcome. *Behavior Research and Therapy, 29*(3), 277–281.

Hanna, F. J., & Ritchie, M. H. (1995). Seeking the active ingredients of psychotherapeutic change: Within and outside of the context of therapy. *Professional Psychology: Research and Practice, 26*(2), 176–183.

Hanna, R. J. (1998). A transcultural view of prejudice, racism, and community feeling: The desire and striving for status. *Journal of Individual Psychology, 54,* 336–345.

Hansen, J., Stevic, R., & Warner, R. (1986). *Counseling: Theory and process* (4th ed.). Boston: Allyn & Bacon.

Hansen, J. T. (2002). Postmodern implications for theoretical integration of counseling approaches. *Journal of Counseling and Development, 80*(3), 315–321.

Harris, A. B., & Harris, T. A. (1985). *Staying ok.* New York: Harper & Row.

Harris, T. A. (1967). *I'm ok—you're ok.* New York: Avon.

Hazan, C., & Shaver, P. (1987). Romantic love conceptualized as an attachment process. *Journal of Personality and Social Psychology, 52,* 511–524.

Hergenhahn, B. R. (1994). *An introduction to theories of personality* (4th ed.). Upper Saddle River, NJ: Prentice Hall.

Herlihy, B., & Corey, G. (1996). *ACA ethical standards casebook.* Alexandria, VA: American Counseling Association.

Herman, L. (1975). One transactional analyst's understanding of Carl Jung. *Transactional Analysis Journal, 5,* 123–126.

Herrera, N. C., Zajonc, R. B., Wieczorkowska, G., & Cichomski, B. (2003). Beliefs about birth rank and their reflection in reality. *Journal of Personality & Social Psychology, 85,* 142–510.

Hill, C. E., & Nakayama, E. Y. (2000). Client-centered therapy: Where has it been and where is it going? A comment on Hathaway (1948). *Journal of Clinical Psychology, 56,* 861–875.

Hill, C. E., & O'Brien, K. M. (1999). *Helping skills: Facilitating exploration, insight, and action.* Washington, DC: American Psychological Association.

Hirschman, L. (1997). Restoring complexity to the subjective worlds of profound abuse survivors. In A. Goldberg (Ed.), *Conversations in self psychology: Progress in self psychology* (vol. 13, pp. 307–323). Hillsdale, NJ: Analytic Press.

Hoffman, E. (1994). *The drive for self: Alfred Adler and the founding of individual psychology.* Reading, MA: Addison-Wesley.

Hoglend, P. (2003). Long-term effects of brief dynamic psychotherapy. *Psychotherapy Research, 13*(3), 271–292.

Holden, J. M. (1993). Transpersonal counseling. *TCA Journal, 21,* 7–23.

Holden, J. M. (1996, April). *Transpersonal perspectives in counseling.* Paper presented at the meeting of the American Psychological Association, Pittsburgh, PA.

Hollon, S. D., & Najavits, L. (1988). Review of empirical studies on cognitive therapy. In A. J. Frances & R. E. Sales (Eds.), *American Psychiatric Press review of psychiatry* (vol. 7, pp. 643–666). Washington, DC: American Psychiatric Press.

Horney, K. (1935). The problem of feminine masochism. *Psychoanalytic Review, 22,* 241–257.

Horney, K. (1939). *New ways in psychoanalysis.* New York: Norton.

Horney, K. (1945). *Our inner conflicts.* New York: Norton.

Horney, K. (1950). *Neurosis and human growth: The struggle toward self-realization.* New York: Norton.

Horney, K. (1967). *Feminine psychology.* New York: Norton.

Horowitz, M., Marmar, C. Krupnick, J., Wilner, N., Kaltreider, N., & Wallerstein, R. (1984). *Personality styles and brief psychotherapy.* New York: Basic Books.

Horvath, A. O., & Symonds, B. D. (1991). Relation between working alliance and outcome in psychotherapy: A meta-analysis. *Journal of Consulting and Clinical Psychology, 38,* 139–149.

Howard, K. I. (1998, August). *Quality assurance in psychotherapy.* Paper presented at the 17th World Congress of Psychotherapy. Warsaw University, Poland.

Howatt, W. A. (2003). Choice theory: A core addiction recovery tool. *International Journal of Reality Therapy, 22*(2), 12–15.

Hutchins, D. E. (1979). Systemic counseling: The T-F-A model for counselor intervention. *Personnel and Guidance Journal, 57,* 529–531.

Hutchins, D. E., & Mueller, R. O. (1992). *Manual for Hutchins Behavior Inventory.* Palo Alto, CA: Consulting Psychologists Press.

Hutson-Comeaux, S. L., & Kelly, J. R. (2002). Gender stereotypes of emotional reactions: How we judge an emotion as valid. *Sex Roles, 48,* 1–10.

Isaacson, E. B. (1990). Neuro-linguistic programming: A model for behavioral change in alcohol and other drug addiction. In C. M. Sterman (Ed.), *Neuro-linguistic programming in alcoholism treatment* (pp. 27–48). New York: Haworth.

Ivey, A. (1986). *Developmental therapy: Theory into practice.* San Francisco: Jossey-Bass.

Ivey, A. E. (1989). Mental health counseling: A developmental process and profession. *Journal of Mental Health Counseling, 11*(1), 26–35.

Ivey, A. E., & Ivey, M. B. (1998). Reframing the *DSM-IV:* Positive strategies from developmental counseling and therapy. *Journal of Counseling & Development, 76,* 334–350.

Ivey, A. E., & Ivey, M. B. (1999). *Intentional interviewing and counseling.* Pacific Grove, CA: Brooks/Cole.

Ivey, A. E., Ivey, M. B., & Simek-Morgan, L. (1997). *Counseling and psychotherapy: A multicultural perspective.* Needham Heights, MA: Allyn & Bacon.

Ivey, A. E., & Rigazio-DiGilio, S. A. (1991). Toward a developmental practice of mental health counseling: Strategies for training, practice and political unity. *Journal of Mental Health Counseling, 13*(1), 21–36.

Jacobi, J. (1973). *The psychology of C. G. Jung.* London: Yale University Press.

Jacobs, L. (1989). Dialogue in Gestalt theory and therapy. *Gestalt Journal, 12,* 25–67.

Jacobson, N. S. (1989). The therapist-client relationship in cognitive behavior therapy: Implications for treating depression. *Journal of Cognitive Psychotherapy, 3*(2), 85–96.

Jakupcak, M., Lisak, D., & Roemer, L. (2002). The role of masculine ideology and masculine gender role stress in men's perpetration of relationship violence. *Psychology of Men & Masculinity, 3,* 97–106.

Jakupcak, M., Salters, K., Gratz, K. L., & Roemer, L. (2003). Masculinity and emotionality: An investigation of men's primary and secondary emotional responding. *Sex Roles, 49,* 111–120.

Jaycox, L. H., Zoellner, L., & Foa, E. B. (2002). Cognitive-behavior therapy for PTSD in rape survivors. *Journal of Consulting and Clinical Psychology, 50,* 891–906.

Jinks, G. H. (1999). Intentionality and awareness: A qualitative study of clients' perceptions of change during longer term counseling. *Counselling Psychology Quarterly, 12,* 57–71.

Johnson, W. B., Ridley, C. R., & Nielsen, S. L. (2000). Religiously sensitive rational emotive behavior therapy: Elegant solutions and ethical risks. *Professional Psychology: Research and Practice, 31,* 14–20.

Jones, E. (1953). *The life and work of Sigmund Freud* (vol. 1). New York: Basic Books.

Jones, E. (1955). *The life and work of Sigmund Freud: Years of maturity, 1901–1919* (vol. 2). New York: Basic Books.

Jones, E. (1957). *The life and work of Sigmund Freud: The last phase, 1919–1939* (vol. 3). New York: Basic Books.

Joyce, A. S., & Piper, W. E. (1998). Expectancy, the therapeutic alliance, and treatment outcome in short-term individual psychotherapy. *Journal of Psychotherapy Practice and Research, 7,* 236–248.

Jung, C. G. (1907/1960). The psychology of dementia praecox. In *The collected works of C. G. Jung* (Vol. 4). Princeton, NJ: Princeton University Press.

Jung, C. G. (1912/1956). Symbols of transformation. In *The collected works of C. G. Jung* (Vol. 5). Princeton, NJ: Princeton University Press.

Jung, C. G. (1921/1971). Psychological types. In *The collected works of C. G. Jung* (Vol. 6). Princeton, NJ: Princeton University Press.

Jung, C. G. (1953). Two essays on analytical psychology. In *The collected works of C. G. Jung* (Vol. 7). Princeton, NJ: Princeton University Press.

Jung, C. G. (1959). Aion: Research into the phenomenology of the self. In *The collected works of C. G. Jung* (Vol. 9). Princeton, NJ: Princeton University Press.

Jung, C. G. (1960). *Collected works 8: The structure and dynamics of the psyche.* New York: Pantheon.

Jung, C. G. (1963). *Memories, dreams, reflections.* New York: Pantheon.

Jung, C. G. (1964). *Man and his symbols.* Garden City, NY: Doubleday.

Kamp, D. (1996). *The excellent training: Putting NLP to work.* Brookfield, VT: Gower.

Katz, A. J. (1991). Renegotiation: What to do when you don't follow your plan. *Journal of Reality Therapy, 11,* 63–65.

Katz, L. Y., Cox, B. J., Gunasekara, S., & Miller, A. L. (2004). Feasibility of dialectical behavior therapy for suicidal adolescent inpatients. *Journal of the American Academy of Child and Adolescent Psychiatry, 43,* 276–282.

Kazdin, A. E. (1994). *Behavior modification in applied settings*. Pacific Grove, CA: Brooks/Cole.

Kazdin, A. E. (1997). Psychosocial treatments for conduct disorder in children. *Journal of Child Psychology and Psychiatry and Allied Professions, 38*(2), 161–178.

Kelly, E. W. (1997). Relationship-centered counseling: A humanistic model of integration. *Journal of Counseling & Development, 75,* 337–345.

Kelly, G. (1955). *The psychology of personal constructs.* New York: Norton.

Kelly, T. A., & Strupp, H. H. (1992). Patient and therapist values in psychotherapy: Perceived changes, assimilation, similarity and outcome. *Journal of Consulting and Clinical Psychology, 60,* 34–40.

Kelly, W. L. (1990). *Psychology of the unconscious: Mesmer, Janet, Freud, Jung, and current issues.* New York: Prometheus.

Kelsch, D. M. (2002). Multiple sclerosis and choice theory: It is a disease and choice theory works! *International Journal of Reality Therapy, 22*(1), 24–30.

Kensit, D. A. (2000). Rogerian theory: A critique of the effectiveness of pure client-centered therapy. *Counseling Psychology Quarterly, 13,* 345–351.

Kern, R. (1992). *Kern lifestyle scale.* Coral Springs, FL: CMTI Press.

Kern, R. M., Wheeler, M. S., & Curlette, W. L. (1997). *BASIS-A interpretive manual.* Coral Springs, FL: CMTI Press.

Kernberg, O. F. (1985). *Borderline conditions and pathological narcissism.* Northvale, NJ: Aronson.

Kernberg, O. F., & Clarkin, J. F. (1992). Treatment of personality disorders. *International Journal of Mental Health, 21,* 53–76.

Kim, B. H. (2002). Church as a self-object environment: A self-psychological psychoanalytic exploration of male members of two Korean immigrant congregations. *Dissertation Abstracts International, 62* (10-A). (UMI No. 3438)

Kirsch, T. B. (1996). A brief history of analytical psychology. *Psychoanalytic Review, 83,* 569–577.

Kirschenbaum, H. (2004). Carl Rogers's life and work: An assessment on the 100th anniversary of his birth. *Journal of Counseling and Development, 82,* 116–124.

Kivlighan, D. M., Patton, M. J., & Foote, D. (1998). Moderating effects of client attachment on the counselor experience-working alliance relationship. *Journal of Counseling Psychology, 45*(3), 274–278.

Kivlighan, D. M., & Schmitz, P. J. (1992). Counselor technical activity in cases with improving working alliances and continuing poor working alliances. *Journal of Counseling Psychology, 39,* 32–38.

Kleinke, C. L. (1994). *Common principles of therapy.* Pacific Grove, CA: Brooks/Cole.

Klerman, G. L., Weissman, M. M., Rounsaville, B. J., & Chevron, E. S. (1984). *Interpersonal psychotherapy of depression.* New York: Basic Books.

Knox, J. M. (2001). Memories, fantasies, archetypes: An exploration of some connections between cognitive science and analytical psychology. *Journal of Analytical Psychology, 46,* 613–635.

Knox, S., Hess, S. A., Petersen, D. A., & Hill, C. E. (1997). A qualitative analysis of client perceptions of the effects of helpful therapist self-disclosure in long-term therapy. *Journal of Counseling Psychology, 44,* 274–283.

Kohut, H. (1971). *The analysis of the self: A systematic approach to the psychoanalytic treatment of narcissistic personality disorders.* New York: International Universities Press.

Kohut, H. (1977). *The restoration of the self.* New York: International Universities Press.

Kohut, H. (1982). Introspection, empathy, and the semicircle of mental health. *International Journal of Psychoanalysis, 63,* 395–407.

Kohut, H. (1984). *How does analysis cure?* Chicago: University of Chicago Press.

Kohut, H., & Wolf, E. S. (1978). The disorders of the self and their treatment: An outline. *International Journal of Psychoanalysis, 59,* 413–425.

Kolden, G. G., Howard, K. I., & Maling, M. S. (1994). The counseling relationship and treatment process and outcome. *Counseling Psychologist, 22,* 82–89.

Korb, M. P., Gorrell, J., & Van de Riet, V. (1989). *Gestalt therapy: Practice and theory* (2nd ed.). New York: Pergamon.

Koss, M. P., & Butcher, J. N. (1986). Research on brief psychotherapy. In S. L. Garfield & A. E. Bergin (Eds.), *Handbook of psychotherapy and behavior change* (3rd ed., pp. 627–670). New York: Wiley.

Kottman, T., & Johnson, V. (1993). Adlerian play therapy: A tool for school counselors. *Elementary School Guidance and Counseling, 28,* 42–51.

Kropf, N. P., & Tandy, C. (1998). Narrative therapy with older clients: The use of a "meaning making" approach. *Clinical Gerontologist, 18,* 3–16.

Kubany, E. S., Owens, J. A., McCaig, M. A., Hill, E. E., Iannuce-Spencer, C., & Tremayne, K. J. (2004). Cognitive trauma therapy for battered women with PTSD (CTT-BW). *Journal of Consulting and Clinical Psychology, 72,* 3–18.

Lachmann, F. M. (1993). Self psychology: Origins and overview. *British Journal of Psychotherapy, 2,* 226–231.

Lachmann, F. M., & Beebe, B. (1995). Self psychology: Today. *Psychoanalysis Dialogues, 5,* 375–384.

Lafferty, P., Beutler, L. E., & Crago, M. (1989). Differences between more and less effective psychotherapists: A study of select therapist variables. *Journal of Consulting and Clinical Psychology, 57,* 76–80.

Lambert, M. J. (1992). Psychotherapy outcome research: Implications for integrative and eclectic therapists. In J. C. Norcross & M. R. Goldfried (Eds.), *Handbook of psychotherapy integration* (pp. 94–129). New York: Basic Books.

Lambert, M. J., & Bergin, A. E. (1994). The effectiveness of psychotherapy. In A. E. Bergin & S. L. Garfield (Eds.) *Handbook of psychotherapy and behavior change* (4th ed., pp. 143–189). New York: Wiley.

Lambert, M. J., & Cattani-Thompson, K. (1996). Current findings regarding the effectiveness of counseling: Implications for practice. *Journal of Counseling and Development, 74,* 601–608.

Lambert, M. J., & Ogles, B. M. (2004). The efficacy and effectiveness of psychotherapy. In M. Lambert (Ed.), *Bergin and Garfield's handbook of psychotherapy and behavior change* (pp. 139–193). New York: Wiley.

Lampropoulos, G. K. (2000). Definitional and research issues in the common factors approach to psychotherapy integration: Misconceptions, clarifications, and proposals. *Journal of Psychotherapy Integration, 10*(4), 415–438.

Landreth, G., Baggerly, J., & Tyndall-Lind, A. (1999). Beyond adapting adult counseling skills for use with children: The paradigm shift to child-centered play therapy. *The Journal of Individual Psychology, 55,* 273–287.

Lankton, S. R. (1980). *Practical magic: A translation of basic neurolinguistic programming into clinical psychotherapy.* Cupertino, CA: Meta.

Lantz, J. (2000). Phenomenological reflection and time in Viktor Frankl's existential psychotherapy. *Journal of Phenomenological Psychology, 3,* 220–228.

Lantz, J., & Gregoire, T. (2000). Existential psychotherapy with couples facing breast cancer: A twenty year report. *Contemporary Family Therapy, 29,* 315–327.

Lanza, M. L., Anderson, J., Boisvert, C. M., LeBlanc, A., Fardy, M., & Steel, B. S. (2002). Assaultive behavior intervention in the Veterans Administration: Psychodynamic group psychotherapy compared to cognitive behavior therapy. *Perspectives in Psychiatric Care, 38,* 89–97.

Lawe, C. F., Horne, A. M., & Taylor, S. V. (1983). Effects of pretraining procedures for clients in counseling. *Psychological Reports, 53,* 327–334.

Lazarus, A. A. (1976). *Multimodal behavior therapy.* New York: Springer.

Lazarus, A. A. (1981). *The practice of multimodal therapy.* New York: McGraw-Hill.

Lazarus, A. A. (Ed.). (1985). *Casebook of multimodal therapy.* New York: Guilford.

Lazarus, A. A. (1989). *The practice of multimodal therapy (update).* Baltimore: Johns Hopkins University Press.

Lazarus, A. A. (1997). *Brief but comprehensive psychotherapy.* New York: Springer.

Lazarus, A. A., & Beutler, L. E. (1993). On technical eclecticism. *Journal of Counseling and Development, 71*(4), 381–385.

Lee, C. W., Taylor, G., & Dunn, J. (1999). Factor structure of the schema questionnaire in a large clinical sample. *Cognitive Therapy and Research, 23,* 441–451.

Lee, J. (1997). Women re-authoring their lives through feminist narrative therapy. *Women and Therapy, 20,* 1–22.

Lega, L. I., & Ellis, A. (2001). Rational emotive behavior therapy (REBT) in the new millennium: A cross-cultural approach. *Journal of Rational-Emotive & Cognitive-Behavior Therapy, 19,* 201–222.

Lennon, B. (2003). Review: "Warning: Psychiatry can be hazardous to your mental health." *International Journal of Reality Therapy, 23*(1), 15–17.

Lesser, J. G. (2000). The group as self-object: Brief psychotherapy with women. *International Journal of Group Psychotherapy, 50,* 363–380.

Levant, R. F., Richmond, K., Sellars, A., Majors, R. G., Inclan, J. F., Rossello, J. M., et al. (2003). A multicultural investigation of masculinity ideology and alexithymia. *Psychology of Men & Masculinity, 4,* 91–99.

Levenson, E. A. (1992). Harry Stack Sullivan: From interpersonal psychiatry to interpersonal psychoanalysis. *Contemporary Psychoanalysis, 28,* 450–466.

Levenson, H. (2003). Time-limited dynamic psychotherapy: An integrationist perspective. *Journal of Psychotherapy Integration, 13,* 300–333.

Levenson, H., Butler, S. F., & Beitman, B. D. (1997). *Concise guide to brief dynamic psychotherapy.* Washington, DC: American Psychiatric Press.

Levenson, H., & Strupp, H. (1999). Recommendations for the future of training in brief dynamic psychotherapy. *Journal of Clinical Psychology, 55,* 385–391.

Lewis, E. (1992). Regaining promise: Feminist perspectives for social group work practice. *Social Work with Groups, 15,* 271–284.

Li, C. (1998). Impact of acculturation on Chinese-Americans' life and its implications for helping professionals. *International Journal of Reality Therapy, 17*(2), 7–11.

Linehan, M. M. (1993). *Skills training manual for treating borderline personality disorder.* New York: Guilford.

Linehan, M. M., & Kehrer, C. A. (1993). Borderline personality disorder. In D. A. Barlow (Ed.), *Clinical handbook of psychological disorders* (2nd ed., pp. 396–441). New York: Guilford.

Littrell, J., Malia, J., & Vanderwood, M. (1995). Single session brief counseling in a high school. *Journal of Counseling and Development, 73,* 451–458.

Livneh, H., & Sherwood, A. (1991). Application of personality theories and counseling strategies to clients with physical disabilities. *Journal of Counseling and Development, 69*(6), 525–538.

Lochman, J. E., White, K. J., & Wayland, K. W. (1991). Cognitive behavioral assessment and treatment with aggressive children. In P. C. Kendall (Ed.), *Child and adolescent therapy: Cognitive behavioral procedures* (pp. 25–65). New York: Guilford.

Locke, S. E., & Colligan, D. (1987). *The healer within.* New York: Mentor.

Lombardi, D. M. (1996). Antisocial personality disorder and addictions. In L. Sperry and J. Carlson (Eds.) *Psychopathology and psychotherapy* (pp. 371–390). Washington, DC: Accelerated Development.

Luborsky, L. (1984). *Principles of psychoanalytic psychotherapy: A manual for supportive-expressive treatment.* New York: Basic Books.

Luborsky, L., & Mark, D. (1991). Short term supportive-expressive psychoanalytic psychotherapy. In P. Crits-Cristoph & J. P. Barber (Eds.), *Handbook of short-term dynamic psychotherapy* (pp. 110–136). New York: Basic Books.

Luborsky, L., Singer, B., & Luborsky, L. (1975). Comparative studies of psychotherapies. *Archives of General Psychiatry, 32,* 995–1008.

Lundin, R. W. (1977). Behaviorism: Operant reinforcement. In R. J. Corsini (Ed.), *Current personality theories* (pp. 177–202). Itasca, IL: Peacock.

Lynch, G. (1997). The role of community and narrative in the work of the therapist: A post-modern theory of the therapist's engagement in the therapeutic process. *Counseling Psychology Quarterly, 10,* 33–363.

Lynch, V. (1991). The treatment process. In H. Jackson (Ed.), *Using self psychology in psychotherapy* (pp. 15–26). Northvale, NJ: Aronson.

Lyons, L. C., & Woods, P. J. (1991). The efficacy of rational-emotive therapy: A quantitative review of the outcome research. *Clinical Psychology Review, 11,* 357–369.

MacGeorge, E. L. (2003). Gender differences in attributions and emotions in helping contexts. *Sex Roles, 49,* 175–182.

Mahalik, J. R., Good, G. E., & Englar-Carlson, M. (2003). Masculinity scripts, presenting concerns, and help seeking: Implications for practice and training. *Professional Psychology: Research and Practice, 34,* 123–131.

Mahoney, M. J. (1988a). Constructive metatheory. I: Basic features and historical foundations. *International Journal of Personal Construct Psychology, I,* 1–35.

Mahoney, M. J. (1988b). Constructive metatheory. II: Implications for psychotherapy. *Journal of Consulting and Clinical Psychology, 61,* 299–315.

Mahoney, M. J. (2003). *Constructive psychotherapy.* New York: Guilford.

Mahoney, P. J. (1998). Freud's world of work. In M. S. Roth (Ed.), *Freud: Conflict and culture* (pp. 32–40). New York: Knopf.

Manfield, P. (1998) *Extending EMDR.* New York: Norton.

Mann, J., & Goldman, R. (1982). *A casebook in time-limited psychotherapy.* New York: McGraw Hill.

Mascher, J (2002). Narrative therapy: Inviting the use of sport as metaphor. *Women and Therapy, 25,* 57–74.

Maslow, A. (1954). *Motivation and personality.* New York: Harper & Row.

Maslow, A. (1968). *Toward a psychology of being* (2nd ed.). New York: Van Nostrand.

Maslow, A. (1971). *The farther reaches of human nature.* New York: Penguin.

Massey, R. F. (1995). Theory for treating individuals from a transactional analytic/systems perspective. *Transactional Analysis Journal, 25*(3), 271–284.

Matlin, M. (1996). *The psychology of women.* Orlando, FL: Harcourt Brace.

Matthews, W. J., & Edgette, J. H. (Eds.). (1997). *Current thinking and research in brief therapy: Solutions, strategies, narratives (Vol. 1).* New York: Brunner/Mazel.

Maultsby, M. C., Jr. (1984). *Rational behavior therapy.* Upper Saddle River, NJ: Prentice Hall.

May, R. (1950). *The meaning of anxiety.* New York: Dell.

May, R. (1969). *Love and will.* New York: Norton.

May, R. (1981). *Freedom and destiny.* New York: Norton.

May, R. (1990a). On the phenomenological bases of therapy. *Review of Existential Psychology and Psychiatry, 20,* 49–61.

May, R. (1990b). Will, decision and responsibility. *Review of Existential Psychology and Psychiatry, 20,* 269–278.

May, R., Angel, E., & Ellenberger, H. F. (Eds.). (1958). *Existence: A new dimension in psychiatry and psychology.* New York: Simon & Schuster.

May, R., & Yalom, I. (1995). Existential psychotherapy. In R. J. Corsini & D. Wedding (Eds.), *Current psychotherapies* (5th ed., pp. 262–292). Itasca, IL: Peacock.

Mayes, L. C., & Cohen, D. J. (1996). Anna Freud and developmental psychoanalytic psychology. *Psychoanalytic Study of the Child, 51,* 117–141.

McCallum, M., Piper, W. E., & Joyce, A. S. (1992). Dropping out from short-term group therapy. *Psychotherapy, 29,* 206–215.

McClendon, R., & Kadis, L. B. (1995). Redecision therapy: On the leading edge. *Transactional Analysis Journal, 25*(4), 339–342.

McClure, F. H., & Teyber, E. (Eds.). (1996). *Child and adolescent therapy: A multicultural-relational approach.* Fort Worth, TX: Harcourt Brace.

McDonald, M. (1996). A midwife of souls. *Maclean's, 109,* 58–61.

McNally, R. J. (2001). Tertullian's motto and Callahan's method. *Journal of Clinical Psychology, 57,* 1171–1174.

McWilliams, J., & McWilliams, P. (1991). *You can't afford the luxury of a negative thought.* Los Angeles, CA: Prelude.

Meares, R. (1996). The psychology of self: An update. *Australian and New Zealand Journal of Psychiatry, 30,* 312–316.

Meichenbaum, D. (1985). *Stress inoculation training.* Elmsford, NY: Pergamon.

Meichenbaum, D. (1993). Changing conceptions of cognitive behavior modification: Retrospect and prospect. *Journal of Consulting and Clinical Psychology, 61*(2), 202–204.

Merrill, K. A., Tolbert, V. E., & Wade, W. A. (2003). Effectiveness of cognitive therapy for depression in a community mental health center: A benchmarking study. *Journal of Consulting and Clinical Psychology, 71,* 404–409.

Mesquita, B., & Walder, R. (2002). Cultural differences in emotions: A context for interpreting emotional experiences. *Behaviour Research and Therapy, 41,* 777–793.

Messer, S. B. (2001). What makes brief psychodynamic therapy time efficient? *Clinical Psychology: Science & Practice, 8,* 5–22.

Messer, S. B., & Warren, S. (1995). *Models of brief psychodynamic therapy.* New York: Guilford.

Metcalf, L. (1998). *Solution focused group therapy: Ideas for groups in private practice, schools, agencies, and treatment programs.* New York: Free Press.

Miars, R. D. (2002). Existential authenticity: A foundational value for counseling. *Counseling and Values, 46,* 218–226.

Miccolis, G. (1996). Sociocultural influences in the theory of Karen Horney. *American Journal of Psychoanalysis, 56,* 141–147.

Miller, C. A., & Capuzzi, D. (1984). A review of transactional analysis outcome studies. *American Mental Health Counselors Association Journal, 6*(1), 30–41.

Miller, N. E., & Dollard, J. (1941). *Social learning and imitation.* New Haven, CT: Yale.

Miller, S., Duncan, B., & Hubble, M (1997). *Escape from Babel: Toward a unifying language for psychotherapy practice.* New York: Norton.

Miller, S., Hubble, M., & Duncan, B. (1996). *Handbook of solution-focused brief therapy.* San Francisco: Jossey-Bass.

Miller, W. R., & Rollnick, S. (2002). *Motivational interviewing: Preparing people for change* (2nd ed.). New York: Guilford.

Milliren, A., & Barrett-Kruse, C. (2002). Four phases of Adlerian counseling: Family resilience in action. *Journal of Individual Psychology, 58,* 225–234.

Minuchin, S., & Fishman, H. C. (1981). *Family therapy techniques.* Cambridge, MA: Harvard University Press.

Miranda, J., Chung, J. Y., Green, B. L., Krupnick, J., Siddique, J., Revicki, D. A., et al. (2003). Treating depression in predominantly low-income young minority women: A randomized controlled trial. *The Journal of the American Medical Association, 290,* 57–65.

Mitchell, S. A. (1986). Roots and status. *Contemporary Psychoanalysis, 22,* 458–466.

Monk, G. (1997). How narrative therapy works. In G. Monk, J. Winslade, K. Crocket, & D. Epston (Eds.), *Narrative therapy in practice: The archaeology of hope* (pp. 3–31). San Francisco: Jossey-Bass.

Moorey, S., & Greer, S. (1989). *Psychological therapy for patients with cancer: A new approach.* Washington, DC: American Psychiatric Press.

Mosak, H. H. (1971). Lifestyle. In A. G. Nikelly (Ed.), *Techniques for behavior change* (pp. 77–84). Springfield, IL: C. C. Thomas.

Mosak, H. H., & Goldman, S. E. (1995). An alternative view of the purpose of psychosis. *Individual Psychology, 48,* 319–323.

Moss, D. P. (1992). Cognitive therapy, phenomenology, and the struggle for meaning. *Journal of Phenomenological Psychology, 23*(1), 87–102.

Mottern, R. (2002). Using choice theory in coerced treatment for substance abuse. *International Journal of Reality Therapy, 22*(1), 20–24.

Mottern, R. (2003). Using the rule of six and traditional American Indian learning stories to teach choice theory. *International Journal of Reality Therapy, 23*(1), 27–34.

Mozdzierz, G. T., Lisiecki, J., Bitter, J. R., & Williams, A. L. (1986). Role functions for Adlerian therapists. *Individual Psychology, 42*(2), 154–177.

Mueller, R. O., Dupuy, P. J., & Hutchine, D. E. (1994). A review of the TFA counseling system: From theory construction to application. *Journal of Counseling and Development, 72*(6), 573–577.

Mulder, C. L., Emmelkamp, P. M. G., Antoni, M. H., Mulder, J. W., Sandfort, T. G. M., & de Vries, M. J. (1994). Cognitive-behavioral and experiential group psychotherapy for asymptomatic HIV-infected homosexual men: A comparative study. *Psychosomatic Medicine, 3,* 271–288.

Murphy, L. (1997). Efficacy of reality therapy in schools: A review of the research from 1980–1995. *Journal of Reality Therapy, 16*(2), 12–20.

Myers, I. B. (1998). *Introduction to type* (6th ed.). Palo Alto, CA: Consulting Psychologists Press.

Myers, I. B., McCaulley, M. H., Quenk, N. L., & Hammer, A. L. (1994). *MBTI manual* (3rd ed.). Palo Alto, CA: Consulting Psychologists Press.

Myers, J. E., Shoffner, M. F., & Briggs, M. K. (2002). Developmental counseling and therapy: An effective approach to understanding and counseling children. *Professional School Counseling, 5*(3), 194–202.

Myers, L. L., & Thyer, B. A. (1994). Behavioral therapy: Popular misconceptions. *Scandinavian Journal of Behavior Therapy, 23,* 97–107.

Najavits, L. M., & Strupp, H. H. (1994). Differences in the effectiveness of psychodynamic therapists: A process-outcome study. *Psychotherapy, 31*(1), 114–123.

Najavits, L. M., & Weiss, R. D. (1994). Variations in therapist effectiveness in the treatment of patients with substance use disorders: An empirical view. *Addiction, 89,* 679–688.

Nance, D. W., & Myers, P. (1991). Continuing the eclectic journey. *Journal of Mental Health Counseling, 13*(1), 119–130.

Neenan, M., & Dryden, W. (1996). The intricacies of inference chaining. *Journal of Rational-Emotive and Cognitive-Behavior Therapy, 14*(4), 231–243.

Neimeyer, G. J., & Neimeyer, R. A. (1994). Constructivist methods of marital and family therapy: A practical precis. *Journal of Mental Health Counseling, 16,* 85–104.

Neimeyer, R. A. (1993). An appraisal of constructivist psychotherapies. *Journal of Consulting and Clinical Psychology, 61,* 221–234.

Neimeyer, R. A., & Stewart, A. E. (1996). Trauma, healing, and the narrative emplotment of loss. *Families in Society, 77*(6), 360–375.

Neukrug, E. S., & Williams, G. T. (1993). Counseling counselors: A survey of values. *Counseling and Values, 38,* 51–62.

Nicholson, B. L. (1991). The treatment process. In H. Jackson (Ed.), *Using self psychology in psychotherapy* (pp. 27–50). Northvale, NJ: Aronson.

Nicoll, W. G. (1994). Developing effective classroom guidance programs: An integrative framework. *School Counselor, 41,* 360–364.

Nielsen, S. L., & Ellis, A. (1994). A discussion with Albert Ellis: Reason, emotion and religion. *Journal of Psychology and Christianity, 13*(4), 327–341.

Norcross, J. C. (Ed.). (2002). *Psychotherapy relationships that work.* New York: Oxford.

Norcross, J. C., & Goldfried, M. R. (Eds.). (1992). *Handbook of psychotherapy integration.* New York: Basic Books.

O'Connell, B. (1998). *Solution-focused therapy.* London: Sage Publications.

Odell, M., & Quinn, W. H. (1998). Therapist and client behaviors in the first interview: Effects on session impact and treatment duration. *Journal of Marital and Family Therapy, 24,* 369–388.

O'Hanlon, B., & Bertolino, B. (1998). *Even from a broken web.* New York: Wiley.

O'Hanlon, B., & Weiner-Davis, M. (1989). *In search of solutions: A new direction in psychotherapy.* New York: Norton.

Orgler, H. (1963). *Alfred Adler: The man and his works.* New York: Liveright.

Orlinsky, D. E., Grawe, K., & Parks, B. K. (1994). Process and outcome in psychotherapy—noch einmal. In B. A. Garfield & S. L. Garfield (Eds.) *Handbook of psychotherapy and behavior change* (4th ed., pp. 270–276). New York: Wiley.

Osborn, C. J. (1999). Solution-focused strategies with "involuntary" clients: Practical applications for the school and clinical setting. *Journal of Humanistic Education & Development, 37*(3), 169–182.

Paris, B. J. (1994). *Karen Horney: A psychoanalyst's search for self understanding.* New Haven, CT: Yale University Press.

Paris, B. J. (1996). Introduction to Karen Horney. *American Journal of Psychoanalysis, 56,* 135–140.

Parker, G., Roy, K., & Eyers, K. (2003). Cognitive behavior therapy for depression? Choose horses for courses. *The American Journal of Psychiatry, 160,* 825–834.

Parker, W. D. (1998). Birth-order effects in the academically talented. *Gifted Children Quarterly, 42,* 29–38.

Parry, A., & Doan, R. E. (1994). *Story re-vision: Narrative therapy in the post-modern world.* New York: Guilford.

Paul, G. L. (1967). Strategy of outcome research in psychotherapy. *Journal of Consulting Psychology, 31,* 109–118.

Paulson, B., Truscott, C., & Stuart, J. (1999). Clients' perceptions of helpful experiences in counseling. *Journal of Counseling Psychology, 46,* 317–324.

Pavlov, I. P. (1927). *Conditioned reflexes* (G. V. Anrep, Trans.) London: Oxford University Press.

Pavuluri, M. N., Graczyk, P. A., Henry, D. B., Carbray, J. A., Heidenreich, J., & Miklowitz, D. J. (2003). Child- and family-focused cognitive behavioral therapy for pediatric bipolar disorder: Development and preliminary results. *Journal of the American Academy of Child and Adolescent Psychiatry, 43,* 528–537.

Perkins, D. (1999, November). The many faces of constructivism. *Educational Leadership,* pp. 6–11.

Perls, F. (1969a). *Gestalt therapy verbatim.* Lafayette, CA: Real Person Press.

Perls, F. (1969b). *In and out of the garbage pail.* Lafayette, CA: Real Person Press.

Perls, F., Hefferline, R. F., & Goodman, P. (1951). *Gestalt therapy: Excitement and growth in the human personality.* New York: Julian.

Perls, L. (1992). Concepts and misconceptions of Gestalt therapy. *Journal of Humanistic Psychology, 32,* 50–56.

Persons, J. B. (1989). *Cognitive therapy in practice.* New York: Norton.

Petersen, S., & Benishek, L. A. (2001). Social construction of illness: Addressing the impact of cancer on women in therapy. *Women & Therapy, 23,* 75–100.

Petrocelli, J. V. (2002). Processes and stages of change: Counseling with the transtheoretical model of change. *Journal of Counseling and Development, 80*(1), 22–30.

Pierce, J. (2003). Mindfulness based reality therapy. *International Journal of Reality Therapy, 23*(1), 20–24.

Pike, K. M., Walsh, B. T., Vitousek, K., Wilson, G. T., & Bauer, J. (2003). Cognitive behavior therapy in the posthospitalization treatment of anorexia nervosa. *The American Journal of Psychiatry, 160,* 2046–2049.

Pikus, C. F., & Heavey, C. L. (1996). Client preferences for therapist gender. *Journal of College Student Psychotherapy, 10,* 35–43.

Poidevant, J. M., & Lewis, H. A. (1995). Transactional analysis theory. In D. Capuzzi & D. R. Gross (Eds.), *Counseling and psychotherapy: Theories and interventions* (pp. 297–324). Upper Saddle River, NJ: Merrill/Prentice Hall.

Polster, E., & Polster, M. (1973). *Gestalt therapy integrated.* New York: Brunner/Mazel.

Polster, E., & Polster, M. (1993). Fritz Perls: Legacy and invitation. *Gestalt Journal, 16,* 23–25.

Powers, R. L., & Griffith, J. (1986). *Individual psychology client workbook.* Chicago, IL: American Institute of Adlerian Studies.

Powers, R. L., & Griffith, J. (1987). *Understanding life-style.* Chicago: American Institute of Adlerian Studies.

Powers, W. T. (1973). *Behavior: The control of perception.* Chicago: Aldine.

Prochaska, J. O., & DiClemente, C. C. (1986). The transtheoretical approach. In J. C. Norcross (Ed.), *Handbook of eclectic psychotherapy* (pp. 163–200). New York: Brunner/Mazel.

Prochaska, J. O., & Norcross, J. C. (2003). *Systems of psychotherapy: A transtheoretical analysis* (5th ed.). Pacific Grove, CA: Brooks/Cole.

Proner, B. (2002). Contemporary transference work and the analytic attitude: Aims and methods—a clinical workshop. *Journal of Analytical Psychology, 47,* 383–395.

Rapport, M. D. (1995). Attention-deficit hyperactivity disorder. In M. Hersen & R. T. Ammerman (Eds.), *Advanced abnormal child psychology* (pp. 353–375). Hillsdale, NJ: Erlbaum.

Raue, P. J., Goldfried, M. R., & Barkham, M. (1997). The therapeutic alliance in psychodynamic-interpersonal and cognitive-behavioral therapy. *Journal of Consulting and Clinical Psychology, 65,* 582–587.

Reis, B. G., & Brown, L. G. (1999). Reducing psychotherapy dropouts: Maximizing perspective convergence in the psychotherapy dyad. *Psychotherapy, 36,* 123–126.

Reker, G. T. (1994). Logotheory and logotherapy: Challenges, opportunities, and some empirical findings. *International Forum for Logotherapy, 17,* 47–55.

Richert, A. J. (2003). Living stories, telling stories, changing stories: Experiential use of the relationship in narrative therapy. *Journal of Psychotherapy Integration, 13,* 188–210.

Rigazio-DiGilio, S. A. (1994). A co-constructive-developmental approach to ecosystemic treatment. *Journal of Mental Health Counseling, 16*(1), 43–74.

Rigazio-DiGilio, S. A., Goncalves, O. F., & Ivey, A. E. (1995). Developmental counseling and therapy: Integrating individual and family theory. In D. Capuzzi & D. R. Gross (Eds.), *Counseling and psychotherapy: Theories and interventions* (pp. 471–513). Upper Saddle River, NJ: Merrill/Prentice Hall.

Rigazio-DiGilio, S. A., & Ivey, A. E. (1991). Developmental counseling and therapy: A framework for individual and family treatment. *Counseling and Human Development, 24,* 11.

Rigazio-DiGilio, S. A., Ivey, A. E., Ivey, M. B., & Simek-Morgan, L. (1997). Developmental counseling and therapy: Individual and family therapy. In A. E. Ivey, M. B. Ivey, & L. Simek-Morgan (Eds.), *Counseling and psychotherapy: A multicultural perspective* (pp. 89–129). Needham Heights, MA: Allyn & Bacon.

Roazen, P. (1985). Helene Deutsch's feminism. *Psychohistory Review, 13,* 26–32.

Roberts, R. L., Harper, R., Caldwell, R., & Decora, M. (2003). Adlerian lifestyle analysis of Lakota women: Implications for counseling. *Journal of Individual Psychology, 59,* 15–29.

Robertson, M. (1979). Some observations from an eclectic therapy. *Psychotherapy, 16,* 18–21.

Rogers, C. R. (1942). *Counseling and psychotherapy.* Boston: Houghton-Mifflin.

Rogers, C. R. (1951). *Client-centered therapy: Its current practice, implications and theory.* Boston: Houghton-Mifflin.

Rogers, C. R. (1955). Person or science? A philosophical question. *American Psychology, 10,* 267–278.

Rogers, C. R. (1959). A theory of therapy, personality, and individual relationships as developed in the client-centered framework. In S. Koch (Ed.), *Psychology: A study of a science* (pp. 184–256). New York: McGraw-Hill.

Rogers, C. R. (1961). *On becoming a person.* Boston: Houghton Mifflin.

Rogers, C. R. (1967). The conditions of change from a client-centered viewpoint. In B. Berenson & R. Carkhuff (Eds.), *Sources of gain in counseling and psychotherapy.* New York: Holt, Rinehart, & Winston.

Rogers, C. R. (1970). *Carl Rogers on encounter groups.* New York: Harper & Row.

Rogers, C. R. (1980). *A way of being.* Boston: Houghton Mifflin.

Rogers, C. R. (1987). Our international family. *Person-Centered Review, 2,* 139–149.

Rossano, F. (1996). Psychoanalysis and psychiatric institutions: Theoretical and clinical spaces of the Horney approach. *American Journal of Psychoanalysis, 56,* 203–212.

Roth, M. S. (Ed.) (1998). *Freud: Conflict and culture.* New York: Knopf.

Rowen, T., & O'Hanlon, B. (1999). *Solution-oriented therapy for chronic and severe mental illness.* New York: Wiley.

Rubin, T. L. (1991). Horney, here and now: 1991. *American Journal of Psychoanalysis, 51,* 313–318.

Sabourin, S., Gendreau, P., & Frenette, L. (1987). The satisfaction level of drop-out cases in a university psychology service. *Canadian Journal of Behavioral Science, 19,* 314–323.

Sanchez, W., & Garriga, O. (1996). Control theory, reality therapy and cultural fatalism: Toward an integration. *Journal of Reality Therapy, 15*(2), 30–38.

Sandler, A. (1996). The psychoanalytic legacy of Anna Freud. *Psychoanalytic Study of the Child, 51,* 270–284.

Sandler, J., & Freud, A. (1985). *The analysis of defense: The ego and the mechanisms of defense revisited.* New York: International Universities Press.

Sands, T. (1998). Feminist counseling and female adolescents: Treatment strategies for depression. *Journal of Mental Health Counseling, 20,* 42–54.

Saner, R. (1989). Cultural bias of Gestalt therapy: Made-in-U.S.A. *Gestalt Journal, 12,* 57–71.

Sapp, M. (1994). Cognitive-behavioral counseling: Applications for African-American middle school students who are academically at risk. *Journal of Instructional Psychology, 21*(2), 161–171.

Sapp, M. (1997). *Counseling and psychotherapy.* Lanham, MD: University Press of America.

Sayers, J. (1991). *Mothers of psychoanalysis: Helene Deutsch, Karen Horney, Anna Freud, Melanie Klein.* New York: Norton.

Schafer, R. (1994). The contemporary Kleinians of London. *Psychoanalytic Quarterly, 63,* 409–432.

Scharff, J. S. (1989). Play with young children in family therapy: An extension of the therapist's holding capacity. *Journal of Psychotherapy and the Family, 5,* 159–172.

Scharff, J. S., & Scharff, D. E. (1992). *Scharff notes: A primer of object relations therapy.* Northvale, NJ: Aronson.

Schatz, A. M. (1995). School reform and restructuring through the use of "quality school" philosophy. *Journal of Reality Therapy, 14*(2), 23–28.

Schwartz, J. P., & Waldo, M. (2003). Interpersonal manifestations of lifestyle: Individual psychology integrated with interpersonal theory. *Journal of Mental Health Counseling, 25*(2), 101–108.

Schwartz, S. E. (1995). Jungian analytic theory. In D. Capuzzi & D. R. Gross (Eds.), *Counseling and psychotherapy: Theories and interventions.* Upper Saddle River, NJ: Merrill/Prentice Hall.

Schwartzberg, S. S. (1993). Struggling for meaning: How HIV-positive gay men make sense of AIDS. *Professional Psychology, 24,* 483–490.

Sedgwick, D. (2001). *Introduction to Jungian therapy.* New York: Brunner-Routledge.

Seeman, J. (1990). Theory as autobiography. *Person-Centered Review, 5,* 373–386.

Seibel, C. A., & Dowd, E. T. (1999). Reactance and therapeutic noncompliance. *Cognitive Therapy and Research, 23,* 373–379.

Seligman, L. (1994). *Developmental career counseling and assessment.* Thousand Oaks, CA: Sage.

Seligman, L. (1996a). *Diagnosis and treatment planning* (2nd ed.). New York: Plenum.

Seligman, L. (1996b). *Promoting a fighting spirit: Psychotherapy for cancer patients, survivors, and their families.* San Francisco: Jossey-Bass.

Seligman, L. (1998). *Selecting effective treatments.* San Francisco: Jossey-Bass.

Seligman, L. (2004a). *Diagnosis and treatment planning in counseling* (3rd ed.). New York: Kluwer/Plenum.

Seligman, L. (2004b). *Technical and conceptual skills for mental health professionals.* Upper Saddle River, NJ: Merrill/Prentice-Hall.

Seligman, M. E. P. (1990). *Learned optimism.* New York: Pocket Books.

Seligman, M. E. P. (1995). The effectiveness of psychotherapy. *American Psychologist, 50*(12), 965–974.

Serlin, I. (1992). Tribute to Laura Perls. *Journal of Humanistic Psychology, 32,* 57–66.

Sexton, T. L. (1995a). Outcome research perspective on mental health counselor competencies. In M. K. Altekruse & T. L. Sexton (Eds.), *Mental health counseling in the 90's* (pp. 51–60). Tampa, FL: National Commission for Mental Health Counseling.

Sexton, T. L. (1995b). Competency survey results. In M. K. Altekruse & T. L. Sexton (Eds.), *Mental health counseling in the 90's* (pp. 25–44). Tampa, FL: National Commission for Mental Health Counseling.

Sexton, T. L., & Whiston, S. C. (1991). A review of the empirical basis for counseling: Implications for practice and training: *Counselor Education and Supervision, 30,* 330–354.

Shainess, M. (1978). Reflections on the contributions of Harry Stack Sullivan. *American Journal of Psychoanalysis, 38,* 301–315.

Shapiro, F. (1989). Efficacy of eye movement desensitization procedures in the treatment of traumatic memories. *Journal of Traumatic Stress, 2,* 199–223.

Shapiro, F. (1994). *Level II: Training manual.* Pacific Grove, CA: EMDR Institute.

Shapiro, F. (1995). *Eye movement desensitization and reprocessing.* New York: Guilford.

Shapiro, F. (2001). *Eye movement desensitization and reprocessing: Basic principles, protocols and procedures* (2nd ed.). New York: Guilford Press.

Shapiro, F. (2002). EMDR and the role of the clinician in psychotherapy evaluation: Towards a more comprehensive integration of science and practice. *Journal of Clinical Psychology, 58,* 1453–1463.

Shapiro, F., & Forrest, M. (1997). *EMDR: The breakthrough therapy for overcoming anxiety, stress and trauma.* New York: Basic Books.

Sharry, J., Darmody, M., & Madden, B. (2002). A solution-focused approach to working with clients who are suicidal. *British Journal of Guidance and Counselling, 30*(4), 383–399.

Sheldon, K. M., Arndt, J., & Houser-Marko, L. (2003). In search of the organismic valuing process: The human tendency to move towards beneficial goal choices. *Journal of Personality, 71,* 835–869.

Sherman, R., & Nwaorgu, A. (2002). Adlerian therapy: A century of tradition and research. In F. W. Kaslow (Ed.), *Comprehensive handbook of psychotherapy: Interpersonal/humanistic/existential.* New York: John Wiley & Sons.

Sherwood-Hawes, A. (1995). Nontraditional approaches to counseling and psychotherapy. In D. Capuzzi & D. R. Gross (Eds.), *Counseling and psychotherapy: Theories and interventions* (pp. 517–556). Upper Saddle River, NJ: Merrill/Prentice-Hall.

Shulman, B. H., & Mosak, H. H. (1988). *Manual for life style assessment.* Muncie, IN: Accelerated Development.

Siegel, B. S. (1990). *Peace, love, and healing.* New York: HarperCollins.

Siegel, L. I. (1987). Sullivan's conceptual contributions to child psychiatry. *Contemporary Psychoanalysis, 23,* 278–298.

Sifneos, P. E. (1979a). *Short-term dynamic psychotherapy: Evaluation and technique.* New York: Plenum.

Sifneos, P. E. (1979b). *Short-term psychotherapy and emotional crisis.* Cambridge, MA: Harvard University Press.

Sifneos, P. E. (1984). The current status of individual short-term dynamic psychotherapy and its future: An overview. *American Journal of Psychotherapy, 38*(4), 472–483.

Silverman, W. H., & Beech, R. P. (1979). Are dropouts, dropouts? *Journal of Community Psychology, 7,* 236–242.

Simkin, J. S. (1975). An introduction to Gestalt therapy. In F. C. Stephenson (Ed.), *Geltalt therapy primer: Introductory readings in Gestalt therapy* (p. 3–12). Springfield, IL: C. C. Thomas.

Skinner, B. F. (1969). *Contingencies of reinforcement: A theoretical analysis.* New York: Appleton-Century-Crofts.

Smith, J. C. (1986). *Meditation.* Champaign, IL: Research Press.

Smith, L. D., & Peck, P. L. (2004). Dialectical behavior therapy: A review and call to research. *Journal of Mental Health Counseling, 26,* 25–39.

Smith, M. L., Glass, G. V., & Miller, T. I. (1980). *The benefits of psychotherapy.* Baltimore: Johns Hopkins University Press.

Snarey, J., Son, L., Kuehne, V. S., Hauser, S., & Valliant, G. (1987). The role of parenting in men's psychosocial development: A longitudinal study of early adulthood infertility and midlife generativity. *Developmental Psychology, 23,* 593–603.

Solnit, S. J. (1983). Anna Freud's contributions to child and applied analysis. *International Journal of Psycho-Analysis, 64,* 379–390.

Solnit, S. J. (1997). A legacy: Anna Freud's views on childhood and development. *Child Psychiatry and Human Development, 28,* 5–14.

Solomon, A., & Haaga, D. A. F. (1995). Rational emotive behavior therapy research: What we know and what we need to know. *Journal of Rational-Emotive and Cognitive-Behavior Therapy, 13*(3), 179–191.

Sperry, L., & Carlson, J. (1996). *Psychopathology and psychotherapy.* Washington, DC: Accelerated Development.

Stafford-Clark, D. (1965). *What Freud really said.* New York: Schocken.

Stalker, C. A., Levene, J. E., & Coady, N. F. (1999). Solution-focused brief therapy—one model fits all? *Families in Society: The Journal of Contemporary Human Services, 80,* 468–489.

Starr, A. (1973). Sociometry of the family. In H. H. Mosak (Ed.), *Alfred Adler: His influence on psychology today* (pp. 95–105). Park Ridge, NJ: Noyes.

Stehno, J. T. (1995). Classroom consulting with reality therapy. *Journal of Reality Therapy, 15*(1), 81–86.

Stein, B. C., Jayoux, L. H., Kataoka, S. H., Wong, M., Tu, W., Elliott, M. N., et al. (2003). A mental health intervention for school children exposed to violence. *Journal of the American Medical Association, 290,* 603–611.

Sterman, C. M. (1990). Neuro-linguistic programming as a conceptual base for the treatment of alcoholism. In C. M. Sterman (Ed.), *Neuro-linguistic programming in alcoholism treatment* (pp. 11–25). New York: Hawthorn.

Stiles, W. B., Startup, M., Hardy, G. E., Barkam, M., Rees, A., Shapiro, D. A., et al. (1996). Therapist intentions in cognitive-behavioral and psychodynamic-interpersonal psychotherapy. *Journal of Counseling Psychology, 43,* 402–414.

Stozier, C. (1985). Glimpses of life: Heinz Kohut (1913–1981). In A. Goldberg (Ed.), *Progress in self psychology* (pp. 3–12). New York: Guilford.

Strauch, I. (2001). An Adlerian reconceptualization of traumatic reactions. *Journal of Individual Psychology, 57,* 246–258.

Strean, H. S. (1994). *Essentials of psychoanalysis.* New York: Brunner/Mazel.

Strumpfel, U., & Goldman, R. (2002). Contacting Gestalt therapy. In D. J. Cain & J. Seeman (Eds.), *Humanistic psychotherapies: Handbook of research and practice* (pp. 189–219). Washington, DC: American Psychological Association.

Strupp, H. H. (1992). The future of psychodynamic psychotherapy. *Psychotherapy, 29*(1), 21–27.

Stuart, R. B. (1998). Updating behavior therapy with couples. *Family Journal, 6*(1), 6–12.

Sullivan, H. S. (1947). *Conceptions of modern psychiatry.* Washington, DC: William Alanson White Institute.

Sullivan, H. S. (1953). *The interpersonal theory of psychiatry.* New York: Norton.

Sullivan, H. S. (1954). *The psychiatric interview.* New York: Norton.

Summers, F. (1993). Implications of object relations theories for the psychoanalytic process. *Annual of Psychoanalysis, 21,* 225–242.

Sweeney, T. J. (1998). *Adlerian counseling: A practitioner's approach* (4th ed.). Philadelphia: Taylor & Francis.

Symonds, A. (1991). Gender issues and Horney theory. *American Journal of Psychoanalysis, 51,* 301–312.

Tallman, K., & Bohart, A. C. (1999). The client as a common factor: Clients as self-healers. In M. A. Hubble, B. L. Duncan, & S. D. Miller (Eds.), *The heart and soul of change: What works in therapy* (pp. 91–131). Washington, DC: American Psychological Association.

Talmon, M. (1990). *Single session therapy.* San Francisco: Jossey-Bass.

Tart, C. T. (1992). *Transpersonal therapies.* San Francisco: HarperCollins.

Taylor, S., Thordarson, D. S., Fedoroff, I. C., Maxfield, L., Lovell, K., & Ogrodniczuk, J. (2003). Comparative efficacy, speed, and adverse effects of three PTSD treatments: Exposure therapy, EMDR, and relaxation training. *Journal of Consulting and Clinical Psychology, 71,* 330–338.

Thomas, K. R., & Garske, G. (1995). Object relations theory: Implications for the personality development and treatment of persons with disabilities. *Melanie Klein and Object Relations, 13,* 31–63.

Thomas, M. B. (1992). *An introduction to marital and family therapy.* New York: Macmillan.

Thompson, N. (1987). Helene Deutsch: A life theory. *Psychoanalytic Quarterly, 56,* 317–353.

Thompson, R. A. (1996). *Counseling techniques.* Washington, DC: Accelerated Development.

Thorpe, G. L., & Olson, S. L. (1997). *Behavior therapy.* Needham Heights, MA: Allyn & Bacon.

Tillich, P. (1961). Existentialism and psychotherapy. *Review of Existential Psychology and Psychiatry, 1,* 8–16, 39–47.

Tinker, R., & Wilson, W. (1999). *Through the eyes of a child.* New York: Norton.

Tori, C. D., & Bilmes, M. (2002). Multiculturalism and psychoanalytic psychology: The validation of a defense mechanisms measure in an Asian population. *Psychoanalytic Psychology, 19,* 701–721.

Tuckey, M. R., & Brewer, N. (2003). The influence of schemas, stimulus ambiguity, and interview schedule on eyewitness memory over time. *Journal of Experimental Psychology: Applied, 9,* 101–118.

Tyson, P., & Tyson, L. L. (1990). *Psychoanalytic theories of development: An integration.* New Haven: Yale University Press.

Van Etten, M. L., & Taylor, S. (1998). Comparative efficacy of treatments for posttraumatic stress disorder: A meta-analysis. *Clinical Psychology and Psychotherapy, 5,* 126–144.

Van Wagoner, S. L., Gelso, C. J., Hayes, J. A., & Diemer, R. A. (1991). Countertransference and the reputedly excellent therapist. *Psychotherapy, 28,* 411–421.

Vernon, A. (1989a). *Thinking, feeling, behaving: An emotional education curriculum for adolescents: Grades 7–12.* Champaign, IL: Research Press.

Vernon, A. (1989b). *Thinking, feeling, behaving: An emotional education curriculum for children: Grades 1–6.* Champaign, IL: Research Press.

Wachtel, P. L. (1977). *Psychoanalysis and behavior therapy: Toward an integration.* New York: Basic Books.

Wachtel, P. L. (1987). *Action and insight.* New York: Guilford.

Wachtel, P. L. (1990). Psychotherapy from an integrative psychodynamic perspective. In J. K. Zeig & W. M. Munion (Eds.), *What is psychotherapy?* (pp. 234–238). San Francisco: Jossey-Bass.

Wachtel, P. L. (2002). Psychoanalysis and the disenfranchised: From therapy to justice. *Psychoanalytic Psychology, 19*(1), 199–215.

Walborn, F. S. (1996). *Process variables.* Pacific Grove, CA: Brooks/Cole.

Walen, S. R., DiGiuseppe, R., & Dryden, W. (1992). *A practitioner's guide to rational-emotive therapy.* New York: Oxford University Press.

Wallerstein, R. S. (1986). *Forty-two lives in treatment.* New York: Guilford.

Walsh, R. (1992). The search for synthesis. *Journal of Humanistic Psychology, 32*(1), 19–45.

Wanigaratne, S., & Barker, C. (1995). Clients' preferences for styles of therapy. *British Journal of Clinical Psychology, 34,* 215–222.

Waterhouse, G. J., & Strupp, H. H. (1984). The patient-therapist relationship: Research from the psychodynamic perspective. *Clinical Psychology Review, 4,* 77–92.

Watson, J. B. (1925). *Behaviorism.* New York: Norton.

Watts, R. E. (2000). Entering the new millennium: Is individual psychology still relevant? *Journal of Individual Psychology, 56,* 21–30.

Watts, R. E., & Holden, J. M. (1994). Why continue to use "fictional finalism?" *Individual Psychology, 50,* 161–163.

Wawrytko, S. A. (1989). The meaning of the moment: The logotherapeutic dimension of everydayness. *International Forum for Logotherapy, 12,* 117–123.

Weakland, J., Fisch, R., Watzlawick, P., & Bodin, A. (1974). Brief therapy: Focused problem resolution. *Family Process, 13,* 141–168.

Webster, S. S. (1985). Helene Deutsch: A new look. *Journal of Women in Culture and Society, 10,* 553–571.

Weiner-Davis, M. (1992). *Divorce busting.* New York: Simon & Schuster.

Weinrach, S. G. (1980). Unconventional therapist: Albert Ellis. *Personnel and Guidance Journal, 59,* 152–160.

Weinrach, S. G. (1995). Rational emotive behavior therapy: A tough-minded therapy for a tender-minded profession. *Journal of Counseling and Development, 73*(3), 296–300.

Weinrach, S. G. (1996). Reducing REBT's "wince factor:" An insider's perspective. *Journal of Rational-Emotive & Cognitive-Behavior Therapy, 14*(1), 53–78.

Weinrach, S. G., & Ellis, A. (1995). Rational emotive behavior therapy after Ellis: Predictions for the future. *Journal of Mental Health Counseling, 17,* 413–428.

Weisberg, I. (1993). Brief, time-limited psychotherapy and the communicative approach. *International Journal of Communicative Psychoanalysis and Psychotherapy, 8,* 105–108.

Weisberg, I. (1994). Linking theory to practice: Melanie Klein and the relational revolution. *International Journal of Communicative Psychoanalysis and Psychotherapy, 9,* 77–84.

Weishaar, M. E. (1993). *Aaron T. Beck.* London: Sage.

Weissmark, M. S., & Giacomo, D. A. (1998). *Doing psychotherapy effectively.* Chicago: University of Chicago Press.

Wessler, R. L. (1986). Varieties of cognitions in the cognitively oriented psychotherapies. In A. Ellis & R. Grieger (Eds.), *Handbook of Rational-Emotive Therapy* (vol. 22, pp. 46–58). New York: Springer.

Wheeler, G. (1991). *Gestalt reconsidered: A new approach to contact and resistances.* New York: Gardner.

White, J., Campbell, L., & Steward, A. (1995). Associations of scores on the White-Campbell Psychological Birth Order Inventory and the Kern Lifestyle Scale. *Psychological Reports, 77,* 1187–1196.

White, M. (1986). Negative explanation, restraint, and double description: A template for family. *Family Process, 25,* 169–184.

White, M. (1988–1989, Summer). The externalization of the problem and the re-authoring of lives and relationships. *Dulwich Centre Newsletter,* pp. 3–20.

White, M. (1989). *Selected papers.* Adelaide, Australia: Dulwich Centre.

White, M. (1992). Deconstruction in therapy. In M. White (Ed.), *Experience, contradiction, narrative and imagination* (pp. 109–152). Alelaide, Australia: Dulwich Centre.

White, M. (1995). *Re-authoring lives.* Alelaide, Australia: Dulwich Centre.

White, M. & Epston, D. (1989). *Literate means to therapeutic ends.* Alelaide, Australia: Dulwich Centre.

White, M., & Epston, D. (1990). *Narrative means to therapeutic ends.* New York: Norton.

Whitmont, E. C., & Perera, S. B. (1989). *Dreams, a portal to the source.* London: Routledge.

Wickers, F. (1988). The misbehavior reaction checklist. *Elementary School Guidance and Counseling, 23,* 70–73.

Wilber, K. (1996). *A brief history of everything.* Boston: Shambhala.

Wilber, K. (1999). Spirituality and developmental lives: Are there stages? *Journal of Transpersonal Psychology, 31*(1), 1–10.

Williams, J. H. (1987). *Psychology of women: Behavior in a biosocial context.* New York: Norton.

Williams, P. S. (1994). Harry Stack Sullivan: Opening the door for a transpersonal vision? *Humanistic Psychologist, 22,* 62–73.

Wilson, G. T. (1995). Behavior therapy. In R. J. Corsini & D. Wedding (Eds.), *Current psychotherapies* (5th ed., pp. 127–228). Itasca, IL: Peacock.

Wilson, S. A., Becker, L. A., & Tinker, R. H. (1995). Eye movement desensitization and reprocessing (EMDR) treatment for psychologically traumatized individuals. *Journal of Consulting and Clinical Psychology, 63*(6), 928–937.

Wimpfheimer, M. J., & Schafer, R. (1977). Psychoanalytic methodology in Helene Deutsch's *The Psychology of Women. Psychoanalytic Quarterly, 46,* 287–318.

Wingerson, D., Sullivan, M., Dager, S., Flick, S., Dunner, D., & Roy-Byrne, P. (1993). Personality traits and early discontinuation from clinical trials in anxious patients. *Journal of Clinical Psychopharmacology, 13,* 194–197.

Winslade, J., Crocket, K., & Monk, G. (1997). The therapeutic relationship. In G. Monk, J. Winslade, K. Crocket, & D. Epston (Eds.), *Narrative therapy in practice: The archaeology of hope* (pp. 158–193). San Francisco: Jossey-Bass.

Winslade, J., & Smith, L. (1997). Countering alcoholic narratives. In G. Monk, J. Winslade, K. Crocket, & D. Epston (Eds.), *Narrative therapy in practice: The archaeology of hope* (pp. 158–193). San Francisco: Jossey-Bass.

Wisdom, J. O. (1990). Helene Deutsch on girlhood and her typology of women. *Melanie Klein and Object Relations, 8,* 1–29.

Witmer, J. M., & Sweeney, T. J. (1992). A holistic model for wellness and prevention over the lifespan. *Journal of Counseling and Development, 71,* 140–148.

Wolf, E. S. (1994). Varieties of disorders of the self. *British Journal of Psychotherapy, 11,* 198–208.

Wolfe, J. L. (1995). Rational emotive behavior therapy women's groups: A twenty year retrospective. *Journal of Rational-Emotive & Cognitive-Behavior Therapy, 13*(3), 153–170.

Wolpe, J. (1969). *The practice of behavior therapy.* New York: Pergamon.

Wong, E. C., Kim, B. S., Zane, N. W. S., Kim, I. J., & Huang, J. S. (2003). Examining culturally based variables associated with ethnicity: Influences on credibility perceptions of empirically supported interventions. *Cultural Diversity & Ethnic Minority Psychology, 9,* 88–96.

Woodman, M. (1982). *Addiction to perfection: The still unravished bride.* Toronto: Inner City Books.

Woollams, S., & Brown, M. (1979). *T. A.: The total handbook of transactional analysis.* Upper Saddle River, NJ: Prentice Hall.

Worrell, J., & Remer, P. (2002). *Feminist perspectives in therapy: Empowering diverse women.* New York: Wiley.

Wubbolding, R. E. (1988). *Using reality therapy.* New York: Perennial.

Wubbolding, R. E. (1990). *Expanding reality therapy: Group counseling and multicultural dimensions.* Cincinnati: Real World.

Wubbolding, R. E. (1991). *Understanding reality therapy.* New York: HarperCollins.

Wubbolding, R. E. (1995a). Integrating theory and practice: Expanding the theory and use of the higher level of perception. *Journal of Reality Therapy, 15*(1), 91–94.

Wubbolding, R. E. (1995b). Reality therapy theory. In D. Capuzzi & D. R. Gross (Eds.), *Counseling and psychotherapy: Theories and interventions* (pp. 385–424). Upper Saddle River, NJ: Merrill/Prentice Hall.

Wubbolding, R. E. (2000). *Reality therapy for the 21st century.* Bristol, PA: Accelerated Development.

Wulf, R. (1998). The historical roots of Gestalt therapy theory. *Gestalt Journal, 21,* 81–92.

Yalom, I. D. (1980). *Existential psychotherapy*. New York: Basic Books.

Yalom, I. D. (1989). *Love's executioner and other tales of psychotherapy*. New York: Basic Books.

Yalom, I. D. (1999). *Momma and the meaning of life: Tales of psychotherapy*. New York: Basic Books.

Yorke, C. (1983). Anna Freud and the psychoanalytic study and treatment of adults. *International Journal of Psycho-Analysis, 64,* 391–400.

Young, M. E. (1992). *Counseling methods and techniques: An eclectic approach*. New York: Macmillan.

Ziegler, D. J. (1999). The construct of personality in rational emotive behavior therapy (REBT) theory. *Journal of Rational-Emotive & Cognitive-Behavior Therapy, 17,* 19–32.

Zimring, R. M., & Raskin, N. J. (1992). Carl Rogers and client/person-centered therapy. In D. K. Freedheim (Ed.), *History of psychotherapy: A century of change* (pp. 629–656). Washington, DC: American Psychological Association.

Zuckerman, L., Zuckerman, V., Costa, R., & Yura, M. T. (1978). *A parent's guide to children: The challenge*. New York: Dutton.

Index